P9-BZM-793

EDUCATIONAL RESEARCH
An Introduction

EDUCATIONAL
RESEARCH

An Introduction

Second Edition

WALTER R. BORG
Utah State University

and

MEREDITH D. GALL
Far West Laboratory for
Educational Research and Development

DAVID McKAY COMPANY, INC.
New York

EDUCATIONAL RESEARCH: An Introduction

Fifth Printing, April 1976

INTERNATIONAL STANDARD BOOK NUMBER: 0-679-30069-4

LIBRARY OF CONGRESS CATALOG CARD NUMBER: 74-135586

MANUFACTURED IN THE UNITED STATES OF AMERICA

Table of Contents

List of Illustrations

List of Tables

Preface

The first edition of this book, published in 1963, has been used widely as an introductory textbook in educational research methods for graduate students enrolled in master's or doctoral programs. In revising it, we have kept to the same goals that guided the writing of the first edition: to cover the essentials needed to carry the student through the entire research process, from identifying the problem to writing the thesis; and to present every research technique commonly used so that the student develops an understanding of the field of educational research as a whole.

The text has been extensively revised, though, because we wished to present the many important developments that have occurred in the field over the past eight years. For example, new types of research institutions have come into existence: the network of research and development centers and regional educational laboratories, ERIC and its various clearinghouses, and the National Center for Educational Research and Development. They are all described here. Campbell and Stanley's classic review of research designs has had a major impact on experimentation in education. Accordingly, we have revised the chapter on experimental research to include their ideas and also to present experimental designs not in the first edition. Another chapter which has been revised extensively is the one on survey research. Educational researchers have been accused of limiting their use of surveys to simple descriptive analysis. Thus, in this edition we present a number of different research designs that can be used in doing survey studies. We have also added a chapter on methods of educational research and development, which may well be the most important new thrust in education over the last decade. The new techniques and issues presented in the revised edition could go on at some length—the use of unobtrusive measures in observation research, a new appraisal of replication in research, the issue of practical versus statistical significance, the National Assessment of Educational Progress, experimenter effects, etc.

Not only have students used the first edition as an introductory text, but because of the completeness of its coverage, many have also found it of value as a reference source in their later graduate work and careers. To increase the book's usefulness in these respects, we have added sections on new career opportunities in educational research and on preparation of research proposals for funding agencies. The annotated references at the end of each chapter have also been updated so that the student can find the best current supplementary information on each research topic. If none of these references meets his requirements, the student is advised to do a systematic search of the literature, following the techniques described in Chapter 3.

As in the first edition, we have tried to make the presentation as simple and practical as possible. Since many research concepts and techniques are difficult for the beginning researcher to understand, we have added more examples from published studies to illustrate how they have been applied in specific situations. The examples also serve the purpose of helping students acquire a background of the kinds of knowledge being generated by educational research. Another revision has been to reorganize the chapters of the book so that they follow more closely the steps needed to carry out a research study. Thus, the introductory chapters deal with formulation of a research problem, initial planning, and review of the literature. The text then turns to a discussion of sample selection, research designs, and techniques of data collection, data processing, and statistical analysis. This is followed by a chapter on report preparation.

Although the book is organized sequentially, the student should read it in its entirety before attempting to plan and carry out his research project. Inasmuch as each phase of a research project is tied rather closely to every other phase, it is not possible to develop a text that permits the student to become fully competent in the initial steps of research before he has gained some knowledge and insight into later steps. He cannot, for example, review the literature adequately until he can evaluate the research of others critically, and this critical evaluation requires knowledge of research design, statistical tools, and, for that matter, insight into almost all aspects of research. In this edition we decided to place the chapter on critical evaluation early in the book since it occurs early in the research process. However, some instructors may wish to assign it after Chapter 18. If they assign it earlier, they are advised to have students review it near the end of the course.

Thus far we have mentioned revisions primarily. It is equally important to stress that we have tried to retain without change the major features of the first edition. Thus, the sections on procedures for carrying out the steps in a research project have been revised only slightly. We have tried to be specific, except when it seemed impractical. For example, a detailed system for preparing note cards has been presented because the student is usually left to his own devices in this area and often arrives at an awkward and inefficient method of taking notes. On the other hand, there seems little justification in presenting details on thesis style and format because most colleges have either adopted one of the published style manuals or developed one of their own that the student must follow.

As was pointed out in the first edition, preparation of a text in research methods poses a problem because it is desirable to give the student a reasonable insight into statistical tools and measurement techniques as they apply to research, but to avoid covering the same ground typically dealt with in courses in elementary statistics and educational evaluation. Thus, we have emphasized the application of measurement and statistical techniques to problems of educational research. An attempt has been made to give the student enough information about such techniques so that he can recognize situations in which each is appropriate. In this edition we have not discussed statistical techniques by themselves, but rather we have tried to relate them to the research designs with which they are commonly associated. For example, correlational statistics are presented in the chapters on prediction and relationship studies, whereas t tests are discussed in the chapter on causal-comparative research. Also, we have described more statistical tests than were covered in the first edition. However, the text does not provide the calculations involved in using each technique; instead, we provide annotated references in which the student can locate this information.

Our recommendations to the student for reading this book are the same as those given in the preface to the first edition. Because it attempts to serve as a handbook as well as a text, brevity has been emphasized and very little material has been included that is not of major importance. Thus, the amount of important information per page is often quite high, and the student will find it difficult to assimilate the information in a single reading. From the standpoint of effective learning, it is recommended that, after a quick reading of the text early in the research course in order to gain perspective, the student try to read a few pages each day, keeping abreast of the instructor's presentation. He should underline or, in some other manner, indicate the most important points and review these points frequently as his reading carries him further into the book. He should make marginal notes to clarify important points, and should mark, for future reference, information that is especially pertinent to his own research plan. Another review of the text will be helpful to the student as he goes through the steps involved in carrying out his own research project. In each step of his research project, the student should pay special attention to the section at the end of the pertinent chapter that lists mistakes often made by graduate students. If he avoids most of them in his research project, he may be sure that his research will be well above average.

We wish to acknowledge our colleague, Mr. Morris Lai, and the junior author's wife, Dr. Joyce Gall, for reading the manuscript critically and offering many suggestions to improve it. We wish also to thank Miss Lisa Hunter, Mrs. Carolyn Amable, and Mrs. Ursula Hoffman for their secretarial assistance.

July 1971   Walter R. Borg
                                                                 Meredith D. Gall

EDUCATIONAL RESEARCH
An Introduction

CHAPTER 1

Education as a Science

A NEW SCIENCE

Education did not begin to emerge as a science until the start of the twentieth century, although a few stirrings were evident during the latter 1800s. Scientific progress is based to a large degree upon the precision of our instruments and upon our ability to measure the phenomena concerned with the science in question. If the student will examine the history of any of the sciences, he will find that development of better tools is almost invariably followed by important gains in scientific knowledge, disproof of some theories, and confirmation of others. The relatively late emergence of education, psychology, sociology, and the other behavioral sciences is due largely to the complexity of the phenomena they attempt to measure and the consequent slow progress in developing measurement tools. Because science is closely tied to measurement, little progress in educational research was possible until some of the early measurement tools were developed. The publication of J. M. Cattell's *Mental Tests and Measurements* in 1890, the development of the intelligence scale by Binet and Simon in 1905, and the development of the handwriting scale by Thorndike in 1910 were among the significant early steps in developing objective tools for educational research.

After an initial negative reaction to early research, such as Rice's study of spelling, most educators embraced the new science and sat back to await the solution to all of their educational problems. Of course, a new science with little theoretical foundation and few satisfactory tools and techniques failed to meet these great expectations. Ralph Tyler recalls for us the disillusionment of educators of the post World War I period:

When I was an instructor at the University of Nebraska nearly forty years ago, there was a great interest in educational research and even in that state, which had previously spent money only on agricultural research, there was established in that university a bureau of educational research with some state support. This was done with the optimistic view following World War I that educational research would give answers to pressing and immediate questions such as: What do you do to get everybody to read in the elementary school? What can you do to get every pupil to spell correctly? What can you do to achieve 100 per cent accuracy in arithmetic? Because of the success of psychological tests in selecting candidates for officer training in World War I and in the use of job analysis for building a short and effective curriculum for bricklayers and carpenters needed in the war effort, many people concluded that a bureau of educational research would quickly solve the immediate, practical problems of the Nebraska schools. But this was an expectation which was not warranted by the later results. The problems of education are not going to be answered in this way.[1]

Because of the pressure of educators in the public schools to get immediate solutions to practical classroom problems, educational research has been slow in developing the theoretical foundations upon which every science must be built. The real value of research is rarely found in its ability to provide quick answers to practical problems. Rather, its value lies in developing theory and advancing knowledge so that the answers it does provide are sound and lead to real gains. Educators, in their impatience to solve their problems, have often adopted new and unproved ideas that later research proved valueless or even detrimental to the educational process. The direct attack on practical problems is not necessarily the best way to arrive at a solution to these problems. Agricultural research provides an interesting illustration of the futility of concentrating too heavily upon direct solutions:

In a certain sense, agricultural researchers reached a kind of impasse when they sought to deal too directly with immediate, practical problems. Agriculture research gained new vitality when different sorts of questions were studied. For example, consider the case of hybrid corn. That hybrid corn existed and many hybrids could be produced was known for many years. But agricultural researchers were not greatly interested in this field because they had a different model to guide their thinking. This model was: We have good corn. How can it best be raised? They were conscious of the amount of water, the quality of seed, the physical and chemical characteristics of the soil, the use of fertilizer, the varying lengths of growing seasons, and these were the variables that were manipulated. When they reached a point where corn production was up to above sixty bushels an acre, this was considered tops; maximum production had been reached. The men working on hybrid corn spent nearly twenty years before they could even get attention by agronomists, because they were geneticists. They were not working on immediate practical problems but on more theoretical ones. When, finally, they got a hearing and corn production jumped, agricultural researchers in large numbers began to study more basic and theoretical problems in order to understand the more immediate ones.[2]

N. L. Gage, a professor of education and psychology at Stanford University, provides another example of how researchers can be led astray

[1] F. W. Banghart (ed.), *First Annual Phi Delta Kappa Symposium on Educational Research* (Bloomington, Ind.: Phi Delta Kappa, 1960), 91. Reprinted by permission of Mr. F. W. Banghart.

[2] *Ibid.*, pp. 91–92.

when they attempt to deal too directly with immediate problems. Educators have always been faced with the practical problem of selecting and training better teachers. The typical research approach to this problem has been to define a general criterion of teaching effectiveness and then to look for differences in the characteristics of teachers who are rated high or low on this criterion. However, this has proved to be an ill-conceived, fruitless strategy. Literally hundreds of studies using this approach have been carried out over the last half century, with few if any positive results. As Gage suggests, the flaw in this strategy is that it assumes teaching effectiveness can be studied as a single, global criterion. Although educators may have to resort to such a criterion for practical matters such as teacher selection and teacher promotion, it has proved to be too simplistic an approach for research purposes. A breakthrough occurred when a number of researchers began to consider the possibility of analyzing teaching effectiveness as a complex phenomenon. Gage, for example, suggested that: "Rather than seek criteria for the over-all effectiveness of teachers in the many, varied facets of their roles, we may have better success with criteria of effectiveness in small, specifically defined aspects of the role." [3] This strategy has led to great advances in recent years in the research investigation of skills that make up effective teaching. For example, now researchers commonly select just one aspect of the teacher's role, such as lecturing or leading group discussions, and attempt to identify or develop teacher skills in that one area of classroom instruction. This research strategy has produced many findings that are now proving to have practical significance for the training of teachers.

The science of education remains weak in theoretical foundation, but a sufficient body of theory has now been developed or borrowed from the other behavioral sciences to permit sound approaches to some of the practical problems of education. The public school administrator is still wanting in an appreciation for basic and theoretical research in education, but today his expectations are much more realistic than those of educators forty years ago. He knows research can provide answers to his problems, because many answers have already been provided. He has gained much insight into the complexities of the educational process, and is resigned to the fact that research moves slowly.

A COMPLEX SCIENCE

Few persons outside of the behavioral sciences have a clear insight into the tremendous problems faced by the research worker in education and the other behavioral sciences. Perhaps the greatest obstacle to progress in

[3] N. L. Gage, "Paradigms for Research in Teaching," in N. L. Gage (ed.), *Handbook on Research in Teaching* (Chicago: Rand McNally, 1963), pp. 94–141.

these sciences is the extreme complexity of the problems. Most laymen think of a science such as nuclear physics as being far more complex than such sciences as education, psychology, and sociology. Actually, the reverse is true. The forces and matter dealt with in physics and chemistry are far easier to understand than the structure of a strange society, the development of the personality, or the processes involved in human thought and problem solving. Living organisms are generally far more complex than the forces and inert matter that make up the content of the physical sciences.

The human being—the subject of most educational research—is by far the most complex of the living organisms. Not only are there many environmental forces acting upon the human individual, but the individual responds actively rather than passively to his environment. In the physical sciences, one can apply a standard stimulus and elicit a predicted reaction under highly generalized conditions of administration (e.g., if one releases any object from a given height, one can predict with great precision how long it will take to fall a given distance). However, in the behavioral sciences such clear-cut cause-and-effect relationships are extremely difficult to establish. Suppose that the researcher wishes to determine the effect of a new textbook on students' reading achievement. Broadly speaking, the new textbook is the stimulus to which the students are to react. Yet the students, because they are active organisms, may react to many other stimuli than the one intended by the researcher. Some students may react primarily to the presence of the researcher in the classroom, and this reaction may affect their reading achievement positively or negatively. Or the teacher may react to the fact that he is participating in an experiment on reading. Thus, he may use nontypical techniques to motivate his students to improve their reading. Some students may actually show a gain in reading achievement, not because of the new textbook but because they are responding to the teacher's use of special motivational techniques. Furthermore, the researcher is faced with the dilemma of measuring the criterion behavior, reading achievement. The reactions of physical objects are typically simple and thus easily measured. The reactions of humans are quite complex; reading behavior, for example, has many aspects such as reading rate, comprehension, fact recall, immediate versus delayed recall, etc. The researcher must decide which of these many aspects of reading behavior his experimental stimulus is likely to affect.

There are three sets of factors, then, that contribute to the complexity of educational research as a science. First, the stimulus to which individuals are exposed is likely to be quite complex. Second, there are wide individual differences in the manner in which each person within a group will process a given stimulus. Third, the reactions of an individual to a stimulus are typically complex. Thus, the educational researcher must deal with many variables simultaneously in a single research study. Whereas the physical scientist can use formal laboratory techniques to obtain rigid control of experimental conditions, the educational researcher must work under conditions that are much less precise. Despite these handicaps, education and the other behavioral sciences have made impressive contributions to our understanding of human behavior.

A VITALLY IMPORTANT SCIENCE

The impact of the behavioral sciences on our society is far greater than most people realize. At one level they are providing technical solutions for important human problems. But at a deeper level they are changing the conception of human nature—our fundamental ideas about human desires and human possibilities. When such conceptions change, society changes.

In the past few generations, many beliefs about such diverse matters as intelligence, child rearing, delinquency, sex, public opinion, and the management of organizations have been greatly modified by the results of filtering scientific fact and theory through numerous layers of popularizing translation.[4]

Nuclear weapons and their threat to humanity are the principal concern of most educated men in our time. Few realize that education and the other behavioral sciences offer us the best hope of controlling this power. Even fewer are aware that knowledge is quickly building up in the behavioral sciences that, if misused, may create a scientific monster potentially more destructive to civilized man than the H-bomb. One of our greatest scientists, Robert Oppenheimer, declared in 1956:

In the last ten years the physicists have been extraordinarily noisy about the immense powers which, largely through their efforts, but through other efforts as well, have come into the possession of man, powers notably and strikingly for very large-scale and dreadful destruction. We have spoken of our responsibilities and of our obligations to society in terms that sound to me very provincial, because the psychologist can hardly do anything without realizing that for him the acquisition of knowledge opens up the most terrifying prospects of controlling what people do and how they think and how they behave and how they feel. This is true for all of you who are engaged in practice, and as the corpus of psychology gains in certitude and subtlety and skill, I can see that the physicist's pleas that what he discovers be used with humanity and be used wisely will seem rather trivial compared to those pleas which you will have to make and for which you will have to be responsible.[5]

[4] Behavioral Sciences Subpanel of the President's Science Advisory Committee, "Strengthening the Behavioral Sciences," *Science,* 136, No. 3512 (April, 1962), 133. Reprinted by permission of *Science.*

[5] Robert Oppenheimer, "Analogy in Science," *The American Psychologist,* 11, No. 3 (March, 1956), 128. Reprinted by permission of the American Psychological Association.

Now, a dozen years after Oppenheimer's speech, some of the terrifying prospects he foresaw are with us. Experiments on the control of animal and human behavior using electrical stimulation of the brain are now being performed. Dr. José M. R. Delgado has recently catalogued the array of behavioral reactions that have already been produced by electrical brain stimulation of animals and humans.[6] These reactions include the following:

1. Different species of animals—including cat, dog, and monkey—have been induced to "move the legs, raise or lower the body, open or close the mouth, walk or lie still, turn around, and perform a variety of responses with predictable reliability, as if they were electronic toys under human control."
2. Retiring young women, upon being electrically stimulated by radio at certain brain sites, have held the hands of their doctors, initiated flirtatious conversation, and even hinted at marriage.
3. An 11-year-old boy, who was normally very quiet and spoke only four to seventeen words every two minutes, became animated when his brain was stimulated; he then talked at an average rate of eighty-eight words in a two-minute interval. The stimulation was repeated seven times. Each time the boy "appeared to be especially optimistic, emphasizing the pleasant side of sensory perceptions and the happy aspects of his memories and ideas." His expression "was spontaneous in character, his usual personal style and phraseology were preserved."
4. In other experiments, brain stimulation has "blocked the thinking process, inhibited speech and movements," and induced "anxiety, feelings of loneliness, distortion of sensory perception, recollection of the past, hallucinations, and other psychic manifestations." [pp. 61–62]

In addition to mind control through electrical stimulation of the brain, researchers are continuing to discover chemicals that achieve similar results. David Krech, a psychologist at the University of California, stated recently in an interview: "With the use of chemical brain control agents, it may be possible to control the individual and the masses, and to do all this unobtrusively and without the active cooperation of the victims."[7] Mind control probably holds for man a greater power for both good and evil than we have ever before dreamed. We are moving into an era of great advances in knowledge in the behavioral sciences that can contribute either to the elevation of mankind to new heights of dignity or to its degradation.

[6] José M. R. Delgado, "Evolution of Physical Control of the Brain," speech delivered at the American Museum of Natural History, New York City. Reviewed in *Saturday Review* (February 5, 1966), 61–68.

[7] John Barbour, "Mind Control is Fact," *Oakland Tribune* (November 20, 1966), 1–2.

THE SCIENTIFIC METHOD IN EDUCATION

Perhaps a major reason for the slow and unsure progress in education has been the inefficient and unscientific methods used by educators in acquiring knowledge and solving their problems. An uncritical acceptance of authority that is not supported by objective evidence and an overdependence upon personal experience have been characteristic of the educator's problem-solving techniques.

Both these techniques have led to many blunders in education. The opinions of authorities should be critically evaluated and checked for supporting evidence before being accepted. Uncritical acceptance of Aristotle's pronouncements greatly retarded the growth of knowledge in the Middle Ages. Uncritical application of Freudian concepts to elementary school education led to amazing blunders in some of the "progressive schools" of the 1920s. Uncritical acceptance of the "sales pitch" of producers of teaching machines and programmed learning materials by today's educators may well lead to another educational fiasco because these techniques, though promising, are far from the level of perfection suggested by the salesmen. A tragic feature of the uncritical acceptance of authority opinion is that it is usually followed by disillusionment and reaction. Thus, many of the useful concepts given to us by men like John Dewey and Sigmund Freud are rejected by educators after the fad of blind acceptance has passed.

Reliance upon personal experience is equally faulty as a means for arriving at solutions to our educational problems. Personal experience almost always constitutes insufficient evidence upon which to make decisions, even if the individual were able to remember and objectively evaluate his experience. We know from psychological research that the individual tends to remember evidence that supports his opinion and to forget or distort evidence that does not. Personal experience often leads the individual to draw conclusions or assume relationships that are false. Yet, personal experience still plays a major role in decision making in the public schools. In recent years one of the authors, in the course of a research project, has discussed ability grouping with a great many teachers and administrators in the public schools. Although nearly everyone in the public schools has strong feelings on this subject, very few have any knowledge of the research evidence concerning it. Education will mature greatly as a science when the majority of educators put aside personal experience and bias and seek scientific evidence as a basis for making decisions.

The scientific method offers the best approach that man has thus far developed for the solution of problems. The steps of the scientific method may be applied not only to the problems of the scientific laboratory but are equally applicable to the problems faced by the school teacher in his classroom. The basic steps of the scientific method are as follows:

1. Recognition of the problem
2. Definition of the problem in clear, specific terms
3. Development of hypotheses
4. Development of techniques and measuring instruments that will provide objective data pertinent to the hypotheses
5. Collection of data
6. Analysis of data
7. Drawing conclusions relative to the hypotheses based upon the data.

As important as these steps are, however, they are less important than the habits of objective and critical thinking that they help the scientist to develop. Few mature scientists follow these steps rigidly in the conduct of their research. This does not mean they are not using the scientific method but merely demonstrates that this method has become so closely bound up with the values and perceptions of the scientist that direct, conscious reference to its steps is no longer necessary.

SOME CONTRIBUTIONS OF EDUCATIONAL RESEACH

Introduction

Although educational research is still in its infancy, it has already produced much useful knowledge and has brought about great changes in educational practice. Benjamin S. Bloom, former president of the American Educational Research Association, calculated that over 70,000 articles have appeared in the *Review of Educational Research* in the short span of 25 years.[8] Among the major methodological contributions made by educational researchers during this period, Bloom mentions the following: statistical tools and research designs (particularly factor analysis, analysis of variance, sampling techniques, and multivariate research designs); use of computers in research; test construction and testing procedures; and instructional procedures (particularly, programmed instruction). Among the substantive contributions mentioned by Bloom are the discoveries that have been made about: the progression of the child through stages of development; the effects of the environment upon development and learning; the predictability and modifiability of human characteristics; and principles of learning (particularly Skinner's contributions).

The following examples are not perhaps the most important contribu-

[8] Benjamin S. Bloom, "Twenty-Five Years of Educational Research," *American Educational Research Journal,* 3 (1966), 211–221.

tions of educational research, but they may serve to illustrate a few areas in which gains have been made.

Promotion of students

Up until the 1920s when extensive research was, for the first time, devoted to the relative merits of promotion and nonpromotion, the vast majority of public schools in the United States employed very rigid promotion standards. These standards were such that, if a pupil failed to attain the level of achievement that had been set for every one of the subjects taught at a particular grade level, he was retained in the grade until this level of achievement had been reached. The success of teachers was judged largely by the number of pupils they succeeded in raising to the level required for promotion. This policy resulted in many children of low ability repeating the same grade several times. These rigid promotion policies were based on the "common sense" notion that, if a person failed to learn the third-grade material satisfactorily, the best way for him to learn it was to repeat the third grade until he did. The student should be very careful in his acceptance of "common sense" solutions. History is filled with instances in which common sense has been proved wrong by science. In the late 1920s and early 1930s, however, a number of studies were conducted on some of the effects of promotion and nonpromotion. Among these were Arthur's study of sixty first-grade repeaters, which showed that the average repeater did not learn more in two years than the average nonrepeater of the same mental age learned in one year.[9]

Another noteworthy study bearing on this question was carried out in the Long Beach public schools. Two groups of potential failures were equated. One of the groups was required to repeat the grade while the other was promoted on trial. When educational tests were administered to both groups, it was found that children of normal ability gained more from trial promotion than children of equal ability who had repeated the grade. Children of less than average ability gained slightly more by repeating the grade than they did by trial promotion.[10]

A study by McKinney found that 53 percent of elementary school repeaters did not improve from repeating a grade. Thirty-five percent showed better work the second time through the grade and 12 percent did poorer work.[11]

[9] Grace Arthur, "A Study of the Achievement of 60 Grade-One Repeaters as Compared with That of Nonrepeaters of the Same Mental Age," *Journal of Experimental Education,* 5 (December, 1930), 203–205.

[10] Vivian Klene and E. P. Branson, "Trial-Promotion vs. Failure," *Educational Research Bulletin,* 8 (January, 1929), 6–11.

[11] D. T. McKinney, "The Promotion of Pupils—A Problem of Educational Administration" (Doctoral dissertation; Urbana, Ill.: University of Illinois, 1928).

Some educators clung to nonpromotion as a device to "get lazy pupils to work," but later studies indicated that the threat of failure had little or no effect as a method of motivation.[12]

The weight of this research caused public schools to move away from rigid promotion standards and the widespread practice of nonpromotion. As is often the case, many schools reacted strongly against their previous practices and established 100 percent promotion programs. At the present time, although few schools subscribe rigidly to a 100 percent promotion policy, the number of failures has been drastically reduced. Exact figures on the percentage of failure are difficult to determine and vary considerably, but all studies concerned with this topic have reported a trend toward a small number of failures.

In all likelihood, the overall promotion rate at the present time in the United States exceeds 95 percent. Teachers, being well aware of the dangers of nonpromotion that have been brought out by research in this area, consider each case very carefully and tend to employ nonpromotion only when considerable evidence seems to indicate that this course of action is desirable in the particular case.[13]

The gifted child

One of the most significant pieces of educational research has been the longitudinal study of gifted children started by L. M. Terman in 1921. This study initially selected some 1,500 superior boys and girls and followed a large proportion of them through school, college, adulthood, and to middle life. Five volumes have been published based on three major field studies, and several mailed follow-ups carried out over a 35-year period. The findings have given us much greater insights into the nature and development of superior individuals and have exploded the once widely held belief that precocious children usually grow up to be inferior adults. Among the results of the latest follow-up, we find that more than 70 percent of Terman's group graduated from college or about ten times as many as would be found in the average population. The requirements for the Ph.D. degree were completed by 14 percent of the men in the study, and these men had produced nearly 2,000 scientific papers, over 60 books and monographs, and at least 230 patents at the time of the 35-year follow-up. The children of the subjects in the original sample have been tested and

[12] J. Henry Otto and Ernest O. Melby, "An Attempt to Evaluate the Threat of Failure as a Factor in Achievement," *Elementary School Journal*, 35 (April, 1935), 588–596.

[13] Ironically, the recent clamor for higher standards has led some public school systems to reinstitute policies leading to nonpromotion of many pupils. Progress in education is not easily gained nor easily maintained. The willingness of some educators to reject scientific evidence in order to gain public approval reflects the immaturity of education as a science. In contrast one is reminded of the many astronomers in the sixteenth century who endured persecution rather than state falsely that the earth was the center of the universe.

30 percent of these children are also gifted.[14] This classic study in educational psychology demonstrates the tremendous amount of knowledge pertinent to education that may be generated through a single research project.

Foreign language teaching

A more recent example of a major improvement in education that has been largely brought about through educational research is found in the teaching of foreign languages. Up until World War II, most foreign language instruction was conducted along the following lines: The teacher, who often had a limited command of the language being taught, carried out the class instruction in English. The usual lesson consisted of a discussion of some grammatical point in the language, an exercise translating a selection from English into the foreign language being studied, another exercise involving translating a selection from the foreign language into English, and a daily vocabulary list to be memorized. Although many educators were dissatisfied with this method of language instruction, little real gains were made until World War II when the need for persons trained in foreign languages was very great and the methods then in use were found to be inadequate. Methods emphasizing conversation and the elimination of grammar and vocabulary lists were developed and tested by research. Many of the changes involved in these new methods were firmly based on principles of linguistics and educational psychology that had been known for many years. The language laboratory, with its use of tape recorders and other electronic equipment and its emphasis upon the oral-aural methods of language instruction, has been the result of this research and development.

Among the significant early studies comparing traditional and oral-aural methods of language instruction is the work of Hohlfeld, who compared college students in two experimental Spanish classes—one emphasizing oral-aural skills and using a series of phonograph records as the chief teaching material, the other emphasizing use of a textbook, grammatical analysis, rapid silent reading, and translation. This study, although involving small samples, was very carefully controlled, subjects being matched with respect to seventeen variables. Hohlfeld's results indicated that in tests aimed primarily at measuring gains made by the traditional method, the oral-aural method was either equal or superior; and in areas such as phonics accuracy and reading, the results were overwhelmingly in favor of the newer method.[15]

[14] L. M. Terman and M. H. Oden, *The Gifted Group at Mid-Life: Thirty-five Years' Follow-up of the Superior Child* (Stanford, Calif.: Stanford University Press, 1959).

[15] John M. Hohlfeld, *An Experiment Employing Two Methods of Teaching Spanish to College Freshmen* (Doctoral dissertation; Philadelphia: University of Pennsylvania, 1950).

A more extensive series of experiments were carried out at the University of Texas by Hamilton and Haden. This work extended over a 3-year period and involved a total of 2,700 students. Results generally reflected a small difference in achievement, using the usual standard tests that are aimed at measuring the skills stressed in the formal program but revealed many features in the oral-aural methods that brought about favorable outcomes not obtained by the formal methods. Among the most interesting results of these studies was the finding that it makes essentially no difference in grammar achievement whether grammar is emphasized in the traditional former manner or whether it is deemphasized and taught inductively as is the case in the newer methods. Later research has supported this finding, and the body of evidence now available indicates that teaching of traditional grammar is essentially a waste of time.[16]

Such early studies, though often weak from a research standpoint, still contained enough significant evidence to indicate strongly the potential of the new methods. Since that time, more carefully controlled studies have generally supported the findings of this earlier work. The efficiency of the oral-aural method has greatly increased since 1950, when the earlier studies had generally established its superiority over traditional methods. Tremendous impetus was given for further research and development on the teaching of modern foreign languages by the National Defense Education Act (NDEA) of 1958. By 1962, the total funds allocated to research dealing with modern language instruction and the development of tests and specialized materials in this field under Title VI and Title VII of the NDEA approached $10 million.

As a result of this research funding, significant advances have occurred in the technology of foreign language instruction over the last decade. Particularly noteworthy is the language laboratory, which has been refined considerably and is now an accepted teaching tool. It is remarkable that there are now well over 10,000 language laboratories in American high schools, compared to the few dozen that were in operation in 1959.[17] The effectiveness of these laboratories should continue to increase as a result of recent research concerning use of programmed film to teach the cultural aspects of language learning. In one such project, students viewed and engaged in conversation with film characters. The 8-mm. sound film was shown in cartridge-loading projectors operated by the student.[18] Another

[16] D. E. Hamilton and E. F. Haden, "Three Years of Experimentation at the University of Texas," *Modern Language Journal,* 34 (February, 1950), 85–102.

[17] Emma Birkmaier and Dale Lange, "Foreign Language Instruction," *Review of Educational Research,* 37 (1967), 186–199.

[18] Louis Forsdale and Gerald Dykstra, "An Experimental Method of Teaching Foreign Languages by Means of 8mm Sound Film in Cartridge-Loading Projectors," *Language Learning,* 13 (1963), 5–10.

mark of progress in foreign language instruction has been the recent development of new tests of foreign language achievement. These include the MLA Foreign Language Proficiency Tests for Teachers and Advanced Students and the MLA Cooperative Foreign Language Tests.

Project TALENT

In the first edition of this book, published in 1963, Project TALENT was described as follows:

This is a highly significant project being sponsored jointly by the University of Pittsburgh and the American Institutes for Research. The study is aimed at obtaining an accurate inventory of the abilities and potentialities of American youth. After tryout and development of measuring instruments on 10,000 high school students, a total of approximately 500,000 students were tested in the spring of 1960. All students in about 1,200 secondary schools including grades 9 to 12 were tested, using a wide range of educational and psychological measures including aptitude and ability tests, measures of educational achievement, interest, and personality characteristics. A follow-up study will be carried out for a number of years in order to determine how closely the potentials of these students match their future accomplishments. The information that has been collected will also be compared with their behavior in a number of areas in later life. All the high school students included in the study will be followed up approximately one year after their graduation from high school and will be contacted at later intervals to obtain information on their occupations, training they have undertaken, success and satisfaction in the activity they have chosen, and many other facts related to their education, career, and adjustment. These data will then be compared with the original measures, using electronic computing equipment. Dr. John T. Dailey is director of this project, and Dr. John C. Flanagan is the national administrative head of the project. Ninety regional coordinators were employed to arrange for the testing and to guide schools in administration of the measures.

Some of the important results of this National Aptitude and Ability Census should be:

A comprehensive counseling guide indicating the patterns of aptitude and ability which are predictive of success in various careers. In the follow-ups after the national examinations and analysis, students who took the test will be located and asked to report on educational and vocational experiences. A young girl may have become a secretary, or a housewife, or she may have gone to college. By studying thousands of student aptitude, interest, and ability patterns and finding out the person's later activities and occupations, we will learn a great deal. This will help students by predicting more precisely what kinds of aptitudes and abilities, what kinds of courses, and what kinds of interests constitute the best basis for various kinds of careers. An artist needs good color sense, a scientist needs mathematical ability, but counselors know that many other factors enter into the qualifications for success in a career. Motivation is a necessary ingredient, but the best use of a student's special talents requires that he identify this talent early and obtain the education essential for the full development and effective use of his powers.

A better understanding of how young people choose their life work. Many people follow their family trade or profession. They tend to think that people know quite early what their life work will be. Other people drift into an occupation, and they tend to think that everyone more or less drifts into a particular trade, business, or profession. Many people feel that they have little choice.

However, many people today do have a choice, and the diversity of occupations and the need for special training continue to increase. We have begun to learn something about the process by which a young person decides that he would like to be a teacher, a lawyer, or an apprentice for a trade. This study and others can help us understand at what ages certain lifetime careers tend to be chosen.

A better understanding of the educational experiences which prepare students for their life work. American education is noted for its diversity. Only through the analysis of detailed information about students, their educational experiences, and their subsequent successes or failures can we hope to make our educational system as flexible and responsible to the individual needs of its students as it must be if our nation is to continue to develop and prosper.

Project TALENT has been carefully designed to fill an important national need for facts regarding the identification, development, and utilization of our human resources. This information is intended as a basis for manpower policies and as a basic resource for the many individuals responsible for the education of our children.[19]

Now, a decade later, we may consider some of the actual contributions that have resulted from Project TALENT.[20] We must be selective in our discussion since Project TALENT has generated literally hundreds of research findings. One of its first published reports concerned characteristics of American secondary schools.[21] This report provides a wealth of data regarding national high school practices, policies, school plant, teaching staff, and community characteristics. It also contains a taxonomy of high schools so that homogeneous groups of schools can be studied and

[19] John C. Flanagan and John T. Dailey, "Project Talent—the Identification, Development, and Utilization of Human Talents," *Personnel and Guidance Journal,* 38 (February, 1960), 504–505. Reprinted by permission of the *Personnel and Guidance Journal.*

[20] Many of these contributions are summarized in John C. Flanagan, "The Uses of Educational Evaluation in the Development of Programs, Courses, Instructional Materials and Equipment, Instructional and Learning Procedures, and Administrative Arrangements," in Ralph W. Tyler, *Educational Evaluation: New Roles, New Means,* 68th Yearbook of the National Society for the Study of Education (Chicago: University of Chicago Press, 1969), 221–241.

[21] J. C. Flanagan, J. T. Dailey, M. F. Shaycroft, D. B. Orr, and Isadore Goldberg, *Studies of the American High School,* Cooperative Research Project No. 226 (Pittsburgh, Pa.: University of Pittsburgh, 1962).

compared. Perhaps the most important data analyses are those relating school characteristics to student outcomes such as achievement, college attendance, and dropout rate. The school characteristics that were found to be most closely related to student outcomes were teacher salaries, teacher experience, number of books in the school library, and per-pupil expenditure. As the researchers point out, teacher salaries may be a good index of teacher quality. Schools with a high salary schedule are probably better able to recruit good teachers and hold them longer than schools with low salary schedules. Project TALENT researchers also identified several school characteristics that demonstrated very little relationship to student outcomes. These characteristics were school size, average size of classes, age of building, and suburban location. Of particular interest is the lack of relationship between class size and student outcomes. Many educators believe that reduced class size is one of the best ways to improve student achievement, yet the Project TALENT data provide very little justification for this belief.

Project TALENT has also given us much important information about high school students and the strengths and weaknesses of the present educational system. For example, Project TALENT tested students' ability to read and understand different kinds of literature. It was found that 85 percent of twelfth-grade students could read and understand satisfactorily the writing of Louisa May Alcott, but only 4 percent could display the same understanding of Thomas Mann's writing. Furthermore, 92 percent of students at this grade level had acceptable comprehension of the content in movie magazines, but only 25 percent could read *Time* magazine with similar comprehension and only 4 percent could read *Saturday Review* satisfactorily. These findings suggest some serious deficiencies in our present instructional program which need correction.

Many findings have come out of Project TALENT regarding students' vocational aspirations and the ability of the schools to meet vocational planning needs. It was found that many high school students have unrealistic plans about their future vocation. Not only do many students aspire to an occupation that seems inappropriate in terms of the intellectual level required, but their vocational plans are very unstable. For example, male students in the twelfth grade were asked to report their choice of occupation. One year later only 31 percent reported the same choice of occupation. Students also recognize that they need assistance in this area. In responding to the questionnaire item, "The main thing I believe I needed which was not provided by this high school was _____," students most frequently stated that guidance and counseling was the largest unfilled need. These important findings clearly indicate the need for educational research and innovation in high school education to improve students' planning for a career and other significant life roles.

Perhaps the most important outcome of Project TALENT is the findings regarding individual differences in student performance in today's schools. One of the project's investigations involved testing a sample of ninth-grade students and then retesting them when they reached the twelfth grade. It was found that almost 30 percent of the ninth-grade students exceeded the performance of the average twelfth-grade student in the subjects of English and social studies. The interpretation provided by Flanagan is that: "These data demonstrate very clearly that a substantial fraction of the Grade 9 students have the ability and information of the typical Grade 12 student and, conversely, that a large proportion of the Grade 12 students are at a level more typical of ninth-grade students." [22] This evidence of broad individual differences in student achievement suggests quite strongly that educational researchers and practitioners need to devote more effort to the problem of individualizing instruction. It is evident that different students progress through a curriculum at different rates, and they probably differ also in their benefit from different pedagogical techniques.

The Project TALENT findings on individual differences in students led directly to the design of another project, Project PLAN.[23] This is a curriculum program designed to bring about significant change in schools in the direction of individualized instruction. In fact, most of the significant new developments in research and curriculum construction have the same goal. These developments, which offer great promise for improving students' learning, are a direct outgrowth of the research findings generated by Project TALENT and similar studies.

The Greater Cleveland Mathematics Program

In the 1963 edition of this book, the Greater Cleveland Mathematics Program was described as follows:

Another research project of major significance is the Greater Cleveland Mathematics Program. The materials for this program were developed by the staff of the Educational Research Council of Greater Cleveland, six of the nation's leading mathematicians, and teachers in twenty-four school districts in suburban Cleveland. The curriculum developed for this program aims at introducing a new mathematics curriculum that systematically presents all the elements of basic mathematical skills. The program emphasizes inductive learning and the mastery of basic concepts rather than giving students specific mathematical tools designed to handle specific skills and problem situations without developing a full understanding of the underlying principles. In a rapidly changing society, the schools have often placed too much emphasis upon specific operations that are appropri-

---

[22] *Ibid.*, p. 231.
[23] An acronym for "A Program for Learning in Accordance with Needs."

ate at the time taught but outdated by the time the pupil is called upon to use his knowledge. This amounts to educating the pupil for yesterday's society instead of tomorrow's. Educating for tomorrow is a difficult task. The Greater Cleveland Mathematics Program appears to be meeting this challenge in one subject area.

Actually, the psychological and educational principles upon which this program is being built are not new and have generally been recognized as superior for a number of years. Taking these principles and combining them with the most advanced educational concepts in a particular subject field, such as mathematics, and then preparing materials and actually putting such a program into effect, however, is new and represents a giant step in closing the gap between research knowledge and educational practice. The first two years of the program have been devoted largely to the development and improvement of the curricular materials and rendering assistance to teachers in the use of these materials. Preliminary experimental materials are now in use in grades four through six, and work is progressing toward the development of suitable materials for the junior and senior high school level. Objective evaluation of pupil progress in classes using these materials was carried out in the spring of 1961, and the results showed the groups using the new materials to be significantly superior to control groups on standardized achievement tests. In addition to their superiority on standardized tests that reflect for the most part a knowledge of operations rather than an understanding of principles (and are thus biased in favor of the older curriculum), the pupils in the experimental groups were also found to be far superior in special tests aimed at dealing with more difficult mathematical concepts and understanding of mathematical principles. In all instances where comparisons have been made, the mean scores for those children who were taught with the materials developed by the Greater Cleveland Mathematics Program were significantly higher than the scores for those children who did not have this material.

A very significant concept introduced in Cleveland is the Educational Research Council of Greater Cleveland that supervised the development of this mathematics program and is carrying out the research. The council was created in 1958 specifically to employ a dynamic approach to research in education and make possible immediate implementation of research findings. Dr. Baird, Executive Director of the Educational Research Council of Greater Cleveland, considers the following elements necessary in order to carry out and implement research findings in the manner done by the council:

1. Full financial backing to avoid the pitfalls of expediency and fiscal shortcoming of amateur, part-time, or ivory-tower research

2. A willingness among regional groups of schools to support immediate active programs of experimentation and implementation.[24]

The Cleveland Council is being sponsored by a group of civic leaders from commerce and industry. Many prominent businessmen from the Greater Cleveland area are actively engaged in raising funds needed for the support of the council. At their instigation the Cleveland Foundation granted $100,000 on a matching basis for the first two years of the program, and a group of leading superintendents from the Greater Cleveland area have enthusiastically supported the council's work.

Because the methods and curricular materials developed in the Cleveland project can be applied to any school system, it is very likely that this study will have a major impact upon mathematics teaching in American public schools. The method established in Cleveland of combining the talents of business leaders, professional educators, subject matter specialists, and educational research workers to make an effective team for conducting research and implementing research results sets a pattern that could lead to great improvements in education and may well solve the nagging problem of closing the gap between research findings and classroom practices. If every greater metropolitan area in the United States of over one million population would develop a council and concentrate upon the improvement of the curriculum in one area or on the solution of one important educational problem, tremendous gains could be made in the next decade.

At the time of this writing, the materials developed through the Greater Cleveland Mathematics Program have been published commercially and are available to all school districts. It is generally recognized that the Greater Cleveland Mathematics Program—along with such other programs as the School Mathematics Study Group Program, the University of Illinois Arithmetic Project, and the Madison Project—has had a major impact on mathematics education in this country. Today's students have a much stronger exposure to the mathematical concepts that underlie the number system and the basic number operations of addition, subtraction, multiplication, and division. Mathematical topics not formerly taught at the elementary school level, such as set theory, are now a standard part of the curriculum. Furthermore, the Greater Cleveland Mathematics Program and similar programs are responsible in part for the recent renewal of interest in the "discovery" approach to teaching.

The organization that sponsored the Cleveland program was formerly known as the Educational Research Council of Greater Cleveland. Now called the Educational Research Council of America, it has a staff of about one hundred research and subject matter specialists in addition to a national corps of consultants. For testing new products the council has

---

[24] George Baird, "Children 'Discover' Own Math," *SRA Insight,* 2, No. 1 (1962), 7.

available an "experimental laboratory" of 26 member school systems representing about 10,000 teachers and 250,000 students. At present the council is developing curriculum improvement programs in eight areas: social science, mathematics, English, humanities, science, physical education, French, and occupational education. The success of the council demonstrates the value of large-scale research and development[25] in bringing about substantial improvements quickly in the nation's schools.

IMPORTANT RESEARCH NOW UNDER WAY

Introduction

More research projects and of larger scope are being carried out now than at any previous time in the history of American education. The dramatic increase in educational research in recent years is a direct reflection of the increased financial support for such activities. Table 1 presents

TABLE 1

EDUCATIONAL RESEARCH EXPENDITURES, 1954–1967 *

	USOE Research	NSF Course Content	Title III, ESEA Dev. and Dem.
1954	$..........	$ 1,725	$........
1955	....	35,000	....
1956	....	18,000	....
1957	1,020,000	650,140	....
1958	2,300,000	750,310	....
1959	6,716,000	6,180,485	....
1960	10,350,000	6,302,055	....
1961	10,117,750	6,167,740	....
1962	11,770,000	9,389,948	....
1963	14,188,400	12,626,771	....
1964	19,820,000	14,157,650	....
1965	37,703,000	14,889,081	....
1966	100,141,241	16,393,383	45,400,000
1967	99,600,000	17,000,000 (est.)	81,000,000 (est.)

* Reprinted by permission of Dembar Educational Research Services, Inc., from *Research and Development Toward the Improvement of Education,* chapter "Research and Development Strategies: The Current Scene," by R. Louis Bright and Hendrik D. Gideonse, 1969.

the yearly expenditures from 1954 to 1967 by three sources of funding—the United States Office of Education, the National Science Foundation, and Title III of the Elementary and Secondary Education Act (ESEA). It can be seen that only a few years ago, USOE support for educational

[25] We shall discuss the concept of research and development later in this chapter.

research increased nearly threefold from about $38 million to over $100 million. Yet even the 1967 expenditure for educational research, about $200 million, was only one half of one percent of what this country spent for education that year—$48.8 billion. Many educators believe that even more dramatic increases in research funding are necessary to bring about a substantial improvement in the total educational process.

Of the many important research projects now under way, we have selected three for discussion. Significantly, two of these projects are in the area of individualized instruction. R. Louis Bright, formerly Associate Commissioner for Research, has expressed the opinion shared by many that individualized instruction "is the real thrust of research programs over the last ten years." [26] The third research project discussed here is concerned with the evaluation of educational outcomes. This project reflects the great interest currently shown for behavioral objectives in education. It also reflects an increasing concern that researchers not only develop more innovative education programs, but that they evaluate objectively the effect, if any, that these programs are having on student achievement.

Individualized instruction programs

Several new curriculum projects based on individualized instruction are under development at this time. More than any other line of current research activity, these projects offer the most promise of bringing about a revolution in the schools. Perhaps the most significant of these projects is Individually Prescribed Instruction (IPI) being developed by the Learning Research and Development Center at the University of Pittsburgh and by Research for Better Schools, Inc. The theoretical rationale for IPI is the research findings and instructional theories that have resulted from work on programmed instruction. The developers of IPI are attempting to apply programming principles to the entire school curriculum in reading, mathematics, and science.

One of the basic elements of IPI which permits individualization of instruction is the specification of sequential curriculum objectives in behavioral terms. The IPI reading curriculum alone contains 400 behavioral objectives in thirteen areas of study. The advantage of analyzing a curriculum area into sequential behavioral objectives is that it enables the teacher to pinpoint how far each student has progressed in the curriculum by measuring the objectives he has achieved. Unfortunately, many current programs have poorly stated, unmeasured objectives. It is very difficult to evaluate or improve such programs, since one cannot measure whether

[26] Leila Sussmann, "Educational Research Programs of the Office of Education: An Interview with Dr. R. Louis Bright, Associate Commissioner for Research," *Sociology of Education*, 40, No. 2 (1967), 158–169.

changes in the program have a specific effect on student achievement. By contrast, in IPI the behavioral objectives permit precise measurement of student achievement, and there is a close relationship between the IPI curriculum materials and these achievement measures.

It is evident that instruction can be individualized in various ways. At present IPI has had most success in individualizing rate of learning. IPI schools are ungraded since each student in a given classroom may be working at different points in the curriculum. The IPI procedure for individualized rate of learning is described by Richardson as follows:

At the beginning of the academic year, a series of placement tests are taken by each student to determine his ability in each IPI subject. After the placement tests indicate the student's position in the curriculum, a pretest is given. This pretest indicates the particular skills of a unit in which the student needs further work in order to attain a mastery criterion. On the basis of these diagnostic tests, prescriptions are developed. These prescriptions list the materials and procedures by which the student is to be taught. The final exercise included in each prescription is a curriculum-embedded test (CET). This test determines whether the student needs more work in the same skill or is ready to progress to the next skill. After progressing through the unit in this manner until all the skills are mastered, the student takes a posttest. If the pupil attains a passing grade in all the sections of this test, he proceeds to the next unit and takes the pretest. If he fails any sections of the posttest, another prescription for that unit is made. These prescriptions continue until the student passes the posttest. This completes the regular cycle that is composed of pretest, prescriptions for teaching materials and CETs, and posttests. With this cycle being repeated by each student, proceeding at his own rate through the curriculum, Individually Prescribed Instruction achieves part of its goal.[27] [pp. 199–200]

This instructional procedure is based on at least two principles of programmed instruction: continuous appraisal of the student's learning and immediate feedback to the student on his performance.

The individualization of rate of instruction is a considerable achievement and a considerable improvement in the education of students. In addition it opens up new areas of investigation for the researcher. Among the questions that may be asked are: Why do some students progress more quickly through the curriculum than others? How can student motivation be improved so that increased learning occurs? Does individualization of rate of instruction lead to superior achievement gains when compared with conventional instruction?

The developers of IPI are also attempting to individualize the materials and techniques of instruction to suit student interests, aptitudes, and learning style. They are acquiring increasing insight into how materials

[27] Robert J. Richardson, "An Information System for Individualized Instruction in an Elementary School," *Educational and Psychological Measurement*, 29 (1969), 199–201.

and instructional techniques can be varied for individual students. Some students may find written materials sufficient for most types of learning; other students may require viewing of pictures, diagrams, and films; and still others may need to physically manipulate something before they can achieve mastery of a concept. With respect to instructional techniques, some students may learn best when they are working alone, whereas other students may require tutorial assistance or small-group instruction. Certainly much important research waits to be done on matching students with appropriate learning materials and instructional techniques. The payoff of this research is bound to be a significant improvement in the educational process.

IPI is one of several individualized instruction programs under development. We have already mentioned Project PLAN, and computer-assisted instruction will be discussed later. Each of these projects has required millions of dollars and years of research effort. Much work needs to be done before any of these programs become operational. They demonstrate clearly that major improvements in education require large-scale research and development efforts involving highly trained staffs and long-term commitments. Yet much of the knowledge and theory that make up the foundation of this large effort was developed by individual researchers who did small-scale but perceptive studies in the area of programmed instruction.

National assessment of educational progress

One of the most ambitious and far-reaching educational research programs currently under way is the National Assessment of Educational Progress, directed by the Committee on Assessing the Progress of Education (CAPE). The goal of this program is to provide census-like data on national educational achievement in ten areas: career and occupational development, citizenship, literature, mathematics, music, reading, science, social studies, and writing. The nation is currently spending about $50 billion a year on education, and many educators and citizens want to know what this expenditure is yielding in terms of educational outcomes. The information provided by the National Assessment program will be useful in appraising national educational progress in much the same way that the gross national product and consumer price index are useful in studying economic development. The initial National Assessment will provide baseline data on how well the nation's educational system is meeting important educational objectives. Future assessments will provide data on how much progress has been made in meeting these objectives.

One of the first steps taken by the National Assessment program was to develop statements of important educational objectives. These objectives were formulated by leading scholars and educators in different fields and then submitted to eleven lay panels for review. The revised objectives were then used by the American Institutes for Research, Educational Testing Service, Psychological Corporation, and Science Research Associates to construct tests by which achievement of each objective could be gauged. The objectives and exercises were rigorously evaluated with respect to three standards: (1) they had to be considered important by scholars; (2) they had to be considered an accepted educational objective of the schools; and (3) they had to be considered desirable by thoughtful lay citizens.

In the next phase of the National Assessment program, the test exercises will be administered to random samples of 32,000 individuals at each of four age levels: 9, 13, 17, and young adult (ages 26–35). Testing began in 1969 and will be completed in 1971. Then a new cycle of testing will begin in order to obtain measures of change in educational achievement.

There are several noteworthy features of the assessment procedure in this program. All group-administered exercises are presented on tape in order to standardize the testing procedure and to assist students with poor reading ability in understanding the exercises. The National Assessment program will provide an opportunity for researchers to determine the effects of this procedure on students' test results as compared with the conventional procedure of having an examiner administer the test to a group. Another feature of the National Assessment program is that students' test results will be reported item by item. In contrast many assessment programs only report students' achievement in terms of a single total score. Thus, it is difficult to determine specifically what a group of students knows about a given subject area. By reporting test results in terms of individual items, the National Assessment program will ensure that these results are readily interpretable by educators and lay persons.

The National Assessment program is a very important research effort. It should bring an increased appreciation to educators of the role that evaluation has to play in educational improvement. As we have already discussed, another large-scale evaluation program, Project TALENT, has produced important findings about educational needs in the areas of individualized instruction and vocational planning for students. However, we must remember that such research efforts, no matter how important they may be, often meet with resistance from certain segments of the educational community. The National Assessment program, for example, was criticized quite severely by some educators during its formative stages. These educators expressed fears that the assessment results would be used to compare schools, teachers would gear their teaching toward the specific assessment exercises, the program would lead toward a national curriculum, and the program would restrict changes in instructional methods and educational goals. None of these fears is justified by the intended purposes of the National Assessment program and the outcomes observed so far. An extensive educational campaign by the National Assessment committee has succeeded in allaying many fears about the program, and most educational groups now endorse its goals. In the next chapter we will discuss possible sources of resistance to one's own research project, particularly if it is carried out in the schools, and techniques for overcoming such resistance.

Computer-Assisted Instruction

Computer-Assisted Instruction, or CAI as it is often called, is one of the most promising and imaginative new developments in education. Essentially, CAI is a method of instruction in which the computer is used to carry out at least some of the educational functions currently served by teachers and textbooks. In the typical CAI arrangement, the student sits at a terminal device linked to a central computer. The simplest terminal device is a typewriter that can type out messages from the computer and on which the student can respond to the computer. The terminal device used in the Stanford-Brentwood project,[28] perhaps the most advanced exploration of CAI, also includes a small television screen that can be used to display letters, numbers, pictures, and other visual symbols; there is also an image projector that projects color pictures from a film strip. In addition earphones are supplied to the student so that he can hear computer-controlled recorded messages that guide him as he progresses through an instructional program. Each student's terminal device is linked to a central computer, which may be located in an adjacent building or even hundreds of miles distant. At present a large central computer can handle up to 6,000 students daily, depending upon the type of instruction offered. The central computer serves several important educational functions: it presents "input," that is, information and questions; it responds to student input, that is, answers to computer questions, by providing feedback and new instructional material; and it keeps track of the student's performance through the course of an instructional program.

The great potential of CAI is that it may someday offer high-quality individualized instruction to all students at relatively low cost. Suppes has delineated several levels of individualized instruction of which CAI is at least potentially capable.[29] The first level is individualized drill-and-practice systems. After the teacher has presented a new concept or skill, the computer can provide practice in its use. The next level is tutorial

[28] A description of this important project can be found in P. Suppes, M. Jerman, and D. Brian, *Computer-Assisted Instruction at Stanford: The 1965–66 Arithmetic Drill-and-Practice Program* (New York: Academic, 1968).

[29] Patrick Suppes, "Computer Technology and the Future of Education," *Phi Delta Kappan*, 49 (1968), 420–423.

instruction in which the computer presents a concept or skill and develops
the student's ability to use it. CAI programs at these two levels have been
successfully developed. The third level of CAI poses some unsolved technological problems; at this level the computer would engage in a genuine
dialogue with the student.

In addition to its practical applications, CAI is an ideal research tool
for the educational researcher, because the computer can be used to maintain close control over the rate and content of what is presented to the
learner. This control is very difficult to attain in the usual laboratory or
field experiment in education. Furthermore the computer can provide the
researcher with response-by-response records of each student's performance,
summarized records for each student, or summarized records for a group
of students. Thus, the data collection and analysis stages of the research
process, which are quite time consuming in most types of research, become virtually automatic when CAI is used. Although most CAI projects
have concentrated on development of curriculum materials and computer
technology, some have generated research studies, also. Among the major
findings to date are the following: Students learn at least as much with
CAI as with conventional techniques of instruction; some studies find
that CAI leads to greater learning gains in less time; CAI can integrate
a wide variety of audio-visual aids into its instructional programs, and
a broad range of courses can be developed in CAI format; students generally have favorable attitudes toward CAI.[30]

There are many questions about CAI that still need to be explored
through research. Bundy has raised some of these questions, including the
following: How effective can CAI be made? Can CAI be used to foster
creative thinking? How can students' time best be divided between CAI
and other forms of instruction? How does CAI affect the teacher's role?
How can the technology of CAI be improved to yield increased student
learning? The answers to these questions will require the dedicated effort
of several generations of researchers in education and other disciplines.

It must be hoped that educators do not embrace CAI with reckless enthusiasm and then abandon it when they find it does not live up to their
expectations. CAI still needs a considerable amount of research and development before it is ready for operational use in the public schools. If educators become disillusioned with CAI, as they have with other promising
innovations such as teaching machines, the funds and support for CAI
may be cut off before it has had a chance to prove itself. Furthermore
already existing negative attitudes toward CAI by some educators must
be overcome. Some educators, for example, believe that CAI is a bad
development because it dehumanizes the educational process. This is in-

[30] A summary of these studies can be found in Robert F. Bundy, "Computer-Assisted
Instruction—Where Are We?" *Phi Delta Kappan,* 49 (1968), 424–429.

deed a possibility, but it is not a necessary aspect of CAI. Properly used, CAI offers the potential of freeing teachers from routine instructional tasks and record keeping so they can spend more of their time in individual work with students.

TYPES OF EDUCATIONAL RESEARCH

Basic versus applied research

The distinction between basic and applied research is not an easy one to make. Nevertheless, it is important to make the distinction since, as we shall discuss later, there is currently strong controversy regarding the relative importance of basic and applied research in bringing about educational improvement.

In a recent discussion of this problem, John Carroll makes four distinctions between basic and applied research.[31] They are relevant not only to educational research but to other branches of science as well. We repeat them here:

With respect to the questions asked, basic research tends to differ from applied research in the fact that it is more concerned with "understanding" and the attainment of knowledge about fundamental variables and their relationships; the prediction of socially important phenomena is of secondary concern, arising solely out of the laws and relationships discovered; and control of phenomena is often of only incidental interest except to verify a finding. Applied research, however, is generally concerned with the control of socially significant phenomena, or if control is difficult or impossible, at least their prediction. It is interested in the "understanding" of phenomena in terms of laws and relationships as a basis for prediction and control. Generally it starts with facts and propositions already established in basic science and proceeds to test them in particular situations and/or in particular combinations such that extrapolation from basic science is risky.

Correlated with this difference is the fact that basic science, in order to gain a better understanding of the workings of phenomena, is more often concerned with detailed, fundamental processes, such as chemical reaction mechanisms, nerve impulses, or isolated learnings; applied research, on the other hand, is more often concerned with gross, higher-order macroprocesses like wine fermentation, social attitudes, or scholastic achievements, because these are the phenomena one wants to predict or control. In the behavioral sciences, we say that basic research has often to do with a "molecular" level of behavior, while applied research has to do with a "molar" level of behavior. For example, basic research in learning is concerned with the precise combinations of stimulus and response variables that produce certain effects, whereas applied research might be concerned with the effects, say, of massive doses of positive reward, which for certain groups of school learners might *on the average* produce significantly beneficial effects. The applied researcher would not necessarily worry about why positive reward works, or why it does not always work for all students, whereas the basic research scientist—if he is worth his salt—will push for understanding of the total dynamics of the phenomena he is studying. (As soon as the applied researcher starts worrying about deeper questions, he becomes a basic scientist.)

In its concern for processes on a "molecular" level, basic research relies to a greater extent on models of functional relationship that involve relatively small error components, while applied research tends to use models that are more probabilistic and error-laden. It is not an accident that statistical procedures were first developed in applied fields of research like certain branches of economics, agriculture, and psychological testing, even though these procedures are, of course, extensively used in basic research even in theoretical physics.

Basic research is more often conducted in the laboratory, or in highly controlled situations, in order to observe the effects of particular variables independently of other possibly relevant variables. Applied research tends to be done in situations that are identical to, or closely similar to, those in which one wants to apply the findings. On the other hand, some basic research is done in relatively uncontrolled situations, and some applied research employs rigorous controls. It is not necessary to suppose that research cannot be basic when it is done in live field situations. In fact, in education there are many arguments for doing certain types of research in such situations. But discussion of this point would take us too far afield.

Basic research is more concerned with the development of theory and of all-embracing models for the explanation of phenomena, while applied research either takes for granted previously established theory and extrapolates from it, or avoids theoretical problems altogether. In any case, basic science stands in a relation of logical priority to applied science. Applied science usually relies heavily upon findings in basic science. It is less often the case that basic science takes off from a finding of applied science; in the instance where this occurs, the purpose usually is to explore the deeper rationale of the finding. Although the essential priority of basic science is not as clear-cut in the behavioral and social sciences as it is in the natural sciences, much is to be gained, I think, by following the model of the natural sciences in giving emphasis to basic research at points where applied research cannot make progress alone. [pp. 271–272]

In the past few years, advocates of basic research have become concerned about the trend toward increased Federal funding of educational development and dissemination at the expense of basic research projects. Cronbach has been one of the most vocal critics of this policy, and he has offered a vigorous defense of the value of basic research in education.[32] He points out, for example, that applied research is concerned only with

[32] L. J. Cronbach, "The Role of the University in Improving Education," *Phi Delta Kappan,* 47 (1966), 539–545.

the assessment of gross effects, for example, is this educational product or procedure better than another educational product or procedure? Cronbach argues that it is necessary to do basic research in order to determine *why* one product or procedure was found to be more effective than the other. Out of such basic research may come new explanatory principles that can be used to develop better educational products or procedures. Cronbach also argues persuasively that the basic researcher must be supported in his work, for he is "the eternal skeptic, the one who finds the slogan of the day a hypothesis rather than a creed." [33] He points out that much applied research and development in education is not objective. The applied researcher and developer may be emotionally committed to find evidence that supports his product or procedure, and will avoid doing research that might yield negative findings. Many innovations in education, unfortunately, have been based on the flimsiest of evidence; they are well promoted, become fads, and then drop out of sight when it becomes apparent that they are no more effective than the procedures they replaced. The basic researcher's orientation toward understanding, rather than practical applications, serves as a healthy corrective to this unfortunate trend in education.

In response to Cronbach's paper on basic research in education, Ebel wrote an article that severely criticized the past results of such research and its future value in helping to solve educational problems.[34] Since Ebel's views are shared by many educators and lay persons, the merit of his arguments is worth considering. First Ebel argues that the record of past performance by basic researchers is "very poor." This is clearly not true. As we discussed earlier, the great advances made recently in individualizing instruction are the direct outgrowth of basic research in programmed instruction and principles of learning. Ebel does admit that there have been many significant research studies in education, but he declines to characterize these studies as basic research. This is a debatable point. Later in his paper Ebel states:

> But knowledge is necessary. Seldom do we have as much knowledge as we need to decide wisely the questions before us. Research can give us this knowledge, but it is the kind of research that educational scientists tend to disdain as mere data gathering. For example, should we launch an extensive program to improve the self-concepts of slum children? No doubt we should if slum children don't learn mainly because they think they can't learn. But is it true that they have poor self-concepts? Is it true that they tend to blame themselves, not society, for their difficulties? Is it true that many of them think of themselves as lacking in ability

[33] *Ibid.*, p. 541.
[34] R. L. Ebel, "Some Limitations of Basic Research in Education," *Phi Delta Kappan*, 49 (1967), 81–84. Reprinted by permission.

to learn? To find the answers to these questions would involve data gathering, not basic research. But it could contribute substantially to the wisdom of our decision on a serious problem. [p. 83]

It is our opinion that Ebel makes a false distinction between "data gathering" and "basic research." The questions that he raises about the self-concepts of slum children are basic research questions, since they are concerned with increasing our *understanding* of an important educational phenomenon.

Another argument raised by Ebel against the value of basic research in education is that the variables which are studied are "so global and encompass such a diversity of specifics as to defy precise definition and exact quantification" [p. 82]. It seems to us that the very complexity of education is all the more reason to support programs of basic research. We know, for example, that all students do not learn at the same rate and with equal effectiveness. We also strongly suspect that the factors underlying learning are complex. But is this any reason to throw up our arms in despair and to state that we should not attempt to understand learning better in order to improve it? A more positive course of action, it seems, would be to acknowledge the complexity of the problem, to tackle small parts of it at a time, and to reconcile oneself to the fact that the fruits of basic research in education will not come overnight.

Ebel also questions the possible contribution that basic research may make in answering the two key questions of education: What shall we try to teach children? How shall we go about getting them to learn it? He contends that the techniques of basic research can only be used to study natural phenomena, not man-made phenomena, such as education, which deal with purposes and values. However, in our opinion this is an untenable position. Basic research is very relevant to questions concerning values and objectives in education. Suppose there were a general consensus among educators that reading *should* begin at age three. Further suppose that through basic research it was found that most children are not ready to begin reading at this age because of physiological and emotional immaturity. This finding should change the opinion of educators regarding the desirability of beginning reading at this age. It is quite clear in this example that basic research can and should have a direct effect in changing the values that educators hold about the proper way to run our educational system.

Ebel does make one statement about basic research that we believe has some merit:

Of course we can, if we wish, do what appears to be basic research on anything, from the distribution of word lengths in Robert Frost's poems to the symbolism in a particular kindergartener's finger painting. But how basic is it, and to what? Basic research is no more free than any other human activity from the necessity of being worthwhile. [p. 83]

Basic researchers do have a responsibility to the larger society which supports their work. If it is true that basic research can be done on virtually any phenomenon, then basic researchers cannot avoid taking a value position in deciding to choose to study one problem rather than another. Although we believe that researchers need freedom to follow their own interests, we are also hopeful that at least a substantial proportion of them will attempt to investigate problems that are relevant to those that currently beset education.

The student who decides to undertake a career in educational research will be confronted by many individuals who will question the value of his work—whether it be basic or applied research. The student is advised to think carefully about the issues we have just considered so that he can respond knowledgeably to criticisms of educational research.

Research and development

One of the most promising changes that has occurred in education is the emergence of significant programs of educational research and development (R & D). Educational R & D programs differ from most basic and applied research projects in four respects. First, the objective of basic and applied research is the search for new knowledge. The outcome of this search is usually a report that appears in a scholarly journal. However, the objective of educational R & D is a finished product that can be used effectively in the schools. The product is typically in the form of textbooks, audio-visual materials, training manuals, and possibly equipment of some sort. (The "product" may also be more encompassing, such as a total system of early childhood education.) Second, basic and applied research are usually small-scale enterprises. The research project is carried out by a single educational researcher with perhaps a few research assistants and consultants. By contrast, relatively large teams of researchers are needed to carry out the objectives of a single R & D program. For example, the authors are working with a team of about 50 other researchers and research assistants on an R & D program in teacher training. Third, basic and applied research projects generally do not last more than a half year or so. However, an educational R & D program will generally extend over a period of years before its objectives are accomplished.

The fourth, and perhaps most critical, difference between basic and applied research and educational R & D is the sequence that is followed. In basic and applied research, the researcher typically begins by developing a hypothesis or problem to be studied. Then the researcher selects a sample of subjects and collects relevant data. These data are analyzed by statistical tools, and subsequently conclusions are reached about the hypothesis or research problem. In educational R & D a quite different sequence is followed. The formulation of this sequence is itself considered a major contribution to the field of educational research. The typical steps in the sequence are:

1. Develop a set of specific behavioral objectives that the eventual product should achieve. For example, if the product is a new curriculum, the researcher should be able to state what knowledge, skills, and attitudes the student will acquire as a result of following the curriculum.
2. Conduct research or review previous research to discover the deficiencies of current products and to identify approaches that are likely to overcome these deficiencies.
3. Develop a new product to the point where one may reasonably expect that it will accomplish its objectives.
4. Test this product in the setting where it will eventually be used and evaluate its effectiveness in meeting its objectives in this setting.
5. Revise the product on the basis of the field-test results.
6. Repeat steps 4 and 5 until the product's objectives have been achieved or until it has been established that the approach being used will not achieve them.
7. If it is successful, put the product into operational use. This often requires further development and testing of a program to train school personnel in the use of the product.

Educational R & D is a very demanding, expensive, and time-consuming strategy for educational improvement through research. However, it is also a very powerful strategy. Educational R & D effectively bridges the gap that has long existed between research and classroom practice. Furthermore, because of its emphasis upon scientific evaluation, the R & D approach provides schools with products of demonstrated effectiveness. All too often products have been adopted in school systems simply because of testimonials or faddism.

The development of a variety of completely new curricula in mathematics and the sciences was among the first educational R & D efforts. Many of these programs were developed by mathematicians and physical scientists rather than professional educators. Among the "new math" and "new science" programs that have gained wide acceptance in the public schools, the Physical Science Study Committee (PSSC) curriculum in physics was the first large-scale effort. The Physical Science Study Committee was made up of a group of physicists initially based at the Massachusetts Institute of Technology. This group developed curricular materials that included a textbook, films, laboratory guides, examinations, and other materials needed to implement a modern course in physics. The program was tested and revised yearly during the period of development, and it required a total investment of approximately $5 million.[35] The Greater Cleveland Mathematics Program, described earlier, was another program developed through the R & D approach.

Developing and testing a new educational program to the point where it is ready for operational use in the schools is a very difficult and costly process. Up until 1965 there were few opportunities to conduct major R & D programs except for the curriculum development projects in mathematics and science just mentioned, which were supported primarily by grants from the National Science Foundation. However, the Elementary and Secondary Education Act of 1965 provided for the establishment of regional educational laboratories and university-affiliated research and development centers. It was hoped that such new organizations could carry out significant R & D programs that have generally been beyond the capacity of all but a few of the R & D facilities that existed before 1965. At this writing it is too early to appraise the full impact of these new organizations. However, some of the regional laboratories and R & D centers have already progressed sufficiently to indicate that they will make significant contributions to education over the next five years. One of the most promising programs to come out of these laboratories and centers is Individually Prescribed Instruction, described earlier.

Although significant R & D efforts are far beyond the capabilities of a single graduate student, there are opportunities for students to make useful contributions to these efforts. All R & D centers and many regional laboratories offer research internships and assistantships for students working on graduate degrees.

Action research

Action research involves the application of the steps of the scientific method to classroom problems. Although it is similar in some respects to applied research, action research differs from applied research principally in the extent to which findings can be generalized beyond a local school situation. Applied research usually involves a large number of cases in order to cancel out some of the random errors that occur in small samples; it involves establishing as much control as possible, consistent with the research goals, over such variables as teaching ability and, perhaps most important, involves more precise sampling techniques than are found in action research. Many action research projects are carried out in a single classroom by a single teacher, while others are carried on by all teachers in a school or even a school district. As action research proj-

[35] The Panel on Educational Research and Development, *Innovation and Experiment in Education* (Washington, D.C.: U.S. Government Printing Office, 1964).

ects become more extensive, they become more similar to applied research. The emphasis in action research, however, is not on obtaining generalizable scientific knowledge about educational problems, but on obtaining specific knowledge concerning the subjects involved in the study. The results of an action research project by a single teacher have important implications for this teacher, but because of the few cases, lack of control and absence of sampling techniques are not generalizable to other similar classrooms. The principal advantage of action research is that it provides the teacher or administrator in the field with objective, systematic techniques of problem solving that are far superior to an appeal to authority or reliance on personal experience, which so often guides decisions in education.

Research designs in educational research

So far we have distinguished four types of educational research: basic research, applied research, research and development, and action research. Educational research studies can also be classified in terms of the research designs they use. The four research designs commonly distinguished are the descriptive method, the causal-comparative method, the correlational method, and the experimental method. These designs will be discussed extensively in a later section of this book.

To give a brief idea of how these research designs differ from one another, suppose that a researcher was interested in the relationship between individual tutoring in reading and student achievement. The researcher could take a number of approaches to study this problem. He might make a survey of teachers to determine how much individual tutoring in reading they do and to determine how useful they believe this technique to be. This is essentially *descriptive* research since the objective is to describe rather than to explain a phenomenon. If he were to use a *causal-comparative* design, the researcher might select a group of teachers who frequently tutor in reading and another group of teachers who rarely tutor in reading. Then the students of these two groups of teachers would be compared to determine whether they differ in their reading achievement. However, the weakness of the causal-comparative method is that it is not really adequate for establishing causal relationships.[36]

The students of teachers who use tutoring may have higher achievement, but this difference could be due to factors other than tutoring. For example, the teachers who do tutoring may also spend more time in reading instruction than the teachers who do not make use of tutoring. It may be the difference in emphasis on reading instruction rather than tutoring per se that accounts for the differences in reading achievement.

[36] The correlational method is similar to the causal-comparative method and has the same limitation regarding inference of causal relationship.

In order to infer causality, it is necessary to use the *experimental* method. This method involves manipulation of one variable and observation of its effect on another variable. For example, the researcher might ask teachers to provide extensive tutoring in reading for one group of students but not to tutor another comparable group of students. If tutoring has an effect on reading achievement, then over time the tutored students should exceed the nontutored students on a measure of this variable. The experimental method is considered the most powerful research design since it alone can be used to establish causal relationships between phenomena with a high degree of certainty.

ANNOTATED REFERENCES

1. American Educational Research Association. "Twenty-Five Years of Educational Research," *Review of Educational Research*, 26, no. 3 (1956). This entire issue of the *Review* is devoted to tracing some of the major trends in educational research between 1931 and 1956. Many significant developments occurring during that period are briefly discussed, and an assessment is made of gains we have made in present knowledge concerning many basic questions in education in such areas as school administration, curriculum research, educational psychology, educational measurement, counseling and adjustment, history and philosophy of education, and research methods. Reading this issue will give the student a brief and useful orientation to the field of educational research.

2. Banghart, Frank W. (ed.). *First Annual Phi Delta Kappa Symposium on Educational Research*. Bloomington, Ind.: Phi Delta Kappa, 1960. This symposium, involving several eminent educational researchers, provides the student with further background in educational research. Among the topics discussed are included: A Survey of Educational Research at Selected Universities, Contributions of the Federal Government to Educational Research Methodology, The Impact of Applied Problems on Educational Research, the Contributions of the Behavioral Sciences to Educational Research, and Philosophy of Educational Research.

3. Behavioral Sciences Subpanel of the President's Science Advisory Committee. "Strengthening the Behavioral Sciences," *Science*, 136 (1962), 233–241. This is a report of the Behavioral Sciences Subpanel of the President's Science Advisory Committee. It contains a number of penetrating observations concerning the development of the behavioral sciences and their present state and probable future role in our society. It discusses some of the difficulties in these sciences in the past and makes a number of recommendations aimed at meeting the requirements for the continuing development of scientific study of human behavior. This article is of importance, not only because it expresses the views of one of the most influential scientific groups in the Federal government, but also because it contains a number of important ideas and insights pertaining to behavioral objectives.

4. Borg, Walter; Kelley, Marjorie; Langer, Philip; and Gall, Meredith. *The Minicourse: A Microteaching Approach to Teacher Education*. Beverly Hills, Calif.:

Macmillan Educational Services, 1970. This book presents the results of a large-scale R & D program in the area of inservice teacher training. The authors provide several examples of each phase of the research and development cycle, and they discuss the implications of R & D for improvement of the educational system.

5. Carroll, J. B. "Basic and Applied Research in Education: Definitions, Distinctions, and Implications," *Harvard Educational Review*, 38 (1968), 263–276. The author presents a good defense of the value of basic research in education. He also presents a review of the distinctions that have been made between basic and applied research.

6. *Educational Technology*. Saddle Brook, N.J.: Educational News Service, 1961 to date. This journal publishes regular articles on educational research and development. It is also recommended for its coverage of new developments in programmed instruction, use of computers in education, and audio-visual techniques.

7. Silberman, H. F., and others. "Effect of Educational Research on Classroom Instruction: A Discussion," *Harvard Educational Review*, 36 (1966), 295–317. In this article several distinguished researchers in education discuss several charges that are often made against the value of educational research. One charge is that educational research has not made a contribution to instructional practice because researchers typically produce articles in journals rather than usable instructional products. Another charge is that researchers participate in the training of teachers who simply accept prevailing practices rather than teachers who are willing to experiment and evaluate.

8. U. S. Office of Education. "Ten Research Lessons That Are Shaking Educational Programs," *Nations Schools*, 81 (1968), 55–64. This article presents ten recent research studies that were selected by USOE officials because of their high quality and relevance to the education of disadvantaged children. These studies are concerned with such variables as teachers' expectations, busing of students, class size, and guidance counseling, and their effect on student achievement.

CHAPTER 2

The Research Problem, Research Plan, and Pilot Study

SELECTING A RESEARCH PROBLEM

Introduction

The selection of a research problem for the Master's thesis is a very important step for the graduate student. Often, in his eagerness to get started on his research work, the student seizes upon the first research idea that comes along. If he commits himself to a research problem before giving his choice much careful study and thought, the student is likely to lose many of the important advantages that he can receive from carrying out his research. The very process of seeking a research problem is an important step in the professional maturation of the student. At the outset of his search, the student usually sees no problems, or from his first explorations into the research literature concludes that research has already solved all the problems in education. His first ideas for research are often naïve and, upon checking, he finds that they have already been thoroughly explored. As the student continues his search, however, his insight into the literature becomes sufficiently broad so that he can see research problems in everything he reads. This point is not reached without a considerable amount of scholarly work in the research literature, but once achieved, the student has made a significant step in his education.

One reason that students seize upon the first idea they encounter is that very often they go too far in their graduate program before starting to search for a suitable research problem. The student has had years of experience in taking courses and thus the classwork involved in his graduate program is a familiar experience and one that he is reasonably confident he can complete successfully. In contrast, the research aspect of his graduate program is new and different and something that he is strongly tempted to put off. Every university has a lengthy list of "allbuts" among its graduate students—those who have completed *all* work for an advanced degree *but* the thesis or dissertation. A great many such students never obtain their advanced degrees. It is usually desirable for the graduate student to obtain some insight into research and to commence his search for a suitable problem as soon as possible after entering graduate work, even if he does not plan to carry out his project until he nears the end of his work.

In looking for a research problem, the student should bear in mind some of the possible outcomes of his research effort in preparing him for his profession. The review of the literature provides the student with an understanding of the work that has already taken place relating to his problem area and prepares him to carry out a project that will add to the facts and information that have been accumulated by previous research workers. Because of the extensive reading he must do in his problem area, the student will usually build up a sizable fund of knowledge. Thus, in order that this knowledge may be of significant future value, the student should attempt to develop a research problem in an area that is closely related to his professional goals. For example, a student who plans to teach elementary school will profit much more from a research project in some area such as child development or the learning of elementary school subjects than in an area involving secondary education, adolescent development, or school administration.

Another reason for the selection of a topic closely allied to the student's interest is that the research project gives him an opportunity to do significant independent work in his problem area that will better prepare him for his professional work and will incidentally make him a more desirable prospect for employment. Although most of them do not produce research findings of major significance, many Master's theses do produce worthwhile information that makes a small but definite contribution to the field of knowledge. Because there are many significant problems in education for which we require further knowledge, the student should resist the temptation to do research that is essentially trivial or that can contribute nothing to educational knowledge. Students often rationalize carrying out a trivial study by saying that the real purpose of the Master's thesis is to provide practice in independent work, and the results cannot be expected to be of any scientific value. Generally, once a significant project has been identified, it requires no more time and effort to carry out than a trivial project or one that repeats work that has already been adequately done. The difference between the trivial project and the significant project is not the amount of work required to carry it out, but the amount of thought that the student applies in the selection and definition of his problem.

Another factor that should be considered by the student in selecting his problem is that he will not only gain valuable knowledge and experience in the problem area he selects, but if he carries out a worthwhile piece of research, it will be possible for him to publish the results in a professional journal. If a student publishes an article based on his thesis, this publication adds significantly to his professional status.

In defining a research problem, the student should not hesitate to entertain ideas and approaches that represent a departure from conventional educational practice. Researchers often overlook or reject promising ideas because they are strange or conflict with some of the individual's biases. Skinner provides us with an excellent example of the degree to which narrow thinking can stifle unusual ideas. During World War II, Skinner worked with a group of psychologists on a project aimed at conditioning pigeons to operate a guidance system for missiles.[1] The pigeons were conditioned to peck at a particular type of target that they viewed on a screen, such as a ship or length of coastline. If the target was not at the center of the screen, the pigeons' pecking provided a guiding signal to change the course of the missile. The device was developed to a high level of efficiency and became nearly foolproof even under unfavorable conditions. It required no materials in short supply, and once the pigeons had been conditioned the behavior persisted for long periods without reinforcement. In several demonstrations before scientific committees the conditioned pigeons performed perfectly, yet the project was abandoned because it was impossible to convince the dozen or so distinguished physical scientists on the evaluation committee that the behavior of a pigeon could be adequately controlled. To these men, who were accustomed to thinking in terms of servomotors, rheostats, and electrical circuits, the idea of using a live organism to carry out the task of missile guidance was too fantastic to be taken seriously, even when they were confronted with evidence that the pigeons could do the assigned task. Although none of us can be completely freed from the shackles of our environment, preconceptions, and prejudices, the researcher seeking a research problem should remain aware of the existence of these impediments and should make a conscious effort to avoid their influence. As Skinner points out, "One virtue in crackpot ideas is that they breed rapidly and their progeny show extraordinary mutations." Thus even the wildest idea can, if pursued, lead eventually to a unique and often practical approach to a scientific problem.

The first step

The first step in locating a specific problem for the Master's thesis is for the student to identify the broad problem areas that are most closely related to his interests and professional goals. The student will find it a profitable experience to write down in as much detail as possible the type of work he wishes to do upon completion of his graduate training and the specific aspects of this work that most interest him. The process of writing

[1] B. F. Skinner, "Pigeons in a Pelican," *American Psychologist,* 15 (1960), 28–37

down this information will help the student clarify his goals and interests. Very often he will find that these goals are somewhat less clear in his own mind than he may have supposed. Typical broad areas of interest that might be listed are high school counseling, teaching art to children in the primary grades, social problems of adolescents, remedial reading in the elementary school, relationships between teachers and principals, and intramural programs in physical education.

After one or more such areas of professional interest have been identified, the student is ready to seek out specific problems in these areas that could form the basis for his thesis.

Working on a team project

Twenty years ago there was almost no money available for the support of educational research. Most research projects were small-scale studies carried out by university faculty members, and in many instances the faculty member himself did all the research including such tasks as administering and scoring tests used in the project. Since that time, however, money available for educational research has increased tremendously. Now most universities are receiving financial support for educational research in the form of contracts and grants from federal agencies and private foundations, and the projects being carried out are much wider in scope and often involve a team of research workers rather than a single scientist. The graduate student often has an opportunity to participate in one of these extensive research projects as a member of a team. As a rule such projects are developed by faculty members, and portions of the project are given to graduate students to complete. Completion of the allotted portion of the project then constitutes the research for the Master's thesis or doctoral dissertation.

Working on team projects has both advantages and disadvantages for the graduate student. Perhaps the most important advantage for most students is that financial support is usually available for the student working on such a project. This support may cover as little as paying for test administration or providing the graduate student with needed materials or clerical assistance, but in many cases also involves a scholarship or research assistantship that is sufficient to meet the student's expenses while he is completing his graduate work. The team project also offers the graduate student an opportunity to participate in a bigger and more sophisticated study than would be the case if he were working independently. These studies usually involve more complex research designs and more advanced statistical procedures, and the student thus learns more about these procedures than he would otherwise. The student also has a chance to learn something about the workings of team research, and because most major projects are now carried out by research teams, this insight will be valuable in his future work. He also can learn a great deal from other members of the research team. Each team member in the project brings a different background of training and experience to bear upon the research problem, and therefore the team can usually produce a more polished research effort than is the case with a single investigator.

Participation in a team research project also has disadvantages for the graduate student. Perhaps the most important of these is that he loses the opportunity to find and develop his own project. In team research, the project is usually created and designed by the faculty member who is directing it. At worst the graduate student involved in a team project is little more than a clerk who carries out various tasks involved in the research without fully understanding what he is doing or why he is doing it. Even in team projects where he does significant independent work—and this is usually the case—the student does not get firsthand experience in all aspects of developing and carrying out a research plan. Another disadvantage of taking part in a team project is that very often the problem being studied is not closely allied with the student's interest nor does it contribute as directly to his future professional work as would be the case if he designed and carried out an independent project.

Whether the student carries out a small independent project or participates in a larger team project, the experience he gains through independent scholarship and research is perhaps the most important aspect of his graduate program. A significant piece of work done at this level can add materially to the student's professional maturity, improve his employment opportunities, and start him on the path to recognition and high professional status.

A reading program

Perhaps the most satisfactory method of locating specific problems within the scope of the student's broad interests is through a systematic program of reading. Let us say, for example, that the student plans to teach in the elementary schools and is particularly interested in problems related to working with bright children at the elementary school level. His first step would be to check the library card catalog in order to locate current textbooks in this field. If he has selected a field in which no complete textbooks have been written, he can usually find chapters dealing with his interest area in some of the introductory textbooks used in general courses in education and psychology. He should select two or three textbooks from those available and review pertinent chapters in each. This gives the student some background of basic information about his area of interest and also gives him insight into various subtopics in the field, a knowledge of current practices, and a brief summary of recent research. This preliminary reading will help the student narrow his attention to one or more specific subtopics. For example, the student whose broad interest is in working with bright children in the elementary school may decide to develop a research problem dealing with the creative abilities of bright children or perhaps to study the social development of bright children in the primary grades. These topics are, of course, still much too broad for a specific research plan, but this narrowing permits the student to explore the selected areas in somewhat greater depth by reading additional material that deals specifically with the more narrow subject. He will also obtain valuable information by checking these topics in such sources as the *Encyclopedia of Educational Research,* the *Review of Educational Research,* and the *Handbook of Research on Teaching.*[2]

This additional reading will usually result in the student identifying a number of tentative research problems that are sufficiently limited and specific to form a possible basis for his research. In the example given, the student interested in studying the social development of bright children in the elementary schools might develop specific research topics such as the following: (1) relationships between intelligence and sociometric choice among sixth-grade children, (2) development of interest in the opposite sex in elementary school children between grades four and six, (3) social activities of bright children as compared with those of average children in ten fifth-grade classrooms, and (4) social adjustment problems of extremely bright children in the intermediate grades.

Research based on theory

Perhaps the approach most likely to produce an outstanding dissertation is for the student to formulate a research problem that will test a theory related to his area of interest.

In simple terms a theory is an explanation of behavioral or physical events. The more "powerful" a theory is, the more events can be explained by it. Psychoanalytic theory is considered by some researchers to be powerful because it provides an explanation for a vast range of behavior from infancy to old age, from the behavior of normal persons through the continuum of mental illnesses. Theories consist of generalizations (in the physical sciences, usually called laws) and constructs. A generalization is a statement of a relationship between two or more events; generalizations can be used to predict events. For example, the statement that individual tutoring results in increased school achievement is a generalization. Assuming it is true, we can predict that a particular student, given tutoring, will show a gain in achievement. A construct is a type of concept used in scientific research to describe events that share similar elements. Motivation, achievement, learning, ability, intelligence, and value are all exam-

[2] Bibliographic information for these references can be found in the annotated references or Chapter 3.

ples of constructs. Constructs are usually defined in operational terms, that is, in terms of the "operations" needed to measure them. For example, the construct "intelligence" is usually defined in terms of scores derived from administration of an intelligence test. Motivation may be defined in terms of changes in subjects' performance after they receive "motivating" instructions. These operational measures of constructs are usually called variables since values or numerals can be assigned to them. Theoretical research usually consists of testing a hypothesis (a speculation about the relationship between two or more variables) that is derived from a theory.

Many areas of education have virtually no theoretical foundation. In areas, however, where the problems of education cut across other behavioral sciences, such as psychology or sociology, an increasing amount of pertinent theoretical work can be found. Some of these areas of overlapping concern are learning, motivation, language development, contingency management, attitude development, and social class. A good example of an educational research problem derived from theory in another behavioral science, psychology, is provided by a recent study of the relationship between anxiety and learning.[3] O'Neill and his colleagues tested a hypothesis derived from a theory formulated by K. W. Spence,[4] a psychologist, relating anxiety (conceptualized as a motivational drive) to learning. This theory includes the generalization, simply stated,[5] that the performance of subjects with high anxiety will be inferior to that of subjects with low anxiety on complex learning tasks. Spence's theory relating anxiety to learning has been tested and confirmed in the psychological laboratory using such tasks as eyelid conditioning, serial learning, and paired-associate learning. The tasks used by O'Neill et al. were drawn from a natural educational situation involving computer-assisted instruction (CAI). College students were asked to work on an easy and a difficult CAI learning task. As predicted, students with high anxiety level did worse than low-anxious students on difficult problems; on easy problems, however, the former group outperformed the latter. Thus, the results confirm Spence's theory.

Several advantages of theory based research can be seen from the preceding example. First, the theory enabled O'Neill and his colleagues to make a prediction about the relationship between three constructs: anx-

[3] Harold F. O'Neill, Jr., Charles D. Spielberger, and Duncan N. Hansen, "Effects of State Anxiety and Task Difficulty on Computer-Assisted Learning," *Journal of Educational Psychology,* 60 (1969), 351–354.
[4] K. W. Spence, "A Theory of Emotionally Based Drive (D) and Its Relation to Performance in Simple Learning Situations," *American Psychologist,* 13 (1958), 131–141.
[5] In the complete statement of the theory, task complexity is defined in terms of strength of competing response tendencies.

iety, learning, and task difficulty. Without the guidance provided by Spence's theory, it might not even have occurred to the researchers to explore the interrelationships of these three constructs. Second, the theory provided a rational explanation of the results. Of course, if the theoretical hypothesis were not confirmed by the experiment, then the theory might require revision and further empirical testing. Still another advantage of good theories is that they enable the researcher to make predictions about a wide range of situations. Considering Spence's drive theory, the student might do a research project testing the theory in other educational contexts. For example, one might hypothesize that high-anxious students would do better than low-anxious students on easy examinations (e.g., multiple-choice tests emphasizing simple fact recall), but that they would do worse on difficult examinations (e.g., essay tests requiring organization of many ideas).

In summary, a valuable technique for defining a research problem is to derive a hypothesis from a theory in one of the behavioral sciences and then to test the hypothesis in a relevant educational context.

Other methods of identifying research problems

If the student still has not located a problem after using the approaches just presented, a number of other approaches may be tried. One of these is to observe carefully the existing practices in his area of interest. For example, a student interested in human relations problems in the public schools may observe faculty meetings, committee activities, and other situations where such problems may arise. These observations will often provide the student with ideas and insights that can lead to a worthwhile research project. The student may observe that in faculty meetings some principals are much more effective than others in enlisting cooperation and developing enthusiasm among teachers. This observation might lead the student to a comparison of the methods of principals who are successful with those who are unsuccessful in obtaining teacher cooperation.

Another valuable source of research ideas is found in the advanced courses that the student takes in his graduate program. In class discussions as well as textbooks, questions are often brought up for which we have no answers. Some textbooks even go so far as to list problems that require additional research. The brief reviews of research in specific educational fields that are published in *The Review of Educational Research* almost always list specific areas in which further study is needed.

The student should not hesitate to consult with professors at his college or researchers at other institutions who are working in areas related to his interests. Because they may have carried out research on a particular problem over a period of years, these people are likely to have developed a sensitivity to important unsolved problems in their field. For

example, the authors have worked over the last several years on the
development of training programs to improve the classroom skills of
inservice teachers. As a result of this experience, we have identified a
number of research problems concerning the teacher's role in the classroom. Little is known, for example, about the effect of many teacher behaviors on student performance. Does the teacher's use of higher cognitive questions in classroom discussions relate to student behavior and
achievement? What is the effect of individual or small-group tutoring
on student achievement? Also, little is known concerning the frequency
with which certain teacher behaviors occur in the classroom, for example, how frequently teachers use tutoring, role playing, or discussion of
controversial issues, and at what grade levels these techniques are most
used. Another type of research problem concerns identification of variables affecting development of teaching skills. We know, for example, that
the use of models facilitates skill development. However, certain variables,
such as sex and status of the model, may enhance or lessen the effectiveness of modeling. By consulting with researchers in his own area of interest, the student may be able to identify problems of similar importance
to the advancement of a particular field of study.

The graduate student in education has the advantage of working in
an area where he has gained much experience during his years as a student. Very often the graduate student can recall problems that he encountered in his own educational experience and from one of these problems
develop a worthwhile research plan. The newspapers and popular magazines are sometimes valuable sources of research ideas. These periodicals
often report at length on educational problems that are currently considered of major importance and usually report the opinions of educators
and other persons in public life concerning these problems. These reports
usually contain assertions, suggestions, and criticisms, the merits of which
can be checked by research. For example, public debate in recent years
concerning the need for changes in the methods of teaching reading has
stimulated many research projects aimed at trying and evaluating some
of the ideas and proposals that have been put forth.

A final source of research ideas is replication of previous work. The
student may sometimes make a valuable research contribution through
repeating a significant research project that someone else has carried out.
The student must be very cautious about selecting a project for replication, however, if he decides upon this approach. In considering replication
of a research project, he should ask the following three questions before
going ahead with his work:

1. Does the project to be repeated make a significant contribution?
2. Will replication clear up doubtful points in the original study?

3. Are there reasons to doubt the accuracy or validity of the results of the original study?

The usual basis for replication is that the research reports significant findings that are in conflict with the results of previous work or theory. In such a case, repeating the project can be extremely valuable. Some persons concerned with graduate education advocate wide use of replications for Master's theses on the grounds that repeating a good study is a better experience for the student than carrying out an original study of poor quality.[6] As replications follow very closely (if not exactly) the procedures of the original study in order that findings between the studies may be directly compared, the graduate student doing a replication has little opportunity for original work. If he is fortunate enough to have a faculty advisor who requires him to think through the procedures of the original study independently and critically, this deficiency is partially overcome. Alas, few advisors can afford to devote enough time to the student to make the replication a creative experience. Thus, in doing a replication, the student loses much of the valuable experience and insight that can be gained only by discovering, planning, and carrying out his own project.

OUTLINING A RESEARCH PLAN

Purpose of the research plan

After having identified a specific project that appears to be satisfactory, the student should outline a research plan in as much detail as possible. The project is still tentative at this point because the student's review of the literature has yet to be carried out, and this review almost always leads to some changes in the research plan. The tentative outline, however, can do much to clarify the student's thinking and will also give focus and direction to his review of the literature. The tentative research plan should contain the following sections: general introduction, statement of objectives or hypotheses, listing of possible tests or measures to be used in the study, description of the proposed sample, procedure to be used in carrying out the project, and plans for carrying out analysis of data to be collected.

The main advantage of a research plan is that it compels one to state all one's ideas in written form so that they can be evaluated and improved upon by others. Even a simple research project contains many elements, and it is easy to overlook some of them unless they are all written down

[6] E. Gloye, E. Craig, and F. Carp, "On Replication," *Psychological Reports*, 3 (1957), 299.

in a systematic manner. The authors recall an instance in which a written plan helped to stop a student from making a serious error in his research project. In discussing the proposed project with the student, we found the research design satisfactory. However, when the research plan was read later, it was discovered that the student planned to have teachers try a new teaching technique with unfamiliar pupils rather than with pupils from their own classes. This procedure would confound the effect of the new teaching technique with the effect of working with unfamiliar pupils. Subsequently the student was advised to change his research design to avoid this error.

Another advantage of a detailed research plan in written form is that it can be easily submitted to several professors and consultants for their comments and suggestions. Furthermore, the final plan can be used as a guide for conducting the research project, otherwise the student will need to rely on memory and may forget important details of the project in carrying it out.

The elements of a research plan are discussed in the next sections. They include general introduction and literature review, hypotheses or objectives, measures, subjects, design, and data analysis.

General introduction to the research plan

The research plan should identify the student's area of interest and describe how the planned research project will contribute to existing knowledge in this area. The student will need, therefore, to provide a brief literature review of research findings and opinion relevant to the student's problem. Previous research studies need not be discussed in detail, but enough information should be given so that the reader can judge whether the proposed research project is likely to make a contribution to existing knowledge.

Stating a research hypothesis or objective

Hypotheses reflect the research worker's guess as to the probable outcomes of his experiment. The principal advantage of a well-thought-out set of hypotheses is that it places clear and specific goals before the research worker and provides him with a basis for selecting samples and research procedures to meet these goals. Many studies carried out in education fail to provide usable knowledge largely because of the lack of specific and well-thought-out hypotheses.

Hypotheses can be stated in a number of different forms. The declarative form usually states a relationship between the variables that the experimenter expects will emerge. For example, the following hypothesis is stated in declarative form: "There will be a significant difference between the scores on a measure of inferiority feelings of low ability pupils in ability-grouped classroom as compared with low ability pupils in random-grouped classrooms." Another form in which hypotheses may be stated is the null form. A null hypothesis states that no relationship exists between the variables concerned. For example, in null form, the aforementioned hypothesis could be stated "There will be no significant difference between the scores on a measure of inferiority feelings of low ability pupils in ability-grouped classrooms and low ability pupils in random-grouped classrooms." The null hypothesis does not necessarily reflect the scientist's expectations, but is used principally because it is better fitted to our statistical techniques, many of which are aimed at measuring the likelihood that a difference found is truly greater than zero. Stated another way— the null hypothesis, in the form usually used in education, states that no difference exists, and the statistical tools test this hypothesis by determining the probability that whatever difference is found in the research subjects is a true difference that also is present in the population from which the research samples have been drawn. The student is sometimes confused by the null hypothesis because it appears to him senseless to hypothesize the exact opposite of his expectations. This is a disadvantage of the null form, because the researcher's expectations, based as they are upon considerable insight into other research and theory, often make the study clearer to the person reading the research report. Some researchers overcome this problem by using both a research hypothesis that reflects their expectations based on theory or previous research and a statistical hypothesis that is usually in the null form and is set up to make evaluations of the research hypothesis statistically more precise.[7]

Hypotheses may also be stated in question form. The aforementioned hypothesis in question form might read "Is there a significant difference between the scores on a measure of inferiority feelings of a group of low ability pupils in ability-grouped classrooms as compared with low ability pupils in random-grouped classrooms?" The question form is often the easiest for the inexperienced research worker to use because it states specifically the question that the research will attempt to answer. In writing the research results, the student may organize his report so as to answer the questions posed in the hypotheses.

In cases where the experimenter has strong reasons to expect a difference to occur in a specific direction, he may state the aforementioned hypothesis as follows: "Pupils of low ability in an ability-grouped classroom will receive significantly higher scores on a measure of inferiority feelings than pupils of low ability in a random-grouped classroom." This hypothesis states a specific expected direction for the finding, and should only be used when there is little or no possibility that the findings will yield a difference in the opposite direction. These two different forms of

[7] Quinn McNemar, *Psychological Statistics*, 3rd ed. (New York: Wiley, 1962).

declarative hypotheses call for different statistical treatment, the first requiring what is called the two-tailed test of significance and the second
requiring a one-tailed test. The two-tailed test assumes that the difference
could occur in either direction—that is, either the ability-grouped or
random-grouped children could have significantly greater inferiority
feelings. The one-tailed test on the other hand assumes that, if a difference
occurs, it can occur in only one direction. The student is referred to Chapter 12 for a discussion of one-tailed and two-tailed tests.

In some research carried out in education, especially descriptive studies,
it is appropriate for the research worker to list objectives rather than
hypotheses. A survey, for example, aimed at determining the extent
of differences in the salaries of university professors in different fields of
learning could list a hypothesis such as "There will be no significant differences between the mean salaries of faculty members of comparable
ranks in different areas of learning." In a study of this sort, however, it
is probably more desirable merely to state the objectives of the study as
follows: "The objectives of this research are (1) to study the salaries
paid professors of comparable academic ranks in different fields of learning and (2) if differences are found to exist, to attempt to identify the
factors that appear to contribute to the observed differences."

Criteria of good hypotheses

If hypotheses are to be useful, they must meet the following criteria:
1. The *researcher should have definite reasons based on either theory
or evidence for considering the hypothesis worthy of testing.* After completing the review of the literature, the research worker will have detailed
knowledge of previous work relating to his research project. In many cases
he will find conflicting research results so that his hypothesis cannot agree
with all available information. In general, however, his hypothesis should
not conflict with the preponderance of previously reported information.

In addition to being in agreement with knowledge already established
within the field, hypotheses should be formulated in accordance with
theories in education or psychology. When this is possible, the results of
the research will contribute to the testing of the theory in question. In
many areas of education so little research has been done that reasonably
conclusive information is not available. In this case educational theory
may form the only basis for developing the hypothesis. The student must
always have some basis in theory and/or fact for his hypotheses. Occasionally, we find a study in education that has used the "shotgun approach." In this approach the research worker tries all the measures he
can in the hope that something he tries will yield useful results. This
approach should be avoided because it uses measures for which no hypotheses have been developed. Many dangers are involved in applying

such research results to educational practice. When we do not have some understanding of why a particular relationship exists, there is always a danger that factors are operating that may be detrimental to the educational program.[8]

2. *A hypothesis should be testable.* Hypotheses are generally stated so as to indicate an expected difference or an expected relationship between the measures used in the research. The relationships or differences that are stated in the hypotheses should be such that measurement of the variables involved can be made and necessary statistical comparisons carried out in order to determine whether the hypothesis as stated is or is not supported by the research. The student should not state any hypothesis that he does not have reason to believe can be tested or evaluated by some objective means. For example, the authors recall a hypothesis prepared by a teacher who wished to evaluate a high school course in civics. It was "to determine whether this course will make the student a better adult citizen." Such an objective would be very difficult to test as it would require: (1) waiting until pupils taking the course had become adult citizens, (2) setting up criteria to determine how good a citizen each pupil had become, (3) evaluating each adult in terms of the criteria established, and then, perhaps most difficult of all, (4) determining what aspects of the adult citizenship of the former pupils could be directly attributed to the civics course. It may be seen from this example that such hypotheses are much easier to state than they are to evaluate by objective means. The hypotheses of inexperienced research workers in education often fail to meet the criterion of testability because relationships are stated that cannot be measured using today's tests. A similar mistake often made by the graduate student is to state his hypotheses in terms that would require many years to test.

3. *The hypothesis should be as brief as possible consistent with clarity.* In stating hypotheses the simplest and most concise statement of the relationship expected is generally the best. Brief, clear hypotheses are easier for the reader to understand and also easier for the research worker to test. The hypothesis "Is a student counseling program desirable and economically feasible at the elementary school level?" reflects the sort of fuzzy thinking often found in the work of graduate students in education. A program can be "desirable" or "undesirable" from a very large number of different viewpoints. No specific guides are given by the hypothesis as to what aspect of the guidance program is to be studied. The second part of the hypothesis dealing with the economic feasibility is determined largely by the individual school district's financial resources. In order to make the aforementioned hypothesis meaningful, it would be necessary to determine first the specific aspects of the elementary school counseling

---

[8] A discussion of the "shotgun approach" will be found in Chapter 13.

program that the research worker plans to study. Let us say he wished to provide counseling for three classes of sixth-grade pupils and not provide counseling for three other classes in a large elementary school and then compare his two groups on such variables as the number of behavior problems reported by the classroom teachers, the incidence of truancy, and the pupils' stated attitudes toward school. In this case perhaps three specific hypotheses would be the best approach. Stated in the null form these might be:

1. Sixth-grade pupils receiving counseling will not be significantly different in the number of behavior problems reported by the teacher from sixth-grade pupils not receiving counseling.

2. Sixth-grade pupils receiving counseling will not be significantly different in incidence of truancy from sixth-grade pupils not receiving counseling.

3. Sixth-grade pupils receiving counseling will not be significantly different in their stated attitudes toward school from sixth-grade pupils not receiving counseling.

It will be noted in the aforementioned example that the broad general hypothesis has been changed to three specific hypotheses, each stating a specific relationship between two variables. It is usually desirable for the student to state his hypothesis in this more precise form. The advantage of stating a hypothesis for each relationship to be studied is that this procedure is simple and clear. The testing of multiple hypotheses involving several relationships leads to some confusion because portions of the hypothesis may be supported by the research evidence and other portions may not be supported. In writing the results of the experiment, the graduate student will find it possible to present a more easily understood picture of his findings if each hypothesis has stated only a single relationship.

Possible measures

The next step in preparing the tentative research plan is to make a listing of possible measures. Most graduate students have had courses in educational measurement that give them some background in the types of measures available and sources of information about educational measures. This topic is covered briefly in Chapters 6 and 7. Very often the process of identifying possible measures will require the student to clarify further his objectives and eliminate hypotheses for which no measures are available or can be developed.

Research subjects

The student should then describe the subjects that will be required for his study. At this point he should carefully consider the chance of obtaining the type and number of subjects that he needs. If his study is concerned with a type of individual who occurs only rarely in the general population, he must be particularly careful to determine whether subjects are available to do the work he has planned. For example, studies of highly gifted children, let us say those with IQ's above 160, are difficult to carry out unless the student has a very large population to draw from because children at this IQ level occur very rarely in the general population. The student's method of selecting his sample should also be considered and tentatively decided upon. Careless selection of cases is an error often found in educational studies. Considerations involved in selecting a sample of subjects are discussed in Chapter 5.

Research design

A tentative research design should be described. The student will become familiar with the various types of research designs in Chapters 12 to 16. The student should be sure that the design he plans to use will permit testing his hypotheses. Students often give little thought to the design of their projects until too late.

Data analysis

A tentative plan for analysis of the research results is very important because this plan may have a considerable bearing upon the number of subjects needed, the measures and scoring procedures used, and the methods of recording the data. Yet many students give no thought to analysis until the data are collected. Then they find that no analysis procedures fit their data very well, and often they discover that the only procedures that can be used to salvage the study are complex ones that they must then learn to use.

In no area is lack of foresight so costly and disastrous as in doing research. Careful planning saves time in the long run and results in much better research. It is emphasized that the student should complete his course in research methods prior to starting the work on his research problem, because much of the knowledge he needs to carry out even the first steps in his research problem requires an understanding of the overall field of educational research.

HUMAN RELATIONS IN PLANNING AND CARRYING OUT RESEARCH

Introduction

In most educational research projects, the subjects used by the researcher are human beings. Without a doubt the human subject is the most complex subject used in any field of research. In planning and carrying out a research project, one must never lose sight of the special requirements and problems involved in working with humans. The "human relations" aspect of educational research is particularly important when the research project is carried out in the public schools. For example, when using school children as subjects, it is necessary to obtain the understanding and cooperation of school administrators, teachers, parents, interested community groups, and the subjects themselves. Thus the student's research plan should include a section describing how he intends to gain school cooperation, potential human relations problems that may arise and how he plans to deal with them, and precautions that will be taken to ensure the confidentiality of research data collected from students or teachers. These topics are discussed in the next sections.

Individual privacy and educational research

In recent years the ethical aspects of behavioral research have been of increasing concern to citizens and to the institutions that support this type of research. In part this concern reflects the great growth of behavioral research and its impact on people's lives. Furthermore, although most researchers have acted in an ethical manner, there have been some unfortunate abuses of the individual's right to privacy. In rare cases data have been collected on subjects without their consent, and confidentiality of data has not been preserved. The problem was considered to be of sufficient severity that congressional hearings were held on psychological tests and invasion of privacy in 1965.[9]

The protection of individual privacy in educational research involves two factors: consent of the individual as to what he shall disclose to the researcher and confidential use of research data collected on individuals.

If at all possible, the researcher should obtain the consent of the individual before gathering data on him. In the case of school children, the consent of parents and appropriate school personnel should be obtained. Ideally the student should receive some explanation of the tests and experimental procedures to be used. This explanation must satisfy the student that his participation is important and desirable and that it is to his advantage to cooperate. There are occasions, however, when it would invalidate the research findings to tell the individual beforehand the purpose of the study and the type of information that he will be expected to provide during the course of the research project. For example, in some experiments it may be necessary to give the individual false information in order to experimentally arouse or decrease his motivation. However, in this situation the researcher should still obtain the individual's consent to be in the experiment, and he can tell the individual that he will be informed of the experiment's purpose *after* the study is completed. Also, if

---

[9] These hearings are discussed in American Psychological Association, "Testing and Public Policy," *American Psychologist*, Special Issue, 20 (1965), 857–993.

possible, the researcher should try to obtain data without using the names of the individuals involved.

Once research data have been collected, the researcher should make certain that no one has access to the data except himself and possibly a few co-investigators. (The research subjects, of course, should be told at the outset who will have access to the data.) Whenever possible the names of subjects should be removed from the data-collection instruments and replaced by a code. This procedure is particularly important to follow when the data are to be stored over a relatively long period of time. The researcher should take particular care with data that could conceivably be subpoenaed. Unfortunately educational research data do not have privileged status (as does communication between husband and wife, lawyer and client, etc.) in most states. The confidentiality of the individual must further be protected by not giving individual names in any publications that may result from the research project.

The student can avoid problems relating to invasion of privacy if he includes controls in his research design for individual consent and preservation of confidentiality and if he carries out his project in an ethically responsible manner. In line with these recommendations, Ruebhausen and Brim have developed a code of ethics for behavioral research based on seven principles:

One: There should be a recognition, and an affirmation, of the claim to private personality.

Two: There should be a positive commitment to respect private personality in the conduct of research.

Three: To the fullest extent possible, without prejudicing the validity of the research, the informed, and voluntary, consent of the respondents should be obtained.

Four: If consent is impossible without invalidating the research, then before the research is undertaken, the responsible officials of the institutions financing, administering and sponsoring the research should be satisfied that the social good in the proposed research outweighs the social value of the claim to privacy under the specific conditions of the proposed invasion. These officials in turn are responsible, and must be responsive, to the views of the larger community in which science and research must work.

Five: The identification of the individual respondent should be divorced as fully and as effectively as possible from the data furnished. Anonymity of the respondent to a behavioral research study, so far as possible, should be sought actively in the design and execution of the study as a fundamental characteristic of good research.

Six: The research data should be safeguarded in every feasible and reasonable way, and the identification of individual respondents with any portion of the data should be destroyed as soon as possible, consistent with the research objectives.

Seven: The research data obtained for one purpose should not thereafter be used for another without the consent of the individual involved or a clear and responsible assessment that the public interest in the newly proposed use of the data transcends any inherent privacy transgression. [pp. 1210–1211] [10]

Questions about one's research

There are several rules that the research worker should observe if he plans to select his subjects from the public schools. First he must have a thorough and detailed research design that he can explain in terms that administrators, teachers, and parents can understand. Many school administrators are doubtful of the value of educational research and are likely to be critical in their appraisal of the research design. If the student has failed to think through his design carefully, he may find himself unable to answer the questions put to him by educators, and this failure will almost certainly lead to a decision by school administrators not to participate in the study.

Before approaching parents or school administrators, the student should have thorough and convincing answers to questions that are likely to arise. Questions he must be prepared to answer include: What is the purpose of the study, what does it hope to find out? Are the findings likely to be worthwhile? Is the study important to education? If the student cannot convince school personnel that the work is worthwhile and likely to produce useful results, it is doubtful whether cooperation can be obtained. Schools generally cooperate in research projects because of a feeling of professional responsibility that exists among educators. Research projects almost always cause school personnel a certain amount of inconvenience and extra work, and unless the research worker can convince these persons that the research to be done is worth this extra effort and inconvenience, cooperation will not be obtained.

Another question that school personnel usually bring up in discussing research is: "Will the results of this research apply directly to our school?" In other words the schools are interested in the direct returns that they may obtain from the research project. One of the direct returns, of course, will be that the research data will have greater application to the schools in which the research is done than it will to other schools. To be of significant value, of course, the research must be designed to obtain findings that can be applied beyond the situation in which the work was carried out. If research could only be applied to the isolated situation and to the specific subjects upon which the experiment were carried out, there would be little value in doing such work. However, the fact remains that a research project will be more applicable to the specific situation in which the experiment is carried out than to similar situations in other schools.

[10] O. M. Ruebhausen and O. G. Brim, "Privacy and Behavioral Research," *Columbia Law Review*, 65 (1965), 1184–1211. Reprinted by permission of The *Columbia Law Review*.

Very often the schools are interested in other possible advantages that they may obtain from the research. These advantages differ depending upon the project, but can include such things as test scores that can be used by the school in guidance and in other of its regular activities, new curricular materials, visual aids, and improved administrative procedures. Some studies also involve the use of special measures that the school cannot afford to administer but that can be useful if administered by the research worker. These include such things as individual intelligence tests, individually administered projective measures, and depth interviews. For example, one of the authors recently carried out a research project that included administering the TAT [11] to a sample of low achieving children. Because this measure was given on an individual basis and required a clinical psychologist for administration and scoring, the cost would have been too great for most school districts. This test identified a number of children who appeared to have serious emotional disturbances. Once identified, the school district was able to arrange for help for these children. Any such possibilities of direct advantage to the schools should be pointed out by the research worker, as this is often a major consideration of school administrators in deciding whether to cooperate with the research.

Administrators will wish to know in considerable detail just what the school's role and responsibility will be in the research project. How much time will be required of the subjects? At what part of the school year must this time be scheduled? Will adjustments to the testing schedule be possible if other school activities interfere? Can subjects be tested in their classroom or will it be necessary to take subjects from their classes to another room? Will teachers be required to administer any of the tests or measures? Will it be necessary for the schools to provide pencils, answer sheets, lap boards, or other materials? Such questions should be thought through carefully by the research worker before approaching the school administrator. The price that the school generally must pay to participate in educational research is measured in the aforementioned terms, and the administrator must weigh the possible advantages to his school and to the profession against the losses in time, extra adjustments that must be made, and possible expenses to the school district. At this point the student should be cautioned against making compromises with the administrator that weaken the research design. For example, if a random sampling of subjects within the school is required for a research project and the school administrator suggests that volunteers be taken instead, the research worker should explain in detail the disadvantages of using volunteers and attempt to win the administrator over to paying the additional price in inconvenience that is required to obtain the random sample. If the ad-

[11] *Thematic Apperception Test*—a projective personality measure in which the subject is shown pictures and makes up a story around each picture.

ministrator insists upon changes that seriously weaken the research design, it is wiser for the research worker to attempt to carry out the study elsewhere than to carry it out with disabling restrictions. In general the research worker should follow the rule that *all* concessions should be made that do not seriously weaken the scientific value of the study and *no* concessions should be made that do so compromise the research.

Another question that the administrator often will not mention but that may concern him greatly is "Will the results of this research reflect unfavorably upon my school?" The research worker should bring this question up and discuss it objectively. As most educational research is aimed at the establishing of general principles and insights rather than the yielding of specific information about the schools or subjects participating, results can usually be prepared in such a way that they will not reflect unfavorably upon the schools used in the study. These results are generally reported in professional research journals, and it is customary to describe the study without identifying the specific schools involved. Such reassurance to the school administrator is especially needed when the study is such that he may have some anxiety concerning the performance of his pupils. Even if research findings reflect unfavorably upon participating schools, the research worker should in all his public statements emphasize that by cooperating in the research, school personnel have shown themselves to be interested in improving their service. It should be pointed out that educators who admit that their schools are not perfect and who are seeking ways to improve are more to be commended than those who are blind to their own shortcomings or those who try to hide deficiencies rather than correct them.

The school administrator will also be concerned with the specific measuring instruments that are to be used in the research. Samples of these measures should be shown to teachers and administrators in order that they may examine them carefully. The research worker should answer any questions concerning the measures and explain the specific purpose of each measure in the research. An exception to this rule occurs in some studies in which a knowledge of the measures can result in teachers' biasing or contaminating the research results. For example, it is sometimes undesirable to allow teachers more than a brief examination of the achievement test to be used in a research project, because some teachers will coach their pupils on the correct answers if they have a copy of the test available. This is usually done by teachers who are insecure and who feel that poor performance of their pupils will reflect unfavorably upon themselves.

Many psychological measures used in educational research projects are difficult for the school administrators to understand. If such measures are to be used, the research worker must be prepared to explain very thoroughly the purpose of these measures and to provide evidence that the measure is a valid and useful one. In examining such measures, the administrators will often have in mind the possible response made by parents to such a measure. If the measure contains items that may cause unfavorable reactions from parents or other community groups, the research worker must have very strong justification for the use of these devices. He should also carry out careful public relations work with the groups concerned prior to the use of these devices. The research worker should avoid the use of measures that he cannot defend on the basis of appropriateness to the study and psychological significance. Prior approval for all measures to be used should be obtained from school authorities before the research is started.

In discussing a proposed research project with school personnel, it is essential that all parties understand specifically what their responsibilities are. Try to bring up and discuss any questions that may lead to future misunderstandings. Keep careful notes during planning meetings. Once you feel that all parties understand their roles in the project, make up a letter that spells out the agreement in specific terms and send this letter to the superintendent or principal involved for confirmation. On major studies it is also desirable to submit your proposal to the school board for approval.

Following channels

It is very important when working with any administrative hierarchy, such as a school district, to follow appropriate channels of authority. If the student plans to use subjects from more than one school, it is generally necessary for him first to obtain approval from the district superintendent or from the assistant superintendent in charge of research. After obtaining such approval, the student must visit each school concerned and present his ideas to the principal. Even though the superintendent has given tentative approval for the project, if the principal objects strongly to testing pupils in his school, the superintendent will usually support the principal. Even if the superintendent were inclined to force the principal to cooperate, such an arrangement would create a situation in which it would be very difficult to carry out effective research. The interest and cooperation of all persons concerned with the research is necessary if it is to be carried through to a successful conclusion.

After the principal and superintendent have been briefed concerning the purposes of the research and the procedures to be followed, it usually will be necessary for the research worker to meet with teachers in the schools and obtain their interest and cooperation. Often a faculty meeting can be devoted to the research topic, and the research worker can present his plans and get the responses of the teachers at this time. Teachers and school administrators frequently will see problems or difficulties in the research plans that the research worker has not recognized. The suggestions of school personnel should be solicited and followed whenever this may be done without compromising some scientific aspect of the research.

In many studies it is also desirable that parents be informed concerning the nature of the study and given an opportunity to express their opinions. This may often be done by having the research worker present his plans at PTA meetings in the schools involved. The purposes of the study and the procedures should be discussed as frankly as possible, omitting only information that could lead to compromising the study in some way. In addition to such a presentation, it is often wise for the research worker to prepare a letter explaining the study. This letter is sent home to parents of all children who will participate as subjects and usually provides a place where the parent may sign to signify his approval of his child's participation in the research.

The degree of rapport that must be built up between the research worker and other community groups is dependent to a great extent upon the nature of the study. Studies dealing with areas such as achievement, which are generally regarded as a major aspect of the school's business, need a less extensive public relations program than studies involving such areas as personality and social adjustment, where the role of the school is less clear and where some of the measures to be employed might be resented or misunderstood by the parent.

It is not only necessary to establish good working relationships before starting your research; it is equally important to maintain these relationships during the time the research is carried on. If they have problems or questions that go unanswered, teachers may refuse to cooperate or may even sabotage your work by doing such things as complaining to parents that your research is interfering with class work, or taking children on field trips on days when you have scheduled testing. It is especially important to keep teachers and other persons who are involved in your project informed of your progress and alerted to coming events in the research plan. In small scale projects, the investigator should personally keep in contact with participating teachers and administrators. In large-scale projects, periodic reports and newsletters should be sent to teachers, parents, and other interested persons. A letter sent to teachers participating in a project conducted by the senior author has been reproduced in Fig. 1 to provide an example.

Much research is only possible because of warm personal relationships between the educational researcher and school personnel. If you develop a sincere interest in the problems of the practitioner and a respect for his ideas and points of view, you will gain insights that will improve your research plans and you will also receive a level of cooperation that makes it possible to complete your project when the going gets rough. The re-

UTAH STATE UNIVERSITY

DARYL CHASE, PRESIDENT

LOGAN, UTAH

COLLEGE OF EDUCATION
JOHN C. CARLISLE, DEAN

May 19, 1960

BUREAU OF EDUCATIONAL RESEARCH

Dear Mrs. Oliver:

With your valued assistance we have just finished collecting data for the second year of the Ogden-Weber ability grouping study. I realize that this research has caused you inconvenience and has taken time from your classes. I assure you that we are aware of the problems that such a study causes in the cooperating schools and shall continue to try to reduce these problems during the remaining two years of the study. I'm afraid that it is inevitable that progressive school districts, such as your own, that choose to support research and strive to find better ways of educating our youth must always pay for their leadership by accepting the problems that major research projects always bring.

I am pleased to tell you that we already have enough important results to indicate that this research is well worth the effort, the problems, and the inconveniences. Our work to date has yielded important new knowledge about ability grouping. The remaining two years of the study will certainly teach us more and will also give us a chance to check the results we have already obtained.

Many educators regard the question of ability grouping a closed issue. This is far from true. Although research of one sort or another has been going on in this field for over 30 years, it has only been in recent years that psychology has developed the measures needed to answer the basic questions that have been raised about the ability grouping technique. Just last month Dean Harold Shane of Indiana University stated in an article on grouping that, "An extensive and definite study of ability grouping remains to be done, and this constitutes an important challenge to the profession."

The work underway in the Ogden-Weber study is the first extensive scientific evaluation of ability grouping and I assure you that through your cooperation you are making a real and important contribution to the teaching profession.

My deepest regret as I look back on the past year's work is that I have had little opportunity to meet with the teachers cooperating in this research. I know that many of you have questions about the study that I could answer. I am also sure that you have suggestions and ideas that would help us to

Fig. 1. Letter sent to a participant in a field research project.

make this research better. I plan to visit each cooperating school next year and hope that you will jot down ideas and suggestions so that we may discuss them at that time.

In closing, permit me to thank you again for your patience and cooperation. I am looking forward to meeting with you and your colleagues in the coming year.

Sincerely,

Walter R. Borg, Director
Bureau of Educational Research

WRB/lr

searcher who is regarded in the schools as a friend and colleague has a much easier time than one who is regarded as an outsider with unknown motives.

Dealing with public relations problems

Public relations problems arise occasionally in educational field studies, in spite of the efforts of the research worker to establish good public relations with concerned groups. The most frequent problem involves a protest over measures used in the research. Such protests are usually made by small but vocal groups of citizens who are primarily interested in obtaining publicity. Often local newspapers, in the quest for more sensational news stories, will encourage such groups by giving their protests wide and sometimes biased coverage. Most of these protests can be traced back to the fact that items occur in many psychological tests, the purpose of which cannot be easily explained to the layman. Many psychological tests in such areas as personality, mental health, social adjustment, attitudes, and interests are still in the early stages of development, and not even their strongest advocates would claim them to be highly valid measures. In many cases, however, such measures are the best available and must be used if research in a particular area is to be carried forward.

We shall discuss this problem further in Chapter 6. However, we may note here that if the researcher's project is given biased coverage in news stories, the researcher should make an attempt to provide newspaper men with his side of the story. He should particularly point out the procedures that are being used to protect individual privacy. These procedures should include obtaining prior consent and assuring confidentiality and anonymity of data.

The pilot study

A preliminary trial of research measures and techniques is essential to the development of a sound research plan. Whenever possible this preliminary trial should be enlarged into a pilot study. In a pilot study the entire research procedure is carried out, including analysis of the data collected. In addition to serving all the purposes of the usual tryout procedures, such as improving data collecting routines, trying scoring techniques, revising locally developed measures, and checking the appropriateness of standard measures, the pilot study provides additional knowledge that leads to improved research:

1. It permits a preliminary testing of the hypotheses that leads to testing more precise hypotheses in the main study. It may lead to changing some hypotheses, dropping some, and developing new hypotheses when called for.

2. It often provides the research worker with ideas, approaches, and clues not foreseen prior to the pilot study. Such ideas and clues greatly increase the chances of obtaining clear-cut findings in the main study.

3. It permits a thorough check of the planned statistical and analytical procedures, thus allowing an appraisal of their adequacy in treating the data. Needed alterations also may be made in the data-collecting methods, so that data in the main study may be analyzed more efficiently.

4. It greatly reduces the number of treatment errors, because unforeseen problems revealed in the pilot study may be overcome in redesigning the main study.

5. It may save the research worker a major expenditure of time and money on a research project that will yield nothing. Unfortunately, many research ideas that seem to show great promise are unproductive when carried out in the field or laboratory. The pilot study almost always provides enough data for the research worker to make a sound decision on the advisability of going ahead with the main study.

6. In the pilot study, the research worker may try out a number of alternative measures, and then select those that produce the best results for the main study with some tentative evidence that they would be productive. If the student plans to continue beyond the Master's degree, his Master's research may sometimes serve as a pilot study for later research to be carried out as part of his doctoral program. The less research experience the student has, the more he is likely to profit from the pilot study. Because of this the student should attempt a pilot study whenever possible, even if it must be limited to only a dozen or so cases.

MISTAKES OFTEN MADE BY GRADUATE STUDENTS

1. Puts off selection of a problem until he has finished all or most of his courses.
2. Uncritically accepts the first research idea that he thinks of or that is suggested to him.
3. Prepares funny or untestable hypotheses.

4. Fails to consider methods or analysis procedures in developing his tentative research plan.
5. Does not make provision in his research plan for a pilot study.
6. Fails to follow proper channels in setting up a study in the public schools.
7. Has not prepared answers for questions likely to be asked by school administrators about his research project.
8. Weakens his research design by making changes for the administrative convenience of the schools from which he is drawing his subjects.

ANNOTATED REFERENCES

1. Brodbeck, May. "Logic and Scientific Method in Research on Teaching," in N. L. Gage (ed.). *Handbook of Research on Teaching.* Chicago: Rand McNally, 1963, pp. 44–93. The author provides an excellent overview of the logic of science and theory construction. Among the concepts which are defined and discussed are: operational definitions, scientific laws, hypotheses, theoretical constructs, causation, and models.
2. Chambers, M. M. "Selection, Definition, and Delimitation of a Doctoral Research Problem," *Phi Delta Kappan,* 42 (3) (1960), 71–73. Offers sound advice to the student starting graduate work and alerts him to many important questions concerning his research plans.
3. Conrad, Herbert S. "Clearance of Questionnaires with Respect to 'Invasion of Privacy,' Public Sensitivities, Ethical Standards, etc.," *American Psychologist,* 22 (1967), 356–359. The author discusses the guidelines used to evaluate questionnaires in research projects supported by the U.S. Office of Education. The article is particularly helpful in identifying the type of questionnaire or personality test item that may be considered as a potential invasion of privacy.
4. Davitz, Joel R., and Davitz, Lois Jean. *A Guide for Evaluating Research Plans in Psychology and Education.* New York: Teachers College Press, 1967. The authors have constructed a very helpful guide for the student to use in evaluating his research plan. The guide presents twenty-five problems that are sometimes encountered in reviewing students' research proposals. There is also a checklist of questions which the student can use to quickly evaluate his plan for soundness of research design.
5. Kohn, Martin, and Beker, Jerome. "Special Methodological Considerations in Conducting Field Research in a School Setting," *Psychology in the Schools,* 1 (1964), 31–46. This article presents a good overview of the many factors that must be considered in planning a research project in the public schools: selection of a school system for the project, parents of students, nature of the community, school board, and school superintendent. The authors point out several techniques to resolve conflicts of interest that often arise between the researcher and school people.
6. Lamke, T. A. "A Primer in Research: Lesson I. Defining the Problem," *Phi Delta Kappan,* 38 (1957), 127–129. This paper emphasizes the importance of translating research ideas into specifics. The author points out that many persons fail in research because they are unable to translate a general research problem into

plan "based on specific operations at specific times in specific places with specific materials." The ideas expressed are particularly pertinent for beginners in educational research.

7. Longstreth, B. "Behavioral Research Using Students: A Privacy Issue for Schools; With Discussion," *School Review*, 76 (1968), 1–40. The author discusses the responsibilities of both the researcher and school authorities in protecting the privacy of students involved in an educational research project. Several good criteria are set forth for determining whether a research project is justified when informed consent of the individuals being studied is not possible.

8. Van Dalen, D. B. "The Role of Hypotheses in Educational Research," *Educational Administration and Supervision*, 17 (1956), 457–460. This article emphasizes the importance of hypotheses in educational research. The functions of hypotheses as a means of stating assumptions, as a basis for explanations, and as an aid in determining the relevancy of facts are discussed. Hypotheses, if well constructed, also help the researcher in determining research design, in presenting the research conclusions, and in formulating new hypotheses.

9. Journals such as *Childhood Education, Elementary English, Educational Leadership,* and *Review of Educational Research* present regular reviews of educational research; these often contain suggestions for future research on significant educational problems. The research division of the National Education Association also publishes frequent extensive reviews of the literature on important problems. Recent publications have appeared on ability grouping (1968), class size (1968), school dropouts (1967), and homework (1966).

CHAPTER 3

Reviewing the Literature

INTRODUCTION

The review of the literature involves locating, reading, and evaluating reports of research as well as reports of casual observation and opinion that are related to the individual's planned research project. This review differs in a number of ways from the reading program often used to locate a tentative research project. First, such a review is much more extensive and thorough because it is aimed at obtaining a detailed knowledge of the topic being studied, while the reading program is aimed at obtaining enough general knowledge and insight to recognize problems in the selected area.

Secondary sources

The reading program generally uses textbooks, encyclopedias, and other secondary source materials. Secondary source materials in education include any publications written by an author who was not a direct observer or participant in the events described. For example, most of the material found in textbooks of Roman history are secondary source materials because the author has merely compiled the reports of others and rearranged these reports into a textbook. Most of the content of textbooks in education and psychology is also secondary source material. Let us suppose that an individual wishes to write a textbook on methods of teaching remedial reading. The prospective author does an exhaustive review of the literature in this field, noting the results of all experiments and weighing and evaluating these results in terms of various approaches to remedial reading instruction. Then, based on his interpretation of the various research reports and articles he has read, he prepares his textbook. If, in the textbook, the author also reports the results of experiments that he himself has carried out, then this portion of the textbook would be considered a primary source. That portion, however, that is based on his interpretations of the work of others would be classified as a secondary source. Secondary sources are useful because they combine knowledge from many primary sources into a single publication. A good textbook, for example, combines the work of many other persons and simplifies or eliminates much of the technical material that is not of interest to the general reader, thus providing a quick and relatively easy method of obtaining a good overall understanding of the field.

Primary sources

The primary source differs from the secondary source in that it is a direct description of an occurrence by an individual who actually observed or witnessed the occurrence. In educational research this generally means the description of the study by the individual who carried it out.

The principal disadvantage to the research scholar of using secondary sources is that it is never possible to be sure what changes have been made by the secondary source author. In the process of simplifying and combining the results of many studies, the author of a textbook or other secondary source report may slant his interpretation of the primary source to agree with his own views, and often he will leave out material that the person reviewing the literature needs to know. Thus a review of the literature should be based, whenever possible, upon primary sources. Most secondary sources, such as textbooks, contain a bibliography listing the sources from which the material was obtained so that the student can generally locate the primary source.

Importance of the review

The review of the literature is an important part of the scientific approach and is carried out in all areas of scientific research, whether in the physical, natural, or social sciences. Such reviews are also the basis of most research in the humanities. In fields such as history, the review of literature not only gives the scholar an understanding of previous work that has been done, but the results of the review actually provide the data used in his research. Historical studies in education, which we will discuss in a later chapter, are based almost entirely upon a careful study of existing printed knowledge in the field.

The review of the literature in educational research provides you with the means of getting to the frontier in your particular field of knowledge. Until you have learned what others have done and what remains still to be done in your area, you cannot develop a research project that will contribute to furthering knowledge in your field. Thus the literature in any field forms the foundation upon which all future work must be built. If you fail to build this foundation of knowledge provided by the review of the literature, your work is likely to be shallow and naïve, and will often duplicate work that has already been done better by someone else. Although the importance of a thorough review of the literature is obvious to everyone, this task is more frequently slighted than any other phase of research. The research worker is always tempted to let a sketchy review of the literature suffice so that he can get started sooner on his own research project. The student, however, should make every effort to complete a thorough review before starting his research because the insights and knowledge gained by the review almost inevitably lead to a better designed project and greatly improve the chances of obtaining important and significant results. Often the insights gained through the review will save the research worker as much time in conducting his project as the review itself required.

PURPOSES OF THE REVIEW

Although the general purpose of the review is to help the research worker develop a thorough understanding and insight into previous work and the trends that have emerged, the review can also help in reaching a number of important specific goals.

Delimiting the research problem

The review of the literature can help in limiting the individual's research problem and in defining it better. Many studies attempted by graduate students are doomed to failure before the student starts because of his failure to limit his problem to an area small enough and sufficiently specific for him to work with satisfactorily. It is far better in research to select a limited problem and treat it well than to attempt the study of a broad general problem and do it poorly. Many graduate students also commit themselves to a research problem before they have thought it out adequately. A fuzzy or poorly defined problem can sometimes result in the student's collecting data and then learning that his data cannot be applied to the problem he wishes to attack. Before he starts his review of the literature, the student should do sufficient background reading from secondary sources to permit a tentative outline of his research problem. The review of the literature will give the student the knowledge he needs to convert his tentative research problem to a detailed and concise plan of action.

Seeking new approaches

In the process of reviewing the literature, the student should not only learn what work has been done but should also be alert to research possibilities that have been overlooked. The unique experience and background of an individual may make it possible for him to see a facet of the problem that other research workers have not seen. Such new viewpoints are likely to occur most frequently in areas where little research has been done, but even in well-researched areas, someone occasionally thinks of an approach that is unique and creative. A good example is Thompson's study of administration of the *Thematic Apperception Test* (*TAT*) to Negro subjects.[1] Prior to this study, many clinicians were administering the standard *TAT* cards to clients regardless of racial background. The persons pictured on the standard *TAT* cards are white, and Thompson saw that the use of these cards with Negro subjects might well lead to different responses because of racial differences. In his research he developed a comparable set of cards in which Negroes were substituted for the whites in the *TAT* pictures and found that his hypothesis was correct. Although hundreds of research projects had been carried out prior to Thompson's work using the *TAT*, his special insight led to a unique and valuable contribution to our knowledge of this important instrument.

Avoiding sterile approaches

In reviewing the literature, the student should also be on the lookout for research approaches in his area that have proved to be sterile. It is not uncommon in doing a review of the literature to encounter several very similar studies done over a period of years, all of which employ approximately the same approach and all of which fail to produce significant results. One or two repetitions of an unproductive approach can be justified on the grounds that these confirm the previous finding that the area is unproductive. Repetitions beyond this, however, serve no useful purpose and generally suggest that the persons repeating the study have not done an adequate review of the literature. In an excellent review of the literature on instructor effectiveness, Morsh and Wilder list eleven studies carried out between 1934 and 1948 in which an attempt was made to relate personality as measured by the Bernreuter Personality Inventory to instructor effectiveness.[2] None of these studies produced correlations sufficiently high to be of any value in predicting instructor effectiveness. In all likelihood additional studies following the same futile approach have been carried out since 1952, the date at which their review terminated.

Insight into methods

The review of the literature can also give the student a great deal of insight into the methods, measures, subjects, and approaches used by other research workers and can thus lead to significant improvement of his design. A mistake made by many graduate students when reading research reports is to give little attention to anything but the results reported. Very

[1] C. E. Thompson, "The Thompson Modification of the Thematic Apperception Test," *Rorschach Research Exchange and Journal of Projective Techniques,* 13 (1949), 469–478.

[2] Joseph E. Morsh and Elinore W. Wilder, "Identifying the Effective Instructor: A Review of the Quantitative Studies, 1900–1952," *AFPTRC Research Bulletin TR-54-44* (Lackland Air Force Base, Tex.: October 1954).

often a study that has little to contribute by way of results can help the student a great deal by suggesting methods and useful approaches. For example, discussion of the various measures used can help the student decide which of these measures would be best suited for his own research. A sampling problem discussed by one research worker can help other research workers in the field avoid the same difficulties. In a study relating the degree of pupil homogeneity in the classroom to achievement, Goldberg, et al. set up 15 different classroom patterns, each having a different level of homogeneity and a different range of ability.[3] Pattern 1, which was to include classes in which all pupils were above 130 IQ, appeared the easiest to obtain because the school system had already set up classes for children at this level. Thus the research workers organized classes that were appropriate for other patterns but assumed that sufficient classes of pattern 1 would be available. On checking, however, it was found that the IQ limit had not been adhered to by schools in setting up these classes and that only one of the ten thought to be available actually met the requirements for pattern 1. Thus in a research project involving 2219 children, only 29 were included in one of the most important groups to be studied. Goldberg's study, although making many valuable contributions to our knowledge of ability grouping, would have been much stronger if the research workers had had available a large number of pattern 1 classes. If he looks carefully at such methodological problems, the student can learn much that will help him improve his own research plan.

Recommendations for further research

The authors of research articles often include specific suggestions and recommendations for persons planning further research in the field. These suggestions should be considered very carefully because they represent the insights gained by the research worker after experience in the problem area. Specific research topics are often suggested that are particularly useful in helping the student delimit his research problem.

Sampling current opinions

Although research reports make up the most important source of information that the student covers in his review, he should also study newspaper accounts, nontechnical articles, and opinion articles related to his topic. Such articles occasionally contain unique ideas that can be tested through research and also help the research worker gain insight into those aspects of the problem area that are considered critical or controversial by educators. For example, a study of opinion articles in the field

---

[3] M. L. Goldberg, Joseph Justman, A. H. Passow, and Gerald Hage, *The Effects of Ability Grouping,* Interim Report (New York: Teachers College, Columbia University, Horace-Mann-Lincoln Institute, 1961).

of ability grouping shows that most of the disputes between educators in this field center around the possible effects of ability grouping on the child's *personality* and *social development*. On the other hand, nearly all the research reported in the field of ability grouping is concerned with the *achievement* of children in the ability grouped situation. These studies contribute valuable knowledge but have had little effect upon the judgments of most educators. Only research that presents objective data concerning the variables that educators consider critical is likely to have any effect upon their decisions concerning whether or not they should establish or support an ability grouping program.

SCOPE OF THE REVIEW

Perhaps the greatest frustration encountered by the graduate student in carrying out his first review of the literature centers around his attempt to determine what he should read and what he should not read. Unfortunately there are no pat formulas that can be given the student to help him make this decision. Obviously the student should read all studies that are closely related to his research problem. The decisions that cause him difficulty involve those studies that are only partially related to his research problem or perhaps only related to one phase of the problem.

Relatively new research areas usually lack an organized body of secondary source information to provide general background and thus require a fairly broad review in which even those studies that are only peripheral to the main area should be read in order to give the student the foundation of knowledge he requires. For example, let us say the student wishes to do research on the use of teaching machines in the training of mentally retarded children. Because widespread interest in teaching machines is fairly new in education, the student should probably read most of the studies that have been done in this field, even if they are not closely related to his topic. For example, a study on the use of teaching machines for inservice training of business executives is quite remote from the student's problem but should probably be scanned in order to check for methods, programming techniques, and so forth that could be applied to his research. The student might also wish to review methods of teaching mentally retarded children other than those employing teaching machines. In such new research areas, the student often finds no more than two or three studies that are reasonably close to his topic.

In more thoroughly explored areas, where research activity has extended over a longer period of time and much of the early work is covered in secondary sources such as textbooks, the student can usually develop adequate insight into the field by reading only those studies that are reasonably close to his research topic. In these more thoroughly explored areas, much greater depth is available and the student can cover a narrower topic range to a greater depth. In new areas little depth is available, and a broad review is therefore necessary to get sufficient insight. A study in a more thoroughly explored area might be concerned with' the effectiveness of high school counseling in bringing about certain personality changes as measured by the *Thematic Apperception Test*. In this area the student would find some studies that relate personality changes to counseling and involve the use of various personality instruments. These should all be covered. In addition, some studies using the *TAT* in other related research areas should be read. For example, if studies were available involving changes in personality during psychotherapy, these studies should be read. As the *TAT* is a well-established instrument that has been used in a great many research projects, it would not be advisable for the student to attempt to read all research involving the use of this instrument. As of 1965 almost 900 studies dealing with the *TAT* had been listed in the *Mental Measurements Yearbooks*. Most of these studies would be of little value to the student carrying out the research described previously. Considerable background reading on the *TAT* in secondary sources, however, would be desirable.

A METHOD OF REVIEWING THE LITERATURE

Although the review of the literature is a preliminary step in all scientific research, the methods of conducting the review differ to some extent from field to field. The method that will be described in detail in this section is one that works well in the field of education. This method has been developed over a number of years, and the student is advised to follow it closely until he has built up sufficient experience to make intelligent adaptations.

Step One—Listing Key Words

In most sciences basic reference books are available that cover most material published in the science in question. In education the most useful source is *Education Index* (see annotated references for complete bibliographical data). *Education Index,* along with the indexes and abstracts published in other sciences, is organized by subject. It is necessary, therefore, that the research worker identify key words related to his topic so that he may look up these key words in the index to locate sources of information related to his topic. For example, let us say that you wish to do a study of the changes in racial attitudes that have occurred in three recently desegregated public schools. Your first step in reviewing the literature would be to make a list of key words that relate to this study. Your first list might include the following: attitudes, civil rights, desegregation integration, prejudice, race relations, racial prejudice, segregation, and tolerance. This preliminary list of key words will almost certainly be incomplete and will be changed when the actual search of *Education Index* begins. It does, however, provide a starting point, and as many possible key words as the student can think of should be listed in order to reduce the likelihood of important studies being overlooked. A useful technique for identifying key words is to consult the *Thesaurus of ERIC Descriptors,* which is described later in this chapter.

Step Two—Checking Preliminary Sources

We will define *preliminary sources* as references, such as indexes and abstracts, which help us find research articles and other primary sources of information. (See annotated references for complete bibliographic data on preliminary sources described in this section.) Many of the preliminary sources that are likely to be of help to the student in reviewing the literature in education and related fields will be discussed in this section.

Education Index

Education Index provides an up-to-date listing of articles published in hundreds of education journals, books about education, and publications in related fields. Until mid-1961, *Education Index* was both an author and subject index—that is, each article was listed once under its subject and again under the name of the author. The author index was dropped for eight years, but as of mid-1969, it was reinstituted. *Education Index* is published monthly (except in July and August). It lists only the bibliographical data concerning each article or book reference. The year for *Education Index* runs from July to the following June. For the current year, each of the monthly issues must be searched, but these monthly issues are combined into a yearly volume for the immediate past year.

Most reviews of the literature in education cover a minimum of ten years. A systematic method of searching *Education Index* for the period of the review should be developed and followed. The author has found that preparing a checklist of key words, such as is shown in Fig. 2 is an effective method for insuring a systematic search. After this checklist has been prepared, the student may start with the most recent issue of the *Education Index* and look up each of his key words. In looking up the key words, he should be alert for other possible key words that may be added to his list to provide more complete coverage.

To check each of these key words in a volume of *Education Index,* the student looks up the word and reads the titles of articles listed under the word. If titles are found that indicate the article deals with some phase of the student's topic, he copies the bibliographical data (author, title, and source of publication) onto a 3 × 5-inch card. A separate card should be

Key words	Education Index	volume						
	10/69	9/69	Vol.19	Vol.18	Vol.17	Vol.16	Vol.15	Vol.14
attitudes (change of)	√*	√						
Civil rights	N†	N						
~~desegregation~~								
~~integration~~								
prejudice	√	√						
race attitudes	√	√						
race relations	√	√						
race ~~racial prejudice~~	√	√						
segregation	√	√						
~~school integration~~								
~~tolerance~~								
Negroes in U.S., segregation	√	N						
Public schools, desegregation	√	√						

Fig. 2. Sample of checklist used in searching the *Education Index*.

  * Indicated volume checked and bibliography cards made.
  † Indicated volume contained no usable references under Key word.

used for each article or reference found. It is often difficult to judge the contents of an article from the title, and many of the articles for which a student prepares bibliography cards will later be found to contain nothing pertinent to the topic being studied. In deciding whether to prepare a bibliography card and check a particular article, the student should generally follow the rule that it is better to check an article that proves of no use than to overlook an article that may be important. Thus, whenever he is in doubt, the student should prepare a bibliography card and check the article in question. After he checks the title under a key word, the student should place a check on his checklist. If, after checking several volumes of the *Education Index,* nothing pertinent to the student's topic has been found under a given key word, this key word can be dropped and not checked in the remaining volumes.

In the aforementioned example, after checking several volumes of *Education Index,* it would be found that some of the original key words are satisfactory and some are unproductive and can be eliminated, and some new ones would be discovered and added. "Attitudes" would become "attitudes, change of"; "desegregation" would be changed to "public schools, desegregation"; and "tolerance" would be dropped because no usable references are found. "Integration" and "school integration" would be dropped because they are not listed at all. "Civil rights" is listed but was found to contain no usable references. "Racial prejudice" would be changed to "race prejudice." New key words added would include "race attitudes," "Negroes in the United States—segregation," and "race prejudice." It will be noted that the revised list of key words is given in Fig. 2.

Psychological Abstracts

Another valuable preliminary source for research workers in education is *Psychological Abstracts.* This reference is published monthly by the American Psychological Association and contains abstracts of articles appearing in over 500 journals in psychology and related areas. Every issue of *Psychological Abstracts* has twelve sections, each covering a different area of psychology. The section on developmental psychology, which includes abstracts on child development and adolescence, and the section on educational psychology, which includes abstracts in areas such as school learning, interest, attitudes and habits, special education, educational guidance, educational measurement, and educational staff personnel, are most pertinent to the research worker in education. The coverage of these areas of psychology is very thorough. For example, many journals such as *Elementary School Journal, Harvard Educational Review,* and *Journal of Reading,* which are predominantly educational journals, are covered in *Psychological Abstracts.* In searching *Psychological Abstracts,* the same key words can be used that you have developed in your search of *Education Index.* Sometimes an additional key word or two will have to be added because of the differences in indexing systems in the two periodicals.

The key word "bibliographies" should always be looked up in *Psychological Abstracts.* Under this heading the student will find a listing of bibliographies on a wide variety of subjects. If he can locate a recent bibliography in his area of interest, it will, of course, be of great help to him in carrying out his review of the literature. We will discuss other sources of bibliographies later in this chapter. The December number of *Psychological Abstracts* contains both an author index and subject index of all articles abstracted in the previous eleven numbers for the year.[4] In using *Psychological Abstracts*, the student turns first to this index number to check his key words. The index number of *Psychological Abstracts* does not contain complete bibliographical data such as are found in *Education Index*, but lists only the subject of the article in the briefest possible terms —usually a word or two. After the subject the student will find one or more numbers. These numbers refer to the numbers of abstracts included during the preceding year or half year. Figure 3 shows a sample of an index number.[5] The student may then check these numbers to obtain the bibliographical data for articles that may be appropriate to his review of the literature. For example, in the index number for January–June 1968, under "prejudice" we find "racial prejudice and urban social participation, white males, 3868." As this article seems pertinent to our study, we look up abstract number 3868, which is in the March 1968 issue. Under this number we find the reference:

Curtis, Richard F., Timbers, Dianne M., and Jackson, Elton F. (U. Arizona). Prejudice and urban social participation. *American Journal of Sociology*, 1967, 73(2), 235–244.

Following the bibliographical data is a brief abstract of the article. These brief abstracts contained in *Psychological Abstracts* are very useful to the research worker because they help him to make a decision as to whether or not a given article actually pertains to his problem. This decision is much easier to make on the basis of an abstract than solely on the basis of the bibliographical data as is found in *Education Index*. After reading the abstract, the research worker decides whether the article is pertinent, and if it is, he records the bibliographical data on a 3 × 5-inch bibliography card so that he may read the entire article later. When the research is on a topic that is exclusively educational, such as the school lunch program, little is gained by checking *Psychological Abstracts*. On the other hand, in areas relating to educational psychology, it is usually desirable to check both *Psychological Abstracts* and *Education Index* in order to be assured of getting a full coverage of the field. When both these preliminary sources are checked, the student should check *Psychological Abstracts* first

---

[4] A semiannual index is also published.

[5] *Psychological Abstracts*, 42 (1968), 41. Reprinted by permission of The American Psychological Association.

Academic Achievement   *SUBJECT INDEX*   Achievement Motivation

interpretation of proverbs, schizophrenics, 12491
knowledge & psychology of theorizing, 17977
letter & digit/relationship between, teaching arithmetic, 11223
paired associate learning, concrete nouns without imagery, 13171
pattern distortions, abstraction of criteria, 14980
pupillary response magnitude & latency during imagery task, stimulus abstractness & imagery ability, 16625
schizophrenics vs. state reformatory inmates, abstract thinking & conception, color form & 3 direction tasks, 15783
speech characteristics in word definition task, audience sensitivity & associational ability, audience presence & stimulus concreteness, 15427
thinking/abstract, psychological & physiological study, paranoid schizophrenics, 14208
visual imagery ability & level of mediator abstractness, 7th graders, 15286
Academic Achievement (SEE Achievement/Academic, Achievement/Academic–College)
Acceleration (SEE Movement)
Acceptance (SEE Social Approval)
Accident (see also Driving, Safety)
cerebrovascular accident, clouding of consciousness & symptoms, 12623
childhood & acculturation, Chinese- & Japanese-Americans, 18660
discrimination/operant, accidental reinforcement, rat, 10271
negative working behavior & productivity, interpersonal processes in small work groups, industrial personnel, 19523
prediction of driving accidents & violations, 11291
Acclimatization (SEE Adaptation)
Acculturation (SEE Conformity, Culture)
Achievement (see also next headings)
counseling vs. noncounseling, & vocational problems & ability & personality & socioeconomic variables, college freshmen, 19322
educational aspirations & academic achievement, parents' educational achievements, high school seniors, 14587
eminence in psychology, chronological & professional age, 17991
& ethnic & socioeconomic status, 2 & 10 yr. olds, Hawaii, 13553
high school physics course, teaching method & achievements of science, 19471
level, small group problem solving & reward distribution, 7th & 8th graders, 15397
motivation, correlation analysis, aspiration level & achievement expectation & performance appraisals, 11198
movie attendance & differential movie appeals, 15434
Music Aptitude Profile vs. Henmon Nelson vs. Iowa Tests of Basic Skills, music achievement, 4th & 5th graders, 15436
n Achievement motive model, trait attribution & verbal reinforcement behavior, counselor personality & counseling process, 12777
occupational motivator orientation, achievement task experiment, employed vs. unemployed, 19496
orientation, social class & community of orientation & sex & religion, 10560
& peer group membership & classroom conduct, teenage boys, 13528
promotion board decisions/predicting, industrial personnel, 17894
reading & Gates & Root Associative Learning Tests, 4th & 5th & 6th graders, 17814
reading, sex differences, elementary students, 17776
reading, word recognition skills, 4th graders, 17789
reading achievement & perceptual training, 1st graders, 13476
self concept & sense of competence & reading achievement & dependency, kindergarten children, 18606
social psychiatry, historical achievements & failures, USSR, 10653
socialization practices, achievement motivation & occupational achievement values, criticism, 13499
socialization practices, achievement motivation & occupational

achievement values, criticism & analysis of data, 13507
socialization practices, achievement motivation & occupational achievement values, reply, 13511
special testing needs & identification of goals & level of achievement, educationally disadvantaged, 12761
success in business, view of business students & middle managers, 12889
training program based on aptitude, learning speed & performance, Army trainees, 17906
Achievement Motivation (see also Achievement/Over & Under)
academic, 11 & 13 yr. olds, 12715
& academic achievement, culturally disadvantaged Negro 5th & 6th & 7th graders, 17770
& academic achievement & monetary incentive, expectancy of success & persistence on insoluble task, 6th grade boys, 13516
academic achievement & occupational choice, adolescents, France, 12702
academic achievement/prediction of, conforming & independent motivation, CPI, college students, 16123
academic aptitude & creativity & motivation & achievement, monozygotic & dizygotic twins & siblings, 15153
adjustment of S in 3 member discussion group, interpersonal & task success & affiliation motive, 13643
& affection need satisfaction & drinking behavior, sex differences, college students, 15447
attitudes toward campus architecture, & achievement, college students, 16002
cheating behavior & attitudes & need achievement, college student, 19252
children's stories, death rate due to ulcer & hypertension 25 yr. later, 16 Western countries, 14245
coronary patients/employed & unemployed, aspiration & need achievement, 19212
correlation analysis, aspiration level & achievement motivation & performance appraisals, 11198
elementary & high school students, & hope of success & academic achievement, 14490
grades/school, verbal ability & attitude toward grade competition & woman's role, high school girls, 12807
group achievement motivation, individual motives to achieve success & avoid failure & seek social approval, 12034
Internal-External Control Scale, correlation with achievement need & test anxiety & social desirability & academic achievement, 12983
& leadership, elementary school principal, 19372
& learner variables, live vs. television lectures, high vs. low achievers, college students, 16147
mental illness & mobility aspiration-achievement discrepancies, 14162
normative & role model & audience reference groups, theory, 10428
& performance & social class learning disabled vs. normal 4th graders, 19439
performance/determination of, & expectation, normals & schizophrenics, 16556
persistance & initiation of achievement-related activities, male college students, 11188
prediction, biography & personality, industry, 16235
professional women vs. housewives of similar ability, TAT Test of Achievement Motivation & Test of Insight, 17253
recall of passed & failed exam questions, Zeigarnik effect, 11686
schizophrenics/good vs. poor premorbid, need achievement & previous school performance & social adjustment, 14229
school completion motivation, disadvantaged high school seniors, 15996
& self concept & independence training, 8–13 yr. old physically handicapped children, 10954
self-rating inventory & teacher rating, & school attainment & verbal reasoning test, 13 yr. olds, 17782
socialization practices, & occupational achievement values, criticism, 13499
socialization practices, & occupational achievement values, criticism & analysis of data, 13507
socialization practices, & occupational achievement values,

41

Fig. 3. Sample from the subject index of *Psychological Abstracts*. Taken from *Psychological Abstracts*, 42 (1968), 41. Reprinted by permission of the American Psychological Association.

because of the advantage of an abstract over bibliographical data only. A checklist such as is shown in Fig. 2 can also be used in searching *Psychological Abstracts*.

A helpful reference for the student searching *Psychological Abstracts* is the *Cumulated Subject Index to Psychological Abstracts, 1927–1960*. This collection of volumes makes it possible for the student to find all references on a given subject in one place, otherwise the student would need to search 34 separate volumes spanning the years 1927 to 1960. If the student wishes to search all references by a given author, there is available a companion set of volumes called *Cumulative Author Index to Psychological Index, 1894–1935 and Psychological Abstracts, 1927–1958*. This reference source has been updated in *First Supplement to the Cumulative Author Index to Psychological Index, 1894–1935 and Psychological Abstracts, 1927–1958*. This reference source has been updated in *First Supplement to the Cumulative Author Index to Psychological Abstracts, 1959–1963*.

Educational Resources Information Center (ERIC)

In the last few years an important new system of information about educational research studies has been developed. ERIC, an acronym for the Educational Resources Information Center, was initiated in 1965 by the U.S. Office of Education to transmit the findings of current educational research to teachers, administrators, researchers, and the public. Although ERIC abstracts some of the same documents as *Education Index* and *Psychological Abstracts,* it includes many documents not abstracted by these services. For example, ERIC abstracts papers presented at education conferences, progress reports of on-going research studies, studies sponsored by the Cooperative Research Program, and final reports of projects conducted by local agencies (school districts, Title III centers) which are not likely to appear in education journals. Thus, ERIC will be valuable to the student in providing an overview of the most current research being done in education. In contrast many of the studies currently referenced in *Education Index* and *Psychological Abstracts* were completed several years previously due to the time lag between completion of the study, publication in a journal, and abstracting by the service.

ERIC provides a variety of services to the researcher through its central office and nineteen clearinghouses.[6,7] Each clearinghouse is responsible for cataloguing, abstracting, and indexing relevant documents in its subject area. In addition, each clearinghouse publishes its own newsletters, bul-

---

[6] New clearinghouses may have been established since the time of this writing.

[7] A complete description of ERIC's services is contained in "How to Use ERIC," which can be purchased by sending twenty cents to the Superintendent of Documents, U.S. Government Printing Office, Washington, D.C. 20402. Specify catalogue no. FS5.212:12037.

letins, bibliographies, research reviews, and interpretive studies. The student is advised to write the clearinghouse in the area of his interest in order to obtain information that may help him in receiving pertinent research literature and in planning his study. The addresses of the nineteen clearinghouses can be found in Appendix A.

The abstracts prepared by each clearinghouse appear in a monthly ERIC publication called *Research in Education*. Approximately 800 document abstracts are included in each issue. Each abstract in *Research in Education* is classified by subject area, author, institution, and accession number. To use *Research in Education* the student should first select key search terms in his area of interest. To assist the user in identifying search terms, ERIC has published the *Thesaurus of ERIC Descriptors*. This volume lists all terms used to classify ERIC documents by subject; for a given subject area, it will provide synonyms, narrower terms, broader terms, and related terms. For example, the general search term "dropouts" is further analyzed into such terms as "high school dropouts," "potential dropouts," "dropout identification," and "dropout teaching." The next step is to search monthly issues of *Research in Education* and the annual cumulative indexes for document abstracts classified under each search term. A sample entry from *Research in Education* with identifying information about each part of the entry is shown in Fig. 4.[8]

If he wishes to obtain the full document that is abstracted in the entry, the student can order it through the ERIC Document Reproduction Service. A Reproduction Service price is listed for each document. The document can be ordered on microfiches, which are small sheets of microfilm, each containing up to 60 pages of text. It can also be ordered in hard copy form at about 70 percent of the document's original size. The advantages of microfiches are their inexpensiveness and small size. However, they require a special microfiche reader which enlarges the image to normal page size. Many libraries now have these special readers. Also, some libraries maintain collections of ERIC microfiches, so it is not necessary to order them through the Reproduction Service.

Other abstracting and indexing sources

In addition to *Education Index, Psychological Abstracts,* and ERIC's *Research in Education,* the student can consult a variety of other preliminary sources for abstracts and indexes of journal articles. (See annotated references for complete bibliographic data on sources mentioned in this section.) Recently ERIC has developed the *Current Index to Journals in Education* (CIJE), which indexes over 200 education journals and journals in related fields. Compared to *Education Index*, CIJE has the

[8] *Research in Education,* 4 (1969), 4. Reprinted by permission of the U.S. Office of Education, Bureau of Research.

ERIC Accession Number—Identification number sequentially assigned to documents as they are processed.

Author(s).

Title.

Organization where document originated.

Date published.

Contract or Grant Number—contract numbers have OEC prefixes; grant numbers have OEG prefixes.

Alternate source for obtaining documents.

EDRS Price—price through ERIC Document Reproduction Service. "MF" means microfiche; "HC" means hard copy. When listed "not available from EDRS" other sources are cited above.

Legislative Authority Code for identifying the legislation which supported the research activity (where applicable).

Clearinghouse accession number.

Sponsoring Agency—agency responsible for initiating, funding, and managing the research project.

Report Number and/or Bureau Number—assigned by originator.

Descriptive Note.

Descriptors—subject terms which characterize substantive content. Only the major terms, preceded by an asterisk, are printed in the subject index.

Identifiers—additional identifying terms not found in the Thesaurus of ERIC Descriptors.

Informative Abstract.

Abstractor's Initials.

ED 013 371   64   AA 000 223
Norberg, Kenneth D.
Iconic Signs and Symbols in Audiovisual Communication, an Analytical Survey of Selected Writings and Research Findings, Final Report.
Sacramento State Coll., Calif.
Spons Agency—USOE Bur of Research
Report No.—NDEA-VIIB-449
Pub Date—15 Apr 66
Contract—OEC-4-16-023
Note —Speech given before the 22nd National Conference on Higher Education, Chicago, Ill., 7 Mar 66.
Available from—Indiana University Press, 10th and Morton St., Bloomington, Indiana 47401 ($2.95)
Descriptors—*Bibliographies, *Communication (thought transfer), *Perception, *Pictorial Stimuli, *Symbolic Language, Instructional Technology, Visual Stimuli.
Identifiers—Stanford Binet Test, Wechsler Intelligence Scale; Lisp 1.5; Cupertino Union School District.
EDRS Price—MF-$0.75 HC-$5.24 129p.
      The field of analogic, or iconic, signs was explored to (1) develop an annotated bibliography and (2) prepare an analysis of the subject area. The scope of the study was limited to only those components of messages, instructional materials, and communicative stimuli that can be described properly as iconic. The author based the study on a definition of an iconic sign as one that looks like the thing it represents. The bibliography was intended to be representative and reasonably comprehensive and to give emphasis to current research. The analysis explored the nature of iconic signs as reflected in the literature and research. The conclusion of the analysis attempted to relate some issues in perception theory to the problem of the development of a theory of iconic signs. Discussions were included on (1) the stimulus-response paradigm, (2) the psychophysical theory of perception, (3) an information theory approach, (4) nonverbal communication and pictic analysis, (5) a theory of pictorial communication and (6) perception and nonlinear signs. (AL)

Fig. 4. Sample entry from *Research in Education* and identifying characteristics. Taken from *Research in Education*, IV (1969), 4. Reprinted by permission of the U.S. Office of Education, Bureau of Research.

advantages of a more comprehensive index (based on the *Thesaurus of ERIC Descriptors*), multidisciplinary journal coverage, and inclusion of an author index as well as a subject index. However, *Education Index* covers a much longer time span of journal publication (1929 to date) than CIJE (April 1969 to date).

The Science Information Exchange (SIE) is an interesting preliminary source that the student may wish to consult.[9] SIE was developed in 1950 to provide research scientists and administrators with information about current research projects being carried out by Federal agencies and by state, university, and private granting, and commercial organizations. All fields of basic and applied research, including education, are covered by

[9] The address of the Science Information Exchange is Smithsonian Institution, Madison National Bank Building, Suite 300, 1730 M. Street N.W., Washington, D.C. 20036.

SIE. In 1965 SIE had about 70,000 current research projects registered on its computer tape. Each project has the following information registered about it: the agency supporting the project, a title, names of the investigators, project location, a 200-word summary of the work in progress, and level of effort. To use the service, which is without charge, the researcher simply writes a letter of inquiry to SIE. The service is particularly helpful for determining what type of research, and how much of it, is being currently undertaken in a given area.

There are many specialized abstracting and indexing sources that may help the student locate articles and materials in a particular area of interest. For example, Buros' *Mental Measurements Yearbooks* are an indispensable aid for the student who wishes to have a bibliography of all references on a particular psychological or educational test. Sources in the areas of child development (*Child Development Abstracts*), college education (*CPSI Abstracts*), sociology (*Sociological Abstracts*), and statistics (*Statistics Sources*) are also available. For other topics the student should consult *Bibliographic Index,* which lists bibliographical materials in about 1500 periodicals. The format is very similar to the *Education Index* except that only references containing a bibliography are listed. If the bibliography is annotated, the abbreviation "annot" is given.

Reviews of the research literature

The student's review of the literature is greatly simplified if someone else has previously prepared a bibliography or literature review on his research topic. The student can consult various sources for pertinent bibliographies and reviews. (See annotated references for complete bibliographic data on preliminary sources described in this section.) Perhaps the most useful of these sources is the *Review of Educational Research,* which is published five times a year by the American Educational Research Association. Each number of the *Review of Educational Research* covers an important educational topic and usually contains several articles dealing with different phases of the topic covered. Each of these articles in turn contains an extensive bibliography that a research worker can check for references pertinent to his project. At present the *Review of Educational Research* summarizes the research literature in twenty-three major topics.[10] Most of these topics are covered every three years, and the majority of the research discussed will have been done since the previous review of the topic. Some topics are covered only once every six years, and a few topics have been treated at irregular intervals. Among the topics covered by *Review of Educational Research* are such areas as adult education, cur-

---

[10] The editorial policy of the *Review* has changed recently; unsolicited manuscripts are now accepted for publication. Thus the topics covered by the *Review* may change over the next few years.

riculum planning and development, educational and psychological testing, and guidance and counseling. In order to use the *Review of Educational Research* as a preliminary source, the student must check the topic list that can be found on the back inside cover to determine when reviews pertinent to his subject have been published. He should then obtain these issues and read the articles that provide a very brief discussion and evaluation of the research. Finally, he should check carefully the bibliographies contained in each issue against the bibliography cards he has previously prepared from his search of *Education Index* and/or *Psychological Abstracts* and make up cards for any pertinent sources he has overlooked.

The *Encyclopedia of Educational Research* (4th edition) is primarily of value as a secondary source that gives the student a brief coverage of the status of research in most educational topics. Most of the articles in the *Encyclopedia*, however, have extensive lists of references that the student may check while doing his review of the literature. Occasionally articles will be found in these reference lists that the student has overlooked in his previous search. The *Yearbooks of the National Society for the Study of Education* contain major overviews of a single educational topic each year. Recent yearbooks have been concerned with reading instruction (1968), programmed instruction (1967), social deviancy among youth (1966), and vocational education (1965). If the student's topic of interest has been the focus of a recent yearbook, it can provide an excellent review of previous research and current approaches to studying the topic. Another useful source of research reviews is the series of pamphlets entitled *What Research Says to the Teacher*, published by the National Education Association. However, some of these pamphlets are several years old and therefore cannot be considered up-to-date sources (in contrast to a source such as *Review of Educational Research*). Titles in this series of pamphlets include *Controlling Classroom Misbehavior* (1965), *Listening* (1964), *Creativity* (1963), and *Anxiety as Related to Thinking and Forgetting* (1964). Education journals also sometimes contain reviews of research on an educational topic. *The School Review, Educational Leadership,* and *The Elementary School Journal,* for example, usually include a literature review in each issue. These journals also provide listings of new books and pamphlets that the student may wish to cover in his review of the literature. For the student concerned with use and evaluation of new products in education, the *Educational Product Report* will be a useful source of information. For example, recent issues have contained extensive listings of available products in the areas of text-based phonics programs, black history, programmed instructional materials, and study carrels.

Some of the literature reviews in the field of psychology are pertinent to educational research topics. The *Annual Reviews of Psychology* are an excellent source of such reviews. In the past this series of annual books has contained many reviews of possible interest to the student in education, covering such topics as counseling, educational psychology, human abilities, cognitive functions, developmental psychology, statistical theory, and instructional psychology. Also, *Psychological Bulletin,* published monthly, contains evaluative summaries of research in specialized areas of psychology.

Preliminary sources covering theses and dissertations

Because many theses and dissertations are never published, a check of the following sources is necessary for a thorough coverage of the research literature:

Dissertation Abstracts, Ann Arbor, Mich.: University Microfilms, Inc. (1955 to date). A monthly compilation of abstracts of doctoral dissertations submitted by over one hundred cooperating institutions. Abstracts in education vary in length up to a full page and usually give a good coverage of the essentials of the dissertation. Any dissertation covered in *Dissertation Abstracts* may be purchased from University Microfilms on either microfilm or Xerox, the price being given at the end of the abstract. University Microfilms also has available a service called DATRIX. The basis of DATRIX is a computer file which stores more than 126,000 post-1938 dissertations. To use DATRIX the student selects words pertaining to his area of interest from a key-word list and sends these words to University Microfilms on an order form available at most libraries. In return the student will receive a bibliography of all relevant dissertations and their location in *Dissertation Abstracts.* This service can save the student considerable time in compiling a personal bibliography of dissertations.

Research Studies in Education, Bloomington, Ind.: Phi Delta Kappa (1953 to date). A yearly compilation of doctoral dissertations completed and underway in education. Contains a subject index of dissertations underway, a subject index of dissertations completed, an author index, and a bibliography on research methods. The coverage of dissertations underway is especially useful in helping the student locate current work and avoid duplicating research someone else is doing. The research methods bibliography gives a good coverage of current trends and problems in education, a listing of library guides, bibliographies, and summaries, as well as many useful references dealing with the collection, analysis, and interpretation of research data. *Dissertation Abstracts* is a more useful source for completed dissertations because of the abstract provided.

Master's Theses in Education, H. M. Silvey (ed.), Cedar Falls, Iowa: Research Publications, Iowa State Teachers College (1952 to date). Master's theses are listed under about forty major educational topics covered in the table of contents, such as Achievement and Progress, Adult Education, Delinquency, and Higher Education. Each volume also contains an

author index, a subject index, and an institutional index where theses
written at a given institution may be located.

Preliminary sources covering periodicals and newspapers

Education is a topic of wide general interest, and as a result much is
written about it in popular magazines and newspapers. If your research
topic is in an area that has received public attention, the following sources
should be checked:

Reader's Guide to Periodical Literature, New York: H. W. Wilson Co.
(1900 to date). An author and subject index similar in format to *Education Index* but covering general and nontechnical periodicals published in
the United States. The magazines that are indexed change from time to
time because the aim is to maintain a good subject balance and overlook
no major field rather than provide exhaustive coverage. At present about
130 magazines are being indexed. *Reader's Guide* is an excellent source for
studying the layman's views on education. Because many of the magazines
covered have wide circulation, their influence upon public opinon can be
signficant.

International Index, New York: H. W. Wilson Co. (1907 to date). An
author and subject index that covers about 170 periodicals in the social
sciences and humanities, including many foreign publications. A good
source of views and reports of other social scientists concerning education.
There is very little overlapping between the journals covered in *International Index* and *Education Index.*

The New York Times Index, New York: The New York Times Co. (1913
to date). Provides an index of news printed in the *New York Times.* This
is primarily a subject index but is extensively cross-referenced; it is also
referenced by the names of persons covered in news stories. Brief summaries of most articles are given along with date, page, and column of the
issue where the story may be found. This index is an excellent source of
current information about education and permits the studying of the
development of educational issues and events that could not be traced as
accurately through any other source. It is recommended that the student
look up some current topic that interests him, such as federal aid to education, school building programs, or racial integration, in order to get some
insight into the value of this index as a source of educational information.

Facts on File, New York: Facts on File, Inc. (1941 to date). A weekly
digest of world news that is indexed yearly and published as a yearbook.
Material from newspapers, magazines, broadcasts, government reports,
and so forth are processed daily to produce the weekly digest. Material is
indexed by subject and names of persons appearing in the news. Date of
the event, page, and location on page in the digest section of the yearbook

are given. Because the yearly index and weekly digests are bound together in one volume, *Facts on File* permits the student to locate and read summaries of important educational news stories without going to another source. It is much easier to use than *The New York Times Index,* but coverage is less thorough.

Step three—taking notes

The bibliography card

During his search of the preliminary sources, the student should prepare a bibliography card for each book or article that he believes might contain material pertinent to his review. Although the bibliographical data for a publication is always about the same, these data can be recorded in many different formats. Before starting his review of the literature, the graduate student should check the rules in effect at his college concerning acceptable format for the bibliography section of the thesis or dissertation. Some schools permit the student to use any format that is generally acceptable in his field of study. Other schools have a specific format that must be followed by all graduate students. If your school permits the use of any form that is acceptable in your field, the easiest approach will be for you to use the format of the preliminary source from which you expect to obtain most of your references. *Education Index* is the most productive source for most students working in education, and therefore its format is advantageous to use when permitted. Most of your references will come from the subject index of the *Education Index,* and articles listed by subject give the title of the book or article before the author's name. For your bibliography card, the author's name (last name first) should be listed before the title. This change is necessary because it is much more convenient for you to maintain your note-card file in alphabetical order by author, and the bibliography as prepared for your thesis normally will be listed in this order. Figure 5 shows a bibliography card in the *Education Index* format. If this format is chosen, the bibliographic data from articles found in other sources, such as *Psychological Abstracts,* should be converted to the *Education Index* format. Let us compare bibliographical data for an article as it appears in *Education Index* and *Psychological Abstracts:*

Education Index. Effects of instructions and age on retention of filmed content. H. W. Stevenson and A. Siegel. *J. Ed. Psychol.,* 60:71–4 F'69.
Psychological Abstracts. Stevenson, Harold W., & Siegel, Alexander. (U. Minnesota, Inst. of Child Development) Effects of instructions and age on retention of filmed content. *Journal of Educational Psychology,* 1969, 60 (1), 71–74.

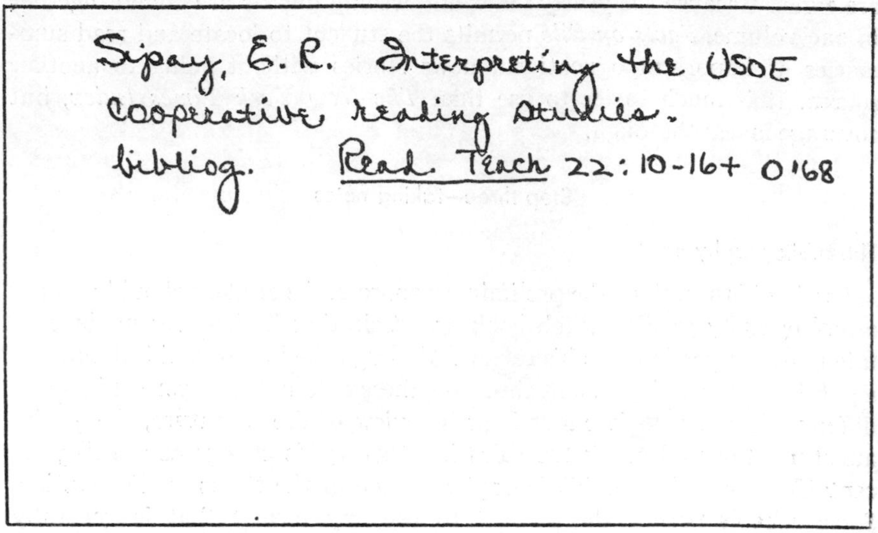

Sipay, E. R. Interpreting the USOE
Cooperative reading studies.
bibliog.   Read. Teach 22: 10-16+ O '68

Fig. 5. Sample bibliography card.

Although these forms are similar, it will be noted that the *Journal of Educational Psychology* is abbreviated differently in the two forms, and the volume number, pages, and year are given in different order; also, the *Education Index* gives month of publication, while the *Psychological Abstracts* form does not. Students reviewing the literature in one of the areas of educational psychology will normally obtain the majority of their references from *Psychological Abstracts,* and, in this case, the *Psychological Abstracts* format may be preferred.

If your college has specified a format for the thesis bibliography that differs from the one used by your preliminary sources, the easiest procedure to follow is to copy the bibliographic data from the preliminary sources in whatever form it is found. Then, when checking the reference in order to determine whether it contains anything pertinent to your review of the literature, you may recopy the bibliographic data in the required school format at the bottom of your bibliography card. You need copy this only for studies that contain pertinent information. Usually, only one out of every three or four references for which the student has prepared bibliography cards will contain material that he wishes to use in his review of the literature.

In preparing bibliography cards, accuracy is extremely important. A mistake made in copying the bibliographic data can often cause the student a great deal of extra work. For example, if he incorrectly copies the name of the journal, date, volume number, or pages, the student will fail to find the article when he checks out the source. On failing to find the article, he is faced with the problem of trying to determine which portion of his bibliographic material is incorrect. Unless the student takes special care, it is easy to make any of these mistakes. After it has been made, the student must usually go back to the preliminary sources in order to find the mistake. As he may well have covered a number of preliminary sources, this search can take much longer than it would have taken to use more care initially. Even if the student makes an error in some portion of the bibliographic data that will not interfere with his finding the material, such as misspelling the author's name, the mistake is still serious because it will probably be repeated in his thesis. Nothing reflects more unfavorably upon the scholarship of the research worker than frequent errors in his bibliographic data.

Using the library

Now that you have completed your search of the preliminary sources in your field and have assembled a set of bibliography cards, it is time to start checking these references in the library. The majority of your references will probably be in professional journals, because this is the principal outlet for primary source research articles.

In using the library to obtain these materials, a great deal of time may be wasted. The student, therefore, is advised to obtain a stack permit and examine the layout of the library to determine what method of obtaining his materials will require the least amount of time. In a library where periodicals in a given field are all shelved in a central location and where study space is available in the stacks, it is usually desirable for the student to work in the stacks. Some libraries, however, do not permit students to enter the stacks, and some, because of space limitations, have journals shelved in such a way that they are difficult to find and cannot be used in the immediate area in which they are shelved. In this case the student can usually save time by making out call slips for about ten periodicals. While waiting for the library clerk to return with these periodicals, the student can make out call slips for his next ten references. The clerk can then look for the second ten references while the student is scanning and making notes on whatever he has received from the first ten call slips. Because a certain percentage of the references that the student wants will be lost, checked out, or in the bindery, it is always advisable to submit call slips for ten or more at a time. Spending a few minutes to determine the most efficient way of obtaining references in his college library will, in the long run, save the student a great deal of time and effort.

Obtaining materials not locally available

The student will almost certainly find that some of the materials he wishes to examine are not available in his college library. There are several ways to obtain these materials, and the student should not give up merely because a source is not available locally. With respect to articles published in professional journals, the quickest and easiest way to obtain those not locally available is to write directly to the author and ask for a reprint of the article. Authors usually receive reprints of their articles and usually are willing to send a reprint to anyone requesting it. Reprints thus received are the student's personal property and should be kept in his file so that he may recheck the article if necessary. The main problem encountered by students in writing for reprints is obtaining the address of the author. If the source has been located in *Psychological Abstracts,* the address is usually given. This information, however, is not available in *Education Index.* A great many authors, however, may be located by checking the various professional directories that are available, such as *Who's Who In American Education, American Psychological Association Directory,* and *American Educational Research Association Directory of Members.* The reference librarian can usually suggest other directories if an individual is not listed in any of the aforementioned.

If the student is unable to obtain a reprint of the article from the author, the next step is to see if the needed journal is available in other libraries in the student's vicinity. In large population centers, where several colleges or universities are located within a small geographical area, the student can usually find the materials he needs at one of the libraries available. In areas where other libraries are not locally available, the student may obtain materials he needs through interlibrary loan. The student should check the policies of his local library regarding interlibrary loan. Many libraries place restrictions upon graduate students in the use of this service because it is rather expensive.

Very often the student wishes to examine several theses and dissertations that are available only in the school library where the work was done. These may be obtained through interlibrary loan, or microfilmed copies of most dissertations may be obtained from University Microfilms, Inc., Ann Arbor, Michigan. Microfilm copies of a dissertation often can be obtained at less expense than borrowing the dissertation through interlibrary loan. Even when more expensive, the microfilm copy is often preferable as it need not be returned and is available for future reference.

The student may usually obtain microfilm or photostatic copies of any reference not locally available. The librarian in his local library will locate needed materials and arrange for their reproduction, but the cost of reproduction and shipping must usually be borne by the student. This cost varies considerably, usually from 15 cents to 35 cents per page. This method is often practical for short articles but expensive for books or lengthy documents. If, however, the needed reference appears to be of major importance, the student should obtain it by some means. The satisfaction of knowing you have done a thorough and scholarly review of the literature will more than compensate for the expense.

Taking notes on research articles

It is advisable for the student to check through his bibliography cards and identify those covering studies that appear most important to his review of the literature. The student should then start his review by checking the most recent of these important studies. The reason for starting with the most recent studies is that these, having the earlier research as a foundation, are likely to be more valuable. By reading the most important articles first, the student quickly builds up a reasonably deep understanding of his problem, and this makes it possible for him to profit more from the subsequent study of articles that are only peripherally related to his topic. After gaining this insight, it is much easier for him to fit these less important studies into the overall picture that he builds of his field through his review of the literature.

When he finally opens the journal to an article he wishes to check, the student should first turn to the summary. The research article almost always contains a short summary, and by reading this the student can usually determine whether the article contains any information that would justify reading the entire article. After reading the summary, if he decides the article is sufficiently pertinent, the student should first check the accuracy of the data on his bibliography card, because the source where he obtained these data could have been in error. He should then record the same bibliographic data on the top of a 5×8-inch note card and take notes on the article as he reads it.

In a research article, the writer attempts to present the essential materials in as brief a form as possible. The student will find that the average research article is only five or six pages in length and thus takes little time to read. The student will also find that the majority of research articles follow a standard pattern that further reduces the time needed to review them. This format usually includes (1) a brief introduction, (2) the hypotheses to be tested, (3) a statement of the procedure including a description of subjects, measures used, and research design, (4) a section giving the findings, and (5) a summary and conclusions. In taking notes the student should be as brief as possible but should not omit anything that he feels he will later use in the design of his study or in the preparation of his research report. A brief outline of the reference using short sentences or phrases with headings for the problem or hypotheses, procedure, findings, and conclusions will usually be sufficient. It is also desirable for the student to record his own evaluation of the study and to note how it may relate to his research while the article is still fresh in his mind. In addition to his outline of the study, it is often profitable to record promising or

Sax, G. and Carr, A., an investigation of response sets on altered parallel forms, Libeiog. Ed + Psychol 7?22 no 2:371-76 Summer '62

Problem: (a) Does response set in subtest format lower reliability? (b) How do subj. responses differ on same test in spiral-omnibus + subtest form?

Procedure: (a) Subj. 335 U. Hawaii freshman, (b) One form Henmon-Nelson Test of mental ability for Col. students adm. in spiral-omnibus form, other converted to subtest form; all subj. to both forms; order of adm. reversed for $\frac{1}{2}$.

Findings: (a) Subj. attempted avg. more items on spiral-omnibus form ($p > .001$), and also got higher scores ($p > .001$). (b) Manual rel. spiral-omnibus 89 vs. 62 for subtest form (act. form); (c) K-R rel. spiral omnibus 81 vs. 85 for subtest form.

Conclusions: Response sets rel. 7ards supporting Cronbach's hyp.

Implications: (a) Increasingly complex items on subtest form discourage students from responding to difficult items. Spiral-omnibus form provides partial reinforcement.

Comments: (a) Pupil rigidity should have been considered as other studies show rigid pupils may do better on subtest form that requires fewer changes in set. (b) K-R doubtful choice for rel. due to speed factor in H.N. test. (c) study generally well-designed.

Fig. 6. Sample note card.

unusual techniques employed in the study, new measures that may be of use, interesting theoretical points, and a critical evaluation including apparent weaknesses that make the results questionable. This critical evaluation of the research is important because the student will often find several research reports that test similar hypotheses but yield different results. Unless the student can make a critical evaluation of the research, it is difficult for him to determine which of the conflicting results is more likely to be correct. Chapter 4 presents a detailed discussion of methods for critically evaluating research articles (see Fig. 6 for a sample note card).

Taking notes on opinion articles

In education many of the articles that the student encounters will not be reports of research projects, but will state the experiences or opinions of the author concerning some educational topic. Opinion articles do not follow the research article format and usually do not contain a summary. When checking the opinion article, the student should first scan the article to get some idea of its content. One method of scanning is to read only the first sentence in each paragraph. After scanning the student should decide whether the article contains material of importance, in which case he should read the entire article. An abstract of the opinion article can usually be prepared most quickly using a sentence outline approach.

Quotations

When reading articles the student should be alert for quotations that might be useful in preparing the review of the literature for his thesis or dissertation. If the student finds material he may wish to quote, the material to be quoted should be copied very carefully on the note card, enclosed in quotation marks, and the page from which the quote was taken noted. Most systems of referencing require that the page be given for direct quotations, and this also facilitates checking the quotation if necessary.

Students often use far too many quotations in their reviews. A good rule to follow is to copy for possible quotations only materials that are stated very skillfully, or in very concise terms, or are typical and clear reflections of a particular point of view the student wishes to illustrate in his thesis. After copying a quotation, the student should recheck to be sure that he has copied it exactly. Inaccurate quotations are a serious reflection on the scholarship of the writer, and it is almost certain that some of the quotations will be checked for accuracy by the faculty members who read the thesis.

Classifying articles you read

In reading articles for your review of the literature, you should keep constantly in mind the objective of your research and should attempt to relate the material you read to your research plan. Do not restrict yourself to the narrow study of only that research that is closely related to the work you are planning. Very often studies that are only partially related to your work will give you new theoretical viewpoints and acquaint you with new tools and methods that can be profitably applied to your research plan.

In doing his review of the literature, the student usually finds that the articles he reads can be classified into several categories. For example, in doing a review of literature in the field of ability grouping, one of the authors found some articles that compare the achievement of students in ability grouping and random grouping systems, some articles that make comparisons of sociometric scores and social status measures between the two systems, some that discuss methods of grouping, and so on. In carrying out his review, the student should be alert for such natural subdivisions because they form a basis for classifying his note cards.

A coding system

As some such pattern for his review emerges, the student should develop a system of coding that will permit him to indicate what type of material is contained on a given note card. The coding system adopted by the research worker will be different for each review of the literature. An example of a coding system used by one of the authors in a recent review of the literature in ability grouping may be helpful to the student in developing his own coding. These codes are generally placed in the upper right hand corner of the note card.

+   An important study
S   Studies dealing with social interaction
A   Studies dealing with achievement of pupils in different grouping systems
G   Studies describing grouping systems and studies discussing problems involved in grouping, such as individual variability, and so forth
B   Studies relating grouping to behavior problems
P   Studies relating grouping to personality adjustment, personality variables, and self concept.

Using such a code is helpful to the student in several ways. It makes him actively aware of the major areas of concentration in his topic. It makes it possible for him to check quickly his notes on a specific portion of the literature, and it makes the job of writing up his review of the literature much easier. The more extensive studies, of course, may contain material relating to two or three subtopics. These are recorded by indicating all the codes for subtopics covered.

MISTAKES OFTEN MADE BY GRADUATE STUDENTS

1. Carries out a hurried review of the literature in order to get started on the research project. This usually results in overlooking previous studies containing ideas that would have improved the student's project.
2. Relies too heavily upon secondary sources.
3. Concentrates on research findings when reading research articles, thus overlooking valuable information on methods, measures, and so forth.
4. Overlooks sources other than education journals, such as newspapers and popular magazines, which often contain articles on educational topics.
5. Fails to define satisfactorily the topic limits of his review of the literature. Searching too broad an area often leads to the student's becoming discouraged or doing a slipshod job. Searching too narrow an area causes him to overlook many articles that are peripheral to his research topic but contain information that would help him design a better study.
6. Copies bibliographic data incorrectly and is then unable to locate the reference needed.
7. Copies far too much material onto note cards. This often indicates that the student does not have a clear understanding of his project and thus cannot separate important from unimportant information.

ANNOTATED REFERENCES

1. Burke, Arvid J., and Burke, Mary A. *Documentation in Education.* New York: Teachers College Press, 1967. A very valuable reference book for any student in education who plans to carry out a review of the literature. Deals with such topics as library searching, making a bibliography, and note taking. Familiarizes the student with many sources that are widely used and are often difficult to find, such as institutional publications, publications of regional educational associations, educational directories, government documents, news items, and others.
2. Gilooly, William B. *The Literature Search.* Somerset, N.J.: Mariner, 1969. The author provides a brief but thorough overview of his subject. Many preliminary sources in fields related to education are discussed, as well as recent innovations in document retrieval.
3. Manheim, Theodore; Dardarian, Gloria L.; and Satterthwaite, Diane A. *Sources in Educational Research: A Selected and Annotated Bibliography.* Detroit, Mich.: Wayne State University Press, 1969. This recent handbook should serve the student as an excellent introduction to the research literature in the various fields of education. Guides, bibliographies, indexes, yearbooks, handbooks, and journals are provided for the general field of educational research as well as the

specific fields of mathematics education, social studies education, library science, comparative education, science education, music education, instructional technology, and language arts.

Abstracting and indexing sources

The following sources are quite useful in locating research articles that have been published in psychology, education, and related fields.

1. *Bibliographic Index*. New York: H. W. Wilson, 1938 to date.
2. Buros, Oscar K. (ed.). *The Sixth Mental Measurements Yearbook*. 5th ed. Highland Park, N. J.: Gryphon, 1965.
3. *Child Development Abstracts*. Washington, D.C.: National Research Council of the Society for Research in Child Development, 1927 to date.
4. *CPSI Abstracts*. Claremont, Calif.: College Student Personnel Institute, 1965 to date.
5. *Current Index to Journals in Education*. New York: CCM Information Sciences, 1969 to date.
6. *Education Index*. New York: Wilson, 1929 to date.
7. *Psychological Abstracts*. Washington, D.C.: American Psychological Association, 1927 to date.
   Cumulated Subject Index to the Psychological Abstracts, 1927–1960. Boston: Hall, 1966.
   Cumulative Author Index to Psychological Index, 1894–1935 and Psychological Abstracts, 1927–1958. Boston: Hall, 1960.
   First Supplement to the Cumulative Author Index to Psychological Abstracts, 1959–1963. Boston: Hall, 1965.
8. *Research in Education*. Washington, D. C.: U.S. Office of Education, 1966 to date.
9. *Sociological Abstracts*. New York: Sociological Abstracts, 1954 to date.
10. *Statistics Sources*. Detroit, Mich.: Gale Research, 1965.

Reviews of research literature

The following sources are helpful to the student in gaining a quick overview of research in education or psychology.

1. Ebel, Robert (ed.). *Encyclopedia of Educational Research*. 4th ed. New York: Macmillan, 1969 (published at ten-year intervals).
2. *Educational Product Report*. New York: Educational Products Information Exchange Institute, 1968 to date.
3. Farnsworth, P. R. (ed.). *Annual Review of Psychology*. Palo Alto, Calif.: Annual Reviews, 1950 to date.
4. Gage, N. L. (ed.). *Handbook of Research on Teaching*. Chicago: Rand McNally, 1963.
5. *Psychological Bulletin*. Washington, D. C.: American Psychological Association, 1904 to date.
6. *Review of Educational Research*. Washington, D. C.: American Educational Research Association, 1931 to date (published five times each year).
7. *The School Review*. Chicago: University of Chicago Press, 1893 to date.

8. *What Research Says to the Teacher.* Washington, D.C.: Department of Classroom Teachers, National Education Association (published at irregular intervals).
9. *Yearbook of the National Society for the Study of Education.* Chicago: University of Chicago Press, 1902 to date (published annually).

Directories

The following directories will help the student locate the addresses of professional workers in education and psychology. This information is needed in order to obtain reprints of articles not available in the local library. If the following directories do not produce the needed information, check under "Directories" in recent issues of *Education Index,* for other sources, or the *Guide to American Directories.* If your library does not have a directory you need, check with faculty members or local educators who may be members of the association publishing the directory.

1. American Educational Research Association. *Directory of Members as of September, 1967.* Washington, D.C.: American Educational Research Association, 1967.
2. *American School Curriculum.* Washington, D.C.: American Association of School Administrators (published each year). Lists names and addresses of over 12,000 members.
3. Klein, Bernard. *Guide to American Educational Directories.* 2nd ed. New York: McGraw-Hill, 1965.
4. Lazo, John A. Q. (ed.). *1968 Directory American Psychological Association.* Washington, D.C.: American Psychological Association, 1968.
5. *Membership Directory and Annual Report.* Washington, D.C.: Department of Elementary School Principals (published each year). Lists names and addresses of over 18,000 elementary school principals, supervisors, and superintendents.

CHAPTER 4

Critical Evaluation of Research

INTRODUCTION

The research worker must build his research upon the knowledge accumulated by previous researchers, and a major goal of the review of the literature is to establish this foundation. Soon after starting his first review of the literature, however, the graduate student will discover that instead of a solid foundation, the previous research appears to provide a foundation of shifting sands. The findings of similar studies will often be contradictory, leaving the student at a loss to decide which, if either, to accept. This problem must usually be resolved by the research worker through a critical evaluation of the research.

The student will find that many of the educational research studies he reviews have such serious flaws and biases that the results must be discounted entirely. The seriousness of this problem should not be underestimated. William Michael, for example, has stated the opinion that only ten percent of the articles that appear in education journals are worth reviewing in *Review of Educational Research*.[1] In 1962 the American Educational Research Association established a Committee on Evaluation of Research to analyze the quality of education journal articles.[2] A total of 125 research reports published in 41 journals during the year 1962 were analyzed by a group of experienced researchers. One of the analyses involved having the researchers take the role of a journal editor and rate each article as acceptable for journal publication, acceptable after revisions were made, or nonacceptable (i.e., reject the article). For the entire sample of articles, all of which had actually been published, only 19 percent were judged acceptable for journal publication! Another 41 percent were judged to be acceptable if they were revised. The remaining 40 percent were recommended for rejection. An interesting finding appeared

[1] William B. Michael, "Teacher Personnel: A Brief Evaluation of the Research Reviewed," *Review of Educational Research*, 33 (1963), 443.

[2] The findings of this committee are reported in Edwin Wandt, "Evaluating Educational Research," in Edwin Wandt (ed.), *A Cross-Section of Educational Research* (New York: McKay), 1965.

when the percentages were computed separately for articles appearing in education journals and articles appearing in journals of related professions, such as psychology. Only 9 percent of education journal articles were rated acceptable, by contrast with 41 percent of related-profession articles. Furthermore, 52 percent of the education articles were recommended for rejection, but only 18 percent of the related-profession articles. This is an unfortunate state of affairs. Hopefully, the present generation of education students is receiving better research training and subsequently will publish journal articles of higher quality. In the meantime the research worker is well advised to review the educational research literature quite critically. This advice is also extended to the teacher or administrator who seeks solutions to his field problems by studying the available research data. The uncritical acceptance of research results by the practitioner can lead to unsound decisions and unjustified changes in educational procedures.

Mistakes, oversights, and biases may occur at any stage of the research process, from the initial steps taken in problem definition to the final phases of statistical analysis. The research worker's effectiveness in detecting these errors is dependent for the most part upon two factors: his knowledge and understanding of the total research process in education and his knowledge in the specific field of his review. Thus, this chapter should properly be studied after one has mastered the next thirteen chapters which cover the entire research process. However, since the chapters are arranged sequentially in terms of the skills required at each step of the research process, it is placed here. Skill in critical evaluation of research is needed early in the research process so that the student can determine the strengths and weaknesses of previous research in his area of interest. The student who cannot properly evaluate the weaknesses of previous research may well repeat them in his own research project. By contrast, the student who can avoid these weaknesses stands a good chance of making a substantial contribution to his area of interest.

Each topic discussed here is covered more fully in a later chapter. Therefore, if he cannot understand a particular topic, the student is advised to look it up in the index and read ahead in the appropriate chapter. Also, the student may profit by supplementing his reading of this chapter with study of the research evaluation check lists presented in Appendices B and C.

FACTORS TO CONSIDER IN EVALUATING RESEARCH

Formulation of the research hypothesis or objective

The first aspect of a research study that should be critically evaluated is the researcher's statement of his hypothesis or objective. Smith found

that weaknesses in this area are a major reason why an average of 70 percent of research proposals submitted to the Cooperative Research Program
are not recommended for funding.[3,4] For example, many researchers set
out to investigate a trivial research problem. Smith provides as an illustration a proposal for an intended study of the role of the high school guidance counselor. This problem in itself is not trivial. However, the researcher's specific objective was to determine how counselors distribute their
time between counseling, group procedures, and student appraisal. Not
only do they overlap, but these categories grossly oversimplify the role of
the high school counselor. No matter how well executed such a study may
be, the findings are likely to be of little significance.

In critically evaluating a research project, the student should also
determine whether the research hypothesis or objective was specific and
clearly stated. An ambiguous, broadly stated hypothesis is a sign that the
researcher has not thought his problem through in sufficient detail. Suppose
the only statement of the researcher's hypothesis is that use of audio-visual
materials in lectures will result in gains in student achievement. This
hypothesis leaves many important questions unanswered. What types of
lectures? What types of student achievement? What is the rationale or
theoretical basis for the hypothesis? The unfortunate consequence of
ambiguous, broadly stated hypotheses is that they yield only ambiguous,
broadly stated conclusions when the study is completed. Suppose that the
hypothesis was not confirmed. What can one conclude about the value of
audio-visual materials in lectures? Very little, since the hypothesis as
stated provided little basis for expecting either positive or negative results.
Therefore, as a first step in evaluating a research project, the student is
advised to examine critically whether the researcher's hypothesis or
objective was developed specifically from theory and previous research
findings.

Deliberate bias or distortion

The goal of research must be the discovery of scientific truth. Unfortunately, many persons who carry out educational research are more interested in obtaining evidence to support a particular viewpoint than in the
discovery of truth. Whenever the researcher has reasons for wanting his
research to support a particular viewpoint, the likelihood of bias is greatly
increased. Occasionally the individual will be so emotionally involved with
his topic that he deliberately slants his findings or even structures his
design to produce a predetermined result. Such cases of deliberate bias are

[3] Gerald R. Smith, "A Critique of Proposals Submitted to the Cooperative Research
Program," in Jack A. Culbertson and Stephen P. Hencley, *Educational Research: New
Perspectives* (Danville, Ill.: Interstate Printers and Publishers, 1963), pp. 277–287.
[4] For a description of the Cooperative Research Program, see Chapter 19.

usually easy to detect because the same emotional involvement that motivates the individual to bias his work is usually reflected in his research report. Studies that are introduced with the phrase "This study was conducted to prove . . ." must be considered suspect. The scientist does not carry out his work to prove a point but to get an answer. The use of emotionally charged words or intemperate language is the most obvious indicator of a biased viewpoint. For example, in reviewing the literature concerned with ability grouping the authors found several articles that referred to ability grouping as "segregation." Inasmuch as this word has strong negative emotional associations for most of us, its use in this context suggests bias. One is not surprised to find that an article entitled "Must We Segregate?" is strongly biased against ability grouping.[5]

Many persons who are emotionally involved with the topic of their research will not deliberately bias their research. Nevertheless, a strong likelihood of bias exists because the person may unconsciously slant his work in a hundred different ways. He may make certain systematic "errors" in sampling, in selecting measures, in scoring the responses of his subjects, and in analyzing and interpreting his results, all of which tend to favor the outcome he wants. Objectivity is always difficult to attain in research in the behavioral sciences and is probably impossible when the researcher is emotionally involved with his topic. Thus the researcher should avoid working in such areas whenever possible.

If his position is such that he must do research in an area where he is involved emotionally, he should have his design checked by several other researchers for omissions or unconscious biases. One of the authors was once directed to conduct a study comparing the effectiveness of air force second lieutenants who had received commissions through the U.S.A.F. Officer Candidate School (O.C.S.) with those who had received commissions through the R.O.T.C. Realizing some bias in favor of the O.C.S. graduate, he had the design carefully checked by other psychologists. One phase of the experiment called for a comparative rating of the effectiveness of officers from the two groups in drilling a company of basic trainees. Officers to be evaluated were to be instructed to report to the drill field in khaki uniform. Raters were not to be told the source of commission of officers being rated. One psychologist, upon reviewing these plans, pointed out that the officers who had graduated from O.C.S. would be immediately recognized as they were required to have their khaki shirts tailored to a close fit, while the R.O.T.C. officers wore loose fitting shirts, which they purchased from the post exchange. Although trying, at least on the conscious level, to avoid bias in this research, the author had "forgotten" this difference in uniforms when designing the research. This clue to source of

[5] C. A. Tonsor, "Must We Segregate?" *National Association of Secondary School Principals' Bulletin,* 37 (1953), 75–77.

commission would have permitted the raters to have reflected their biases in their ratings. In summary, the student should look for the following clues when attempting to locate possible biases of the research worker in a research report:

1. Does the phraseology used suggest that the research worker is inclined to favor one side of the question?
2. Is emotional or intemperate language of either a favorable or unfavorable nature employed?
3. Does the person hold a position or does he belong to a group (racial, vocational, religious, political, ethnic, etc.) that would predispose him in a given direction about the subject of his research?

Sampling bias

All the points that must be remembered in setting up the procedures for selecting a sample for your own research should be applied to evaluating the sampling techniques used by other researchers. Sampling bias in one form or another probably weakens more educational studies than any other factor. Sampling techniques will be discussed in Chapter 5. Let us review some types of sampling bias that should be looked for in evaluating the research of others.

1. *Did the study use volunteers?* Volunteer groups are rarely representative, differing at least in motivation level from nonvolunteers. Motivation is, of course, an extremely important variable in most educational research. A basic weakness of most questionnaire studies is that the persons responding are essentially "volunteers" who may differ greatly from the nonresponding subjects. The results of studies using volunteer subjects can probably be safely applied to other volunteer groups, but *not* to the population from which the volunteers were drawn.

2. *Have subjects been lost?* Studies reporting large losses of subjects in one or more of the groups involved can usually be expected to have sampling bias. The reason for this bias is that subjects are not lost on a random basis. The subjects lost will generally be different from the ones who remain with the study until its completion. The nature and magnitude of these differences, and therefore their effect upon the research results, are difficult to estimate.

3. *In an effort to get subjects who differ in the variable being studied have groups been selected who also differ in other important respects?* Causal-comparative studies often suffer from this form of sampling bias. Some of the early studies of relationships between cigarette smoking and lung cancer illustrate such bias. The "heavy-smoker" sample was obtained in large cities while the "nonsmoker" sample came from rural areas. These two groups were vastly different in many factors other than smoking, such

as living habits, amount of impurities in the air breathed, and pressures of daily life. With sampling biases of this magnitude, it would be difficult for such studies to link lung cancer to smoking with any degree of confidence.

4. *Are subjects extremely nonrepresentative of the population?* Few educational studies are able to employ truly random or representative samples of national populations. Yet, unless samples are extremely biased, the results often have important implications for the large population. For example, although no one would assert that a sample of poor readers taken from the different school districts in Los Angeles County was representative of the nation as a whole, a study involving this sample may well have national implications. This is because most American public schools have much in common, and pupils in one large heterogeneous area such as Los Angeles County who are having reading problems are probably quite similar to pupils in other areas of the country. As the sample becomes less heterogeneous and less representative, however, the general significance of the findings diminishes. Subjects from a single district may lead to a less useful study because of unique district policies concerning reading instruction. On the other hand, such a study using subjects from an obviously nontypical school district, such as one with a large Latin-American population, may have no general implications because of the nonrepresentative nature of the group and the relationship between bilingualism and reading difficulties. Similarly, a study of attitudes toward Negroes using a sample from New Orleans, or a study of attitudes toward smoking using a sample from Salt Lake City, would produce little information of general significance, although such studies might throw much light on the situation in the area sampled.

In some studies a great deal more care is devoted to obtaining a representative experimental group than a representative control group. This difference probably stems from the erroneous notion of inexperienced researchers that the experimental group is far more important and that any subjects will serve for the control group. Because the performance of the experimental group must be weighed against the control group, a biased control group can obviously lead to erroneous results. Thus, careless selection of the control group should be watched for. In reviewing the research of others, it must be remembered that nonrepresentative samples do not produce data of general significance and often yield results that are misleading, and can lead to serious blunders if applied to the general population. If such a study is read, the findings must be interpreted with the sampling bias in mind.

Have important variables been overlooked?

Many studies are found in education that have overlooked or failed to control important variables. Such studies usually produce misleading results because the influence of the uncontrolled variable upon the dependent variable cannot be assessed. For example, many of the early studies comparing the effectiveness of televised instruction with conventional classroom instruction failed to control teaching ability. The usual procedure was to select the best teacher available and give this person the full day to prepare his TV lesson. Progress of TV pupils was then compared with progress of pupils in conventional classrooms having average teachers who taught the usual four to six classes daily. The results, which were loudly hailed as proof that television had some intrinsic merit that greatly increased learning, were in fact nothing more than a demonstration that better teachers who have more preparation time do a better job. Better controlled studies concerned with TV instruction showed little or no difference as compared with conventional classroom instruction.

Inasmuch as each of us brings a different background of perception and experience to focus upon a given problem, it is not surprising that one person may overlook the importance of a variable that is immediately apparent to another. The best way to avoid overlooking important variables in your own research is to have your design studied and criticized by several other researchers before starting to collect data. The previous research exposes the research worker to a number of different viewpoints about his research area and reduces his chances of overlooking or failing to control an important variable. Many such oversights can be traced to a careless and inadequate review of the literature.

Critical evaluation of measurement techniques

Many of the weaknesses and limitations of educational research can be attributed to the inadequacies of our measures. Many tools and techniques of educational measurement are crude and of doubtful validity. We will discuss the procedures for evaluating measurement tools in Chapter 6. Let us review these and related concepts with special attention to applying these methods to the critical evaluation of research.

A thorough check of all measuring instruments and techniques reported in all studies reviewed would be a very time-consuming task, and it is not recommended for the student doing his first review of the literature. The student should make such a check, however, of the measures used in any studies that are of major importance in his review. Any study that has yielded findings that make an important contribution to the area of the review or have an important bearing on the researcher's own design should be thoroughly checked. If standard measures are cited with which the student is not familiar, he should study a specimen set, consult the *Mental Measurements Yearbook,* and check other sources of information to be discussed in Chapter 6. If the measures used are new or have been developed for the research being evaluated, the student should obtain a copy and weigh the measure carefully against his knowledge of test development techniques and the theoretical constructs upon which the measure is based. The findings of research that the student reads can only be evaluated after the measurement tools that produced these findings have been carefully appraised and the probable effects or flaws in these instruments have been considered.

Let us briefly summarize some of the questions that the student should ask when evaluating the measurement tools employed in research closely pertinent to his own topic.

1. *What reliability data are available?* The type of reliability calculated and the reliability coefficient should both be checked. Tests of very low reliability often lead to negative results even though the use of more reliable instruments would have given positive results. Thus the student should consider carefully the possible effects of low reliability upon the reported results of studies he evaluates and should not reject a promising hypothesis from his own study because of negative findings based on small samples of unreliable measures.

2. *What validity evidence is available?* As discussed in Chapter 6, there are four important types of validity. The validity evidence should be studied carefully because interpretation of the research results hinges on the validity of the measures upon which these results are based. The absence of extensive validity data in a new measure does not mean the measure lacks validity but definitely limits the interpretations that can be made. Many inexperienced research workers accept standardized educational measures at face value and assume that these measures are valid, although little evidence is put forth by the test publisher to support this assumption. It is generally safer in the case of measures of dubious validity to consider the results reported to be tentative at best.

3. *Is the measure appropriate for the sample?* In evaluating the research of others, it should be remembered that even a well-standardized and generally accepted measure will have little value if applied to an inappropriate sample. A typical mistake made by inexperienced researchers is to use a measure that is more appropriate for some subsamples of the research group than others, therefore biasing results in favor of the subsamples whose background gives them an advantage on the measure. Occasionally tests are employed that are either too easy or too difficult for the majority of the sample measured. For example, a study of achievement of children at different ability levels will have little meaning if the measures used have too low a ceiling, thus limiting the level of achievement that a superior student can display.

4. *Are test norms appropriate?* Many educational research projects compare the performance of the research sample with normative data that

have been provided with the measure. If normative data are to be used, the comparability between the research group and the test norm group should be checked. Some tests, although generally applicable to the sample tested, have single items that are invalid. Some of the older intelligence tests, for example, have drawings of such objects as automobiles, airplanes and telephones that are so different in appearance from the form familiar to today's children that the test item so illustrated has lost much of its validity. Such errors, although not immediately apparent to most adults have a significant influence on test scores.

Many more subtle forms of measurement bias may also make significant differences in research findings. For example, the authors recently encountered a questionnaire being used in an educational followup study in which the respondent was to rate various aspects of a school he had attended using five quality levels. The quality levels provided were "excellent," "superior," "very good," "average," and "below average." It will be noted that, on this scale, average is not located in the middle of the alternate choices. When asked why the choices were arranged in this way the research worker stated that he had observed in previous questionnaire that more responses occur above the average line of the scale and he had therefore, provided an extra classification on the above average side. He was surprised to find that the ratings he had obtained in this followup study were somewhat higher than those obtained in previous studies of the same school. When using the quality levels just mentioned, the mean response fell between the "superior" and "very good" categories as compared with a mean response between "average" and "very good" in previous studies. This suggested a higher evaluation of the course of study being followed up. Actually, however, the errors of leniency and central tendency (see Chapter 9) would lead most respondents to rate a course of study average or slightly above average if they had no strong feelings about one way or the other. Because most people consider the average rating to be the one that falls in the middle, when the research worker changed the names of his categories, the respondents continued to check the middle category or the one adjacent to and higher than the middle. Thus, in terms of the mean position of the responses on a 5-point scale, no change occurred, but in terms of the adjectives employed, there was an apparent improvement in the respondents' evaluation of the school. Use of unbalanced response choices in which more opportunities are available for favorable response than for an unfavorable response will tend to yield responses with a favorable bias. The danger of such biases is well known to experienced measurement specialists and, therefore, errors of the sort just described are more likely to be found in measures developed specifically for the research project by an inexperienced researcher. If the use of such measures is reported in research projects pertinent to the student field of interest, he should request copies in order that he may study them for biases of the sort previously described.

Observer bias

Human beings have a disturbing tendency to see what they want to see, hear what they want to hear, and remember what they want to remember. Observer bias has been recognized as a problem by workers in the physical sciences for centuries, and techniques to control such bias are routinely included in physical science experiments. Workers in the behavioral sciences have not only attempted to control observer errors, but have studied these biases and found them to be much more subtle and complex than physical scientists had imagined.

Rostand [6] tells us a remarkable but true story that illustrates the dangers of observer bias, even in scientific areas such as physics that deal with phenomena that are much simpler, more concrete, and more adaptable to measurement than are the elusive substances of the behavioral sciences. This example deals with the N ray, which was discovered by a distinguished French physicist, René Blondlot, while investigating X rays that had been discovered a short time earlier by Röntgen. After discovering the N ray, Blondlot went on to study its characteristics. He found the ray increased the brightness of any luminous object. A Nernst filament was found to be a rich source of N rays and produced a radiation so intense that Blondlot doubted that anyone with eyes could fail to see it. In fact, of the many persons who were permitted to observe these rays, Blondlot reports only three or four who failed to see them. As his experiments continued, Blondlot discovered that the sun was a source of N rays. He learned that N rays could be stored in certain substances such as quartz and later reemitted. Further experiments revealed that external stresses caused certain substances to emit N rays. Finally, Blondlot set up a series of careful experiments using three independent measures that resulted in measuring the wavelength of the N ray. The results of measurements using the three different approaches were highly consistent. By February 1904, photographs had been taken that showed the effect of N rays on an electric spark. Upon this discovery Bordier, lecturer at Lyons Medical School, rebuked the few doubters who had not been able to see the N ray by pointing out:

Such observers have only themselves to blame; no doubt they used faulty techniques or else the source of radiation was impaired; in any case, the existence of N rays will never again be put in doubt, particularly now that their action has been recorded *photographically*, i.e. by a purely objective method.[7]

[6] Jean Rostand, *Error and Deception in Science* (New York: Basic Books, 1960). Reprinted by permission of Basic Books, Inc.

[7] *Ibid.*, p. 18. Reprinted by permission of Basic Books, Inc.

Other researchers now began to report extensive findings from their experiments on the N ray. The experiments of one scientist revealed that sound vibrations gave rise to N rays; another found N rays emitted from a magnetic field, another from liquefied gasses, and so on.

Charpentier, Professor of Biophysics at Nancy, discovered that N rays were liberated from the muscles and nerves of living animals and concluded that these rays might play a fundamental role in biology. Many other experiments were stimulated by this discovery. Because N rays were emitted from nerves, studies of the anatomy of the nervous system became possible and were started. This technique, of course, had very important implications for medical science. For example, research workers soon discovered that changes in N radiation occurred as a consequence of certain diseases of the nervous system.

In 1904, less than two years after Blondlot had reported his original work, an imposing body of knowledge had been amassed concerning the N ray. Yet, we hear nothing about N rays today. The fact is that *the N ray does not and never did exist,* and within a few short months after these later discoveries, the entire edifice erected by Blondlot and his colleagues had tumbled down.

Doubting voices had been raised from the very beginning of Blondlot's discovery and some specialist objections had never been silenced effectively. Still, no amount of doubting or criticism had been able to halt the triumphant progress of the new science. All the world had clearly observed a phenomenon that had never existed. Then, almost over night, the hypnotic spell was broken.

The Nancy group and some of its faithful managed to put up some slight resistance, but the whole business was dropped and buried once and for all. N-rays, N_1-rays, and physiological radiations would never again grace the pages of scientific journals, in which they had cut so marvellous a figure. . . .

The most astonishing facet of the episode is the extra-ordinarily great number of people who were taken in. These people were not pseudoscientists, charlatans, dreamers, or mystifiers; far from it, they were true men of science, disinterested, honourable, used to laboratory procedure, people with level heads and sound common sense. This is borne out by their subsequent achievements as Professors, Consultants and Lecturers. Jean Becquerel, Gilbert Ballet, Andre Broca, Zimmern, Bordier—all of them have made their contribution to science.

No less extraordinary is the *degree of consistency, and of apparent logic that pervaded the whole of this collective delusion;* all the results were consistent, and agreed within fairly narrow limits. . . .

While we have no evidence that flattery or deception was at the roots of the discovery of N-rays, we may take it that the urge to make new discoveries, so powerful in all men of science, played a considerable role from the very start. Coupled with this urge were *preconceived ideas, and autosuggestion* together with the desire to break new ground.

The remarkable history of N-rays is full of morals both for the individual, and also for the social, psychologist.[8]

Although observations are sometimes deliberately biased by the researcher with an ax to grind, the more serious danger is from biases of which the researcher is unaware such as those that occurred in research on the N ray. These undeliberate and unconscious observer biases are often undetectable from the usual research report that appears in the professional journal. For example, an interviewer may unconsciously give the subject subtle signs of approval and disapproval to different responses that will tend to encourage the subject to give the approved answer whether it is true or not. Although the information available to the student is too limited for him to expect to detect many such biases, he should, nonetheless, search carefully for evidence of their existence, and weigh their possible effects when they are discovered.

The methods of descriptive research, especially interview and observation studies, are perhaps most susceptible to observer bias. Let us review some of the main sources of such bias that the student should watch for in critically evaluating descriptive research:

1. Does the interview guide contain leading questions? Is it structured in such a way as to give the subject clues as to the preferred answer?

2. Does the observer's or interviewer's method of recording behavior or responses permit undue emphasis upon behavior that is in accordance with observer biases or expectations? Use of tape recordings greatly reduces danger of this bias.

3. Do methods of recording behavior require that the observer or interviewer draw inferences about the meaning of the behavior he is observing? In general, the more inferences the observer must draw, the more the likelihood of bias.

4. Are questions asked that might threaten, embarrass, or annoy some respondents, thus leading them to give false or unsatisfactory replies?

Hawthorne effect

In experiments involving human subjects, a great many subtle influences can distort research results. If the individual is aware that he is participating in an experiment, for example, this knowledge may alter his performance and therefore invalidate the experiment. A series of studies carried out at the Hawthorne Plant of the Western Electric Company first called attention to some of these factors.[9] In this study the illumination in three departments in which employees inspected small parts, assembled

[8] *Ibid.*, pp. 27–29. Reprinted by permission of Basic Books, Inc.
[9] Fritz J. Roethlisberger and W. J. Dickson, *Management and the Worker* (Cambridge, Mass.: Harvard University Press, 1940).

electrical relays, and wound coils was gradually increased. The production efficiency in all departments generally went up as the light intensity increased. It was found, however, that upon decreasing the light intensity in a later experiment, the efficiency of the group continued to increase slowly but steadily. Further experiments, with rest periods and varying the length of working days and weeks, were also accompanied by gradual increases in efficiency whether the change in working conditions was for the better or for the worse. It appears that the attention given the employees during the experiment was the major factor leading to these production gains. This phenomenon is referred to by psychologists as the "*Hawthorne effect*." The factory workers who carried out the same dull, repetitive task month after month were stimulated and motivated by the attention and concern for their well-being that was displayed by the research workers. A new element had been added to their dull existence—not illumination or the other variables that the researchers were studying—but the researchers themselves. The term "*Hawthorne effect*" has come to refer to any situation in which the experimental conditions are such that the mere fact that the subject is participating in an experiment or is receiving special attention will tend to improve his performance. Certainly many educational experiments report changes and improvements that are due primarily to *Hawthorne effect*. Studies involving methods, for example, in which one group of teachers continues with the same teaching methods it has previously employed while another group is trained in a new method and receives considerable help and attention in implementing this method will usually result in changes in teacher performance or pupil achievement favorable to the new methods. Many school districts, in the process of trying out new methods, frequently set up a one-year experiment in which the new method is introduced to a limited number of pupils. The results of such experiments are almost certainly influenced by *Hawthorne effect* because teachers usually approach a new method with some enthusiasm, and the students, being aware that they are being taught by a new and different method, are also likely to display more interest and motivation than usual. The influence of *Hawthorne effect* can be expected to decrease in the school situation as the novelty of the new method wears off and therefore, studies extending over a period of two or three years can be relied upon somewhat more in evaluating the effectiveness of a new technique.[10]

Placebos

A placebo is a chemically inert substance that is administered in the same manner as the drug or active substance under investigation. Placebo

[10] *Ibid.*

are employed in medical research and in educational and psychological studies in which the effects of various substances on human behavior are being tested. The purpose of the placebo is to make it impossible for the subject to determine whether or not he is receiving the active substance under study as this knowledge may have an effect upon his behavior. Many studies have demonstrated that if one group of subjects receives some sort of attention, such as the administration of a drug, while the control group receives no comparable attention, some of those receiving the drug will react in various ways that cannot be explained by the chemical or medical effects of the drug. Although relatively little is known about the psychological factors causing such reactions, it seems likely that the human contact with the researcher and the subject's expectation that something will occur as a result of the substance he has received contribute significantly. The results of such studies that do not use placebos are always subject to doubt because the proportion of the results that are attributable to psychological factors and the proportion caused by the drug cannot be determined. The placebo, in effect, acts as a control permitting the psychological factors to operate. The physical or behavioral changes brought about by the active substance cannot operate in control group subjects because the active substance is not present in the placebo. Even when using placebos, it has been found that if the experimenter knows which subjects receive the active substance and which subjects receive the placebo, this knowledge can lead to observer bias or can result in the researcher's unconsciously giving the subject subtle clues, such as watching for reactions more attentively in cases where the subjects have received the active substance. Therefore, most studies aimed at evaluating the effects of drugs or other substances now employ what is called the "double-blind" technique, in which neither the experimenter nor the subject knows when the active substance or when the placebo is being taken. Obviously, in order to attain this situation, the placebo must be identical to the active drug in those characteristics that may be compared by the subject, such as appearance and taste.

Although placebos play a useful role in helping control psychological variables, many researchers fail to recognize that the control attained is still subject to error. Medical studies have demonstrated that there is considerable individual difference in reaction to placebos. Some individuals tend to react to placebos while others do not. For example, some hospital patients will consistently report a reduction in pain following the administration of an inert substance while others will not. Persons may show either a positive or negative reaction to the placebo. Beecher found that the incidence of relief reported in 15 studies involving medical placebos ranged from 15 to 58 percent. However, he also found thirty-five different toxic effects that occurred after the administration of placebos.[11]

Persons who react to placebos are referred to as *placebo reactors.* In small sampling studies, there is always a possibility that the control group will contain a larger number of *placebo reactors* than the experimental group. If this is the case, the results of the experiment may be negative even though the active substance being tested has a definite effect upon the experimental subjects. Some studies have shown that if *placebo reactors* are screened out, significant differences sometimes emerge that would not show up otherwise.[12] As yet we know very little about the degree to which some persons are consistently placebo reactors or whether such persons are different from individuals who do not react to placebos in terms of personality and other variables. Some evidence suggests that such differences do exist, and until we know more about placebo reaction, differences in this variable can considerably distort research findings involving small samples.[13]

Observer and statistical contamination

Faulty research design often permits contamination to occur in educational studies. Contamination refers to any situation in which data that should be kept independent to satisfy the requirements for sound research have in some way become interrelated. We will discuss various ways in which contamination can enter the research design in later chapters. Let us mention some of these briefly here.

Observer contamination

Observer contamination usually arises when the research worker has knowledge of the subject's performance on the dependent variable, and this knowledge influences his observation of the behavior of the subject on the independent variable. Let us suppose, for example, that we are doing a study of the relationship between the amount of conflict present in the home environment of the child and behavior in the classroom involving direct and indirect aggression. If the observer collected data on conflicts in the home prior to carrying out his classroom observations, there would be a strong possibility that his knowledge of the child's home environment

[11] H. K. Beecher, "The Powerful Placebo," *Journal of American Medical Association,* 159 (1955), 1602–1605.

[12] H. K. Beecher, A. S. Keats, F. Mosteller, and L. Lasagna, "The Effectiveness of Oral Analgesics (Morphine, Codeine, Acetylsalicylic Acid) and the Problem of Placebo 'Reactors' and 'Nonreactors,'" *Journal of Pharmacology and Experimental Therapeutics,* 109 (1953), 393–400.

[13] L. Lasagna, J. Mosteller, J. M. von Felsinger, and H. K. Beecher, "A Study of the Placebo Response," *American Journal of Medicine,* 16 (1954), 770–779.

would influence his interpretation of the child's aggressive behavior in the classroom. In other words, if he had hypothesized that children coming from home environments involving conflicts would display more direct aggression in the classroom, he would tend to look for signs of direct aggression in these children and would be likely to see more direct aggression and interpret questionable behavior as direct aggression. Observer contamination, of course, is not limited to studies in which the person uses observational techniques. Any research situation that involves subjective evaluations, drawing implications, or making judgments on the part of the research worker is subject to this form of contamination. In any situation where a knowledge of one aspect of the research can influence the research worker in his appraisal of other aspects of his research data, the possibility of contamination is present.

Statistical contamination

Statistical contamination occurs when data that have in some way become related are treated as being independent in the statistical analysis. An example of statistical contamination was recently encountered by one of the authors in the work of one of his doctoral candidates. The student was carrying out a study of characteristics related to success of elementary school principals. The design called for the participation of each person to be evaluated in six role-playing situations. In each situation the subject was evaluated independently by two raters on a number of pertinent behaviors. These specific evaluations were combined in order to provide an overall evaluation of the individual as a principal. In carrying out his analysis, the student found a high correlation between observer ratings in the specific area of "human relations skills" and the overall evaluations of the individual's effectiveness. From this correlation he concluded that "human relations skills" constituted by far the most important factor in the effective performance of elementary school principals. He had failed to realize, however, that because the overall rating also included the rating of human relations skills, which was the most heavily weighted of the specific rating areas, he was in effect correlating human relations skills with itself to the extent that it was part of the overall rating. Such correlations are, of course, spurious and indicate statistical contamination.

Critical evaluation of statistical analyses

As part of Wandt's study of the quality of educational research articles, a panel of experts was asked to identify shortcomings of articles that were rated "revise" or "reject." [14] The two most frequently cited shortcomings

[14] Edwin Wandt, *Educational Research*, ibid.

were that the results of statistical analyses were not clearly presented and that incorrect statistical methods were used to analyze data. Therefore, the student is advised to be particularly critical of statistical analyses presented in journal articles.

Many types of errors may be present in the statistical analysis of research data. As he acquires more training and experience with statistical tools, the student will become increasingly able to detect such mistakes. Often statistical errors occur simply because the researcher does not know how to use a particular statistical technique. For example, the researcher may do a t-test to determine the statistical significance of a difference between mean scores and, in the process of doing the computations, he will compute the wrong degrees of freedom. Also the wrong statistical technique may be selected. The researcher may select a parametric statistical technique even though the distribution of scores is badly skewed; when this situation occurs, a nonparametric technique should be used. Another weakness of some statistical analyses is that they are carried out only for the total sample and not for subgroups as well. For example, the researcher may find a significant correlation between two variables in a sample of students. Assuming adequate sample size, the researcher should then determine whether the correlation also exists for selected subgroups, such as boys versus girls and students at different grade levels.

Errors frequently occur in the interpretation of statistical findings. Researchers often have a tendency to confuse the statistical significance of research results with their practical significance. An illustration of this point can be found in a recent study of readability of science materials.[15] In this generally well-designed study, the investigator determined the effect on student comprehension of rewriting a sixth-grade science textbook to a third-grade level of readability. The experimental group received the rewritten reading material, while the control group received the original text. On a test of comprehension of the reading passages, it was found that the experimental group scored significantly higher ($p < .05$) than the control group. There is no problem with the statistical analysis so far. However, on the basis of this finding, the investigator recommends that sixth-grade science textbooks be rewritten by publishers and by teachers during summer writing conferences. Is this recommendation, which entails a good deal of work for educators, warranted by the statistical findings? When we look at the data more closely, we find that the comprehension test administered to all students contained 129 items. The mean scores of the experimental and control groups on this test were 76.97 and 73.48, respectively. Thus, there is only a difference of 3.5 items between the two

[15] David L. Williams, "Rewritten Science Materials and Reading Comprehension," *The Journal of Educational Research,* 61 (1968), 204–206.

groups on a test containing 129 items. The difference is statistically significant, but this can be attributed to the fact that a very large sample (417 students) was used. Even a very small difference between mean scores is likely to be statistically significant with this large a sample. In short, the research results do achieve statistical significance, but they can hardly be said to have significance for educational practice. In critically evaluating research, the student should make a point of checking that the investigator has not "overinterpreted" the results of his statistical analyses.

SUMMARY

This chapter has attempted to alert the student to some of the factors that must be considered in critically evaluating the research of others. By carrying out the critical evaluations of research pertinent to his problem thoroughly and carefully, he will not only gain a sounder insight into this work but will also develop a better understanding of the entire field of educational research that will steadily improve the quality of his own work. At best, an introduction to research such as is presented in this text can do little more than start the student on the road to maturity as a research worker. After gaining this foundation, the student must work with more experienced researchers and do research of his own if he is to progress further.

This chapter is far from an exhaustive coverage of all the elements that must be considered in critical evaluation of research. Although guides and checklists are available, it is doubtful that a truly exhaustive evaluation could be written because scholars and researchers in the behavioral sciences are discovering new sources of research error and new methods of doing research almost daily. Thus, even the experienced research worker will almost certainly overlook some errors and biases when he evaluates research. The goal of both the beginning graduate student and the research worker with many years of experience is thus the same in critically evaluating research—to do the best job that he can. The student who does a careful and sincere job in this phase of his review of the literature will find himself repaid by significant growth in maturity and research sophistication.

ANNOTATED REFERENCES

1. Allen, E. M. "Why Are Research Grant Applications Disapproved?" *Science*, 32 (1960), 1532–1534. This article discusses why research projects submitted to the National Institutes of Health were disapproved, and, based on an analysis

of the minutes of evaluation meetings carried out in 605 of these disapproved proposals, the author has constructed a table classifying the major reasons for disapproval. This article gives the student many insights into common short-comings of research design as seen by scientists who sit on advisory boards, and can assist the student in evaluating his own research ideas.

2. Eysenck, H. J. "The Effects of Psychotherapy: An Evaluation," *Journal of Consulting Psychology*, 16 (1952), 319–324. This classic article presents a critical evaluation of the research literature on the effectiveness of psychotherapy. On the basis of his critique, the author concluded that about two thirds of psychiatric patients improve over time, with or without therapy. The education student will find this article a masterful example of the critical evaluation technique. Also, the student may be interested in reading critiques by other authors who reached different conclusions on the basis of their reviews of the same literature. A list of these critiques can be found in Sundberg, Norman D., and Tyler, Leona A. *Clinical Psychology*. New York: Appleton-Century-Crofts (1962), p. 301.

3. Orlansky, H. "Research on the Series of Infant Care as Related to Personality," *Psychological Bulletin*, 46 (1949), 1–48. This article provides a critical evaluation of research relating to Freudian and neo-Freudian theories concerning the relationship between infant care and later personality development. The article provides an excellent example of how critical evaluation techniques can be applied to gain a clearer picture of the status of knowledge in the scientific field.

4. *Psychological Bulletin*. Washington, D. C.: American Psychological Association, 1904 to date. This journal presents critical reviews of the research literature on psychological topics. The student should read some of these reviews in order to observe some techniques of critical evaluation in practice.

5. Sells, S. B. "Psychological Aspects of Research Design." Taken from Collier, R. O., and Elam, S. M. (eds.), *Research Design and Analysis, 2nd Annual Phi Delta Kappa Symposium on Educational Research*. Bloomington, Ind.: Phi Delta Kappa, 1961. Sells emphasizes in Chapter 5 the importance of situational variables in influencing research results in the behavioral sciences and the need for developing methodological tools for properly recognizing these variables. The value system of the experimenter and the subject and their frames of reference are also discussed as factors influencing the outcome of research in the behavioral sciences.

6. Smith, Gerald R. "A Critique of Proposals Submitted to the Cooperative Research Program," in Jack A. Culbertson and Stephen P. Hencley. *Educational Research: New Perspectives*. Danville, Ill.: Interstate Printers and Publishers, 1963, 277–287. This article provides insight into the criteria that experts use to critically evaluate research proposals for possible funding by the Office of Education. The four main criteria discussed are significance of the problem for education, soundness of the research design, personnel and facilities available to conduct the investigation, and economic efficiency of the investigation.

7. Stinnett, T. M. "Check That Statistic!" *Educational Record*, 38 (1957), 83–90. This article demonstrates ways in which the professional reader and the general public may be misled by biased reporting of statistical information. Many inter-

esting examples from the field of education are given. The student who has been disturbed by the many shocking statistics about education quoted by public figures in the last few years would do well to study this article carefully. The type of critical questioning advocated by the author is one of the most important characteristics of a competent research worker.

CHAPTER 5

Selecting the Sample

THE NEED FOR SAMPLING TECHNIQUES TO SELECT SUBJECTS

A common mistake in educational research is to use whatever persons are available as research subjects. For example, a researcher might select all his subjects from one school because he happens to know the school principal and is sure that the principal will grant permission to do the study in his school. The problem with this strategy is that the research results cannot be generalized reliably to another sample of subjects. Suppose that the researcher who has selected all his subjects from one school finds that teaching method A results in significantly better learning than teaching method B. A principal in another school can legitimately raise the question: How do I know that teaching method A will be superior in *my* school?

Generalization from one school to another or from one sample of students to another is a risky business—unless the researcher has selected subjects by means of appropriate sampling techniques. The method of selecting a sample is critical to the whole research project. If research findings are not generalizable to some degree beyond the sample used in the study, then the research cannot provide us with new knowledge, cannot advance education as a science, and is largely a waste of time.

The proper selection of research subjects is important for another reason. If an adequate number of subjects is not included in the sample, then one's confidence in the research findings will be shaky. Research findings based on a sample of two or three subjects are apt to be highly unreliable. If we studied another sample of this size, it is quite likely that different findings would be obtained. It is important to select a sample of adequate size in order to produce research data that reliably approximate the data that would be obtained if the entire population were studied.

In this chapter we shall discuss sampling techniques that enable the researcher to select a sample that is representative of a larger population. Since proper sampling is such an important element of a good research study, we shall continue to discuss this topic in later chapters too. Al-

114

though our discussion will be concerned primarily with the selection of subjects for a research project, the student should note that the sampling techniques discussed here also pertain to the selection of events or objects for research. For example, sampling techniques would be used if the researcher wished to select a random sample of class periods for systematic observation, or a random sample of textbooks in order to do a content analysis.

DEFINING THE POPULATION

Sampling means selecting a given number of persons from a defined population as representative of that population. By population, also called "universe," we mean all the members of a real or hypothetical set of persons, events, or objects. The advantage of drawing a small sample from a large population is that it saves the researcher the time and expense of studying the entire population. If the sampling is done properly, the researcher can reach valid conclusions about an entire population by studying only a small sample drawn from that population.

The first step in sampling is to define the population from which the sample is to be drawn. Typical populations from which educational research samples might be drawn include: school superintendents in the state of Utah, practice teaching supervisors in state-supported teacher's colleges, bilingual children in the primary grades of the San Antonio City School District, pupils failing algebra in Hoover High School, and seniors graduating from American public high schools in June of 1963. It may be seen from the previously mentioned examples that the population to be sampled may represent a large group scattered over a wide geographical area or a rather small group concentrated in a single school.

If the research worker defines his population narrowly, the results of his research on a sample of this population will be generalizable only to the narrow population, although the results may have implications for a broader population having similar characteristics. For example, let us say that we wish to study the reading ability of fifth-grade pupils in American public elementary schools. This is a broadly defined population, and in order to obtain a satisfactory sample of this population, a complex method of identifying and selecting cases from different areas, different sized communities, and different types of schools would have to be developed. Obviously the selection of such a sample and collection of data would involve a tremendous amount of work. Opinion polls such as those that attempt to predict the outcome of national elections must use such complex techniques in order to have some assurance that their samples are representative. On the other hand, the aforementioned population could be defined as all fifth-grade pupils in a selected state. Now, because the population is much smaller, the problem of obtaining a sample of this population would be easier. However, the research results based on this sample would be generalizable only to fifth-grade students in the state from which the sample was selected. To the degree to which these fifth-grade pupils were similar to the fifth-grade pupils in other states, the findings of the research could have implications for a broader population. Often the financial limitations or the nature of the research area limit us to sampling the student population of a single school district. Studies based upon this narrow population are, of course, less generalizable but may still have important implications for other educators.

It is beyond the scope of most research projects to identify all the members of a defined population. For example, the identification by name of all fifth-grade teachers in even a single state would be a major undertaking. Thus, researchers usually rely on published lists of various populations which are of interest to educators. The researchers responsible for Project TALENT, which we discussed in Chapter 1, used the *Directory of Public Secondary Day Schools* [1] in order to define the population of American high schools from which their random sample was drawn.[2] Most researchers will only be able to define populations at the state or district level. In these cases the state or district education office should be contacted to find out if they have a list defining the population in which you are interested. State and district education departments usually maintain complete lists of several different school characteristics (e.g., schools, principals, teachers, buildings) for administrative purposes. In certain instances the researcher may wish to contact a national association or national directory, even though the defined population is at the state or district level. For example, suppose one wished to survey a random sample of educational researchers in a given state. One might obtain a national directory, such as the *National Register of Educational Researchers,*[3] and go through it, marking all the educational researchers residing in that state. Then, from the defined subpopulation, a random sample of educational researchers can be selected. The *Guide to American Educational Directories* [4] is a helpful source for locating directory lists that can be used to define populations.

In using any published list to define a population, the student should check to determine whether it is complete and up-to-date. School enroll-

[1] Leah W. Ramsey, *Directory of Public Secondary Day Schools 1958–59*, publication no. OE-20031 (Washington, D.C.: Government Printing Office, 1961).

[2] F. G. Cornell and E. P. McLoone (see annotated references) mention lists that have been used in other research studies to define a national population.

[3] Bureau of Educational Research, the Ohio State University, *National Register of Educational Researchers* (Bloomington, Ind.: Phi Delta Kappa, 1966).

[4] Bernard Klein, *Guide to American Educational Directories*, 2nd ed. (New York: McGraw-Hill, 1965).

ment and memberships of organizations are constantly changing, so frequent updating of population lists is necessary. Also it should be realized that membership in most organizations is voluntary. Thus, if the student uses an organization directory to define a population, he faces the risk of selecting a biased sample, since joiners of organizations may differ in important respects from nonjoiners. Should this be the case, the student should probably define his population as all members of a given organization, rather than as all members of the profession or group which the organization serves.

SAMPLING TECHNIQUES

Introduction

As we have already mentioned, sampling involves the selection of a portion of a population as representative of that population. To help insure that the sample is representative, researchers generally try to select a random sample from a population. (A random sample is one in which each individual in the defined population has an *equal* chance of being included.) We shall discuss here the random sampling techniques most commonly used by educational researchers.

It should be noted that the use of sampling techniques can be quite complicated. This is particularly true when these techniques are used to draw a random sample from a national population. However, sampling from a national population usually occurs only in survey research, such as public opinion polls. Samples used in experimental, causal-comparative, or correlational research are generally drawn from a much more limited population, for example, all the elementary school teachers in a particular school district.

The main purpose for using random sampling techniques is to select a sample that will yield research data that can be generalized to a larger population. Sampling techniques are also needed so that the researcher can apply inferential statistics to his research data. Inferential statistics enable the researcher to make certain inferences about population values (e.g., mean, standard deviation, correlation ratio, differences between population means) on the basis of obtained sample values. However, if a random sample has not been drawn from a defined population, the logic of inferential statistics is violated. We shall discuss the relationship between sampling and inferential statistics later in this chapter and in Chapter 12.

Simple random sampling

In simple random sampling, all individuals in the defined population have *equal* and *independent* chances of being selected as a member of the sample. (By "independent" is meant that the selection of one individual does not affect in any way the selection of any other individual.) A variety of techniques can be used to derive a simple random sample. Let us say, for example, that the research director in a large city school system wishes to obtain a random sampling of 100 pupils currently enrolled in the ninth grade from a population of 1,000 cases. First, he would obtain a copy of the district census for ninth-grade pupils. Then he might use a table of random numbers to draw a sample from the census list. Tables of random numbers can be found in the appendix of some statistics books.[5] Generally these tables consist of long series of five-digit numbers generated randomly by a computer. Here are ten such numbers:

$$21736$$
$$05805$$
$$55067$$
$$99264$$
$$21634$$

$$88757$$
$$61100$$
$$21238$$
$$78016$$
$$37415$$

To use the table of random numbers, the researcher picks an arbitrary starting place in one of the table columns and then selects all the numbers that follow in that column. Since there are 1,000 cases in our illustrative city school system, it is only necessary to use the last three digits of each five-digit number. If the above column of random numbers were used, the researcher would select the 736th pupil on the census list, the 805th pupil, the 67th pupil, and so on. This procedure would be followed (with a much larger table of random numbers, of course) until a sample of 100 pupils had been selected.

If a small population is used, another method of selecting a simple random sample is sometimes followed. This method involves placing the name of each individual in the population in a container, mixing the container thoroughly, and then drawing the required number of names. Another method that is sometimes used, but not recommended, is to select the required number of individuals as they appear on the population list. In the example just described, the researcher might select the first 100

[5] See also Rand Corporation, *A Million Random Digits with 100,000 Normal Deviates* (Glencoe, Ill.: Free Press, 1955).

names from the census list of 1,000 pupils. The problem with this method is that if the list is in alphabetical order, a biased sample might result since certain ethnic groups might be grouped disproportionately under certain letters of the alphabet. (Even if the list is not in alphabetical order, it might still have been compiled nonrandomly, e.g., by each school in the district.) To lessen the possibility of a biased sample, it is much more advisable to use a table of random numbers or a container.

The procedures and problems of simple random sampling are well illustrated by a recent study involving the collection of a national random sample of secondary school physics teachers.[6] The researchers responsible for this curriculum evaluation study wished to avoid using a nonrandom sample consisting largely of "volunteer" teachers. This procedure, typical of many curriculum evaluation studies, makes it difficult to generalize the findings of the curriculum evaluation to other groups of teachers, particularly nonvolunteers, who might be required to teach the new curriculum. The researchers first purchased a list of the names and addresses of 16,911 physics teachers compiled by the National Science Teachers Association. They point out in their report that this is the most comprehensive population list of high school physics teachers available, although it is not complete; it was based on responses received from 81 percent of all secondary schools in the United States. Thus, their population was not "all high school physics teachers" but rather "all high school physics teachers on the 1966 NSTA list." Each teacher on the population list was assigned a number according to his ordinal position on the list. Then a table of random numbers was used to select a total of 136 teachers. These 136 teachers were sent letters inviting them to participate in the study, but it was only possible to contact 124 of them.

It turned out eventually that 72 of the original 136 teachers agreed to participate in the study according to the conditions specified. Another 46 teachers were unable to participate for various reasons. In order to determine whether their final sample was biased, the researchers decided to compare several characteristics of the 72 accepting teachers against those of the 46 nonacceptors. When this comparison was made, the researchers found that significantly more acceptors than nonacceptors worked in larger schools and taught the Physical Science Study Committee (PSSC) physics course. The researchers interpreted these differences as indicating that the accepting teachers were more likely to be those who taught in large schools where previous innovations had been accepted. Thus, although they attempted to obtain a truly "random" sample, their actual

[6] Wayne W. Welch, Herbert J. Walberg, and Andrew Ahlgren, "The Selection of a National Random Sample of Teachers for Experimental Curriculum Evaluation," *School Science and Mathematics*, 69 (1969), 210–216.

sample was somewhat biased in favor of teachers working in innovative schools. Nevertheless, the researchers' final sample was more representative than the samples used in most curriculum studies, and it was possible to generalize the study's findings to a national population of physics teachers, with certain qualifications.

Incidentally, the study just described illustrates another problem that sometimes occurs with research samples. Of the 72 accepting teachers, 46 were assigned to the experimental group teaching the new physics curriculum, and the remaining 26 were assigned to the control group. During the course of the year-long evaluation study, ten teachers were lost from the experimental group and five were lost from the control group for various reasons—death, quitting one's job, transfer to a new position, and so forth. Whenever a research project extends over a considerable period of time, there is likely to be attrition of subjects. Not only can attrition lead to bias in the research sample (since those who leave the study may differ in important ways from those who persist), but the reduced sample size can make it more difficult to find statistically significant differences. Thus, if the research study makes considerable demands on subjects or lasts over a long period of time, it is advisable to include more subjects in the random sample than are needed in order to correct for possible attrition.

In summary, simple random sampling is a powerful technique for selecting a sample that is representative of a larger population. It is probably the sampling technique most frequently used by educational researchers. Also we should note that most of the conventional formulas for the various statistical tools described later in this book assume that simple random sampling was used to select the sample.

Systematic sampling

As with simple random sampling, the technique of systematic sampling is used to obtain a random sample from the defined population. This technique can be used if all members in the defined population have already been placed on a list in random order. Consider, for example, the research problem previously described in which the researcher selected a random sample of 100 pupils from a census list of 1,000 pupils. To use systematic sampling, the researcher first divides the population by the number needed for the sample (1,000 ÷ 100 = 10). Then the researcher selects at random a number smaller than the number arrived at by the division (in this example, a number smaller than 10). Then, starting with that number (e.g., 8), he selects every eighth name from a list of the population.

Systematic sampling is an easier procedure to use than simple random sampling. It differs from simple random sampling in that each member of the population is not chosen *independently*. Once the first member has been selected, all the other members of the random sample are automatically determined. Systematic sampling can be used instead of simple random sampling so long as one is certain that the population list is in random order. If there is any possibility of periodicity in the list (that is, if every *n*th person on the list shares a characteristic that is not shared by the entire population), then simple random sampling should be used instead.

Stratified sampling

In many educational studies, it is desirable to select a sample in such a way that the research worker is assured that certain subgroups in the population will be represented in the sample in proportion to their numbers in the population itself. Such samples are usually referred to as stratified or representative samples. Let us say, for example, that we wish to conduct a study to see if there are significant differences on *TAT* aggression scores of pupils at different ability levels selected from ability grouped sixth-grade classrooms. Under this grouping system, pupils are classified into three levels on the basis of general intelligence and placed in classrooms accordingly. In this case, if we were to define the population as all sixth-grade pupils in the district being studied and select a random sample, our random sample may not include a sufficient number of cases from one of the three ability levels. In this research we must also consider the possibility that girls will react differently in terms of aggression scores than boys. In order to avoid samples that do not include a sufficient number of pupils of each sex at each ability level, a stratified sample could be selected. In order to obtain a stratified sample in this case, all sixth-grade pupils in the district would be divided into one of the following six groups: superior boys, superior girls, average boys, average girls, slow boys, and slow girls. Subsamples of the desired size would then be selected at random from each of the six groups. Using this technique, we would predetermine the number of cases that would be available in each of the subgroups, but would randomly select the cases that would be used in the sample. Stratified samples are particularly appropriate in studies where part of the research analysis is likely to be concerned with comparisons between various subgroups. In summary, stratified sampling procedure assures the research worker that his sample will be representative of the population in terms of certain critical factors that have been used by the research worker as a basis for stratification, and also assures him of adequate cases for subgroup analysis.

Cluster sampling

In cluster sampling the unit of sampling is not the individual but rather a naturally occurring group of individuals. Cluster sampling is used when it is more convenient to select groups of individuals than it is to select

individuals from a defined population. Suppose, for example, that one's
defined population consists of all residents over the age of 18 in a particular city. Simple random sampling or systematic sampling could be used
if there is available an up-to-date, complete census of all the city's individuals and their ages. If not, then cluster sampling is advisabie. The city
might be divided into areas containing 16 square blocks. (Each block may
be viewed as "a naturally occurring group of individuals.") Each area
would be numbered, and the areas to be sampled would be drawn at random. All individuals in each sample area would be studied, excepting those
who cannot be reached or who are uncooperative. Thus, the unit of sampling is a 16-square-block area rather than the individual citizen. Multi-
stage sampling is a variant of cluster sampling. Once the square block
areas have been randomly selected, the researcher can further reduce the
sample size by only studying a random sample in each square block area.
For example, the researcher might study the residents of every tenth
house in each 16-block area included in the sample.

Cluster sampling is sometimes used in educational research with the
classroom as the unit of sampling. Suppose that one wishes to administer
a questionnaire to a random sample of 300 pupils in a population defined
as all sixth graders in four school districts. Let us say there are a total
of 1,250 sixth graders in 50 classrooms, with an average of 25 pupils in each
classroom. One approach is to draw a simple random sample using a census
list of all 1,250 pupils. In cluster sampling, though, one would draw a
random sample of 12 classrooms from a census list of all 50 classrooms.[7]
Then one would administer the questionnaire to every pupil in each of
the 12 classrooms.

The main advantage of cluster sampling is the saving in time and money
it allows. The use of this sampling technique enables one to confine questionnaire administration to 12 of the 50 classrooms. If simple random
sampling were used, one might have to arrange for access to all 50 of the
classrooms, even though in some of these classrooms one might only need
a few students for the sample. The disadvantage of cluster sampling is
that one cannot use the conventional formulas for computing statistics on
one's research data.[8] Also, the statistics are less sensitive to population
differences. Nevertheless, these disadvantages must be weighed against
the considerable savings in time and money which can result from using
cluster sampling.

[7] One would select 12 classrooms because there are an average of 25 pupils in each classroom and the desired sample is 300 pupils.

[8] For statistical formulas to be used with data obtained from a clustered sample, the
student is advised to consult Kish (1965). See annotated references for complete bibliographic information.

SAMPLE SIZE

A problem that must be faced in planning every research project is to determine the size of the sample necessary to attain the objectives of the planned research. The general rule is to *use the largest sample possible*. The reason for this rule is that although we generally study only samples, we are really interested in learning about the population from which they are drawn. The larger the sample, the more likely are their means and standard deviations to be representative of the population mean and standard deviation. Sample size is also closely connected with statistical hypothesis testing. The larger the sample, the less likely is the researcher to obtain negative results or to accept the null hypothesis when it is actually false. We will discuss this relationship between sample size and hypothesis testing in more depth in Chapter 12, when we consider the theory underlying statistical hypothesis testing.

In most research projects, there are financial and time restrictions which limit the number of subjects that can be studied. Generally in correlational research it is desirable to have a minimum of 30 cases. In causal-comparative and experimental research, it is desirable to have a minimum of 15 cases in each group to be compared. These are just guidelines, however, and under certain conditions larger samples are necessary. These include the following:

1. *When many uncontrolled variables are present.* In many educational research problems, it is impossible for the research worker to control some of the important variables that could have an effect upon the research findings. Under these conditions the research worker can have more confidence in his findings if he employs large random samples. The large random sample insures to some extent that the uncontrolled variables will themselves be operating randomly for the different groups being studied and therefore will not have a systematic effect upon the results. Teaching ability, for example, is a difficult variable to control but is important in many educational studies. If a study of teaching methods involves only two teachers, one using method A and one method B, teaching ability differences may cause more change in achievement than method differences. On the other hand, if we have a dozen or more teachers using each method, teaching ability differences will probably "randomize out," thus permitting us to appraise method differences.

2. *When small differences are anticipated.* In research projects in which only small differences on the dependent variable are expected among the various groups being studied, it is desirable to use large samples. For example, a teacher may have developed a set of visual aids to help in teach-

ing certain mathematical concepts. Such aids usually cannot be expected to make large differences in achievement. In order to evaluate these aids, large comparable samples of pupils using and not using the aids would have to be compared. In this case the reason for using large samples is that if small samples were used the larger standard errors attending such samples could obscure small but important relationships that would be found to be significant in a large sample study.

3. *When groups must be broken into subgroups.* Many educational research projects involve not only general comparisons between the major groups studied but can also contribute additional worthwhile knowledge if these major groups are divided into subgroups and further comparisons are made. For example, let us suppose that we were carrying out a study of the possible effects of an extracurricular program upon the attitudes of high school students toward school. Ten schools having no organized extracurricular programs could be selected, and in five of these schools such a program could be developed. A pretest of student attitudes could be administered before the extracurricular program was introduced, and after a period of one or two years final measures could be administered to determine what changes had taken place in student attitudes toward school. Attitude changes occurring in the schools that had adopted an organized program could then be compared with the changes that occurred in the schools in which no extracurricular program had been present. After an overall analysis of these results had been made, however, the research worker might wish to compare the effects of the extracurricular program upon different groups in order to develop some theoretical framework that fits his results. For example, he may hypothesize that girls' attitudes would be changed more markedly than boys' by the introduction of such a program because they value social activities more highly at the high school level. This would require dividing the groups studied by sex and making further comparisons. It may then occur to the researcher that students at different socioeconomic levels might respond differently to the organized program. Perhaps such a program would lead to favorable attitude changes on the part of middle-class children and unfavorable changes on the part of lower-class children. Again it would be necessary to subdivide the original sample on the basis of social class in order to conduct this further analysis. Such analyses often provide us with worthwhile knowledge and interesting theoretical constructs but can only be carried out if the original groups are large enough so that, after such divisions are made, the subgroups still have sufficient numbers of cases to permit a statistical analysis. In the preceding example, a group of 100 students might be adequate to make the overall comparisons of the effects of the extracurricular program. However, in dividing the 100 cases into groups on the basis of sex and socioeconomic status, it may be found that only

seven of the subjects can be classified as lower-class girls. This would indicate that 100 cases are not sufficient if such subgroup analysis were planned.

A mistake commonly made by inexperienced research workers is to select a random sample that would be large enough for division into the anticipated subgroups only if the subgroups are equally represented in the sample. The research worker then discovers that he has an unequal representation, such as is given in the previously mentioned example, which leaves him with an insufficient number of cases to carry out the analysis that he planned. This problem usually can be avoided by stratified sampling, but because the research worker cannot always predict all subgroups he may want to study, a large number of cases reduces the chances of disappointment.

4. *When the population is highly heterogeneous on the variables being studied.* If every person in the population were exactly alike on the variable studied, a sample of one would be sufficient. As the population becomes more variable, however, larger samples must be used in order that persons at different levels of skill or having different amounts of the characteristic in question will be satisfactorily represented.

In many educational research projects, small samples are more appropriate than large samples. This is often the case in studies in which role playing, depth interviews, projective measures, and other such time-consuming measurement techniques are employed. Such techniques cannot be used in large sample studies unless considerable financial support is available. However, a study that probes deeply into the characteristics of a small sample often provides more knowledge than a study that attacks the same problem by collecting only shallow information on a large sample. For example, a number of studies have attempted to learn the reasons why many superior college students drop out of college. Most of these studies have consisted of little more than classifying the one-sentence responses made by students on the dropout cards they completed for the registrar. Our knowledge of related studies in sociology and social psychology would lead us to doubt whether the student gives his true reasons for dropping out of college on such a card. Many students write down a convenient or socially acceptable reason regardless of their true reason for withdrawal. Other students are not themselves aware of the true reasons why they are dropping out. The senior author once participated in a research project in which superior students dropping out of Utah State University were given a carefully planned depth interview. These interviews, carried out by a trained psychologist, revealed that the student's true reasons for dropping out of college were almost always different from the reasons stated on the registrar's dropout card. Although it involved fewer than 50 superior dropouts, this study produced insights into the reasons for withdrawal from college that probably could never be obtained by the shallower approach employed by other studies.[9]

In other studies very close matching of subjects on the critical variables concerned in the study is possible, and under these conditions, small sampling studies often yield the information sought more efficiently than large sampling studies. The research by Newman, Freeman, and Holzinger on the intelligence of identical twins is a good example of such a study.[10] One phase of this study, although concerned with only nineteen pairs of separated identical twins, provided information on the relative influences of heredity and environment upon intelligence that would have been difficult to obtain with large samples of less closely matched subjects.

SAMPLING ERRORS

In selecting random samples, some degree of difference may be expected to occur between groups even though statistically acceptable methods of selection are used. For example, one group may contain subjects that are more intelligent, more highly motivated, or in other ways different from the subjects in other groups in the experiment. Such errors may be large in groups made up of few cases, but may be expected to decrease as the number of subjects increases. Let us say, for example, that we wish to compare the achievement of a group of ninth-grade pupils taught algebra using an inductive method with the achievement of another group taught algebra using a deductive method. We could randomly assign 70 pupils who wish to take algebra to two classes at the start of the term and assign algebra teachers of comparable experience to teach the classes. In this experiment errors due to sampling may be expected to be large because only one class of 35 pupils is involved in each group. If, among the 70 subjects, there were two very brilliant students, and if these two students were both assigned to the same group (as could easily occur in the random process), the achievement of these students could be high enough to raise the mean achievement of their entire group by several points. If, however, we could repeat our study ten times, and if ten classes of 35 subjects were to be included in each group instead of one class, the chances of the twenty brightest students all being assigned to groups being taught by the same method would be very remote.

Even if groups are made up by random selection from the available subjects, another problem arises from the fact that the available subjects may comprise a rather limited defined population. In the example given, the schools from which ninth-grade algebra classes are selected may differ in

---

[9] This study was conducted by Luna Brite.

[10] H. H. Newman, F. N. Freeman, and K. J. Holzinger, *Twins: A Study of Heredity and Environment* (Chicago: University of Chicago Press, 1937).

certain important ways when compared to all schools that offer ninth-grade algebra. For example, the schools may be located in predominantly middle-class neighborhoods, may be in college towns where academic work receives greater emphasis, or may be located in an area where the dominant religious group has certain values that are reflected in pupil attitude. Such a difference can lead to findings that are valid for the schools studied but not generally valid in other schools where ninth-grade algebra is taught. In most educational studies, this type of error cannot be entirely avoided. The research worker can do his best to select his sample from representative schools and can describe the source of his sample in detail so that other educators can compare his research subjects with the pupils in their schools to decide whether the research findings may be applied. In a few major projects, samples have been studied that represent a large number of schools selected from different sized communities of different socioeconomic levels in different geographical areas. Unfortunately, few research projects have sufficient financial support to permit obtaining samples of this type.

SAMPLING BIAS

The problems involved in obtaining random or stratified random samplings of human subjects, even for a narrowly defined population, are often considerable. Because of these difficulties, many research workers fall into one or another of several pitfalls when selecting their sample, resulting in sampling biases that invalidate the results of their research.

Perhaps the most common sampling mistake made in educational research is to use volunteers as research subjects. Volunteers can rarely be used as a research sample because the very fact that they volunteer makes them different from persons in the population who did not volunteer. Therefore, samples of volunteers can be assumed to be biased, and the results of studies employing volunteers must usually be discounted or applied only to other volunteers drawn from the same population. For example, the authors are familiar with a study in which an attempt was made to determine the success of college football players in later life as compared with other college graduates. In this study questionnaires requesting such information as the person's occupation and income were sent to football players who had graduated from a particular college. Only a small percent of these questionnaires were returned. The results were most encouraging when compared with the income of large samples of unselected college graduates taken from other surveys. Before accepting these data, however, let us look at the possible biases of this study. The small percentage of persons returning the questionnaire were, in effect, volunteers. Who is most likely to volunteer information concerning his financial status?

In most cases this information is most freely volunteered by persons who are financially successful. Thus, the results of such a questionnaire can tell us little about the population—in this case all football players graduating from the university in question. In studies involving achievement, volunteers are equally inappropriate because they generally represent a group that is somewhat more highly motivated than those members of the population not volunteering.

Still another problem encountered in studies using volunteer samples is that individuals who are participating in a research project on a voluntary basis usually feel free to withdraw from the study before all data are gathered if they lose interest or find further participation inconvenient. The authors are familiar with a study that clearly illustrates the problems that can be encountered under these circumstances. The purpose of this research was to determine whether college freshmen who were very poor spellers could be helped significantly by special spelling instruction using teaching machines. Volunteers from the poor spelling group were called for, and these were randomly divided into a control group that received no special instruction and an experimental group that received weekly instruction on the teaching machine. As the study progressed, students in the experimental group began dropping out because they became bored with the teaching machine or found the study schedule inconvenient. No withdrawals occurred in the control group because no demands were made on this group. By the end of the study, more than half the experimental group had dropped out. A final spelling test was then administered to the experimental and control groups, and the results showed significantly greater spelling gains for the experimental group. The question, of course, arises as to whether this gain was due to the special instruction using the teaching machines or whether it was due to the fact that only the more highly motivated students in the experimental group remained until the end of the study. Studies with sampling biases of this type generally produce results that are meaningless and, in many cases, can lead the naïve reader into drawing faulty or unjustified conclusions from the data.

Another procedure that often leads to a biased sample is the use of subjects, merely because they happen to be available, who are not appropriate for the research. College sophomores have been the subjects for so much research in education and psychology that the use of sophomores in research projects finds its way into many of the jokes about research workers in these fields. Some studies suffer relatively little from using available subjects. For example, exploratory studies on the effects of drugs upon learning and other forms of behavior are not seriously damaged by the use of such subjects. Whenever the research worker wishes to generalize his results to specifically defined populations, however, the use of subjects merely because they are available is inappropriate.

Many educational field studies are biased because the research worker chose his experimental and control groups from different populations. For example, some of the early studies on the effectiveness of TV instruction used high school students receiving conventional instruction as a control group, but used adults who wanted to complete their high school education in home study as an experimental or TV-instruction group. The age, interests, motivation, and dropout rates for the two groups are very different, thus making the results of such studies meaningless.

Occasionally the methods the research worker must use to identify the subjects he wants are sufficiently time consuming and expensive to warrant the use of shortcuts. Terman's famous study of "gifted children" provides us with an example of a sampling shortcut.[11] In this study Terman wished to locate 1,000 children with IQs over 140 on the *Stanford-Binet* test. Because the *Stanford-Binet* is expensive and time consuming to administer, he decided that rather than test many pupils who had little chance of obtaining a score of 140, he would ask teachers to suggest the names of students whom they considered to be superior, and would test only these. The difficulty with this procedure was that teachers tend to underestimate the intelligence of pupils who create disturbances and are not cooperative in the classroom. Thus, Terman's sample does not include this type of individual, and, as a result of this apparently small blunder in selecting his original sample, all the findings of his important study must be qualified. This means that a preponderance of the children Terman selected came from middle-class families where education is valued, and conformity to the school situation and respect for the teacher are expected. Thus, Terman's results, rather than being applicable to gifted children in general, refer primarily to a particular type of gifted child.

Often the research worker is under considerable pressure to alter his sampling techniques in order to fit administrative convenience. This problem is particularly common when working with the public school populations. In selecting a sample of fifth-grade students in a given school district, for example, it is much easier administratively to test all the fifth-grade children in one school than to test a few cases from each of several schools in the district. This process, however, significantly weakens the sample because there is little reason to believe that the pupils in one school are representative of the district as a whole. The degree to which such changes can damage the research design depends on the nature of the research problem. It should again be emphasized that if the student feels that certain changes cannot be made in the sampling procedures without seriously weakening the study, it is better for him to attempt to obtain his

[11] Lewis M. Terman (ed.), *Genetic Studies of Genius, Volume I, Mental and Physical Traits of a Thousand Gifted Children* (Stanford, Calif.: Stanford University Press, 1926), p. 21.

sample elsewhere or give up the study altogether than to devote his time, effort, and money to a study with serious sampling flaws.

MISTAKES OFTEN MADE BY GRADUATE STUDENTS

1. Student fails to define his research population.
2. Uses a sample too small to permit statistical analysis of interesting subgroups.
3. Fails to use the stratified sampling technique to select random samples of subgroups.
4. Attempts to conduct his research using only volunteer subjects.
5. Changes his sampling procedure in order to make data collection more convenient for the schools involved.
6. Does not allow for attrition in selecting his sample size.
7. Selects a sample that is not appropriate for the research project.

ANNOTATED REFERENCES

1. Collier, Raymond O., Jr. and Elam, Stanley M. (eds). *Research Design and Analysis*. Second Annual Phi Delta Kappa Symposium on Educational Research. Bloomington, Ind.: Phi Delta Kappa, 1961. This published symposium contains several good papers on educational research design. The paper by Leslie Kish, "The Design of Sample Surveys," describes the various sampling techniques and the sampling errors associated with each technique. The paper by Francis G. Cornell, "The Sampling Problem in Educational Research," describes some of the uses that can be made of sampling techniques in educational research and educational administration.
2. Cornell, Francis G., and McLoone, Eugene P. "Design of Sample Surveys in Education," *Review of Educational Research,* 33 (1963), 523–532. This article includes a helpful summary of published lists used to define populations, and descriptions of major research projects that relied heavily on use of sampling techniques. The authors also mention mistakes often made by researchers in using sampling techniques.
3. Furno, Orlando F. "Sample Survey Designs in Education—Focus on Administrative Utilization," *Review of Educational Research,* 36 (1966), 552–565. This article, written with the school administrator in mind, presents a useful overview of sampling theory and its application to survey studies. Numerous examples of published studies employing sampling techniques are cited; these may help the student in planning his own research project.
4. Kish, Leslie. *Survey Sampling*. New York: Wiley, 1965. This book is an authoritative reference on the use of sampling techniques in the social sciences. The discussion is fairly technical, but it is well worth consulting before the student attempts to use one of the sampling techniques presented in this chapter.
5. National Education Association, Research Division. "Small-Sample Techniques," *NEA Research Bulletin,* 38 (4) (1960), 99–104. This article is concerned with the selection of a random sample from a large population. A formula is presented that permits the researcher to determine the size of a sample needed to attain a

given degree of accuracy. The use of the formula is illustrated in the selection of a sample of male public school teachers who are to respond to a questionnaire. This article is extremely valuable to the research worker faced with the problem of selecting a sample from a large population.

6. Selvin, Hanan C. "A Critique of Tests of Significance in Survey Research," *American Sociological Review*, 22 (1957), 519–527. This article discusses the difficulty involved in obtaining random samples in sociological research and points out that tests of significance are not appropriate with nonrandom groups. This article gives the student valuable insight into some important sampling problems.

CHAPTER 6

Selection and Administration of Standardized Tests

CHARACTERISTICS OF STANDARDIZED TESTS

The standardized test (also called "standard test") can be defined as *any instrument for assessing individual differences along a given dimension of behavior*. Not only have standardized tests become a basic part of methodology in educational research, but also their practical applications have become increasingly important in our society. Think, for example, of the many tests that you yourself may have taken as you progressed through the American school system—intelligence tests, teacher-made and published measures of school achievement, the Scholastic Aptitude Test, and the Graduate Record Examination. Perhaps at some point you sought guidance in deciding upon an academic major and career; in the process you probably completed tests pertaining to vocational interests and personality. In a somewhat different context, it is possible that your physician at some time has found it necessary to give you a battery of standard medical tests as an aid to diagnosis.

It should be evident that standardized tests, as used for the classification, selection, evaluation, and diagnosis of persons, have a number of important social applications. However, our discussion will focus only on their uses in educational research. We may begin by considering some of the defining characteristics of a standardized test.

1. *Objectivity*. The objectivity of a standardized test depends on the degree to which it is uninfluenced or undistorted by the beliefs or biases of the individual who administers it. Prescientific measures and the measures used in the less mature sciences tend to have relatively little objectivity. Two individuals may use the same measure and arrive at two different observations or scores. In fact, the development of a science may be traced in terms of the progress it has made in recognizing the possibility of personal errors in measurement and in ruling them out to a greater and greater degree.

A classic example of personal error in scientific measurement occurred in the late eighteenth century at the Greenwich Observatory. Maskelyne, the astronomer royal at the observatory, dismissed his assistant, Kinnebrook, because of inaccuracies in his observations of the movement of stars across the sky. Kinnebrook's observations were "inaccurate" because they lagged behind Maskelyne's own measurements. Twenty years later, at Konisberg, an astronomer named Bessel made a study comparing his observations of stellar transits with those of other reputable astronomers. He found that differences in observations were actually fairly frequent. Thus, Kinnebrook's disagreement with his superior's observations probably reflected the state of measurement in astronomy at that time rather than personal carelessness or lack of ability. To increase the objectivity of measurements of stellar transits, Bessel developed what is known as "personal equations," or adjustments that individual astronomers could use to control their idiosyncrasies in amount and direction of observation bias.[1]

The degree of objectivity of standardized tests in education can usually be determined by analyzing whether the administration and scoring procedures permit bias to occur. In our later discussion of individually administered tests (particularly projective techniques such as the Rorschach Inkblot Technique and the Thematic Apperception Test), we shall show how the conditions of administration and scoring provide a number of opportunities for bias to occur. Not surprisingly then, these techniques usually do not yield high estimates of interrater and test-retest reliability.[2] In contrast, multiple-choice tests are generally considered much more objective since they are self-administered in large part, and all scorers can apply a scoring key and agree perfectly. In fact, these types of standardized tests are often called "objective tests."

2. *Conditions of administration.* Cronbach (1960) points out that a test can be "standardized" by establishing specific conditions of administration or by collection of normative data.[3] It should be apparent that a test is of limited value if its developers do not specify all the directions to be given in administering the test. These directions usually include specification of how much personal interaction (e.g., establishing rapport) is allowed between the tester and his subjects, how much time is allowed for the test, whether guessing is penalized, and whether instructions can be repeated. One of the basic principles of research methodology is that procedures are

---

[1] Other classic examples of the lack of objectivity introduced by personal error in the history of the physical, biological, and behavioral sciences can be found in Robert Rosenthal, *Experimenter Effects in Behavioral Research* (New York: Appleton-Century-Crofts, 1966).

[2] These terms will be defined in the next section.

[3] Lee J. Cronbach, *Essentials of Psychological Testing*, 2nd ed. (New York: Harper, 1960).

specified exactly so that researchers in other laboratories can duplicate the same conditions in order to replicate research findings obtained by the original investigator. In fact, an important advantage of using standardized tests in your research is that if you produce significant research findings other researchers will be able to replicate and expand on your work, since they can create the same conditions of administration by consulting the test manual.

3. *Normative data.* The process of collecting normative data on a test is called standardization. Therefore, a standardized test is one for which normative data are available. Generally a test developer will administer his test to a carefully defined sample (or several samples, usually varying in sex and age) and collect a set of raw scores. Individual scores are then related to the performance of the group as a whole by compiling a table of norms. Often the raw scores are converted to percentile ranks. Given a particular raw score, the table of norms based on percentile ranks enables one to determine the percentage of individuals in the standardization group who received the same or a lower raw score. Table 2 shows norms based on percentile ranks.

TABLE 2

NORMS BASED ON PERCENTILE RANKS

Raw Score	Percentile Rank	Raw Score	Percentile Rank
48		34	44
47		33	40
46		32	36
45	99+	31	30
44	96	30	22
43	93	29	18
42	90	28	15
41	87	27	11
40	81	26	7
39	76	25	4
38	71	24	3
37	65	23	1
36	56	22	1−
35	49		

The table of norms is very helpful to the researcher since usually he is interested in a subject's performance relative to the group rather than in the subject's absolute performance. However, the researcher should observe several precautions in using tables of norms prepared by developers of standardized tests. First, the researcher should check to determine whether his sample is comparable to the standardization group on which the table of norms is based. Suppose that the researcher tests a sample of 12-year-olds with an aptitude test standardized on a group of high school seniors. If he uses the table of norms for that group, he will seriously underestimate the average level of aptitude of his group.

A second concern of the researcher should be the conversion of percentile scores to standard scores if the table of norms does not provide them. Although percentile scores are useful because they are easily understood by the layman, they cannot be used for the computation of statistics. This is because percentile ranks are not linear transformations of raw scores.[4]

Many standardized tests in use today are provided with a table of norms based on standard scores. Essentially, standard scores are a set of transformed scores weighted by the mean and standard deviation of the raw scores. The topic of standard scores will be developed further in our discussion of analysis of research findings in Chapter 11.

The student has probably noted that the degree of confidence that can be placed in a table of norms depends on the care with which standard conditions of administration and scoring have been specified by the test developer. For example, if the tests on which normative data are based are scored by two individuals, one of whom is biased to assign lower scores, the resulting table of norms will reflect this bias and therefore will present an inaccurate picture of the distribution of test scores within a given population.

4. *Reliability and validity.* In addition to the characteristics of objectivity, standard conditions of administration, and normative data, standardized tests can also be described in terms of their reliability and validity. These important test characteristics are discussed next.

WHEN IS A TEST VALID?

In selecting a standardized test for use in a research project, the student will want to make a thorough review of the evidence regarding the test's validity. A commonly used definition of validity is that it is the degree to which a test measures what it purports to measure. However, this definition does not take into account the fact that there is more than one kind of test validity. The prospective test user should not ask, "Is this test valid," but "Is this test valid for the purposes to which I wish to put it?"

An illustration of the multidimensional nature of test validity is provided by the General Aptitude Test Battery (GATB). The GATB was produced by the U.S. Employment Service and is most often used to guide high school students into suitable lines of work. Nine aptitudes are measured by the test battery, which contains eight paper-and-pencil tests and

---

[4] See Chapter 11 for further discussion of this point.

four apparatus tests. Is the GATB a valid test? Bemio recently reviewed 424 validity studies that researchers have conducted on the GATB.[5] Bemio found that, on the average, the GATB aptitudes predicted training criteria better than they did job-proficiency criteria. It seems then that the validity of the GATB, like the validity of any other standardized test, cannot be determined in an absolute sense, but rather is a relative characteristic depending on the purposes to which the test will be put.

Without standards regarding validity, it is apparent that tests can be misused and may actually have deleterious effects on the person being tested. For example, an unscrupulous test developer might claim, without benefit of supporting evidence, that a particular test measures intelligence, predicts vocational success, or is a good indicator of psychopathology. Also, the value and meaning of educational research would be seriously weakened if tests were used without evidence of validity. For this reason professional associations in psychology and education have published guidelines for determining test validity.[6] In this publication and in the field of educational measurement generally, four types of test validity are recognized—content, concurrent, predictive, and construct.[7] Since the typical graduate student is probably conversant with these terms, our discussion will emphasize their relevance to the design of a research project.

Content validity

Content validity is the degree to which the sample of test items represents the content that the test is designed to measure. One type of content validity is face validity, which refers to the evaluator's appraisal of what the content of the test measures. For example, if a test purports to measure reading achievement and if the items appear to deal with relevant content in this area, the test can be said to have face validity. A related type of content validity is called sampling validity, or the degree to which the test serves as an adequate sample of the total universe of content that one wants to measure.

Content validity is important primarily in achievement testing and various tests of skills and proficiency, such as trade tests. For example, a test of achievement in ninth-grade mathematics will have high content validity if the items covered on the test are closely representative, in type and proportion, of the content presented in the course. If test items cover topics not taught in the course, ignore certain important concepts, and unduly

[5] Stephen E. Bemio, "Occupational Validity of the General Aptitude Test Battery," *Journal of Applied Psychology*, 52(3) (1968), 240–244.

[6] *Standards for Educational and Psychological Tests and Manuals*, 1966—see annotated references.

[7] Concurrent and predictive validity are sometimes grouped together and called "criterion validity."

emphasize others as compared with their treatment in the course, the content validity will be lower. Unlike the other types of validity, the degree of content validity is not expressed in numerical terms as a correlation coefficient (sometimes called a "validity coefficient"). Instead, content validity is appraised usually by a subjective comparison of the test items with curriculum content and the skills that they purport to teach. Often the test manual will describe the techniques used to arrive at the test content. Thus, if he is interested in selecting a measure of ninth-grade mathematics achievement that is appropriate for his particular sample, the researcher will want to determine, if possible, whether the test developer derived test items from the same textbook or one similar to it that was studied by his sample.

Content validation is a particularly important consideration in selecting a test for experiments involving the effect of training methods on achievement. Suppose, for example, you are interested in doing a research project to determine whether an inquiry method of teaching social studies concepts is superior to a noninquiry method. The research project may involve training two groups of sixth-grade teachers to use one or the other method for one school term. At the end of the semester, a test of social studies achievement will be administered to determine if the two teaching methods lead to different amounts of learning. To make a proper comparison, the researcher should administer an achievement test that is representative of the content covered during the term; in other words, the test should have high content validity, otherwise one cannot confidently draw conclusions from the study. If the hypothesis states that an inquiry approach leads to superior learning, but the specific content that was learned is not measured by the achievement test, the hypothesis has not been given a fair test.

The first research projects comparing the "new" math with the traditional curriculum often yielded nonmeaningful findings because the content validity of the achievement tests used to assess outcomes was not carefully considered. The usual finding was no difference between the two curricula. However, the content of most mathematics achievement tests about a decade ago emphasized computational skills. With the development of new achievement tests with more emphasis on test items sampling basic concepts, research studies began to show that both curricula lead to similar achievement in computational skills but that students in the "new" math curriculum show superior achievement in their understanding of mathematical concepts.[8] If you are planning a similar project involving comparison of the effects of several treatments (e.g., different teaching

[8] This research is reviewed in Vincent J. Glennon and Leroy G. Callahan, *Elementary School Mathematics: A Guide to Current Research,* 3rd ed. (Washington, D.C.: Association for Supervision and Curriculum Development, NEA, 1968).

methods) on achievement, then you should select a test whose content is similar to that used in the treatments. In other words, the test should have high content validity.

Predictive validity

Predictive validity is the degree to which the predictions made by a test are confirmed by the later behavior of the subjects tested. The usual method of determining predictive validity is to administer the test, wait until the events that the test attempts to predict have occurred, and then correlate the occurrence of the event with the scores of the subjects on the test. Let us take an algebra aptitude test as an example. Suppose that such a test were designed to be administered near the end of the eighth grade to predict success in ninth-grade algebra. In order to determine the predictive validity of this test, it would be administered to a large random sample of eighth-grade pupils. The scores of these pupils would then be kept until the pupils had completed ninth-grade algebra. At the end of ninth grade, the test scores would be correlated with a measure of algebra achievement, such as grades in the algebra class or an algebra achievement test. In this case the algebra grades or the achievement test scores would be called the criterion measure, that is, it is the measure that the aptitude test is attempting to predict. The correlation between the algebra aptitude test and the algebra achievement test would give us a measure of the predictive validity of the aptitude test, that is, the degree to which its prediction of the student's success in algebra was borne out by his performance. Much educational research is concerned with the prediction of success in various courses of study.

It is important to assess the predictive validity of a standardized test in deciding whether to use it in making practical decisions, such as selecting students for college. Predictive validity is also an important consideration in many research projects. As an illustration, suppose that you are interested in planning a research project to identify variables that predict success among high school students in doing remedial tutoring with younger students. In deciding which tests to include in your test battery, you might well look for measures that have been shown to have predictive validity in similar situations. For example, you might find that the *Strong Vocational Interest Blank* is a good predictor of which high school students will choose to major in education at college. On the basis of this evidence, you might include this vocational interest inventory in your test battery in expectation that it would predict this new criterion.

In reviewing evidence pertaining to a test's predictive validity, the researcher should carefully evaluate the criterion predicted by the test. Suppose one is interested in predicting performance in graduate school. A study might be found that shows that a particular test has poor predictive validity against this criterion. However, closer examination of the study might indicate that the criterion consisted of ratings made by faculty advisors after the students had been in graduate school one semester. The meaningfulness of this criterion is open to doubt for several reasons: faculty advisors may not know the students well and therefore may not be able to make sound judgments; performance in the first semester of graduate school may not be representative of performance later on (such as the passing of qualifying exams or the merit of the dissertation). Should this be the case, the student might still consider including this measure in his battery of tests if his criterion is sufficiently different from the one for which poor predictive validity was found.

The student who plans to assess the validity of a test in predicting a particular criterion should be familiar with the concepts of base rate and cross-validation. Base rate is the proportion of persons who meet the criterion out of the total number of persons in the population. To illustrate, suppose that a researcher's project involves the use of personality tests to predict students who will be arrested for delinquency during a particular school year. Suppose further that the incidence of delinquency is five percent of the particular student population in which the researcher is interested. Thus, in a sample of 100 students it is likely that 5 will become delinquent and 95 will remain nondelinquent. Now one can see that with this base rate, one can predict delinquency correctly 95 percent of the time simply by predicting that everyone in the sample will be nondelinquent. Although it has been demonstrated that a valid personality test can further increase the predictability of delinquency under these conditions, the practical value of the test will be slight.[9] The implication of this example is that the student should only attempt to predict a criterion whose base rate of incidence is not exceptionally high or low.

In many prediction studies, a number of tests are used to predict a specific criterion. The researcher can then develop a prediction equation (see Chapter 14) based on some or all of these tests which will yield a higher validity coefficient than the correlation between any one test and the criterion. However, this prediction equation may be spuriously high because it capitalizes on chance fluctuations in the data. Therefore, to determine the value of the prediction equation it is necessary to *cross-validate* by administering the same tests to a new sample drawn from the same population. Generally the validity coefficient yielded by the prediction equation will shrink somewhat in the new sample. Whether it shrinks to the point where it is useless in a practical prediction situation will depend on a number of factors.[10]

[9] E. Cureton, "A Recipe for a Cookbook," *Psychological Bulletin*, 54 (1957), 494–497.
[10] See Helmstadter, pp. 131–133 (listed in annotated references).

Concurrent validity

The concurrent validity of a test is determined by relating the test scores of a group of subjects to a criterion measure administered at the same time or within a short interval of time. The distinction between concurrent and predictive validity depends on whether the criterion measure is administered at the same time as the standardized test (concurrent) or later, usually after a period of several months or more (predictive).

In designing a research project, the student will often be interested in locating a short, objective test that has high concurrent validity with a criterion and that is easily administered. For example, if the student is interested in measuring his pupils' intelligence, it would be quite impractical to use the Wechsler Intelligence Scale for Children or the Stanford-Binet, each of which must be individually administered and requires one or more hours of testing time, even though these tests have considerable standardization data and predictive and construct validity. Instead it is much more economical to administer one of several brief, objective, group tests of intelligence whose concurrent validity against the Stanford-Binet or the Weschsler scales has been demonstrated to be of a high magnitude.

Tests with high concurrent validity can often be used as a substitute for ratings of a particular personality characteristic. One of the authors planned a research project to determine whether anxious college students showed more preference for female role behaviors than less anxious students.[11] To identify contrasting groups of anxious and nonanxious students, it might have been necessary to have a large sample of students evaluated for clinical signs of anxiety by experienced clinical psychologists. However, the author was able to locate a quick, objective test, the Taylor Manifest Anxiety Scale, which has been demonstrated to have high concurrent validity with clinical ratings of anxiety in a college population.[12] The author saved considerable time conducting the research project by substituting this quick, objective measure for a procedure that is time consuming and subject to personal error. However, if the test's concurrent validity had been established with groups other than students, such as military personnel or psychiatric inpatients, then the author would have had no justification for substituting this test for clinical ratings or other measures of anxiety. If you are planning a research project involving measurement of subjects, you should seriously consider using a brief standardized test before resorting to measures that require complicated administration procedures.

[11] Meredith D. Gall, "The Relationship Between Masculinity-Femininity and Manifest Anxiety," *Journal of Clinical Psychology*, 25 (1969), 294–295.

[12] See, for example, D. P. Hoyt and T. M. Magoon, "A Validation Study of the Taylor Manifest Anxiety Scale," *Journal of Clinical Psychology*, 10 (1954), 357–361.

In evaluation of a test's concurrent validity, it is important to assess the adequacy of the criterion (as is true in evaluation of a test's predictive validity). Occasionally a test will be validated against another test rather than against a meaningful real-life criterion. It is of little value to know that one test of anxiety, for example, correlates highly with a criterion test of anxiety, unless the criterion test itself has been demonstrated to have significant construct and predictive validity. If the criterion is valid, so presumably is the other test that correlates highly with it.

Construct validity

Construct validity is the extent to which a particular test can be shown to measure hypothetical constructs. Psychological concepts—such as intelligence, anxiety, creativity—are considered hypothetical *constructs,* since they are not directly observable but rather are inferred on the basis of their observable effects on behavior. To better understand construct validity and its importance in research, suppose that a test developer publishes a test that he claims is a measure of anxiety. How can one determine whether the test does in fact measure the construct of anxiety? A first step might be to look at the test items. A sample item might be, "I worry a great deal, often for no apparent reason." While items such as these suggest that the test measures anxiety, this is far from conclusive evidence. A next step might be to determine whether the test differentiates between psychiatric and normal groups, since theorists have hypothesized that anxiety plays a substantial role in psychopathology. If the test does in fact differentiate the two groups, then we have further evidence that it measures the construct of anxiety.

A variety of procedures are needed to establish the construct validity of a test, yet many published tests have only a limited amount of evidence to indicate that they are indeed measuring the constructs that they purport to measure.[19] Construct validity is a particularly important factor to consider in planning a research study that proposes to test a hypothesis. For example, suppose that one plans to test the hypothesis that creative children will be able to state more meanings of a word than noncreative children. To test this hypothesis, the researcher will need to ask himself whether his hypothesis presupposes a particular concept of creativity, for example, potential or actualized creativity, artistic or scientific creativity, creativity as process or creativity as product.

On occasion the student may plan a research project in which it is not

[19] For a good example of the variety of procedures that can be used to establish the construct validity of a test, the reader is recommended to read this review of studies on the socialization scale from the *California Psychological Inventory:* H. G. Gough, "Conceptual Analysis of Psychological Test Scores and Other Diagnostic Variables," *Journal of Abnormal Psychology,* 70 (1965), 294–302.

important to consider construct validity. This is the case when the primary purpose of the research is to find predictors of a criterion on an empirical basis without resort to theory.[14] Here the concern is to identify tests that have predictive validity for a particular purpose. The construct validity of the tests is not necessarily relevant. In fact, it is not uncommon for a researcher to determine a test's predictive validity in one study and then investigate the test's construct validity in later studies. As an illustration, in the field of psychological research, Barron empirically developed a test scale that predicted response to psychotherapy.[15] Since the test predicted an important criterion, Barron conducted additional studies and found that the test appeared to have construct validity as a measure of ego strength, an important concept derived from psychoanalytic theory.

DETERMINING TEST RELIABILITY

Reliability, as applied to educational measurements, may be defined as the level of consistency of the measuring device. Suppose we wished to measure students' knowledge of physics. A physics achievement test consisting of one multiple-choice item would be highly unreliable. Some students may know quite a bit about physics, yet may not happen to know the answer to this particular test item; by contrast, some students whose achievement level in physics is low may happen to know or guess the correct answer. Thus, the one-item test is susceptible to many chance factors and therefore is not a "reliable" index of the student's true level of achievement in physics.

Reliability is an extremely important characteristic of tests, and it must be considered carefully in selecting measures for research purposes. The level of reliability that the research worker should expect from a test is determined largely by the nature of the research in which he plans to use the measure. If the research project is such that the research worker can expect only small differences between his experimental and control groups on a variable measured by the test, it is necessary that a test of high reliability be used. Conversely, if large samples are to be used and if the test scores are expected to differ materially for the experimental and control groups, the research worker may select a measure of relatively low reliability and still be assured that the test will discriminate adequately. The reason a test of high reliability is required in the first situation and not the second is that when only small differences are likely to be found, a test of low reliability may be too crude to reveal these differences. For example, let us say we wished to measure the height of two samples of

---

[14] This approach to research is sometimes called "dust-bowl empiricism."
[15] Frank Barron, "An Ego-Strength Scale Which Predicts Response to Psychotherapy," *Journal of Consulting Psychology,* 17 (1953), 327–333.

adult men, but had only a crude measuring device, such as the span.[16] Let us further suppose that the true mean difference in height between the groups is one-half inch. One is unlikely to detect this small a difference because the span is a fairly unreliable measure; a person may not extend his hand to the same length each time, and if more than one person does the measuring, their hands probably will not be of the same size. However, if the true mean difference in heights between the two groups of men is four inches, it is much more likely that the taller group will be accurately distinguished from the shorter group despite the unreliability of the span as a measuring device.

It is much easier to establish the reliability of a test than to establish its validity. Therefore, if no specific information on reliability is provided in the test manual, the research worker may safely assume that the reliability of the test is low. A helpful list of representative reliabilities of standardized tests has been prepared by Helmstadter,[17] and is reproduced in Table 3. It should be noted that the values of the reliabilities vary with the type of intellectual and personality characteristic being measured.

TABLE 3

RANGE AND MEDIAN VALUES OF RELIABILITIES REPORTED FOR VARIOUS TYPES OF MEASURES

Type of Test	Number of Reliabilities	Value of Reported Reliabilities		
		Low	Median	High
Achievement Batteries	32	.66	.92	.98
Scholastic Ability	63	.56	.90	.97
Aptitude Batteries	22	.26	.88	.96
Objective Personality	35	.46	.85	.97
Interest Inventories	13	.42	.84	.93
Attitude Scales	18	.47	.79	.98

A point that must be watched for in evaluating test reliability is that many tests yield a number of subscores in addition to a total score. This is the case for some intelligence and achievement tests that provide subscores in order to give a profile of the student's performance in the various areas making up the test. However, reliability is often reported only for the total score. Therefore, the subscores must be used cautiously unless reliability data are available for them. When such data are not available, the research worker will have difficulty making an intelligent appraisal of the worth of the subscores. He may be sure that all or most of these subscores

[16] The space from the tip of the thumb to the tip of the little finger when extended.

[17] Table 8 from *Principles of Psychological Measurement* by G. C. Helmstadter. Copyright © 1964. Reproduced by permission of Appleton-Century-Crofts, Educational Division, Meredith Corporation.

will have lower reliabilities than the total test reliability. The reliability coefficients of the subscores, however, may differ considerably, with some being as reliable as the total test and others being of such low reliability that they should not be used in the planned research.

The reliability of a standardized test is usually expressed as a coefficient. The reliability coefficient reflects the extent to which a test is free of error variance. Error variance may be defined as the sum effect of the chance differences between persons that arise from factors associated with a particular measurement. These factors might include wording of the test, the person's mood on the day the test is administered, the ordering of the test items, or the content that is used. The more closely a reliability coefficient is to the value of 1.00,[18] the more the test is free of error variance and instead is a measure of the true differences among persons in the dimension assessed by the test.

Reliability coefficients can be obtained by several different approaches, and each type has a somewhat different meaning. A description of the four types in common use follows:

Coefficient of internal consistency

This type of reliability is based upon estimates of the internal consistency of the test. The most widely used method of estimating internal consistency is through the split-half correlation. In this method the test for which reliability is to be calculated is administered to an appropriate sample. It is then split into two subtests, usually by placing all odd-numbered items in one subtest and all even-numbered items in another subtest.[19] The scores of the two subtests are then computed for each individual, and these two sets of scores are correlated. The correlation obtained, however, represents the reliability coefficient of only half the test, so that a correction must be applied in order to obtain the reliability of the entire test. The Spearman-Brown prophesy formula is used to make this correction.[20]

The method of rational equivalence

The method of rational equivalence is the only widely used technique for calculating reliability that does not require the calculation of a correlation coefficient. This method gets at the internal consistency of the test through an analysis of the individual test items. A number of formulas have been developed to calculate reliability using this method. These are

[18] Reliability coefficients vary between values of .00 and 1.00.
[19] Other methods of splitting the test are sometimes used, such as a logical division of the test into two sets of comparable items.
[20] See Henry Garrett, *Statistics in Psychology and Education,* 5th ed. (New York: McKay, 1958), chap. 13.

generally referred to as the Kuder-Richardson formulas (after the authors of an article in which these formulas were first discussed).[21] The formulas in this article are numbered, and the two most widely used are numbers 20 and 21. Formula 20 is considered by many specialists in educational and psychological measurement to be the most satisfactory method of determining reliability. This formula is being used to an increasing degree to determine the reliability of standardized tests.

Formula 21 is a simplified approximation of formula 20, and it is of value primarily because it provides a very easy method of determining a reliability coefficient. The use of formula 21 requires so much less time than other methods for estimating test reliability that it is highly appropriate for use in teacher-made tests and short experimental tests being developed by a research worker. One desirable aspect of the Kuder-Richardson formulas is that they generally yield a lower reliability coefficient than would be obtained by using the other methods described. Thus they can be thought of as providing a minimum estimate of reliability and, if used, tend to reduce the danger of overestimating reliability of a test.

Coefficient of equivalence

This method of calculating reliability may be used whenever two or more parallel forms of a test are available. This method is often called "alternate form reliability" and is computed by administering two parallel forms of the test to the same group of individuals and then correlating the scores obtained on the two forms in order to yield a reliability coefficient. Some interval between the administration of the forms is usually desirable, especially if the alternate forms are nearly identical, as is the case with some achievement measures. This interval tends to reduce practice effects that may be an important factor if the two forms of the test are administered at the same sitting. At the present time, the coefficient of equivalence is the most commonly used estimate of reliability for standardized tests. It is very widely used with standardized achievement and intelligence tests.

Coefficient of stability

This form of reliability is useful when alternate forms of the test are not available or not possible to construct. To calculate the coefficient of stability, sometimes called "test-retest reliability," the measure is administered to a sample of individuals, and then after a delay the same measure is again administered to the same sample. Scores obtained from the two administrations are then correlated in order to determine the coefficient of

[21] M. W. Richardson and G. F. Kuder, "The Calculation of Test Reliability Coefficients Based upon the Method of Rational Equivalence," *Journal of Educational Psychology*, 30 (1939), 681–687.

stability. The most critical problem in calculating this form of reliability is to determine the correct delay between the two administrations of the measure. If the retest is administered too quickly after the initial test, students will recall their responses to many of the items, and this will tend to produce a spuriously high reliability coefficient. On the other hand, if the retesting is delayed for too long a period, there is a good possibility that the student's ability to answer some items will change. For example, he may pass through a period of development or learning and thus be better prepared to answer questions on the retest.

LONG VERSUS SHORT FORMS OF TESTS

The amount of time available to test research subjects is usually limited. Suppose that a total of one hour is available for testing. The researcher may want to administer several measures; however, one of these measures requires an hour to complete. If he reads the test manual and reviews the literature, the researcher might learn that a short form of the test, requiring perhaps half the time of the long form, is available. This savings in time permits the researcher to administer one or more additional measures, which may make an important contribution to his research.

The reliability of a test is dependent on its length. The more items in a test, the better estimate we can make of the person's true score, which would be his score on a test of infinite length. Since the reliability coefficient indicates the extent to which a test reflects true score variance, it follows that the shorter form of a test will be less reliable.[22] However, the student may well consider using the short form of a test if the saving of time is significant and if the loss of reliability is not substantial. For example, the total test reliability of the *California Short Form Test of Mental Maturity* (*Junior High Level*) using Kuder-Richardson Formula 21 is .87, while the reliability of the long form of the same test is .92.[23] The short form requires 51 minutes to administer, while the long form requires 88 minutes. In view of the relatively small difference in reliability, it would be advisable in most cases to use the short form, thus saving 37 minutes.

It should be noted, too, that in addition to affecting reliability, shortening a test affects its validity. It can be demonstrated mathematically that the correlation between a test and a criterion cannot exceed the square root of the correlation between two forms of the test (which provides an

[22] The student may recall that the Spearman-Brown prophesy formula, in correcting the reliability coefficient based on only half a test, increases the magnitude of the coefficient.
[23] See *Manual, California Short-Form Test of Mental Maturity, Junior High Level, 1957 S-Form*, p. 4, and *Manual, California Test of Mental Maturity, Junior High Level, 1957 Edition*, p. 5.

estimate of reliability). Therefore, the student should not use a short form of a test if the reliability is drastically reduced, because the test's validity will also be adversely affected. Small losses of reliability, however, will not affect validity appreciably.

INDIVIDUALLY ADMINISTERED VERSUS GROUP TESTS

For many intellectual and personality characteristics, both group tests and individually administered tests are available. A group test is one that has been constructed so that a sample of subjects can take the test all at one time; the test giver distributes the tests, reads directions, and may time it if it is a speed test. Such tests usually yield objective scores of the yes-no, multiple-choice, or true-false type. By definition the individually administered test is one in which the tester measures one subject at a time. Most projective tests, such as the Rorschach Inkblot Technique, and some measures of intelligence, are of this type.

Individually administered measures should only be selected when they make an essential contribution to the research project. This is usually the case when the researcher is interested in studying *process* rather than *product*. Most standardized tests represent a product approach to measurement. An achievement test in mathematics, for example, usually yields a single score or set of scores that sums up an individual's performance on the test. Of course, it is very important to have an index of the outcomes of performance, but there are also situations in which it is important to know the process by which an individual earned a particular score on the test. Why did the individual miss particular items on an arithmetic test? Did he guess, or was he careless in his computations, or did he lack understanding of basic mathematical concepts, such as regrouping as used in subtraction exercises (e.g., $38 - 19 = \Box$)? The test would need to be individually administered in order to assess these aspects of a subject's performance. Tests developed in a clinical setting, such as the Rorschach Inkblot Technique and the Thematic Apperception Test, often are individually administered so that the clinician can measure not only a subject's responses, but also learn why the subject gave a particular response. Thus, if you are interested in topics such as the comparison of problem-solving techniques of fifth graders and eighth graders, or identification of reading disorders in low achieving students, it may well be that you will need to use individually administered tests in your research.

The nature of the sample will also determine whether individually administered tests are necessary. Very young children, for example, cannot often be tested as a group because their attention span is limited and they do not have the reading skills usually required by group tests. Other groups, such as the retarded or physically handicapped, may also need to be individually tested. Delinquents and potentially recalcitrant groups may require individual testing if there is reason to believe that their performance on a group test will be unreliable.

Individually administered tests generally have a number of disadvantages for the graduate student. First, specialized training is often required to administer such tests. If he is unable to administer the test himself, the student probably will have to incur the expense of hiring experienced testers. This in itself presents a problem since it is well established that, for most projective measures, the tester affects the results.[24] As we shall find later in this chapter, it is usually necessary to employ more than one tester to control for a possible examiner effect. Second, these tests generally cannot be scored with the objectivity of group tests. Therefore, you will need more than one scorer in order to increase reliability. Third, scores yielded by many individually administered tests are not immediately interpretable, but require interpretation by a trained educational or clinical psychologist.

The fact that individually administered tests have a number of disadvantages compared to group tests does not mean that the student should rule out using them in his research project. However, since they are difficult to use, they should be selected only when they make an essential contribution to the research.

SELECTING BETWEEN MEASURES OF THE SAME VARIABLE

It is not uncommon for a student to search for a measure of a particular variable, only to find that there is more than one measure available. Which measure should the student select? The answer to this question is complex. Some alternative measures can be ruled out because they are unsuitable for one's sample of subjects. Perhaps others will be found deficient in test reliability and validity. Yet occasionally situations arise when the student has a number of seemingly appropriate measures from which to select.

To consider an example of such a situation, suppose that the student wishes to investigate the hypothesis that creative college students will do better than noncreative students in courses in which grades are based primarily on essays, but no difference in grades is expected between the two groups in college courses that rely primarily on multiple-choice exams for grading purposes. To test this hypothesis, the student will need to measure individual differences in creativity among college students. A review of the literature would indicate that creativity in college students has been measured by a number of tests, including the Remote Associates Test, the Barron-Welsh Figure Preference Test, and the Myers-Briggs Type Indi-

[24] Joseph M. Masling, "The Influence of Situational and Interpersonal Variables in Projective Testing," *Psychological Bulletin*, 57 (1960), 65–85.

cator. These tests all have favorable evidence regarding their reliability and predictive validity. Therefore, which of these tests should the student select for his research project? If he has not already done so, the student should examine the rationale of his hypothesis more closely. Perhaps his rationale is that grades on essays reflect in part the ability to generate novel ideas about a given topic, whereas grades on multiple-choice tests emphasize the ability to assimilate facts. In this case the Remote Associates Test may be the best test to use, since it measures the ability to generate remote associations to words. (Of course, if another test could be located that had been demonstrated to predict creativity in essay writing, this would be the test to use.) If, on the other hand, he cannot arrive at an exact definition of creativity, then perhaps the student should consider doing an empirical study rather than a hypothesis-testing study. In this case he might want to select several measures, including those mentioned here, to correlate with grades in the two types of courses.

To summarize, selecting between alternate measures of the same or ostensibly the same variable involves several considerations: suitability for one's sample of subjects, evidence regarding the tests' reliability and validity, and the way in which each test measures the variable with which one is concerned.

IS THE TEST APPROPRIATE FOR YOUR RESEARCH SAMPLE?

The student will need to evaluate a test carefully before deciding on its appropriateness for his research sample. Some of the considerations involved in this evaluation have been discussed already under other headings.

It is important to check the reading level of the test, particularly if it will be used by elementary school children. Occasionally one finds a test that the manual describes as usable at a particular grade level but that includes many words not generally known by students at that level. Such a test would be invalid since a person's score will depend to some degree upon his vocabulary and reading ability rather than on his ability in the characteristic the test purports to measure.

In selecting an aptitude or achievement test, the student should judge its appropriateness in terms of the general aptitude or achievement level of his research sample. Each test is designed to work most efficiently at a particular level. Some tests claim to be usable over a fairly wide age or grade range, but such measures are generally more accurate at the center of their range than at the extremes. If it is not appropriate for the level of subjects to be tested, a test will not discriminate, that is, it will fail to reflect differences that exist among the subjects. A test that is too easy discriminates poorly because most subjects will receive perfect or near perfect scores. For example, if we administer a third-grade arithmetic test to ninth-grade pupils, all but the poorest ninth-grade pupils will obtain nearly perfect scores. Therefore, it is impossible to determine from this test how much arithmetic a ninth-grade pupil knows. Average students, above average students, and highly superior students will all receive about the same score on the test. The same, of course, is true of a test that is much too difficult or advanced for the subjects. In this case, all but a few superior students will receive very low scores.[25]

In many research projects, the test norms provided by the publisher are used in some phase of the research. If they are to be used, these norms must be based on subjects who are reasonably comparable to the research subjects. Also, the test's reliability and validity data should have been collected on samples comparable to the one that will be used in the research. The importance of this point is illustrated by a study using the California F-Scale, a measure of authoritarianism, to predict plant workers' performance.[26] The researchers noted that most of the construct validity studies on the F-Scale were based on urban, middle-class Americans. They predicted that this measure would not be valid for subjects born and reared in rural environments. To test this prediction, the researchers measured plant workers' productivity before and after an experimental treatment in which the workers were extensively interviewed and observed by so-called "researchers." The hypothesis was that increases in productivity would be positively correlated with presence of authoritarian trends, as measured by the F-Scale, in urban but not in rural workers, since the so-called "researchers" would be perceived as authority figures toward whom authoritarian personalities would be likely to respond positively. As hypothesized, a statistically significant correlation of $+.39$ was found between the F-Scale and productivity increases for the workers born and reared in an urban environment. However, for the subsample *born and reared in a rural environment*, a nonsignificant correlation of $+.04$ was found.

This study makes the point that a test may be valid for one population but not for another. Therefore, the student should make certain that a particular test's validity data are appropriate for his sample of subjects before deciding to use it in his research project.

IF NO SUITABLE TEST IS AVAILABLE

Occasionally a research worker will need to measure a variable for which no suitable standardized test is available. An illustration of such a situa-

[25] To get a sense of how tests are designed to be appropriate for particular populations varying in ability, the student is recommended to read Lee J. Cronbach, *Essentials of Psychological Testing* (New York: Harper & Row, 1960), pp. 228–233.

[26] Stephen M. Sales and Ned A. Rosen, "Subcultural Variations in the Validity of the California F-Scale," *Educational and Psychological Measurement* (1967), 1107–1114.

tion is provided by Fisher's study of the effect of reading and discussion on attitudes toward the American Indian.[27] The purpose of the study was to determine whether children's attitude toward Indians would change as a result of reading literature about them; also, the effect of discussions following reading was investigated. To conduct the study it was necessary to construct a test, the *Test of Attitude Toward American Indians,* for children in the upper elementary grades, since, as Fisher noted, "None was found which would do the specific job required for this study."

Standard techniques for developing attitude scales were used to determine the items for this test. Then the scores of the first eight items were correlated with the second eight to arrive at a split-half reliability coefficient, corrected for attenuation by the Spearman-Brown formula. A test of the measure's construct validity was made by administering it to groups assumed to differ in their attitudes toward American Indians. The attitude scale differentiated between three groups (children in a school that was over 90 percent Indian; non-Indian children in a school surrounded by an Indian community; and children living in a metropolitan area) as predicted, thus lending support to the validity of this scale as a measure of attitude toward American Indians. Fisher then used the scale to measure change in attitude in his sample of subjects as a result of reading and discussing literature about Indians.

It should be evident that the nonavailability of a suitable measure complicated and lengthened this research project. Therefore, the student designing his own project should make a thorough search of the literature for a suitable measure before deciding to develop his own test. If this decision is made, then the student should be prepared to pretest his measure several times, to perform item analyses, and to collect data with which to evaluate the measure's construct validity. It is recommended that the student, before attempting to develop his own test, become quite familiar with test development procedures. Skills in these procedures can be gained by taking a course in educational measurement, by study of measurement textbooks,[28] and by expert consultation, perhaps with a professor in one's department who specializes in this field.

HOW TO LOCATE INFORMATION ABOUT TESTS

Before he selects a particular standardized test, a student should accumulate as much information as possible about it. It is not uncommon for a student to hastily decide upon a test in planning his research and

[27] Frank L. Fisher, "Influences of Reading and Discussion on the Attitudes of Fifth Graders Toward American Indians," *Journal of Educational Research,* 62(3) (1968), 130–134.

[28] Some standard textbooks in this field are described in the annotated references.

then find himself plagued with difficulties in using the test and interpreting the findings. For example, suppose that one wishes to test the hypothesis that empathy is an important trait for the successful school counselor to possess. Two groups of counselors rated as successful and unsuccessful are formed, and a test of empathy is administered. Since a measure of empathy is crucial to testing the hypothesis, if the measure is found to be invalid by those who might evaluate the research—such as editors of educational journals and professional counselors—then the findings that result from such a study are immediately cast in doubt.

The student will want to know how to obtain information about tests for another reason. In reviewing the research done by others, the student cannot make sound judgments concerning the findings without having access to information about the tests used to measure the research variables. The following are widely used, accessible sources of information about tests.

The test manual

The test manual provides the student with much of the information that he needs to evaluate the standardized test.[29] Among the questions that the manual usually answers are the following:

What validity data are available? What types of validity have been studied? Is the evidence of validity sufficient for use in the planned research?

What reliability data are available? Is the measure sufficiently reliable to meet the needs of the planned research?

For what types of subjects is the test appropriate?

What conditions of administration are necessary to use the test?

Does the test require special training for interpretation?

Is a shorter form of the test available that will yield substantially the same results?

While test manuals can provide much useful information to the student interested in evaluating a particular standardized test, the student must be able to evaluate the test manual itself. For example, test manuals will occasionally omit evidence regarding validity or reliability that is unfavorable to the test and that might dissuade potential purchasers.

Some standardized tests, particularly those that have been extensively researched, are likely to pass through several revisions. Therefore, the student should be certain that his test manual is appropriate for the test version that he is evaluating.

[29] Details about obtaining copies of manuals for standardized tests are given on pages 158–159.

The *Mental Measurements Yearbooks*

A very important source of information on standardized tests is the *Mental Measurements Yearbooks*. Over the past thirty years, Oscar K. Buros has edited this series of very useful references to standard tests in psychology and education. The most recent of the series is the *Sixth Mental Measurements Yearbook,* published in 1965. This is a complete new work that supplements the earlier editions. The current edition lists 1,219 tests. There are 795 critical test reviews and 8,001 references on the construction, use, and limitations of the specific tests included in this edition. Another section of the *Yearbook* lists and reviews books and monographs on measurement and related fields. The current edition lists 527 books, and many of the more important ones have several reviews.

The *Mental Measurements Yearbooks* can be used to obtain information on specific tests that the student has located elsewhere or they can help the student locate tests that are available in a particular field. The *Yearbooks* are also very valuable tools for evaluating the research of others.

In using this reference, the student first refers to the Classified Index of Tests. Here he will find the tests classified under a number of broad categories such as "achievement batteries," "character and personality," "foreign language," and "intelligence." Under each category he will find the pertinent tests listed alphabetically by title. Thus he may quickly check the tests available in his area of interest. Upon locating tests in the classified index that interest him, he may note the number of the test and check each number in the Tests and Reviews section of the book. Under the test number, he will find a brief listing of practical information, such as the types of subjects that may be administered the test, the scores yielded by it, administration time, cost, and publisher. Following these data he will usually find a number of references containing information about the test. For the more widely used tests, several hundred references may be available. A quick examination of these references will often reveal several that are of particular relevance to the student's research project. Reviews are available for many of the tests listed. These reviews are perhaps the most valuable feature of the *Mental Measurements Yearbooks* because they give the student an evaluation of the test by one or more authorities in the field. They are generally written by persons who have worked extensively in the field with which the test is concerned and are written specifically to provide test users with appraisals that can help them in evaluating the test. The reviews are generally critical and treat most of the essential elements important in test evaluation, thus providing the student with a sounder evaluation than he could make for himself.

Psychological Abstracts

Occasionally the student will want to obtain information on a new test not reviewed in the *Mental Measurements Yearbooks*. This situation may arise when the thesis topic is in the area of test development. For example, the student may decide to investigate the construct validity of a promising new test that has been described in an educational or psychological journal. In addition to the *Yearbooks,* the *Psychological Abstracts* should be checked for possible information on the test. If there is a specific test on which information is sought, the subject index at the end of each monthly issue (or the annual cumulative index) may be checked. If the student does not have a specific test in mind, then these headings under the table of contents of the *Abstracts* can be checked:

METHODOLOGY & RESEARCH TECHNOLOGY
  Test construction and validation
PERSONALITY
  Intelligence
  Creativity
  Personality measurement
EDUCATIONAL PSYCHOLOGY
  Testing

The test developer

If the test has been developed fairly recently, it is advisable to write the test developer requesting any information that has not appeared in print. If the student's letter explains the purposes for which he wants to use the test, it is likely that the test developer will be cooperative. One reason for this cooperation is that the test developer may be able to add the findings from the student's research project to those he has already collected.

The authors know from personal experience the value of this method for obtaining information about newer tests. For example, several years ago one of the authors was searching for information about a new measure of creative thinking, The Remote Associates Test,[30] for possible use in a research project on this subject. The author was able to contact a psychologist who had been active in the development of the test. Through this source it was possible to obtain valuable normative and validity data that had not yet appeared in print. With these data the author was able to make a sounder evaluation of the test than if he had only consulted the publications already listed.

[30] Described in S. A. Mednick, "The Associative Basis of the Creative Process," *Psychological Review,* 69 (1962), 220–232.

The test itself

One of the most important sources of information about standardized tests is a copy of the test in which you are interested, particularly if you are concerned about content validity or the appropriateness of the test for your sample. For example, the test manual may claim that a particular test is appropriate for students in the fifth and upper grades. However, your examination of a copy of the test may reveal that the reading level is beyond that of the fifth graders whom you are planning to test. Or suppose that your research project entails the evaluation of two methods for teaching reading. In selecting a criterion test of reading achievement to evaluate the effectiveness of the two methods, you may find that the test manual and the *Yearbooks* do not provide information about the reading content covered by the test. To determine whether the reading content covered by the test is representative of that included in your training materials, your best source of information will probably be a copy of the test itself.

In addition to the sources of information already listed, there are other reference works that may be helpful to the student. These are listed in the annotated references at the end of the chapter.

THE SOCIAL SIGNIFICANCE OF TESTING

In the last fifty years the testing movement has had a major impact on American society. Each year literally millions of tests are administered for the purpose of making important decisions about individuals—Who shall be admitted to college and to what college? Who shall be selected to fill a particular job opening? Who needs to be hospitalized for mental illness? Therefore, the researcher planning to use standardized tests needs to realize some of the ethical issues that have arisen in connection with the testing movement.

The early 1960s witnessed a rash of books attacking tests.[31] Chief among their criticisms of testing were these:

1. Invasion of privacy. Some tests, particularly those dealing with personality, ask individuals to reveal information usually considered personal. The individual's right to privacy is generally considered to be a basic American value.
2. Accessibility of test data. Test scores are not usually made available to the individual tested, yet important decisions about him are often made on the basis of these scores. This situation gives testers a po-

[31] Among those authors who criticized the testing movement most severely were H. Black, *They Shall Not Pass* (New York: Morrow, 1963); M. L. Gross, *The Brain Watchers* (New York: Random House, 1962); and B. Hoffman, *The Tyranny of Testing* (New York: Crowell-Collier, 1962).

tentially large degree of power over an individual's destiny and may make the individual feel helpless and under the control of testers.

3. Rigid use of test scores. Critics complain that testers make no allowance for change in the individual or in the environment. Although an individual may earn low achievement scores during a particular school year, this does not mean necessarily that he will continue to be a low achiever. Also, the individual's environment is often a changing one, and therefore test predictors may only be valid for a short period of time and within a limited environmental setting.

4. Types of talent selected by tests. Tests generally sample only a few of the aptitudes and personality traits important for success in a given area. Thus, if aptitude tests alone are used to select individuals for college, this practice may discriminate against individuals who do not have high scores on the aptitudes measured by these tests but who do have a high level of creativity or artistic aptitude. A related criticism is that tests can perpetuate the status quo rather than encourage change. For example, if college admission is determined only by scholastic aptitude tests, only persons of high scholastic aptitude will complete college. These graduates, now in a position of power, may continue the use of the same tests to select students who are similar to themselves. This approach to test use may keep individuals out of college who might bring about productive changes in the college system.

5. Unfairness to minority groups. It has been claimed that some aptitude and intelligence tests are unfair to minority groups since they contain test items pertaining to experiences that these groups may not have enjoyed. Therefore, minority groups will earn undeservedly low scores on these tests and not be selected for schools and jobs that would help them improve their social and financial status.

Although they are primarily addressed to situations in which tests are used to make practical decisions affecting individuals' lives, these criticisms are sometimes applied to research projects involving testing. This is particularly true when tests are administered in the public schools. In one unfortunate episode in Houston, Texas, the answer sheets to six sociometric and psychological measures that had been administered to some 5,000 ninth-grade students were ordered burned by the school board. In this instance accounts indicated that parents objected to having their children respond to such items as: "I enjoy soaking in the bathtub." "Sometimes I tell dirty jokes when I would rather not." "Dad always seems too busy to pal around with me." [32]

[32] Gwynn Nettler, "Test Burning in Texas," *The American Psychologist*, 14 (1959), 682–683.

In a more recent episode, in spite of a thorough and well-planned public relations program, a similar problem arose. In this case the research program dealt with mental health and was being carried out by a foundation that was well established and had good rapport in the community. An extensive public relations program was carried out, including meetings and discussions with school boards, superintendents, administrative personnel, school nurses and teachers, religious leaders, P.T.A. groups, the Lions Club, and other civic groups. The research worker's difficulty started because a local right-wing group was currently involved in a campaign opposing the "mental health movement."

The man who spearheaded this opposition was also a member of the American Legion and later read a statement along the same lines at a P.T.A. panel on which members of the research team appeared. He accused us of implanting "Red" ideas in children's minds and said our "Guess-Who" technique was a way of "fingering" certain children (designating them at an early age so they would be marked for life for our own ulterior motives).[33]

The authors have had some experience with a similar protest movement, and when this experience is compared with the previously described situations, it appears that all three have a number of things in common. First, individual test items are generally attacked without reference to their context or psychological foundations. Second, such attacks are usually led by small extreme groups of one sort or another. In the authors' experience, the protest group was made up almost entirely of a close-knit group of health food faddists. Another characteristic of all three of these situations is that although it was vigorous and noisy, the protesting group did not represent any significant parent group. In the Houston episode, tests were returned to a number of small school districts—the Spring Branch Board of Education decided to destroy the answer sheets only of pupils whose parents objected to the testing. Six weeks after that decision, only eleven parents out of the possible 750 requested that the answer sheets be destroyed. In the second episode discussed, a similar offer was made and only three parents, those who started the original protest, requested that their children's records be destroyed. In the authors' experience, approximately 5,000 children were tested, and in spite of the considerable bedlam raised by the small protesting group, only one parent came forward to request that her child's test papers be destroyed.

In dealing with such problems, a number of points might be worth mentioning. First, remember that in many instances these protests are led by demagogues who are not truly concerned about the testing but wish to use it merely as a vehicle to gain publicity or gratify some personal need.

[33] L. D. Eron and L. O. Walter, "Test Burning II," *The American Psychologist*, 16 (May 1961), 239.

Second, it is impossible to explain adequately to a lay group the function of many items used on psychological tests. It is doubtful whether the research worker should ever attempt to debate the merits of specific test items. Instead, he should explain how the test was developed and attempt to demonstrate that the test as a whole is valid and useful. Third, it is important to take all action that seems appropriate at the very outset of any such protest. If the research is well designed and the measures are justified, those parents who are truly concerned can generally be convinced of the value of the study, thus depriving the extreme group of their support. The researcher should work closely with the newspapers and do everything possible to acquaint them with his side of the question. Finally, it is wise to offer to withdraw children from the study if the parents examine the tests and make a written request that their children be withdrawn.

It should be clear to the student by this point that the use of tests in a research project is not a matter to be taken lightly. He should be aware of the main criticisms of testing and realize that tests can be used to advance scientific knowledge, or can be abused by those who are unethical or who are poorly trained. Therefore the sections ahead on proper techniques for administering tests should be read with care.

HOW TO OBTAIN COPIES OF TESTS

Once he has decided on the standardized test (or tests) to be used in his research project, the student will need to obtain a number of copies of each test. If the test is distributed through a test publisher, such as Science Research Associates or California Test Bureau, the student should purchase copies of the test through them. The publisher and purchase costs of a particular test can be found in the most recent edition of Buros' *Mental Measurements Yearbook*. The college counseling or testing center often has catalogues issued by test publishers which give information about purchasing tests.[34] Under no circumstances should a student obtain a single copy of a test and then duplicate the items in order to make mimeographed copies, since this would constitute a violation of copyright.[35] Occasionally a test with all its items will appear initially in a professional publication. If this is the case and if the author makes no reference to copyright, the test can be duplicated for purposes of a research project. In this situation it is a good practice to write the test developer to inform

[34] Anastasi's book on testing (see annotated references) contains the names and addresses of the major test publishers.

[35] If he wants to use only part of a published test or alter its format for research purposes, the student should consult a professor or other qualified person. It may be necessary to have the publisher's permission before the test can be altered.

him of your project and to request any information not in the published article pertaining to the test's validity, reliability, administration, and scoring.

In order to insure that tests are used only by qualified personnel, test publishers have the ethical responsibility of checking a prospective purchaser's qualifications. The American Psychological Association has specified the qualifications needed to administer three levels of tests:

Level A. Tests or aids that can adequately be administered, scored, and interpreted with the aid of the manual and a general orientation to the kind of institution or organization in which one is working (e.g., achievement or proficiency tests).

Level B. Tests or aids that require some technical knowledge of test construction and use, and of supporting psychological and educational fields such as statistics, individual differences, psychology of adjustment, personnel psychology, and guidance (e.g., aptitude tests, adjustment inventories applicable to normal populations).

Level C. Tests and aids that require substantial understanding of testing and supporting psychological fields, together with supervised experience in the use of these devices (e.g., projective tests, individual mental tests).

The manual might identify a test according to one of the foregoing levels, or might employ some form of statement more suitable for that test.[36]

Generally, a test categorized at any of these levels can be used in a bona fide research project. However, some tests, particularly measures of personality, may require sponsorship by a psychologist or educator holding the doctorate. The student's thesis chairman or committee members are likely candidates to serve as sponsors.

ESTABLISHING STANDARD CONDITIONS OF ADMINISTRATION

Part of the meaning of the term "standardized test," as we noted earlier, is that the test developer has specified the same conditions (directions, materials, timing, etc.) for every person who will take the test. Without standard conditions of administration, tables of norms and studies reporting validity and reliability would be worthless to the user. Similarly, the student's research findings can make no scientific contribution if he does not insure standard conditions of administration for the tests used in his project.

The importance of this aspect of research procedure can be illustrated by a study investigating tester effects on the Stanford-Binet Intelligence Scale.[37] Six female and seven male testers administered the Stanford-Binet

[36] "Ethical Standards for the Distribution of Psychological Tests and Diagnostic Aids," *American Psychologist*, 5 (1950), 620–626. Reprinted by permission of the American Psychological Association.
[37] V. J. Cieutat, "Examiner Difference with the Stanford-Binet IQ," *Perceptual and Motor Skills*, 20 (1965), 317–318.

to a sample of four-year-old minority group children. It was found that the children tested by females earned significantly higher mean IQ (89.61) than those tested by males (83.19). Thus, it appears that some of the variance in these children's IQ scores is attributable to the testers rather than to "true" individual differences in intelligence. In this sense, the IQ scores are unreliable. The purpose of establishing standard conditions of administration is to reduce error variance (such as that attributable to tester characteristics) and at the same time increase true score variance.

The problem of tester effects is a particular concern with individually administered tests, since this situation provides the tester with ample opportunity to bring his personality into the testing relationship.[38] To control for tester effects, the student is advised to employ experienced testers. Second, it is advisable to employ more than one tester. The data collected by each tester can then be compared to determine whether the findings have been influenced by tester effects. For example, suppose one is interested in comparing the intelligence of 30 sixth-grade students nominated as showing signs of creativity with 30 students nominated as noncreative. Further, suppose that 4 experienced examiners are employed to test the subjects. Each examiner will then test 15 students, half (7 or 8) in each group. Then, using analysis of variance (see Chapter 15) the student can determine whether the testers affected the results. One may find that some testers yield higher IQ scores than others, or that there is an interaction, that is, for some testers creative children score higher on the Stanford-Binet, while for others the creative child may score lower on the Stanford-Binet. In summary, to create standard conditions of administration when the tester is a potential source of variance, it is important to employ more than one tester.[39]

Standard conditions of administration are, of course, also extremely important for group tests. The test manual will usually provide specific directions for the tester to read to the group that he is testing. These directions should be read carefully before he enters the test session, otherwise he may find himself in the situation of being unable to answer subjects' questions, even though the answers are contained in the test manual. Or he may use a test procedure that he finds afterwards to be nonpermissible.

Although tests vary widely in conditions of administration (e.g., speededness versus nonspeededness, encouragement or discouragement of guessing), two sets of conditions remain constant across tests. First, subjects

[38] For a review of studies on examiner effects, see Joseph M. Masling, "The Influence of Situational and Interpersonal Variables in Projective Testing, *Psychological Bulletin*, 57 (1960), 65–85.
[39] The problem of tester effects is similar to the problem of experimenter effects discussed in Chapter 15.

should be tested in a comfortable physical environment. An overcrowded classroom, poor lighting, and excessive outside noise may all contribute to error variance in subjects' scores. Second, the state of the person or persons being tested should be a paramount concern. The overly anxious or fatigued person is not likely to turn in a representative performance on a standardized test. To rule out such effects on subjects' performance, the researcher should take care not to test subjects at unusual times (e.g., orientation week, examination week, end of the school year), and he should not administer more than one or two tests in a single session.

MOTIVATING AND GAINING SUBJECTS' COOPERATION DURING TESTING

The subjects' cooperation is important if test results are to be meaningful. Before administering a test, the researcher needs to ask himself the questions: How can I enhance the amount of cooperation I will receive from my subjects? What might motivate students to turn in a maximal or typical performance on the measures I will administer?

Some answers to these questions have been given in the previous section. A comfortable physical environment and consideration for subjects' mental and physical state are likely to increase the cooperation they will give. Another important consideration is that the tester be very familiar with the test directions. It can be very annoying for a subject to be tested by someone who fumbles with materials, who appears unsure of himself, or who makes obvious errors. Subjects are likely to feel that if the research were of any importance, the tester would be more conversant with test materials and directions. Feeling that the research lacks significance, subjects may take a haphazard approach to the testing; as a consequence their test scores will be unreliable.

An obvious way for the researcher to gain familiarity with a particular test outside of a formal research testing session is to "pretest" the measure. The researcher can enlist the cooperation of a few friends or subjects and practice the testing procedures on them. One of the authors had to train eight experimenters to individually administer a test as part of a research project. Since none of the experimenters was familiar with the test, they were asked to study the directions first and then asked to practice administering it to the author until their proficiency reached an acceptable level.

If he wants to increase the likelihood that he is sampling subjects' maximal performance (as on tests of aptitude or achievement), the researcher should attempt to make the testing a reinforcing event for the subject. In the case of elementary and high school students, he can often do this by gaining the cooperation of the students' teacher beforehand.[40] Students often have a strong need to please their teacher; thus, you might request the teacher to tell her students that the test is important and that they should try to do their best on it. College and graduate students are usually intrinsically motivated to do well on tests. To increase the cooperation of these groups, the authors have found that a good technique is to tell them that you will reveal the purpose of the research after the testing is finished. This technique appeals to subjects' sense of curiosity and serves as a reinforcer for them to cooperate in taking the tests. Another good technique is to make the testing appear important; the use of a stopwatch and reading directions from a manual are likely to make subjects feel that their performance is of significance to the tester.

In administering tests of personality, questionnaires, and attitude scales, the tester is often faced with the problem of having subjects depict themselves in a typical, honest manner. Some items in these tests may ask subjects to give personal information which they may feel uncomfortable about revealing. (The problem of response sets in personality assessment is discussed in the next chapter.) Therefore, the tester should make it clear before the testing session begins that under no circumstances will data collected on any individual be revealed to anyone. It is also helpful to remind subjects that test scores will be reported in group form only. To further protect subjects' sense of privacy and anonymity, it is recommended that the researcher assign code numbers to all subjects. If the researcher plans beforehand, he should be able to arrange the testing session so that subjects can write a code number on the test instead of their names.

The testing of preschool and primary grade children will present special problems for the researcher. Trained testers should be employed to administer the research measures to these groups, otherwise the resulting test scores are likely to be quite unreliable. Test manuals will often contain special directions to be used when testing these age groups. Also, a number of helpful suggestions have been given by Goodenough for individual testing of young children.[41] These include keeping test materials at hand but out of sight, not requiring the child to respond before he is ready, and praising adequately.

Older students will often ask whether it is appropriate to guess on a test of aptitude or achievement. Usually the test manual will contain directions which can be given to subjects on this matter. However, if a subject persists in asking questions about guessing after the directions have been

[40] Procedures for gaining the cooperation of school and other officials are discussed in Chapter 2.
[41] F. L. Goodenough, *Mental Testing: Its History, Principles, and Applications* (New York: Rinehart, 1949), pp. 298–304.

ead, or if no directions are contained in the test manual, the tester should ot attempt to influence the subject. When this situation arises, the tester's esponse should be something like, "Do what you think is best," or "Use our judgment." [42]

Occasionally after a testing session is ended, one or two subjects will ask they can have access to their test results. The researcher should not rovide subjects with this information. Most subjects will be satisfied if ney are told that the tests were administered for a research project, and nerefore they can only be used for this purpose. However, if a subject ersists in wanting to learn his test scores, the researcher can recommend hat the subject go to the school counselor or campus counseling center vhere he will be able to receive professional assistance.

SCHEDULING AND ADMINISTERING TESTS IN THE SCHOOLS

If the student plans to administer tests in the schools as part of his esearch project, his success will depend on how carefully the scheduling f tests meets the conditions that prevail in most schools. First, do not chedule excessively long testing sessions. The nature of the test and the notivation of the students must be considered in setting up the length of he testing session, but it is doubtful whether children in the upper ele- nentary grades should be tested more than 90 minutes in a single session nd whether single sessions should extend beyond three hours for students t the secondary level. The ideal testing times for most materials are prob- bly about one half these limits. If testing is to be scheduled for more han one school period, it is usually necessary and desirable to schedule reaks. These breaks may be scheduled between tests or even during a ontimed test. It is usually sufficient to permit the students to stand at heir chairs, stretch, and talk for two or three minutes.

In setting up the schedule, the research worker should attempt to com- lete all testing within a reasonably short period. If the testing program s stretched out over a period of several weeks, as is sometimes the case vhen large samples must be tested, there is some danger that the testing ituation will be somewhat different for those persons tested last as com- ared to those persons tested first. In the case of achievement measures, or example, students tested last will have had additional time in which to chieve, and may therefore earn higher scores than pupils tested early in ne program. The research worker should avoid testing near holidays or too lose to the end of the school year. The excitement attending the holiday an make a significant difference in the attitude of students concerning ne testing. Testing during the last month of the school year often causes

[42] For a discussion of the effects of guessing on subjects' test scores, see Lee J. Cronbach, *Essentials of Psychological Testing*, 2nd ed. (New York: Harper & Row, 1960), pp. 49–51.

problems because students are less likely to be attentive to the test, and it may be difficult to arrange makeup tests prior to the end of the term. Also, because numerous special programs and extracurricular activities are scheduled at this time, many students will be absent from the testing.

Whenever possible, students should be tested in small groups. The regular classroom unit is probably the most desirable group to test because the students are in a familiar environment and the group is small enough so that the test administrator can maintain good control over the situation. Testing in large groups, on the other hand, makes it difficult for the administrator to answer questions or to collect materials, and a single giggle can result in the test situation degenerating into chaos and confusion.

Although he will often be unable to achieve an ideal testing situation, the research worker should attempt to set up the most favorable situation possible. If experimental and control groups are to be tested separately, as is often the case, he should also attempt to equalize as much as possible the situation faced by the two groups. For example, it would be undesirable to test all experimental subjects in the morning and all control subjects in the afternoon because students are often less alert and less highly motivated during the afternoon session. It would be similarly undesirable to test all experimental subjects during the first week of the testing program and all control groups during the second week. To whatever extent such scheduling variables can be equalized between the experimental and control groups, this should be done.

During the scheduling session, the research worker should also come to an agreement with the school principal involving such questions as: What help will the schools provide for the testing program? How will makeup tests be scheduled and who will administer them? What role will the classroom teacher play in the testing program? How will disciplinary problems that occur during the testing period be handled? This latter question is especially important because a prompt and efficient means of handling disciplinary problems often makes the difference between maintaining or losing control of the testing situation. If the testing is to be carried out in the classroom, the research worker should also visit each teacher who will be involved and discuss the teacher's role during the testing. Under certain conditions it would be more desirable for the teacher not to be present during the testing session, while in others the teacher might assist as a proctor and be responsible for disciplinary problems. The role of the teacher must be decided on the basis of the needs of the specific study, but should always be fully understood prior to the start of the session.

If he has done a thorough job of pretesting and preparing for the testing program in which he will collect his research data, the research worker has little to do during the actual session except follow closely the procedure he has developed and tried. In the event that some unusual or some unfore-

en situation arises during a testing period, the research worker should
ake careful notes of what occurred in order to determine later whether
e occurrence has introduced factors or biases that will reduce the value
the data.

USING TEST DATA COLLECTED BY SCHOOLS

The student is often under pressure in carrying out research for the
aster's thesis to use test data already collected by the schools. This is
nerally not advisable for several reasons. First, the measures available
e often not those that are most appropriate for the research project. Sec-
d, there will probably be some subjects whom the student wishes to
clude in his sample who will not have taken the test. Third, the research
orker does not know the conditions under which the test was admin-
tered and, of course, had no control over these conditions. The student
therefore urged to select and administer the measures that seem most
ppropriate for his research whenever this is possible and to avoid using
ata not collected under his control.

MISTAKES OFTEN MADE BY GRADUATE STUDENTS

1. Student fails to evaluate measures thoroughly before selecting those to be used
   in his research. This often leads to the use of invalid or inappropriate measures.
2. Uses a table of norms that is inappropriate for his research sample.
3. Does not evaluate carefully the criteria that have been used to determine the
   validity of a particular test.
4. Does not consider the problem of base rate in determining a test's predictive
   validity.
5. In attempting to measure a particular construct, selects a test on the basis of
   its name rather than on the basis of its construct validity.
6. Selects measures of such low reliability to use in his research that true differences are hidden by the errors of the measure.
7. Fails to consider the human relations aspect of testing.
8. Does not attempt to control for possible tester effects, particularly when a
   test is administered individually.
9. Does not study the test manual carefully before administering a test.
0. Attempts to administer too many tests in a single testing session.

ANNOTATED REFERENCES

Characteristics of standardized tests

American Psychological Association. *Standards for Educational and Psychological Tests and Manuals.* Washington, D.C.: American Psychological Association, 1966. This booklet is a revision of two earlier publications: *Technical
Recommendations for Psychological Tests and Diagnostic Techniques,* published

by the APA in 1954, and *Technical Recommendations for Achievement Tests,* issued by the National Education Association in 1955. In the current booklet, professional organizations concerned with the procedures and ethics of test development (APA, American Educational Research Association, National Council on Measurement in Education) set forth standards for test validity, reliability, administration, scoring, and norms. The student will find these standards helpful in the evaluation of tests that he plans to use in his research project.

2. Helmstadter, G. C. *Principles of Psychological Measurement.* New York: Appleton-Century-Crofts, 1964. The author provides a technical but readable treatment of many of the topics covered in this chapter. The student will find this book particularly helpful if the main focus of his research project is concerned with test development, validation, or standardization.

3. Anastasi, Anne. *Psychological Testing.* 3rd ed. New York: Macmillan, 1968. This textbook is recommended for the student who is unfamiliar with the field of psychological and educational measurement. In addition to providing an easy-to-read coverage of the characteristics of standardized tests, it also will serve the reader as a comprehensive introduction to the main types of tests in use today.

Test theory and research

4. Jackson, Douglas N., and Messick, Samuel (eds.). *Problems in Human Assessment.* New York: McGraw-Hill, 1967. This volume includes a comprehensive selection of classic papers in the field of test theory and assessment procedures. The student may want to refer to these primary sources for an in-depth treatment of topics that are presented in general textbooks on measurement.

5. Payne, David A., and McMorris, Robert F. (eds.). *Educational and Psychological Assessment: Contributions to Theory and Practice.* Waltham, Mass.: Blaisdell, 1967. This collection of papers deals with a number of measurement topics that have particular relevance to educational research. Many of th papers deal specifically with the design, construction, and applications o achievement tests in education.

6. "Educational and Psychological Testing," *Review of Educational Research* 38 (1) (1968). This issue of the *Review* gives the student a brief coverage o most of the recent developments in educational and psychological testing. Th literature on this topic is reviewed in 3-year intervals, and the student ma wish to refer to the previous *Review* 32 (1) (1962) for additional information

7. Lavin, David E. *The Prediction of Academic Performance: A Theoretical Analysis and Review of Research.* New York: Russell Sage Foundation, 1965. This book contains a thorough review of the literature on one of the most important topics of educational research. The student planning a research project in this area will find this book most helpful, and indeed may find in it many ideas that might be used as a basis for a research project.

The ethics of testing

8. American Psychological Association. "Special Issue: Testing and Public Policy. *American Psychologist,* 20 (1965), 857–993. In this publication a number

psychologists express their views on congressional hearings held in 1965 on personality tests and the invasion of privacy of government employees.

9. Willingham, Warren W. (ed.). "Invasion of Privacy in Research and Testing," *Journal of Educational Measurement,* supplement to vol. 4, no. 1, Spring 1967. This publication presents the contributions of seven researchers who participated in a symposium, supported by the National Council on Measurement in Education, on invasion of privacy in research and testing.

CHAPTER 7

Types of Standardized Tests

INTRODUCTION

It is important in planning a research project to be familiar with the wide variety of standardized tests that have been published. The student who has this familiarity is likely to select a better test than the student who selects the first measuring instrument that he is able to locate.

As we pointed out in the previous chapter, the sixth edition of Buros' *Mental Measurements Yearbook* lists over 1,200 tests. An organization of these tests by type is provided in the *Yearbook's* table of contents, part of which is reproduced in Fig. 7.[1] Table 4 is another helpful item from the *Yearbook*.[2] It lists the number and percentage of tests in each of the major

TABLE 4

SIXTH MMY TESTS BY MAJOR CLASSIFICATIONS

Classification	Number	Percentage
Personality	196	16.1
Vocations	179	14.7
Intelligence	131	10.7
Miscellaneous	108	8.9
English	99	8.1
Mathematics	96	7.9
Reading	87	7.1
Foreign languages	77	6.3
Science	74	6.1
Social studies	61	5.0
Business education	29	2.4
Achievement batteries	28	2.3
Sensory motor	27	2.2
Multiaptitude	16	1.3
Fine arts	11	0.9
Total	1219	100.0

[1] *The Sixth Mental Measurements Yearbook* (Highland Park, N.J.: Gryphon, 1965), pp ix–x. Reprinted by permission of Gryphon Press.

[2] *Ibid.*, p. xxx. Reprinted by permission of Gryphon Press.

classifications. Reference to this table indicates that the largest number of published tests are found in the areas of personality, vocations, and intelligence.

In this chapter standardized tests are classified into ten main types. Because the number of tests is so many, we will mention only a few of those used frequently in educational research.

Table of Contents

* * * * *

Fig. 7. *The Sixth Mental Measurements Yearbook* (1965), pp. ix–x. Reprinted by permission of The Gryphon Press.

THE SIXTH MENTAL MEASUREMENTS YEARBOOK [x

INTELLIGENCE TESTS

Intelligence tests provide an estimate of a person's general intellectual level by sampling his performance on a variety of tasks. These tasks may include word definition, mathematical problem solving, general knowledge, and short-term memory of digits. Most intelligence tests yield a single global score of performance on these tasks. This score is called the IQ (intelligence quotient). Some intelligence tests also yield subscores such as verbal IQ and nonverbal IQ; subscores may also sometimes be obtained for specific intellectual functions, such as spatial relationships, verbal ability, numerical reasoning, and logical reasoning. However, if he plans to use subscores in his research analysis, the student should carefully check to determine if they are supported by sufficient evidence of construct validity and reliability.

Intelligence tests are held in high regard by educational researchers and school personnel because of their success in predicting school achievement. In fact, they are often called scholastic aptitude tests because the majority of them measure those aspects of intelligence that appear to be required for success in school learning.

Measures of intelligence may take the form of group or individually administered tests. The group intelligence tests have the advantage of low cost, and these tests provide a measure of scholastic aptitude that is satisfactory for most research purposes. Perhaps the most serious weakness of the group intelligence test is its inability to identify pupils in the group who are ill, negative toward the test, or suffer from some handicap that will cause them to make spuriously low scores. The individual tests overcome this difficulty because the examiner can usually determine by the student's answers and his general behavior whether extraneous factors that would tend to lower the student's score are entering the testing situation. Another disadvantage of the group test that can seriously distort research results in studies involving young children or children of below average achievement is that most of these tests depend to a considerable degree on the student's ability to read, and students whose reading ability is low will generally receive a spuriously low score on the test.

The disadvantage of the individual test, of course, is its expense. A trained examiner requires about an hour to administer the usual individual intelligence test to a single pupil. The individual tests also require considerable training to score and take much longer to score than the group tests, most of which are machine scorable. In spite of these disadvantages, however, the research worker should use an individual intelligence test whenever his subjects are such that he has reason to doubt the accuracy of results obtained from group tests. It is better for the research worker to reduce the size of his sample to permit individual testing than to test a large sample with a group measure of questionable validity.

Of the individually administered measures of intelligence, the Stanford-Binet is perhaps the best known. It is more suitable for the testing of children than of late adolescents and adults. A primary reason for the usefulness of the Stanford-Binet in educational research and practice is the considerable amount of evidence that has been collected regarding its validity and reliability. In recent years, though, the Wechsler Scales have achieved increasing prominence in the field of testing. This is perhaps due to the fact that these scales yield a number of useful subscores in addition to an overall IQ score. The Wechsler Adult Intelligence Scale (WAIS) is suitable for the testing of late adolescents and adults. The Wechsler Intelligence Scale for Children (WISC) is a downward extension of the WAIS and is suitable for the testing of children between the ages of five and fifteen. The most recent test in this series is the Wechsler Preschool and Primary Scale of Intelligence (WPPSI), which was published in 1967. It was designed for the testing of children between the ages of four and six and a half. The Peabody Picture Vocabulary Test (PPVT) has been used extensively as a measure of intelligence in Project Headstart research studies. In administering the PPVT, the examiner says a word, and then the child points to the one picture in a display of pictures that represents

that word. The main advantages of the PPVT are that it can be administered quickly and it can be used when individual testing is required but
a trained examiner is not available.

A number of group tests of intelligence are available. Some of these are
actually batteries of tests. The reason for developing a battery of tests is
that a single group test can usually sample only a restricted range of
difficulty in content. For example, a group test to assess the intellectual
performance of fifth-graders would be totally inadequate to assess high
school seniors: the items would be so easy that the test would not discriminate differences in intellectual level for the latter group. Therefore,
a series of tests comparable with regard to type of content are developed
for various grade levels. As an illustration, the Cooperative School and
College Ability Tests (SCAT) have forms available for grades 4–6, 6–8,
8–10, 10–12, 12–14, and 15–16. Since they are comparable in content and
in unit of measure, these forms make it possible for the researcher to study
intellectual development over many years in school and also to compare
the intellectual performance of children at different grade levels. Other
widely used batteries of group tests beside the SCAT are the California
Test of Mental Maturity, the Henmon-Nelson Tests of Mental Ability,
the Kuhlmann-Anderson Intelligence Tests, and the Otis-Lennon Mental
Ability Test.

Culture-fair tests of intelligence

As we pointed out previously, tests have been criticized because they
may discriminate unfairly against minority groups within a culture. Test
developers have responded to this criticism by constructing tests that
purport to be culture fair. By "culture fair" is meant that words and facts
that are culturally linked have been eliminated from the test. Consequently, most of these tests do not require the individual to use language.
The Culture-Fair Intelligence Test, published by the Institute for Personality and Ability Testing (IPAT), is one of the most widely used of
such tests. Various forms are available for testing individuals from age four
on up. Other tests designed to be culture fair are the Raven Progressive
Matrices and the Goodenough Draw-A-Man Test.

Although the culture-fair testing movement has been gaining increasing
favor by educators, there is reason for some caution in accepting the concept of a culture-fair test. For example, there is a growing body of evidence that verbal tests may actually be more culture-fair than nonverbal
tests.[3] Also, some psychologists and educators have argued that it is meaningless to construct tests that eliminate differences between groups, if these

[3] For a critical discussion of the concept of the culture-fair test, see Nadine Lambert,
'The Present Status of the Culture-Fair Testing Movement," *Psychology in the Schools,*
ι(3) (1964).

are true differences. Instead, training such as that provided by Project Headstart should be used to eliminate these differences.[4]

APTITUDE TESTS

Aptitude tests are aimed at predicting the student's later performance in a specific type of behavior. Tests are available to measure aptitudes for many specific school subjects, such as foreign language, art, music, and mathematics. Examples of such tests are the Modern Language Aptitude Test, the Orleans-Hanna Algebra Prognosis Test, and the Metropolitan Readiness Tests. Aptitude tests to measure skills needed in various occupations are also available. These include tests of sensory capacities, mechanical aptitude, and aptitude for selling.

A major trend in educational testing has been the development of test batteries that measure a wide range of aptitudes that are related to vocational and scholastic success. For example, the General Aptitude Test Battery (GATB) developed by the United States Employment Service measures these aptitudes: verbal, numerical, spatial, form perception, clerical perception, motor coordination, finger dexterity, and manual dexterity. The student's scores on these aptitudes yield a profile that can be compared with profiles of successful persons in various occupations in order to locate types of work for which the student has the aptitude required for success. The Differential Aptitude Tests (DAT) are another frequently used test battery for counseling and research with high school students and adults. Eight aptitudes are measured by the DAT: verbal reasoning, numerical ability, abstract reasoning, clerical speed and accuracy, mechanical reasoning, space relations, language use I—Spelling, and language use II—Grammar. Validity studies have demonstrated the value of the DAT in predicting students' scholastic success and vocational choice.

The usual evaluation procedures should be followed by the research worker in the selection of aptitude tests for research purposes. Predictive validity is especially important in aptitude tests because they are primarily concerned with prediction of future behavior. Aptitude tests are often used in educational research initially to equate groups that are to receive two different experimental treatments. For example, let us say we wish to compare the effectiveness of two methods of teaching ninth-grade algebra. If the students to be used in the experiment are initially different in terms of algebraic aptitude, the group with the higher aptitude might learn more regardless of the method. Therefore, in order to evaluate the

[4] A. R. Jensen, "Social Class and Verbal Learning," in M. Deutsch, I. Katz, and A. R. Jensen (eds.), *Social Class, Race, and Psychological Development* (New York: Holt, Rinehart & Winston, 1968), chap. 4.

effectiveness of the two methods, it would be desirable either to equate the two groups being studied by matching students on algebraic aptitude or to make statistical adjustments for initial differences found by the aptitude test. If either of these methods was employed, the experimenter could be more confident that achievement differences measure at the end of the study were due to differences in method than he could if he had no knowledge of the initial aptitude of the two groups.

Aptitude tests are also used in research to identify students of a particular aptitude level for special study. For example, the research worker may wish to identify students who have very low aptitude for learning a foreign language in order to determine whether a method could be developed to teach foreign language effectively to students at this level.

ACHIEVEMENT TESTS

Inasmuch as achievement is one of the major goals of education, measures of achievement are often used in educational research. Many standardized achievement tests are available to the research worker. Some are essentially aimed at measuring the student's knowledge of specific facts, while some of the more recent tests attempt also to measure the student's understanding and mastery of basic principles related to the subject. Administration time for different achievement tests varies greatly; some test batteries take as little as 50 minutes, while others require two days of testing to administer the entire battery. Achievement test batteries also differ in the subject matter areas covered. The California Achievement Test Battery,[5] for example, contains tests in the areas of reading, language, and arithmetic, and requires only an hour and a half for the primary battery. The Sequential Tests of Educational Progress (STEP) Battery, on the other hand, includes tests on essay writing, listening comprehension, reading comprehension, writing, science, mathematics, and social studies, and requires over nine hours to administer.

In selecting an achievement test or battery for his research project, the student should first decide what areas of achievement he wishes to measure, and then evaluate the tests that purport to measure achievement in these areas. Because he usually has a limited time available for testing in the public schools, it is often necessary for the student to administer single achievement tests rather than an entire test battery. As a rule the research worker will administer only tests measuring achievement in the specific areas concerned with the research. In addition to studying the evaluations available in the *Mental Measurements Yearbooks* and evaluating the test manual, the student should also administer the test to himself (even if it

[5] Further information on tests referred to in this chapter may be found in Oscar K. Buros, *Sixth Mental Measurements Yearbook* (Highland Park, N.J.: Gryphon Press, 1965).

is at the elementary school level) in order to check the instructions and gain an insight into the specific content covered. A major problem in developing achievement tests is to select content sufficiently common to the curriculums of most school systems so that the test will have a satisfactory level of content validity. It is much more difficult to achieve content validity in areas such as social studies than in areas such as arithmetic where the sequence and content is reasonably standard. A test may be very well constructed and receive good reviews in the *Mental Measurements Yearbooks* and still be inappropriate if it does not fit the content covered in the schools to be used in the research. In selecting an achievement test or battery to be used in more than one school district, the problem of content validity is increasingly acute because tests may fit the curriculum of one district better than the other. In this case obtained differences in achievement may be due to differences in content validity rather than actual differences brought about by the research conditions. Very often, some of the newer achievement batteries, which place more emphasis upon principles and less upon specific facts, are more appropriate for use in studies involving more than one district. Another aspect of content validity that the student should check when examining the test is the degree to which the test is up-to-date. Some achievement tests that were excellent several years ago are considerably less valid today. A common weakness found in the older tests is that illustrations of devices that have changed in physical appearance, such as the airplane, the automobile, and the telephone, may be so outdated that many students in today's schools would not even recognize them.

Another factor to be considered in selecting achievement measures for research is the test battery already being used by the schools from which the research sample will be drawn. Nearly all school districts now administer achievement tests on a regular basis as part of their program of self-evaluation and improvement. It is generally undesirable to use the same battery for research that is being used for other purposes in the public schools unless a very close control of the testing situation is possible. Achievement testing is psychologically threatening to many teachers because they fear that unless their students do well on the tests, it will be a reflection on the teacher's ability. Thus, it is not uncommon, if teachers have copies of the test at their disposal, for them to give their pupils special preparation in areas and sometimes even on specific items covered by the test. If the research worker selects his own measures, there is much less likelihood of the teacher's being able to give this sort of special assistance to his pupils.

When the research conditions call for measures of very specific knowledge, it is often necessary for the research worker to develop an achievement test for use in the research project. The principal advantage of the locally developed achievement test is that it can be tailored to the precise content area with which the research worker is concerned. The disadvantages are the additional time required to construct such a test and the fact that most research workers cannot bring a locally developed test to the high technical level attained by standardized tests.

DIAGNOSTIC TESTS

Occasionally the aim of a research project will be to evaluate the effectiveness of a remedial program. In this situation the researcher may find it helpful to use one of the variety of diagnostic tests that are available to identify students in need of remediation.

Diagnostic tests are a form of achievement test. However, an achievement test typically yields a single score indicating the student's general level of achievement in a given subject, such as reading or arithmetic. By contrast, diagnostic tests typically yield several scores which indicate the student's strengths and weaknesses in a given subject. Some diagnostic tests in common use are the Stanford Diagnostic Reading Test, the Stanford Diagnostic Arithmetic Test, and the Durrell Analysis of Reading Difficulty. There are several advantages to administering diagnostic tests in research or remedial programs. First, students who share a specific deficiency in a subject can be identified; otherwise students might be selected whose deficiencies vary widely, even though they earn the same score on a general achievement test. Second, the use of diagnostic tests is helpful in planning individualized remedial instruction, an approach advocated by many educators. A disadvantage of some diagnostic tests, however, is that the subscores have low reliabilities and are highly intercorrelated with one another.

MEASURES OF CREATIVITY

The identification and nurture of creative talent has become a major concern of educational researchers in the last two decades.[6] Not surprisingly, many new measures of creativity have been developed during this same period of time. A primary reason for this upsurge of research in creativity is that educators have become increasingly interested in the role of nonintellectual factors, such as creativity and personality characteristics, in school achievement.[7]

Most measures of creativity are intended to assess the aptitudes and per-

[6] See, for example, C. W. Taylor (ed.), *Creativity: Progress and Potential* (New York: Wiley, 1964).

[7] It should be noted, however, that some measures of creative aptitude have been found to be highly correlated with traditional measures of scholastic aptitude.

sonality traits that contribute to creative achievement. They are not direct measures of creative achievement itself. One of the major contributors in this area is J. P. Guilford, who has constructed a number of tests measuring divergent thinking processes. Some of these tests are Word Fluency (the person writes words each containing a specified letter); Brick Uses (the person lists uses for a common brick); Expressional Fluency (the person composes 4-word sentences, given only the initial letters, e.g., H_____ r_____ t_____ s_____); Plot Titles (the person composes plot titles, which are rated for their cleverness). Another major research effort is that of E. P. Torrance, who has developed a battery of ten tests of creative thinking. Since they were developed within a school context, these tests are frequently used by educational researchers in projects involving students at all grade levels.

MacKinnon and his colleagues have developed and studied a number of personality measures that differentiate between various creative and noncreative groups.[8] One of their best predictors of creativity has proved to be the Barron-Welsh Art Scale. This test is constructed so that the person taking it records whether he "likes" or "dislikes" a series of black-and-white drawings. The high scorer is one whose preferences agree with those expressed by a criterion group of artists. Since it does not require language, the Art Scale can be administered to a wide variety of groups whom the educational researcher may be interested in studying. Other measures that MacKinnon and his fellow researchers have found to predict creativity are the Mosaic Constructions Test and certain scales of the Strong Vocational Interest Blank and the Myers-Briggs Type Indicator.

SELF-REPORT MEASURES OF PERSONALITY

Many measures of personality rely on self-report to assess individual differences in traits, needs, adjustment difficulties, and values. These measures are used frequently in educational research to describe the personality characteristics of different groups of concern to educators, such as underachievers, minority groups, exceptional children, and members of a particular profession. They are also used to identify certain personality types for use in studies concerned with interrelationships between personality characteristics and other variables, such as intelligence, school achievement, or popularity.

Some of these measures are referred to as "general inventories" because a single instrument is used to measure a variety of personality traits. The inventory seeks information about the individual's personality by asking him questions or requiring him to respond to statements. Since a number

[8] The findings from their investigations are discussed in D. W. MacKinnon, "The Nature and Nurture of Creative Talent," *American Psychologist*, 17 (1962), 484–495.

of variables are assessed at the same time, there are usually at least several hundred of these statements. Consequently, most subjects will require an hour or two to complete a general inventory. One of the principal advantages of the personality inventory is its low cost and ease of administration and scoring. The questions or statements are almost always in dichotomous form (e.g., "I enjoy listening to popular music: TRUE-FALSE"), and therefore can be scored by computer or with a template. However, a few of these measures require training in order to interpret particular variables. For example, the student would have no difficulty administering the Minnesota Multiphasic Personality Inventory (the MMPI), since it is virtually self-administering and can be objectively scored. But suppose the student found that one of his research groups scored significantly higher on the Pt scale (psychasthenia) than a comparison group. Unless he has had training in the MMPI or can consult with someone who has had this training, the student probably will be unable to interpret the significance of this finding.

One of the potentially serious disadvantages of personality inventories stems from the fact that they are based on self-report. Like most self-reporting devices, they are only accurate to the degree that the self-perceptions are accurate and to the degree that the person is willing to express them honestly. This problem has been, and continues to be, a matter of concern to many educational and psychological researchers.

If self-report inventories are to be used effectively in practical applications and in research settings, it is important to investigate the extent to which subjects are responding to the content of each item and the extent to which their responses are determined by a general "set." Three types of "response sets" have been extensively researched: social desirability, or the set to present oneself in a favorable light; acquiescence, or the set to respond "true," no matter what the content of the inventory item may be; and the set to respond deviantly.[9] It should be noted that the extent of contamination of personality inventories by response sets is still an active research problem. For example, Block (1965) has presented evidence indicating that the MMPI is relatively free of response sets, even though previous researchers had reached just the opposite conclusion.[10] As a practical matter, though, if the student has good reason to believe that his research sample will fake or give atypical answers, then a self-report inventory should not be selected.

It was pointed out in the previous chapter that there has been an increasing frequency of attacks on tests as an invasion of privacy. This is

[9] A critical review of the research evidence on these response sets can be found in Irwin A. Berg (ed.), *Response Set in Personality Assessment* (Chicago: Aldine, 1967).

[10] Jack Block, *The Challenge of Response Sets: Unconfounding Meaning, Acquiescence, and Social Desirability in the MMPI* (New York: Appleton-Century-Crofts, 1965).

particularly true of personality measures. Therefore, the student should carefully review the personality inventory he is considering to see if items are present that might cause public relations difficulties with parents or community groups. For example, administering an inventory that contained questions dealing with sexual conduct to junior high school students might cause serious repercussions in the community and make it impossible to complete the research. If such items are essential to the research objectives, very extensive public relations work must be carried out before and during the study.

We will now briefly describe self-report measures of personality that are used frequently in educational research.

General inventories

Minnesota Multiphasic Personality Inventory (MMPI). This inventory was developed by determining which items out of a 550-item pool differentiated empirically between particular psychiatric groups and normal groups. In addition to the original scales (e.g., Hypochondriasis, Depression, Schizophrenia), many other variables can be assessed, including response sets and scales of ego strength, anxiety, and repression-sensitization. The sixth edition of the *Mental Measurement Yearbook* lists 1,394 research projects involving the MMPI, many of them relevant to educational research. The MMPI may be an appropriate instrument to use when the student is interested in measuring various aspects of personality adjustment in late adolescents and adults.

The California Psychological Inventory (CPI). Although the CPI draws heavily on the MMPI item pool, its aim is to measure traits thought to be relevant to interpersonal behavior and intellectual functioning. Whereas the MMPI was developed for use in psychiatric settings, the CPI is oriented primarily to the assessment of normal persons. Some of its 18 scales are dominance, sociability, responsibility, good impression, flexibility, intellectual efficiency, and achievement via independence. The CPI can be used with high school and adult populations.

The Edwards Personal Preference Schedule (EPPS). This inventory measures 15 needs based on Henry Murray's need system. One of the merits of the EPPS is that an attempt has been made to control for the response set of social desirability by having subjects decide between pairs of statements of equivalent social desirability. Some of the 15 scales are autonomy, dominance, intraception, and abasement. Norms on the EPPS are available for college students and adults.

The Sixteen Personality Factor Questionnaire (16 P.F.). This inventory is different from those already described in that its scales were developed by the method of factor analysis. Some of the personality dimensions measured by the scales are reserved versus outgoing, affected by feelings versus emotionally stable, practical versus imaginative, relaxed versus tense. Primarily used for research purposes, the 16 P.F. can be administered to adolescents and older age groups.

Specific inventories

In addition to the general personality inventories just described, there are available a group of inventories that measure a single personality variable or small set of related variables.

Rokeach Dogmatism Scale. Although designed to measure the variable of closed-mindedness, this scale is often used in educational and psychological research as a measure of general authoritarianism. A sample item is: "When it comes to differences of opinion in religion we must be careful not to compromise with those who believe differently from the way we do." (Agreement with this item is scored in the direction of closed-mindedness.)

Fundamental Interpersonal Relations Orientation-Behavior (FIRO-B). This brief inventory is based on Schutz's theory of small group behavior.[11] It measures the strength of the individual's expressed inclusion, control, and affection, and the extent to which he wants these behaviors from others. FIRO-B can be used with high school students on up.

Allport-Vernon Study of Values. This inventory attempts to determine the predominant value system of the person tested. The Study of Values yields six scores indicating the relative strengths of the dominant values that shape the individual's personality: theoretical, economic, aesthetic, social, political, and religious.

Checklists

Some self-report measures of personality take the form of check lists. A collection of items is presented to the individual, and he is asked to check off those items that are applicable to himself.

The Adjective Check List (ACL). This measure consists of 300 adjectives such as "imaginative," "stubborn," "relaxed." The person checks as many of these adjectives as are self-descriptive. The ACL data can be used to compare groups with regard to the frequencies with which they endorse particular adjectives. The ACL can also be scored on 24 scales that assess personality variables, such as defensiveness, self-confidence, dominance, and need for change. The ACL is a useful research instrument, since it yields a considerable amount of information in a relatively short period of time (it can be completed in 15 or 20 minutes). Also, the ACL can be used by a person to describe himself or to describe another person or group.

Mooney Problem Check List. This measure contains a list of problems

[11] William C. Schutz, *FIRO: A Three-Dimensional Theory of Interpersonal Behavior* (New York: Holt, Rinehart & Winston, 1958).

that a student may have. The student simply checks off those problems applicable to himself. This checklist is used with some frequency in educational research and may be administered to students in grade seven on up.

PROJECTIVE TECHNIQUES

The term "projective technique" was popularized by L. K. Frank.[12] It was his contention that the use of instruments such as the Rorschach Inkblot Technique, with its amorphous stimuli and freedom of response, would reveal the individual's inner thoughts, fantasies, and idiosyncratic structuring of reality. One of the purported advantages of projective techniques over self-report inventories is that they are less subject to faking.

A review of the literature by Crenshaw, Bohn, Hoffman, Mathews, and Offenbach (1968) indicates that the Rorschach, the Thematic Apperception Test, and various types of Human Figure Drawings are the most frequently used research instruments among projective techniques.[13] Well over 3,000 research studies have been conducted on the Rorschach alone. In spite of their popularity, however, the authors would caution their use in a research project. Jensen (1965) has summed up the opinion of many educational and psychological researchers in this fashion:

The question of why the Rorschach still has so many devotees and continues to be so widely used is still quite another problem and is beyond the scope of this review. A satisfactory explanation of the whole amazing phenomenon is a task for future historians of psychology and will probably have to wait upon greater knowledge of the psychology of credulity than we now possess. Meanwhile, the rate of scientific progress in clinical psychology might well be measured by the speed and thoroughness with which it gets over the Rorschach. [p. 509] [14]

However, should he find need to administer the Rorschach or similar projective techniques in his project, the student should employ carefully trained testers, as we have noted before.

A recent development in the field of projective techniques is the construction of group-administered instruments to measure classic Rorschach variables. The most widely used of these instruments is the Holtzman Inkblot Technique (HIT) which, from a psychometric point of view, is far superior to the Rorschach. Unlike the Rorschach, where the subject

[12] L. K. Frank, "Projective Methods for the Study of Personality," *Journal of Psychology*, 8 (1939), 349–413.

[13] David A. Crenshaw, Suzanne Bohn, M. R. Hoffman, J. M. Mathews, and S. G. Offenbach, "The Use of Projective Methods in Research: 1947–1965," *Journal of Projective Techniques and Personality Assessment*, 32(1) (1968), 3–9.

[14] Arthur R. Jensen, review in Oscar K. Buros, *The Sixth Mental Measurements Handbook* (Highland Park, N.J.: Gryphon, 1965), 501–509.

may give as many or as few responses to each stimulus as he chooses, the number of responses which the subject can give to each Holtzman card is controlled. Most of the Holtzman scoring variables have satisfactory reliability. The disadvantages of the HIT are that training is needed to interpret the scoring variables and that some of these variables seem to reflect verbal productivity rather than basic personality characteristics.[15]

MEASURES OF SELF-CONCEPT

The *self* or *self-concept* may be defined as the set of cognitions and feelings which each of us has about ourself. Researchers may want to measure the self-concept for various reasons. For example, it is sometimes important to investigate the effect of various educational practices on students' self-concept,[16] or one may want to investigate whether students' self-concept is a determinant of school performance.

In a sense all self-report inventories are measures of self-concept. The Adjective Check List,[17] for example, requires the individual to check those adjectives that are self-descriptive, and thus it is sometimes administered simply to obtain a measure of self-concept. However, the scales of this instrument measure traits such as aggressiveness, dominance, and nurturance. When scale scores are obtained, the researcher is not interested in how the individual views himself per se, but is primarily interested in the concurrent validity of the self-report against the criterion of behavioral observations or ratings. Of the self-report inventories, the Adjective Check List seems best suited for the study of self-concept.

The Semantic Differential, which we will discuss later as a technique for measuring attitudes, can also be applied to the measurement of self-concept. The individual describes himself on a series of 7-point scales with bipolar adjectives at each end (e.g., good-bad, tense-relaxed, large-small). The three main factors that these scales yield indicate whether the individual views himself as good or bad (evaluation), strong or weak (potency), and active or passive (activity). A somewhat different technique is the Q sort. The individual is given a set of cards, each containing a descriptive statement (e.g., "I enjoy going to parties"). He is asked to sort the cards into piles with a predetermined distribution, ranging from "most characteristic" to "least characteristic." The researcher may make up a set of cards to meet the specific needs of his research project, but

[15] Regarding this last criticism of the Holtzman Inkblot Technique, see E. I. Megargee, "The Relation of Response Length to the Holtzman Inkblot Technique," *Journal of Consulting Psychology,* 30 (1966), 415–419.
[16] In a study conducted by the senior author, the effect of an ability-grouping system on students' self-concept was determined.
[17] See p. 180.

often a published set of cards such as the California Q sort is employed. To date the Q sort technique has perhaps found its widest use in research on changes in self-concept as a result of Rogerian counseling and psychotherapy.[18]

It should be noted that each of these techniques for measuring self-concept can also be used to measure how the individual perceives his "ideal self," how he thinks certain others perceive him, or how he perceives others, such as his parents, teachers, and so forth.

ATTITUDE SCALES

Scales are frequently developed to measure the individual's attitude toward a particular group, institution, or institutional practice. An attitude is usually thought of as having three components: an affective component, which consists of the individual's feelings about the attitude object; a cognitive component, which is the individual's beliefs or knowledge about the attitude object; and a behavioral component, which is the individual's predisposition to act toward the attitude object in a particular way.

Several different procedures have been used to develop measures of attitude. On a Thurstone-type scale, the individual expresses whether he *agrees* or *disagrees* with a series of statements about the attitude object. On a Likert-type scale, the individual checks one of five possible responses to each statement: strongly agree, agree, undecided, disagree, strongly disagree. Sometimes the Semantic Differential is used to assess attitudes. The individual gives a quantitative rating of an attitude object on a variety of bipolar adjectives, such as fair-unfair, valuable-worthless, and good-bad. Guttman scaling, interviews, and open-ended questionnaires are examples of other methods used to measure attitudes.

Attitudes are often measured in educational research because of their possible predictive value. For example, a researcher may be interested in measuring students' attitude toward high school, since this variable might predict which students will be high school dropouts. An important study concerned with this use of attitude scales was done by Tittle and Hill.[19] They compared the effectiveness of various types of attitude scales (Likert, Guttman, Semantic Differential, Thurstone, Self-Rating) in predicting objective indices of voting behavior. The Likert scale was superior to all the other scale types; it yielded a mean correlation coefficient of .54 with the objective indices of voting behavior.

[18] C. R. Rogers and R. F. Dymond (eds.), *Psychotherapy and Personality Change* (Chicago: University of Chicago Press, 1954).

[19] Charles R. Tittle and Richard J. Hill, "Aptitude Measurement and Prediction of Behavior: An Evaluation of Conditions and Measurement Techniques," *Sociometry*, 30 (1967), 199–213.

In reviewing the research literature, the student may come across an attitude scale that he can use in his project.[20] For example, in the previous chapter, a research study was mentioned in which a scale to measure attitudes about American Indians had been developed by the researcher. One of the frequently administered attitude scales in educational research is the Minnesota Teacher Attitude Inventory, which measures the individual's attitudes toward teaching.

Sometimes the student will wish to measure an attitude for which no scale is available. For example, the senior author found it necessary to develop a scale to measure teachers' attitudes toward ability grouping. Satisfactory attitude scales can be developed by the research worker if he follows closely the procedures outlined in textbooks on this subject (see annotated references). The Likert technique is usually the easiest method of developing scales needed in research projects.

Attitude scales are direct self-report measures and so have the usual disadvantages of this type of instrument. The primary disadvantage is that we can never be sure of the degree to which the subject's responses reflect his true attitudes. Under certain conditions, for example, when the individual's attitude is in conflict with the social norm, he may go to considerable lengths to hide his true attitude. Less direct attitude measures are needed to overcome this difficulty, but to date few such measures have been developed.[21]

MEASURES OF VOCATIONAL INTEREST

Vocational interest inventories have proved to be of considerable value to educational researchers. They are used to investigate how students come to develop specific vocational interests, and they also provide an indirect assessment of personality characteristics (e.g., an individual interested in banking is likely to have a different personality structure than an individual interested in art as a career).

Vocational interest inventories typically require the individual to express his interest in various types of people, sports, hobbies, books, and other aspects of daily life. The Strong Vocational Interest Blank (SVIB), one of the most thoroughly researched and widely used of these inventories, was constructed by determining how the interests of a given occupational group differed from "men in general" or "women in general."

[20] Also, Shaw and Wright (see annotated references) have made a useful compilation of published attitude scales.

[21] For examples of "disguised" techniques to measure attitudes, see David Krech, Richard S. Crutchfield, and Egerton L. Ballachey, *Individual in Society: A Textbook of Social Psychology* (New York: McGraw-Hill, 1962), pp. 161–167. See also the discussion of unobtrusive measures in Chapter 9.

The SVIB is scored by comparing the individual's interests with those of men or women in different occupations. To date the men's form can be scored on 54 occupational scales, and the women's form can be scored on 32 scales.

Since the SVIB primarily measures interest in professional and business occupations, this instrument is probably not appropriate for the researcher investigating the interests of students who are not college-bound. The Minnesota Vocational Interest Inventory is likely to be more useful in such cases, since it measures the individual's interest in various skilled and semiskilled occupations. The construction of this inventory was similar to that of the SVIB.

The Kuder Interest Inventory-Vocational was developed to measure the individual's interest in various broad occupational areas rather than in specific occupations. These occupational areas are outdoor, mechanical, computational, scientific, persuasive, artistic, literary, musical, social service, and clerical. Recently the Kuder General Interest Survey was developed to measure the interests of students, sixth through twelfth grades, in these occupational areas.

MISTAKES OFTEN MADE BY GRADUATE STUDENTS

1. Student selects the first test he is able to find rather than systematically selecting the test most appropriate for his research problem.
2. Uses subscores from a test without checking their validity and reliability.
3. Does not check the content of an achievement test to determine whether it corresponds to the content covered in the schools that will be used in the research.
4. Selects a test instrument, such as the Minnesota Multiphasic Personality Inventory, that he is not qualified to administer and interpret.
5. Fails to check the content of personality tests to determine whether it is likely to cause public relations difficulties.

ANNOTATED REFERENCES

General

1. Anastasi's textbook on psychological testing (see annotated references for Chapter 7) provides excellent coverage of all the types of tests presented in this chapter. In addition, the most important tests in current use are carefully described with regard to content, norms, reliability, and validity. The *Mental Measurements Yearbooks* and psychology and educational journals are also helpful sources of information about specific types of tests.
2. "Educational and psychological testing," *Review of Educational Research*, 38 (1), February 1968. This issue of the *Review* presents the main trends in testing exceptional students and students at various grade levels. The researcher

planning an investigation of a particular student population will find the individual reviews helpful in selecting appropriate tests.

Achievement tests

3. Gronlund, Norman E. *Constructing Achievement Tests.* Englewood Cliffs, N.J.:
   Prentice-Hall, 1968. This book provides specific techniques for the student who
   finds it necessary to develop a measure of achievement for his research project.

Measures of creativity

4. Golann, Stuart E. "Psychological Study of Creativity," *Psychological Bulletin,*
   60 (1963), 548–565. This article provides a good review of the main issues in
   the study of creativity and the types of tests that have been devised to measure
   various aspects of creativity.

Self-report measures of personality

5. Kleinmuntz, B. *Personality Measurement: An Introduction.* Homewood, Ill.:
   Dorsey, 1967. This book presents a comprehensive description of the major types
   of personality measures. Sections on test administration, scoring, and interpretation are included.

Projective techniques

6. Murstein, Bernard I. (ed.). *Handbook of Projective Techniques.* New York:
   Basic Books, 1965. This volume provides a useful service in pulling together the
   most important studies from a body of research literature that includes several
   thousand titles. The Rorschach Inkblot Technique, Thematic Tests, the Draw-
   A-Person Test, the Bender Gestalt, and the Sentence Completion Test are each
   represented by several classic studies.

Measures of self-concept

7. Wylie, Ruth C. *The Self Concept: A Critical Survey of Pertinent Research Literature.* Lincoln, Nebraska: University of Nebraska Press, 1961. The author
   critically reviews research pertaining to theories and measures of self-concept.

Attitude scales

8. Shaw, M. E., and Wright, J. M. *Scales for the Measurement of Attitudes.* New
   York: McGraw-Hill, 1967. This volume is a compilation of attitude scales that
   have been constructed by research workers over the years. It is a valuable reference for students who need to measure a particular attitude for their research
   project.

CHAPTER 8

The Methods and Tools of Survey Research

OVERVIEW

The survey as a form of educational research

Survey research is a distinctive research methodology that owes much of its recent development to the field of sociology. Considered as a method of systematic data collection, though, surveys have a long historical tradition. As far back as the time of the ancient Egyptians, population counts and surveys of crop production have been conducted for various purposes, including taxation. The contribution of twentieth-century sociologists, such as Lazarsfeld, Hyman, and Stouffer, was to link instruments of data collection (e.g., questionnaires and interviews) to a logic and to statistical procedures for analyzing these kinds of data.

The information collected by surveys can be of various types. The Gallup poll is probably the best known survey used to sample public opinion. Market researchers employ surveys to evaluate product acceptance and use. Among the scientific disciplines, researchers in economics, anthropology, psychology, and public health make frequent use of surveys to collect information relevant to interests and problems in their fields.

Studies involving surveys account for a substantial proportion of the research done in the field of education. For example, Lazarsfeld and Sieber did a content analysis of educational research appearing in 40 journals in 1964, and found that about a third of them involved use of the survey method.[1] A wide range of educational problems can be investigated in survey research, as illustrated by this list of recent studies:

G. T. O'Hearn and R. L. Doran, "Survey of State Supervisors of Science," *Science Education,* 52 (1968), 204–208.

G. F. Shearron and H. Wait, "Nongraded Elementary Schools: A Survey of Practices," *National Elementary Principal,* 47 (1967), 39–42.

[1] Paul F. Lazarsfeld and Sam D. Sieber, *Organizing Educational Research* (Englewood Cliffs, N.J.: Prentice-Hall, 1964).

M. D. Shipp, "Teacher Aides: A Survey," *National Elementary Principal*, 46 (1967), 30–33.

M. M. Anapol, "Survey of Graduate Study in Speech," *Speech Teacher*, 16 (1967), 253–258.

J. P. Dipps, "Health Class Project: Smoking Survey," *Journal of School Health*, 38 (1968), 169–176.

W. O. Covert, "Illinois Junior High Schools: Survey of Sizes and Types," *Illinois Education*, 56 (1967), 110–111.

Local school districts sometimes have need to do surveys. The comprehensive school survey explores and evaluates many aspects of the school system, such as buildings, maintenance, administrative procedures, financial support and procedures, teaching staff, learning objectives, curriculum, and teaching methods. Such surveys are usually carried out by a team of visiting specialists from universities and other school systems. Another type of survey, the school census, is conducted so that administrators can predict the educational needs their schools will be called upon to meet in future years. Local surveys are also used for the purposes of internal evaluation and improvement.

The student who must perform a research project for completion of an advanced degree might well consider employing the survey approach to investigate a particular educational problem. However, the student should be aware that surveys involve considerably more than administering a questionnaire to describe "what is." It is unfortunate but true that many research workers in education hold surveys in low esteem because they believe that surveys are limited to description. In fact, though, survey research utilizes a variety of instruments and methods to study relationships, effects of treatments, longitudinal changes, and comparisons between groups. In this chapter we shall discuss the basic design in survey research, the cross-sectional survey, and methods for conducting it.

Data-collection tools in surveys

Data-collection tools are used in survey research to obtain *standardized* information from all subjects in the sample. If he wishes to determine his subjects' socioeconomic status, for example, the researcher must administer the same instrument to all subjects. He cannot determine the socioeconomic status of half the sample by questionnaire, and then use an interview to collect the same information for the remaining sample. Also, the conditions of administration must be as similar as possible for each subject in the sample.

It is assumed that the information collected by survey instruments is quantifiable. In the case of multiple-choice questionnaire items, the information is quantified at the time it is collected. If open-ended questions are used, the "open-ended" information that is obtained must be codified so that it can be analyzed and reported quantitatively.

The questionnaire and individual interview are the most common instruments for data collection in survey research. Accordingly, detailed steps in constructing and administering questionnaires and interview schedules are presented in this chapter. However, the student should be aware of the other methods that can be used to collect survey information. The telephone interview is one such method.[2] The advantage of the telephone interview is that it is a relatively quick method for obtaining certain kinds of information. Assuming that the questions asked of the respondent are not highly personal or too numerous, the researcher will probably be able to collect information from a high percentage of his sample in a relatively short time. By contrast with the questionnaire and personal interview methods, he need not arrange for appointments in advance, travel to subjects' residences, or leave it to subjects to mail in survey information at their leisure. The obvious disadvantages of the telephone interview are that relatively few questions can be asked, questions are not usually answered in depth, certain groups of respondents cannot be reached easily by phone, and the method becomes fairly expensive if a large, widely dispersed sample is surveyed.

Another technique for collecting survey information is to examine records. For example, students' files often contain much information of interest to the researcher: parents' ages, income, occupations, marital status, the student's school attendance, course grades, extracurricular activities. Examination of records has the advantage of being relatively complete and quick, since all the relevant information is usually stored in one location. Of course, the student should be sensitive to the issue of invasion of privacy if this technique is used. Clearance from all involved groups should be obtained before proceeding to examine records. Depending on the situation, these groups may include the research subjects, the subjects' parents, and the administrators who have compiled the records.

The cross-sectional survey

In the cross-sectional survey, standardized information is collected from a sample drawn from a predetermined population. (If information is collected from the entire population, the survey is called a census.) As we discussed in Chapter 5, the sampling techniques most commonly used in educational surveys are simple random, stratified, or cluster sampling. Another basic feature of the cross-sectional survey is that the information is collected at one point in time (although the actual time required to complete the survey may be one day to a month or more).

[2] One application of the telephone interview has been to determine what percentages of a sample are viewing particular television programs on a given hour and day of the week.

Survey data from a cross-sectional survey can be analyzed by a variety of methods. The particular method or methods that the researcher selects will depend on the types of inferences he wishes to make from his data.

Descriptions of single variables

The simplest use to which survey data can be put is a description of how the total sample has distributed itself on the response alternatives for a single questionnaire item. These are sometimes called the "marginal tabulations." For example, newspapers often report the results of public opinion polls in terms of marginal tabulations, for example, 50 percent of the sample were in favor of a particular governmental policy, 30 percent disagreed with it, and 20 percent were unsure or had no opinion.

Survey research in education often yields this type of normative description. As an illustration, we may consider a study by Trenfield which was designed to investigate the degree of interest of high school students in participating in adult civic activities.[3] A Likert-type scale of 30 items, each describing a different civic activity, was administered to a sample of 300 students randomly drawn from a population of approximately 4,000 high school students in a Texas school district. Students were asked to describe their degree of interest in participating in each activity on a 5-point scale. In the data analysis, the mean score of the entire sample on each attitude item was determined. This form of data analysis provides an interesting description of students' civic interests. We find, for instance, that these students are most likely to express their civic interest by voting in national elections and by signing a petition to be presented to a public official. They are least likely to express interest in running for public office and in attending night classes to improve their ability as a citizen.

Descriptions of this type may provide important leads in identifying needed emphases and changes in school curricula. Also, we should note that since proper sampling procedures were employed, Trenfield was able to generalize his descriptive findings from the sample to the population from which they were drawn.

Exploring relationships

In addition to their value for determining the distribution of a sample on a single variable, surveys can be used to explore relationships between two or more variables. The student who is aware of the possibilities for investigating relationships in his survey data will make a more substantial

---

[3] W. G. Trenfield, "An Analysis of the Relationships Between Selected Factors and the Civic Interests of High-School Students," *Journal of Educational Research*, 58 (10) (1965), 460–462.

research contribution than the student who limits his data analysis to single variable descriptions.

Questionnaire items may refer to past, present, or future phenomena. If he studies relationships between questionnaire items that refer to the same point in time, the researcher is engaging in what is known as "time-bound association." If the items can be temporally ordered relative to each other, then the data analysis is referred to as "time ordered association."

One type of time-bound association occurs when the researcher relates two or more questionnaire items to each other because they are thought to be measures of the same phenomenon. In the Trenfield study, the 30 attitude statements of civic interest were intercorrelated to determine the extent to which they measured the same underlying concept. This type of time-bound association is equivalent to the reliability estimates for standardized tests which we discussed in Chapter 6. Since the internal reliability of the civic interests scale was found to be satisfactory (.90), a summary score on the scale for each subject could be used in further data analyses. Whenever more than one item is included in a questionnaire to measure the same attitude or variable,[4] the interrelationship of the items should be examined by computing a reliability coefficient. If the coefficient is sufficiently high, the items can be combined to form a summary measure.

A second type of time-bound association occurs when the researcher determines the relationship between questionnaire items measuring *different* variables. The questionnaire items may refer to the same point in time, or they may be assumed to refer to the same point in time if the researcher does not wish to assume that they are related to each other in a causal-temporal order. In the Trenfield study of civic interests, several instances of time-bound association can be found. Students' scores on the scale of interest in participation in adult civic activities were correlated with three different variables: parents' interest in civic participation (measured by the same scale that was administered to the students), students' participation in extracurricular activities, and students' grades in social studies. The correlation of students' interest scores with each of these latter variables was, respectively, .46, .33, and .30. It should be noted that Trenfield did not hypothesize a causal relationship between any of these variables; or, to state it another way, he did not engage in time-ordered association. For example, Trenfield did not hypothesize that parents' interest in civic participation would *cause* their sons and daughters to be interested in civic participation. The results are simply presented as empirical relationships between different variables.

---

[4] Socioeconomic status, for example, is often measured by combining items that are based on different indices of status, such as occupational level, income, and amount of education.

When survey data refer to different points in time, analysis of these data is called "time-ordered association." Two types of time-ordered association may be distinguished. The first type, called "differentiated description," involves breaking down the total sample into different subgroups and then examining how their responses are distributed on selected variables. Subgroups may be formed on the basis of age, income, sex, education, or other demographic factors. For example, it would have been of interest in the Trenfield study to take the total sample and form subgroups of males and females. Then questionnaire items could have been analyzed to determine whether there are sex differences in the civic interests of high school students. Subgroups could also have been formed on the basis of students' academic and vocational goals, socioeconomic status, or age, and the questionnaire data analyzed accordingly. It should be apparent that analysis in terms of differentiated description provides a more interesting and complete survey than would be provided by simply computing distributions on single variables for the entire sample.

Thus far we have been concerned only with the descriptive uses to which survey data can be put. If survey data are time orderable, then hypotheses can be tested. As an illustration, Huettig and Newell [5] used the survey method to investigate whether amount of training in modern mathematics would result in more positive attitudes toward this subject. A sample of 115 elementary school teachers was administered a questionnaire designed to collect information about their teaching experience and attitudes about modern mathematics. They responded to 31 Likert-type attitude statements, and the data were analyzed in terms of whether 60 percent or more of each subgroup had a positive or negative attitude on each item. The hypothesis was considered confirmed, since it was found that teachers with more training in modern mathematics were likely to respond favorably to more attitude items than teachers with little or no training (see Table 5).

It would be erroneous to conclude from these results alone that training in modern mathematics *results in, leads to,* or *causes* these more favorable attitudes. Only an experiment with appropriate controls can determine with a high degree of certainty that the relationship between these two variables is causal. In survey research, though, there is a strategy that can be used to strengthen one's confidence that two variables that are correlated with each other (such as amount of training and positiveness of attitudes toward modern mathematics) are also causally related. This strategy consists of attempting to find another variable that explains the relationship between the two original variables. If we cannot find a variable that explains away the relationship, then we can be more confident, though not

[5] A. Huettig and J. M. Newell, "Attitudes Toward Introduction of Modern Mathematics Program by Teachers with Large and Small Number of Years' Experience," *Arithmetic Teacher,* 13 (February 1966), 125–130. Reprinted by permission.

TABLE 5 *

AMOUNT OF TRAINING IN MODERN MATHEMATICS AND ATTITUDE TOWARD
MODERN MATHEMATICS

Amount of Training	Number of Positive Attitudes	Number of Negative Attitudes	Number of Neutral Attitudes
Two courses	22	3	6
One course	20	4	7
One-half course	16	8	7
One workshop	11	11	9
No training	9	18	4

* *Ibid.*

certain, that the relationship is causal-temporal. This strategy could be
applied to Huettig and Newell's study. As we have already discussed, these
researchers found a substantial relationship between amount of training
in modern mathematics and positiveness of attitudes toward this subject.
What antecedent variable might explain this relationship? One possibility
is suggested by another data analysis, presented in Table 6, in which
Huettig and Newell found that amount of teaching experience bore a strong
negative relationship to the frequency of favorable attitudes toward modern mathematics.

TABLE 6 *

TEACHING EXPERIENCE AND ATTITUDE TOWARD MODERN MATHEMATICS

Teaching Experience	Number of Positive Attitudes	Number of Negative Attitudes	Number of Neutral Attitudes
1–2 years	18	2	11
3–9 years	13	10	8
10–20 years	7	18	16
21–48 years	5	17	9

* *Ibid.*

Perhaps, then, the variable of teaching experience would explain away
the relationship between favorable attitudes and training in modern mathematics. Since Huettig and Newell did not do this data analysis, we will
work with hypothetical data as shown in Table 7.

We see from this table of hypothetical data that irrespective of training
in modern math, inexperienced teachers are likely to have positive attitudes toward modern mathematics. Also irrespective of training in modern
math, very experienced teachers are likely to have negative attitudes. Thus,
in our hypothetical situation, teaching experience "explains away" the
original relationship that was found between training and attitudes. Ac-

TABLE 7 *

AMOUNT OF TRAINING, TEACHING EXPERIENCE, AND ATTITUDE TOWARD MODERN
MATHEMATICS (BASED ON HYPOTHETICAL DATA) †

Training	1–2 Years Experience		21–48 Years Experience	
	Positive Attitudes	Negative Attitudes	Positive Attitudes	Negative Attitudes
Two courses	18	5	5	20
No training	18	5	5	20

* *Ibid.*

† To simplify matters, only two levels of training in mathematics are shown,
although in the actual study five levels of training were distinguished.

cordingly, we can reject the hypothesis that these two variables are
causally related to each other.

Now let us suppose that the original relationship is maintained after the
third variable is introduced. If this is the case, *replication* of the original
relationship is said to have occurred. Replication is illustrated by the hypothetical data of Table 8.

TABLE 8 *

HYPOTHETICAL DATA ILLUSTRATING REPLICATION

Training	1–2 Years Experience		21–48 Years Experience	
	Positive Attitudes	Negative Attitudes	Positive Attitudes	Negative Attitudes
Two courses	18	2	18	2
No training	5	17	5	17

* *Ibid.*

The data of Table 8 indicate that irrespective of teaching experience,
training is related to attitudes toward modern mathematics. If replication
occurs, then we have further support for the hypothesis that training and
attitudes are causally related.[6]

It should be noted that replication has no bearing on the problem of
direction of causality, that is, we still have no way of knowing whether
training in modern mathematics leads teachers to form more positive attitudes toward this subject (irrespective of their original attitudes) or
whether teachers with positive attitudes toward modern mathematics seek
out training in the subject. To answer these questions an experimental

[6] Of course, there is always the possibility that another "third" variable could be found
which explains this relationship. Also, it is possible that a "third" variable only *partially*
explains away the original relationship. For example, it might be that both teaching experience and training affect the positiveness of attitudes toward modern mathematics.

approach is necessary. The experimental design would involve measurement of attitudes before and after training in an experimental and control group.[7]

In summary, the value of survey research of the type carried out by Huettig and Newell is that while it cannot establish causal relationships with any degree of certainty, it can be used to explore a variety of relationships (e.g., between training and attitudes) in a relatively economical way. If important relationships are found, then questions about causality can be resolved by means of an experiment.

STEPS IN CONDUCTING A QUESTIONNAIRE SURVEY

Defining the questionnaire objectives

The first step in carrying out a satisfactory questionnaire study is to list specific objectives to be achieved by the questionnaire. It is not uncommon for a graduate student to develop a questionnaire before he has a clear understanding of what he hopes to obtain from the results. Unless you are able to state specifically and in detail what information you need, what you will do with this information after you get it, and how each item on the questionnaire contributes to meeting your specific objectives, you have not thought through your problem sufficiently.

In preparing your objectives, you should keep in mind the methods of data analysis that you will apply to the returned questionnaires. Suppose that you are interested in surveying the extent of usage of ability grouping in the schools of your state. The first objective of your study might be to determine the percentage of schools in the state that are using some form of ability-grouping. Therefore, you should include items in the questionnaire that will elicit reliable information from each school regarding its use of ability-grouping systems. Of course, the objectives of your study need not be limited to describing the current situation in the schools. You might consider surveying your sample on such questions as: how administrators of schools with ability-grouping think their grouping practices can be improved, whether administrators of schools without ability-grouping have previously tried to institute an ability-groupng system, and how the community has reacted to the idea of ability-grouping in its schools.

In our discussion of the cross-sectional survey, we pointed out that survey data can be used to achieve objectives other than description of how the responses of the total sample are distributed on each questionnaire item. In a survey of ability-grouping practices, one objective may be to investigate differences between types of schools. For example, the survey

[7] This type of research design is discussed in Chapter 15.

data may be analyzed to determine whether urban schools are more or less likely than suburban or rural schools to have an ability-grouping system. The study of descriptive relationships between variables may also be an objective. As an illustration, one could investigate the relationship between the schools' achievement test norms and the presence or absence of an ability-grouping system. As we discussed earlier in this chapter, it is possible to describe such relationships as instances of time-bound association, that is, no inference is made about a causal relationship between the two variables. However, the testing of causal hypotheses can be an objective of your study if the data are time-orderable. For example, one may hypothesize that schools which send a large proportion of their students to college will be more likely to institute an ability-grouping system than schools in which the percentage of college-bound students is low. To test this hypothesis, data should be collected about presence or absence of an ability-grouping system in each school and the percentage of college-bound students in each school.[8]

To summarize, surveys can have a variety of objectives. However, these objectives need to be identified at the outset of the study, otherwise you will find it very difficult to make sound decisions regarding selection of a sample, construction of the questionnaire, and methods for analyzing the data.

Selecting a sample

The most obvious consideration involved in selection of subjects for a questionnaire study is to get people who will be able to supply the information you want. Very often the group who will have the data you want is immediately apparent. But in some cases, if you do not have a thorough knowledge of the situation involved, you may send your questionnaire to a group of persons who do not have the desired information. For example, a graduate student seeking data on school financial policies sent questionnaires to principals of a large number of elementary schools. Many of the questionnaires returned were incomplete, and few specific facts of the sort wanted were obtained. This study failed because the trend in recent years has been for the superintendent and his staff to handle most matters concerning school finance. Inasmuch as the principals who received the questionnaire had little specific knowledge concerning this topic, they were unable to supply the information requested on the questionnaire.

Most questionnaire studies conducted in education are aimed at specific professional groups. Once you have established that the professional group

---

[8] If such a study were to be done, the percentage of college-bound students should be based on data collected by the schools *prior* to the institution of an ability-grouping system.

selected actually has access to the information you wish to obtain, you can survey the entire group or you can select a random sample from the population.[9] Many professional groups in education have special organizations or societies, and in some cases a random selection of names from the directory of organization members gives a satisfactory group. This type of selection, however, must be used cautiously, as there may be a tendency for the more competent members of the professional group to belong to the organization, thus leading the researcher to select a biased sample.

State public school directories are more satisfactory for selection of subjects because they list all persons involved in public education in the state and are usually up-to-date. When the population is very large, such as all elementary school teachers in the United States, and no complete name list is available, it is usually necessary to use a two-stage procedure to obtain a random sample. The first stage in obtaining a nationwide sample could be to select randomly a specified number of school districts. Since most districts print rosters of their teachers, the next step would be to request a copy of the rosters from districts selected in the first stage. A specified number of teachers could then be randomly selected by name from each roster.

As we have discussed previously, it is often desirable to obtain responses from several specific categories of persons within the professional group being sampled. For example, you may wish to compare responses dealing with use of pupil-centered instruction gathered from teachers with different amounts of professional experience. If this is your objective, then it is desirable to use stratified sampling in order to select equal-size subsamples from different levels of the population (e.g., 100 inexperienced teachers, 100 teachers with one-to-three years experience, and 100 teachers with four or more years experience).

Constructing questionnaire items

Many of the questionnaires that are received by principals, superintendents, and other educators appear to have been thrown together by the graduate student during the short break between lunch and his two o'clock class. This type of questionnaire has led many school administrators to develop negative attitudes about the questionnaire as a research approach. Some of the more harassed administrators deposit the questionnaires they receive in the wastebasket with little more than a quick glance. This attitude, of course, presents an obstacle that the graduate student planning to use this technique must and can overcome by the careful construction and administration of his questionnaire. Each item on your questionnaire must

[9] Random sampling techniques are discussed in Chapter 5.

be developed to measure a specific aspect of one of your objectives or hypotheses. You should be able to explain in detail *why* you are asking the question and *how* you will analyze the responses.

Questions may be of either the closed form in which the question permits only certain responses (such as a multiple-choice question), or the open form in which the subject makes any response he wishes in his own words (such as an essay question). Which form will be used is determined by the objective of the particular question. Generally, though, it is desirable to design the questions in closed form so that quantification and analysis of the results may be carried out efficiently. Let us suppose you wish to know the size of the teacher's home town so that you can compare teachers from different-sized towns in terms of interests and vocational goals. There are several ways that this question could be asked. Perhaps the poorest technique would be to ask "What is your home town?" This question requires that you be able to read the person's reply and look it up in an atlas to determine the population. A technique that would be somewhat better would be to ask "What is the population of your home town?" In this case you could classify the responses into population categories such as those used by the U.S. Census Bureau. A still better means of obtaining this information would be to ask "What is the population of your home town? (Check one.)"

        _____ rural, unincorporated
        _____ incorporated, under 1000
        _____ 1,000 to 2,500
        _____ 2,500 to 5,000
        _____ 5,000 to 10,000
        _____ 10,000 to 50,000
        _____ 50,000 to 250,000
        _____ over 250,000

This latter technique would provide you with the information you want in immediately usable form, thus requiring less effort on your part, while requiring no more effort by your subjects.

Perhaps the best method of determining the multiple-choice categories to use in closed questions is to ask the question in essay form of a small number of respondents, and then use their answers to develop the categories for the multiple-choice item that will be included in the final form of the questionnaire. In multiple-choice areas where a certain number of unexpected responses might occur, an "other" choice can be used along with a space for explanation. For example, suppose that you are interested in provisions made for gifted pupils in elementary schools. First, you could ask a small number of respondents the question, "How are gifted pupils in your school identified and what provisions are made for them? Please be specific and indicate the extent to which each technique was employed during the past school year." Examination of the respondents' answers will probably suggest a limited number of categories which can be incorporated into multiple-choice items, for example:

1. Do you have a systematic program for identifying gifted children in your school? _____ _____ If yes, what means of identification do you use?

      yes   no

_____ *a*. Group intelligence test

_____ *b*. Individual intelligence test

_____ *c*. Achievement battery

_____ *d*. Aptitude battery

_____ *e*. Teacher ratings

_____ *f*. Other   (specify) _____

2. What provisions were made for gifted pupils in your school during the school year 1960–61? (Check appropriate answers.)

_____ *a*. Acceleration (grade skipping)

_____ *b*. Ungraded program

_____ *c*. Ability grouping

_____ *d*. Enrichment

_____ *e*. Special classes

_____ *f*. Other   (specify) _____

Depending on the specific objectives of the questionnaire, other questions could be added concerned with such matters as the number of pupils at each grade level who skipped a grade, the number of pupils in special classes, the criteria for establishing ability-grouped sections, and others.

Under certain circumstances it is not desirable to substitute multiple-choice items for open-ended questions. A case in point is provided by Colfax and Allen, who compared the relative efficacy of open-ended and multiple-choice items when used by students to report their father's occupation.[10] A sample of 67 sixth graders, 85 ninth graders, and 86 twelfth-grade students were asked to respond to these open-ended items, "What is your father's job or occupation?" and "As best you can, write exactly what your father does when he is at work." The students also responded to a multiple-choice item in which they were asked to check one of ten occupational categories that described their father's job most closely. It was found that only 6 percent of the sixth graders did not respond to the open-ended

---

[10] J. D. Colfax and I. L. Allen, "Pre-Coded Versus Open-Ended Items and Children's Reports of Father's Occupation," *Sociology of Education*, 40 (1967), 96–98.

items, but one third of them gave unusable answers on the multiple-choice item (they left the item blank, checked the "don't know" category, or checked two or more categories). All the ninth graders and twelfth graders responded to the open-ended item, but 14 percent and 8 percent of them, respectively, gave unusable answers on the multiple-choice item. Furthermore, when the open-ended answers were used as the criterion of the father's occupation, it was found that the error rates on the multiple-choice item rose to 52 percent (sixth graders), 20 percent (ninth graders), and 15 percent (twelfth graders). Colfax and Allen conclude that the open-ended form is preferable to a multiple-choice item in this situation, even though the former is a more expensive and time-consuming method. Besides illustrating the value of open-ended questions in some situations, this study indicates the need to pretest questionnaires before administering them to one's primary sample.

Another rule you should observe in constructing questionnaire items is to avoid questions that may in some way be psychologically threatening to the person answering. For example, a questionnaire sent to school principals concerning the morale of teachers at their schools would be threatening to some of the principals because low morale suggests that the principal is failing in part of his job. When he receives a questionnaire containing threatening items, a person usually does not return it. If he does return it, little confidence can be placed in the accuracy of his reply because of his ego involvement in the situation.

Finally, it is very important that an effort be made to avoid leading questions. If the subject is given hints as to the type of answer you would most prefer, there is some tendency for him to give you what you wish. This tendency is especially strong when the letter of transmittal that accompanies the questionnaire has been signed by someone whom the subject is eager to please.

Attitude measurement in questionnaires [11]

Most questionnaires deal with factual material, and in many cases each item is analyzed separately to provide a specific bit of information that contributes to the overall picture that you are attempting to obtain. Thus, it is possible to look upon the questionnaire as a collection of one-item tests. The use of a one-item test is quite satisfactory when one is seeking out a specific fact, such as teacher salary, number of baseball bats owned by the physical education department, or number of students failing algebra. When questions get into the area of attitude and opinion, however, the one-item test approach is extremely unreliable. A questionnaire dealing with attitudes must generally be constructed as an attitude scale

[11] A discussion of the attitude scale as a type of standardized test can be found in Chapter 6.

and must use a number of items (usually at least ten) in order to obtain a reasonable picture of the attitude concerned.

The attitudes measured in a questionnaire can cover a wide range of topics. For example, earlier in this chapter, we reviewed two survey studies in which attitudes toward modern mathematics and participation in civic activities were measured. The student who is planning to collect information about attitudes should first search the literature to determine whether a scale suitable for his purposes has already been constructed.[12] If a suitable scale is not available, it will be necessary to develop one. Thurstone and Likert scales are probably the most common types of attitude scales that are constructed. If the student develops an attitude scale for his survey project, it should be pretested in order to collect reliability and validity evidence. Also, the student should investigate in his pretest whether the sample of subjects has sufficient knowledge and understanding to express a meaningful opinion about a particular topic. For example, you might want to learn the attitudes of a sample of teachers or administrators toward some of the newer developments in education, such as microteaching, Individually Prescribed Instruction, and the Fenton social studies curriculum. If a sizable proportion of the sample is not adequately familiar with these developments, its attitude responses will be of questionable value.

One method of dealing with subjects who are not familiar with a particular topic is to include a "no opinion" category as one of the response alternatives for each attitude item. The disadvantage of this method is that subjects with little or no information about a particular topic will often still express an opinion in order to conceal their ignorance or because they feel social or professional pressure to express an opinion. This point is illustrated by an interesting study dealing with interview surveys.[13] A total of 625 respondents in three Iowa urban communities were interviewed about their attitudes regarding nine persons (e.g., Barry Goldwater, John F. Kennedy) and seven organizations (e.g., CORE, John Birch Society). The respondents could express a favorable or unfavorable attitude on six Likert-type categories, or they could use a seventh category to express no knowledge of a particular person or organization. To determine whether respondents would express an attitude toward an organization about which they were uninformed, the interviewers asked for their opinion of a nonexistent organization called the League for Linear Programs. To their surprise the interviewers found that ten percent of the sample expressed a favorable or unfavorable attitude toward this organization about which it was impossible for them to have any knowledge! It was also found that this same

---

[12] See annotated references for Chapter 6.

[13] Irving L. Allen, "Detecting Respondents Who Fake and Confuse Information About Question Areas on Surveys," *Journal of Applied Psychology*, 50(6) (1966), 523–528.

ten percent of the sample were also more likely to express attitudes toward the other organizations and persons rather than check the "don't know" category. They also were more likely to express favorable attitudes and to have less formal education than the rest of the sample.

The implication of these findings is that the respondents' knowledge and expertise is an important factor in interpreting attitude data. Therefore, the student planning a questionnaire survey involving attitude measurement should investigate his respondents' familiarity with each attitude object covered in the survey. One technique for doing this is to administer an information test to a small sample of respondents (similar to those to be queried in the main survey) to determine whether they are capable of expressing an informed opinion about the persons, organizations, or educational practices mentioned in the attitude scales.

Effect of anonymity on questionnaire responses

In most educational studies, the respondent is asked to identify himself. Anonymity is sometimes called for if data of a personal nature or data that may be threatening to the individual are requested. A questionnaire dealing with sexual behavior, for example, may receive more honest responses if anonymous.

The anonymous questionnaire poses many research problems. Followups are difficult and inefficient because nonresponding individuals cannot be identified. Furthermore, it is usually not possible to make some of the statistical breakdowns of the group that may be desirable. For example, in a study of teacher-principal relationships, it may be desirable to divide the respondents into men and women teachers, married and unmarried teachers, and teachers with different amounts of experience, and then compare the responses of these different groups. In the anonymous questionnaire, breakdowns of this sort that were not anticipated and provided for in the questionnaire cannot be made. Often the desirability of analyzing certain subgroups separately is not apparent until the data are collected.

The essential question that must be answered, however, is whether anonymity is necessary to get accurate replies. In a study of 400 military officers, one half were given a questionnaire requiring that they identify themselves by name, while the other half were given the same questionnaire but were not required to identify themselves by name. Significant differences in response were found in only two percent of the 118 items with no trend favoring either subjects who identified themselves or subjects who remained anonymous. Persons who signed their names took a longer period to answer their questionnaire, which may indicate that they were more careful in their responses. No significant differences, however, were found between the groups in either the quality or the quantity of their responses as measured by "degree of careless thinking," "number of omitted questions," or "number of ideas represented in open-ended questions." [14] This study suggests that mature adult respondents tend to answer the questions whether they are asked to identify themselves or not. The factors to be considered in deciding whether identification is to be asked for are the importance of identification in the analysis of results, the level of maturity of the respondents, the degree to which questions involve answers that the respondent might be reluctant to give if he is identified, the probable effect of anonymity on the number of returns, and the procedures that can be used in the analysis of results.

Pretesting the questionnaire

In addition to the preliminary check that you make of your questions in order to locate ambiguities, it is very desirable to carry out a thorough pretest of your questionnaire before using it in your study. For the pretest you should select a sample of individuals from a population similar to that from which you plan to draw your research subjects. For example, if you were concerned with mechanical aids used for teaching foreign languages in California high schools, you could pretest your questionnaire using a sample of foreign language teachers employed in another state. The pretest form of the questionnaire should provide space for the respondents to make comments about the questionnaire itself so they may indicate whether some questions seem ambiguous to them, whether provisions should be made for certain responses that are not included in the questionnaire, and other points that can lead to improving the instrument. The techniques for administering the questionnaire during the pretest should be essentially the same as planned for the main study, except when there is some doubt as to which of two questions or two approaches might be most useful; both can be tried on portions of the pretest sample. The number of cases in the pretest sample need not be large. If the subjects are taken from a well-defined professional group, such as school superintendents, as few as twenty cases will often be sufficient. For more heterogeneous groups, such as persons paying property taxes or parents with one or more children in elementary school, a larger pretest group is advisable.

When the pretest results are in, first check the percentage of replies obtained. Educational studies generally can be expected to yield a higher percentage of replies than questionnaires sent to random samples of the general population because the educational questionnaire usually aims at a reasonably homogeneous group, and this makes it possible to prepare an appeal to the group for cooperation, which is more likely to be successful.

[14] Francis J. DiVesta, "Problems in the Use of Questionnaires for Studying the Effectiveness of Programs," *Educational and Psychological Measurement*, 14 (1954), 138–150.

If, in checking the percentage of replies, you have received less than 75 percent of the pretest sample, it is probable that major changes will be needed in the questionnaire or in the procedures for administering it. The next step is to read the subjects' comments concerning the questionnaire. These comments often give specific information on how the questionnaire can be improved. Then, check the responses item by item. If you find items that are often left blank or answered in ways that you did not predict, it is very likely that the item was misinterpreted by some of the subjects.

It is now possible to do a brief analysis of the pretest results. This will give you a chance to determine whether the methods you have planned to use for summarizing and quantifying the data will work satisfactorily. Also, the pretest results may suggest additional questions to you. For example, if sharp disagreement is found in the responses to a particular item of the questionnaire, it may be desirable to construct additional items that will help you understand the reasons for this disagreement.

After the preceding procedure has been completed and all improvements made in the pretest questionnaire, you are ready to proceed with the administration of your questionnaire to the sample you have selected.

The letter of transmittal

The student's major problem in doing a questionnaire study is to get a sufficient percentage of responses to use as a basis for drawing general conclusions. Perhaps the most important single factor in determining the percentage of responses you will obtain is the letter of transmittal used with your questionnaire. This letter must be brief but yet must convey certain information and impressions to the subjects if you are to obtain a satisfactory percentage of responses. First, it is essential that you give the subjects good reasons for completing your questionnaire and sending it back to you. Whenever possible, the purposes of the study should be explained briefly and in such a way as to make the subject feel that the study is significant and important. If your questionnaire is aimed at a group with specific professional ties, such as mathematics teachers, it is usually desirable to make some reference to the person's professional status and his feelings of affiliation with this group. In some cases a certain amount of subtle flattery is also useful in preparing the letter of transmittal. This is usually accomplished by stressing the importance of the subjects' professional group and the value of the information the group can supply. An offer to send the respondent a copy of the results is often effective. If made, however, such a promise should be honored because neglect of such matters is not ethical and will weaken future studies involving persons in your sample.

If possible, it is also desirable to associate your study with some professional institution or organization with which individuals in your sample might be expected to value or identify. For example, superintendents within a particular state might be expected to respond favorably to a letter signed by the state superintendent, the state or national president of a superintendents' association, or the dean of education at the state university. If your study is well-designed and deals with a significant problem, it is usually possible to have someone sign your letter of transmittal who will represent a favorable authority symbol to the persons responding.

If your questionnaire is not aimed at a specific professional group, it is much more difficult to obtain responses, because specific appeals cannot be made. Under these conditions you might slant your appeal along lines in which you might expect even the members of a widely diversified group to have common views, such as patriotism, desire to improve the community, and so on. However, if your study is one where these general appeals are obviously inappropriate, the best approach is probably an appeal to the individual's sense of humor. For example, several years ago a national magazine wished to obtain information from its readers on the extent to which they used commercial flying in pursuing their sports activities. As the subscribers were a highly heterogeneous group having very little in common except subscription to this periodical and as the topic was not one where a general appeal could be expected to work, the magazine sent their very brief questionnaire along with a letter of transmittal on which was glued a dime. The letter of transmittal started out by asking the person to take a coffee break at the expense of the magazine and while drinking the coffee to check off answers on the attached postcard. This sort of approach is likely to get good response because it amuses the subject while making very modest demands upon his time.

One of the items contained in the letter of transmittal is a request that the questionnaire be returned by a particular date. It is important to set this date so that the subject will have sufficient time to fill out and return the questionnaire without rushing or inconvenience, but on the other hand, will not be likely to put it aside to do later as is the tendency if too generous a time allowance is given. A satisfactory rule of thumb would be to calculate the probable mailing time and allow the individual an additional week or less to complete the questionnaire and return it. Included with the questionnaire and the letter of transmittal should be a stamped, self-addressed envelope so that the individual can respond with a minimum of inconvenience.

The neatness and composition of your questionnaire and accompanying material is an important factor in determining the number of replies. The more expensive methods of duplication are usually worth the extra cost. A letter of transmittal reproduced by the offset process on letterhead paper and signed with a different color ink will command more attention than one poorly dittoed on cheap paper. A poorly reproduced questionnaire indicates to the respondent that the study is of little importance to you or anyone else in spite of your protestations to the contrary. A sample letter of transmittal is shown in Fig. 8.

Sample Letter of Transmittal

Letterhead paper⟶ **OKLABAMA STATE UNIVERSITY**
Collegetown, Oklabama
M. A. Brown, President

College of Education
I. B. Smith, Dean

February 1, 1963

Typed with same
machine used in ⟶ Mr. A. B. Jones
cutting offset stencil Superintendent of Schools
Mediumtown, Oklahoma

Dear Sir:

Duplicated using offset
process to look like ⟶ The attached questionnaire con-
individually typed cerned with procedures used in selec-
letter ting elementary school principals is
Purpose of study part of a state-wide study being carried on cooperatively by the State Department of Public Instruction and Oklabama State University. This project
is concerned specifically with determining the present status of principal
Importance of ⟶ selection in our state. The results
study of this study will help to provide preliminary criteria to be used for developing better selection procedures and for
improving the administrator training program at Oklabama University.

Importance of We are particularly desirous of ob-
respondent ⟶ taining your responses because your experience in principal selection will contribute significantly toward solving some
of the problems we face in this important
area of education. The enclosed questionnaire has been tested with a sampling of
school administrators, and we have revised
it in order to make it possible for us
to obtain all necessary data while requiring a minimum of your time. The average
time required for administrators trying
out the questionnaire was 9½ minutes.

Fig. 8. Sample letter of transmittal.

Reasonable but specific time limit ———→ It will be appreciated if you will complete the questionnaire prior to February 10th and return it in the stamped,

Special delivery further stresses importance ———→ special delivery envelope enclosed. Other phases of this research cannot be carried out until we complete analysis of the questionnaire data. We would welcome any comments that you may have concerning any aspect of principal selection not covered in the questionnaire. We will be pleased to send you a summary of questionnaire

Offer results ———→ results if you desire. Thank you for your cooperation.

Sincerely yours,

Printed different color to appear personally signed ———————————→ I. B. Smith

Signed by important educator rather than graduate student ———→ I. B. Smith, Dean

Enc.
sjc

Follow-up techniques

A few days after the time limit that you have set in your letter of transmittal, it is usually desirable to send a follow-up letter along with another copy of the questionnaire and another self-addressed envelope to individuals who have not responded. The follow-up letter must generally assume the tone that you are certain the individual wished to fill out the questionnaire, but perhaps due to an error on your part or some oversight, it was overlooked. The follow-up letter should then go on to point out again the importance of the study and value of the individual's contribution to this important project.

As a rule, if careful attention is given to the design of the questionnaire, the letter of transmittal, and follow-up letter, a sufficient percentage of subjects will respond. In cases where a very high percentage of response is required, it may be necessary to conduct a further follow-up using a different approach. A second follow-up letter will generally produce little result, but if a new approach is used, it might bring in the additional cases needed. On some occasions as many as three follow-up letters are used. Figure 9 shows the pattern of responses to one questionnaire study in which three follow-ups were used.[15] It will be noted that in this study the first follow-up brought in an additional 20 percent of the sample, the second about 15 percent, and the third about 2 percent. The effectiveness of the

[15] National Education Association, Research Division, "Small-Sample Techniques," *NEA Research Bulletin,* 38 (December 1960), 102. Reprinted with permission of the NEA Research Division.

second and third follow-ups in this study was greater than average, probably because these were sent as telegrams, which are more likely than letters to command attention. On some occasions a telephone call is effective if the first follow-up letter does not yield sufficient returns.

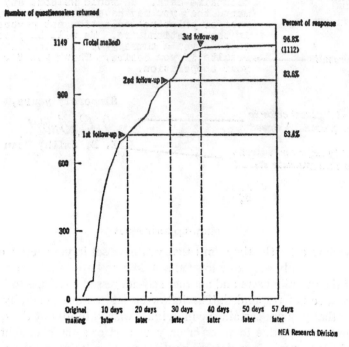

Fig. 9. Pattern of response to Opinion Poll No. 1. Taken from National Education Association, Research Division, "Small-Sample Techniques," *NEA Research Bulletin* XXXVIII (December, 1960), 102. Reprinted by permission of the NEA Research Division.

The effectiveness of follow-up techniques in increasing the percentage of questionnaire returns is illustrated by another study.[16] The researcher was particularly interested in whether follow-up techniques would increase the percentage of college dropouts responding to a questionnaire. This questionnaire was mailed to all college men who had enrolled at a large state university a number of years prior to the study. Three waves of mail resulted in a 67 percent mail-back response. In the first wave, respondents were sent a questionnaire, a cover letter, and a stamped return envelope. The second wave of mail came twenty days later, when the nonrespond-

[16] B. K. Eckland, "Effects of Prodding to Increase Mail-Back Returns," *Journal of Applied Psychology*, 49 (1965), 165–169.

ents were sent the same enclosures again except for a new cover letter. The third wave of mail resulted when a reminder card was sent out. At this point different follow-up techniques were used to encourage mail-backs by the 383 resistant nonrespondents. All nonrespondents whose phone number could be located were telephoned. Those who could not be reached by phone were sent a certified letter and a new questionnaire. The investigator points out:

Certified mail, coupled with a postal receipt, is a relatively inexpensive means of verifying delivery by requiring the recipient to affix his signature upon a card which is then returned to the sender. It serves the same purpose as a registered letter, except there is no insurance coverage on the contents of the letter (and, thus, about one-third the cost).

The use of the telephone and certified mail as follow-up techniques resulted in an 82 percent mail-back return from the 383 resistant nonrespondents in this study. The total mail-back return was thereby raised to 94 percent of the original sample, which is an unusually high percentage for this type of survey study. One further point is worth noting regarding respondents who had been college dropouts. Had follow-up techniques been discontinued after the first three waves of mail-back response, college dropouts would have comprised 23 percent of the respondents. After the telephone calls and certified mailings, college dropouts accounted for 31 percent of the total number of respondents. Since college dropouts possessed special characteristics of interest to the investigator, it was worth the additional follow-up time in order to get a more adequate representation of them.[17]

What to do about nonrespondents

After the responses have been obtained, the research worker faces the problem of analyzing his results. The question that usually arises at this point is "How would the results have been changed if all subjects had returned the questionnaire?" If only a small percentage of your subjects failed to respond, this question is not critical. If more than 20 percent are missing, however, it is very likely that most of the findings of the study could have been altered considerably if the nonresponding group had returned the questionnaire and had answered in a markedly different manner than the responding group. This could be the case if the nonresponding group represents a biased sampling, that is, if those people who did not respond to the questionnaire are in some measurable way different from those who did respond. A common sampling bias of this type is that per-

[17] We shall find later in this chapter that nonrespondents in questionnaire surveys tend to be less academically successful than respondents.

sons having a good program are more likely to respond than those having a poor program. For example, a questionnaire dealing with the physical education program at the elementary school level will get a higher percentage of responses from those schools having programs that the respondents believe to be above par. School administrators are often reluctant to admit the deficiencies of their schools and therefore fail to return questionnaires in which these deficiencies would be revealed.

Several recent studies have investigated whether personality and intellectual differences exist between respondents and nonrespondents.[18] The general finding of these studies is that respondents and nonrespondents do not differ on any significant personality dimensions. However, nonrespondents tend to have achieved less academic success than respondents.

If more than 20 percent of the questionnaires are not returned, it is desirable to check a portion of the nonresponding group even though this checking usually involves considerable effort. The ideal method of checking is to select a small number of cases randomly from the nonresponding group, and then interview these subjects in order to obtain the necessary information. If the questionnaire has been sent over a wide geographical area, interviewing a random selection of nonresponding cases is usually not possible. Under these circumstances the student can get some insight into the nature of the nonresponding group by checking those persons who are within a reasonable distance. In most educational studies of the sort conducted by graduate students, 20 cases are adequate to check the nonresponding group. After data have been obtained from these cases, the responses of this group to each item are compared with the responses of those who replied initially to determine whether the nonresponding sample is biased. If this sample of nonresponding subjects answers the questions in about the same manner as the responding group, it is probably safe to assume that the responding group is an unbiased sample of those to whom you mailed the questionnaire. If this sample, however, is considerably different in their responses, these differences should be noted and their significance discussed in reporting the results of the responding sample. Also, serious consideration should be given to using some of the follow-up techniques that were discussed earlier in this chapter. Telegrams, telephone calls, and certified mailings can be effective devices for substantially increasing the percentage of responding subjects.

[18] R. G. Cope, "Nonresponse in Survey Research as a Function of Psychological Characteristics and Time of Response," *Journal of Experimental Psychology,* 36 (1968), 32–35; D. L. Thistlewaite and Norman Wheeler, "Effects of Teacher and Peer Subcultures upon Student Aspirations," *Journal of Educational Psychology,* 57 (1966), 35–47; Carson M. Bennett and Robert E. Hill, "A Comparison of Selected Personality Characteristics of Responders and Nonresponders to a Mailed Questionnaire Study," *Journal of Educational Research,* 58 (1964), 178–180.

THE INTERVIEW AS A RESEARCH TOOL

Introduction

The steps in conducting an interview study are essentially the same as those for conducting a study that uses the mailed questionnaire as the primary data-collection tool. Therefore, only the main points of the previous section will be repeated here.

The first step is to write a statement describing the general purpose of the research. In writing this statement, the student should be aware of the various research designs that can be used in the cross-sectional survey. These designs make it possible to describe the distribution of the sample's responses on a single variable, to make differentiated descriptions of selected groups (e.g., male versus female, college-educated versus non-college-educated), and to study time-bound and time-ordered relationships.

Next, a sample of respondents should be selected using random sampling techniques. A serious weakness of interview studies done by graduate students is the usual necessity of using small samples. The research worker should remember that the dangers of a biased sample are particularly serious when only a small number of individuals can be included in the research. After a random sample has been selected, it is advisable to obtain some commitment of cooperation from these individuals before the interviewing starts. Every effort should be made to obtain the cooperation of all individuals initially selected. If some of the subjects selected refuse to cooperate, this refusal will almost certainly lead to some biasing of the research results. The random selection of substitutes for these non-cooperating individuals does not remove the possibility of this bias.

In the first part of this chapter, we described in detail the complexities involved in constructing a sound research questionnaire. The construction of an interview guide and the conduct of the interview are similarly complex. Therefore, these topics are given extensive treatment in the next sections.

Advantages and disadvantages of the interview

The interview as a research method in descriptive research is unique in that it involves the collection of data through direct verbal interaction between individuals. This direct interaction is the source of both the main advantages and disadvantages of the interview as a research technique. Perhaps its principal advantage is its adaptability. The well-trained interviewer can make full use of the responses of the subject to alter the interview situation. As contrasted with the questionnaire, which provides no immediate feedback, the interview permits the research worker to follow-up leads and thus obtain more data and greater clarity. The interview situation usually permits much greater depth than the other methods of collecting research data. A serious criticism of questionnaire studies is that they are often shallow, that is, they fail to dig deeply enough to provide a true picture of opinions and feelings. In contrast, the skilled interviewer, through the careful motivation of the subject and maintenance of rapport, can obtain information that the subject would probably not reveal under any other circumstances. The reason why such information may be difficult to obtain is that it usually concerns negative aspects of the self or negative feelings toward others. Respondents are not likely to reveal this type of information about themselves on a questionnaire and will only reveal it in an interview situation if they have been made to feel comfortable by a skillful interviewer.

The advantages of the interview over the mailed questionnaire in certain situations were shown in a study by Jackson and Rothney.[19] These investigators conducted a follow-up study of 890 high school students, some of whom had received intensive counseling. The entire sample was sent a 4-page mailed questionnaire five years after its high school graduation. A subsample of 50 cases was then drawn for a personal interview in which the same items as appeared on the questionnaire were asked. The information collected by means of the two techniques was then compared. It was found that a higher proportion of the sample completed each interview item than the corresponding questionnaire item. Also, 98 percent of the planned interviews were completed, compared with 83 percent of the mailed questionnaires. Two experienced counselors read and evaluated the questionnaire and interview data for evidence of personal problems. The mean number of problems yielded by the interview data was 8.82, whereas the corresponding figure for the questionnaire data was only 2.82. Thus, it appears that under favorable conditions the interview tends to yield more complete data and also more data regarding negative aspects of the self.

Another finding of this study was that respondents were fairly consistent when their interview and questionnaire responses to fact or yes-no items were compared. A study by Walsh [20] yielded a similar finding. This investigator compared the relative accuracy of the interview and questionnaire in collecting factual data from a college sample (e.g., grade-point average, number of failed courses, quarter hours completed). The interview and questionnaire proved to be of comparable accuracy when the data collected by each method were compared with the records on file

[19] Robert M. Jackson and J. W. M. Rothney, "A Comparative Study of the Mailed Questionnaire and the Interview in Follow-Up Studies," *Personnel and Guidance Journal*, 39 (1961), 569–571.

[20] W. B. Walsh, "Validity of Self-Report: Another Look," *Journal of Counseling Psychology*, 15 (1968), 180–186.

at the university.[21] Since it is considerably less expensive than interviewing, the mailed questionnaire is the technique of choice when factual,
unambiguous information is to be collected. However, as the study by
Jackson and Rothney indicates, the interview is likely to yield more complete information when open-ended questions pertaining to negative aspects of the self need to be asked.

Although it has a number of important advantages over other data-
collection tools in certain situations, the interview does have definite limitations as a research tool. Most important, the very adaptability gained
by the interpersonal situation leads to subjectivity and possible bias. The
interactions between the respondent and the interviewer are subject to
bias from many sources. Eagerness of the respondent to please the interviewer, a vague antagonism that sometimes arises between the interviewer
and the respondent, or the tendency of the interviewer to seek out answers
that support his preconceived notions are but a few of the factors that may
contribute to biasing of data obtained from the interview. Another problem of the interview method that seriously limits the graduate student in
education is that considerable training is required before the individual
can successfully carry out an interview study. The student must gain a
thorough knowledge of interview procedures and must obtain practice in
interviewing before he can expect to collect usable data through this technique. This chapter will acquaint the student with the basic information
needed to plan an interview study, but he should study carefully some
books on interviewing before attempting to use this technique in research.
The interview is also time-consuming and therefore limits the number of
subjects from whom the graduate student can expect to obtain data.

The interview guide

It is necessary to develop a tentative guide to be used during the interview. This guide makes it possible to obtain the data required to meet the
specific objectives of the study and to standardize the situation to some
degree. The guide lists, in the desired sequence, the questions that are to
be asked during the interview. The form that these questions will take
depends upon the level of structure of the interview, that is, the amount
of direction and restriction imposed by the interview situation. An interview can be thought of as being highly structured, semistructured, or
unstructured. Of course, within a single interview, the questions asked by
the interviewer may vary along this entire continuum. Certain types of
information, such as the limited specific facts or opinions collected in
public opinion polls, call for a highly structured interview situation. In
these studies the interviewer usually asks each respondent a brief series

---

[21] When such records are available, the researcher should use them, since they are nearly
always more accurate and accessible than questionnaire or interview data.

of questions that can be answered either "yes" or "no," or by selecting one of a set of alternate choices. The respondent's answers are not followed up to obtain greater depth, and the level of structure in this case is such that the data could be collected quite satisfactorily with a mailed questionnaire. The only advantage of the interview over the mailed questionnaire for this type of data collection is that the interviewer is likely to get responses from more of the persons in the sample selected. The disadvantage, of course, is the greater expense of collecting data.

Interviewers in educational research will generally include some highly structured questions in their interview guide, but they will aim primarily toward a semistructured level. At this level the interviewer first asks a series of structured questions and then probes more deeply, using open-ended questions in order to obtain more complete data. Suppose the interviewer is trying to understand the relationship between the student's high school experiences and his college achievement. First he may ask a sample of college students structured questions having to do with the size and location of their high schools, their grades, extracurricular activities, courses taken, and so forth. Then he may probe by asking open-ended questions, such as, "How well do you think your high school experience prepared you for college?" and "If you could repeat your high school experience, would you want to do anything different on the basis of what you have learned in college so far?" After the respondent gives his initial reaction to these questions, the interviewer can use the resulting information to probe deeper for additional insight into his central concern, namely, the relationship between high school experiences and college achievement. The semistructured interview, therefore, has the advantage of being reasonably objective while still permitting a more thorough understanding of the respondent's opinions and the reasons behind them than would be possible using the mailed questionnaire. The semistructured interview is generally most appropriate for interview studies in education. It provides a desirable combination of objectivity and depth and often permits gathering valuable data that could not be successfully obtained by any other approach.

The unstructured interview is best illustrated by the client-centered approaches used in clinical psychology and psychiatry. In this type of interview, the interviewer generally has some specific objectives, but these objectives are such that they can be met better in a situation in which the individual freely expresses his feelings without restriction. In the unstructured interview, the interviewer does not employ a detailed interview guide but has a general plan and usually asks questions or makes comments intended to lead the respondent toward giving data to meet the interviewer's objectives. Unstructured interviews are generally called for in situations where the type of information sought is difficult for the subject to express or is psychologically distressing to the individual. Because of the threatening nature of topics usually covered by unstructured interviews, this procedure must constantly adapt to the respondent and is highly subjective and time consuming. The graduate student can very seldom employ the unstructured interview in his research because skillful use of this technique requires a great deal of training and experience.

Recording the interview

Note taking or tape recording are the usual methods for preserving the information collected in the interview. Before choosing one of these methods, the interviewer will need to consider carefully the advantages and disadvantages of each.

If note taking is employed, the interviewer should ditto a supply of interview guides containing the questions to be asked during the interview, with space for recording responses. As each question is asked, the interviewer simply jots down the information that the respondent provides. The interview guide should of course, allow more space after open-ended questions than after closed-form questions which can be answered in a few words. The chief advantage of the note-taking method is that it facilitates data analysis, since the information is readily accessible. The respondents' answers are recorded beside the appropriate questions on the interview guide, and so it is easy for the researcher to go through the guides, processing all the data for each question separately in a relatively short period of time.

One disadvantage of the note-taking method is that it may disrupt the effectiveness of the communication between interviewer and respondent. Whether this happens is to some extent dependent on the type of question being asked:

There is some consensus that, if the respondent is giving statistical or factual information which is not confidential, he is unlikely to feel threatened, and he may be somewhat surprised and even offended if the interviewer does not take down the facts and figures he presents. On the other hand, if the respondent is talking about some highly confidential matter, taking notes may distract or upset him and prevent him from giving information which he otherwise might have given. [p. 234] [22]

If confidential information is desired, the interviewer should carefully prepare the respondent. It is particularly important to stress the fact, before the formal interview begins, that the information provided by the respondent will be anonymous and reported only in group form (that is, combined with the data of other respondents). Another way to avoid the possibly disruptive effect of note taking is for the interviewer to consider

[22] Stephen A. Richardson, Barbara S. Dohrenwend, and David Klein, *Interviewing: Its Forms and Functions* (New York: Basic Books, 1965).

delaying this procedure until after the interview is completed and the respondent has left the setting. However, the delay may lead the interviewer to forget important details, for instance, details that disagreed with the interviewer's expectations. Of course, even if the note taking is done during the interview, the interviewer may unconsciously emphasize responses that agree with his expectations and fail to record responses that do not.

The use of tape recorders has several advantages in recording interview data for research. Most important perhaps is that it reduces the tendency of the interviewer to make an unconscious selection of data favoring his biases. The tape recorded data can be played back more than once and can be studied much more thoroughly than would be the case if data were limited to notes taken during the interview. It is also possible to reanalyze the taped interview data to test hypotheses not set up in the original study. For example, interview data originally taped to study the interests of college freshmen could be reanalyzed to study their grammatical errors. Finally, it is possible with tape recorded data for a person other than the interviewer to evaluate and classify the responses. This permits calculation of a reliability coefficient for the interview data. Reliability estimates can be made by comparing interviewer evaluations with evaluations of another research worker using the tape only, or by comparing initial interviewer evaluations with evaluations made by the same interviewer at a later date based on playback of the taped interview. In well-designed interview studies, these reliability coefficients may be as high as .90.[23] The tape recorder also speeds up the interview process because there is no necessity for extensive note taking, although some minimal notes may be desirable. For example, some record of gestures might be appropriate in certain interview situations.

The principal disadvantage of the use of the tape recorder with the interview is that the presence of the tape recorder changes the interview situation to some degree. In interviews involving information of a highly personal nature, the respondent may be reluctant to express his feelings freely if he knows that his responses are being recorded. The interviewer should carefully explain the purpose of the recording and gain the confidence of the respondent, so as to minimize any undesirable effects of having the interview recorded. In interviews not aiming primarily at the collection of research data, it is seldom necessary to tape record the results. The opportunity to calculate reliability coefficients and the gain in objectivity provided by the taped record are very important factors, however, in research, and therefore the use of the tape recorder should be seriously considered for research interviews.

[23] Robert C. Anderson, "The Guided Interview as an Evaluative Instrument," *Journal of Educational Research*, 48 (1954), 85.

Effective communication in interviews

Interview questions must be framed in language that ensures effective communication between the interviewer and the respondent. The respondent must fully understand the language in which the question is framed. In those educational research studies where the respondents are professional educators, the problem of phrasing questions in language common to both interviewer and respondent is not usually serious, but for studies involving interviews with laymen, the educational jargon we in the profession know and use can seriously block effective communication. For example, if a question such as "What is your opinion of homogeneous grouping in the public schools?" were asked, it is likely that many of the persons answering would not have a clear understanding of the term "homogeneous grouping." Often the respondent is reluctant to admit that he doesn't understand the meaning of the question. The fact that he has been asked the question implies that he should understand it, and rather than admit his ignorance, he may give an evasive or noncommital answer.[24] To avoid this difficulty, the interviewer should explain technical terms in plain language before asking for the respondent's opinion. Also, it is advisable to ask a few information questions about the topic first. If the respondent cannot answer the information questions, then the opinion item can be skipped since the respondent's answer will have little value or meaning.

Occasionally a graduate student is carried away by his enthusiasm for a research idea and asks for information that no one could reasonably be expected to have. An example of this was an interview study proposed recently by a graduate student that would ask college students to recall conversations the students had during their childhood with teachers or other adults that exerted a major influence on the moral values and educational and vocational goals of the students. The graduate student believed that there are certain critical moments in everyone's childhood when the words of a parent or teacher become a major factor in determining the future goals and behavior of the child. Such a theory may be valid, but the line of questioning planned by the graduate student called for a level of recall as well as a level of insight that few persons could be expected to possess. Another error frequently made in educational studies is to ask parents to comment on technical aspects of education about which they have little or no knowledge. For example, an interview study carried out to learn the parents' opinions of different methods of teaching reading could produce very little useful information. Many of the parents would probably have opinions concerning the teaching of reading, but for

---

[24] The student may recall our discussion of the study by Allen (p. 201), who found that ten percent of a sample expressed an opinion about a bogus organization, the League for Linear Programs, rather than check the "don't know" category.

the most part these opinions would have little foundation except the limited personal experiences of the respondents.

Effective communication between the interviewer and the respondent is facilitated if the respondent appreciates the purpose of each question that he is asked. With the help of the interviewer, the respondent develops an idea of the purpose of the interview, and if he can see no connection between his perception of the purpose and a question that is asked, he is likely to react negatively. He may become suspicious of the interviewer and wonder whether the interview actually has some purpose other than the one he has been told. Inasmuch as he cannot be sure of what this hidden purpose is, his suspicions are aroused, and he is immediately placed on his guard. Under these circumstances his answers will be evasive and his attitude guarded or hostile. On the other hand, he may consider such a question as indicative of a lack of ability or poor planning on the part of the interviewer. In this case he is likely to feel that his participation is a waste of time. This loss of confidence in the interviewer is serious in that it is often followed by a refusal to cooperate. If the status of the respondent is higher than that of the interviewer, a special effort must be made to avoid questions that the respondent can interpret as wasting his time. The problem of questions that appear irrelevant arises often in studies involving psychological data, such as personality. Indirect questioning is often necessary in this area, and unless considerable groundwork is laid by the interviewer, resistance by the respondents will be encountered.

There are a number of other techniques which the skillful interviewer can use to promote effective communication with the respondent. Before the formal interview begins, he engages the respondent in a few minutes of small talk to help him relax and to establish rapport. The interviewer also assures the respondent that all his statements will be held in strictest confidence and be used for research purposes only. In some instances it may be desirable to use subtle social pressure to impress on the respondent the importance of the interview. For example, the interviewer might make a statement such as, "I am doing this study in collaboration with Dr. _____ at the state university in order to learn how men in your position feel about these issues." Once the interview has been initiated, other techniques may be helpful in maintaining respondent cooperation and participation. After the respondent has completed an answer, the interviewer can sometimes elicit additional information by pausing before asking the next question or by saying, "Tell me more about that." Of course, it is undesirable to contradict or appear to cross-examine the respondent, since he may become threatened and deceptive in answering further questions. If the respondent does appear to be threatened by a particular question, then the interviewer should change the subject; at a later point in the interview, it may be possible to raise the subject again in such a way that the respondent is not threatened. Finally, it is inadvisable to ask too many closed-form questions in succession or to change the subject of the interview too frequently. Otherwise a respondent may feel that the interview is not necessary and that the interviewer is not interested in obtaining his views in depth.

Leading questions

A factor that often biases the results of interview studies is the use of leading questions by the interviewer. A leading question is any question that, because of the phrasing of the question, leads the respondent to consider one reply more desirable than another. Let us say, for example, that we were interviewing a random sampling of voters concerning their attitudes toward federal aid to education. After establishing whether the respondent was familiar with the issue of federal aid to education, a reasonable question might be, "What is your opinion of federal aid to education?" A question that might be classified as moderately leading would state "Do you favor federal aid to education?" This question is a little easier for the respondent to answer in the affirmative than the negative. A more serious attempt to lead the respondent would result in a question such as "In view of the dangers of federal control, do you feel that federal aid to education is advisable?" Here the respondent is strongly motivated to give an unfavorable response to federal aid. Questions can be slanted even further by the use of emotionally toned words to which the individual is inclined to react for or against with little thought for the basic issue involved. Such a question might be, "Do you favor federal aid to education as a means of providing each child with an equal educational opportunity?" In this case the concept of "an equal opportunity for all" is likely to elicit favorable replies.

The respondent's frame of reference

Each person is the product of an environment that is unique. Words recall different experiences and have different shades of meaning for each of us. Unless the interviewer establishes a common ground for communication—a common frame of reference—these differences can seriously interfere with the communication process. If the respondent's frame of reference is different from that of the interviewer, his replies are likely to be misinterpreted. For example, if a group of mothers were asked, "What do you think of the teacher your child has this year," one might answer in terms of the teacher's personal appearance, another may think of the teacher's willingness to help on a P.T.A. committee, another may have never seen the teacher but may feel that her child is not getting proper reading instruction, while another may have had a conference with the teacher the day before about her child's misbehavior and think of nothing but this meeting in making an evaluation. Thus, we can see that unless the interviewer and respondent are using the same frame of reference, many difficulties can arise when obtaining interview data. In research perhaps the most desirable solution to this problem is to specify the frame of reference wanted by the interviewer. The preceding question could be placed in a specific frame of reference by asking, "What do you think of the way your child's teacher handles parent-teacher conferences?"

Pretest of the interview procedures

Although the interview can provide us with valuable data, the research worker must remember that it is a highly subjective technique. When this technique is used in research, all possible controls and safeguards must be employed if we expect to obtain reasonably objective and unbiased data. A careful pilot study is the best insurance the research worker has against bias and flaws in design. After the interview guide has been developed, a pilot study should be conducted to evaluate and improve the guide and the interview procedure and help the interviewer develop experience in using the procedure before any research data for the main study are collected. The number of subjects interviewed in the pilot study need not be large—10 to 20 are sufficient for most educational studies. The interviewer can usually determine from the progress of his last few pilot interviews whether more are needed to improve his procedures further. The subjects interviewed in the pilot study should be taken from the same population as the main study sample whenever possible and from a very similar population when research design does not permit drawing from the main study population.

The pilot study should be carried out with specific objectives in mind. The interviewer should determine from the pilot study whether the planned procedures actually produce the data desired. The interviewer should be alert to communication problems, evidence of inadequate motivation, and other clues that suggest a rephrasing of questions or revision of procedure. Several methods of opening the interview should also be tried and perfected. Unwillingness of the respondent to cooperate generally indicates that the techniques that have been established are not sufficient for motivation and maintenance of rapport. The pilot study also gives the interviewer an opportunity to evaluate his methods of recording the interview data, to determine whether adequate information is being recorded, whether the recording method causes excessive breaks in the interview situation, and whether the mechanics of reporting can be improved.

During the pilot study, the research worker also should assess carefully the methods he has planned to use for quantifying and analyzing his interview data. If the pilot study results indicate that data obtained cannot be quantified or are not falling into the areas anticipated, the interview procedures must be revised until satisfactory quantification and analysis are possible.

Tape recording of pilot study interviews is especially important even if the tape recorder is not to be used during the regular interview procedure. By playing back the interview, the interviewer can gain many insights into his handling of the questions and will be made aware of problems that may have escaped him during the interview situation itself.

MISTAKES OFTEN MADE BY GRADUATE STUDENTS

Survey research in general:

1. Student does not formulate clear, specific objectives for his research.
2. Relates his data-gathering procedure to his objectives in only a general way and thereby fails to get quantitative data specific to his problem.
3. Selects his sample on the basis of convenience rather than attempting to obtain a random sample.
4. Analyzes survey data one variable at a time rather than analyzing relationships, longitudinal changes, and comparisons between groups.

Questionnaire studies:

5. Student uses a questionnaire to investigate problems that could be better studied with other research techniques.
6. Gives insufficient attention to the development of his questionnaire and fails to pretest it.
7. Asks too many questions, thus making unreasonable demands on the respondent's time.
8. Overlooks details of format, grammar, printing, and so on that, if observed, give the respondent an unfavorable first impression.
9. Fails to check a sample of nonresponding subjects for possible bias.

Interview studies:

10. Student does not adequately plan the interview or develop a detailed interview guide.
11. Does not conduct sufficient practice interviews to acquire needed skills.
12. Fails to establish safeguards against interviewer bias.
13. Does not make provisions for calculating the reliability of his interview data.
14. Uses language in the interview that is not understood by the respondents.
15. Asks for information that the respondent cannot be expected to have.

ANNOTATED REFERENCES

1. Glock, Charles Y. (ed.). *Survey Research in the Social Sciences*. New York: Russell Sage Foundation, 1967. This edited volume provides a good introduction to the uses and potential of survey research in the social sciences. Glock's introduction and his chapter "Survey Design and Analysis in Sociology" provide extensive treatment of the types of analytic procedures that can be applied to survey research data. The chapter by Martin Trow discusses the relevance of survey research to educational practice, past misuse of surveys by educational researchers, and some problems that could be fruitfully investigated by means of surveys.

2. Sieber, S. D. "Case of the Misconstrued Technique: Survey Research in Education," *Phi Delta Kappan*, 49 (1968), 273–276. The author critically analyzes why survey research is held in low esteem by researchers and educators. He points out that most survey research in education reports distributions on one variable at a time rather than treating survey data analytically. This article lends support to the case that we made in this chapter for exploiting the various descriptive and explanatory uses of the cross-sectional survey when planning a study of this type.

3. Furno, Orlando F. "Sample Survey Designs in Education—Focus on Administrative Utilization," *Review of Educational Research*, 36 (5) (1966), 552–565. This review of the literature was intended for the administrator who must make decisions on the basis of survey findings. However, it should also be helpful to any student planning a survey study. Among the topics treated are sampling techniques, statement of objectives, data collection, survey measurement methods, data processing and analysis.

Questionnaires

4. Oppenheim, A. N. *Questionnaire Design and Attitude Measurement*. New York: Basic Books, 1966. This book should prove helpful to the student who wishes a sophisticated, comprehensive treatment of questionnaire design. Topics include question wording, attitude-scaling methods, projective techniques in attitude study, and quantification of questionnaire data.

Interviewing

5. Hyman, H. H., *et al. Interviewing in Social Research*. Chicago: University of Chicago Press, 1954. This volume contains a wealth of data on the interviewer and reports much important research on the interviewer and the interview process. The main emphasis is upon the sources of error in the interview. Such variables as respondent's perception of the interviewer, interviewer opinions and beliefs, interviewer expectation, situational effects, effects of racial differences between interviewer and respondent, and many others are discussed, and research evidence is presented. This text is required reading for anyone planning an interview study. The final chapter on reduction and control of error merits very careful study.

6. Richardson, S. A.; Dohrenwend, B. S.; and Klein, D. *Interviewing: Its Forms and Functions*. New York: Basic Books, 1965. This book gives a thorough, up-to-date treatment of the interview as a research instrument. Parts 2 and 3, concerned with respondent participation and the question-answer process, respectively, contain many specific techniques that should be helpful to the student planning to conduct his own interviews or to train personnel in interviewing.

CHAPTER 9

The Methods and Tools of Observational Research

STEPS IN COLLECTING OBSERVATIONAL DATA

Introduction

In preceding chapters we discussed standardized tests, survey questionnaires, and interviews as methods for collecting research data. These methods are similar in their reliance on self-report as the basic source of data. Although as a rule self-reports can be obtained easily and economically, people often bias the information they offer about themselves, and sometimes they cannot accurately recall events and aspects of their behavior in which the researcher is interested. The observational method, if used properly, overcomes these limitations of the self-report method. Sechrest, for example, has argued that social attitudes, such as prejudice, should be studied by means of naturalistic observations, since self-reports of these attitudes are often biased by the set to give a socially desirable response.[1] Prejudice has been studied naturalistically by observing the seating patterns of black and white students in college classes.[2] Even when bias is not present in self-report data, the observational method usually yields more accurate quantitative data than could be obtained by self-report. For example, many educators have noted that in class discussions teachers dominate the talk at the expense of student participation. But what are the actual percentages of teacher and student talk in these discussions? It is unlikely that teachers or students could provide accurate information on this question. However, an observational study in which an audiotape or videotape recorder was used could yield precise quantitative data.

[1] Lee Sechrest, "Naturalistic Methods in the Study of Social Attitudes," paper presented at APA Annual Convention, 1966.
[2] D. T. Campbell, W. H. Kruskall, and W. P. Wallace, "Seating Aggregation as an Index of Attitude," *Sociometry,* 29 (1966), 1–15.

Although they overcome some limitations of self-report instruments, observational techniques have potential limitations of their own. It is not uncommon in observational studies to find the experimenter attempting to study complex behavior patterns but finding that the more straightforward behaviors, which can be objectively observed and recorded, are only slightly related to the complex behaviors he wishes to study. Thus, he is faced with the choice of getting objective data that is of little value because of its limited relationship to a complex behavior or getting data more closely related to the complex behavior he is studying but finding it of limited value because of its subjectivity. Obtaining data related to complex behavior that is objectively observable and yet pertinent to the problem requires careful planning.

Another problem that must be faced in conducting the observational study is to determine the degree to which the presence of the observer changes the situation being observed. In observations of classroom behavior, for example, a change in the behavior of both the teacher and class members usually occurs when an observer enters the room. Classrooms in laboratory schools are often provided with adjacent rooms fitted with one-way screens so that observations can be carried on without disturbing the situation. Occasionally studies are conducted in which the observer visits the classroom a number of times before recording any observational data so that the class will become accustomed to his presence and will react normally when the research data are actually collected. Very often the graduate student with limited control over the situations that he wishes to observe finds it difficult to solve this problem satisfactorily.

The time factor often makes observational research difficult for the graduate student. This method of gathering data is time consuming, and the student usually finds it difficult to make enough observations of a sufficiently large sampling of individuals to provide reliable data. To provide reasonably sound data and to permit reliability estimates, observational studies usually require that at least two independent observers evaluate the situation being observed. This again poses a problem for the graduate student, who must often rely entirely on his own resources for obtaining research data.

Defining observational variables

Developing observational measures for one's research project is difficult. This section presents some techniques for developing and simplifying observational measures. To illustrate these techniques, we will use as an example a research problem that requires observation of behavior. Suppose our research problem is to determine whether a particular type of workshop in modern mathematics affects what teachers do in their classrooms.

This broad statement of the problem suggests that some type of classroom observation should be used. However, the nature of these observations cannot be specified until several decisions are made.

First, it is necessary to limit the number of observations that will be made. Because of the problem, observations will be limited to teachers' daily mathematics class, probably an hour or less. This still includes too broad a range of behavior. It would be quite unrealistic to expect an observer to record everything that transpires in a classroom for an hour. Even in a minute's time many different kinds of activities may occur. In order to determine what the observer should look for, it is useful to develop hypotheses or expectations about the effect of the workshop on classroom teaching. At this point one should be able to limit the focus of the observations considerably. Suppose that one's main hypothesis is that teachers who have had workshop training in modern mathematics will spend more time explaining new mathematical concepts than teachers without this training. If this is the case, the observation process is simplified considerably, since the observer need only focus on the teacher rather than on students and teacher simultaneously. However, the total length of observation may need to be increased beyond a single class period. Teachers with workshop training may spend as much time as teachers without training in explaining a new concept on the first day, but they may spend more days developing a complete explanation. To detect this difference, observations over a period of several days, perhaps a week, may be necessary.

The first step then is to limit the number of one's observations by referring to one's hypotheses or expectations for the pertinent variables to be observed and recorded. The next step is to define a behavioral and a time unit. This process may in turn result in a still more focused range of observation. For the present example, it would be necessary to decide what behavior or behaviors constitute an "explanation of a new mathematical concept." One may decide to define explanation as "all teacher statements that define some aspect of the new concept, that present examples of the concept, or that direct students to perform tasks pertaining to the concept." In this case one might decide to make the individual sentence the basic unit of observation. This unit of observation would enable one to express research findings in the form: "Teachers with workshop training uttered _____ sentences to explain the new mathematical concept compared with _____ sentences of teachers without this training." [3] Next, it is necessary to define a precise time unit based on the total length of the observation. In our example the time unit might reflect a week's period

[3] To simplify the process of recording, it might be desirable to just observe the time spent uttering such sentences. Thus, minutes and seconds become the basic unit of observation.

of instruction in mathematics class, or about four hours. Thus, research findings would now be stated in the form, "Teachers with workshop training uttered _____ sentences in four hours of observed mathematics instruction, compared with _____ sentences for teachers without this training, in an equivalent time period." Now ratios can also be expressed, for example, "Ten explanatory sentences were uttered per hour of class time."

Three types of observational variables may be distinguished: descriptive, inferential, and evaluative. Descriptive variables have the advantage that they require little inference on the part of the observer. Consequently, they generally yield reliable data. For the present research example, it might be desirable to have observers record all utterances of certain key phrases as each teacher explains a mathematical concept, such as regrouping. (These phrases might include "place value," "base ten," "expanded notation," "renaming.") This is a purely descriptive task, and thus there would be high agreement between observers recording the behavior of a given teacher. Other observational variables require the observer to make an inference before a variable can be scored. For example, observers may be asked to record the self-confidence with which a teacher explains a mathematical concept. Some teachers may speak with a good deal of confidence, while others may appear uncertain, confused, or anxious because their understanding of the topic is weak. Confidence, uncertainty, confusion and anxiety are not behaviors but rather are inferences made from behavior. It is much harder to collect reliable data when observers are asked to make inferences from behavior. To increase the reliability with which inferential variables are scored by observers, the researcher should provide the observer with several examples of each variable. Ideally the reseacher might videotape instances of behavior illustrating points of the continuum that define the variable (e.g., videotape teachers who are very confident, teachers who are somewhat sure of themselves, and teachers who are confused and anxious). The observer would study these examples before attempting to record observations for the main study. Related to inferential variables are evaluative variables, since they also require an inference from behavior on the part of the observer. For example, the researcher may be interested in obtaining ratings of the quality of the teacher's explanation of a mathematical concept. Quality ratings are not behavior but rather are inferences made from behavior. Since it is difficult to make reliable observations of evaluative variables, the researchers should collect examples of behavior that define points along the continuum of excellent-to-poor explanations.

To ensure accurate recording, observers should be required to score only one or two behaviors at a given point in time. For example, most observers would find it quite difficult to record certain aspects of the teacher's talk and at the same time record the percentage of children who appear to be paying attention to the teacher. Consequently, the reliability of both sets of observations is apt to be low. To prevent this problem, the researchers should consider using the technique of time sampling. For example, the observer's task can be simplified by having him alternate between observations of the teacher and the students each minute of class time. Since they are collected on a time sampling basis, the data can be considered representative of the students' and teacher's behavior during the entire class hour.

Recording observations

Once the observational variables to be used in the research study are identified, it is necessary to develop a form on which they can be recorded. A paper-and-pencil observational form can accommodate a variety of scoring procedures. Perhaps the most common scoring procedure is to use a form that describes the behaviors to be observed in considerable detail so that the observer can check each behavior whenever it occurs. This form of scoring requires a minimum of effort on the part of the observer and can usually be developed so as to require the observer to make few inferences. The first item of the observation form presented in Figure 10 is

1. Check each question asked by the teacher into one of the following categories (observer for the first fifteen minutes of the class hour):

	Frequency	Total
a. Asks student to solve an example at blackboard	x x x x	4
b. Asks student to solve an example at his seat	x x x x x x x	7
c. Asks students if they have any questions or if they understand	x x	2
d. Other	x x x x x	5
	Grand Total	18

2. Each time the teacher asks a student to solve an example, rate its level of difficulty on a 5-point scale.

	Frequency	Total
1. Difficult	x x x	3
2.	x	1
3. Average	x x x x x	5
4.	x	1
5. Easy	x	1
	Grand Total	11*

* The sum here should equal the sum of categories "a" and "b" in Item 1.

Fig. 10. Sample observation form.

of this type. This scoring procedure is fairly easy for the observer to use, particularly if the categories are well defined and do not require a high level of inference.

Some studies require that the observer not only record the behavior as it occurs, but also evaluate it on a rating scale. Item 2 of the sample observation form is of this type. It is obvious that this scoring procedure requires more work and a higher level of inference on the part of the observer. The observer must not only record the behavior, he must also evaluate it, and this is much more difficult to do objectively. If he uses a rating scale as part of his scoring procedure, the research worker should avoid the common mistake of attempting to obtain excessively precise discrimination from the observer. Most human behavior studied in educational research cannot be reliably rated on more than five levels. The 3-point rating scale, breaking the behavior observed into such categories as "above average," "average," and "below average," is often as fine a discrimination as can be made with satisfactory reliability. Five-point rating scales, however, are often used in educational research and can be employed effectively in observing well-defined behavior. It is almost never advisable to attempt to obtain ratings for finer than a 5-point scale. Furthermore, the more inference the observer must use in making the rating, the fewer rating levels should be employed. The "Officer Effectiveness Report" employed by the U.S. Air Force provides the ultimate example of attempting fine discriminations in the evaluation of characteristics that, at best, can only be differentiated roughly. This instrument, for example, requires the senior officer to make an evaluation on the individual's cooperativeness. Fifteen levels of cooperativeness are provided by the scale. It is doubtful that a complex behavior requiring as high a level of inference as "cooperativeness" can be accurately discriminated at more than three levels by most observers.

Another form of observation involves checking the occurrence of a particular category of behavior and then describing the specific action that has occurred. This approach is generally impractical if the behavior being observed occurs frequently or if the observer is responsible for recording data on several individuals. Another problem with this type of observation is that the descriptions eventually must be converted to quantitative data. A preliminary study will usually yield a system for classifying the behavior observed. This classification can then be set up as a check list that is more convenient and more reliable than requiring the observer to record lengthy behavior descriptions.

Figure 10 illustrates the way the observers' recording task can be made more simple and accurate by providing a check list. The first item of the sample observation form in Fig. 10 might require the observer to write down each question that is asked by the teacher. Since teachers ask ques-

tions fairly frequently, the observer would need to do much writing; if
the writing demand is excessive, the accuracy of the observer's report is
likely to be affected adversely. The use of the four categories which appear
in the sample observation form is preferable since the observer's task is
simplified and the resulting data are in quantitative form.

Standard observational schedules

Instead of developing his own observational schedule for a research
project, on occasion the researcher may prefer to use one of the many
standard observational schedules that have been developed by educational
researchers. In planning an observational study, you should consider the
various advantages of using one of these schedules. First, as is true of
standardized personality and aptitude tests, standard observational schedules have usually reached a stage of development where they are valid and
reliable measuring instruments. Second, use of a standard schedule saves
you the considerable amount of time that it takes to develop your own
schedule. Third, since most of these standard schedules have been used in
a number of research studies, it is possible to compare your findings with
those obtained by other researchers using the same instrument. The obvious disadvantage of standard schedules is that they sometimes do not
include all the variables that you are interested in measuring. However,
in this case you can use just the part of the schedule that you need.

The standard observational schedules that have been developed vary in
complexity, the type of behavior they record, and the settings in which
they can be used. Recently Boyd and DeVault have provided a helpful
listing and classification of these schedules.[4] Their table of representative
observation schedules is presented in Fig. 11.[5] Each schedule is classified
according to whether social-emotional behavior, cognitive problem solving,
and/or overt behavior is to be observed. Also, Boyd and DeVault's table
enables one to identify which schedules have been developed for observation of classrooms, small groups, children's behavior, and counselor and
family interaction.

A good illustration of the research contribution that standard observational schedules can make is provided by Herman's study of how a 6-week
social studies unit was taught in classrooms of above average, average,
and below average ability students.[6] Flanders' system of interaction analysis and Medley and Mitzel's OScAR (Observation Schedule and Rec-

[4] See annotated references.

[5] R. D. Boyd and M. V. DeVault, "Classification of Representative Observation Systems," *Review of Educational Research,* 36 (December 1966), p. 533. Copyright by American Educational Research Association. Reprinted by permission.

[6] Wayne L. Herman, Jr., "An Analysis of the Activities and Verbal Behavior in Selected
Fifth-Grade Social Studies Classes," *Journal of Educational Research,* 60 (1967), 339–345.

Author	Social-Emotional	Cognitive Problem Solving	Overt Behavior (only)	Comments
CLASSROOM				
Withall (1949)	X	X		Primarily concerned with the social-emotional aspects of teacher and pupils.
Withall (1956)			X	Time-lapse photography.
Medley and Mitzel (1958)	X		X	Overt behavior categories are employed on pupils' behaviors.
Kowatrakul (1959)			X	Classroom activity organization.
Smith (1958)		X		
Wright (1959)		X		
Withall (1960)	X	X		Primarily concerned with the social-emotional aspects of teacher and pupils.
Perkins (1964)	X	X		Has both teacher categories and pupil categories—also type of instruction.
Flanders (1965)	X	X		Primarily concerned with the social-emotional aspects of teacher and pupils.
SMALL GROUP				
Chapple and Arensberg (1940)			X	
Bales (1950)	X	X		
Schutz (1958)	X			
Thelen (1959)	X			
Borgatta (1962)	X	X		Very similar to Bales.
Borgatta (1963) (BSs System)	X			Group work categories are included.
Longabaugh (1963)	X	X		Problem-solving categories are very broad; similar to Bales.
Sawyer and Friedell (1965)	X	X		Problem-solving behavior perceived in the light of Resource and Rewards.
CHILD STUDY				
Bonney (1955)	X		X	Has 25 major categories and many subcategories.
Moustakas, Sigel, and Schalock (1956)	X			Child-adult interaction—34 categories.
Smith (1958)	X	X		
Schaefer, Bell, and Bayley (1959)	X			There are 2 forms; one has 32 items and the other 28 items.
Fanshel, Hylton, and Borgatta (1963)	X			Certain categories directed at intellectual inabilities, self-destruction.
Schaefer (1965)	X			Children's reports of parental behavior—26 categories.
INTERPERSONAL				
Fine and Zimet (1956)	X	X		Based heavily on work of Bales.
Riskin (1963)	X	X		Family interactions.
Meyer, Borgatta, and Fanshel (1964)	X			7 categories for counselor, 6 categories for client (behavior variables).

Fig. 11. Classification of representative observation systems.

ord) were used to observe classroom interaction. Several interesting differences in teachers' instructional style were found between the three types of classrooms. Analysis of the observational data collected using Flanders' system (which classifies all classroom verbal behavior) showed that teachers of above average students tend to use more indirect techniques [7] than teachers of average and below average students. Also, teachers very infrequently criticize above average and average students, but criticize below average students to a moderate extent. Another finding was that above average students tend to talk more than average and below average students, who, in turn, do not differ from each other in talkativeness. The OScAR data provided somewhat different insights into classroom interaction. The reason is that this observational schedule classifies different behaviors (primarily classroom activities) from Flanders' system. Analysis of the OScAR data indicated that teachers of above average students spend only half as much class time (7.7 percent) using illustrations [8] as teachers of average students (20.8 percent). Teachers of below average students rely on illustrations most of all (41.5 percent of class time). Herman's interpretation of this finding is that "This progression should appear because as the intelligence level of the groups decreases there is more need for concrete instructional materials of a visual nature, such as maps, pictures, blackboard, and three-dimensional activities" (pp. 342–343). Further analysis of the OScAR data indicated that students of above average ability spend more total class time (30.8 percent) in independent seatwork than do students of average (10.6 percent) or below average (12.6 percent) ability. This finding suggests that above average students are more independent and less in need of teacher direction.

It should be apparent from this summary of Herman's research project that use of standard observational schedules, such as Flanders' system and OScAR, can yield important insights into the nature of classroom interaction. Since classroom interaction is becoming a topic of increasing interest to educational researchers, the use of these observational schedules should become more prevalent in the future.

Use of audiotape and videotape recorders

In some situations it is impractical to collect observational data at the same time the critical behavior is occurring. If several of the behaviors to be rated occur at the same time or closely together, the observer's task can be complicated to the point that his observations lose validity. For example, the observer may be required to rate each teacher and student response on one or more dimensions. If teacher-student interaction occurs

---

[7] Indirect techniques include accepting feelings, praising students, accepting student ideas, and asking questions.

[8] Illustrations include maps, pictures, and blackboard activities.

with high frequency, the observer is likely to be frustrated in his attempts to record all the necessary observational data. Also, we have already noted that observational ratings differ in the extent of inference required of the observer. When ratings require a high level of inference, an observer will probably want an opportunity to study the behavior carefully before making a rating. However, in a live observational setting, there is no chance to have several "instant replays" of a critical event. Another situation in which it may be impractical to collect observational data at the time the behavior occurs is when the researcher wants to check on the reliability of observers' ratings. We have discussed elsewhere the desirability of reporting the interrater reliability of observational data, otherwise one has no way of knowing the extent to which observations reflect the biases and idiosyncrasies of a single observer. However, it is not always possible to have two or more observers present at the same time to observe the events on which ratings are to be made. A similar situation occurs when one wishes to have specially qualified observers rate samples of behavior. As an illustration, suppose that one wishes to describe and rate the techniques that children use in the process of drawing pictures. Art teachers are probably the best qualified to make such observations, but they may not be free to observe at the time the children are working on their pictures.

It is obvious that all the situations just described present obstacles to the researcher's using the observational method. Audiotape and videotape recorders overcome these obstacles. When recorders are used, it is no longer necessary for observers to make ratings at the time particular events are occurring. These events may be recorded on audiotape or videotape so that they can be replayed several times for careful study or for several observers to rate at their convenience. Therefore, you should consider carefully the advantages of these recording techniques if you are planning to do an observational study. At the same time you should note certain disadvantages. Videotape recorders provide a fairly complete record of behavior, but they are not easy to obtain, and videotape is fairly expensive. Audiotape recorders are much more accessible, but they are limited to recording verbal behavior; also, it is often hard to identify and differentiate among speakers when listening to audiotape. In certain situations technical competence is required in order to obtain satisfactory video/audio recording. For example, it is usually necessary to have more than one microphone and to adjust the camera frequently so that a reasonably complete record of classroom behavior can be obtained.

If these disadvantages are overcome, it is highly desirable to record behavior so that it can be observed and rated at a later time. Sometimes it is not possible to obtain enough videotape or audiotape recorders to use in the main data-collection phase of one's study. However, if they are available, one or two recorders can be used to collect samples of behavior to facilitate the development of an observation form. The recordings can be replayed as often as necessary, thus making it easier to develop observational categories and to test the reliability with which observers can use these categories in rating behavior.

Another possibility when a limited amount of videotape is available is to make typed transcripts of the videotaped records. Once the transcript has been made, the videotape can be erased and reused. This approach is especially useful when sophisticated analysis of language is required or when the observer is working with a complex category system or one requiring a high level of inference. Typed transcripts of videotape have been used in many of the Stanford studies of microteaching and have yielded highly reliable scores.[9]

Training observers

After it has been developed and tried out on a small scale to correct its more serious deficiencies, the observation form should be employed to train the individuals who will conduct the observations required by the research. The first step in the training is to discuss the observation form with the observers, describing each item sufficiently to develop a thorough understanding of what is to be observed and how it is to be recorded.

Then, set up practice observations in which all observers complete the observation form. These practice observations should be discussed by the observers immediately after the observation. If appropriate, the situation should be tape recorded and played back immediately so that scoring differences between observers can be discussed and resolved. This technique, of course, cannot be applied to observations of behavior where speech is not the major factor, such as observations of social behavior among nursery school children. Tape recording, however, is very useful in training observers for situations involving verbal interaction, such as counseling. In the more advanced observational studies, observers are often trained through the use of motion pictures that present practice observation situations. Although these methods are usually beyond the resources of the graduate student, the training system he develops for observers must involve some provision for immediate review of the training observations and for comparisons between the data recorded by the different observers. These comparisons lead to the development of a common frame of reference among the observers that is necessary if the observational data are to have satisfactory reliability. If each observer interprets and records the same behavior differently, it is obvious that no objective information will be produced.

[9] These studies are described in Walter Borg, Marjorie Kelley, Philip Langer, and Meredith Gall, *The Minicourse: A Microteaching Approach to Teacher Education* (Beverly Hills, Calif.: Macmillan Educational Services, 1970).

During the training period, interrater reliability should be calculated after every ten practice sessions in order to estimate the degree to which observers are developing a common frame of reference. Interrater reliabilities should reach at least .70, and much higher reliabilities can be obtained if training is adequate and the observations are of specific behavior. During the training period, it is likely that some observers will be found who cannot develop a reliable frame of reference. Some persons seem to be unable to interpret the behavior they observe consistently, or in the same light as the rest of the group. After a reasonable training period, it is usually advisable to replace these persons with other observers.

During the training period, an effort should be made to further improve the observation form. Some items may be found for which the objective scoring procedures established do not work. Other types of behavior on the form will be found to occur so rarely as to contribute little or nothing to the overall record. Descriptions of behavior used in the observation form usually undergo considerable change during this period in order to make them more specific and usable.

When the main data collection occurs it sometimes happens that observers drift apart in their frames of reference concerning the behavior they are observing, particularly when observations are made over a long period of time. During the course of the study, therefore, efforts should be made to maintain a common frame of reference among observers. This may be done by having observers occasionally evaluate and discuss a practice observation, such as was done during the training period. These discussions help the observers maintain a common basis for reporting behavior on the observation form and thus increase the reliability of the observational data.

Reducing observer bias

It is well documented that observers are sometimes not very objective in their use of observational schedules. When this situation occurs, the research data will reflect the biases and characteristics of the observer rather than the observational variables that one seeks to measure. It is also well documented that the presence of the observer can affect the behavior of those being observed. As a consequence, the research data reflects atypical rather than naturally occurring behavior.[10] The student planning an observational study should be aware of these unwanted observer effects and take steps to remove them.

1. *The effect of the observer on the observed.* Unless he is concealed, the observer is likely to have an impact on the observed. For example, an

---

[10] Evidence for various types of observer bias is reviewed in Eugene J. Webb, Donald T. Campbell, Richard D. Schwartz, and Lee Sechrest, *Unobtrusive Measures: Nonreactive Research in the Social Sciences* (Chicago: Rand McNally, 1966), chap. 1.

observer entering a classroom for the first time probably will arouse the curiosity of the students and possibly the teacher. The resulting inattentiveness of the students to the teacher may not reflect their usual behavior and thus may provide nonrepresentative observational data. To prevent this situation the observer should not record any observations for the first five or ten minutes that he is in the classroom. It is also advisable for the teacher to prepare his students beforehand for the observer's visit and to introduce the observer when he enters the classroom. This procedure is usually sufficient to satisfy students' curiosity and to restore the normal classroom situation.

A more serious problem caused by the presence of the observer occurs when the person or persons being observed are influenced in their behavior by the observer's intentions. Suppose the purpose of an observational study is to record the number and length of dyadic interactions between teacher and student in art classes. If they learn that this is the purpose of the study, teachers will probably increase the frequency of their dyadic interactions, particularly if they are led to believe that this is desirable behavior. As a result, the research data based on recorded observations will be nonrepresentative of the teachers' actual classroom behavior and thus possess little or no validity. It is therefore advisable to meet with the teachers before observations are made. At this meeting the teachers should be informed candidly that they cannot be told the nature of the research project because this might affect their behavior. However, it is good procedure to also tell the teachers that after the observational data have been collected, they will be informed of the study's purpose. Occasionally while the study is in progress a teacher will attempt to learn the purpose of the research from the observer or to secure a copy of the observation form. The training of observers should include directions not to give this information to teachers while the study is in progress.

2. *Observer bias.* It is doubtful whether any observations that we conduct are completely free from bias. In the observation process, the observer brings to bear all his past experience, and, as this past experience will differ for each observer, it will lead to different perceptions of the situation, different emphases, and different interpretations. Biases, of course, have a much greater chance of operating when the observer is called upon to draw conclusions or make involved inferences from the behavior he has observed. Possible sources of bias should be looked for and eliminated if they are found. For example, it would be unwise to use an observer who was prejudiced against blacks in a study in which he would observe the creative ability of black and white children in a nursery school. His bias would almost certainly lead him to see more creative behavior among white children and either ignore, misinterpret, or minimize the creative efforts of black children in this group.

To control for the possible presence of observer bias, two or more raters should be used to make observations of each behavior. Generally the combined records of two or more observers provide more reliable data than the record of a single observer. The extent of interobserver agreement can be determined by computing the appropriate statistic. Usually a measure of correlation is obtained. (Correlational statistics are discussed in Chapter 11.) When more than one observer is used, each should work independently, except when doing a practice observation to maintain a common frame of reference. If observers work together, one usually influences the others, and the judgments of this observer are therefore given more weight since they are reflected in the ratings of his colleagues. Also, when observers work together, each observer's ratings are contaminated by the judgments of the other observers, thus making reliability coefficients spuriously high.

3. *Rating errors.* In our discussion of standardized measures of personality, we noted that the validity of these measures is sometimes weakened by the presence of response sets. Some persons will give a socially desirable response or "acquiesce" to a personality item irrespective of the item's content. Thus, the person's score on the test is more a reflection of his response set than whether he possesses the personality trait measured by the test. A similar situation is found sometimes with observational rating scales. Some observers assign the same rating to the majority of research subjects even when there are obvious individual differences among them. For example, some observers have a tendency to rate most individuals at the high end of the scale. This tendency is called the "error of leniency." In studies where the research worker has an opportunity to train his observers thoroughly and has complete control over the situation, the error of leniency is rarely a problem. In many observational studies, however, research workers have relied upon observers over whom they have little control. As an illustration, studies of teacher effectiveness often use the school principal as an observer. It is rarely possible in studies of this sort to train the observers sufficiently to rule out errors of leniency and other rating errors. Therefore, if at all possible the research worker should attempt to train impartial observers.

Another error common in observational ratings is the "error of central tendency." This error is caused by the inclination of the individual to rate the person he has observed at the middle of the scale. This error is often made in cases where some of the behaviors to be rated have not occurred during the observation. The observer, feeling the need to register some sort of information on the form, rates the individual at the average, or center, of the rating scale.

Still another error frequently encountered is the so-called "halo effect." This is the tendency for the observer to form an early impression of the person being observed and to permit this impression to influence his ratings on all behaviors involving the given individual. For example, if he forms an initially favorable impression of the person being observed, the observer will tend to rate the individual favorably in subsequent performance areas. An initially unfavorable impression can lead to the opposite effect. "Halo effect" is most serious when the observer must evaluate abstract qualities rather than record specific behaviors. Thus, it is much easier for the "halo effect" to occur when the observer rates such characteristics as "cooperativeness," "integrity," and "interest in the job," than it is when he rates specific behavior, such as "shakes hands with the visitor," "rises from his chair when the visitor enters the room," and "offers the visitor a chair."

4. *Contamination.* A frequent flaw in observational studies is contamination. The most common source of contamination is the influence of the observer's knowledge concerning the performance of the subjects on one of the variables being studied on his observation of another variable. Let us say, for example, that we are doing a study of the human relations skills of successful elementary school principals. Unsuccessful and successful principals could be identified by a composite evaluation made by teachers, parents, and school superintendents. It may then be possible to observe the performance of the successful and unsuccessful principals in faculty meetings and evaluate them on certain human relations skills. If, however, the persons observing the faculty meetings are aware of which principals have been classified as successful and which as unsuccessful, this knowledge will almost certainly influence their perceptions of the principal's behavior. This type of influence is called contamination because knowledge of one aspect of the study tends to corrupt by contact the data recorded in another aspect of the study. Contamination is an especially serious problem in Master's degree studies because one graduate student often collects all data involved in the study. If he is aware of the dangers of contamination, however, the student can usually avoid it. For example, if we are studying relationships between academic achievement and leadership in the classroom, observations of leadership behavior could be carried out before achievement data are gathered; or the achievement test could be administered, if necessary, but not scored until leadership ratings are completed.

A similar problem arises when some form of pre-post observations are to be made. If he knows the expected outcomes of the experimental treatment, the observer may watch more closely for these outcomes on the post-treatment observations. This effect can be avoided by having the observer score tape recordings or typed transcripts of the classroom situation. Under these conditions the investigator should wait until both pre-

and post-treatment recordings have been made and then assign tapes or transcripts to observers in random order. An even better method is the "double blind" technique in which all tapes or transcripts are number coded and neither the observers nor the person distributing them to the observers knows which tapes or transcripts were made at the beginning and which at the end of the study.

Unobtrusive measures

Thus far in this chapter we have been concerned with observations of ongoing behavior. For example, to study classroom interaction a researcher might train observers to record behavioral events (such as verbal statements and movements of students and teacher) that occur in the course of a specified time period. However, there are other indices of classroom interaction that do not require behavioral observation. Writing on the blackboard, teacher-made materials (assignments, tests, teaching devices), students' written work, arrangement of the classroom furniture—all provide information about what has transpired during the class hour. These have been called "unobtrusive measures" [11] since they do not involve direct observation of a person and thus are not as susceptible to the distortion often found in such observations. For instance, to observe the arrangement of the furniture in a teacher's classroom, the observer need not be present while the class is in session.

In planning an observational study, the researcher should be alert to unobtrusive measures that can be used to assess relevant variables. As an illustration, suppose that you are interested in studying how teachers individualize instruction. To measure this variable you might train observers to record teacher statements that suggest individualization of instruction. Of course, it may be difficult to devise such an observation schedule and to train observers in its use. Also, the data may be distorted by the observers' biases and by the influence of the observer on the teacher. A simpler approach to this measurement problem would be to look for "unobtrusive" signs of individualized instruction. One possibility would be simply to record the variety of textbooks and workbooks in use in each classroom. If he is individualizing instruction, a teacher should be using a wider variety of curriculum materials than a teacher who instructs his class as an undifferentiated group. Another unobtrusive measure would be the written work that students complete during a class period. In a classroom that has individualized instruction, students will be working on different assignments, whereas in a conventional classroom all students will be working on the same assignment. Therefore one can measure the extent of individualization in the classroom by counting the number of

[11] Eugene J. Webb *et al.*, *ibid.*

different assignments being worked on by students during a particular point in time.

Educational researchers have not exploited the uses of unobtrusive measures to a significant degree, yet the classroom and other educational settings contain many artifacts which can be used to measure research variables. Webb and his coworkers have collected many examples of unobtrusive measures which have been used in research studies. Some of them are listed here to suggest their usefulness as a substitute for behavioral observations, interviews, or questionnaires:

The floor tiles around the hatching-chick exhibit at Chicago's Museum of Science and Industry must be replaced every six weeks. Tiles in other parts of the museum need not be replaced for years. The selective erosion of tiles, indexed by the replacement rate, is a measure of the relative popularity of exhibits.

The accretion rate is another measure. One investigator wanted to learn the level of whiskey consumption in a town which was officially "dry." He did so by counting empty bottles in ash cans.

The degree of fear induced by a ghost-story-telling session can be measured by noting the shrinking diameter of a circle of seated children.

Chinese jade dealers have used the pupil dilation of their customers as a measure of the client's interest in particular stones, and Darwin in 1872 noted this same variable as an index of fear.

Library withdrawals were used to demonstrate the effect of the introduction of television into a community. Fiction titles dropped, nonfiction titles were unaffected.

The role of rate of interaction in managerial recruitment is shown by the over-representation of baseball managers who were infielders or catchers (high-interaction positions) during their playing days.

Sir Francis Galton employed surveying hardware to estimate the bodily dimensions of African women whose language he did not speak.

The child's interest in Christmas was demonstrated by distortions in the size of Santa Claus drawings.

Racial attitudes in two colleges were compared by noting the degree of clustering of Negroes and whites in lecture halls. [p. 2.] [12]

The senior author has worked with a number of unobtrusive measures in school settings. In one project where the objective was to estimate student attitude toward school authority, the principal mentioned over the school public address system that there was a great deal of littering in the school halls and urged students to use waste baskets. The weight of litter collected from halls the day before the announcement was compared with that collected the day after the announcement. A reduction was considered indicative of a favorable attitude toward the principal, while an increase suggested a negative attitude. Samples of such measures may be found in Appendix D.

[12] Eugene J. Webb et al., ibid.

SITUATIONAL TESTING AS AN OBSERVATIONAL TECHNIQUE

Introduction

In situational testing the research worker devises a situation and assigns appropriate roles to the subjects, who are asked to play these roles to the best of their ability. The situations are aimed at bringing out the specific types of behavior that the researcher is interested in evaluating. Originally developed by social psychologists to study leadership behavior and small group interaction, situational testing has many applications for the educational researcher. For example, many studies have attempted to identify the factors related to successful teaching or successful administrative behavior through the use of personality inventories and other paper-and-pencil measures. The results of these studies have been disappointing, probably because it is difficult to break down the complex behavior patterns that teachers or principals display in their work and study it piece by piece. Situational testing permits a study of the total behavior pattern and thus seems more likely to provide insight into the characteristics required for success in complex activities.

Situational testing also has advantages over the observation of behavior in natural settings. By setting up the situation, the research worker can control, to a considerable degree, the types of behavior that are likely to occur. This permits him to focus the observation on behavior that appears to be critical in the area being studied. In order to observe such critical behavior in a natural situation, it might be necessary for the observer to be present for weeks or even months. The artificial situation also permits much more careful training of the observers. Inasmuch as he has a good idea of the types of behavior that will occur, the research worker can develop observational rating forms that fit the situation specifically and can train his observers in the specific situations that they will later observe in the collection of research data. Because a number of subjects can be exposed to the same role-playing problem (although each, of course, will respond differently), it is much easier to obtain comparable data on the behavior through this technique than through observations of behavior in natural situations.

The principal criticism of situational testing is that the situation itself is artificial and therefore may not give an accurate indication of how the individual would behave in a natural situation. In using role-playing situations in research, however, the authors have been impressed by the degree to which the subjects appear to forget that they are involved in an artificial situation. Particularly in situations that involve emotional interaction between the subject and actors, it appears that most subjects become deeply involved in the situation, and many seem to forget, at least for the moment, that the situation is an artificial one.

Perhaps the principal disadvantage of situational testing for the graduate student is the time involved in developing and carrying out a project using this technique. Small-scale situational studies, however, can be carried out by the graduate student. For example, parent-teacher conference situations could be developed and used in a study of teacher behavior. In research problems concerned with human relations, situational testing offers perhaps the best chance of producing meaningful data.

There are several types of situational tests that might be adapted to educational research. We will briefly discuss three of these: the leaderless group discussion, team problem-solving activities, and individual role-playing situations.

Leaderless group discussion

In a leaderless group discussion, a group of subjects (usually six or eight) is given a problem by the research worker and asked to discuss this problem and arrive at possible solutions. Observers record the behavior of the different group members. The technique of the leaderless group discussion is said to have been developed originally around 1925 to study leadership behavior in the German Army.[13] More recently, this technique has been used to study decision making and interaction in various types of military groups, student groups, and executive groups in business. Its value is that it provides a good simulation of important situations that occur in real life. For example, the behavior of school board members in a leaderless group discussion working on a problem presented them by the researcher is probably quite similar to the behavior of these same individuals as they tackle the problems they confront in real-life school board meetings. Consequently, ratings of leadership, cooperation, and teamwork made on the basis of observations of leaderless group discussions have been found to have high predictive validity.[14] In education this technique could be used to study such problems as decision making by school boards, leadership behavior among school children at different levels, and teacher interaction in faculty meetings.

Team problem-solving activities

Team problem-solving activities usually involve a situation where a team is presented with a problem that it is called upon to solve. These problems differ from the leaderless group discussion in that in addition

[13] H. L. Ausbacher, "History of the Leaderless Group Discussion," *Psychological Bulletin*, 48 (1951), 383–391.

[14] For a review of these studies, see B. M. Bass, "The Leaderless Group Discussion," *Psychological Bulletin*, 51 (1954), 465–492.

to discussing solutions, the team arrives at a solution and attempts to carry it out. Problems involving the escape of the team from a prison compound or getting the team across a difficult physical barrier have been used in research by military psychologists. Observers may be assigned to evaluate total team activities or to evaluate the behavior of individual members of the team. This technique has been used for the most part in the study of military leadership.[15] However, it could be applied to research in a number of educational areas, such as studies of player interaction in team sports, studies of group behavior in high school clubs, and studies of work groups in parent-teacher projects.

Individual role playing

The individual role-playing situation is generally aimed at collecting research data in a situation where only one research subject is involved, usually in a key role. The situation may also involve actors who are trained to play other roles necessary to bring out the subject behavior that is to be evaluated. The subject is usually given material that describes the situation in which he is to work and sometimes discusses the nature of the problem he will attempt to solve and the identity of other persons who will participate. He studies this material prior to the start of the situation, arrives at his solution or method of handling the problem, and then attempts to carry out this solution in the role-playing situation. In observing his behavior in the situation, it is possible to evaluate his decisions, but more important, it is also possible to evaluate his skill in carrying them out. For example, one of the authors recently participated in a study aimed at developing criteria for measuring the effectiveness of elementary school principals.[16] In this study each subject played the role of a principal in several different situations aimed at revealing different aspects of the behavior important in the elementary principal's position. Six situations were developed. In each of these the person being tested took the part of the principal. Actors were trained to take other roles called for. In one of these situations, the person tested was given the following instructions:

Instructions to Principal

You are the principal of a large elementary school of about 1,000 pupils, from kindergarten to sixth grade, in a city of about 30,000 population. The schools in the city are up-to-date, progressive, and have a high rating. The people in the community are proud of their schools and support them enthusiastically.

[15] E. Tupes, W. R. Borg, and A. Carp, "Performance in Role-Playing Situations as Related to Leadership and Performance Measures," *Sociometry*, 21 (1958), 165–179.

[16] W. R. Borg and J. A. Silvester, "Playing the Principal's Role," *Elementary School Journal*, 64 (1964), 324–331.

There is a Mr. Jones waiting to see you about getting his son registered in school. Mr. Jones is a successful businessman who is active in civic affairs, is well liked, and has a lot of influence in the community. He is proud of his children (two of them are already in school), and he is interested in giving them every opportunity to grow and develop.

It seems that, when he attempted to enroll his son in kindergarten, the son was turned down because he was five hours too young. Miss Roberts was so busy enrolling new pupils that she did not have time to discuss the matter with Mr. Jones and just told him that his son did not come up to the age requirement. Mr. Jones was a little disturbed and has asked you for an appointment to discuss the matter. He will probably try to get you to make an exception for his child.

You have had problems before on the age requirements for enrollment, so take a few minutes to think it through. The superintendent is out of town for ten days, and a decision has to be made before he returns.

Main Points:
1. Mr. Jones is an important man in the community.
2. Entrance age requirements or some other entrance requirements are necessary.
3. You are proud of your school and its high rating.
4. You cannot afford to have the public unhappy about the school.
5. You have 15 minutes to spend with Mr. Jones, and you should make a decision within the time limit.

The actor trained to play the role of Mr. Jones had the following instructions:

Instructions to Actor

You are a successful businessman in a community of about 30,000 population. You are active in civic affairs and interested in the progress of the community. You are generally well liked and have considerable influence.

You are the father of three children and are very proud of your family and interested in their welfare. Two of your children are already in school and are well adjusted and doing very good work. You have your own set of cumulative records on each child that you keep up-to-date. These records are complete and show that your children are superior.

Your youngest boy, Edward, was just turned down when you tried to get him enrolled in the kindergarten because he was five hours too young. This disturbed you because the records you received from the private nursery school Edward has been attending show that his IQ is 136; he is well above the average in physical size and development; he is socially well adjusted; he is in excellent health; and is an active, alert, and happy boy.

You know he is ready for school and that he will make a good adjustment. You feel that it is in the child's best interest to start now, and if they will not take him into the public schools you will have to enroll him in a private school. You do not want this extra expense, and besides you are a taxpayer and have donated a lot of time and money for public welfare and feel that your children have a right to public education.

You think that the chronological age rule used to determine who is ready for school is old-fashioned and silly, and you know that your boy is more ready to enter kindergarten than 90 percent of the children being enrolled.

You did not like the way Miss Roberts turned you down when you tried to get Edward enrolled because she did not take time to listen to the reason why you thought Edward was ready for school. So you decided to go to the principal about it. This bothers you because you are a busy man, and you do not like to waste time over something that seems so unreasonable and wrong.

You are not acquainted with the principal, Mr. Smith, but you are well acquainted with the superintendent of schools. You know the superintendent is a reasonable man and you tried to see him, but he is out of town for a few days, and this enrollment has to be taken care of now or it will be too late.

When you go to the principal's office, you present your problem and wait for his reaction.

There are several possible approaches the principal might follow:

1. He might dogmatically say no. If he does, threaten to make a public issue of it. You have rights as a taxpayer; your boy is superior, and so forth. Just do not take no for an answer. Do not hesitate to show your anger under those circumstances.
2. He may try to win you over without yielding—here again you should point out that your boy is better prepared for kindergarten than most of the children who were accepted because he has been in private nursery school and the test results show him to be superior.
3. He may refuse to yield but agree to study the policy and see how exceptions could be made. But your boy is ready now and the policy could be studied and rules made for exceptions later.
4. He may accept Edward if it is kept quiet, as a special favor, and so on. You do not want any underhanded admission because the boy is qualified to go in the "front door," on his own merits, and so on.
5. He may accept Edward without qualifications. If he does, tell him that your neighbor has a boy that has been in the same nursery school

that Edward attended. There is a complete set of records showing that this boy is superior also. He is only 15 days younger than Edward, and his parents would like to get him enrolled also.

Keep in mind that you are an important man, that the records show that Edward is superior, that his experience in the private nursery school gives him an added advantage, that you think the chronological age rule is no good, and that other superior children should also be allowed in.

Situations such as these seem to provide a better basis for evaluating some of the complex human-relations skills needed by a principal than any number of trait-oriented personality, aptitude, or interest measures.

A highly significant study using role-playing situations to study school administrator behavior was carried out at Columbia University.[17] In this study the subjects were introduced to a mythical school district through the study of handbooks, motion pictures, and participation in meetings, and then played the role of a principal attempting to solve administrative problems related to the school and district.

OBSERVATIONS MADE BY UNTRAINED GROUPS

Introduction

Most of our discussion of observational studies to this point has been concerned with closely controlled scientific observation. In many educational studies, however, it is not possible to maintain this control over the observational situation. We will now discuss techniques that provide less precise scientific data and are to some extent less direct, as they are based on the observations and recollections of special groups whom we cannot train thoroughly or control closely. This type of observation is much more likely to be subjective and biased. Nevertheless, in many instances the very subjectivity of the observations may be of value to the researcher. For example, the leadership ability of students could be determined by trained adult observers. However, nominations of leadership ability by a student's peers may be of more value in predicting a student's later standing in his peer group, even though these nominations are not based on objective observations.

The anecdotal record

One technique used quite commonly in education is the anecdotal record. Anecdotal records are generally based on teacher observations and

[17] John K. Hemphill, Daniel E. Griffiths, and Norman Fredericksen, *Administrative Performance and Personality: A Study of the Principal in a Simulated Elementary School* (New York: Teachers College, Columbia University, 1962).

involve descriptions of behavior that the teacher considers typical of the individual described. With some training teachers can produce anecdotal records of considerable value to the scientist. The anecdotal record should be an objective description of the child's behavior without interpretations by the observer. In preparing the instructions and forms for anecdotal records, the research worker should strive toward as great objectivity as possible. The most serious danger in anecdotal records is that the teacher will write these records while emotionally upset about the incident being described. For example, in compiling anecdotal records dealing with disciplinary problems and misbehavior, the teacher is much less likely to be objective than an observer who is not directly involved in the disciplinary situation.

Sociometric techniques

Sociometric techniques are designed to measure the social structure of a group and to appraise the social status of each individual with respect to other members of his group. A number of different techniques can be used to collect these data. In the usual approach, each group member is asked to select persons in the group most preferred by him on the basis of a specific criterion. For example, he may be asked to indicate the three persons with whom he would most like to work on a committee assignment. In studies involving classroom groups, pupils are often asked to indicate persons with whom they would most like to do an assignment, near whom they would prefer to have their desks, and so on. Moreno, in the earliest development of sociometric measurement, used such methods as a means of rearranging groups of school children so that they could study together more harmoniously.[18] Occasionally selections of least preferred individuals are also made. In another version of the sociometric technique, the individual is asked to identify persons whom he believes have chosen him. The choices that he believes were made can then be compared with actual choices in order to obtain an indication of his insight into his social position. Still another type of sociometric measure is the "guess who test." These measures contain descriptions of various social roles, and subjects are asked to indicate the group member who best fits each role. For example, the researcher might present a group of students with these descriptions:

"This student would make a good class president."

"This student would be the most fun at a party."

"This student is the smartest in my class."

"If I had difficulty with arithmetic, I would ask this student for help."

The instructions would direct each student to write down the names of one or two students who fit each description.

[18] J. L. Moreno, *Who Shall Survive?* (New York: Beacon, 1953).

Sociometric techniques are often used to measure popularity among students in a classroom. Since popularity among one's peers is an important personal attribute, many researchers have investigated factors that might be related to popularity as measured by sociometric techniques. An interesting study of this type was carried out by McDavid and Harari.[19] They investigated whether people, like objects, tend to be judged favorably or unfavorably by their labels, that is, by their first name. Their sample consisted of 59 fourth and fifth graders who belonged to one of four youth groups at a community center. These students were asked to indicate on a 3-point scale how much they liked or disliked each of 49 different names (being all the first names of those children in the sample). Two social desirability ratings were completed for each name. One rating (SDI) was the mean of the ratings made by the members of the youth group to which a particular student belonged. The other rating (SDO) was the mean of the ratings made by nonmembers of the youth group; the purpose of this rating was to minimize the possibility that a student would rate a name in terms of an actual person whom he knew rather than as a label. Once these social desirability ratings of names had been obtained, the popularity status of each student was established by the sociometric technique of having students nominate others with whom they would like to play together, and so on. The correlation between a student's popularity and the social desirability of his or her name was high (r for SDI was .63, and r for SDO was .49), leading McDavid and Harari to conclude "that the child who bears a generally unpopular or unattractive name may be handicapped in his social interactions with his peers" (p. 458).

Supervisory ratings

Ratings, such as those made of teachers by their principals or of principals by their superintendents, provide a commonly used method of gaining data concerning the behavior of subjects in educational research. Supervisory ratings, of course, are difficult to conduct on a scientific and tightly controlled basis. In some studies the supervisor makes special observations as part of the research plan, but as he has already formed an opinion of his subordinates prior to the time these observations are made, this opinion will inevitably have an effect upon his observational ratings even if he tries to be objective. Under these conditions we may be sure that observed behavior that agrees with the observer's bias is most likely to be noted and recorded. "Halo effect" also operates strongly in this type of evaluation. In many cases, however, the behavior of the individual as seen through the eyes of his supervisor, although different perhaps from the objective behavior of the individual, still has an important meaning

[19] J. W. McDavid and H. Harari, "Stereotyping of Names and Popularity in Grade-School Children," *Child Development*, 37 (1966), 453–459.

in educational research. For example, a researcher may be interested in studying factors related to promotion or nonpromotion of teachers. Principals' ratings of the teacher's competence may be an important factor in predicting promotion and therefore should be obtained, even though in some instances these ratings may not be objective.

The critical-incident technique

One form of observational rating that has been employed to a considerable degree in recent years is the critical-incident technique developed by Flanagan.[20] This technique, as usually applied, requires an interview with the supervisor of the individual to be evaluated. The interviewer attempts to obtain from the supervisor descriptions of the subject's specific behavior patterns that are considered to be critical to the skills being studied. Some studies of military leadership ability, for example, have used the critical-incident technique. One of the authors once had the opportunity to read hundreds of the critical incidents collected by Flanagan in his research on military leadership. In reading these incidents, it was apparent that many of the incidents recorded would not be considered "critical" by a psychologist, because many were global evaluations and general comments about the subject's performance rather than specific incidents involving the subject. Perhaps the most serious problem encountered in using the critical-incident technique is to obtain incidents from the individuals interviewed that seem to be truly critical to the behavior or skills being studied. If incidents can be collected that are truly critical, that truly differentiate between successful and unsuccessful behavior, then this method can be a very useful research approach.

The critical-incident technique seems to be well suited to many educational problems, particularly those involving the qualifications of school administrators and teachers. In one such study, the researcher was interested in how educators viewed professionalism in the field of education.[21] Specifically, Leles was concerned with whether educators have the same notion of professional and nonprofessional behaviors as do other occupational groups. The critical-incident technique permitted collection of a large amount of data on this subject. Leles asked teachers, administrators, counselors, and others to recall an incident that involved nonprofessional conduct on the part of an educator. The use of the critical-incident technique was a simple, yet effective alternative to training observers and having them carry out lengthy observations of professional and nonpro-

[20] John C. Flanagan, "The Critical-Incident Technique," *Psychological Bulletin*, 51 (1954), 327–358.
[21] Sam Leles, "Using the Critical Incidents Technique to Develop a Theory of Educational Professionalism: An Exploratory Study," *Journal of Teacher Education*, 19 (Spring 1968), 59–69. Reprinted by permission of the *Journal of Teacher Education* and Sam Leles

fessional conduct in a variety of educational settings. To give an idea of
the data that can be collected by this technique, some of Leles' reported
incidents are presented in the following paragraphs:

Running time clock at basketball games.

In coaching, we are often asked to do things for administrators. Once last year,
a friend of mine who was a coach had to chauffeur women around to various schools.
These women were very influential, and the administrators were afraid of them, so
the coaches more or less became ambassadors of goodwill to them. We hated every
minute of it.

My principal took a master copy from my files (book report form), had copies
made, and then presented them to our faculty meeting as his own idea. This was
done without my knowledge or permission, although the form was original with me.
Other teachers reported similar incidents with the same principal.

A teacher was reprimanded severely by a principal in front of the students for not
following a school rule about fire drills.

A teacher who, while chairman of the Salary Committee, used classroom time to
carry on duties related to that position. This was an elementary situation, and the
children were put to work at busy work. This same teacher, who exercises a good
deal of control over many of the personnel, voices long and loud protests over teachers associating with custodial help, etc. This, she says, is unprofessional.

Many teachers in my building have children standing in the halls because they are
unable to cope with their behavior in the classroom. I believe that much of this
stems from the failure to provide for individual differences and the discipline in the
classroom.

Reprimanding and insulting a teacher (by the principal) in front of other teachers
and parents.

Many teachers with below-standard training teaching in system. (Cadet certifi-
cates, etc.).

Several instrumental music teachers in the area are receiving 10 percent kickbacks
from the musical instrument dealers who sell instruments to their students. Such
awards (in confidence of course) are made in a direct cash handout or accumulated
into something like a grand piano, etc.

A teacher, after talking to another teacher outside in the hall, comes into the
classroom and criticizes that teacher before students in the room.

I consider using school time to study for law exams unprofessional.

What seems to me to be unprofessional behavior is the discussion by teachers in
the teachers' lounge. By this I mean discussing students in a derogatory manner.

Arriving late and leaving early. There have been examples of teachers who do
not show up at the school at an appropriate time—time enough to enable students
to talk with the teacher if necessary before classes—and they leave immediately
after the last bell—again not permitting the students an opportunity to talk with
the teacher.

Film for use with a class project was needed by the teacher. She went to her
principal and was told that he had some old outdated film that would be good
enough for school. He then bought new film for himself and was reimbursed for his
film.

Teachers gossiping and making fun of students in the teachers' lounge; usually for the glorification of the teachers.

A teacher repeatedly dismissed his class from normal classroom activities and kept them out of the classroom so that he could finish writing his thesis for the M.A. degree. The administrative officer was made aware of this by the students and their parents; even the staff discussed the problem with an official. However, the teacher was offered a contract for the following year.

English teacher approaches superintendent and board of education with regard to large classes and the lack of time to work with children on their writing of themes. She wanted more help or fewer students. Superintendent answered by accusing her in presence of board of education of not being able to handle classes. Some superintendents do not want problems to exist and will deny their existence. [pp. 67–68]

CONTENT ANALYSIS

Types of studies employing content analysis

"Content analysis is a research technique for the objective, systematic, and quantitative description of the manifest content of communication." [22] The raw material for the research worker using the content-analysis technique may be any form of communication, usually written materials, but other forms of communication such as music, pictures, or gestures should not be excluded. Textbooks, high school compositions, novels, newspapers, magazine advertisements, and political speeches are but a few of the sources available. Content analysis is often used in conjunction with observational studies. The researcher tape records classroom verbal behavior, for example, and makes a typed transcript from the audiotape. The content of the transcript is then analyzed in order to measure variables formulated by the researcher.

Most content analyses in education have been aimed at answering questions directly relating to the material analyzed. These analyses have generally been concerned with fairly simple classifications or tabulations of specific information. Content analyses of pupil compositions, for example, can give us a classification of grammatical and spelling errors as well as information on the frequency of different types of errors. This information can be directly applied to the revision of English courses or the development of remedial programs. A content analysis of current textbooks in first-year algebra can tell us such things as: What topics are covered by all books? What emphasis is placed on each topic? In what sequence are topics usually presented? What mathematical terms are introduced? What system of symbols is most frequently used? Such textbook analyses are often carried out by test publishing companies that produce standardized

[22] Bernard Berelson, *Content Analysis in Communication Research* (Glencoe, Ill.: Free Press, 1952), p. 18.

achievement tests in order that their tests can be constructed to have high content validity. Among the important early content analyses carried out in education were simple frequency counts of words in order to identify those words most commonly used in the English language.[23] Such word lists then formed the basis for determining the readability of textbooks and for the development of elementary reading textbooks and spelling lists. However, readability is a function of other factors besides frequency of word occurrence. Therefore, later researchers attempted a more complex content analysis of textbook materials in developing readability formulas.[24] Other areas of education that have been studied using content analysis include analysis of propaganda, sociological effects of reading, treatment of the Negro in history textbooks, the Soviet Union in American textbooks, nationalism in children's literature, analysis of television programs, analysis of readability of books and newspapers, and the social ideas in McGuffey readers.[25] It may be seen from these examples that content analysis can be a valuable tool for obtaining certain types of information useful in identifying or solving educational problems.

Whereas most early studies employing content analysis relied on simple frequency counts of objective variables (e.g., spelling errors, type/token ratios [26]), recent studies frequently aim at using content analysis to gain insights into complex social and psychological variables. Such studies are much more difficult to carry out than the simple frequency studies and often depend on a high level of sophistication of the researcher in psychology, sociology, or other behavioral sciences. An example of such a study is Ralph Tyler's investigation of officer education at the U.S. Air Force Air University.[27] The various officer training programs at the Air University had no clear-cut objectives prior to Tyler's study, and the relationship between the objectives that had been prepared and the needs of the Air Force had not been clearly established. One of the functions of Tyler's study was to develop statements of objectives for the various Air University courses. In order to do this, a large number of documents relat-

[23] Edward L. Thorndike, *A Teacher's Word Book of the Twenty Thousand Words Found Most Frequently and Widely in General Reading for Children and Young People*, rev. ed. (New York: Teachers College, Columbia University, 1932).

[24] Irving Lorge, "Predicting Readability," *Teachers College Record*, 45 (1944), 404–419, and Rudolf Flesch, *How to Test Readability* (New York: Harper & Row, 1951).

[25] See Berelson, op. cit., pp. 199–220, for an extensive listing of research using content analysis.

[26] The type/token ratio is the ratio of number of different words to total word count for a given communication.

[27] Ralph W. Tyler, *Analysis of the Purpose, Pattern, Scope, and Structure of the Officer Education Program of Air University* (Maxwell Air Force Base, Alabama Officer Educational Research Laboratory, May 1955) (OERL Technical Memorandum 55–56).

ing not only to the Air University programs but to many aspects of officer performance and job requirements were analyzed at the University of Chicago. One of the results of this complex analysis was the development of objectives that established the educational goals of the Air University on a very broad and comprehensive basis. These specific objectives formed a sounder foundation for further curriculum development and evaluation than had ever been previously available.

A recent trend in content analysis studies is to consider not only content frequencies but also the interrelationships among several content variables, or the relationship between content variables and other research variables. An illustration of this trend in content analysis is provided by Zahorik's study of the types of feedback statements that teachers use to inform students about the adequacy or correctness of their responses.[28] Teacher feedback includes statements such as "All right," "Fine," "Why did you say that?" and "Could anyone give us another point?" To study teacher feedback behavior, Zahorik tape recorded and transcribed discussion lessons of third-grade and sixth-grade teachers. The content of these discussions was then analyzed by means of an instrument developed for the study, which contained 25 categories for classifying teacher feedback. In the first part of the data analysis, Zahorik simply computed the frequencies with which different types of teacher feedback were given. Then, more sophisticated analyses of the content data were made. Teachers' use of different types of feedback was related to grade level of the classroom, purpose of the lesson (introduction-readiness discussions versus development discussions), teachers' use of questions, and quality of student answers. Such analyses can yield valuable insights into the nature of classroom interaction. One of the main findings of Zahorik's study, for example, was that teachers' verbal feedback tends to be rather limited in variety and depth: "Only a few types of feedback are used with regularity and these types may be less informational than others which are used infrequently" (p. 149). Such a finding might serve as the basis for improving teachers' instructional practices. Zahorik raises the possibility that a wider variety of types of feedback, including types that seem to carry more information, would benefit learners. He suggests that teachers develop wide feedback repertories, including more emphasis on elaborate types of praise, direct negatives such as simple reproof-denial, reasons or explanations as to why a comment had or lacked value, and clues or prompts regarding what to do next to improve a response. These types of feedback should improve the learning process, since they give the learner a clearer idea of the worth of his responses.

[28] John A. Zahorik, "Classroom Feedback Behavior of Teachers," *Journal of Educational Research*, 62(4) (1968), 147–150.

Planning a content analysis study

The first step in planning a content analysis study is to establish specific objectives to be achieved or hypotheses to be tested. The study might be concerned with a description and classification of the content in a particular type of communication (e.g., the questions found in elementary school textbooks), a comparison of content (e.g., types of questions found in first-, third-, and fifth-grade textbooks), or investigation of relationships (e.g., the relationship between ratings of question difficulty and readability indices of the textbook content).

Content analyses can be misleading or biased if the research worker does not use satisfactory methods for selecting the sample of content to be studied. In many content analyses, all content specifically pertinent to the research problem is studied. For example, an analysis concerned with the educational theories of a single author would usually be conducted by analyzing all the writing of the author in question. Content analyses dealing with topics that draw from a very large body of documentary materials, however, usually select material to be analyzed by some sampling technique. A study of trends in educational philosophy as reflected in newspaper editorials over the past fifty years would involve a very large volume of "raw material." In this case a sampling technique would be used to reduce the content to be analyzed to manageable size. One might, for example, limit one's selection to newspapers published every fifth year; thus only ten years of newspaper publishing need be considered rather than all fifty years. Next, one might use a table of random numbers. If the numbers 125, 5, 300 appeared, one would examine newspapers published on the 125th, 5th, and 300th day of the year. One could go through the table of random numbers until a specified number of editorials on educational philosophy had been selected for each year.

Once the content has been selected using appropriate sampling techniques, a classification system needs to be developed for analyzing the content. It is necessary to define content categories that measure the variables indicated by the research objectives or hypotheses. For example, if one were interested in the frequency of positive and negative self-references in first and last counseling interviews, it would be necessary to develop a set of categories and rules for deciding what types of statements are to be scored. Objective categories such as specific words (e.g., all occurrences of the word "I") are relatively easy to develop and score. Content categories involving inference or evaluation on the part of the rater are more difficult to develop. Since content analysis usually depends on frequency counts, it is very important to control for the length of the communication. For example, one may find that clients of student counseling services make more negative self-references in the first interview than in the last interview. Before interpreting this finding, one must examine the length of interviews to make sure they are comparable. It may be that clients talk more in the first interview than in the last interview. Thus, the apparent change in frequency of negative self-references can be attributed to the change in clients' talkativeness.[29]

After initial development of the content classification system, one should determine whether several raters can use it with a high degree of inter-rater reliability. If interrater reliability is low, it will be necessary to identify points of ambiguity in the content classification system and to clarify them. Sometimes it is helpful to develop a set of scoring rules in order to increase the reliability with which the classification system can be used. This was the case in a study carried out by one of the authors.[30] It was hypothesized that creative persons would be more sensitive to aesthetic, dynamic, and affective properties of objects than noncreative persons. To test the hypothesis, the frequency with which creative persons used certain kinds of noun modifiers (adjectives, participles, predicate adjectives) in describing Rorschach inkblots was compared with the frequency of noun modifier use by noncreative persons.[31] In order to ensure that raters would reliably tally appropriate noun modifiers, it was necessary to make up a set of rules for scoring noun modifiers to resolve the ambiguities which had become apparent in initial development of the classification system. The following lists the rules for scoring noun modifiers:

Rule 1: Noun modifiers usually immediately precede or follow a noun, or they immediately follow: is, are, looks, appears, seems.

Rule 2: Words immediately preceding or following nouns are almost always scored as a noun modifier if they end in: -ed, -ing, -en, -y, -some, -like, -ful.

Rule 3: Do not score these adjectives or adjectives of their type: a, an, the, this, that, these, those, his, her, our, your, my, its, their, some, any, no, other.

Rule 4: Do not score adjectives having to do with number, such as: first, second, one, two, few, many, each, both, every.

Rule 5: Do not score adjectives referring to location on the blot (e.g.,

---

[29] The factor of talkativeness (measured by word count or number of sentences, for example) can be removed as a possibly contaminating variable by a statistical technique called "analysis of covariance," which we shall discuss in Chapter 15.

[30] Meredith D. Gall, "An Investigation of Verbal Style in Creative and Noncreative Groups" (Unpublished doctoral dissertation; University of California, Berkeley, 1968).

[31] For example, in describing one of the Rorschach inkblots, a creative architect said, "It's *live* and *growing, soft* and *fragile* . . . could move in the wind." By contrast, a noncreative person might say, "Just looks like an inkblot . . . side things look like two animals."

"the *top* part of the blot looks like. . . .") or on an object-percept (e.g., "looks like the *top* part of a beetle"), such as: top, bottom, upper, lower, side, back, entire, whole.

Rule 6: Score such adjectives as "huge," "tremendous," "tiny," but do not score these specific words: big, large, small, little.

Rule 7: Do not score color words, such as white or black. The exceptions are combination colors, such as "blue-gray" (which is scored as one word) and words like "reddish."

Rule 8: Do not score adjectives that are an integral part of a noun phrase, such as praying mantis, United States. However, the adjective "high" in the phrase "high heels" is scored, since it refers to a particular style of shoes.

Rule 9: Only those noun modifiers that reflect one or more of the seven qualities previously stated are to be scored. This means that several types of adjectives are not scored, such as: location (e.g., "marine life"), general class of human, animal, or inanimate (e.g., "human figures," "bearskin rug," "cloud formation," "anatomical shape"), critical-evaluative words (e.g., "obvious," "strange," "appropriate," "fantastic").

Rule 10: The noun modifiers that are not usually scored because of Rule 9 are scored if they modify a quality noun (e.g., "a sense of *anatomical* form," "an *underwater* quality").

By the use of such rules, it was possible to achieve near-perfect agreement between raters in scoring Rorschach protocols for appropriate noun modifiers.

A recent development in content analysis has been the application of the computer to analyze communications. The *General Inquirer,* a computer program, enables the researcher to analyze a large body of data economically for various types of content variables.[32] For example, by punching spelling lists from different textbooks onto IBM cards, one can have them stored in the computer. Then by using appropriate retrieval routines, one could have the computer print out a variety of research data such as a set of words common to every spelling list, a set of words unique to each spelling list, a readability index computed for each spelling list, and even a classification of the words in each list by themes and types (e.g., sports, science, adjectives, number of syllables). As the *General Inquirer* and similar computer programs become more available, the sophistication and use of the content analysis technique should likewise increase.

In closing we should like to note that the content analysis technique is

[32] Philip J. Stone, Dexter C. Dunphy, Marshall S. Smith, and Daniel M. Ogilvie, *The General Inquirer: A Computer Approach to Content Analysis* (Cambridge, Mass.: M.I.T. Press, 1966).

very well suited for small-scale educational research projects, and it is surprising that more students do not carry out content analysis studies. It is usually much easier to obtain communications such as textbooks and newspapers than it is to obtain research subjects. There is less opportunity to bias the data collection process, since communications are usually "nonreactive." Also, communications can be analyzed directly, whereas one generally needs to collect data first from subjects by means of interview, standardized test, or observation before proceeding to the data analysis phase of the research project. In short, many graduate students may find that the content analysis technique can provide for their research project a basis that is significant, yet economical in terms of time and money. Although we have learned much about word frequency, spelling and grammatical errors, and textbook content, we know almost nothing about the more subtle effects of the different forms of educational communication upon the personality, goals, and values of our youth.

MISTAKES OFTEN MADE BY GRADUATE STUDENTS

1. Student does not sufficiently train his observers and thus obtains unreliable data.
2. Uses an observation form that requires too much from the observer.
3. Fails to take adequate precautions to avoid having the observer disturb or change the situation he is to observe.
4. Asks observers to make excessively precise discriminations among behaviors.
5. Does not use at least two observers in order to determine interrater reliability.
6. Does not ensure that observers work independently of each other.
7. Allows contamination of his data collection to occur.
8. Does not use random sampling techniques when appropriate.

ANNOTATED REFERENCES

General observation

1. Boyd, Robert D., and DeVault, M. Vere. "The Observation and Recording of Behavior," *Review of Educational Research*, 36 (5) (1966), 529–551. This review article contains about 100 references covering the literature on observational methods from 1960 to 1966. It will be helpful to the student concerned with the role of the observer, types of observational schedules, selection of behavior units, sampling techniques, and analysis of verbal behavior.
2. Webb, Eugene J., Campbell, Donald T., Schwartz, Richard D., and Sechrest, Lee. *Unobtrusive Measures: Nonreactive Research in the Social Sciences.* Chicago: Rand McNally, 1966. This book is a major contribution to the methodology of observational studies. The authors point out various sources of error that can weaken the validity of observations. They then show how these errors can be overcome by use of "nonreactive" measures. They give many examples of nonreactive measures that the student might adapt to his own research project.

Classroom observation

3. Biddle, Bruce J. "Methods and Concepts in Classroom Research," *Review of Educational Research,* 37 (3) 1967, 337–357. The author reviews the recent literature on observation of classroom interaction. He discusses the types of classrooms that have been studied; what aspects of classroom interaction have been focused on; and the observer rating systems, methods of recording, anl units of measurement that have been employed.

4. Meux, M. O. "Studies of Learning in the School Setting," *Review of Educational Research,* 37 (1967), 539–562. This author presents a useful overview of recent developments in classroom observation systems. Three types of observation systems are differentiated and discussed: multi-aspect, cognitive, and affective. The author also discusses some of the methodological problems associated with these systems.

5. Medley, Donald M., and Mitzel, Harold E. "Measuring Classroom Behavior by Systematic Observation," in N. L. Gage (ed.). *Handbook of Research on Teaching.* Chicago: Rand McNally, 1963. This review includes a sophisticated discussion of the major classroom observational schedules and of the considerations involved in carrying out an observational study. It should be particularly helpful to the student planning a research project in which teacher behavior is to be observed and measured.

6. Remmers, H. H. "Rating Methods in Research on Teaching," in N. L. Gage (ed.). *Handbook of Research on Teaching.* Chicago: Rand McNally, 1963. This paper provides a good overview of the main types of rating scales used in studying teacher behavior. Topics include format of rating scales, sociometric methods, Osgood's Semantic Differential, Q-Technique ratings, and rating bias.

Observation of children

7. Wright, H. F. "Observational Child Study," in P. E. Mussen (ed.). *Handbook of Research Methods in Child Development.* New York: Wiley, 1960, Chap. 3. The author provides a comprehensive overview of methods that have been used to study the behavior of children. In addition to reviewing types of observational methods, the author discusses problems of observer influence, reliability of observation, instrumental aids, and descriptive categories. The student is well advised to consult this paper before attempting research in this area.

Sociometry

3. Grouland, Norman E. *Sociometry in the Classroom.* New York: Harper, 1959. Any researcher planning a sociometric study in an educational setting should consult this text. The author presents a thorough treatment of the following topics: construction of sociometric tests, typical sociometric patterns, validity and reliability of sociometric tests, and correlates of sociometric choice. The last section of the book, "Applying Sociometric Results to Educational Problems," suggests a number of research problems that might be investigated by means of sociometric methodology.

Situational testing

9. Hemphill, John K., Griffiths, Daniel E., and Fredericksen, Norman. *Administrative Performance and Personality: A Study of the Principal in a Simulated Elementary School.* New York: Teachers College, Columbia University, 1962. The study described in this book is the most extensive use of situational testing in educational research that has been completed to date. Chapters dealing with the development and evaluation of the situational measures are particularly pertinent for students contemplating research in this area.

Content analysis

10. Berelson, Bernard. *Content Analysis in Communication Research.* Glencoe, Ill.: Free Press, 1952. This book provides the student with a practical treatment of the use of content analysis as a research tool. Both quantitative and qualitative content analysis techniques are discussed, along with many examples of their application to various types of content. Technical problems involved in content analysis, including reliability, sampling, and presentation of data are also covered. An extensive bibliography of content analysis studies published since 1950 is included.

11. Pool, Ithiel deSola (ed.). *Trends in Content Analysis.* Urbana, Ill.: University of Illinois Press, 1959. An excellent source for the student planning a content analysis study. Discusses the qualitative and quantitative approaches, the research methods applicable to content analysis studies, and the application of content analysis techniques to several different fields of learning. Contains an extensive bibliography.

CHAPTER 10

Techniques of Historical Research

INTRODUCTION

Historical research is the systematic and objective location, evaluation, and synthesis of evidence in order to establish facts and draw conclusions concerning past events. Many students consider the pursuit of a historical study as being completely divorced from science and, therefore, not demanding the rigor and objectivity of scientific methods. Such studies are often selected as an "easy way out" by students who are afraid to attempt an experimental study.

A critical analysis of a large sample of historical studies in secondary education published between 1900 and 1948 revealed that fewer than one half met the requirements of historical research.[1] Actually, the demands for objectivity are as high in historical research as in other scientific methods, and these demands are much more difficult to meet because of the nature of historical data. Although historical research is perhaps the most difficult type of educational research to do well, it is important and necessary because it gives us an insight into some educational problems that could not be gained by any other technique. The historical study of an educational idea or institution gives us a perspective that can do much to help us understand our present educational system, and this understanding in turn can help to establish a sound basis for further progress and improvement. Historical research also can give us an insight into human behavior that can be very valuable in arriving at practical solutions for educational problems. For example, a careful historical study of the school bond elections in a given school district might give us broad insights into the human interactions involved in these elections, critical factors contributing to the success or failure of the issue, clues to obtaining support for future bond elections in the district, and finally a general understanding of variables operating in such elections that could be applied to

[1] Philip W. Perdew, *A Critical Analysis of Research in the History of Secondary Education in America* (Unpublished doctoral dissertation; Los Angeles: University of California, 1948).

other districts as well. In this chapter the student will find an introduction to the fundamentals of historical research. If he plans to carry out this type of project, he should take a course in historical research methods (usually offered by the history department) or should study one of the texts devoted to this topic.

DESIGNING THE HISTORICAL RESEARCH PROJECT

Appropriate problems for historical research in education may be identified using most of the same approaches suggested in Chapter 2 for locating other types of research problems. Perhaps the most fruitful problems, however, develop from a knowledge of current practices and an interest in how these practices developed. At the present time, for example, there is much dispute as to whether the age-grade form of grouping currently in effect in most of our public schools provides a desirable setting for learning. Certainly, a historical study that traced the development of the present system and weighed the various factors contributing to the establishment of this system would provide us with an understanding of age-grade grouping that could be of considerable value in evaluating the effectiveness of this system for present-day instruction. Historical studies often reveal that current practices were originally developed to fit situations and meet needs that no longer exist.

The essential steps of historical research are defining the problem, gathering the data, and evaluating and synthesizing the data into an accurate account of the subject investigated. It will be noted that these steps are essentially the same as those involved in other types of research projects. There are, however, important differences in the way that these steps are carried out between the historical research project and other educational research methods. In historical research, it is especially important that the student carefully defines his problem and appraises its appropriateness before committing himself too fully. Many problems are not adaptable to historical research methods and cannot be adequately treated using this approach. Other problems have little or no chance of producing significant results either because of the lack of pertinent data or because the problem is a trivial one.

A fact that many students fail to realize is that historical research usually requires the setting up of specific, testable hypotheses. Without such hypotheses, historical research often becomes little more than an aimless gathering of facts. In searching the materials that make up the source of historical research data, unless the student's attention is aimed at information relating to specific questions or concerned with specific hypotheses, he has little chance of extracting a body of data from the available documents that can be synthesized to provide new knowledge or new understanding of the topic studied. Even after specific hypotheses have been established, the student must exercise strict self-control in his study of historical documents, or he will find himself collecting much information that is interesting but is not related to his area of inquiry. If the student's hypotheses are not sufficiently delimited and specific, it is an easy matter for him to become distracted and led astray by information that is not really related to his field of investigation.

GATHERING DATA

Perhaps the major difference between historical research and other forms of scientific research is that historical research must deal with data that are already in existence. Hockett points out that:

History is not a science of *direct* observation, like chemistry and physics. The historian like the geologist interprets past events by the traces they have left; he deals with the evidences of man's past acts and thoughts. *But the historian, no less than the scientist, must utilize evidence resting on reliable observation.* The difference in procedure is due to the fact that the historian usually does not make his own observations, and that those upon whose observations he must depend are, or were, often if not usually untrained observers. Historical method is, strictly speaking, a process *supplementary* to observations, a process by which the historian attempts to test the truthfulness of the reports of observations made by others. Like the scientist, he examines his data and formulates hypotheses, i.e., tentative conclusions. These conjectures he must test by seeking fresh evidence or reexamining the old, and this process he must continue until, in the light of all available evidence, the hypotheses are abandoned as untenable or modified until they are brought into conformity with the available evidence.[2]

Sources of historical data

Historical sources may usually be classified as either documents or relics. Documents include a wide range of written and printed materials recorded for the purpose of transmitting information. Relics include physical objects related to the period or the institution being studied. In education these might include such materials as school furniture or various physical objects used in teaching, such as flash cards, multiplication tables, and so on. Textbooks, although printed, may be regarded as relics if they are studied as physical objects, and the printed content is not the source of the information being sought. For example, in a study of printing methods used in textbooks, the textbook could be classified as a relic. On the other hand, a study of the viewpoints concerning some phase of American history presented by textbooks of different periods would use the textbooks

---

[2] Homer C. Hockett, *The Critical Method in Historical Research and Writing* (New York: Macmillan, 1955), pp. 7–8. Reprinted by permission of The Macmillan Co.

as documents. In historical research concerning education, there has been relatively little use made of relics.

Primary sources and secondary sources are defined in historical research in basically the same terms as in the appraisal of scientific research. In historical research, primary sources are generally defined as those documents in which the individual observing the event being described was present. Secondary sources are those in which the person describing the event was not present but has obtained his description from someone else who may or may not have directly observed the event. Occasionally, the number of times that the writing is removed from the observer is indicated, but generally all levels of removal are lumped together as secondary sources.

Search for historical data

In other forms of educational research, the review of the literature is considered a preliminary step to gathering data and is aimed at providing the student with a knowledge of previous research that he can apply to the improvement of his own research plan. In historical research, however, the review of the literature actually provides the research data. In reviewing research literature, most of the information the student seeks will be contained in research articles published in the professional journals. These articles describe in brief and concise terms the procedures and findings of a single research project. Many of the documents that will be studied by the student in a historical research project, in contrast, will be much longer, but only a small portion of each document may relate to the specific hypotheses of the historical research project. Because of these differences in the nature of the materials searched, the search and note-taking procedures required in historical research are somewhat different and more difficult than those carried out by a student who is concerned with a review of the literature in a limited research topic. A difference already stated is in the length and breadth of content of historical documents as compared with research articles. Another difference is that documents required in historical research often date back much further than those that must be searched in order to carry out a review of the literature in a specific research area. Still another difficulty arises because historical documents used in education are often unpublished materials such as school-board reports, curriculum plans, records of physical examinations, and personal letters, and therefore are not classified in such source books as *Education Index*.

Note-taking

Effective note-taking procedures are extremely important in historical research. In fact, many of the inaccuracies found in histories produced up until recent times are considered to be largely the result of unwieldy or ineffective note-taking techniques. The system used by early historians of compiling notes in chronological order in a bound note ledger made it impossible to arrange these notes into logical sequence after they had been collected. Laborious indexes were often developed to make use of the bound volumes of notes, but such an approach was a great deal less effective than the use of a note-card system or looseleaf system in which notes may be arranged in any order desired.[3] While the student whose review of the literature is limited to brief research articles may usually outline the entire article on a single card, authorities in historical research recommend placing only one item of information on each note card. The difference in procedure is necessary because of the fact that many small bits of information relating to the various hypotheses of the research worker may be obtained from one important document such as an auto-biography or a diary. If all notes from a single major document such as a diary were copied on a single card, the process of rearranging the information would be much more difficult and complicated. Each card may be coded to indicate the hypothesis or subtopic to which the note relates.

EVALUATION OF DATA

The historical research worker, while in the process of gathering research data, concurrently carries on an evaluation of these data. Inasmuch as the pertinent documents provide the sole source of information for historical research, the evaluation of these documents is of critical importance in helping the research worker to place each bit of information in its proper perspective and draw sound conclusions from the total picture obtained. The evaluation of historical evidence is usually referred to as historical criticism. It is in the process of historical criticism that the historical research worker leans most heavily upon scientific methods and frequently upon other sciences that can assist him in making a valid appraisal of the authenticity and accuracy of his data. Historical criticism is generally divided into two major categories—external criticism and internal criticism.

External criticism

The methods of external criticism are primarily aimed at determining whether the evidence being evaluated is authentic. External criticism is therefore aimed primarily at the document itself rather than the statements contained in the document. A careful study of a document can give us a great many clues concerning its authenticity. Analyses of the physical materials such as the paper used can often permit an approximate dating of the document. Other clues such as references to place-names can also be

[3] Hockett, *op. cit.*

helpful in establishing dates. Since place-names frequently change over the years, many forgeries are uncovered because they contain incorrect place-names for the places referred to at the time the forged document was supposed to have been written. Forgeries are constantly being uncovered by historians through the use of techniques of internal and external criticism. Hockett [4] discusses the "False Decretals," religious documents that were allegedly written in the third and fourth centuries but were actually forged in the ninth century. These forgeries, however, were accepted as genuine until subjected to historical criticism in the latter part of the nineteenth century. The student of educational history is less likely to encounter forged and spurious documents than would be the historical research worker studying in some political or religious area where stronger motivations usually exist for creating forgeries.

Internal criticism

After the authenticity of a document has been established, the task of evaluating the accuracy and worth of the data contained in the document must be undertaken. Internal criticism is usually much more difficult than external criticism because it involves evaluating the writer, his biases, and his possible motives for distortion. This evaluation requires an extensive knowledge of the individual concerned, as well as the training in psychology necessary to interpret this knowledge. In testing the competence of an observer, we also must attempt to determine what opportunities the individual had for knowing the facts. If he witnessed the events that he described, do we have evidence from these observations or others that he is a reliable observer? Many studies in psychology have demonstrated that eyewitnesses can be extremely unreliable, especially if they are emotionally aroused or under stress at the time of the event. Even under conditions where no emotional involvement occurs, some individuals are a great deal more competent as observers than others. The location of the individual, his ability to take notes, and his understanding of the events that he is observing are all factors that can affect the accuracy of his observation. If several observers have described the same situation differently, it is obvious that someone has recorded the event inaccurately.

The person who has an ax to grind or has strong motives for wanting a particular version of a described event to be accepted can usually be expected to produce biased information. For example, a school superintendent, when writing an account of a school-board meeting in which a dispute occurred between himself and members of the school board, will tend to present his own side of the argument in the most favorable light, may subconsciously alter his position to agree with facts that have become apparent since the meeting, and may forget or deliberately omit state-

[4] *Op. cit.*

ments of his opponents that have been found to have merit since the meeting occurred. Many historical research projects in education are concerned with fairly recent events, and under these conditions the research worker may supplement the information available from documents with information he may obtain by interviewing some of the participants in the event in question. The evidence collected through such interviews, however, must be evaluated carefully and checked whenever possible against other witnesses or other documentary evidence. The individual's recollection of even fairly recent events may be considerably in error. If the events involve a dispute, differences in opinion, or argument, one may be sure that each witness' report of the event will be somewhat distorted to support his own views. This may not be a deliberate distortion but merely reflects the well-known tendency to remember best those things that agree with our own opinions and biases.

Historical research workers must put much of their documentary evidence to the test of truthfulness as well as competence. Even a competent observer, if sufficiently biased in the direction of a given point of view, may record an untruthful record of the occurrences in question. If the author of a document or maker of a statement has some interest to be promoted by the acceptance of a particular point of view, one may expect that this viewpoint will be put forth, whether truthful or not. Historians must often delve to a considerable degree into the race, political party, religious group, and social status of the observer in an effort to appraise the likelihood of prejudices or biases. The use of emotionally charged or intemperate language whether of a favorable or unfavorable nature usually suggests bias and should be watched for.

Persons often exaggerate their own roles in important affairs. This exaggeration frequently is not deliberate but merely reflects the occurrences from the point of view of the individual concerned. Much material that is basically untruthful can be traced to the tendency of many individuals to elaborate or color their description of events in order to make a more interesting story or to call more attention to their own role or importance in the events being described. Sometimes, on the other hand, the social or political position of the individual is such as to require him to make conventional statements rather than honest ones. For example, a school superintendent faced with internal difficulties with principals or other members of his organization might, upon being questioned, give the usual answers indicating the high morale and level of agreement of his staff, because he may feel that airing the internal difficulties of the school district can serve no useful purpose. People in public life frequently make conventional statements concerning political opponents or in eulogizing other individuals that may have little or no bearing upon the true feelings of the individual making the statement.

There are, of course, many documents in educational history that are essentially neutral in character and in which it is difficult to imagine anyone having a motive to distort the facts deliberately. Such documents may, of course, be in error because of the incompetence of the observer.

COMMON ERRORS IN HISTORICAL RESEARCH

Historical research projects carried out by graduate students in education often contain one or more of the following errors:

1. *A research area is selected in which sufficient evidence is not available to conduct a worthwhile study or test the hypotheses adequately.* The vast majority of documents available to the student carrying out historical research in education relate to events that are not of major importance and have usually been recorded by persons unaware that their observations might have any future historical significance. For example, let us say that we are conducting a historical study tracing the development of a student-teaching program in a particular university. The minutes of faculty meetings in which the program was discussed would be an important source of data for the research worker. In all likelihood, however, minutes would have been kept by only one person and, because such minutes are often kept by a secretary who is unable to recognize significant points in the discussion, the information available may be very sketchy. Furthermore, most historians follow the rule that the statement of one person should not be regarded as establishing the truth of details described in the document. Essential agreement in the statements of independent witnesses is considered to establish truth beyond a reasonable doubt, while identical statements are generally considered to prove that the various documents are not independent.

2. *Excessive use of secondary sources of information is frequently found in studies not dealing with recent events.* The student often discovers that the time and expense involved in locating and examining primary sources is so great that he has little or no chance of covering these sources thoroughly. Primary source documents are often located at distant libraries, and they are generally not available through interlibrary loan. Thus, students must either visit the libraries or obtain photostatic copies of the needed documents. Both of these procedures are expensive, and because the pertinence of a document cannot be determined accurately until it has been examined, the student often must pay for photostating much material that will be of little or no use to him. In selecting a problem, the availability of primary sources should be carefully considered, and if needed sources are not available, the study should not be attempted. Studies of recent local history are most practical for the graduate student in education. If the student attempts a study beyond these limitations, he will

almost surely be forced to rely too heavily on secondary sources. For example, one article, "Teacher Education in the Fifteenth Century," was based entirely upon secondary sources, the earliest of which was published in 1841.[5]

3. *Attempts to work on a broad and poorly defined problem.* The failure to establish specific hypotheses and the failure to delimit the research problem often go hand-in-hand. Poorly defined hypotheses make it impossible for the student to decide what documents are pertinent to his problem. If the student persists in too broad a problem in historical research, the result is almost inevitably a cursory or slipshod treatment of the evidence available. It is much more satisfactory for a student to carry out a thorough study dealing with a small, specific problem than attempt to work with a problem that is beyond the scope of his time, money, and ability.

4. *Fails to evaluate adequately his historical data.* Although the student doing historical research in education rarely encounters forged documents, he should be prepared to apply the principles of external criticism to documents where some doubt as to their authenticity exists. The more difficult application of internal criticism, however, is appropriate for most of the historical evidence the student in education will collect. Failure to apply the principles of internal criticism is perhaps the most serious weakness found in historical studies in the field of education.

5. *Allows personal bias to influence his research procedures.* Because many historical studies in education deal with recent events and with questions and procedures about which the research worker might have definite feelings and opinions, the possibilities for personal bias are great. It is inadvisable for the student to attempt to test hypotheses in historical research that are concerned with topics about which he already has strong feelings or convictions. Such convictions will almost surely influence his selection and interpretation of the evidence available. Historical research, like all other forms of research, must be aimed primarily at gaining new knowledge rather than proving a point. Important evidence is easily overlooked or ignored in the study of historical documents. Thus, bias has a greater opportunity to operate in historical research than in experimental studies.

6. *The student's report recites facts but does not synthesize or integrate these facts into meaningful generalizations.* Many students consider that the historical research study is complete when the facts related to the topic have been assembled. The mere recitation of facts is not historical research and without synthesis and interpretation cannot provide us with the better understanding and perspective that is the usual goal of historical research.

---

[5] Clara P. McMahon, "Teacher Education in the Fifteenth Century," *Journal of Educational Research*, 44 (1950), 134–137.

CRITERIA FOR RESEARCH IN EDUCATIONAL HISTORY

Perdew lists the following criteria for research in educational history. If the student follows these criteria and avoids the errors already stated, he is likely to produce worthwhile historical research.[6]

a. Purpose. One of the common concepts in the definitions of research is that research has the purpose of extending, correcting, or verifying knowledge. Some reports using historical data may merely restate knowledge already the common property of scholars in the field. This is usually true of textbooks, which commonly have the purpose of instructing students, and are not designed to add to the knowledge of scholars.

b. Presentation of facts. It is difficult to conceive of a report of historical research which does not deal with facts. The second measure of a publication which uses historical data is the extent to which it presents facts.

c. Generalizations. History is dependent upon the synthesis of facts or small-scale generalizations and interpretations, and it does not lead to universal laws nor a philosophy of history. Reports which do not recognize the necessity for the proper balance between fact and interpretation do not qualify as historical research. Critical or philosophical articles which use historical data to illustrate and strengthen the argument, although good in themselves, are not historical research.

Except as an investigation meets in full the first three criteria listed above, it cannot be classified as historical research in education.

d. Demonstration of sources. Since, obviously, past events cannot•be repeated or brought in for experimentation, the historian turns to sources contemporary with the events. A report of historical research, then, must show evidence of being based upon such sources. This evidence may be in the text of the publication, in footnotes, or in the bibliography. There is room for historical writing which is largely interpretative and done by men whose reputation justifies their recognition, but, in doing such writing, one hazards his reputation as an historian.

e. Selection of sources. The selection and evaluation of sources is a delicate task requiring training and judgment. Every subject has its own special sources. In general the student should attempt to locate sources as close in time and place as possible to the event, in other words, to use as extensively as possible the primary sources.

f. Statements of problems. The good research report shows evidence of delimitation in the problem studied. An occasional work sets for itself too large a problem for the space allotted to it, leading to generalization without supporting data. Sometimes a title with a large scope is given whereas the publication deals with only a small aspect of it. These tendencies weaken the quality of research publications.

g. Logical organization. Weaknesses in the logical organization of a report of historical research suggest weaknesses in the author's understanding and analysis of the problem.

[6] Philip W. Perdew, "Criteria of Research in Educational History," *Journal of Educational Research,* 44 (1950), 217–223. Reprinted by permission of the *Journal of Educational Research.*

h. Social forces. Since historians of education generally support the view that education is to be shown in its interrelation with other social institutions and forces, proper recognition of such relationships is a characteristic of a good research report.

i. Development of cause and effect relationships. History is not a listing of events. That is the area of the annalist or the chronicler. To be history, the events must be brought into causal relationships.

j. Language and style. Language and style are significant aspects of a report of historical research. A clear lucid style is imperative if communication between the writer and the reader is to be established. Beyond this is the style of the consummate artist with words, who charms and interests his audience to a greater extent than the subject and material alone justify. The historical geniuses have the gift of language in large measure. It must not be forgotten by even the humble monographer that history is a great subject and warrants the grand style.

ANNOTATED REFERENCES

1. Garraghan, Gilbert J. *A Guide to Historical Method.* New York: Fordham University Press, 1946. This textbook provides the student planning a historical research project with a firm foundation in historical research method. A general orientation to history and the historical method, and its relationship to other sciences is presented. The section on locating sources gives the student an introduction to the types of historical sources, as well as information on note-taking systems and the use of libraries. Sections dealing with historical criticism and presentation of the results of historical research are very useful, the former borrowing heavily from Bernheim's *Lehrbuch der Historischen Methode,* which is generally recognized as the classic work in the field of historical research method.

2. Good, Carter V. *Introduction to Educational Research.* New York: Appleton-Century-Crofts, Inc., 1959. The student is referred to Chapter 4, which describes the processes of historical research and the major steps in carrying it out, including collection of data, evaluation of data, and preparation of the report. Although this chapter provides a good coverage of basic principles, the student planning a historical research project should consult more complete sources, such as Gottschalk or Hockett (see References 3 and 5). The student may find other references pertinent to his specific interest in historical research in the extensive reference list provided.

3. Gottschalk, Louis. *Understanding History: A Primer of Historical Method.* New York: Alfred A. Knopf, Inc., 1951. This book is written primarily for the student who wishes to do historical research and writing in the college or university and is strongly oriented toward "how to do it." Treatment of internal and external criticism is somewhat less thorough than Hockett (see Reference 5). Contains more emphasis on such practical subjects as choosing a subject, use of footnotes, note-taking, use of quotations, preparing a draft, and others.

4. Handlin, Oscar; Schlesinger, Arthur; *et al. Harvard Guide to American History.* Cambridge, Mass.: Harvard University Press, 1954. This book is a comprehensive treatment of American history. The first five chapters, however, provide the student with extensive information on research and historical writing, historical

materials, aids to historical research, and historical sources. The student planning a historical research project can learn much from these chapters.

5. Hockett, Homer C. *The Critical Method in Historical Research and Writing.* New York: The Macmillan Co., 1955. This textbook orients the student to the role of history, traces the development of the historical method, and presents a thorough coverage of historical criticism. Because it has been prepared primarily for the use of graduate students, emphasis is also given to the preparation of the Master's thesis and doctoral dissertation. It contains a very extensive bibliography on historical methodology, writing and teaching, and other topics important to the historical research worker. This text is highly recommended as basic reading for the student planning a historical research project in education.

6. Perdew, Philip W. "Criteria of Research in Educational History," *Journal of Educational Research,* 44 (1950), 217–223. The author discusses criteria for research from various sources and develops ten criteria that can guide students in conducting historical research in education. He points out that, of over 900 historical writings published in the field of secondary education since 1900, less than half can rightfully be considered historical research. This article calls the attention of the graduate student interested in historical research to factors that he must consider in developing and carrying out his project.

7. Woody, Thomas. "Of History and Its Method," *Journal of Experimental Education,* 15 (1947), 175–201. Provides a brief but useful background in history and historical method, including philosophy of history, historical method, qualifications needed to carry out historical research, selection of a subject, internal and external criticism, documentation, note-taking, and other related topics. Contains a great deal of useful information in very brief form.

CHAPTER 11

Introduction to Statistical Analysis and Research Design

PRELIMINARY CONSIDERATIONS

Most research in education can be classified as one of two types—descriptive studies and those aimed at discovering causal relationships. Descriptive studies are primarily concerned with finding out "what is." Examples of questions that might be studied by means of a descriptive approach are: Do teachers hold favorable attitudes toward "new" mathematics? What kinds of activities occur in sixth-grade art classes, and how frequently do they occur? What have been the reactions of school administrators to innovations in teaching the social sciences? Have first-grade textbooks changed in readability over the last fifty years? Observational and survey methods are frequently used to collect descriptive data.

Although description is an important aspect of the scientific approach in education, most research studies are concerned primarily with discovering causal relationships. Typical causal problems investigated by educational researchers are: What factors determine choice of college major? What causes underachievement? Does this new instructional strategy lead to increased learning when compared with conventional instructional strategies? We may distinguish between research designs in terms of their effectiveness in establishing causal links between two or more variables. The causal-comparative method is aimed at the discovery of possible causes for the phenomenon being studied by comparing subjects in whom this variable or characteristic is present with similar subjects in whom it is absent. However, this research design can only be used to explore causal relationships, not confirm them. Suppose that one is interested in testing the hypothesis that anxiety impairs performance on timed aptitude tests. If a causal-comparative design were used, one might select contrasting groups of high- and low-anxious students, and then compare their performance on a timed aptitude test. Suppose we found that the high-anxious group did indeed have lower test scores on the average than the low-anxious group. Although this finding is consistent with the research hypothesis, an alternative causal hypothesis is possible, namely, that poor performance on timed aptitude tests (and perhaps other academic tests) is likely to cause anxiety. Thus, the research results do not tell us whether anxiety causes impaired performance or whether impaired performance causes anxiety.

A similar problem occurs with the correlational research design. Correlational studies include all of those research projects in which an attempt is made to discover or clarify relationships through the use of correlation coefficients. Although the correlation coefficient tells the researcher the magnitude of the relationship between two variables A and B, it cannot be used to determine whether A causes B, B causes A, or whether a third variable X causes both A and B.

The experimental research design is ideally suited to establish causal relationships if proper controls are used. Taking the research problem just mentioned, one might first select a sample and divide it randomly into two groups. Then one would manipulate the independent variable, level of anxiety, by raising it in one of the two groups (for example, one could tell them that they are about to be administered a test that will be used to determine scholarship awards or college selection). The other group, called the "control group," would not receive this treatment. Then the timed aptitude test would be administered to both groups. If the experimental group scored significantly lower on the test than the control group, one could safely infer that their impaired performance was the direct result of increased anxiety. It should be apparent that the experiment is the most powerful research design for testing theories about causal relationships.

In doing his research for the master's or doctoral degree, the student will probably use one of these three research designs—causal-comparison, correlation, or experiment. Therefore, in this and the next four chapters we will discuss at length how to use each design properly. Analysis of the data is also part of one's research design; therefore we will discuss the statistical techniques most commonly used with each research design.

We may distinguish between two main types of statistical techniques. As the name implies, "descriptive statistics" (also called "summary" statistics) are used to "describe" the data we have collected on our research sample. The mean, median, and standard deviation are the main descriptive statistics; they are used to indicate the average score and the range of scores for the group. Inferential statistics, the second type of statistical technique, are used to make inferences from sample statistics to the population parameters.[1] Inferential statistics are extremely important in educational research, since we rarely study a whole population, but rather a sample or samples randomly drawn from the population. In this chapter we shall discuss the rationale of inferential statistics and how they can be used to answer questions such as, "If I find a difference of 5 I.Q. points between the mean of sample A and the mean of sample B, how likely is it that I would find the same difference if the entire populations A and B (from which the two samples were randomly drawn) were studied?" In later chapters we shall discuss a variety of inferential statistics and how they are used to analyze one's research data.

WHAT YOU SHOULD KNOW ABOUT STATISTICS

To effectively analyze research results, the student needs to have four kinds of information about statistical tools. This information can be summarized in the following four questions: (1) What statistical tools are available? (2) Under what conditions is each tool used? (3) What do the statistical results mean? and (4) How are the statistical calculations made? Let us take a brief look at these questions and see how they will be handled in this and the next chapters.

What statistical tools are available?

One of the most serious weaknesses of research reports written by inexperienced research workers is that they often fail to make maximum use of the data collected. It is not uncommon for the student to limit his analysis to two or three comparisons between the experimental and control groups. In many instances a more thorough analysis would produce valuable results that the student loses through his lack of ability to make use of statistical tools. Often the student compares final mean scores for his experimental and control groups and finds no significant results but overlooks the possibility that significant differences in variability, as measured by the standard deviation, may have occurred as a result of the experiment. For example, one teaching method emphasizing drill and the mastery of basic operations may result in a reduction of variability in student performance from the beginning to the end of the experiment. This reduction might occur because the teaching method, with its thorough coverage of concrete materials, is well within the grasp of the less able students in the class. These students may consequently gain more than would normally be expected. The bright students might have little opportunity in this

---

[1] Descriptive values such as the mean, median, and standard deviation are usually referred to as statistics if they are computed from the scores of a sample of subjects. The same values are referred to as parameters if they are computed from the scores of the entire population.

teaching situation to take full advantage of their superior ability and thus may gain little more than the less able students. The relatively large gain by slow students and small gain by bright students would make the group less variable. On the other hand, a teaching method that emphasized the understanding of abstract principles and attempted to cover a large content area in a short time might result in an increase in the variability between the initial and final testing. In this case the bright students would probably learn much more than they would under the first method described, while the slow students would learn very little because they could not master the complex content in the time available. If we were to conduct a learning experiment using these two teaching methods, we might find no significant difference between the mean achievement gains of groups of pupils taught by the different methods, but marked differences might occur in standard deviation. The statistical significance of these variability differences can be calculated and can provide valuable insights.

Many useful statistical tools are not covered in the elementary statistics course usually required for master's degree candidates. Therefore, in this and the next four chapters we will discuss some of these tools and how they are used in various research designs. The calculations required to apply these statistical techniques do not usually involve complex or difficult mathematics and can easily be mastered by the graduate student for the treatment of his research data. Mastering the mathematics involved is much less important than knowing what tools exist and how to apply them to research problems.

Under what conditions are statistical tools appropriate?

To develop a sound research plan, the student should select appropriate statistical tools prior to the collection of data. Different statistical tools may require that the data be collected in different forms. Also, the selection of statistical tools at an early stage in the research planning will help in determining an appropriate sample size. For example, consider the case of a research worker who plans to do a correlational study to determine whether two variables are related to each other. Since his data analysis will include the testing of correlation coefficients for their statistical significance, he would do well to consult a significance table.[2] This table shows that for a sample size of 10 a correlation of .63 is necessary to achieve statistical significance. For a sample of 20 subjects, the value is .44, whereas for 30 subjects it is .36. Suppose now that the true correlation between the two variables to be studied by the research worker is .37. If he chose to study only ten subjects or fewer, it is extremely unlikely that he would obtain a correlation of .63 (if the true population value is

[2] This is a table found in the appendix of most statistics textbooks. It contains the values of correlation coefficients and sample size required for different levels of significance.

.37) necessary for statistical significance. Thus he would conclude that there is no evidence for a linear relationship between the two variables when, in fact, there is a true relationship.[3] Obviously the research worker needs to select the appropriate statistical tools and appropriate sample size before collecting data. Once data have been collected, it is poor research design and quite impractical to increase the sample size in order to lower the value of the correlation needed for statistical significance.

On many occasions inexperienced research workers use a tool that is completely inappropriate for the data they are attempting to analyze. A common mistake, for example, is to use the incorrect formula to calculate the standard error of the difference between means. If the final mean scores of the experimental and control groups are correlated, as they usually are if matched groups have been used, a special form of this formula must be used. On many occasions, however, the simpler formula for uncorrelated means is used instead. This error lowers the apparent significance of the results and often leads the student to report his results as not significant, when he would have found them to be significant if the correct formula had been used.

Another common error is to use a statistical tool when the data to be analyzed do not meet the conditions required for the tool in question. For example, most tests of statistical significance are based on the assumption that the characteristics we have measured are normally distributed in the population. This assumption of normality is justified for most of the variables we use in education, but when not justified, nonparametric or "distribution free" methods should be used because these techniques make no assumptions about the shape of the distribution. We will discuss these topics further in later chapters.

What do the statistical results mean?

After he has decided what statistical tools are most appropriate for the analysis of his research data and has applied these tools, the student must interpret the research results. On many occasions research results are misinterpreted, even though the student has selected the correct statistical tool and has made his calculations without error. For example, a common misinterpretation is to confuse statistical significance with practical significance. A survey reported by Dunnette provides a good illustration of this point.[4] Dunnette studied a random sample of the statistical analyses reported in four psychological journals having high publication standards. The results of t tests and analyses of variance were converted to correlation

---

[3] Generally it is desirable to use a sample of 30 to 40 subjects in a correlational study in order not to overlook small but statistically significant findings.

[4] Marvin D. Dunnette, "Fads, Fashions, and Folderol in Psychology," *American Psychologist*, 21(4) (1966), 343–352.

ratios (*eta*) so that the degree of relationship between the variables measured in each study could be determined.[5] In nearly a third of the studies, Dunnette found that the correlation ratio failed to reach .30; in a sixth of the studies the correlation ratio failed to reach .25; and five percent of the studies yielded correlation ratios below .20. Although all these correlations indicated that a statistically significant relationship existed between the variables that were measured, the relationships were so small as to be of little or no value for most practical applications. The lesson to be learned from Dunnette's survey is that in interpreting your own research results and those obtained by others, you should consider not only the statistical significance but also the practical significance of findings based on the *t* test, F test, or other statistical test that was used.

How are calculations made?

This is the question that demands the majority of time in most statistics courses and is not within the scope of this book. It is concerned with the mathematical procedures involved in the use of statistical formulas. In this chapter as few references as possible will be made to statistical calculations. Most of the calculations are not difficult, and it is generally a more practical procedure for the student to direct his attention to learning what statistical tools are available, when they are used, and what the results mean after they are used. With this knowledge he can make most of the decisions he will be called on to make during his review of the research literature and the development of his own research plan. Inasmuch as most of us rapidly forget formulas and calculation techniques, it is doubtful whether much time should ever be spent on this aspect of statistics until the research worker is ready to use specific statistical tools. Then, with a reasonable foundation in elementary statistics and the help of a statistics text, he can learn how to make the calculations required for his analysis.[6]

DESCRIPTIVE STATISTICS

Measures of central tendency

Though a number of measures of central tendency can be found in most elementary statistics books, the only ones used to any extent in educational research are the mean and the median. These measures are sometimes called descriptive statistics because they give a very brief description of the sample that has been measured. For example, if one has the scores of

---

[5] *Eta* is discussed further in Chapter 13.
[6] See annotated references for textbooks recommended for their clear presentation of statistical computations and theory.

one hundred pupils on a test of algebraic ability, it is hard to get even a crude picture of the level of the group by examining these individual scores. Calculating the mean or median, however, gives a rough description of the group in terms of the average score attained. The mean is generally considered the best measure of central tendency.

Computing the mean is one of the initial steps in applying many of the more advanced statistical tools, such as standard deviation, analysis of variance, and correlation. One advantage of the mean over the median is that it is more stable. Thus, if we study several samples drawn from the same population, the mean scores are likely to be in closer agreement than the median scores. Another advantage of the mean is that it is more susceptible to mathematical manipulation.

The mean, calculated by dividing the sum of the scores by the number of scores, weights each score in direct proportion to its distance from the mean. In other words, scores that are extreme are weighted more heavily in calculating the mean than scores that are less extreme. The median, by comparison, is merely the middle score in the distribution and is not affected by the magnitude of scores at either end of the distribution. When a distribution of scores is symmetrical, the mean and the median are located at the same point. When the distribution has more extreme scores at one end than the other, that is, when it is skewed, the mean will always be in the direction of the greater number of extreme scores (see Fig. 12). Let us say that you have collected data on the reading rates of 1,000 college students. Such a distribution will generally be skewed with most students reading at rates between 200 and 500 words a minute. Relatively few will be found reading at less than 200 words a minute, but a few will read at much higher rates, ranging to over 2,000 words a minute. If the purpose of your study is to reflect the amount of reading one might expect from the average college student, the median would probably be a more accurate measure than the mean. In this case the mean score would be raised several words a minute merely because of the presence of the few extreme cases of students reading over 1,000 words a minute.

Because of the difference between the median and mean in skewed distributions, the two measures can have considerably different implications. Have you ever noticed when reading about labor disputes in the newspaper that the average wage reported by the labor union is usually somewhat different from the average wage reported by management? This difference is sometimes due to the fact that the management representatives are more likely to calculate the *mean* wage of all persons employed by the company, including high-level executive personnel, thus giving a skewed distribution. The union, on the other hand, is more likely to use only union members (thus excluding highly paid executives), and then to calculate the *median*. This would usually result in a figure considerably

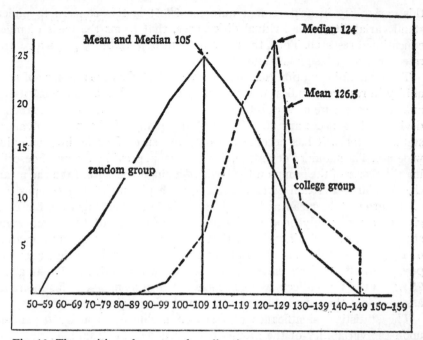

Fig. 12. The position of mean and median in symmetrical and skewed distributions. The IQ distributions of 100 randomly selected adult males and 100 graduate students.

lower than that calculated by the company. The motive of the persons calculating such figures is, of course, to support their own cause. In research, the purpose of statistics is to provide the most accurate picture of the data being studied. In most cases the median gives a more accurate description of the group when the distribution is considerably skewed.

Measures of variability

Most statistics texts describe several measures of variability, including the range, quartile deviation, average deviation, and standard deviation. Variability is usually thought of as the amount of dispersion of scores about a central value, such as the mean. Measures of variability provide information regarding the extent of individual differences on a given measure, for example, an intelligence test. If all persons had the same score on an intelligence test, this dimension would hold little interest for educational researchers. However, the fact that there is usually variability about a mean score leads researchers to ask, "Why do some subjects earn low intelligence scores, while others earn high scores? What accounts for this variability?" or "This educational program leads to increased achievement for some students but not others; what factors might account for this variability in achievement outcomes?" It is this concern to understand variability, or individual differences, that forms the basis of much educational research. Thus, the measurement of variability plays a central role in research design and statistical analysis.

The standard deviation is almost always selected as the measure of variability in research studies. It is generally considered to be the most useful and stable measure of variability, and because the calculation of standard deviation is a necessary step for applying many of the more advanced statistical tools, it has become the only measure of variability enjoying wide use. The standard deviation, like the mean, provides a way of describing the scores of the group on the basis of a single measure. Like the mean, the standard deviation gives a rather rough picture of the composition of the group. The mean and standard deviation taken together, however, give us a reasonably good description of the nature of the group being studied. For example, if we know that a group of subjects had a mean score of 10 on a test and a standard deviation of 2, we can infer that about 68 percent of the subjects earned scores between 8 and 12, and that about 95 percent of the subjects earned scores between 6 and 14. (This inference assumes that the scores approximate a normal distribution.)

The statistical significance of research findings is usually dependent upon the variability of the groups being studied. For example, the more variable the group is on the measures that are administered, the higher will be correlations between related test scores obtained from the group. It may be easier to understand why this is the case if we consider the following illustration. Research correlating success in school with IQ generally yields correlations around .55 to .70 at the elementary school level.[7] At the high school level, however, the correlations reported between intelligence and school success are usually .40 to .60, and at the college level, correlations between these variables are usually under .40.[8] This lowering of the correlation reflects the fact that as we move up into the higher school grades, students become less and less variable in terms of intelligence. Students of low intelligence start dropping out of school during the elementary years, and as the scholarship demands become greater through the high school and college years, an increasing proportion of the less intelligent students are unable to remain in school. Thus, a sample of one hundred first-grade pupils will be much more variable in intelligence than a sample of college seniors. As the students become more similar in intelligence, other variables, such as motivation and study habits, become more important in determining success in school.

[7] A. N. Frandsen and J. W. Grimes, "Age Discrimination in Intelligence Tests," *Journal of Educational Research,* 51 (1957), 229–233.

[8] H. L. Hendersen, "Predictors of Freshmen Grades in a Long Island College," *Educational and Psychological Measurement,* 17 (1957), 623–627.

Standard deviation and the normal curve

Many characteristics of human behavior, including most of those measured by educational tests, have been found to be distributed along a bell-shaped curve similar to that shown in Fig. 13. This curve is a frequency polygon—that is, the height of the curve at a given point indicates the

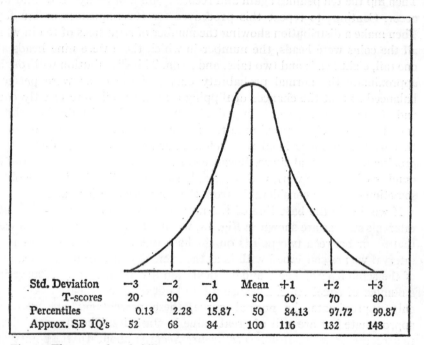

Std. Deviation	−3	−2	−1	Mean	+1	+2	+3
T-scores	20	30	40	50	60	70	80
Percentiles		0.13	2.28	15.87	50	84.13	97.72	99.87
Approx. SB IQ's	52	68	84	100	116	132	148

Fig. 13. The normal probability curve.

proportion of cases at that point. This curve shows that the majority of individuals whom we have measured are clustered close to the mean, and as we move farther and farther from the mean, we find fewer and fewer cases. Take, for example, a characteristic such as the height of adult men. The average height of American adult men is approximately 5 ft. 9 in., and the vast majority of adult men are of heights between 5 ft. 6 in. and 6 ft. As we move farther from the mean, we find fewer and fewer individuals until we reach a point in the vicinity of 7 ft. where cases are extremely rare. On the other side of the distribution, we find very few adult men of heights under 5 ft. The curve that we obtain when we plot such things as height of adult males, intelligence test scores, time required to swim 100 yards, and, for that matter, most measures of complex human characteristics and behavior, usually has a shape similar to that shown in

Fig. 14. This bell-shaped curve is known as the normal curve or normal probability curve. The exact normal curve has a mathematical formula, just as is the case for other geometrical curves, such as the parabola and the circle. This normal curve can be developed by any technique that involves chance occurrences. If you would like to develop a normal curve, flip ten pennies and record how many heads and how many tails occur. Then flip the ten pennies again and record again how many heads and tails occur. Continue to repeat this procedure for 100 sequences of ten flips. Then make a distribution showing the number of sequences of ten in which all the coins were heads, the number in which there were nine heads and one tail, eight heads and two tails, and so on. This distribution will roughly approximate the normal probability curve. If the coins were perfectly balanced so that the chances of flipping a head or tail were exactly equal and if the ten coins were flipped 10,000 times, the distribution plotted would very closely approximate the normal curve. Most of the measures that we use in educational research are such that their distributions approximate the normal curve. Because our measures are not precise and the number of cases we work with is usually small, the distributions we obtain sometimes deviate considerably from the normal curve formula.

If we divide the base line of the normal curve into a number of equal intervals such as are shown in Fig. 13, we find that the percentage of cases that occur between two points on the base line is always the same if the interval we are concerned with is at the same distance from the mean and of the same length. The standard deviation divides the normal curve into a number of equal units. Because most of our data in educational research only approximate the normal curve, these percentages are also only approximate but are still of great value in statistics. The standard deviation of the *Stanford-Binet Intelligence Scale* is about 16 IQ points (see Fig. 13).[9] Thus, a person with an IQ of 116 would be at approximately the 84th percentile. This percentile is easily arrived at if we remember that 50 percent of the cases would occur up to the mean and that the interval between the mean and a point one standard deviation above the mean (116 IQ) contains approximately 34 percent of the cases.

In analysis of research data, the standard deviation is an intermediate step that is computed as part of other statistical calculations. The standard error of measurement, product-moment correlation, and many other statistical tools are based partially on the standard deviation. The standard deviation also forms the basis for various types of standard scores, such as Z scores, T scores, and Stanine scores. Standard scores are discussed later in this chapter.

[9] Lewis N. Terman and Maud A. Merrill, *Measuring Intelligence* (Boston: Houghton Mifflin, 1937), p. 40.

Standard error of measurement and the normal curve

Every measure used by man is subject to error. The measures used in the more mature sciences, such as physics, often are accurate within very small tolerances. The atomic clock, for example, is capable of measuring time intervals to the nearest billionth part of a second.[10] You will note, however, that even though it is highly accurate, this device is only accurate to a certain fraction of a second. This indicates that errors in its measurements, though very small, do occur. The measurement devices that we use in education are subject to much larger errors than those that we find in the physical sciences.

If it were possible to administer the same test to the same student on 100 occasions without his gaining any knowledge from practice, we would still not obtain the same score for each of the 100 administrations of the test. Many of the student's scores would be considerably higher or lower than this mean. If we were to construct a frequency polygon showing the distribution of these 100 different scores, its shape would approximate the normal curve. Measurement errors are normally distributed. Relatively small errors occur with considerable frequency, but as the size of the error increases, the frequency decreases. If we were to calculate the standard deviation of the curve showing the errors in measurement based on repeating the same test 100 times, this standard deviation would give us an estimate of how frequently an error of a given magnitude might be expected to occur in using this particular test. This standard deviation of the error curve is called the "standard error of measurement." Fortunately, we need not employ the procedure described previously in order to obtain the standard error of measurement. A simple formula for estimating standard error of measurement may be found in most textbooks in elementary statistics.

Many published tests in education report the standard error of measurement. This information can be of value in interpreting test scores. For example, the standard error of measurement on the *Stanford-Binet Intelligence Scale* is reported by Terman to be 4.5 IQ points for persons whose scores range between 90 and 109 IQ.[11] The standard error, being the standard deviation of the error curve, includes the same percent of cases between standard deviation intervals as any other normal curve (see Fig. 13). Thus, if a pupil receives a score of 100 on the *Stanford-Binet Intelligence Scale,* we can estimate that there are about two chances out of three ($\pm$ 1 SD = 68 percent) that his true score will be 100 + 4.5 or will be be

[10] Leonard A. Stevens, "They're Slicing the Second into Billionths," *Think,* 26(8) (1960), 12–16.

[11] Terman and Merrill, *op. cit.,* p. 46.

tween 95.5 and 104.5. Similarly there are about 95 chances out of 100 that his true score will be within two standard errors of his obtained score of 100. Two standard errors would equal 9 IQ points, so we could assume that his true score would very likely be between 91 and 109 IQ (100 ± 9).

Standard error of measurement helps us to understand that the scores we obtain on educational tests are only estimates and can be considerably different from the individual's "true score." With this in mind we can avoid the blind faith in test scores that many teachers seem to have. We can see, for example, that there may be no real intelligence difference between two pupils who receive IQ scores of 97 and 102. Standard error of measurement can also be regarded as an index of a test's reliability. In fact, the standard error of measurement can be determined directly from the reliability coefficient of a test and the standard deviation of the test scores. However, the standard error of measurement cannot be used to compare the reliability of different tests, although the reliability coefficient can be used for this purpose.

Standard error of the mean and other statistics

In addition to the standard error of measurement, a measure of standard error can be calculated for statistics such as the mean, standard deviation, and the correlation coefficient. As is the case with individual scores, these statistics are subject to error, and the errors follow the distribution of the normal curve. For example, suppose that we randomly selected 100 individuals from a large population, such as American sixth-grade children, administered a test to those 100 children, and calculated their mean score. If we repeated this procedure 100 times, each time selecting a new random sample of 100 cases from the defined population, we would find that the 100 means we had calculated would not all be the same. If we calculated the average of these, we would find that most of the means clustered close to this average, but an occasional mean would differ considerably from the average. That is, an occasional group of 100 randomly selected children would score considerably higher or considerably lower on the test than most of the other groups. If we were to plot these 100 group averages on a frequency polygon, we would obtain a figure that approximated in shape the normal probability curve. The standard deviation of this curve would give us the standard error of the mean. The standard error of the mean tells us the amount we might expect our group mean to fluctuate if we repeated our study with other random samples.

As we shall see in the next section, it is necessary to calculate a measure of standard error in order to determine whether two or more statistics (e.g., the mean achievement scores of samples of urban versus rural students) differ from one another or from the population parameters.

STATISTICAL INFERENCE

The null hypothesis

As we discussed previously, it is rare in educational research to study every member of a specified population, for example, all sixth-grade students in the United States. Generally measurements are made only on a sample of subjects randomly drawn from a defined population. However, the research findings based on a random sample are not of value unless they can be used to make *inferences* about the defined population. For example, suppose that we are interested in testing the hypothesis that girls have greater verbal aptitude than boys. To collect data a measure of verbal aptitude is administered to random samples of 100 sixth-grade boys and 100 sixth-grade girls drawn from a specified population.

The first step in the statistical analysis is to calculate descriptive statistics. Means (M) and standard deviations (SD) would be calculated for the boys and girls separately. Suppose that we obtain the following results:

	N	M	SD
Boys	100	80	4
Girls	100	85	5

The mean verbal aptitude score for sixth-grade girls is five points higher than the mean score for sixth-grade boys. Thus we might conclude that girls at this grade level have greater verbal aptitude than boys. However, at this point the researcher must ask himself the following questions: "Is this a chance finding? Is it probable that if I studied a new random sample of sixth-grade boys and girls, no differences in verbal aptitude scores would be found? If I inferred that this is a 'true' difference between the entire population of sixth-grade boys and girls, how likely would it be that my inference is false?"

Statisticians have evolved a theory of statistical inference and a set of procedures based on this theory that enables the researcher to answer these questions. The initial step in statistical inference is to establish a null hypothesis. The null hypothesis states that *no* difference will be found between the descriptive statistics compared in one's research study.[12] In this example the null hypothesis would be that the population of sixth-grade girls does not have a higher or lower mean verbal aptitude score than the population of sixth-grade boys. After stating the null hypothesis, the researcher carries out a test of statistical significance to determine whether the null hypothesis can be rejected (i.e., whether there actually is a differ-

---

[12] In contrast, the research hypothesis usually states that there *is* a difference between the descriptive statistics being compared.

ence between the groups). As we shall find in the next section, this test enables us to make statements of this type: "If the null hypothesis is correct, we would find this large a difference between sample means only once in a hundred experiments. Since we have found this large a difference, it is quite probable that the null hypothesis is false. Therefore, we will reject the null hypothesis and conclude that the difference between sample means reflects a *true* difference between population means." Let us now determine the statistical basis that permits us to make these inferences from samples to the populations from which they were drawn.

The test of statistical significance

A test of statistical significance is made to determine whether the null hypothesis can be rejected. In the example we have been considering, suppose that the null hypothesis is correct, that is, the mean verbal aptitude scores for the populations of sixth-grade boys and sixth-grade girls are the same. However, even if there were no true difference between the two populations, we would probably find a difference if we measured a random sample from each population. In fact, if we selected many random samples of a given size, the differences between mean scores would approximate a normal curve. These difference scores would have a mean of zero and a standard deviation whose value depends on the population standard deviations. Assume that the standard deviation of difference scores in our example is 2. Thus, if we studied many samples of sixth-grade boys and girls, and each time subtracted the mean verbal aptitude score of the boys from that of the girls, about 68 percent of the time these difference scores would have a value between +2 and −2 (one SD above and below the mean). About 95 percent of the time the difference scores would have a value between +4 and −4.

In our example we have selected just one sample of sixth-grade boys and girls and have found a difference between the means of five points (85–80). How often would a difference score of this magnitude or larger be found between two populations whose means are the same? Since we do not know the population means or standard deviations that are necessary to answer this question, we must estimate them using the sample means and standard deviations. These sample statistics are combined in such a way as to yield a z value [13] (or Student's t if the samples are small). The z indicates what percentage of the time a difference score of a given magnitude between samples of a given size would occur when there is no true population difference. For our sample of boys, N = 100, M = 80, SD = 4. For our sample of girls, N = 100, M = 85, SD = 5. Thus we obtain a z of 7.81. This large a z indicates that if there were no difference between the population means for sixth-grade boys and sixth-grade girls, we would

---

[13] Also called a "critical ratio."

obtain this large or a larger difference (five points or more) less than once in every thousand samples we studied. Since this is an extremely unlikely event, the researcher would reject the null hypothesis in favor of the alternative hypothesis, that is, there is a true population difference between sixth-grade boys and sixth-grade girls.

The z distribution (or Student's t) is used to determine a significance level. If the magnitude of z is 1.96 or larger, it indicates that the difference between means (or other statistics being compared) is significant at the .05 level, that is, there is one chance in 20 (.05) that this large or a larger difference would occur if there were in fact no difference between population means.[14] Generally educational researchers will reject the null hypothesis if the z is significant at the .05 level. Occasionally the more stringent .01 level is chosen, and in exploratory studies the .10 level may be used to reject the null hypothesis. However, the student should note that when the .10 level is chosen, there is one chance in ten that the researcher will reject the null hypothesis when, in fact, it is correct. However, if the significance level of .01 is chosen, there is only one chance in a hundred that this would occur. The rejection of the null hypothesis when it is correct is called a Type I error. Obviously, if we lower the significance level required to reject the null hypothesis, we reduce the likelihood of a Type I error. At the same time, we increase the likelihood of a Type II error, that is, the acceptance of the null hypothesis ("no difference") when there is, in fact, a difference.

The test of statistical significance, then, permits the researcher to measure the differences between two samples and to make an inference about the populations from which they were drawn. Given the finding that a random sample of sixth-grade boys earns a mean verbal aptitude score of 80 and girls a mean score of 85, the researcher would ask, "How likely is this difference of five points to be true of the total populations of sixth-grade boys and girls?" The test of statistical significance enables the researcher to answer the question in the following form: "Given sample means of 80 and 85, standard deviations of 4 and 5, respectively, and 100 subjects in each group, there is less than one chance in a thousand that this large a difference would occur if the population means are equal; therefore, we conclude that the population means do indeed differ."

Interpretation of tests of significance

Statistical tests of significance are frequently misinterpreted both by inexperienced and experienced research workers.[15] Because the test of sig-

---

[14] The problem of one-tailed versus two-tailed tests of statistical significance will be discussed in the next chapter.

[15] For a review of this problem, read David Bakan, "The Test of Significance in Psychological Research," *Psychological Bulletin,* 66(6) (1966), 423–437.

nificance plays such a large role in research design, we will consider its
proper interpretation and common misinterpretations.

It is not uncommon for researchers to establish the level of significance
(usually .10, .05, or .01) after the statistical analyses have been completed.
A z or t will be computed, and the researcher will refer to a significance
table to determine how "significant" it is. However, the logic of statistical
inference dictates that the significance level be established *before* a z or
t is computed. The researcher should make a decision at the outset of his
study that if he finds a difference between his samples that exceeds a given
significance level (for example, .05), the null hypothesis will be rejected.
He cannot properly wait until after the statistical analysis to reject the
null hypothesis at whatever significance level the z happens to reach.

As we have seen, the level of significance is expressed as a probability
value p. The p value has been subject to a number of misinterpretations.[16]
Some researchers believe that the p value indicates the probability that
the differences found between groups can be attributed to chance. For
example, if one found that a mean difference of five IQ points between
groups of subjects was significant at the .01 level, one might erroneously
conclude that there is one chance in a hundred that this is a chance difference. The proper interpretation of such a finding is that the null hypothesis
can be rejected (assuming that the .01 level of significance had been established beforehand), since the mean difference of five points exceeds the
mean difference that we would find once in a hundred samples if the population mean difference was zero. Another misinterpretation is that the
level of significance indicates how likely it is that one's research hypothesis
is correct. For example, suppose that one had hypothesized that inquiry
teaching will result in greater student achievement than expository teaching. If the difference between the mean achievement scores is found to be
significant at the .01 level, one might conclude that the probability is 99
percent $(1.00 - .99 = .01)$ that one's hypothesis is correct. However, the
level of significance only helps us to make a decision about rejecting the
null hypothesis; it has only an indirect bearing on the confirmation of
one's research hypothesis.[17] For example, one may find a significant difference between two groups but not for the reason suggested by one's hypothesis. Similarly, one may find too small a difference between groups to
reject the null hypothesis, but one's research hypothesis may still be correct; a Type II error may have occurred, or the measures used to test
the hypothesis may have been inadequate.

Still another misinterpretation of p values is to think that they indicate

[16] *Ibid.*, p. 429.

[17] As we stated previously, the research hypothesis usually states that a difference between groups will be found, whereas the null hypothesis states that no difference will be
found.

the probability of finding the same research results if the study were repeated. One might think, for example, that if a difference between the means of two groups is significant at the .05 level, a comparable difference will be found 95 times in every 100 repetitions of the study. However, even if the difference between means that we obtained in our study is a true population difference and is highly significant, we might still find considerable variations in the amount of difference from repetition to repetition of the study. In short, the level of significance cannot be used to predict the results of future studies (in which all conditions of the original study are replicated); it can only be used to make a decision about rejecting the null hypothesis.

Perhaps the most common and most serious misinterpretation of the test of significance is to confuse the level of significance (i.e., the p value) of the research results with the practical and theoretical significance of the research results. It should be realized that the level of significance is influenced to a considerable degree by the number of individuals tested in the research project. Thus, the larger the sample size, the smaller the difference needed to reach a given level of significance. For example, with a sample of 1,000 subjects, a correlation coefficient of .081 is significant at the .01 level. Thus, the researcher would reject the null hypothesis (that the correlation coefficient for the population is .00) if he had established a p of .01 as the level of significance. The relationship in this case, however, is extremely slight and would be of no practical value in working with the types of educational problems that we attempt to solve with correlational studies.[18] For example, if we studied 1,000 subjects and found a correlation of .081 between school grades and a new aptitude test, the findings would be statistically significant, but they would not merit further development of the test. Also, this level of relationship would not be of any use in helping to predict school grades from aptitude test scores.

As we have already observed, the test of significance is concerned with the inferences that we wish to make from sample statistics to population parameters. Thus, a test of significance is made when we wish to determine how probable it is that the differences we have found between our samples will also be found in the populations from which they were drawn. Therefore, to use the test of significance properly, one should use it only with samples randomly drawn from a specified population. However, researchers sometimes do not specify the population or do not use random sampling

---

[18] Actually, in a negative sense a correlation coefficient this small might have practical or theoretical significance. It would indicate to researchers that future investigation of the relationship between the two variables under study would not be warranted (thus saving research time and money). Also, if only a small relationship were found when a large one had been predicted by one's theory, the finding might have the effect of leading one to revise the theory.

techniques, and thus the sample may not be representative. Also, on occasion they use the test of significance when the entire population has been studied. For example, suppose that a researcher defined all males and all females at a particular college as two populations. Then suppose he finds, as hypothesized, that the females have higher grade-point averages than the males. In this situation it is meaningless to use a test of statistical significance. The difference between grade-point averages is a *true* difference because the entire populations have been studied rather than samples drawn from their respective populations.

The importance of replication

It should be clear to the student at this point that the test of significance is only one approach to the interpretation of research results, albeit an important one. Some educational researchers consider replication of research results to be equally important in assessing their significance. For example, Bauernfeind has stated that the principle of replication is "the cornerstone of scientific inquiry." [19] Bauernfeind also observed that although replication is a vital aspect of research design and interpretation, "The principle of replication was largely ignored in educational research until around 1950, and even today it is not viewed as a major criterion of quality research" (p. 126). The principle of replication holds that if one's research findings represent a true phenomenon (e.g., the finding that measures of aptitude predict school achievement), these findings should be obtained in each repetition of the study.

If possible the student should attempt to replicate his research project, particularly if the first data collection and analysis yield findings that show promise of making a contribution to educational research. If the researcher is able to replicate his findings, they are of much more "significance" to other educational researchers than a statistically significant but weak finding (e.g., a correlation of .20 significant at the .01 level) obtained in the original study. A replicated finding is strong evidence against the possibility that a Type I error (rejection of the null hypothesis when it is true) occurred in the original study. Replication also provides other kinds of evidence, depending upon the type of replication study that is carried out. Lykken has distinguished three types of replication:

Literal replication . . . would involve exact duplication of the first investigator's sampling procedure, experimental conditions, measuring techniques, and methods of analysis; asking the original investigator to simply run more subjects would perhaps be about as close as we could come to attaining literal replication and even this, in psychological research, might often not be close enough.

[19] Robert H. Bauernfeind, "The Need for Replication in Educational Research," *Phi Delta Kappan*, 50(2) (1968), 126–128.

In the case of *operational replication,* on the other hand, one strives to duplicate exactly just the sampling and experimental procedures given in the first author's report of his research. The purpose of operational replication is to test whether the investigator's "experimental recipe"—the conditions and procedures he considered salient enough to be listed in the "Methods" section of his report—will in other hands produce the results that he obtained.

In the quite different process of *constructive replication,* one deliberately avoids imitation of the first author's methods. To obtain an ideal constructive replication, one would provide a competent investigator with *nothing more than* a clear statement of the empirical "fact" which the first author would claim to have established . . . and then let the replicator formulate his own methods of sampling, measurement, and data analysis. [pp. 155–156] [20]

Literal replication, which the student can carry out himself, can be used to evaluate whether a Type I error might have occurred in the original study. Operational replication is particularly important for experiments in which the researcher must determine the effectiveness of a procedure to improve learning. For example, suppose a researcher trained teachers in the use of the inquiry method and found that this method led to greater student achievement than conventional teaching methods. If other researchers can then use the first researchers' training procedures and materials and find similar achievement gains, we may conclude that the inquiry method is a superior instructional strategy. However, if operational replication is not possible, then we would probably conclude that the effectiveness of the training procedure and materials is limited to the original researcher. Obviously, an educational procedure or product that holds up after an operational replication has more practical significance for the improvement of education than one that works only in the hands of the original researcher. The third type of replication, constructive replication, increases the validity of theoretical studies in education. Suppose one hypothesizes that the presence of anxiety leads to a decrement in academic performance. To test this hypothesis, it is necessary to select or construct measures of anxiety and of academic performance. The hypothesis becomes increasingly credible when it is demonstrated that the relationship between the two variables holds up after several constructive replications in which different operational measures of the same two variables are used each time. For example, if a given measure of anxiety predicts decrement in grade-point average for each year of college, decrement in performance on a particular examination, and decrement in scores on untimed and timed aptitude tests, the hypothesis is much more compelling than if anxiety predicted only one of these variables.

[20] David T. Lykken, "Statistical Significance in Psychological Research," *Psychological Bulletin,* 70(3) (1968), 151–159.

TYPES OF SCORES

Introduction

Measurements in educational research are usually expressed in one of five forms: the continuous score, the rank, the artificial dichotomy, the true dichotomy, and the category. It is important to recognize the differences between these scores, since the form in which the data are expressed usually determines one's choice of a statistical tool. For example, if he had collected continuous scores on two groups, the researcher would probably analyze group differences by calculating mean scores and by computing a z or Student's t. However, if the measurements were in the form of categories, the researcher would analyze group differences by a chi-square (χ^2) test in which relative frequencies of category occurrence are compared.

Before deciding on a method of statistical analysis, the student should determine the form of his research data. The five forms of scores are discussed in the next sections.

The continuous score

The continuous score is the type of score that we obtain from intelligence tests, achievement tests, and most other standardized tests employed in educational research. When we say a variable is in continuous form, it means that scores on the variable could theoretically occur at any point along a continuum. For example, in the measurement of IQ, it is possible theoretically for a person to obtain a score at any IQ point within the broad range of IQ's possessed by human beings. This not only means it is possible for a person to obtain a score of 101 while another person obtains a score of 102, it also means that theoretically it would be possible to find a person who would perform slightly better than a person at 101 and slightly lower than a person at 102 IQ, thus earning a score between the two. In practice, scores on continuous variables are usually limited to whole numbers, but the continuous variable, in theory, must be such that it would be possible to construct tests that would measure at any fractional point along the continuum.

Besides raw scores in continuous form, percentiles and standard scores (which are derived from raw scores) are the two main types of continuous scores. Percentiles are obtained by computing the percentage of persons whose score falls below a given raw score. For example, if 50 percent of the sample obtain a raw score of 16 or below, then anyone obtaining a raw score of 16 would be at the fiftieth percentile. Manuals for published tests sometimes contain percentile equivalents for raw scores based on the standardization sample.

Although they have the advantage of being easily computed and interpreted, percentile scores are not commonly used in statistical analysis because of the inequality of units. For example, if he refers to the normal curve on page 281 (see section "Standard Deviation and the Normal Curve"), the student will find that there is the same range of scores from the fifteenth percentile (actually the 15.87th percentile) to the fiftieth percentile as there is from the second precentile to the fifteenth percentile.[21] Thus, if the mean of a test is 50 and its standard deviation is 10, a person with a score of 50 and a person with a score of 40 would be about 35 percentiles different from each other. However, two other persons with the same raw score difference of 10, but having raw scores of 40 and 30, would only be about 13 percentiles different from each other.

Because of the inequality of percentile units when applied to most variables in education, standard scores are most frequently used in statistical analysis. We have already discussed one type of standard score, the Z score. A Z score is obtained by subtracting from a person's raw score the mean score of the total group $(x-\bar{x})$ and then dividing the result by the standard deviation of the group. For any distribution of raw scores, Z scores have a mean of zero and a standard deviation of 1.00. Also, Z scores are continuous and have equality of units. Thus, a person's relative standing on two or more tests can be compared by converting the raw scores to Z scores. Since Z scores can yield negative numbers (e.g., a person who is one standard deviation below the group mean would earn a Z score of -1.00), researchers sometimes convert raw scores to standard scores yielding only positive numbers. For example, T scores have a mean of 50 and a standard deviation of 10. The Stanine scale, developed by the United States Air Force, has a mean of 5 and standard deviation of 2. The 1960 version of the Stanford-Binet Scales yields standard scores having a mean of 100 and a standard deviation of 16.

The rank score

In some types of educational research, it is easier to rank individuals than to assign quantitative scores to them. For example, ranking procedures are used very commonly in the evaluation of teachers. A researcher may ask principals or teacher supervisors to rank a given group of teachers in terms of their effectiveness. The rank scores may then be used to form subgroups of effective and ineffective teachers, or the scores may be correlated with another variable thought to be related to teacher effectiveness. Some forms of educational data are available only as ranks, such as the student's high school graduation rank, which is often used in educational studies. The ranks used in education are often another form of

[21] This presentation of the inequality of percentile units assumes that the raw scores are normally distributed.

continuous variable because it may be assumed that, if a greater number of persons were studied, cases would fall between the ranks already assigned. Continuous scores, such as IQ, can be converted to ranks, and this is often done in order to simplify analysis of research results.

The artificial dichotomy

Sometimes educational information that at least theoretically could be expressed in terms of continuous scores is available in two categories only. For example, a common division of a continuous variable into two categories is found in what is called the "pass-fail dichotomy." Taking any group of students who complete a given course of study, it is possible to divide these students into those who passed and those who failed. The term "dichotomy" refers to any division into two distinct groups. In the case of a pass-fail dichotomy, the criterion for dividing the individuals into two groups is artificial or arbitrary. In other words, someone must specify the point we will use to divide passing from failing pupils. In some schools, this point is 70 percent, in others 60 percent, and in others no specific criterion such as a percentage point is employed. The division of individuals into two categories on the basis of performance on a continuous variable is called an "artificial dichotomy." It is easy to see that the pass-fail dichotomy is artificial because we know that if we very carefully tested the individuals who complete a given course of study, we would find that their test scores, reflecting the amount learned, would make a continuous distribution ranging from those persons who learned a great deal to those persons who learned little or nothing. The point at which we divide this continuous variable into pass-fail groups is based upon an arbitrary cutting point or criterion. If we compare the person who barely passes and the person who barely fails, we find that these individuals are very similar and do not have any characteristic except their score or grade in the course of study to indicate that one person belongs in the failing group and the other person in the passing group.

The true dichotomy

Occasionally in education we encounter groups that are different because of some distinct and recognizable trait. When individuals are divided into two groups on the basis of a true difference, the dichotomy resulting is referred to as a "true dichotomy." The true dichotomy differs from the artificial dichotomy in that it is not necessary to establish any arbitrary cutting point for dividing the cases into two groups. Members of each group have some distinct characteristic that makes it possible to differentiate them from members of the other group. Perhaps the true dichotomy most frequently used in educational research is sex. Many studies are concerned with differences between the performance of boys and girls in learning patterns, verbal fluency, personality, and other measurable characteristics. In these studies one of the variables studied is usually of a continuous nature, such as scores on a verbal fluency test. The other variable is sex, which is a true dichotomy.

Categories

Variables in education occasionally are expressed in more than two categories. (If there were only two categories, the variable would be an artificial or true dichotomy.) Student participation in high school athletics, for example, could be recorded in such categories as (1) earned letter in varsity sports, (2) participated but did not earn letter, (3) participated in intramural sports, (4) participated in physical education classes, or (5) did not participate in any athletics. Occasionally, data we wish to use in research studies are available only in categories. For example, studies in eye-hand dominance usually classify individuals in such categories as left-left, left-right, right-left, and right-right. Such data cannot usually be obtained in any of the other score forms.

MISTAKES OFTEN MADE BY GRADUATE STUDENTS

1. Student selects a statistical tool that is not appropriate or correct for the proposed analysis.
2. Collects research data before deciding on a statistical tool for analyzing them.
3. Uses only one statistical procedure when several can be applied to the data. This mistake often leads to overlooking results that could make a significant contribution to the study.
4. Uses inferential statistics even when the data fail grossly to meet the necessary assumptions.
5. Overstates the importance of small differences that are statistically significant.
6. Does not define the population to which the sample results are to be generalized.

ANNOTATED REFERENCES

1. Garrett, Henry E. *Statistics in Psychology and Education.* 5th ed. New York: David McKay, 1958. This text provides an excellent coverage of most of the statistical tools used in the behavioral sciences and is especially recommended to students whose background in mathematics is limited. Garrett employs very simple statistical terminology and provides clear and detailed explanations of every step involved in carrying out each statistical operation. These explanations are usually given in conjunction with an example, which is worked out for the student in step-by-step fashion. This book places statistics within the reach of any student who has mastered the basic operations of arithmetic.
2. Hays, William L. *Statistics for Psychologists.* New York: Holt, Rinehart and Winston, 1963. This book provides a more thorough, sophisticated treatment than Garrett's text. It is for the student who wishes a deeper understanding of

the theoretical and mathematical bases of statistics. It is a fine reference book, having a well-organized, comprehensive table of contents covering the major topics in statistics: sets, probability theory, descriptive statistics, hypothesis testing, chi-square, analysis of variance, correlation, and nonparametric statistics.

3. Meredith, William. *Basic Mathematical and Statistical Tables for Psychology and Education.* New York: McGraw-Hill, 1967. This book is a valuable reference for statistical analysis of data. It contains all the tables that are normally needed when doing *t* tests, analysis of variance, nonparametric tests, and correlation. It also contains tables needed for some of the less frequently used statistical tests.

4. Kerlinger, Fred N. *Foundations of Behavioral Research: Educational and Psychological Inquiry.* New York: Holt, Rinehart and Winston, 1966. This text will be useful to the student seeking a more extensive discussion of the topics in research design and statistical analysis covered here. The author's writing style is quite readable, and many examples are provided. Since the logic of research design and statistical analysis is fairly complicated, the student will profit by reading several sources including this one. The use of statistics in educational research is presented particularly well.

CHAPTER 12

The Causal-Comparative Method

PLANNING A CAUSAL-COMPARATIVE STUDY

Advantages and limitations

The causal-comparative method is aimed at the discovery of possible causes for a behavior pattern by comparing subjects in whom this pattern is present with similar subjects in whom it is absent.[1] In using the causal-comparative method to study juvenile delinquency, for example, Glueck and Glueck located subjects who were juvenile delinquents and compared their behavior with that of similar subjects who were not juvenile delinquents.[2] Characteristics that were present more frequently among the delinquent subjects than among the nondelinquent subjects were examined as possible causes of juvenile delinquency.

The causal-comparative method is often used instead of the experimental method to test research hypotheses about cause-and-effect relationships. The reason is that many of the relationships that we wish to study in education and the other behavioral sciences do not permit experimental manipulation. For example, suppose that one wishes to test the hypothesis that aggressiveness is a cause of juvenile delinquency. To test this hypothesis experimentally, it would be necessary to randomly select two groups of children. The environment of one of these groups would be manipulated so as to provoke aggressive behavior in them over a prolonged period of time. The environment of the other group (the control group) might be manipulated so as to minimize the occurrence of aggressive behavior. If the hypothesis is correct, a significantly greater percentage of the children in the aggression-provocation group should become juvenile delinquents than children in the control group. Of course, such an experiment could not be carried out because of ethical considerations. However, the hypothesis could be tested using a causal-comparative de-

---

[1] This method is sometimes called ex post facto research, since causes are studied after they have presumably exerted their effect on another variable.

[2] Sheldon Glueck and Eleanor Glueck, *Unraveling Juvenile Delinquency* (New York: Commonwealth Fund, 1950).

sign. A group of juvenile delinquents and a group of nondelinquent youth would be selected, and their aggressiveness measured by standardized personality tests, observational ratings, or other assessment techniques. If the hypothesis is correct, the delinquent group should earn significantly higher scores on measures of aggressiveness than the group of nondelinquents. The limitation of causal-comparative research is that one cannot infer that aggressiveness *causes* juvenile delinquency on the basis of this finding. All that can be concluded is that a *relationship* between these two variables exists.

This limitation of causal-comparative research arises out of the fact that the research worker must start with observed effects and then attempt to discover the antecedents (causes) of these effects. In this process of discovery it is often difficult to determine whether a variable found to be related to the behavior being studied has been a contributing cause or has been a result of the behavior pattern. For example, the Gluecks' study of juvenile delinquency found that delinquent boys displayed more aggression than did nondelinquent boys. We do not know the aggression patterns that were present in either group *before* any of the boys became delinquent. Thus, in attempting to interpret the findings we are faced with the questions: Do boys who are more aggressive more often become delinquents? Do boys become more aggressive in the process of becoming delinquent? Or does some third factor such as social frustration cause both the aggression and the delinquency? A similar dilemma has occurred in causal-comparative studies aimed at identifying possible effects of acceleration or grade skipping. These studies usually compare pupils who have been accelerated two or more years with pupils matched for intelligence who have not been accelerated. The results usually show higher achievement for the pupils who have been accelerated, but the question arises: Did the accelerated students achieve more because they were accelerated? Were they accelerated because they had developed patterns of high achievement before they were accelerated? Or does some third factor, such as high parental intelligence, cause both a pattern of high achievement and school acceleration (thus leading to a relationship between these latter two variables, even though they are not causally related)? Selecting the correct answer to such questions on the basis of causal-comparative data is either very difficult or impossible.

However, the causal-comparative method can be used to identify possible causes and thus give direction to later experimental studies that are more likely to produce clear-cut results. As an illustration, suppose that one were interested in developing instructional techniques to increase the achievement of students in remedial reading classes. If he decided to use the experimental method, the research worker could only test the effectiveness of one or two instructional techniques at a time. It might be necessary to conduct a sizable number of experiments, requiring a large commitment of time and money, before one or two effective techniques were found. For such a research problem, the causal-comparative method might yield more results in less time. The researcher would first collect two samples from remedial reading classes—one sample of classes that has increased reading achievement and one sample of unsuccessful reading classes. Then these two samples of classes would be compared on a relatively large number of instructional variables. Hopefully, the researcher would discover several techniques that differentiated the two types of classes. For example, it might be found that teachers with high-achieving remedial reading classes had used individualized instruction, but teachers in the less successful classes had not made any efforts in this direction. The next step would be to conduct an experiment to determine whether individualized instruction, when introduced into a random sample of remedial reading classes not already using this technique, increases the reading achievement of students. If the experiment were successful, then we could be fairly certain that there is a causal relationship between individualized instruction and student achievement in remedial reading classes.

Although mainly used to search for possible causes, the causal-comparative method can also be used for descriptive purposes. Studies such as those comparing normal with handicapped groups are not aimed primarily at investigating causes, but rather at obtaining a better understanding of the relative characteristics of the groups compared. A study by Howe, for example, compares the motor skills of mentally retarded and normal children.[3] This study has implications largely in terms of developing and adapting physical education to the mentally retarded child, and is concerned more with the effects of retardation than with its causes.

Causal-comparative studies bridge the gap between descriptive research studies and experimental studies. In its simplest form, the causal-comparative design involves identifying subjects with some particular characteristic and studying them in comparison with a normal or control group. A project, for example, that identified a group of "under-achievers" in high school and studied their characteristics would be a causal-comparative design as test scores or other data collected would be compared with norms or other estimates of "normal" behavior. Such an approach, however, is much less rigorous because of the absence of a specific comparison group and is essentially similar to the descriptive study. On the other hand, the selection of a closely comparable control group in causal-comparative research can produce results that approach the precision of a well-designed experiment.

[3] C. E. Howe, "A Comparison of Motor Skills of Mentally Retarded and Normal Children," *Exceptional Children*, 25 (1959), 352–354.

Selecting a defined group

After the research problem or hypothesis has been stated, the next step in a causal-comparative study is to define the group that possesses the characteristic we wish to study. The nature of the group selected will not only determine the meaning and applicability of the results but may also determine whether meaningful results are possible. Under-achievers, for example, might be defined conceptually as pupils whose achievement is less than would be expected from their measured aptitude. Our operational definition, however, must be much more precise. It must specify the measure of achievement to be used, the measure of aptitude to be used, and the degree of difference between them that is to be considered indicative of under-achievement. One such definition might be: an under-achiever is any pupil whose T score on the total STEP Achievement Battery is five or more points lower than his T score on the *California Test of Mental Maturity*.[4] Obviously, a study using the aforementioned definition of an under-achiever will yield different results from one defining the under-achiever as any pupil whose grade placement score on an achievement test is more than one year below his current grade placement. This latter definition, which is sometimes used, ignores the aptitude factor and will result in a sample that includes few pupils of high aptitude even if they are working well below their potential. Thus, studies that appear at first glance to be very similar may really be different because of differences in defining the samples.

Another problem that must be considered before selecting an under-achiever sample is whether under-achievers obtained by applying our operational definition are likely to be reasonably homogeneous in terms of factors causing under-achievement. Can we identify types of under-achievers that are under-achieving for different reasons, or are the same causes likely to be operating for all under-achievers? This is an important question for the researcher to ask. Suppose that the researcher's hypothesis is that a basic cause of high school under-achievement is poor personal adjustment. Further suppose that, in actuality, under-achievement in English is due to difficulties in personal adjustment, but that under-achievement in mathematics is totally unrelated to this factor. If he fails to discriminate between English and mathematics under-achievers in selecting his sample, the researcher will seriously weaken his chances of finding any support for his hypothesis. Having treated all under-achievers as a homogeneous group, the researcher will probably find no difference between them and a comparison group (e.g., a normally achieving or over-achieving group) on a measure of personal adjustment. However, had he

---

[4] T scores are specified so that direct score comparisons may be made. See Chapter 11 for a discussion of T scores.

tested his hypothesis using only under-achievers in English, the researcher would probably have found significant differences between English under-achievers and an appropriate comparison group on a measure of personal adjustment. Even in this instance it may be necessary to further define one's group. For example, it may be that there are sex differences in the factors leading to under-achievement in English. Thus we might find that problems in personal adjustment are a factor in under-achievement for females but not for males. If this were the case, further data analysis would reveal pronounced differences between female under-achievers in English and an appropriate comparison group of females. However, no differences would be found for male under-achievers in English.

It should be evident from the preceding discussion that the success of a causal-comparative study depends on the investigator's skill in selecting groups that are homogeneous with respect to certain critical variables.

After a group has been selected that possesses the characteristic one wishes to study, it is essential to ask the question: Is this a homogeneous group or can further subgroups be defined? A few examples of subgrouping follow:

Initial Defined Group	Further Subgrouping
1. first-grade teachers	1. male versus female teachers
2. juvenile delinquents	2. delinquents who commit crimes against property versus delinquents who commit crimes against persons
3. mathematics instructors	3. instructors who have had training in new math versus those who have not
4. school administrators	4. school superintendents versus assistant school superintendents

Sometimes it is necessary to consider several factors simultaneously in order to arrive at homogeneous groups. For example, one may wish to study differences between college-bound and noncollege-bound students. One may find it first necessary to distinguish between college-bound students planning to attend public colleges and those planning to attend private colleges. Then these students could be differentiated further in terms of sex and social class. In analyzing the data, we would consider each subgroup separately. We might find, for example, that lower-class male students planning to attend a public college differ from an appropriate comparison group, that is, lower-class male students planning to attend a private college, whereas none of the other subgroups differ from their comparison groups on the factors measured by the researcher.

Often one's review of the literature will provide ideas about the types of subgroups that need to be formed if one is to find significant differences. For example, if previous research showed a different pattern of factors leading to under-achievement in male and female students, you should be sure to study male and female students separately if you are planning to do research in this area. If you are studying a characteristic that has not been researched previously, common sense and psychological reasoning can be used to form homogeneous subgroups. In studying teachers, for example, it would seem reasonable to consider forming subgroups on the basis of age, sex, grade, and subject matter taught.

Selecting comparison groups

Once he has selected a homogeneous group having the characteristic he wishes to study, the research worker must next select a group not having this characteristic in order to permit comparisons. The population from which the control sample is to be taken is usually defined so as to be similar except for the variable being studied. This control group may either be selected at random from the defined population, or control subjects may be matched with experimental group subjects on the basis of one or more variables. Random selection is usually preferred. The process of matching "controls" the variables matched for by holding them constant. For example, the Gluecks matched their delinquent and nondelinquent boys for ethnic origin, IQ, and age, thus producing closely comparable groups with respect to these variables.[5] Even if ethnic origin, for example, were an important factor related to delinquency, the Gluecks' study would not show this because, by matching for this variable, the research has eliminated any chance of its emerging as a possible cause.

Occasionally it is desirable to form multiple comparison groups. For example, we have already considered a research problem in which it was necessary to define several subgroups of college-bound students. Each subgroup can be compared with a control group of noncollege-bound students randomly selected from a defined population. However, subgroups can also be contrasted with each other. Thus, we might first compare middle-class male students planning to attend a public college with a general control group of noncollege-bound students. Next we might contrast middle-class male students planning to attend a public college with a group similar in all respects but sex. Obviously many such comparisons are possible. Sometimes hypotheses are stated so that only a few comparisons are required. In an exploratory study, however, it may be desirable to compare several subgroups with one another in various combinations.

Data collection

Since causal-comparative research usually seeks past causes for present conditions, there is generally considerable emphasis upon biographical

[5] Glueck, *Juvenile Delinquency*, op. cit.

data. Knowledge of a pupil's family relationships, school behavior, and other biographical information during the time he was developing his current behavior patterns often tells us more than test scores and other data that describe his *present* personality, attitudes, or behavior. The latter type of information is also used, however, and the degree of emphasis placed upon the two types of data is determined by the nature of the study.

It should be noted that several types of measuring instruments can be used in causal-comparative studies. Standardized tests, questionnaires, interviews, and naturalistic observations are all useful for collecting data bearing on causal factors.

STATISTICAL ANALYSIS OF CAUSAL-COMPARATIVE DATA

Introduction

A variety of statistical tools are used in causal-comparative studies. The first step in data analysis is to compute descriptive statistics for each comparison group in the study; these generally will include the group mean and standard deviation. Next, use of one or more parametric (or nonparametric) [6] statistics is made depending on whether the researcher is interested in comparing groups with respect to mean score, variance, median, rank scores, or category frequencies. The student should be familiar with the whole range of these statistical tools, presented in the next sections, so that he can choose the appropriate ones for analyzing his research data. Also, the student should note that many of the same statistical tools can be used in analyzing data from experiments.

The *t* test for differences between two means

The basic rationale for testing the significance of the difference between two sample means was worked out in the previous chapter. The student may wish to reread the sections concerned with the standard error of the mean, the null hypothesis, and the test of statistical significance. In discussing the use of these statistical procedures in causal-comparative studies, we made up the following problem: To test the hypothesis that girls have greater verbal aptitude than boys, a measure of verbal aptitude is administered to random samples of 100 sixth-grade boys and 100 sixth-grade girls. Suppose the following results are obtained:

	N	M	SD
Boys	100	80	4
Girls	100	85	5

We showed that the z distribution, which follows the normal curve distribution of differences between sample means, can be used to test the null

[6] Nonparametric statistics are described later in the chapter.

hypothesis that there is no difference between population means. It is appropriate to use the z distribution when large samples are studied ($N = 30$ or larger). However, when small samples are studied ($N = 29$ or smaller), it is necessary to use the t test instead.

The t test is probably the most commonly used statistical tool in causal-comparative studies. This is due in part to the fact that educational researchers usually work with small samples. Many research problems require a great deal of time and money, and so it is not possible to study many research subjects. For example, one may wish to compare the performance of creative and noncreative adolescents on individually administered intelligence tests. If the researcher's resources are limited, it may only be possible to work with a total sample of 20 or 30 subjects in each group. If the researcher's criterion of creativity is very restrictive (e.g., the production of work that is of high artistic or scientific merit), the sample size may be even smaller because of the difficulty in finding subjects who meet the criterion. In this situation the t test is the appropriate statistical tool to determine whether the sample means differ significantly from one another.

The t distribution is similar to the z distribution except that it takes into account the nonnormal distribution of standard errors when the sample size is small. The importance of using t instead of z when studying small samples is illustrated by Hays in his statistics textbook.[7] Suppose that a test of significance based on a sample of five subjects yields a t of 2.13. The probability of obtaining a t this large when there is no difference between population means is one in twenty ($p = .05$). However, as Hays observes, if the t is interpreted as a z value, then the probability of obtaining a z value this large when there is no difference between population means is one in a hundred ($p = .01$). Thus, if one chose .01 as the level of significance for testing the null hypothesis, he would reject the hypothesis in this example if the z distribution were used, but not if the t distribution were used. Since the t test provides a more accurate estimate of the significance level of one's findings when small samples are studied, you should use this test rather than the z distribution when your N is less than 30. Most statistics textbooks provide separate tables listing values for the z and the t distributions.

The t test makes three assumptions about the scores obtained in causal-comparative research. The first assumption is that scores form an interval or ratio scale of measurement. The second is that scores in the populations under study are normally distributed. The third is that score variances for the populations under study are equal. In the example we just considered, a t test could not be used if the population of sixth-grade boys

---

[7] William L. Hays, *Statistics* (New York: Holt, Rinehart, and Winston, 1963), p. 307.

had verbal aptitude scores that were markedly more variable than the scores of sixth-grade girls. In this case a nonparametric statistical technique (discussed later in this chapter) would be used. Generally we do not know the population distribution of scores or the population variance; instead our information about the population is based on inferences from sample statistics. It has been found empirically that even if the assumptions underlying the t test are violated, the t test will still provide in most instances an accurate estimate of the significance level for differences between sample means.[8]

Correlated and uncorrelated means

It is important for the student to realize that there are two kinds of t tests for determining the significance of differences between sample means. The researcher's choice of one of these t tests depends on whether the mean scores of the two groups are correlated or independent. Suppose that one is interested in testing the hypothesis that juvenile delinquents earn lower achievement test scores than a nondelinquent control group. One approach to testing this hypothesis is to select random samples of delinquent and nondelinquent students and to administer achievement tests to them. If this approach is used, the difference between the mean scores for the two groups can be tested by the t test for independent means. In this example the samples are independent, since there is no reason to expect that the two sets of achievement test scores are correlated with each other.

Another approach is to first select a random sample of delinquent students. One then *matches* each student with a control student who shares certain pertinent characteristics (e.g., intelligence, social class, grade level). Thus, the control group is not a random sample, but rather is a matched sample; each control student has a counterpart in the delinquent sample who has approximately the same intelligence score, social class status, and grade placement. As a result, it is likely that the achievement test scores for the two groups will be correlated (since the achievement scores should be correlated with at least one of the matching variables, e.g., intelligence). If this approach is used, the difference between the mean scores for the two groups should be tested by the t test for correlated means. The advantage of this t test is that it results in a smaller standard error than the t test for independent means. Consequently, one's chances of detecting a significant difference between mean scores for samples of a given size are increased. To think of it another way, the t test for correlated means is less likely than the t test for independent means to lead to a Type II error (accepting the null hypothesis when it is false).

[8] For an extended discussion of this problem, see C. A. Boneau, "The Effects of Violations of Assumptions Underlying the t Test," *Psychological Bulletin.* 57 (1960), 49 61.

One-tailed versus two-tailed tests of significance

The ends of a normal curve where it approaches the base line are called the tails of the distribution. In effect, when we compare two means to determine whether they are significantly different, we are checking the degree of overlap between the tails of the standard error curves of these two means. In Fig. 14 (a), for example, Mean A is significantly higher

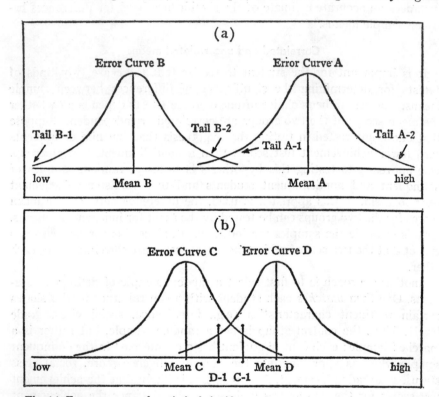

Fig. 14. Error curves and statistical significance.

than Mean B because there is almost no overlap between the two error curves. In Fig. 14 (b), however, there is some overlap. If the experiment were repeated, there is a good chance that Mean C would be higher than Mean D in some repetitions. For example, on repetition of the experiment, Mean C may move to C-1 and Mean D to D-1, thus reversing the relationship between C and D. This is the situation that exists when two means are not significantly different.

In most educational research, such as a study comparing two teaching methods, we may expect Method B to produce greater achievement gains than Method A, but we must not ignore the possibility that the reverse will be true. In Fig. 14 (a) we are comparing the overlap between Tail B-2 of Error Curve B and Tail A-1 of Error Curve A to determine if the means are significantly different. If Mean A had been higher, however, we would compare the overlap between Tail B-1 and Tail A-2. Under these conditions, a "two-tailed" test of significance is used in which both tails of the error curve are considered. In a few studies, however, we can be almost positive that any change to take place will be in the hypothesized direction. For example, suppose we did a study of the effect upon school achievement of administering vitamins and dietary supplements to undernourished school children. In such a study, we would randomly divide a sample of undernourished children into two groups, give one group dietary supplements and the other group placebos. In this study it seems extremely unlikely that these nutritional aids would lead to *lower* achievement as compared to a control group. In such cases a one-tailed test can be used that, in effect, makes the assumption that if any difference is found it will be in favor of the children who received the dietary supplement rather than the children who received a nutritionally worthless placebo. In this case we need consider only one tail of the error curve because the difference can occur in only one direction. The main advantage of the one-tailed test of significance is that a smaller critical ratio (*t* test) is needed to be statistically significant. Inexperienced researchers often use the one-tailed test under circumstances where it is not justified in order to make their results appear more significant. The student should avoid the one-tailed test unless he is quite certain that its use is justified in his study.

The *t* test for a single mean

In most causal-comparative research, one is interested in comparing the mean scores of two samples to determine whether they are significantly different from each other.

The *t* tests for independent means or for correlated means are used for this purpose. However, occasionally the researcher is interested in whether a sample mean differs significantly from a specified population mean. For example, suppose the researcher investigates a sample of twelfth-grade students who share a particular characteristic (such as being college bound). Further suppose that the researcher administers the Wechsler Adult Intelligence Scale [9] to each student and finds the mean IQ score to be 109. As part of the data analysis, the researcher may wish to determine whether this sample mean deviates significantly from the population mean. Assuming a population mean of 100, we may use the *t* test for a single mean to determine whether this difference (109–100) is statistically significant.

Generally population means are not known in educational research.

[9] See Chapter 7.

However, some standardized tests provide norms based on very large samples; the means of these samples are generally close approximations of their respective population means. Also, population norms are available for some physical measures (e.g., height, weight, strength) that may be of interest to the educational researcher.

Comparison of more than two means (analysis of variance)

As we have already discussed, causal-comparative research may occasionally involve the study of more than two groups. For example, a researcher may wish to determine whether a relationship exists between school achievement and personality factors. A 2-group design might involve a comparison of high achieving students with low achieving students (with achievement level defined, say, as scores in the top 30 percent and bottom 30 percent on a standard achievement test). Another design might involve three or more comparison groups—for example, high achievers (top 20 percent), middle achievers (middle 20 percent), and low achievers (bottom 20 percent). These three groups could be compared to determine whether their mean scores on a particular personality factor differ.

One approach to the statistical analysis of these data would be to perform several t tests to compare (1) high achievers with middle achievers, (2) high achievers with low achievers, and (3) middle achievers with low achievers. Of course, the total number of required t tests increases considerably with each additional comparison group. Rather than using this approach, most researchers start by doing a simple analysis of variance. The purpose of analysis of variance in this situation is to determine whether any of the groups differs significantly from any other.[10] If the analysis of variance yields a nonsignificant F ratio (the ratio of between-groups variance to within-groups variance), the computation of appropriate t tests is unnecessary, since none will reach a level of statistical significance. If the F ratio is statistically significant, the researcher can do t tests to determine which group means differ significantly from one another. However, the student should note that a special form of the t test is used following analysis of variance. The standard error of this t test is derived from the variances of all the groups rather than from the variances of the two specific groups being compared. Also, if the student has not planned to make specific comparisons *before* undertaking the research, then a t test for multiple comparisons should be used.[11] These special

---

[10] In more technical terms, analysis of variance is used to determine whether the between-groups variance is significantly greater than the within-groups variance.

[11] Of the several available t tests for multiple comparisons, such as Newman-Keuls', Tukey's, and Scheffe's, Duncan's multiple range test is probably most frequently used. Computational procedures for these statistical tests can be found in B. J. Winer, *Statistical Principles in Experimental Design* (New York: McGraw-Hill, 1962).

t tests take into account the probability that the researcher will find a significant difference between mean scores simply because many comparisons are made on the same data.

The test for differences between variances

The standard deviation and its square, the variance, are two statistics for describing the variability of scores obtained from a sample of subjects. The researcher will often want to do a statistical test to determine whether the variances for two samples differ significantly from each other, just as he might want to determine whether the mean scores differ significantly. There are two main reasons for doing this test. The first reason is that most of the commonly used statistical tests (including the t test for differences between means) assume the variances of the two samples to be roughly equal. If the variance of scores for two samples differs markedly, then one of the nonparametric tests, discussed later in this chapter, should be used. The second reason for testing variance homogeneity between two samples is that the researcher's hypothesis may concern the variability of sample scores. For example, the researcher might hypothesize that college graduates are more like one another in scholastic aptitude than college dropouts. The rationale might be that all college graduates are apt to be fairly intelligent but that, for various reasons, both students of high and low aptitude may leave college before graduation. To test this hypothesis in a causal-comparative study, the researcher would administer a measure of scholastic aptitude to a sample of college graduates and a sample of college dropouts. Next the researcher would do a statistical test to determine whether college graduates have less variable scores on the aptitude measure than do the college dropouts.

The statistical tool used to test for significance of differences between variances is analysis of variance (which is the same tool used to test for differences between several means). The larger the F ratio, the less likely is it that the variances of the populations from which the samples were drawn are equal. Usually if the F ratio exceeds the five percent significance level, the researcher will reject the null hypothesis (stating equality of variances) and conclude that the obtained difference between the sample variances is a true one.

The student should be aware that there are several statistical tests to compare differences between variances. If the two sets of scores are obtained from independent samples, the test for homogeneity of independent variances is done. If the two sets of scores are obtained from repeated measures on a single sample or from two matched samples, then the test for homogeneity of related variances is done. Should the student wish to determine whether the variances of more than two sets of scores differ significantly from one another, the F maximum test for homogeneity of variance can be used.[12]

Controlling for initial differences (analysis of covariance)

In doing causal-comparative studies, researchers sometimes need to determine whether a difference between two groups on a particular variable can be explained by another difference that exists between the two groups. Suppose, for example, the researcher plans to test the hypothesis that seventh-grade boys make more grammatical errors in writing class papers than seventh-grade girls. A sample of papers written by the two groups is scored for grammatical errors, and it is found by t test that the mean number of errors is significantly greater for the boys than for the girls. At this point the researcher needs to ask the question, "Can this obtained difference be explained in terms of some other variable on which the groups might differ?" In this example the researcher should consider the length of the students' papers as a possible other variable. Suppose it is found that the sample of boys wrote significantly longer papers than the sample of girls, thus increasing their opportunity to make grammatical errors. The researcher now needs to determine whether controlling for initial differences in writing productivity eliminates the obtained difference in mean number of grammatical errors. To control for initial differences, the statistical technique of analysis of covariance is used.[13] The effect of analysis of covariance is to make the two groups equal with respect to one or more control variables. If a difference is still found between the two groups, one cannot use the control variable to explain the effect of one's research variable. In our example, if he found that boys still made significantly more grammatical errors than girls after using analysis of covariance to control for initial differences in writing productivity, the researcher would conclude that the grammatical error difference cannot be attributed to the fact that boys write longer papers. Analysis of covariance is quite useful in causal-comparative studies, since one cannot always select comparison groups that are matched with respect to all relevant variables except the one that is the main concern of the researcher's investigation. Analysis of covariance provides a post-hoc method of matching groups on variables such as writing productivity, age, intelligence, education, and socioeconomic class.

---

[12] Computational procedures for these statistical tests can be found in Bruning and Kintz (see annotated references).

[13] In the next chapter we shall find that similar statistical techniques, partial and part correlations, are available to determine whether a correlation between two variables is the result of their mutual relationship to one or more other variables.

NONPARAMETRIC TESTS OF SIGNIFICANCE

Advantages and disadvantages of nonparametric tests

The statistical tests discussed up to this point are known as parametric statistics. A parameter, you will recall, is a population score, whereas a statistic is a score for a sample randomly drawn from the population. Parametric statistics make certain assumptions about population parameters. One assumption is that the scores in the population are normally distributed about the mean; another assumption is that the population variances of the comparison groups in one's study are approximately equal. When extremely large deviations from these assumptions are present in the research data, parametric statistics should not be used. Instead, one of the nonparametric statistics should be selected since, as their name implies, they do not make any assumptions about the shape or variance of population scores.

Still another assumption of parametric statistics is that the scores are derived from a measure that has equal intervals. The student will recall from our discussion in the previous chapter that most continuous scores meet this criterion. Thus, if one were doing a causal-comparative study in which two groups were being compared for differences in mean IQ score, parametric statistics could be used. However, when scores are dichotomous or in the form of categories or ranks, one of the nonparametric statistics should be used for data analysis. In the next sections we shall discuss the common types of nonparametric statistics used to analyze data in the form of ranks, frequency counts, or dichotomies.

When research data meet the assumption of being interval scores but do not meet the assumptions of normal distribution and variance homogeneity, it is still advisable to use the parametric statistics we have discussed earlier in the chapter. The main reasons for recommending the use of parametric statistics in these situations are: (1) studies have shown that moderate departure from the theoretical assumptions have very little effect upon the value of the parametric technique; [14] (2) nonparametric statistics are generally less powerful, that is, they require larger samples in order to yield the same level of significance; (3) and for many of the problems encountered in educational research, suitable nonparametric tests are either not available or are complicated and difficult for the student to obtain.

---

[14] Refer to our discussion regarding the effects of violating the assumptions underlying the t test.

The chi-square test

Chi-square (χ^2) is a nonparametric statistical test often used in causal-comparative studies, particularly when the research data are in the form of frequency counts. These frequency counts can be placed into two or more categories. For example, suppose that a researcher is interested in determining whether bright students, average students, and slow students who have been placed in "homogeneous" classroom groups on the basis of intelligence have each developed favorable or unfavorable attitudes toward ability grouping. To investigate this research problem, we might observe the *frequency* with which each of the three groups endorses categories reflecting a very favorable, favorable, indifferent, unfavorable, or very unfavorable attitude toward ability grouping. Then we would ask, "Does the

TABLE 9

DISTRIBUTIONS OF ATTITUDES TOWARD ABILITY GROUPING
OF BRIGHT, AVERAGE, AND SLOW PUPILS

| | Bright pupils | | | | |
	Very favorable	Favorable	Indifferent	Unfavorable	Very unfavorable
Observed attitude	32	39	14	12	3
Expected attitude	20	20	20	20	20
	Average pupils				
Observed attitude	19	21	30	23	7
Expected attitude	20	20	20	20	20
	Slow pupils				
Observed attitude	10	21	27	31	11
Expected attitude	20	20	20	20	20
	Contingency table				
Bright pupils	32	39	14	12	3
Average pupils	19	21	30	23	7
Slow pupils	10	21	27	31	11

frequency with which each of the five categories is endorsed by each group of students differ from the frequencies that could be expected by chance?" This question can be answered by means of a chi-square test. Table 9 presents hypothetical data regarding distributions of attitudes toward ability grouping of bright, average, and slow students. It can be seen that bright and slow students deviate considerably from the frequency distribution expected by chance; on the other hand, there appears to be a fairly close relationship between the observed and expected frequencies of average students' responses. The greater the difference between the expected and observed frequencies, the larger the chi-square value will be. A chi-square table can be consulted to determine whether a particular chi-square value has reached the level of significance decided upon by the researcher.

In the preceding research example, the distribution of students' actual responses was compared to an expected distribution of responses. The chi-square test can also be used to compare research groups directly with one another. At the bottom of Table 9 a contingency table shows the relative frequencies with which each of the student groups has endorsed each of the five attitude categories. A chi-square test can be computed from this frequency data, and the resulting chi-square value tells the researcher whether the distribution of frequencies differs significantly from group to group.

The student should be aware that there are several types of chi-square tests from which one can choose. A simple chi-square test can be done when the frequencies are in the form of a fourfold table. In the preceding example, we might have studied only bright and slow pupils, and classified their attitudes as either favorable or unfavorable. This research design would have yielded this fourfold table for chi-square analysis:

		ATTITUDES	
		Favorable	Unfavorable
STUDENTS	Bright	71	15
	Slow	31	42

When the frequency data are grouped into more than four cells (as is the case with each of the chi-square tables in Table 9), a more complex chi-square test is done. The student should also be aware that when the expected frequency in any cell is less than five, a correction needs to be applied to the regular chi-square test. (The student can apply Yates' correction, or he can do a Fisher exact test.) In the process of doing a chi-square test, the student might also compute a phi coefficient (for a fourfold table) or a contingency coefficient (for more than four cells).[15]

[15] These correlation coefficients are discussed more completely in the next chapter.

These correlation coefficients provide an estimate of the magnitude of the relationship between the variables in a chi-square table.

The chi-square test is most often used when the categories into which frequencies fall are discrete rather than continuous. For example, let us assume we want to determine whether large families contribute more or fewer than the expected proportion of children appearing before juvenile courts. The number of children is a discrete variable (because a family can have 3 or 4 children but never 3½). Appearance before juvenile court is similarly a situation that has either occurred or not occurred and is also discrete. Under conditions such as these, chi-square is often the only analysis technique available to the graduate student with a limited statistical background.

Chi-square, however, is equally useful when the traits or characteristics being considered are actually continuous variables that have been categorized. The school system, for example, may provide the researcher with categories by the placement of children into ability-grouped classrooms. In some instances the research worker has data in the form of a continuous score, but divides it into categories in order to permit the use of chi-square or because chi-square analysis seems to be most likely to yield meaningful results in terms of the hypotheses being tested. For example, in sociometric measurement the popularity score of a child is a continuous variable. In practice the child's popularity score is usually taken as the sum of favorable choices given him by other members of the class. Research workers using sociometric data, however, often categorize pupils into several groups, such as "stars," "isolates," and "neglectees," based upon the number of choices each pupil receives. The sociometric category into which the individual is classified sometimes provides a more meaningful basis for analyzing the data than his popularity score, and in this case analysis using chi-square would be appropriate.

Other nonparametric tests

Of the nonparametric tests of significance, chi-square is probably the most frequently used by educational researchers in causal-comparative studies. However, other nonparametric tests may be of service, particularly when the research data are in the form of rank-order scores or interval scores that grossly violate the parametric test assumptions of normality and homogeneity of variance.

The Mann-Whitney U test may be used to determine whether the medians of two independent samples differ significantly from each other. It is analogous to the t test for uncorrelated means, except the group medians rather than the group means are compared. The Wilcoxon signed-rank test is used to determine whether two samples differ significantly from each other when the samples are related (either through matching or because repeated measures are taken on the same sample). The Wilcoxon test is analogous to the t test for correlated means except that it makes no assumptions regarding the shape of the score distribution or homogeneity of variance between the two sets of scores. If more than two groups of subjects are to be compared, a nonparametric one-way analysis of variance (the Kruskal-Wallis test) can be used.

MISTAKES OFTEN MADE BY GRADUATE STUDENTS

1. Student assumes the results of causal-comparative research are proof of a cause-and-effect relationship.
2. Does not form homogeneous groups to be compared. After the initial group has been defined, does not form subgroups on the basis of age, sex, socioeconomic status, and so on.
3. Uses the wrong sampling distribution (should use the t test, not the z distribution) when testing the statistical significance of data obtained from small samples.
4. Does not use the correct t test when comparing independent means or correlated means.
5. Does a one-tailed test of statistical significance when a two-tailed test should be done.
6. When comparing several means, does not do an analysis of variance prior to determining which group means differ significantly from each other.
7. Does not control for initial differences between groups that might explain the differences that are found.
8. Neglects to use a nonparametric test of significance when the data grossly violate the assumptions of parametric statistical tests.

ANNOTATED REFERENCES

1. Bruning, James L., and Kintz, B. L. *Computational Handbook of Statistics.* Glenview, Ill.: Scott, Foresman, 1968. A step-by-step computational guide is given for these statistical tests frequently used in causal-comparative studies: t test for a difference between a sample mean and a population mean, t test for a difference between two independent means, t test for a difference between two correlated means; one-way analysis of variance; test for difference between variances of two independent samples, test for difference between variances of two related samples, test for differences among several independent variances; Duncan's multiple-range test; test for significance of difference between two proportions; Mann-Whitney U Test for independent samples; Wilcoxon signed-rank test for related samples; simple and complex chi-square tests, phi coefficient and contingency coefficient.

. Gaito, John. "Nonparametric Methods in Psychological Research," *Psychological Reports*, 5 (1959), 115–125. This paper is concerned with the effects of failure to meet the assumptions of the analysis of variance technique on the subsequent test of significance. The assumptions are discussed and examples are given of the results of failure to meet them. The article also discusses in considerable detail the advantages and disadvantages of nonparametric techniques as compared with parametric methods. This discussion is particularly useful to the graduate student who is faced with a research situation in which nonparametric methods appear appropriate.

3. Siegel, Sidney. *Nonparametric Statistics for the Behavioral Sciences.* New York: McGraw-Hill, 1956. Nonparametric techniques have a number of advantages that make them particularly well suited for certain data of the behavioral sciences. These techniques make no assumptions concerning the population distribution, are easy to compute, and are particularly useful with small samples such as are often used by the graduate student. This text presents nonparametric techniques in a form that can be understood by the average behavioral scientist who lacks advanced mathematical training. Siegel's emphasis is upon research application of these techniques, and he strengthens his presentation with many interesting examples taken from the behavioral sciences. Although some of the techniques presented such as chi-square and the Spearman's *Rho* are treated in most textbooks in educational and psychological statistics, many of the techniques covered in this text are not generally found in these sources.

CHAPTER 13

The Correlational Method—Part I

THE NATURE OF CORRELATION

Correlational studies include all those research projects in which an attempt is made to discover or clarify relationships through the use of correlation coefficients. Since an understanding of correlation coefficients is essential to what follows, we will briefly discuss their meaning in nonmathematical terms.

Individual differences are of prime importance to the researcher. If everyone had the same school achievement, for example, there would be little interest in studying the determinants of school achievement, in predicting school achievement, or in measuring school achievement. Yet people do *vary* with respect to this attribute, and the researcher is interested in understanding this variability. Why do scores on a particular test of achievement vary, let us say, from 40 to 100? Or to state it another way, what factors are related to these variations in scores? The correlation coefficient is a statistical tool that was designed to help researchers answer such questions.

To understand how the correlation coefficient helps us in this situation, consider an achievement test on which a group of students earned scores varying from 40 to 100. How would we know if students' scores on some other measure, such as an intelligence test or personality inventory, are related to their scores on the achievement test? Suppose that students who earned a score of 40 on the achievement test had an IQ of 85 on an intelligence test; those with an achievement score of 41 had an IQ of 86; and so on through the range of scores, so that students with achievement scores of 100 had IQ's of 145. If this were the case, we could say that there is a perfect relationship, or correlation, between the two variables. Suppose, by contrast, that for any given achievement score there are students with widely varying IQ's. Then we would conclude that there is little relationship, or correlation between the two variables. Of course, too, there could be a negative relationship between achievement test scores and IQ, if students with progressively higher achievement scores earned progressively lower IQ scores.

The purpose of the correlation coefficient is to express in mathematical terms the degree of relationship between any two variables. If the relationship is perfectly positive (for each increment in one variable there is a corresponding increment in the other), the correlation coefficient will be 1.00. If the relationship is perfectly negative, it will be −1.00. If there is no relationship, the coefficient will be zero. If two variables are somewhat related, the coefficients will have a value between zero and 1.00 (if the relationship is positive) or between zero and −1.00 (if negative). Thus, the correlation coefficient is a precise way of stating the extent to which one variable is related to another. To express the idea another way, the correlation coefficient tells us how effectively persons' scores on one variable (e.g., an intelligence test) can be used to predict their scores on another test (e.g., an achievement test).

There are several types of correlation coefficients. Different coefficients are necessary, we shall find, because certain variables (e.g., most measures of intelligence) are in the form of interval scales or ratio scales, whereas other variables are in the form of rank orderings (e.g., ranking of teachers in terms of their effectiveness) or dichotomies (e.g., true-false data). Also, the relationship between two variables is not always linear, as we shall find in our discussion of the correlation ratio later in the chapter.

The basic design in correlational research is very simple, involving nothing more than collecting two sets of scores on the same group of subjects and computing a correlation coefficient. We might, for example, select a group of college freshmen and attempt to predict their first-year grades on the basis of their overall Scholastic Aptitude Test scores. Many valuable studies in education have done little more than follow this simple design. Some studies, however, employ more sophisticated correlational techniques in order to obtain a clearer picture of the relationship being studied. As is the case with most research, however, the quality of correlational studies is determined not by the complexity of the design or the sophistication of the correlational techniques used, but by the level of planning and the depth of the theoretical constructs going into the development of the hypotheses. In the past many correlational studies in education have involved little more than locating available scores on a group of pupils, and then correlating these scores in hopes that some meaningful relationship would emerge. Such studies cannot be classified as scientific research because they have no theoretical foundation and test no hypotheses. Instead they employ the prescientific trial-and-error approach. Occasionally such an approach will produce usable bits of information, but the chances of gaining significant knowledge are far less than if the individual employs careful research methods. Such trial-and-error techniques are not acceptable for thesis research in most colleges of education today.

ADVANTAGES OF THE CORRELATIONAL APPROACH

The correlational approach is highly useful in studying problems in education or in other behavioral sciences. Its principal advantage is that it permits one to measure a great number of variables and their interrelationships simultaneously. The usual experimental technique, in contrast, permits the manipulation of only a single variable and is most applicable to the problems of the physical sciences in which simple causal relationships are found much more frequently than in the behavioral sciences. In the behavioral sciences, instead of a single direct cause, we are frequently confronted with situations in which a large number of variables are contributing causes of a particular pattern of behavior. Thus, the classical experimental method, which manipulates one variable and attempts to hold others constant, often introduces a high level of artificiality into research situations encountered in the behavioral sciences. In contrast, the correlational approach, though less rigorous, permits the studying of behavior in a far more realistic setting. The forms of physical control and manipulation often required in experimental design frequently change the behavior being studied to an extent that makes it doubtful whether the results have any implications to the field situations in which the behavior will normally occur. Partial correlation is often preferable to experimental design in situations where control is necessary, as it permits the statistical control of variables that we wish to hold constant and does so without changing the field situation.[1]

Another advantage of the correlational approach is that it provides us with information concerning the degree of relationship between the variables being studied. Inasmuch as few behavioral phenomena can be logically divided into the type of all-or-none dichotomy most appropriate for the causal-comparative approach, the ability of the correlational technique to specify the degree to which the different variables concerned are related often gives the researcher an understanding of the way in which the variables are operating that cannot be gained through other designs. For example, causal-comparative studies of teaching ability generally start with the identification of a group of good and poor teachers. Comparisons are then made between the two groups on a number of dependent variables in order to identify possible causes for differences in teaching ability. It is obvious, however, that such a dichotomy is artificial because, within both of these groups of teachers, some will certainly be better than others, and these

---

[1] Partial correlation is discussed later in this chapter.

differences in degree are ignored when using the causal-comparative approach. In reality what we have in this population is not two groups of teachers of distinctly different ability, but a single group ranging in degree of teaching ability from very poor to very good. Furthermore, certain characteristics might be more important at some levels of teaching ability than at others. A knowledge of the degree of relationships, as provided by the correlation coefficient, can therefore give us deeper insights into the relationships we are studying than are possible with research designs that do not yield some estimate of degree. In addition to the sounder insights given us by the correlation coefficient in relationship studies, this technique also permits carrying out prediction studies and making close estimates of the probable accuracy of our predictions.

CORRELATION AND CAUSALITY

Many graduate students make the error of inferring cause-and-effect from correlation coefficients. For example, a correlation found between amount of education and level of interest in cultural activities might suggest the interpretation that each year of formal schooling is likely to *cause, determine,* or *result in* greater interest in cultural activities. However, two other interpretations are equally plausible. Level of interest in cultural activities may determine how much education a student will seek for himself. Also, some third variable may determine both amount of education and level of interest in cultural activities, thus creating a relationship between these two variables. Parents' education is a possible third variable. Parents who are college graduates may encourage their children to stay in school longer *and* to develop more cultural interests than parents with less formal education. If this is the case, then the relationship between education and cultural interests is not a cause-and-effect relationship in either direction, but rather is the result of their common determination by a third variable.

Occasionally a correlational relationship between two variables will be due to an "artifact." For example, if one correlates two scales scored from the same personality inventory, a significant relationship between the scales may be found because both scales contain some of the same items, not because the personality dimensions that they measure are causally related. In such cases a statistical technique can be used to correct the correlation coefficient for covariation due to overlapping test items.[2] Also, when raters are used to collect data, relationships between variables may be found because the same rater scores both variables. This is particularly

[2] This statistical technique can be found in W. Grant Dahlstrom and G. S. Welsh, *An MMPI Handbook: A Guide to Use in Clinical Practice and Research* (Minneapolis, Minn.: University of Minnesota Press, 1960), p. 83.

likely when there is rater bias due to halo effect (see Chapter 9). One may find, for example, interrelations between several positive traits if raters form an initial positive or negative impression of a person. If the impression is positive, they will probably score the person high on all the traits; if negative, they will probably assign him low scores. Then the relationships found between traits may be due to this artifact rather than to a possible causal relationship.

In summary, correlation coefficients cannot be used to determine cause-and-effect relationships, although they may be used to explore relationships between two variables A and B. A correlation between A and B can mean that A is a determinant of B, B is a determinant of A, a third variable X determines both A and B, or the relationship between A and B is due to an artifact. Only an experiment can provide a definitive conclusion about cause-and-effect. Correlation coefficients are best used to measure the *degree* of relationship between two variables and to explore *possible* causal factors that can later be tested in an experimental design.

PLANNING A RELATIONSHIP STUDY

The basic research design

Relationship studies are concerned primarily with gaining a better understanding of complex behavior patterns (e.g., school achievement) by studying the relationships between these patterns and variables to which they are hypothesized to be related (e.g., intelligence). This research design is especially useful for exploratory studies in areas where little or no previous research is available. To understand the steps involved in conducting a relationship study, we will consider a study by Henriette Lahaderne on the correlates of children's attention in class.[3]

The problem

The first step in a relationship study is to attempt to identify some of the specific variables that appear to be important in the complex characteristic or behavior pattern to be studied. Past research and a knowledge of pertinent theory usually gives the researcher the insight he needs to identify such variables. In Lahaderne's study the behavior pattern was children's attention in class. Attention is an important behavior since, as the researcher notes, teachers often evaluate students and their teaching on the basis of the child's apparent involvement in classroom activities. Therefore, it seems worthwhile to identify the factors that are related to

[3] Henriette M. Lahaderne, "Attitudinal and Intellectual Correlates of Attention: A Study of Four Sixth-Grade Classrooms," *Journal of Educational Psychology*, 59(5) (1968), 320–324.

attention to increase our understanding of this behavior pattern. In this study it was possible to locate previous research findings that suggested that classroom attention is related to intelligence, school achievement, and attitude toward school.

Selection of subjects

The next step in a relationship study is to select subjects who can be measured on the variables with which the research is concerned. As we pointed out in our discussion of causal-comparative studies, it is very important to select a group of subjects drawn from a narrowly defined population, otherwise relationships between variables may be obscured by the presence of subjects who differ widely from each other. In Lahaderne's study only sixth-grade pupils were selected. Furthermore, correlation coefficients were computed separately for boys and girls since, as we shall find later, relationships between variables may be obscured by treating the two sexes as a homogeneous group.

Data collection

Data for relationship studies can be collected by various methods. Standardized tests, questionnaires, interviews or observational techniques can be used, the only requirement being that the data are in quantified form. In Lahaderne's study several of these techniques were used. The state of students' attention was measured by an observation schedule. Each student was observed on many occasions over a period of several months. On each occasion the observer checked the student's state of attention in one of four categories: attentive, inattentive, uncertain whether the student was attentive or inattentive, student's attention nonobservable. Attitude toward school was measured by two questionnaires, and standardized tests were used to assess students' achievement and intelligence.

Data analysis

In a simple relationship study, the data are analyzed by correlating (1) measures thought to be related to a complex behavior pattern with (2) a measure of the behavior pattern itself. In Lahaderne's study the measures of attitude toward school, school achievement, and intelligence were each correlated with the measure of attention. These correlations are presented in Tables 10, 11, and 12.[4] The findings indicate that there is a lack of relationship between students' attention and their attitude toward school. Thus, knowing whether a student has a positive or negative attitude toward school tells us very little about how attentive he is likely to be in

---

[4] Lahaderne, "Attitudinal and Intellectual Correlates of Attention," Tables 1–3. Reprinted by permission of the American Psychological Association and the author.

class (at least for the sample of students observed in this research project).
The situation is somewhat different for achievement and intelligence. The
pattern of positive and negative correlations for each variable indicates
that the brighter the student and the more he has achieved in school, the
more likely he is to be attentive in class. One should note, too, that the
relationship of attention to achievement and intelligence is generally
greater for boys than for girls.

TABLE 10

CORRELATION BETWEEN ATTENTION AND
STUDENTS' ATTITUDES

Attention	Attitudes			
	Student Opinion Poll II		Michigan Student Questionnaire	
	Boys[a]	Girls[b]	Boys[c]	Girls[d]
Attentive	.12	−.13	.02	−.09
Inattentive	−.07	.10	.00	.03
Uncertain	−.08	.10	−.02	.11
Nonobservable	−.16	.19	−.09	.22

[a] $N = 62.$
[b] $N = 63.$
[c] $N = 61.$
[d] $N = 63.$

TABLE 11

CORRELATIONS BETWEEN ATTENTION AND MEASURES OF ACHIEVEMENT

Attention	Achievement							
	Scott-Foresman		Stanford					
	Reading		Reading		Arithmetic		Language	
	Boys[a]	Girls[b]	Boys[c]	Girls[d]	Boys[e]	Girls[d]	Boys[e]	Girls[d]
Attentive	.51**	.49**	.46**	.39**	.53**	.39**	.48**	.37**
Inattentive	−.47**	−.53**	−.42**	−.44**	−.52**	−.39**	−.47**	−.38**
Uncertain	−.28*	−.33**	−.37**	−.24	−.36**	−.37**	−.34**	−.31**
Nonobservable	−.23	.07	−.08	.05	−.06	.17	−.03	.11

[a] $N = 61.$
[b] $N = 63.$
[c] $N = 56.$
[d] $N = 55.$
*$p < .05.$
**$p < .01.$

TABLE 12

CORRELATIONS BETWEEN ATTENTION AND IQ

Attention	IQ	
	Boys[a]	Girls[b]
Attentive	.48**	.44**
Inattentive	−.35**	−.46**
Uncertain	−.49**	−.33**
Nonobservable	−.20	.07

[a] $N = 61$.
[b] $N = 63$.
$* p < .05$.
$** p < .01$.

Other considerations

The basic research design in relationship studies is actually fairly simple from the viewpoint of data collection and analysis, which is probably the main reason that the correlational method is so often used by graduate students in their thesis or dissertation research. However, there are special correlational techniques and certain problems in interpreting correlational data which the student should know about if he is to use this method effectively. We shall now discuss these topics.

The shotgun approach

As we have already noted, one advantage of the correlational approach is that it permits us to study the relationship between several variables simultaneously. However, this potential advantage can become a weakness if the researcher administers a very large number of measures to a sample of subjects in the hope that some of these measures will turn out to be related to the complex behavior pattern being studied. In the shotgun approach, measures are included even though the researcher can think of no theoretical basis or common-sense rationale to justify their inclusion.

It is not uncommon in correlational studies for the researcher to correlate 20 or more variables with a criterion measure. Sometimes there are several criterion measures, and if they are each related to all the other variables the number of correlation coefficients can become quite large. Some computer programs enable the researcher to correlate up to 120 variables with one another simultaneously. A total of 7200 different correlation coefficients would result from such a data analysis. Although the shotgun approach of correlating this many variables with one another sometimes yields significant relationships, it should be avoided by the research worker. Because of the large number of measures that must be administered, this approach is costly and inefficient. Finding tests that correlate with a given criterion is not enough because these tests may correlate for entirely irrelevant reasons, and, upon repeating the study, many of these correlations will normally disappear. The only situation in which this approach may be justified is when a quick research solution is required without regard to cost in an area where previous work is insufficient to form the basis for a more scientific approach.

Limitations of the relationship study

We have already discussed the fact that correlations obtained in a relationship study cannot establish cause-and-effect relationships between the variables correlated. Also, many researchers have criticized relationship studies because they attempt to break down complex behavior into simpler components. Although this atomistic approach is appropriate for many research areas in education and psychology, there is some question as to whether a complex characteristic, such as artistic ability, can be meaningful if broken into its elements. It is not uncommon to find artists who seem to possess all or most of the specific skills that appear related to artistic ability and yet are unable to produce creative art work. On the other hand, many of the recognized masters in the graphic arts have been notably deficient in some specific skill related to their media and yet have produced masterpieces. The correlational approach has failed in the study of some complex behavior patterns, such as teaching ability, where a great many studies have been done without materially advancing our knowledge. Another problem involving the use of the correlational technique to identify variables related to complex skills or abilities is that success in many of the complex activities that interest us can probably be attained in a number of different ways. For example, a study attempting to relate success of high school principals to specific independent variables might fail because of the lack of any set of characteristics common to all successful principals. For one group of administrators, for example, forcefulness might be significantly correlated with success, while for another group of administrators who employ different administrative techniques, this characteristic might be negatively correlated with success. We know so little about certain behavior patterns, and many of these patterns are so highly complex, that only the most careful interpretation of correlational data can provide us with some understanding of the phenomenon being studied.

CORRELATIONAL STATISTICS IN RELATIONSHIP STUDIES

Two-variable correlational techniques

In this section we will discuss ten correlational techniques that can be used to analyze the degree of relationship between two variables. The form of the variables to be correlated and the nature of the relationship determine which of these ten statistics is used. Variables in relationship studies are usually expressed in one of five forms: continuous score, rank, artificial dichotomy, true dichotomy, and category.[5] Table 13 lists the ten correlational techniques and the conditions under which they can be used.

TABLE 13

APPROPRIATE CORRELATIONAL TECHNIQUES FOR DIFFERENT FORMS OF VARIABLES

Technique	Symbol	Variable 1	Variable 2	Remarks
Product-moment correlation	r	Continuous	Continuous	The most stable technique, i.e. smallest standard error
Rank-difference correlation (rho)	ρ	Ranks	Ranks	Often used instead of product-moment when number of cases is under 30
Kendall's *tau*	τ	Ranks	Ranks	Preferable to *rho* for numbers under 10
Biserial correlation	r_{bis}	Artificial dichotomy	Continuous	Sometimes exceeds 1—has a larger standard error than r—commonly used in item analysis
Widespread biserial correlation	r_{wbis}	Widespread artificial dichotomy	Continuous	Used when you are especially interested in persons at the extremes on the dichotomized variable
Point-biserial correlation	r_{pbis}	True dichotomy	Continuous	Yields a lower correlation than r_{bis}
Tetrachoric correlation	r^t	Artificial dichotomy	Artificial dichotomy	Used when both variables can be split at critical points
Phi coefficient	ϕ	True dichotomy	True dichotomy	Used in calculating inter-item correlations
Contingency coefficient	C	2 or more categories	2 or more categories	Comparable to r_t under certain conditions—closely related to chi-square
Correlation ratio	η	Continuous	Continuous	Used to detect nonlinear relationships

Product-moment correlation, r

The product-moment correlation r is used when both variables that we wish to correlate are expressed as continuous scores. For example, if we

[5] These five types of scores are described in Chapter 11.

administer an intelligence test such as the *California Test of Mental Maturity* and an achievement test such as the *STEP Social Studies Test* to the same group of individuals, we will have two sets of continuous scores, each individual having a score on each of the two tests. Because most educational data are expressed in continuous scores, this is the most frequently used correlational technique. The product-moment correlation is subject to a smaller standard error than the other techniques we will discuss in this chapter and is generally preferred when its use is possible. It should be noted that continuous scores can be converted to ranks, categories, or artificial dichotomies. Thereupon, other correlational techniques may be used. Such conversions are rarely made since *r* provides a more stable measure of relationship than the other correlational techniques.

Rank difference correlation, rho

The rank difference correlation *rho*, developed by Spearman, is a special form of the product-moment correlation. The rank difference correlation is used to correlate two variables under the special condition that the data for one or both of these variables are available only in rank form. For example, studies comparing various measures of intelligence with graduation standing in high school would generally employ the rank difference correlation because the individual's graduation standing is expressed as a rank. To use this correlational technique, however, both variables must be expressed as a rank, so in this case the scores of the subjects on the other variable (intelligence test), which is available in the form of a continuous score, would have to be converted to ranks before the correlation could be calculated. Converting continuous scores to rank scores involves the simple procedure of listing the continuous scores in order of magnitude and then assigning ranks.

As a rule one would expect the product-moment correlation to be slightly more precise than the rank difference correlation. Let us refer to the data presented in Table 14. Students A and B, who have consecutive ranks, differ 15 IQ points when their scores are expressed in intelligence quotients. On the other hand, Students N and O in the same group also have consecutive ranks but differ by only one IQ point. Thus, it may be seen that rank scores do not reflect the differences between subjects nearly as accurately as do continuous scores. Although the rank difference correlation reduces the precision of the data, this reduction is usually slight. For example, if we calculated a product-moment correlation between scores made by a group of pupils on two continuous variables, then converted these continuous scores to rank scores and calculated a rank difference correlation with the same data, we would find that the two correlations obtained would be very close to the same.

Although the rank difference correlation is valuable when data are available only in ranks, its main use is in studies where the experimenter must calculate a large number of correlations on moderately small samples of individuals. With fewer than 30 subjects, the rank difference correlation is far quicker and easier to calculate than the product-moment correlation and yields results that are very similar. When the number of cases becomes large, however, the ranking procedure becomes laborious, and *rho* cannot be calculated as quickly as *r*.

TABLE 14
CONTINUOUS SCORES AND RANKS OF 20 SUBJECTS
ON AN INTELLIGENCE TEST

Student	IQ Score	Rank
A	150	1
B	135	2
C	121	3
D	120	4
E	118	5
F	115	6
G	108	7½
H	108	7½
I	105	9
J	99	11
K	99	11
L	99	11
M	92	13
N	90	14
O	89	15½
P	89	15½
Q	86	17
R	82	18
S	80	19
T	69	20

Kendall's *tau*, τ

Tau is another form of rank correlation that has some theoretical advantage over the better known Spearman's *rho*. Like *rho*, it is used to correlate two sets of ranks. Data not in rank form can be converted to ranks if it is desired to use *tau*. Its principal advantage is that it has a more normal sampling distribution than *rho* for numbers under ten. It is somewhat more difficult to calculate than *rho* and yields lower correlation coefficients when computed from the same data. As *rho* very closely approximates the Pearson *r* calculated from the same data, it is less likely than *tau* to be misinterpreted by the educator

The biserial correlation, r_{bis}

The biserial correlation r_{bis} is used when one of the variables we wish to correlate is in the form of continuous scores and the other variable is in the form of an artificial dichotomy. For example, if we wish to determine the relationship between success and failure in algebra and scores on an algebra aptitude test, we would use the biserial correlation. In this case the aptitude test yields continuous scores, while the record of each subject as having passed or failed algebra takes the form of an artificial dichotomy. Unlike the rank-difference correlation, the biserial correlation is not a form of the product-moment correlation. The results of the two techniques are roughly comparable, but as a rule, the correlations obtained using the biserial technique are somewhat higher than those obtained for comparable data using the product-moment technique.

Although the theoretical limits of any correlation are $+1$ to -1, it is mathematically possible to obtain biserial correlations greater than one if the variables are not normally distributed. This fact should be kept in mind by the research worker when employing the biserial technique. If he is unaware of this characteristic of the biserial and obtains a correlation greater than one, he will spend a great deal of time looking for an error that does not exist. In addition to yielding higher correlations, the biserial technique is somewhat less precise than the product-moment correlation and has a larger standard error reflecting this lesser degree of accuracy. Therefore, if we wished to conduct a study relating success in school to IQ, it would be better to employ a continuous variable as a measure of school success, such as grade-point average, rather than use the pass-fail dichotomy. With this approach we would have two continuous variables and could use the product-moment correlation. In many instances, however, information cannot be obtained in continuous form for one of the variables. Under these circumstances the research worker should not hesitate to use the biserial correlation.

The point biserial correlation, r_{pbis}

The point biserial correlation r_{pbis} is used when one of the variables we wish to correlate is in the form of a continuous score and the other variable is in the form of a true dichotomy. This type of correlation is used very widely in studies relating sex to different continuous variables, such as intelligence, verbal fluency, reading ability, and achievement. In such studies sex provides the true dichotomy, and the other measure provides the continuous variable. The point biserial correlation is a form of the product-moment correlation and therefore differs from the biserial and the widespread biserial. As a rule the correlation coefficients obtained when using

the point biserial will be somewhat lower than if the same data were analyzed using the biserial correlation. This technique has several advantages over the biserial correlation. It does not yield correlations greater
than 1.0. Its standard error is easier to calculate and, being a product-
moment correlation, its statistical significance can be determined using
the significance tables for the regular Pearson correlation that are found
in most elementary statistics texts. In situations in which an artificial
dichotomy is not based upon a normally distributed continuous variable,
the point biserial is often used in preference to the biserial.

The widespread biserial correlation, r_{wbis}

There are many instances in educational research where it is desirable
to correlate scores on a continuous variable, such as intelligence, with extreme scores on some other characteristic. Let us say, for example, that
we wished to determine whether teaching success was correlated with certain personality traits. The measurement of teaching success is a difficult
task for which satisfactory measures are not easily obtained. Evaluations
of teaching ability are usually based on a composite evaluation made by
two or more raters. In making ratings raters usually find it relatively
easy to pick out the extremes, that is, the better and poorer teachers in
the group. The real difficulty in making such ratings arises when we attempt to discriminate among teachers who are within the average range
of teaching ability. For example, if five raters were used to evaluate 100
teachers, we would find that the raters would agree much more closely in
their identification of the ten best teachers and the ten poorest teachers
than they would agree on the relative ability of teachers close to the
average. This situation occurs in many studies where ratings are used as
a basis for evaluation.

In addition to those research situations where it is difficult to obtain
reliable scores except for persons at the extremes, there are also many
situations in educational research where, even though it is possible to
obtain a range of scores over the entire continuum, the nature of the
variable studied is such that a more meaningful interpretation can be
made by studying extreme cases. For example, in studying personality
traits related to over-achievement and under-achievement in school children, it is possible to classify all students as being either over-achievers,
under-achievers, or normal achievers. A correlational technique that left
out the normal achievers and used over-achievers and under-achievers as
the two ends of a dichotomy would be more useful than one that divided
all individuals into either over-achievers or under-achievers, including those
whose achievement was actually not sufficiently extreme to be considered
other than normal. When only those individuals whose scores are at the
two extreme ends on a dichotomized variable are used, we have a wide-

spread dichotomy. In research situations where we wish to correlate a continuous score with a widespread dichotomy, we use the widespread biserial correlation.[6]

The widespread biserial is closely related to the biserial correlation and always involves artificial dichotomies. In most situations in which the widespread biserial correlation is used in educational research, the cutoff points for identifying extreme cases are defined in such a way that the two extreme groups are equal in number of cases. For example, let us assume that we wish to determine whether popularity in high school is related to certain personality characteristics, such as introversion, ascendency, inferiority feelings, and cooperativeness. In this case the various personality traits probably would be measured with a personality inventory that would yield continuous scores. A study of very popular and very unpopular persons (perhaps the top and bottom 10 percent) on these personality characteristics using the widespread biserial correlation would probably give us better insights into student popularity than an approach using the product-moment correlation in which all students would be included. If we used the latter technique, the scores of the preponderance of students who are neither very popular nor very unpopular might obscure personality differences that existed between the extreme groups.

It is not necessary, however, that these extreme groups be equal in size in order to calculate a widespread biserial correlation. One way of establishing each individual's popularity would be to obtain friendship nominations for each person in the sample on a sociometric measure. This would give us a popularity score for each individual equal to the number of nominations he had received from his peers. In establishing the widespread dichotomy in the preceding example, we could either select a percentage of cases from each extreme that would give us equal groups or we could define our popular and unpopular groups in terms of specific criteria that would give us unequal groups. Some research workers define individuals who receive more than a certain number of the possible sociometric choices as "stars," while those receiving a somewhat smaller number are defined as "neglectees."[7] It would be possible to use these two defined terms as the limits for our widespread groups, and if this were done, the size of the two groups would usually be different.

The tetrachoric correlation, r_t

Occasionally we encounter a situation in educational research where both variables that we wish to correlate are in the form of artificial di-

---

[6] See Charles C. Peters and Walter R. Van Voorhis, *Statistical Procedures and Their Mathematical Bases* (New York: McGraw-Hill, 1940), pp. 384–391.

[7] See Chapter 7 for a definition of these terms.

chotomies. Under these conditions the tetrachoric correlation is used. It is assumed that, if continuous scores could be obtained, the variables underlying the dichotomies in the tetrachoric correlation would be continuous and normally distributed. The tetrachoric correlation is sometimes employed, however, even though continuous scores are available on one of the variables. For certain variables, such as aptitude test scores, the research worker may be more interested in whether or not the student reaches a critical cutoff point on the test than he is with the precise score earned by the student. If this is the case, the continuous scores are converted into an artificial dichotomy using the critical point of the test as the basis for dichotomizing the scores.

An example of this approach is found in validation studies of the *General Aptitude Test Battery* (*GATB*) currently used by the U.S. Employment Service. This test measures a number of aptitudes related to different occupations. Cutoff points have been established for each aptitude. In using the test, the principal concern is to determine whether the counselee obtains scores above or below the cutoff point in those aptitudes required for a given occupation. If above the cutoff, the person is considered to have sufficient aptitude, and if below, insufficient aptitude. Thus, the cutoff point constitutes a critical score and is the only point that is considered in advising the counselee. In validating the *GATB*, there is another critical point to consider—the point separating success or failure in the occupation in question. Thus, in validating this test, two artificial dichotomies are used, the cutoff point on the aptitude test and success or failure in the occupation. This situation makes the tetrachoric correlation ideally suited for validation of the *GATB,* and it has been used extensively for this purpose.[8]

In any situation where a critical score point exists for a continuous variable, conversion to an artificial dichotomy often provides a more useful basis for analysis than use of the variable in continuous form. This is because the dichotomy ignores all differences except the critical point of difference. If he has continuous data available on the variables he wishes to correlate, however, the research worker should not use the tetrachoric correlation unless he has a well-defined reason for doing so. The tetrachoric correlation is considerably less stable than is the Pearson product-moment correlation, having a standard error that is 50 to 100 percent larger than the standard error for the product-moment correlation under similar conditions. The standard error of the tetrachoric correlation is also quite difficult to compute, which means that considerable effort

[8] United States Department of Labor, *Guide to the Use of General Aptitude Test Battery, Section III: Development* (Washington, D.C.: Bureau of Employment Security, 1952).

is required to determine whether the correlation obtained is significant. The tetrachoric correlation is most stable when a large number of cases is used and when the dichotomies divide the sample into approximately equal groups.

The phi coefficient, ϕ

The *phi* coefficient is employed in the case where both variables that we wish to correlate are true dichotomies. Because we deal with relatively few true dichotomies in education, *phi* coefficients are used rarely in educational research. Perhaps the widest use of this technique is to determine the correlation between two items on a test during item analysis. Each subject's response to each item can be classified as either correct or incorrect, thus giving us two true dichotomies. In general, when we are dealing with fairly large numbers of cases and when we are confident that the variables underlying our dichotomies are continuous and normally distributed, the tetrachoric correlation is preferred. When the aforementioned conditions cannot be met to a reasonable degree, the *phi* coefficient is preferable. The *phi* coefficient yields a somewhat lower correlation coefficient than does the tetrachoric correlation but is somewhat more stable, and its level of significance is easily determined.

The contingency coefficient, C

The contingency coefficient C may be used when the variables to be correlated are in the form of categories. Although C can be used when the variables are divided into dichotomies, the *phi* coefficient or tetrachoric correlation is preferable under these conditions. When either or both variables are classified into more than two categories, however, ϕ or r_t cannot be applied, and C should be used to measure the degree of relationship. C is closely related to chi-square and is computed using a contingency table. If chi-square has been computed, C can easily be derived from chi-square. Conversely, chi-square can be computed from C, and this is usually done when C is computed because chi-square provides the easiest method of determining the statistical significance of C.

The contingency coefficient yields correlations closely comparable to the Pearson r if each variable is split into at least five categories and if the sample is large.

C should not be used unless the data are available only in categories or unless converting the scores to categories presents the data in a more logical or understandable form. For example, sociometric data obtained as continuous scores are often divided into categories such as stars, above average, below average, neglectees, and isolates, because these classifications have meaning among persons using sociometric techniques.

SCATTERGRAMS AND THE CORRELATION RATIO (η)

We have observed that the magnitude of the relationship between two variables can be represented by a correlation coefficient. The magnitude of the relationship can also be pictorially represented by making a scattergram. All that is required is to draw an X axis and Y axis representing the score ranges of the two variables involved. The two scores of each individual in one's sample can then be represented by a single point (i.e., coordinate) on the graph. Figure 15 illustrates some scattergrams. The

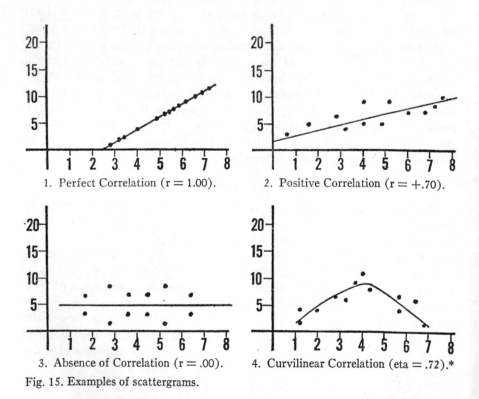

1. Perfect Correlation ($r = 1.00$).   2. Positive Correlation ($r = +.70$).

3. Absence of Correlation ($r = .00$).   4. Curvilinear Correlation (eta $= .72$).*

Fig. 15. Examples of scattergrams.

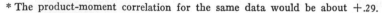

* The product-moment correlation for the same data would be about $+.29$.

first scattergram shows a perfect correlation, indicated by the straight line, since each unit of increment in the X-axis variable is accompanied by a unit of increment in the Y-axis variable. The correlation is 1.00, since if we know a person's score on one variable, we can predict perfectly his score on the other. The second scattergram indicates a fairly high degree of positive correlation between the two variables. If we know a person's score on the X-axis variable, we cannot predict his score on the Y-axis variable perfectly, but the score given by the straight line ("the line of best fit") will yield a fairly accurate prediction.[9] If the line that described the relationship between two variables slanted down from left to right (instead of down from right to left, as in the second scattergram), the correlation coefficient would be negative. The third scattergram is a graphic representation of a complete lack of relationship between two variables. Knowing a person's score on the X-axis variable is of no value at all in predicting his score on the Y-axis variable.

Using a scattergram to represent graphically the relationship between the variables involved in a correlational study is particularly helpful when the relationship is nonlinear. The correlation techniques described previously assume that the relationship is linear, in other words, that a straight line best describes the relationship between the two variables. However, sometimes the relationship is nonlinear, as in the fourth scattergram of Figure 15. In this example a curved line rather than a straight line best describes the relationship between the two variables and, therefore, leads to better predictions from scores on the X axis to scores on the Y axis.

Sometimes nonlinear relationships are "discovered" in correlational studies only after the analyses have been made, but occasionally they are hypothesized to describe the relationship between two variables. For example, some researchers have hypothesized a curvilinear relationship between anxiety and intellectual performance. The rationale for this hypothesis is that persons low in anxiety will not be motivated to do well on a performance task and thus will earn low scores. Persons with a moderate amount of anxiety will be motivated by their anxiety to perform well, and since their anxiety is moderate, it will not disrupt their performance. Therefore, they should earn higher scores than the non-anxious group. By the same reasoning, highly anxious persons should be even more motivated to perform well. If high motivation were the only factor operating, highly anxious persons should earn the highest scores, and the relationship between anxiety and performance would be linear. However, it has been hypothesized that highly anxious persons, though well-motivated, are disrupted by their anxiety and thus will earn low performance scores. Consequently, the hypothesized relationship between anxiety and performance is curvilinear with high- and low-anxiety groups hypothesized to have low performance scores, and the middle-anxiety group hypothesized to have high performance scores.

If the scatterplots for one's research data indicate that the relationship between two variables is markedly nonlinear, then one should compute

<hr>

[9] A straight line equation of the form $Y = ax + b$, is used to predict scores on the Y-axis variable from the scores on the X-axis variable.

the correlation ratio *eta*. The advantage of the correlation ratio is that it provides a more accurate index of the relationship between two variables than other correlational statistics when the relationship is markedly non-linear. Other types of correlation coefficients will generally underestimate the degree of relationship when nonlinearity exists.[10] The disadvantage of the *eta* coefficient is that it is relatively difficult to compute. However, this disadvantage has been virtually eliminated by the advent of computer programs designed to compute *eta*'s and scattergrams with little researcher effort needed.

FACTOR ANALYSIS

Factor analysis is a tool of considerable value in helping us understand the relationships found in exploratory studies. In a factor analysis, tests that might measure different aspects of the complex characteristic or behavior pattern under study are administered and a correlation matrix is computed.[11] The factor analysis is then carried out in order to determine whether "factors" can be identified that are related to the behavior being studied. The factors that emerge from a factor analysis are somewhat different from the test scores that are collected and used in the intercorrelational matrix. A factor is a mathematical construct that represents a basic behavior pattern or characteristic. The test, in contrast, may measure portions of a number of factors. Once factors have been identified, it is often possible to develop tests that are predominantly measures of a single factor and are therefore more easily understood and interpreted than tests that measure certain elements of a number of undefined or only partially defined factors. Thurstone's classic study on mental ability factors is a typical example of the use of factor analysis in improving the understanding of complex variables.[12] In this study Thurstone administered a battery of 56 tests to a sample of his students at the University of Chicago. The tests dealt with such variables as reading, word classification, word grouping, and figure classification. An intercorrelational matrix was then developed for the 56 measures, and a factor analysis was conducted. A number of major factors of mental ability emerged from this factor analysis and were identified by Thurstone as Verbal-Meaning, Number, Word Fluency,

[10] Researchers sometimes perform a special statistical test to determine whether the *eta* statistic yields a coefficient that is of significantly greater magnitude than the coefficient yielded by a linear correlation statistic.

[11] A correlation matrix is a table on which all variables to be correlated are listed on both the horizontal and vertical columns. At the point where two variables intersect, the correlation between them is given; thus the matrix shows the correlation between each test and all other tests administered in the battery.

[12] L. L. Thurstone, "Primary Mental Abilities," *Psychometric Monographs*, 1 (1938), 110–112.

Perceptual Speed, Memory, Space, Motor, Inductive and Deductive Reasoning. Based upon these results, Thurstone developed his *Tests of Primary Mental Abilities* aimed at measuring the various factors that had emerged. The factor analysis therefore led to the development of a series of valuable measures of mental ability in addition to contributing to our theoretical knowledge and understanding of mental abilities.

CORRECTIONS FOR ATTENUATION AND RESTRICTION IN RANGE

A number of corrections may be applied to correlation coefficients. The most important of these are correction for attenuation and correction for restriction in range. When we correlate two test scores, the correlation coefficient obtained is lowered to some extent by the fact that the tests or other measures we have correlated are not perfectly reliable. This lowering of the correlation coefficient due to unreliability of the measures employed is called attenuation. Correction for attenuation provides us with an estimate of what the correlation between the variables would be if the tests employed had perfect reliability. In prediction studies correction for attenuation is not usually applied because we must make predictions on the basis of the measures we have, and the reliability of these measures, even if low, must be accepted as a limitation. This correction is used, however, in exploratory studies. In these studies crude measures of low reliability are often used, and the correction for attenuation helps us determine whether usable relationships would exist if we improved the reliability of these exploratory measures. Correction for attenuation also is used to give us some inkling of the possible relationship between traits. Because correction for attenuation is only an estimate, it sometimes yields corrected correlations above one. These are spurious and are usually dropped to .99 in research reports. Finally, one should remember that a correlation corrected for attenuation tells us "what might have been" rather than "what is."

Correction for restriction in range is applied to correlation coefficients when we know that the range of scores for our sample is restricted on one of the variables being correlated. Restriction in range leads to a lowering of the correlation coefficient. For example, if we study the correlation between IQ and college achievement, it is sometimes appropriate to correct the correlation we obtain for restriction in range. A group of college students represents a restricted range of intelligence that includes very few persons with IQ's below 100. By knowing the variability of the group we are studying and the variability of an unrestricted group on the measure in question, it is possible to make a correction for restriction in range that will give us a more accurate picture of the true relationship between the variables we have correlated.

PARTIAL CORRELATION

Partial correlational techniques are sometimes employed in exploratory relationship studies. This approach is most valuable when we wish to rule out the influence of one or more variables upon the criterion behavior pattern in order to clarify the role of other variables. The usefulness of partial correlation is illustrated by Lahaderne's study of classroom attention. If he refers back to Tables 12 and 13, the reader will find that attention is related to achievement. This means that students who pay attention in class are likely to have a higher level of school achievement than their nonattentive peers. But the findings also indicate that students who pay attention in class tend to be more intelligent than their nonattentive peers. Thus, one can argue that the attentive students achieve more, not because of their attentiveness, but simply because they are more intelligent. To determine whether this argument has merit, we can use the statistical technique of partial correlation. In this instance partial correlation serves the purpose of removing the influence of intelligence both on school achievement and on attention.[13] In Lahaderne's study the partial coefficient between achievement and attention for boys, with IQ held constant, was .31 using the Scott-Foresman Reading Test as the measure of achievement, and .26 using the Stanford Arithmetic Achievement Test. Although they are statistically significant,[14] these coefficients are considerably less than the coefficients obtained when intelligence is not held constant (the coefficients are .51 and .53, respectively). Thus it appears that attentive male students have a higher level of school achievement primarily because they are more intelligent than their nonattentive peers. However, the statistically significant partial coefficients indicate that attention does play a minor role, independent of intelligence, in school achievement. The situation is somewhat different for girls. Partial coefficients between achievement and attention for girls, with intelligence held constant, indicate that attentive female students have a higher level of achievement than their nonattentive peers almost entirely because they are brighter.

In using partial coefficients, the researcher must keep in mind the difficulties associated with making causal assumptions based upon the correlational method. In the preceding example, we were assuming that it was necessary to hold intelligence constant since intelligence may *determine*

[13] If a researcher were just interested in removing the influence of intelligence from one of the factors (e.g., the influence of intelligence on attention), then the statistical method of part correlation would be used instead of partial correlation.

[14] That is, the difference between these coefficients and coefficients of .00 (which indicates there is no relationship between the two variables) is greater than would be expected by chance.

both how well the student attends in the classroom and how well he does on measures of school achievement. But one can also assume another causal chain, namely, that the capacity to attend to intellectual tasks *determines* how well the student performs both on intelligence tests and on measures of school achievement. If the latter is the case, then it is meaningless to hold intelligence constant by using partial correlation. Use of the partial correlation rests on the assumption that the factor held constant has a causal influence on the other two variables. Faced with this situation of two plausible causal linkages between attention, school achievement, and intelligence, the researcher reported the partial coefficients (in which intelligence was held constant to remove its causal influence) but also raised "the question of whether it is proper to search for the effect of attention independent of IQ. Maybe the ability to attend is an integral part of intelligent performance and contributes as much to a child's performance on an IQ test as to achievement in school" (p. 323).

DIFFERENTIAL ANALYSIS

In discussing causal-comparative studies, we stressed the importance of forming well-defined groups with which to study causal factors. The same principle also applies to relationship studies. The formation of homogeneous subgroups may uncover relationships that are obscured when correlations are computed for the total sample. The importance of this point was impressed on the authors recently in a study of the relationship between personality and teaching behavior.[15] This study was part of a larger study to investigate gains in teachers' use of classroom skills as a result of an inservice teacher education program ("the minicourse") that incorporates microteaching. Before the sample of 16 male and 32 female elementary school teachers took the minicourse, they were administered the Edwards Personal Preference Schedule and the Rokeach Dogmatism Scale. In addition each teacher taught a 20-minute lesson that was videotaped and later scored on several indices of teaching behavior. The relationship of the personality scales to two measures of teacher behavior (percentage of teacher talk in a class discussion and frequency with which a teacher asks a question and then answers it himself) is presented in Table 15. First examine the correlations for the entire sample of 48 teachers. Percentage of teacher talk is related to only three of the personality variables at the .10 level of statistical significance, and frequency

[15] Meredith D. Gall, Walter R. Borg, Philip Langer, and Marjorie L. Kelley, "The Relationship Between Personality and Teaching Behavior Before and After Inservice Microteaching Training," Paper presented at the Annual Meeting of the California Educational Research Association, Los Angeles, March 1969.

of answering one's own questions is significantly correlated with but one personality variable. The correlation coefficients are of quite low magnitude.

However, it should be noted that the total sample includes both male and female teachers. The authors thus decided that it might be worthwhile to compute the correlation coefficients separately for both groups of teachers. This data analysis is also presented in Table 15. Many sizable correlation coefficients at a high level of statistical significance are found for male teachers. By contrast, the data for female teachers yield few significant relationships between teacher behavior and personality variables. This research study illustrates the importance of forming subgroups for data analysis when exploring relationships between variables. Had the data not been analyzed separately by sex, the authors might have reached the erroneous conclusion that there is little relationship between the personality variables and teacher behaviors measured in the study.

Two other points should be made about the data analysis presented in Table 15. First, it is important to take into account the number of correlation coefficients that were computed in order to properly interpret their statistical significance. Thirty-four coefficients were computed for the total sample. By chance alone three of these coefficients should reach statistical significance at the .10 level. The results indicate that three of the coefficients were significant at the .10 level and one at the .05 level. Thus, one should be wary about concluding that there is a relationship between the personality variable of deference and percentage of teacher talk (for the total sample), since this is likely to be a chance finding. However, it is quite clear that the number of statistically significant correlation coefficients for male teachers far exceeds the number that would be expected by chance alone. For example, four of the coefficients are significant at the .01 level, whereas the operation of chance would dictate that less than one of the 34 computed coefficients should be significant at this level. The second point regards the interpretation of the difference between two correlation coefficients. For example, considering the relationship between need achievement and percentage of teacher talk, we find that the correlation coefficient for male teachers ($r = .65$) is significantly different from zero, but the corresponding coefficient for female teachers ($r = .29$) is not significantly different. But is the difference between the correlation coefficients for male and female teachers statistically significant, that is, can the difference be accounted for by the operation by chance? The student should be aware that there is a statistical test available for answering this question.[16]

In selecting subgroups for differential analysis, the investigator should

[16] See the Bruning and Kintz reference at end of chapter.

TABLE 15

RELATIONSHIPS BETWEEN PERSONALITY VARIABLES AND TEACHER BEHAVIOR

EPPS[a] Scales	Percentage Teacher Talk			Answering Own Question		
	Total Sample N = 48	Males N = 16	Females N = 32	Total Sample N = 48	Males N = 16	Females N = 32
Achievement	.40	.65***	.29	.30**	.74***	.11
Deference	—.25*	—.46*	—.14	—.05	—.18	.04
Order	.12	.14	.11	.16	.35	.07
Exhibition	.10	.36	—.02	.00	.16	—.09
Autonomy	.09	.70***	—.27	—.15	.15	—.31*
Affiliation	—.21	—.68***	.10	—.10	—.47*	.16
Intraception	—.21	—.13	—.30*	.11	.21	.15
Succorance	.01	—.08	.05	—.14	—.44*	.04
Dominance	—.10	—.33	.06	—.07	.06	—.19
Abasement	.25*	.19	.27	.08	.04	.11
Nurturance	.03	—.47*	.32*	—.08	—.56**	.18
Change	—.16	—.16	—.19	.00	.10	—.01
Endurance	—.02	.04	—.04	.13	—.10	.19
Heterosexuality	—.19	.17	—.36**	—.07	.12	—.22
Aggression	.08	.53**	—.11	.03	.13	.04
Consistency	.25*	.54**	.15	.12	.68***	—.01
Rokeach Dogmatism	—.01	.51**	—.20	.08	.12	.05

[a] Edwards Personal Preference Schedule
* p < .10
** p < .05
*** p < .01

consider not only such obvious variables as sex, grade level, and so on; he should also be alert for more subtle relationships. For example, the senior author, in a correlational study concerned with the nature of artistic ability, hypothesized that the artist is likely to be a careful observer of his environment. The Bennett-Fry Test of Mechanical Comprehension was selected to test this hypothesis. The items on this measure consist of pictures illustrating various physical principles and questions about the pictures. For example, one picture shows two wagons on a sharply slanted road. One wagon has a very high level while the other does not. The student is asked which wagon is more likely to tip over. The correlation between scores on this test and the criterion, a quality rating of each subject's artistic products at an art college, was .22. At this point the author hypothesized that a student could arrive at the correct answers on the Bennett-Fry test either by being a careful observer or by knowing the physical principles involved. He found that some of the subjects had taken physics in high school. Since training in physics would obscure the hypothesized relationship, the students who had taken physics were removed and the correlation recomputed. A correlation of .47 was obtained. This supported the hypothesis and added to our knowledge of the nature of artistic ability.

A useful strategy for identifying variables for differential analysis is to ask yourself what characteristics or relationships, other than the one you have hypothesized, could have contributed to the correlation you have obtained. Then select subjects from your sample that have the characteristic and recompute the correlation for the two subgroups, that is, those having and those not having the characteristic in question. If the resulting correlations are about the same, you may conclude that the characteristic in question has not contributed to your initial correlation, but if these two correlations are significantly different, you have gained a new insight into the relationship you are studying.

MISTAKES OFTEN MADE BY GRADUATE STUDENTS

1. Student assumes the results of correlational research to be proof of a particular cause-and-effect relationship.
2. Selects variables for correlation that have been found unproductive in previous studies.
3. Fails to make use of educational and psychological theory in selecting variables for study in correlational research.
4. Uses simple correlational techniques in studies where partial correlation, differential analysis, and corrections for attenuation or restriction of range are needed to obtain a clear picture of the way the variables are operating.
5. Applies tables giving significance levels of Pearsonian correlation coefficients to non-Pearsonian correlations, which often leads to reporting nonsignificant relationships as being significant.
6. Uses the "shotgun" approach in exploratory relationship studies.
7. Fails to develop satisfactory criterion measures for use in correlational studies of complex skills or behavior patterns.
8. Uses the incorrect correlation technique, such as the biserial correlation when the widespread biserial correlation is called for.

ANNOTATED REFERENCES

1. The mathematical basis of the correlational techniques discussed in this chapter can be found in most statistics textbooks. A textbook that provides a thorough treatment of correlation is William L. Hays, *Statistics for Psychologists*. New York: Holt, Rinehart, and Winston, 1963.
2. Bruning, James L., and Kintz, B. L. *Computational Handbook of Statistics*. Glenview, Ill.: Scott, Foresman, 1968. This book provides easy-to-follow computational procedures for these correlation techniques: Pearson product-moment correlation, Spearman rank-order correlation, Kendall rank-order

correlation, point-biserial correlation, the correlation ratio, and partial correlation. Also, tests for determining the statistical significance of differences between correlations are presented.

3. Kerlinger, Fred N. *Foundations of Behavioral Research: Educational and Psychological Inquiry*. New York: Holt, Rinehart and Winston, 1966. The author provides a clear, easy-to-understand introduction to factor analysis. Unlike most other discussions of this topic, the author's discussion of factor analytic principles is descriptive rather than mathematical and emphasizes the application of factor analysis to educational research problems.

CHAPTER 14

The Correlational Method—Part II

PLANNING A PREDICTION OR SELECTION STUDY

Introduction

Educational researchers carry out many prediction studies, usually with the aim of identifying variables that forecast academic and vocational success. The scope of prediction studies can be illustrated by the titles of these recent journal reports:

Patricia S. Faunce, "Personality Characteristics and Vocational Interests Related to the College Persistence of Academically Gifted Women," *Journal of Counseling Psychology*, 15(1) (1968), 31–40.
H. G. Gough, G. W. Durflinger, and R. E. Hill, Jr., "Predicting Performance in Student Teaching from the CPI," *Journal of Educational Psychology*, 59(2) (1968), 119–127.
Robert Tanofsky, R. Ronald Shepps, and Paul J. O'Neill, "Pattern Analysis of Biographical Predictors of Success as an Insurance Salesman," *Journal of Applied Psychology*, 53(2) (1969), 136–139.

Prediction studies provide the researcher with three types of information: the extent to which a criterion behavior pattern can be predicted; data for theory building about possible determinants of the criterion behavior pattern; and evidence regarding the predictive validity of the test or tests that are correlated with the criterion.

Prediction studies can be differentiated in terms of which of these types of information the researcher is most interested in obtaining. In some studies the emphasis is on a particular criterion behavior (e.g., first-year college grades), and one or more personality and aptitude tests are used to predict this criterion. Those tests that are good predictors are then applied to practical problems, such as selection of students for college admission. In other studies a similar research design is followed, but the researcher is primarily concerned with the theoretical significance of his findings. Finally, researchers may carry out prediction studies for the

344

purpose of test development. The emphasis is on writing test items and determining the test's predictive validity; the behavioral criterion used for prediction is of secondary importance.

Prediction research has made a major contribution to educational practice. Many prediction studies have been aimed at short-term prediction of the student's performance in a specific course of study, and others have been aimed at long-term prediction of general academic success. The findings of these studies have greatly aided school personnel in choosing students most likely to succeed in a particular academic environment or course of study. Also, prediction studies provide the scientific basis for the counselor's efforts to help students plan their academic future. Another type of prediction research has been concerned with establishing methods of predicting vocational success. As we discussed in Chapter 7, vocational interest tests have proved highly effective in predicting a person's future occupation. Also, as the cost of training new personnel for today's complex vocational skills increases, the saving to be realized by effective selection and prediction procedures also increases. For example, a selection system such as that employed by the U.S. Air Force for prediction of success in pilot training can save vast sums of money because it eliminates a certain number of persons who would fail during the training program. Because such training is extremely costly and because the cost of training the unsuccessful candidate up to the point of failure must be added to the per capita cost of training successful candidates, it may be seen that a prediction program that will reduce the number of failures can be of great value.

The basic research design

Prediction studies are similar to relationship studies in that both involve computing correlations between a complex behavior pattern (the criterion) and variables thought to be related to the criterion. However, in prediction studies the other variables (sometimes called "predictor variables") are measured some time before the criterion behavior occurs. By contrast, in relationship studies the criterion behavior and other variables need not be measured in a particular order; they are usually measured at the same point in time. Also, prediction studies, as compared to relationship studies, are more often concerned with maximizing the correlation between the criterion and predictor variables.[1]

The problem

As we have already observed, researchers may carry out prediction studies for different purposes. They may be interested in testing the pre-

---

[1] As we shall see, correlations can sometimes be increased by means of multiple correlation and moderator variables.

dictive validity of a particular test, in predicting a behavior criterion for use in an applied situation, or in predicting a behavior criterion to test a theoretical hypthesis. An example of the first type of research is Holtzman and Brown's study of the *Survey of Study Habits and Attitudes* (SSHA).[2] The main purpose of the study was to determine the validity of the SSHA for predicting the grade-point average of junior high and high school students. The researchers already had some reason to believe that the SSHA would predict this criterion, since the college version of the test, developed earlier, correlated significantly with college grades (*r* ranged from .27 to .66 for several samples).

Another important aspect of prediction studies is the proper definition of one's criterion behavior pattern. It is likely that many studies have failed to find predictive relationships because a poor criterion was specified. For example, grade-point average is sometimes used as a criterion, as in Holtzman and Brown's study. However, a grade-point average usually includes a person's grades in several subjects, such as mathematics and literature. Since it is likely that different aptitudes, skills, and interests are required for success in each subject, grades for each subject need to be predicted separately in order to obtain maximum correlations between the predictor variables and the criterion grade-point score. For example, study habits may be a critical determinant of success in mathematics, but not in literature. If the correlation is computed between a test such as the SSHA and the combined grade-point average for both academic subjects, the predictive relationship between study habits and grades in mathematics is obscured.

Selection of subjects

As we have discussed with respect to other research designs, it is important to draw subjects from the specific population most pertinent to your study. To meet this requirement, Holtzman and Brown formed separate groups of students for each grade level from the seventh through the twelfth grade. The correlational data were analyzed separately for each group. It should be noted that the researchers might have made their groups still more specific by forming separate subgroups of male and female students at each grade level.

Data collection

Standardized tests, questionnaires, interviews, or observational techniques can be used to measure predictor variables and the criterion behavior pattern in a predictor study. Of course, the predictor variable

[2] Wayne H. Holtzman and William F. Brown, "Evaluating the Study Habits and Attitudes of High School Students," *Journal of Educational Psychology,* 59(6) (1968), 404-409.

must be measured a period of time before the criterion occurs. Otherwise, one cannot claim that a particular test has "predicted" the criterion. In Holtzman and Brown's study, the SSHA was administered at the beginning of the fall semester in grades seven through twelve of various schools. Students' scores on scholastic aptitude tests administered by each school system were also obtained. At the end of the fall semester, students' grade-point averages were computed and used as the criterion behavior.

Generally speaking, prediction of events or behaviors that are to occur in the immediate future is easier and can be done more accurately than prediction of events or behaviors to occur in the more distant future. This is because in short-term prediction, more of the factors leading to success in the behavior being predicted are likely to be present. Furthermore, short-term prediction allows less time for important predictor variables to change or for the individual to gain experience that would tend to change his probability of success in the predicted behavior. Prediction through the use of the correlational technique is based on the assumption that at least some of the factors that will lead to the behavior we wish to predict are present and measurable at the time that we make the prediction. For example, if we wish to predict the probable success of individuals in a management training program, we would normally start with variables that we have found in previous research to be related to later success in management positions. This type of test battery might include such factors as verbal intelligence, social attitudes, emotional maturity, and so on. The degree to which these predictor variables correlate with the specific behavior we are attempting to predict, of course, determines the accuracy of our prediction. In such an area as success in management positions, certain variables important to success could not possibly be predicted because they are not present at the time the prediction must be made. For example, the individual's ability to work well with his superiors in the management hierarchy could not be predicted if these future superiors were unknown. Similarly, as success in some management positions is thought to be dependent to some degree upon the ability of the individual's wife to fit into the situation, it would not be possible to predict this variable if the individual were not married.

Data analysis

The basic form of data analysis in a prediction study consists of correlating each predictor variable with the criterion. In the study we have been describing, the SSHA and scholastic aptitude test scores (the predictor variables) were each correlated with students' grade-point average. The correlations are shown in Table 16 [3] in columns three and five. It

[3] Holtzman and Brown, op. cit., Table 1, p. 107. Reprinted by permission of W. H. Holtzman, W. F. Brown, and the American Psychological Association.

TABLE 16

MEAN CORRELATION OF SURVEY OF STUDY HABITS AND ATTITUDES (SSHA), FORM H;
SCHOLASTIC APTITUDE (SA); AND GRADE-POINT AVERAGE (GPA) TOGETHER
WITH MULTIPLE (R) AND PARTIAL (r) CORRELATIONS OF SCORES
WITH GRADE-POINT AVERAGE

Grade	N	SSHA (1) with GPA (3)	SSHA (1) with SA test (2)	SA test (2) with GPA (3)	$R_{3.12}$	$r_{31.2}$	SSHA total M	Study Orientation score SD
7	1,684	.55	.32	.61	.72	.47	106.5	33.1
8	1,628	.52	.29	.59	.69	.45	107.0	32.8
9	2,005	.49	.29	.52	.63	.41	101.6	31.5
10	2,064	.49	.29	.62	.70	.41	97.9	31.6
11	1,840	.47	.24	.57	.67	.42	97.7	30.9
12	1,667	.46	.20	.53	.66	.43	102.9	30.3
Total	10,888	.49	.27	.57	.67	.43		

NOTE—Mean correlations were obtained by converting each r into its Fisher's z function, weighting by the appropriate number of cases, averaging the values, then reconverting. Multiple and partial coefficients were derived from the weighted averages.

can be seen that both predictor variables yield rather high correlations; both tests would be considered valid for use in counseling and in selecting students who have academic promise.

In prediction studies multiple correlation may be used to determine whether two or more of all the predictor variables in the study can be combined to predict the criterion better than any one predictor variable does alone. Reference to column six in Table 16 indicates that the SSHA and the Scholastic Aptitude Test can be combined by a multiple regression equation to yield a better prediction of grade-point average than either test alone.[4] On the average the tests combined account for 45 percent of the variance in the criterion (.67 squared), as compared with the 24 per cent accounted for by the SSHA (.49 squared) or the 32 percent accounted for by the Scholastic Aptitude Test (.57 squared). Since researchers are interested in maximizing correlations in prediction studies, the technique of multiple correlation is often used.

Another technique for maximizing correlation is moderator or differential analysis, which we have discussed previously with respect to relationship studies. Although this technique was not used intentionally in the Holtzman and Brown study, we can see that the SSHA and the Scholastic Aptitude Test predict the criterion differentially for various subgroups, that is, grade levels, within the entire sample of students. For example, in grade seven the SSHA accounts for 30 percent of the variance

[4] The multiple regression equation uses the subject's scores on two or more tests to predict his performance on the criterion measure.

in students' grade-point average, whereas in the twelfth grade the amount of explained variance drops to 21 percent.[5] The purpose of moderator analysis is to identify a subgroup for whom the correlation between a criterion and a predictor variable is significantly greater than the correlation for the total sample from which the subgroup was formed.

CORRELATIONAL STATISTICS IN PREDICTION-SELECTION STUDIES

Multiple correlation

In certain educational research problems, particularly those involving prediction, it is desirable to determine the correlation between the behavior we wish to predict (such as success in school) and a combination of preliminary tests or measures, each of which correlates to some extent with the predicted behavior. For example, we may find that grade-point average in college is correlated with general intelligence, study skills, motivation, and reading rate. Because we can obtain scores on these four prediction measures prior to the student's entry into college, it would be possible to make a prediction based on the combination of these four measures that will estimate the student's college grade-point average before he enters college. This sort of prediction is often used by colleges that accept only a small number of those applying for admission. Inasmuch as each of the prediction measures correlates with college grade-point average, it follows that a prediction based on all four of these measures will be more accurate than a prediction based on only one measure. In order to determine the correlation between the combined variables and grade-point average in college, a multiple correlation would be employed. Closely related to multiple correlation is the multiple regression equation. The multiple regression equation combines the predictive value of several tests or measures into a single formula in order to make an improved prediction. Several predictive instruments, each having 15 percent or more variance in common with the behavior being predicted, can, when combined, yield a satisfactory prediction provided that they measure different aspects of the predicted behavior.[6] The multiple regression equation weights each variable in terms of its importance in making the desired prediction. The

---

[5] The reader might note the generally decreasing correlations between the SSHA and Scholastic Aptitude Test scores with grade-point average from grades seven to twelve, and also the increasing restriction of the standard deviation for SSHA. This is an illustration of restriction in range, which we discussed in the previous chapter. Holtzman and Brown observe that "The slight but regular drop in the correlation between SSHA and grade-point average is probably due to gradual loss of extremely poor students who drop out of high school before finishing."

[6] By 15 percent "common variance" we mean that the predictive test measures 15 percent of whatever goes into the behavior we are trying to predict.

scores of each applicant on the prediction measures can be placed in the formula, and those who have the highest weighted scores are most likely to succeed in the predicted behavior. A study by Webb illustrates a typical prediction study using the multiple correlation and multiple regression equation.[7] In this study Webb wished to develop a battery to predict the success of applicants to a dental school. Webb correlated sixteen prediction measures with grade-point average using regular product-moment correlations. Then, based on these correlations, he selected five of his prediction measures, which he combined using multiple correlation. It may be seen in Table 17 that the multiple correlation with grades based on these variables is .503 as compared with the product-moment correlation of .402 for predental grade average, the best single predictor.[8] Although the R of .503 does not permit highly accurate prediction, it indicates that the combined predictor battery has about 25 percent of common variance (R^2) with dental school grades, while the best single predictor has only 16 percent common variance (r^2) with this criterion. Better gains are usually obtained with multiple correlation when individual predictors correlate .35 or more with the criterion and when these predictors are not closely related to each other.

TABLE 17

CORRELATIONS BETWEEN FIVE PREDICTORS AND FIRST YEAR GRADE POINTS
IN DENTAL SCHOOL

	r	R^a
Predental grade average	.40	.402
Carving score	.27	.463
Biology score	.21	.493
Chemistry score	.28	.500
Object visualization score	.16	.503

[a] The multiple correlation on each line involves the variables named in the same and preceding lines.

Shrinkage

In using correlations for prediction, the usual procedure is to select a test or battery of tests that we believe will predict the behavior with which we are concerned. These tests are then tried out on a sample in order to determine their predictive validity, that is, the degree to which they will predict the behavior that we wish them to predict. The correlation between the prediction made by the test and the later behavior of the individual

[7] Sam C. Webb, "The Prediction of Achievement for First Year Dental Students," *Educational and Psychological Measurement*, 16(4) (1957), 543–548. Reprinted by permission.
[8] Webb, *op. cit.*

gives us an estimate of the predictive validity of the test. This correlation, however, especially if it is based upon a predictive instrument of low predictive validity and was validated on a small sample, will almost certainly become smaller if we repeat the experiment with a new sample. The tendency for predictive validities to decrease when the experiment is repeated is referred to as shrinkage. Webb's previously cited study of success in dental school provides a good example of shrinkage.[9] His five predictor measures gave an R of .503 in his initial study. Upon repeating this study with another sample, this R shrank to .425. The validity of his best single predictor, predental grade average, shrank from .402 to .309.

Shrinkage is due primarily to the fact that when we initially validate our measures, some of them will yield significant correlations by chance. In other words, characteristics unique to the group of subjects we have tested tend to yield a maximum predictive validity for some of our predictive measures. Upon repetition of the study, however, these same chance variables are not likely to be present in our new sample, and in this case the correlation initially obtained becomes smaller or disappears. As it is not possible to carry out predictions on the basis of correlations that only apply to one sample of subjects, it is always advisable to conduct a cross validation of predictor instruments before using them in practical prediction situations. Thus, after preliminary validation of the battery, the predictive validity of each prediction instrument should be cross-checked using another sample, and those correlations that have dropped to the level that makes them impractical for inclusion in the regression equation should be eliminated.

Moderator variables and differential prediction

Sometimes a test is more effective in predicting the behavior of certain subgroups than in predicting the behavior of other subgroups. In this situation we can use differential prediction, which is a form of differential analysis (see previous chapter). For example, it has been found that aptitude test scores generally predict school grades better for females than for males.[10] In this instance sex is designated a moderator variable since it moderates the predictive validity of a test. Sex, education, and socioeconomic status are frequently used as moderator variables. Also, one test is often used as a moderator variable to improve the predictive validity of another test. In one study the Taylor Manifest Anxiety Scale (TMAS) was used as a moderator variable to improve the correlation between scores on the School and College Aptitude Test (SCAT) and college grades. TMAS scores of a total sample of 210 students were used to form sub-

[9] Webb, *op. cit.*
[10] See H. G. Seashore, "Women Are More Predictable Than Men," *Journal of Counseling Psychology*, 9 (1962), 261–270.

groups of high-, intermediate-, and low-anxious students. Then separate correlations between SCAT scores and school grades were computed for each anxiety subgroup. The findings, shown in Table 18, indicate that anxiety is an effective moderator variable.[11] It is possible to make much better predictions with the SCAT for students low in anxiety than for students intermediate or high in anxiety. The total SCAT score explains 44 percent of the variance in grades for low-anxious students, 20 percent for intermediate-anxious students, and only 3 percent for high-anxious students. These results suggest an interesting problem for further investigation: If aptitude does not have predictive validity for high-anxious stu-

TABLE 18

CORRELATIONS BETWEEN GRADES AND SCAT SCORES
(V = Verbal, Q = Quantitative, T = Total)

Group	N	V score and Grades	Q score and Grades	T score and Grades
Total population	210	.377**	.266**	.334**
High anxiety	42	.252	—.034	.158
Middle anxiety	42	.279	.407**	.447**
Low anxiety	42	.577**	.507**	.644**

** Significant at .01 level.

dents, then what other variables might predict school achievement within this subgroup?

To identify possible moderator variables, the student should undertake a careful analysis of how various factors interact in determining academic or occupational success. An example of this kind of analysis occurred in a study by Air Force psychologists to determine whether success in pilot training could be predicted from the cadet's interest in aviation. The psychologists developed a test containing many items of general information about aviation. It was hypothesized that an individual interested in aviation would have gained the information needed to answer the questions, while persons not interested would not have this information. The test was tried on a sample of aviation cadets and found to correlate moderately with later success in pilot training. It was then hypothesized that the test would be a more satisfactory predictor for individuals with low interest in reading than individuals with high interest in reading. This hypothesis was based upon the premise that the individual who did a great

11 Lawrence R. Malnig, "Anxiety and Academic Prediction," *Journal of Counseling Psychology,* 11(1) (1964), 72–75. Reprinted by permission of L. R. Malnig (St. Peter's College, N.J.) and the American Psychological Association.

deal of reading might have gained much of the information called for without having a strong interest in aviation. On the other hand, individuals who had little interest in reading would almost surely not have the information on the test unless they had a strong interest in aviation. Further research proved this hypothesis to be correct.

Taylor-Russell Tables in group prediction

The goal of many prediction studies is to develop measures with sufficient predictive validity to be used in practical selection programs in education or industry. The efficiency of a measure for selection purposes, however, is not determined solely by its predictive validity. Two other factors influence this efficiency in practical selection problems. The first is the selection ratio. This is the proportion of the available candidates that must be selected. A predictive measure gives better results if only the few candidates scoring highest need be chosen than if all but the few who score lowest must be chosen. In other words, the smaller the proportion of candidates that must be chosen, the more of those chosen will be successful. The other factor influencing the proportion of successful candidates who will be obtained by the selection system is the proportion of candidates who would be successful if no selection were applied. In most vocational applications, this is the proportion of employees hired for the given activity, prior to the selection system, whose work was satisfactory. In educational selection it would be the number of students who succeeded in the given course of study prior to the use of selective admission. This number provides a base line, and a selection system, even one with low predictive validity, should improve to some degree the proportion of successful candidates.

The Taylor-Russell Tables combine the three factors of predictive validity, selection ratio, and proportion successful without selection. If these three factors are known, the research worker can predict the proportion of the candidates selected who will be successful. Table 19 is a sample page of the Taylor-Russell Tables,[12] this sample being usable when 70 percent of the candidates were successful prior to the selection system. A page is provided for each 5 percent interval on this variable from 5 percent to 95 percent. After the correct page is located, the predictive validity is located in the left hand column under r. We then locate the selection ratio in the top row and read the figure at the intersection of the row containing the predictive validity and the column containing the selection ratio. For example, let us assume that a college of engineering has received 500 appli-

[12] H. C. Taylor and J. T. Russell, "The Relationships of Validity Coefficients to the Practical Effectiveness of Tests in Selection: Discussion and Tables," *Journal of Applied Psychology*, 23 (1939), 565–578. Reprinted by permission of the American Psychological Association.

TABLE 19

SAMPLE TAYLOR-RUSSELL TABLE [a]

(Selection Ratio: Proportion Selected on Basis of Tests)

r	.05	.10	.20	.30	.40	.50	.60	.70	.80	.90	.95
.00	.70	.70	.70	.70	.70	.70	.70	.70	.70	.70	.70
.05	.73	.73	.72	.72	.72	.71	.71	.71	.71	.70	.70
.10	.77	.76	.75	.74	.73	.73	.72	.72	.71	.71	.70
.15	.80	.79	.77	.76	.75	.74	.73	.73	.72	.71	.71
.20	.83	.81	.79	.78	.77	.76	.75	.74	.73	.71	.71
.25	.86	.84	.81	.80	.78	.77	.76	.75	.73	.72	.71
.30	.88	.86	.84	.82	.80	.78	.77	.75	.74	.72	.71
.35	.91	.89	.86	.83	.82	.80	.78	.76	.75	.73	.71
.40	.93	.91	.88	.85	.33	.81	.79	.77	.75	.73	.72
.45	.94	.93	.90	.87	.85	.83	.81	.78	.76	.73	.72
.50	.96	.94	.91	.89	.87	.84	.82	.80	.77	.74	.72
.55	.97	.96	.93	.91	.88	.86	.83	.81	.78	.74	.72
.60	.98	.97	.95	.92	.90	.87	.85	.82	.79	.75	.73
.65	.99	.98	.96	.94	.92	.89	.86	.83	.80	.75	.73
.70	1.00	.99	.97	.96	.93	.91	.88	.84	.80	.76	.73
.75	1.00	1.00	.98	.97	.95	.92	.89	.86	.81	.76	.73
.80	1.00	1.00	.99	.98	.97	.94	.91	.87	.82	.77	.73
.85	1.00	1.00	1.00	.99	.98	.96	.93	.89	.84	.77	.74
.90	1.00	1.00	1.00	1.00	.99	.98	.95	.91	.85	.78	.74
.95	1.00	1.00	1.00	1.00	1.00	.99	.98	.94	.86	.78	.74
1.00	1.00	1.00	1.00	1.00	1.00	1.00	1.00	1.00	.88	.78	.74

[a] For use when 70 percent are successful without the selection system.

cations for admission to their freshmen class but can only take 250 students. They have a test battery that has been tried for two previous years when no selection system was used and found to have a predictive validity of .60 when correlated with freshmen grades. During the previous two years, 70 percent of the freshmen accepted had received passing grades. If the test battery is administered to the 500 applicants and the top 250 accepted, how many of these will succeed? If we enter the Taylor-Russell Table, using the page for 70 percent success of previous students, a selection ratio of .50 (the number to be selected, 250, divided by the number available, 500), and a predictive validity r of .60, we find that 87 percent, or 217 of the 250 selected, will be successful. If the predictive validity of the battery had been only .40, 81 percent or 202 of the 250 selected would be successful. Thus, even with a battery of low predictive validity, the selection system yields 27 more successful candidates than the 175 (70 percent of 250) that would be obtained if the 250 were selected by some random means. Thus, it may be seen that with a favorable selection ratio, measures with predictive validities lower than normally needed for group prediction can make worthwhile increases in the number of successful candidates selected.

Test development and item statistics

Sometimes a researcher hypothesizes that a personality characteristic or aptitude will predict a specific criterion, but no standardized test is available to measure the predictor variable. In this situation researchers may decide to develop a new test to predict the criterion. The first step in test development is to write a variety of items that appears to measure the personality characteristic or aptitude in which one is interested. This step is sometimes bypassed by using an already existing pool of items in a published test. Item analysis is then applied to determine which items best predict the criterion for inclusion in the final form of the test.[13] Item analysis is for the most part carried out using correlational statistics.

To select the items with the most predictive validity from an item pool, each item is usually correlated with scores on the criterion variable. Since items usually yield dichotomous scores (right-wrong, agree-disagree, etc.), the correlational techniques most often used in item analysis are biserial correlation, point-biserial correlation, tetrachoric correlation, and the phi coefficient. The procedure for selecting the appropriate correlational technique from these four has already been discussed in the previous chapter. Occasionally extreme criterion groups are used in item analysis. For example, suppose that one wished to determine which items from a collection of items best predict ratings of success in graduate school. Instead of correlating each item with the entire continuum of success ratings, one might use just the ratings of students at the upper and lower ends of the rating continuum. It has been found that when this procedure is used, it is best to select subjects who are at the upper and lower 27 percent of the continuum. After extreme groups are formed, one determines whether different proportions of subjects in each group endorse or answer correctly a particular item. For example, 55 percent of graduate students in the extreme group of high ratings may endorse a particular item, while only 20 percent of the students in the lower extreme group endorse it. The difference in percentages yields a value, .35, which is known as the index of discrimination (D). The values of D can vary from +1.00 to −1.00. Items yielding a D closest to +1.00 or −1.00 are those which are most valid for predicting a criterion based on extreme groups. A widespread biserial correlation can also be used in this situation to determine item validity.

The selection of predictive items in test development is analogous to the

---

[13] Item analysis is not limited to use in selecting test items which have predictive validity. This analytic procedure can also be applied to the selection of test items having construct validity, concurrent validity, and content validity.

selection of a battery of tests with high predictive validity by means of multiple correlation. In Holtzman and Brown's study, discussed earlier, a multiple regression equation based on the SSHA and a Scholastic Aptitude Test correlated more highly with grade-point average (the criterion) than each test separately. The reason is that the tests were negligibly correlated with each other, but both were moderately correlated with the criterion. Similarly, in item analysis one should select test items that correlate as little as possible with one another, but which have the highest index of validity. These items, when combined into a single test, will yield a measure having high predictive validity. However, item analysis capitalizes on chance factors in the same fashion as multiple correlation. Therefore, it is necessary to cross-validate the selected items with a new sample of subjects in order to determine whether shrinkage occurs. Otherwise, one's estimate of predictive validity of a new test based on a single item analysis is apt to be spuriously high.

Item statistics may be used for other purposes besides determining item validity. In developing aptitude and achievement tests, researchers usually compute an index of item difficulty. This index is the percentage of persons that passes a particular item. If it is too difficult or too easy, as determined by the percentage of persons answering correctly, then an item is of little value in measuring individual differences and thus is usually discarded from the item pool. Generally items at the .50 difficulty level (half the sample answer it correctly) provide the best discrimination. An exception to this rule occurs when one wishes to use the test items to select a specified percentage of individuals. For example, if one wants to develop a test to be used in selecting the top quarter of applicants for a particular academic program, then it is recommended that items having a difficulty level of about .25 (one fourth of the sample answer it correctly) be selected.

Item statistics also provide an approach to the development of test reliability. Each item can be correlated with the total score derived by summing scores on all items. Then one selects those items having the highest item-total correlation. This item analysis procedure can be used to develop a test having high internal consistency, or reliability. The advantage of a test with this property is that it is easily interpreted, since it usually measures a single personality or aptitude factor. However, the student may recall that to develop a test with strong predictive validity it is desirable to select items that have low correlations with one another (in effect, a low item-total correlation). Thus, item statistics can be put to cross-purposes. The researcher may use item analysis to select items so that the final test will have maximal internal consistency but low predictive validity, or to select items so that the final test is low in internal consistency but has high predictive validity. The decision to maximize the former or latter property depends on the researcher's purpose in constructing the test. If he wishes to develop a test that measures a single factor, then the researcher will compute item-total correlations to maximize internal consistency. If instead he wishes a test to have strong predictive validity, the researcher will select items having a high correlation with the criterion and a low correlation with other items.

INTERPRETING SIMPLE CORRELATION COEFFICIENTS

Statistical significance in correlational studies

Students often have a difficult time interpreting the correlation coefficient after computing it. Because correlations are expressed in decimals, students often incorrectly assume that they are similar to percentage points. A simple correlation is a mathematical way of expressing the degree of relationship between two variables or, to state it another way, the amount of variance that the two variables have in common. Although a correlation of .50 does not mean that the two measures have 50 percent in common, the square of the correlation does give this "common variance." Two tests that are correlated .50 have $.50^2$ or .25 of their variance in common. The concept of common variance is a useful one in helping us interpret correlations.

Correlation coefficients are usually interpreted either with reference to their statistical significance in exploratory relationship studies or their value as predictive devices in prediction studies. These two interpretations are considerably different because a correlation that is highly significant is often of little or no value for most purposes of prediction. Statistical significance when referred to a correlation usually describes whether or not the correlation obtained is different from zero at a given level of confidence. If the correlation is not significantly different from zero, it must be assumed that no relationship exists between variables (or that the sample size was not large enough to detect the difference). Most statistics texts include a table from which the statistical significance of a Pearson product moment correlation may be determined directly. The level of statistical significance of the correlation is determined to a great degree by the number of cases upon which the correlation is based. For example, with 22 cases, a Pearson correlation of .54 is needed to be significant at the one percent level. If we have 100 cases, however, a correlation of .25 is significant at the one percent level, and with 1,000 cases a correlation of only .08 is significant at the one percent level.

When we say that a correlation coefficient is statistically significant we mean that this coefficient is sufficiently high so that we may be reasonably confident that a true relationship exists between the variables we have correlated. If the correlation is significant at the one percent level, it may be interpreted as indicating that there is only one chance in 100 that the correlation is due to chance errors in sampling. We have seen that if we have a reasonably large number of cases, the correlation coefficient may be significant even though it is quite low. The size of the correlation coefficient is indicative of the degree of relationship between the variables, and a low correlation indicates a low relationship even if the correlation is significant at the one percent level. Relationship studies are aimed primarily at gaining a better understanding of the complex skills or behavior patterns being studied. In studies of this sort, low correlations are often useful because they give us clues about the nature of the behavior we are studying. These clues can then be followed up by prediction studies or by studies using experimental research designs.

Prediction studies are concerned with the use of correlation techniques to predict certain kinds of future behavior and require higher correlations than those usually found in exploratory relationship studies. In prediction studies statistical significance is of little consequence because correlations must far exceed this point to be of practical value in most prediction problems. Correlations are also interpreted somewhat differently in problems involving individual prediction than in problems involving group prediction.

In individual prediction we administer a test or battery of tests, and on the basis of the test scores predict the likelihood that certain individuals will succeed in the predicted activity. An algebra aptitude test, for example, is generally used for individual prediction. Another type of prediction used in educational problems is group prediction. In group prediction we predict, on the basis of our test scores, that at certain score levels a given percentage of our subjects will fail and the remainder will pass. For example, in establishing an intelligence cut-off point for selecting college students, it may be found that students below 105 IQ would have only one chance in ten of completing college. Students between 105 and 115 IQ might have three chances in ten of completing college, and students between 115 and 130 IQ might have six chances in ten of completing college. If we have a reasonably valid test to predict the behavior with which we are concerned, it is possible to predict how many persons between certain score intervals will succeed and how many will fail. The difficulty with group prediction is that we cannot predict *which* members of a given score interval will succeed and *which* ones will fail. Group prediction is often used in college admissions programs; the college usually adopts the principle that it is not feasible to accept ten students who score in a given intelligence range if it is known from past experience that nine of these ten will fail. Group prediction is also used in many of the training schools operated by the military services. The test battery used by the U.S. Air Force to predict success in pilot training is used to make group predictions.

It is known from prediction studies of previous aviation cadets what percentage of cadets at each score level on the test battery will succeed in pilot training. Thus, it is possible for the Air Force to determine how many students at the score levels available must be entered into the program in order to have the number of graduates required to man the aircraft planned for at a given future date.

The correlation coefficient may thus be interpreted in terms of two major dimensions. First the correlation is either statistically significant or not significant. Secondly, the correlation has a meaning for prediction, either group or individual. The following rules provide the student with a basis for roughly interpreting correlation coefficients obtained in his research. These data are, of course, only a general guide but will be approximately correct for most situations. Let us assume that we are dealing with correlations based on 100 or more subjects.

Correlations ranging from .20 to .35

Correlations at this level show a very slight relationship between the variables, although this relationship may be statistically significant. A correlation of .20 indicates that only 4 percent of the variance in the two measures that have been correlated is common to both. Correlations in this range may have limited meaning in exploratory research where relationships are being sought using crude measures. Correlations at this level, however, are of no value in either individual or group prediction.

Correlations ranging from .35 to .65

Correlations in this range are statistically significant beyond the one percent level. With correlations around .50, crude group prediction may be achieved. As a correlation of .50 between a test and the performance predicted only indicates 25 percent common variance, it is obvious that predictions based on a correlation this low can be expected to be frequently in error.

Correlations within this range, however, are useful when combined with other correlations into a multiple-regression equation. Combining several correlations in this range can in some cases yield individual predictions that are correct within an acceptable margin of error. Correlations at this level used singly are of little or no use for individual prediction because they yield only a few more correct predictions than could be accomplished by guessing or by using some chance selection procedure. The exception is when a very favorable selection ratio may be applied (see Table 19).

Correlations ranging from .65 to .85

Correlations at this level make possible group predictions that are accurate enough for most purposes. As we move toward the top of this range, group predictions can be made very accurately, usually predicting the proportion of successful candidates in selection problems within a very small margin of error. Near the top of this correlation range individual predictions can be made that are considerably more accurate than would occur if no such selection procedure were used.

Correlations over .85

Correlations at this level indicate a close relationship between the two variables correlated. A correlation of .85 indicates that the measure used for prediction has about 72 percent variance in common with the performance being predicted. Prediction studies in education very rarely yield correlations this high. When obtained at this level, however, correlations are very useful for either individual or group prediction.

RELIABILITY COEFFICIENTS

Test reliability

Correlational techniques are often used to determine the reliability of a test or of observers' ratings. We have already discussed in Chapter 6 the various methods by which test reliability can be estimated using a correlation coefficient. The coefficients yielded by these methods are interpreted in the same way as are other correlations. For example, the method of test-retest reliability involves administration of a test to a sample of individuals, and then after a delay the same test is administered again to the same sample. The correlation between the scores on the two test administrations, the coefficient of stability, provides a measure of test reliability. If this coefficient were .90 for a particular test, it would mean that 81 percent of the variance in the second test is accounted for by the variance in the first test. Since reliability is defined as the proportion of true variance in a test, the coefficient can also be interpreted as indicating that 81 percent of the test variance is "true" variance attributable to stable individual differences. The remaining 19 percent of the variance is due to error (e.g., conditions of administration, the subject's health on a particular day). Generally reliability coefficients of .90 or over are required for a test to be considered a reliable measuring instrument. This level is reached by most standard aptitude and achievement tests. In some of the areas that are more difficult to measure, such as personality, reliability coefficients typically range from .60 to .80. Such measures, although of limited value for individual diagnosis or prediction, can be very useful in research studies where analysis is concerned with groups rather than individuals.

Interrater reliability

In previous chapters we have discussed the importance of determining reliability of scores whenever human judgment is involved in the scoring process. Human judgment usually enters into content analysis, use of observational schedules, interviewing, and personality ratings, and it is desirable to assess the reliability of such judgments. Correlation is the statistical method most often used to determine interrater reliability, that is, the extent to which two observers agree in their assignment of scores to the same group of students.

If the research data are in the form of discrete categories, then interrater reliability can be determined by computing π.[14] For example, in Flanders' Interaction Analysis system, observers need to code particular instances of classroom behavior into one of ten discrete categories. When two observers are used to code the same classroom behavior, their reliability in assigning particular instances of behavior to the same category can be determined by computing π.

Often observers are asked to rank subjects on a particular trait. The extent of agreement between judges in their rankings can be determined by computing a rank difference correlation ρ. When research data are in interval-scale form, then a product-moment correlation r can be used to determine the reliability of two observers' scores. For example, the researcher might ask observers to make a frequency count of instances of a particular theme in students' compositions. The reliability of the frequency count scores can be determined by computing r. However, this correlational technique only measures the extent to which the two sets of observers' scores are linearly related. It does not provide a measure of the exact agreement in the two sets of scores. Two observers might agree highly with each other in terms of an r, yet one might assign higher scores and a wider range of scores than the other. To determine precise agreement in scores, it is necessary to compute the intraclass correlation coefficient ρ.[15] Generally, ρ yields a lower coefficient than would be obtained using product-moment correlation.

MISTAKES OFTEN MADE BY GRADUATE STUDENTS

1. Student does not identify a specific meaningful behavior criterion that is to be predicted.
2. Does not use multiple correlation to maximize correlations in prediction studies.

[14] Computational procedures for π can be found in William A. Scott and Michael Wertheimer, *Introduction to Psychological Research* (New York: Wiley, 1962), pp. 194–196.

[15] Computational procedures for ρ can be found in Scott and Wertheimer, op. cit.

3. Does not carry out a cross-validation study in order to determine shrinkage of predictive correlations obtained in the original study.
4. Develops a new test without using item analysis.
5. Does not interpret obtained correlation coefficients accurately.

ANNOTATED REFERENCES

1. Jackson, Douglas N., and Messick, Samuel (eds.) *Problems in Human Assessment*. New York: McGraw-Hill, 1967. Many of the articles reprinted in this book will be of assistance to the student planning a prediction or selection study. Among them are: Robert L. Thorndike, "The Analysis and Selection of Test Items," pp. 201–216; J. P. Guilford, "Some Lessons from Aviation Psychology," pp. 335–345; David R. Saunders, "Moderator Variables in Prediction," pp. 362–367; Edward E. Cureton, "Validity, Reliability, and Baloney," pp. 372–373.
2. Guilford, J. P. *Psychometric Methods*. New York: McGraw-Hill, 1954. Guilford's classic work discusses the mathematical basis of the statistical techniques discussed in this chapter. The chapters on test theory, reliability and validity, and item analyis will be particularly helpful to the student planning to develop his own test for use in a relationship or prediction study.
3. Bruning, James L., and Kintz, B. L. *Computational Handbook of Statistics*. Glenview, Ill.: Scott, Foresman, 1968. Easy-to-use computational procedures are presented for several of the statistical techniques discussed in this chapter: multiple correlation; reliability of measurement (test-retest, parallel forms, split-half, Kuder-Richardson).

CHAPTER 15

Experimental Designs

INTRODUCTION

The experiment is the ultimate form of research design, providing the most rigorous test of hypotheses that is available to the scientist. Although correlational and causal-comparative designs can uncover relationships between variables, the experiment is needed to determine whether the relationship is one of cause-and-effect.

Most experiments carried out by educational researchers are concerned with testing the effect of new educational materials and practices on students' learning. Thus, the results of educational experiments may have a direct impact on the adoption of new curriculum materials and teaching methods in the schools. The scope of present-day experimentation in education is illustrated by the titles of some recent journal articles:

Harry E. Anderson, Jr. and W. L. Bashaw, "An Experimental Study of First Grade Theme Writing, *American Educational Research Journal*, 5(2) (1968), 239–247.
Burl J. Brim, "Impact of a Reading Improvement Program," *Journal of Educational Research*, 62(4) (1968), 177–182.
John H. Litcher and David W. Johnson, "Changes in Attitudes Toward Negroes of White Elementary School Students After Use of Multiethnic Readers," *Journal of Educational Psychology*, 60(2) (1969), 148–152.
Graham Nuthall, "An Experimental Comparison of Alternative Strategies for Teaching Concepts," *American Educational Research Journal*, 5(4) (1968), 561–584.
Harold W. Stevenson and Alexander Siegel, "Effects of Instructions and Age on Retention of Filmed Content," *Journal of Educational Psychology*, 60(1) (1969), 71–74.

Most experiments in education employ some form of the classic single-variable design. All single-variable experiments involve the manipulation of a single treatment variable followed by observing the effects of this manipulation on one or more dependent variables. The variables to be manipulated will be referred to in this chapter as the "experimental treatment." (It is sometimes also referred to as the "independent variable," "experimental variable," or "treatment variable.") The variable that is measured to determine the effects of the experimental treatment is usually referred to as the "posttest," "dependent variable," or "criterion variable." In this chapter we will use the term "posttest" to describe this measure. (Occasionally, a variable is measured prior to administering the experimental treatment; it is called the "pretest.") For example, let us suppose we wished to design an experiment to determine the effects of anxiety upon ability to memorize mathematical formulas. In this experiment the posttest would be the measurement of the subject's performance in memorizing mathematical formulas, while the experimental treatment would be the steps taken by the experimenter to vary the amount of anxiety experienced by the subjects. In single-variable experiments, different groups are exposed to different experimental treatments while an attempt is made to hold constant all variables except the experimental treatment. Differences between the experimental treatments can then be attributed to effects of the experimental treatment plus errors. Depending on the experimental design used, there may be a control group, which is a sample of subjects, used for comparison purposes, that does not receive the experimental treatment.

The key problem in experimentation is establishing suitable control so that any change in the dependent variable can be attributed only to the independent variable that was manipulated by the researcher. As we shall find in the next sections, there are many extraneous variables that need to be controlled in order to allow an unequivocal interpretation of experimental data. Also, we shall find that there is no single correct approach to designing and carrying out experiments. Rather, different experimental designs can be used depending upon the variables that the researcher wishes to "control," that is, rule out as possible causes of changes on the posttest.

DIFFICULTIES IN DOING EXPERIMENTAL RESEARCH

Holding variables constant

The most difficult task in applying experimental methods to educational problems is holding all variables in the educational situation constant except the administration of the experimental treatment. In the physical sciences, where the classic single-variable experiment was first developed and where it has been most fruitful in the production of knowledge, the material worked with is much more adaptable to the rigorous requirements of the experimental laboratory. In the behavioral sciences and particularly in those experiments involving human subjects, it is doubtful whether the rigorous control of the physical science laboratory can ever be achieved.

Campbell and Stanley (1963) have distinguished between experimental designs in terms of their internal validity.[1] Experiments are more or less internally valid depending on how well extraneous variables have been controlled by the researcher. If extraneous variables are not controlled in the experiment, we cannot know whether observed changes in the experimental group are due to the experimental treatment or to an extraneous variable.

To demonstrate the importance of controlling for extraneous variables, we will consider a simple research problem amenable to experimental analysis. Suppose a researcher wishes to evaluate the effectiveness of a newly developed program in remedial reading. At the beginning of the school year, he selects 100 students for participation in the program; all these students meet the requirement of scoring at least two grades below age norm on a standard test of reading achievement. After participation in the remedial program for a school year, the students are once again given a reading achievement test. Suppose the researcher finds that a large, statistically significant gain (as determined by t test for correlated means) in reading achievement has occurred. Can the researcher conclude that this achievement gain was caused by the experimental treatment, that is, the remedial reading program? He cannot safely infer cause-and-effect unless extraneous variables have been adequately controlled. Campbell and Stanley have identified eight classes of extraneous variables, some of which are pertinent to the experiment that we have been considering. They are as follows:

1. *History.* Experimental treatments extend over a period of time, providing opportunity for other events to occur besides the experimental treatment. The students in our example participated in the remedial program over the period of a school year. It is conceivable that other factors, such as the students' regular instruction from teachers, could have accounted for all or part of their achievement gain.

2. *Maturation.* While the experimental treatment is in progress, biological or psychological processes within the student are likely to occur. He may become older, stronger, fatigued, elated, or discouraged. During the year of the remedial program the students were developing physically, socially, and intellectually. Possibly maturation in one of these areas, rather than the remedial program, enabled the students to overcome their reading deficiency.

[1] Donald T. Campbell and Julian C. Stanley, "Experimental and Quasi-Experimental Designs for Research on Teaching," in N. L. Gage (ed.), *Handbook of Research on Teaching* (Chicago: Rand McNally, 1963).

3. *Testing.* In most educational experiments a pretest is administered, followed by the experimental treatment and then a posttest. If the two tests are similar, students may show an improvement simply as an effect of their experience with the pretest, that is, they have become "test-wise." In the case of our research example, it is unlikely that this extraneous variable is operating because of the long period of time between pre- and posttesting.

4. *Instrumentation.* A learning gain may be observed from pretest to posttest because the nature of the measuring instrument has changed. Suppose that in our research example the students had been administered a different, easier posttest of reading achievement compared to the pretest. The gain in achievement could be attributed to the testing instruments rather than to the effect of the experimental treatment. In experiments involving observational measurements, instrumentation effects can be a special problem: observers who assess teachers or students before and after an experimental treatment may be disposed to give more favorable ratings the second time simply because they "expect" a change to have occurred.

5. *Statistical regression.* Whenever a test-retest procedure is used to assess change as an effect of the experimental treatment, the possibility exists that statistical regression can account for observed gains in learning. We will not present the mathematical basis for statistical regression here, but simply describe its effects on test scores.[2] In our research example, a group of students was selected who fell below the 15th percentile on a test of reading achievement. If the same students are tested again on a similar test (i.e., one that is correlated with the first test), they will earn a higher mean score because of statistical regression, with or without an intervening experimental treatment. Furthermore, if another group of students was selected who earned very high scores on the first test, for example, above the 85th percentile, these students would earn a lower mean score when retested on a similar measure, again as a result of statistical regression. The researcher should be alert to the confounding effects of statistical regression whenever students have been selected for their extreme scores on a test and are retested later on a measure that is correlated with the first test. Upon retesting, regression always tends to move the subject's score toward the mean. The probable regression can be estimated and considered in the results.

6. *Differential selection.* In experimental designs in which a control group is used, the effect of the treatment can sometimes be confounded because of differential selection of students for the experimental and control groups. Suppose that in our research example students need to meet

[2] A discussion of statistical regression can be found in Campbell and Stanley, "Experimental Designs," pp. 180–182.

the requirements of falling below the 15th percentile in reading achievement and of *volunteering* to participate in the program. Further suppose that the achievement gains of this group are compared with a control group of students that has equivalent reading deficiencies but that did not volunteer for the program. If the experimental group shows greater achievement gains than the control group, the effect could be attributed to "volunteer" characteristics rather than to the experimental treatment itself. To avoid this confounding effect, the experimenter needs to select experimental and control groups that do not differ except for exposure to the experimental treatment.

7. *Experimental mortality* (sometimes referred to as attrition). This extraneous variable might be operative in our research example if there were a systematic bias in the type of students who dropped from the remedial program during the school year. For example, some students might leave the program because they perceived they were not making any achievement gains. If the researcher only measures the achievement gains of those students who completed the program, the effectiveness of the experimental treatment will be exaggerated. It is necessary first to measure the achievement gains of all students who entered the remedial program irrespective of whether they completed it or not; then their achievement gain should be compared to that of a suitable control group.

8. *Selection-maturation interaction*. This extraneous variable is similar to differential selection (see number 6), except that maturation is the specific confounding variable. Suppose that first-grade students from a single school district are selected into the remedial program previously described. The control group is drawn from the population of first-grade students in another school district. Because of differential admissions policy the average age of the control group is six months older than that of the experimental group. Now suppose the research results show that the experimental group makes significantly greater achievement gains than the control group. How should we explain these results? Do they reflect the effectiveness of the experimental treatment, or do they show that reading gains in younger students are more influenced by maturational factors than in slightly older students? Because of differential assignment of students varying in maturation to the experimental and control groups, it is not clear which of these alternative explanations is correct.

We have seen now how eight different kinds of extraneous variables can threaten the internal validity of an experiment. It is necessary for the researcher to select an appropriate experimental design that controls such factors, so that any observed changes can be attributed with a high degree of confidence to the experimental treatment rather than to one or more of these extraneous variables.

Generalizing results of experiments

As we learned in the previous section, the educational researcher faces many potential threats to the internal validity of his experiment. A variety of controls is needed so that the effect of the experimental treatment is not confounded by other variables. However, the educational researcher is faced with the dilemma that, as more rigorous controls are applied to the experiment, less carry-over can be expected between the experiment and related field situations. In other words, the behavioral sciences are constantly faced with the choice of obtaining rigorous laboratory control at the cost of realism or of maintaining realistic experimental situations, so that findings may be readily transferred into practical field application, at the cost of losing scientific rigor in the process. Most educational studies aim at a compromise between these goals; they attempt to attain sufficient rigor to make the result scientifically acceptable while maintaining sufficient realism to make the results reasonably transferable to educational situations in the field.

Campbell and Stanley have identified four factors that affect the generalizability of findings from experiments—what they call the experiment's "external validity." The first of these factors is the *reactive effect of testing*. In some instances the pretest may act as part of the experimental treatment and thus affect one's research results. Thus, if the experiment is repeated without the pretest, different research results will probably be obtained. Let us consider a hypothetical experiment in which this reactive effect might operate. Suppose a researcher is interested in the effect of point of view in a film on students' attitudes. For example, the researcher might develop a film in which the narrator takes a strongly slanted, positive view of controversial decisions made by a contemporary politician. To assess the effect of the film, the researcher might administer a pretest and posttest of students' attitudes toward the politician. Suppose there is a significant positive shift in students' attitudes, which the researcher attributes to the experimental treatment, that is, the film. Can the researcher generalize this finding and assert that this film will have the same effect when used in other situations? The generalization is not warranted unless the researcher can demonstrate that the pretest has no effect on the experimental treatment. The possibility exists that the pretest activates students' awareness of their attitudes toward this politician, and sensitizes them to the narrator's attitude. It may be that this sensitization, induced by the pretest, is the factor that interacts with the film to produce the attitude shift. By contrast, if they are shown the film alone, students might be most sensitized to learning the facts presented in the film. Thus, they might show little or no attitude shift since they did not have a set to attend to the narrator's point of view. This example illustrates the fact that, if a "reactive" pretest is administered, the researcher cannot safely generalize his findings about a particular experimental treatment to a situation in which the treatment is administered without a pretest. If one wishes to make this kind of generalization, it is necessary to use an experimental design in which a pretest is not administered or employ at least one treatment that does not receive the pretest.

The second factor that influences the external validity of experiments is the *interaction of the experimental treatment with particular student characteristics, measuring instruments, and the time of the study*. To illustrate, suppose that a researcher is concerned with determining whether a programmed instructional format leads to greater achievement gains than conventional textbook presentation of curriculum materials. The researcher performs the experiment on a sample of seventh-grade students, and he finds that programmed instruction leads to greater achievement gains. Although the researcher might wish to generalize his findings to the population of "all" students, strictly speaking he can only generalize to the population from which his sample was drawn—namely, seventh-grade students. Until other experiments are carried out, the researcher does not know whether instructional format interacts with student characteristics. That is, although programmed instruction was found to be superior to conventional textbook presentation for seventh-grade students, quite different results might be obtained with students at other grade levels. Similarly, the generalizability of the experiment may be limited by the particular pretest and posttest designed to measure achievement gains. Suppose that the superiority of a programmed instruction format was demonstrated using multiple-choice tests. The experiment does not permit the researcher to generalize his findings to other measuring instruments; for example, no difference between instructional formats might be found if essay-type pretests and posttests were administered. Finally, in a strict sense one cannot generalize beyond the time period in which the experiment was done. An experiment evaluating an innovative educational method might be done at a time when teachers are particularly disenchanted with a corresponding conventional method. They might be exceptionally motivated to demonstrate the superiority of the new method. At a later time, a researcher might repeat the experiment and find no difference because teachers no longer see the method as "innovative."

Although most experiments sample only a limited range of student characteristics, evaluation instruments, and time periods, there is a great tendency for researchers and professional educators to make far-reaching generalizations on the basis of findings from single experiments. As the preceding example demonstrates, generalizations to educational situations not represented in the experiment should be made quite cautiously. Ideally, a new experiment would be performed each time there is a significant change in the educational situation to which one wishes to generalize the findings of an experiment.

③ The third factor affecting the external validity of experiments is the *possible artificiality of the experimental treatment and the students' knowledge that they are involved in an experiment.*[3] In Chapter 5 we discussed how the Hawthorne effect and the placebo effect often occur when researchers perform experiments to determine the effectiveness of innovative educational practices. Researchers often give participating teachers and students special attention, and this factor, not the experimental treatment itself, may cause a change in their behavior. Should the Hawthorne effect or the placebo effect occur, the external validity of the experiment is jeopardized, since usually educators will be unable to generalize the findings from the experiment to a situation in which researchers or similar personnel are not present.

The fourth factor that may affect the external validity of an experiment is *multiple treatment interference.* Occasionally a researcher will use an experimental design in which each subject is exposed to more than one experimental treatment. Suppose that each subject in the experiment receives three different treatments: A, B, and C. Treatment A is found to produce significantly greater learning gains than treatments B and C. Because of the experimental design that was used, the researcher cannot safely generalize his finding to a situation in which treatment A is administered *alone*. It is possible that the effectiveness of treatment A depends on the coadministration of the other two treatments. Whenever it appears that multiple-treatment interference will affect the generalizability of one's findings, the researcher should choose an experimental design in which only one treatment is assigned to each subject.

We have now discussed four factors that may lessen the generalizability of experimental research findings. In our discussion of the various types of experimental designs, we will find that some designs enable the researcher to control for one or more of these factors.

Random selection and random assignment

We have previously discussed randomization in terms of selecting a sample of persons to participate in one's study. Briefly stated, randomization means that each person in a defined population has an equal chance of being selected to take part in the study. When doing an experiment, the researcher needs to consider another type of randomization, namely, *random assignment* of persons to experimental treatments. Suppose that a researcher wishes to compare the effectiveness of two teaching methods —conventional textbook versus programmed instruction. First he selects

[3] Campbell and Stanley refer to this factor as "reactive arrangements."

a random sample of 50 students. Next he should randomly assign each student to either the textbook treatment or the programmed instruction treatment, that is, each student should have an equal chance of being exposed to one or the other of the experimental treatments.

In the design of laboratory experiments, it is usually possible for the researcher to randomly assign persons to treatments. However, random assignment is frequently not possible in field experiments, particularly when the experiment is done in the public schools. The reason is that students within a given classroom cannot easily be assigned to different treatments. Not only are there sticky logistical problems to overcome; it is possible for students to form biases in favor of one treatment (a bias they could not form if they were aware only of the treatment to which they are exposed). Faced with this situation, the researcher would probably want to break up the class and form two classes, one for each experimental treatment. Students would be randomly assigned to each of the two new classes. However, it is usually quite difficult for the experimenter to manipulate the classroom structure established by public school administrators. The experimenter is forced to deal with students, not as individuals, but as members of an intact group. This intact group is usually defined in terms of a particular grade level, teacher, and classroom (e.g., the fourth-grade class taught by Miss Jones in room 16).

Given this situation, the researcher might do the experiment in two classrooms. For example, students in the fourth-grade class of school A and the fourth-grade class of school B are assigned conventional instruction and programmed instruction, respectively. The integrity of the public school structure is thus preserved. Most field experiments in education use this procedure to compare the effectiveness of different experimental treatments. However, there are several problems with this procedure because students have not been randomly assigned to the experimental treatments.[4] Consider, for instance, what would happen if students in school A came from predominantly upper middle-class families and students in school B came from lower-class families. Since scholastic achievement is correlated with social class, it is likely that students in school A will have higher achievement scores than students in school B with or without the intervention of the experimental treatment. Thus, we cannot conclude on the basis of the findings that conventional instruction (administered only to students in school A) is superior to programmed instruction (administered only to students in school B). An equally plausible interpretation is that the differential achievement gain results from the differences in the composition of the experimental groups.

---

[4] That is, each student in school A must receive conventional instruction, and each student in school B must receive programmed instruction. Each student is not free to be assigned to either treatment.

Although it presents a simplified situation, the preceding illustration typifies the thorny problems encountered by the researcher doing a field or laboratory experiment in which random assignment to experimental treatments is not possible because the subjects are members of intact groups. Nonetheless, it is possible to design an experiment in which the limitations of nonrandom assignment are partially or wholly overcome. Experimental designs of this type have been designated "quasi-experiments" by Campbell and Stanley to distinguish them from "true" experiments, that is, experiments having random assignment. Later in this chapter, we shall discuss procedures for developing equivalence between intact groups receiving different experimental treatments.

Experimenter bias

Robert Rosenthal's studies of experimenter bias effects have made a significant contribution to experimental methodology.[5] It is likely that researchers will have expectancies about the outcomes of their experiments, and Rosenthal has demonstrated that these expectancies are sometimes transmitted to subjects in such a way that their behavior is affected. This phenomenon is known as the experimenter bias effect. It should be noted that the phenomenon occurs outside the awareness of the experimenter. The experimenter bias effect does not refer to situations in which an experimenter, with full awareness of his actions and intentions, manipulates subjects' behavior or falsifies data in order to yield an "expected" finding.

Rosenthal and his associates have carried out many experiments on the experimenter bias effect, and we shall describe one of them here.[6] A group of undergraduates was trained to run albino rats through a simple T maze and to train these rats in a discrimination learning problem. The student experimenters were told that, as a result of generations of inbreeding, some rats they would train were "maze-bright" while others were "maze-dull." They were then given instructions regarding expected findings:

> Those of you who are assigned the Maze-Bright rats should find your animals on the average showing some evidence of learning during the first day of running. Thereafter performance should rapidly increase.
> Those of you who are assigned the Maze-Dull rats should find on the average very little evidence of learning in your rats. [p. 159]

In fact, though, a homogeneous group of albino rats (not varying on the dimension of maze brightness-dullness) were randomly assigned to the

[5] Robert Rosenthal, *Experimenter Effects in Behavioral Research* (New York: Appleton-Century-Crofts, 1966).
[6] R. Rosenthal and K. L. Fode, "The Effect of Experimenter Bias on the Performance of the Albino Rat," *Behavioral Science,* 8 (1963), 183–189.

experimenters for training. Nevertheless, Rosenthal and Fode found that rats trained by experimenters who thought their rats were maze-bright earned significantly higher learning scores than rats trained by experimenters with the opposite expectancy. The differential learning gains were the result of an experimenter bias effect rather than genetic differences between groups of rats.

The implication of this finding for educational experiments is obvious. An educational researcher might do an experiment to determine whether a technique or product he has developed is superior to conventional practice. If the researcher has a strong expectancy that his innovation is superior to conventional practice, his experiment might yield this finding. In this case the finding is attributable to an experimenter bias effect rather than to the innovation per se. Should impartial researchers carry out further experiments to evaluate the innovation, they are not likely to replicate the original finding since the experimenter bias effect is no longer operating.

The method of transmission of the experimenter's expectancy to the subject is not clearly understood, although Rosenthal and others have conducted studies directed at this problem.[7] Yet the experimenter bias effect does appear to be a real threat to the validity of experiments. The researcher should take steps to avoid the operation of this effect in designing and carrying out an experiment. One effective technique is to train naïve experimenters to work with students or teachers participating in the study. Whenever possible the researcher himself should not work directly with the subjects. Also, the researcher should avoid suggesting to his experimenters, directly or indirectly, that one experimental treatment is better than another.

To some degree the tools used to measure the dependent variables can be selected so as to reduce the chance of experimenter bias. For example, if the rats in the Rosenthal and Fode experiment had been trained in mazes having sensitized pathways so their progress was measured and recorded automatically, there would have been much less chance of observer bias influencing the results. Observer expectations are most likely to influence research results when scores on the dependent variable rely upon subjective judgment by the observer, or when the investigator can make inputs (often subconsciously) into the experimental treatment itself.

[7] Rosenthal and Lenore Jackson have also recently reported an experimental study of how teachers' expectancies affect their students' behavior in *Pygmalion in the Classroom* (New York: Holt, Rinehart and Winston, 1968). Although Rosenthal's experimental procedure has provoked some controversy, his book has stimulated much interest and concern regarding whether teachers' expectancies about their students' potential (based on knowledge of their I.Q. scores) can actually affect student achievement.

Strong versus weak experimental treatments

One of the major problems of experimental research is producing a treatment that is strong enough to have an effect on the dependent variable. For example, a researcher may do an experiment to determine whether a particular teaching method affects student achievement. The experimental design might require a group of teachers to use the method for a period of one month, with student achievement measured at the beginning and end of this time period. Also, there might be a control group of teachers that used a conventional teaching method for the same period; the achievement of their students would be measured in the same way as that of the experimental students. Suppose no differences were found between the experimental and control groups. Should the researcher conclude that the experimental teaching method does not produce greater achievement gains? If he did, others might raise the criticism that he used a "weak" treatment. That is, one might argue that the experimental teaching method would have produced greater achievement gains had it been used over a longer time period, perhaps an entire school year. Of course, as the researcher increases the strength of the treatment, the experiment is likely to increase in complexity, time, and cost. Thus, many educational problems amenable to an experimental approach cannot be tackled by student researchers. They require a well-funded and well-staffed organization in order to be investigated properly. Before doing an experiment the student should determine whether he has the resources necessary to design a treatment that can reasonably be expected to have an effect on student achievement or other dependent variables.

Two other related factors must be considered by the researcher as he designs an experiment. One of these is the quality of the experimental treatment. In evaluating the preceding research example, the student should ask how the teachers were trained to use the experimental teaching method, and whether checks were made to see that they used the method every day of the experiment. The length of the treatment might be adequate, but the researcher might have done a poor job of training teachers to use the experimental method, or the training materials might have been of poor quality and thus not successful in arousing the interest of participating teachers. Also, once the experiment started, the researcher may not have exerted sufficient "quality control" to insure that all teachers in the experimental and control groups did what was required of them.

A third factor that the researcher should consider is whether the experimental treatment adequately operationalizes the concept it is intended to represent. Many educational concepts are not clearly defined and are susceptible to a number of interpretations. For example, some of the experiments designed to test the effectiveness of teaching by discovery (sometimes called "inductive teaching") have been criticized on the grounds that their treatments are inadequate representations of this teaching method.[8] Sometimes it is impossible to obtain a consensus among educators regarding the meaning of a particular concept or method. Faced with this situation, the researcher is advised to state *his* definition of the concept or method. Then the experimental treatment can be evaluated with respect to how well it operationalizes this particular definition.

EXPERIMENTAL DESIGNS AND STATISTICAL ANALYSIS TECHNIQUES

In this section we shall discuss 16 types of experimental designs that may be used in educational research. Table 20 provides a schematic presentation of these designs. Some designs are much more complex than others. They vary in use of random assignment, use of control groups, and administration of a pretest. Table 20 shows that some experimental designs are much more likely than others to possess high internal and external validity. However, as we shall find, with a few exceptions all have application in educational research. The selection of a particular design

TABLE 20[a]

EXPERIMENTAL DESIGNS AND THEIR SOURCES OF INVALIDITY

Design	Sources of Invalidity	
	Internal	External
Single group design		
1. One-shot case study X O	History, maturation, selection, mortality	Interaction of selection and X
2. One group pretest-posttest design O X O	History, maturation, testing, instrumentation, interaction of selection and other factors	Interaction of testing and X; interaction of selection and X

[a] This table was adapted from Tables 1, 2, and 3 in the Campbell and Stanley study. Please note that only definite weaknesses in various experimental designs have been indicated here. In Campbell and Stanley's tables, some invalidating factors have been shown as possible sources of concern in certain designs, but they are not shown here.

Key: R = Random assignment
  X = Experimental treatment
  O = Observation, either a pretest or posttest of the dependent variable

[8] The research on teaching by discovery is reviewed and discussed in L. S. Shulman and E. H. Keislar (eds.), *Learning by Discovery: A Critical Appraisal* (Chicago: Rand McNally, 1966).

TABLE 20 (Continued)

EXPERIMENTAL DESIGNS AND THEIR SOURCES OF INVALIDITY

	Sources of Invalidity	
Design	Internal	External

Control group designs with random assignment

3. Pretest-posttest control group design

R   O   X   O
R   O   O

Internal	External
None	Interaction of testing and X

4. Posttest-only control group design

R   X   O
R   O

Internal	External
Mortality	None

5. Solomon four-group design

R   O   X   O
R   O   O
R   X   O
R   O

Internal	External
None	None

Quasi-experimental designs

6. Static-group comparison [b]

    X   O

        O

Internal	External
Selection, mortality, interaction of selection and maturation, etc.	Interaction of selection and X

7. Nonequivalent control group design

    O   X   O

    O   O

Internal	External
Interaction of selection and maturation, etc.	Interaction of testing and X

8. Times series design

O   O   O   OXO   O   O   O

Internal	External
History	Interaction of testing and X

9. Counterbalanced designs

X_1O X_2O X_3O
X_3O X_1O X_2O
X_2O X_3O X_1O

Internal	External
None	Multiple-treatment interference

[b] Broken lines indicate that the experimental and control groups are not formed randomly.

Key: R = Random assignment
     X = Experimental treatment
     O = Observation, either a pretest or posttest of the dependent variable

will depend upon the type of problem the experimenter is attempting to solve and the conditions under which he must work.

In presenting each experimental design, we shall briefly discuss the statistical procedures used to analyze the data yielded by the design. Most of these procedures were first introduced in Chapter 12, when we discussed causal-comparative research. Since the experimental designs presented here often involve the measurement of change, which poses some tricky methodological problems, we shall discuss this topic later at some length.

SINGLE GROUP DESIGNS

The one-shot case study

The one-shot case study hardly qualifies as an experimental design. In this design an experimental treatment is administered, and then a posttest is administered to measure the effects of the treatment. As Table 20 shows, this design has poor internal validity. Suppose one selects a group of students, gives them remedial instruction (the experimental treatment), and then administers a measure of achievement (the posttest). How can one determine the influence of the treatment on the posttest? Unfortunately, there is no way of making this determination. The students' scores on the posttest could be accounted for by their regular school instruction or by maturation, as well as by the treatment. Also the fact that students were tested only once makes it impossible to measure change in their performance. Without a measure of change, it is impossible even to determine whether the students' achievement improved over time, regardless of whether this change was due to the treatment or to some other variable. In short, the one-shot case study, although relatively simple to carry out, yields meaningless findings. If he is limited to studying a single group of subjects, the investigator should administer at the very least both a pretest and a posttest. This is the design that we shall discuss next.

One group pretest-posttest design

This design involves three steps. The first step is the administration of a pretest measuring the dependent variable. The second step is the application of the experimental treatment (independent variable) to the subjects, and the final step is the administration of a posttest measuring the dependent variable again. Differences due to application of the experimental treatment are then determined by comparing the pretest and posttest scores.

F. T. Smith's study of changes in college student attitudes toward the

Negro provides a good example of a study that employed this design.[9] In this study Smith administered his pretest, an attitude scale measuring attitudes toward the Negro, to a sample of 354 college students at Columbia University. Of this sample he selected 46 students who were representative of the larger group tested. These students were then exposed to the experimental treatment, that is, a series of favorable contacts with Negroes, such as having dinner with a Negro family, visiting a Negro church, and meeting leaders of the Negro community in Harlem. These contacts extended over a 4-day period. Smith's hypothesis was that these contacts with Negroes would change the attitudes of his research subjects in a favorable direction. Ten days after the last planned contact with Negroes, Smith posttested his group using the same attitude measure and found that the mean attitude had changed significantly in favor of Negroes. Then, after waiting ten months, Smith administered still another posttest to determine how much of the favorable attitude change had persisted.

The major limitation of the single-group design is that, as no control group is used, the experimenter must assume that changes between the pretest and posttest were brought about by the experimental treatment. There is always some chance, however, that one or more extraneous variables brought about all or part of the change noted between the pretest and the posttest scores. For example, in the case of Smith's study, let us assume that after the pretest was administered, but some time prior to the posttest, a Negro committed some especially vicious crime in Harlem and this crime received broad and highly emotional coverage in the New York newspapers. Smith then would have been faced with the problem of trying to determine how much of the attitude change observed on the posttest could be attributed to the planned application of the independent variable and how much was due to reactions to this crime. Although situations such as highly publicized crime quite obviously might have an effect upon the subjects, there is also a possibility that some subtle factors unrelated to the experimental treatment have operated on all or some of the research subjects and have led to a change on the posttest.

Because of the assumption that the changes on the dependent variable are not due to extraneous factors, the one group pretest-posttest design is limited to the study of characteristics or behavior patterns that are reasonably stable, that is, are not likely to change unless some direct action by the experimenter is taken to bring about such a change. The single-group design, for example, is often used for studying changes in racial and religious attitudes of adults because these attitudes are known to be quite stable in most individuals by adulthood and are unlikely to change unless

[9] F. T. Smith, "An Experiment in Modifying the Attitudes Towards the Negro," *Teachers College Contributions*, 887 (1943).

some significant effort is made to change them. In fact, the attitudes are sufficiently stable so that most of the studies that have devoted considerable effort to changing attitudes have failed to bring about significant changes. The single-group design is completely inappropriate for studies where the dependent variable is not stable or where it is likely to change due to maturation. For example, a study aimed at testing the effect of teaching methods on the creative thinking of elementary school children could not be done using the single-group method because the abilities of children at this level are developing rapidly and a significant gain between the pretest and posttest might be due primarily to maturation rather than to the effect of the teaching methods employed in the experiment.

In order to reduce the likelihood of extraneous variables altering the posttest results, most studies employing this design attempt to keep the interval between the pretest and the posttest as short as possible. For example, studies that attempt to measure the effect of motion pictures upon racial or religious attitudes are frequently designed so that the pretest is administered immediately before the subjects are shown the motion picture and the posttest is administered immediately following the motion picture. Under these conditions there is very little likelihood that extraneous variables have entered into the situation. Such an approach, however, has its drawbacks because immediate posttest scores are often a poor indicator of whether permanent attitude changes are brought about by the experimental treatment.

In summary, the research worker should use the one group pretest-posttest design only when the dependent variable is reasonably stable, when the interval between the pretest and the posttest can be kept short, and when it is impossible to obtain a control group.

Statistical analysis

The statistical analysis of data obtained using this design is fairly simple. Usually the pretest and posttest means are compared for statistical significance using the t test for correlated means (this t test is used since the same subjects take both the pretest and posttest). If the scores on either the pretest or posttest show marked deviation from the normal distribution, a nonparametric statistic should be used. Most likely the research worker would select the Wilcoxon signed-ranks test.

CONTROL-GROUP DESIGNS WITH RANDOM ASSIGNMENT

Pretest-posttest control group design

Nearly any study that can be conducted using a single-group design can be carried out more satisfactorily using one of the control-group designs, which we will now discuss. The essential difference between the single-group design and the control-group design is that the latter employs at least two groups of subjects, one of which is called the "control group" and is included primarily to make it possible to measure the effect of extraneous factors upon the posttest. The treatment of the experimental and control groups is generally kept as close to identical as possible with the exception that the experimental group is exposed to the experimental treatment. If extraneous variables have brought about changes between the pretest and posttest, these will be reflected in the scores of the control group. Thus, only the posttest change of the experimental group that is over and above the change that occurred in the control group can be attributed to the experimental treatment. If properly carried out, this experimental design effectively controls for the eight threats to internal validity identified by Campbell and Stanley [10]: history, maturation, testing, instrumentation, regression, selection, mortality, and interaction effects. However, Table 20 indicates that the external validity of this design may be affected by an interaction of the pretest with the experimental treatment, that is, it may be that the experimental treatment produces significant effects, but only because a pretest was administered. When it is tried on a group that has not been pretested, the treatment does not work. If he thinks that his experimental treatment is affected by pretesting, then the researcher should use the posttest-only control group design or the Solomon 4-group design.

An essential feature of this experimental design is random assignment of subjects to the experimental and control groups, that is, every subject has an equal chance of being assigned to either group. Random assignment of subjects to groups can be obtained by using a table of random numbers or by a mechanical system, such as flipping a coin or drawing names from a hat. Random assignment is used in order to cancel out initial differences between treatment groups.[11] For example, suppose that the mean pretest achievement score for 100 students is 50. If these students are randomly assigned to the experimental and control groups, the mean pretest score for each group should be about 50. Now suppose that the posttest mean for the experimental group increases to 70, whereas the posttest mean for the control group remains at about 50. Since both groups started at the same initial level and since there was no systematic bias in selecting sub-

---

[10] Campbell and Stanley, op. cit.

[11] The student should note the distinction between random selection and random assignment. Random selection of a sample from a defined population enables the researcher to generalize findings beyond the sample studied. Random assignment does not permit this generalization (unless random selection is also used in the experiment), but it does enable the researcher to assume that there are no systematic initial differences between treatment groups.

jects into each group, we are able to attribute the differential increase in achievement only to the effect of the experimental treatment, not to an extraneous variable, such as history, maturation, and so on.

In situations where more than 50 subjects are to be assigned to each group, it is likely that the subjects will be equivalent in all major respects, assuming random assignment has occurred. However, when a smaller number of subjects is used, it is possible that the groups may differ significantly from each other on the pretest (or on some other variable, such as age, intelligence, socioeconomic status) simply by chance. In the preceding example, if a smaller sample had been used, it is conceivable that the pretest means of the experimental and the control group would be significantly different from each other. Suppose that the pretest means are 40 and 60, respectively. Then suppose that the posttest means are 60 and 60, respectively. We might conclude that the experimental treatment has no effect, since the posttest means of the two groups are the same. However, the pretest means differed significantly from each other, even though random assignment occurred. When this situation occurs, analysis of covariance can be used to control for initial differences. In our example it might well be that there are differences on the posttest favoring the experimental group when initial differences are controlled.

The pretest-posttest control group design is one of the most commonly used experimental designs by educational researchers. It involves the following steps: (1) random assignment of subjects to experimental and control groups, (2) administration of a pretest to both groups, (3) administration of the treatment to the experimental group but not to the control group, and (4) administration of a posttest to both groups. It is important to realize that the experimental and control groups must be treated as nearly alike as possible except for the treatment variable. For example, both groups must be given the same pretests and posttests and be tested at the same time.

It should be noted that these steps apply to a special case of the pretest-posttest control-group design. This is the case where the control group receives no treatment from the experimenter except a pretest and a posttest. However, in certain situations the experimenter may want to administer an alternative experimental treatment to the control group. Suppose, for example, a researcher wishes to determine the effect of a film about race relations on student attitudes toward minority groups. To determine the film's effectiveness, the researcher might have the experimental group view it while the control groups go about their regular school work. If the researcher was interested instead in the relative effectiveness of the film as compared to a discussion group (in which students meet as a group to discuss their attitudes about race relations), a different experimental design would be used. The experimental group would view the film while the control group would hold a discussion. Thus, both groups receive a treatment. Of course, there can be more than two treatment groups. Thus, in the preceding example, the researcher can form several groups depending on the comparisons he wishes to make. He might, for example, compare the effectiveness of the film-viewing group with a discussion group, a group that reads about race relations, and a group that receives no treatment.

An illustration of the pretest-posttest control group design is provided by Taylor and Hoedt's study of the effect of praise upon the quality and quantity of creative writing in fourth-grade students.[12] Random assignment was achieved as follows:

> Pupils in three science classes, homogeneously grouped according to general achievement, were assigned numbers and randomly placed in either experimental group A or B. Each class was evenly divided so that half the pupils were in group A and half were in group B. [page 80]

The effectiveness of random assignment in equating the experimental and control groups is shown by their near equal IQ scores (mean IQ scores were 94.16 and 93.87, respectively). The purpose of the experiment was to determine the effect of praise (the experimental treatment) versus criticism (the control treatment) on various aspects of students' creative-writing themes: quality, quantity, creativity, and attitudes toward creative writing. Praise or criticism were given in the form of teacher-made written comments upon students' creative-writing papers. Examples of praise statements used were "Excellent work!" "What an expressive phrase," "Good word choice!". By contrast, criticism was expressed using such statements as: "I'm sure you can do much better!" "Is this your best work?" "Your word choice could be better." Students' creative writing was subjected to these comments for ten weeks and then analyzed for differences. It was found that praise did not produce greater gains in quality or creativity of theme writing than criticism. However, the group receiving praise wrote significantly more words per theme than the group receiving criticism ($t = 2.42$, $p < .01$). The experimental and control treatments had other pronounced effects on students' behavior. For example, the criticized students more often came to the teacher's desk to elicit praise statements ($t = 2.38$, $p < .05$). Also, the children were asked to respond to a checklist question, "Written comments placed on my papers by the teacher made me feel ————," with these results:[13]

[12] Winnifred F. Taylor and Kenneth C. Hoedt, "The Effect of Praise Upon the Quality and Quantity of Creative Writing," *Journal of Educational Research,* 60 (1966), 80–83.

[13] It would have been of interest to analyze these data separately by sex. For example, it seems reasonable to expect that, within the criticized group, boys would show different reactions than girls.

	Group A (praise)	Group B (criticism)
Happy	41	4
Very angry	2	18
Like crying	2	24
Like giving up	4	22
Insulted	2	11
Angry with myself	4	11
Angry with teacher	4	12

Taylor and Hoedt's experiment demonstrates that teachers' written feedback has a definite impact on students' theme writing, classroom behavior, and emotional state. Since the experimental and control groups were randomly assigned, we can be fairly certain that these effects were due to the experimental treatments, not to prior differences between students in each group.

Statistical analysis

The pretest-posttest control-group design typically yields four scores, as illustrated by these hypothetical data:

	Pretest Mean	Posttest Mean
Experimental group	45	95
Control group	50	80

Campbell and Stanley have pointed out that researchers often use the wrong statistical procedure to analyze such data.[14] The incorrect procedure is to do a separate t test on the pretest and posttest means of the experimental group (45 versus 95) and of the control group (50 versus 80). If the t test is statistically significant for the experimental group but not for the control group, it would be concluded that the experimental treatment led to a significant change in subjects' performance. However, this method of statistical analysis is inadequate in that it occasionally produces significant differences that do not really exist between the experimental and control groups. The best statistical method to use is analysis of covariance, in which the posttest means (95 versus 80) are compared using the pretest means (45 versus 50) as the covariate.

Pretest-posttest control-group design with matching

A variation on the pretest-posttest control-group design is the use of the matching technique to obtain additional precision in the statistical analysis of the data. Matching in such designs refers to an attempt on the part of the research worker to place his subjects into experimental and

---

[14] Campbell and Stanley, op. cit., p. 192.

control groups in such a manner that they are closely comparable on a pre-test that measures the dependent variable or variables correlated with the dependent variable. The main purpose of matching is to reduce initial differences between the experimental and control groups on the dependent variable or a related variable.

Matching is most useful in studies where small samples are to be used and when large differences between an experimental and control group on the dependent variable are not likely to occur. Under these conditions the small differences that do occur are more likely to be detected if sampling errors are reduced by the use of matching. The more closely the matching variable correlates with the dependent variable, the more effective the matching will be in reducing these errors. Thus, it is necessary, if matching is to be employed, to have available a matching variable that correlates highly with the dependent variable. This circumstance occurs in many educational studies. For example, in studies concerned with achievement gains that occur under different conditions of learning, alternate forms of the same achievement test can usually be used for the initial matching and for posttesting of the dependent variable. Inasmuch as these alternate forms usually correlate highly, standard error is reduced considerably by the matching technique. This increase in precision is reflected, for example, in the standard error of the difference-between-means formula used for correlated means versus the formula used for uncorrelated means. The formula for the standard error of the difference between uncorrelated means is $\sigma_D = \sqrt{\sigma^2_{m_1} + \sigma^2_{m_2}}$ while the formula for the standard error of the difference between correlated means for matched groups is $\sigma_D = \sqrt{\sigma^2_{m_1} + \sigma^2_{m_2} - 2r_{12}\sigma_{m1}\sigma_{m2}}$. The two formulas are identical except for the last factor in the matched-group formula and, as this factor is subtracted, it always reduces the standard error (the size of the reduction increasing as the size of the correlation increases).

Another advantage of matching is that it permits the division of experimental and control groups into subgroups on the basis of the matching variable in order to determine whether the experimental treatment has had a different effect on subjects at different levels. For example, let us consider an experiment aimed at determining the relative effectiveness of teaching algebra using an inductive method as compared with a deductive method. Subjects are given an algebra aptitude test at the outset, pairs of individuals who are closely comparable in aptitude are identified, and one member of each pair is randomly assigned to each of the two groups. This will produce groups that are closely comparable on the matching variable. At the conclusion of the algebra course (experimental treatment) an algebra achievement test could be given, and the mean score of the group taught by the inductive method could be compared with the mean score of the group taught by the deductive method. Let us assume that in this hypothetical experiment, no significant difference was found in the overall comparison (see Table 21). Because of the data available on the matching variable, however, subgroups could be identified and a further analysis could be made. Based on scores on this variable, each group could be divided into three subgroups—high, average, and low aptitude students. Comparisons of these three subgroups might indicate that high aptitude students achieve more when taught by the inductive method, while low aptitude students achieve more when taught by the deductive method (see Table 21). Significant findings are often revealed in subgroup comparisons that would not even be suspected if the analysis were limited to overall comparisons.

TABLE 21

COMPARISON OF INDUCTIVE AND DEDUCTIVE METHODS IN TEACHING ALGEBRA

	Treatment	
	Inductive Method	Deductive Method
High-aptitude students Mean achievement (N = 25)	78.6	67.2
Average-aptitude students Mean achievement (N = 25)	56.4	58.1
Low-aptitude students Mean achievement (N = 25)	41.5	51.2
Overall mean achievement (N = 75)	58.8	58.8

Steps

The usual steps in carrying out a study using the pretest-posttest control-group design with matching are as follows:

1. Administer measures of the dependent variable or of a variable closely correlated with the dependent variable to the research subjects.
2. Assign subjects to matched pairs on the basis of their scores on the measures described in step 1.
3. Randomly assign one member of each pair to the experimental group and the other member to the control group.
4. Expose the experimental group to the experimental treatment and if appropriate administer a placebo to the control group.
5. Administer measures of the dependent variable to the experimental and control groups and compare in order to determine the effect of the experimental treatment upon the dependent variable.

A study by Yang provides an example of the use of this experimental design.[15] The purpose of this study was to determine whether a drug (Deanol) would bring about changes in the efficiency of the mental functioning of college students. A total of 150 subjects was taken from four sections of a general psychology course. The *School and College Ability Test* (SCAT) was administered, and subjects were matched on the basis of the initial test scores and placed in three experimental groups and one control group. The experimental groups received different dosages of the drug while the control group received a placebo. Over a period of seven weeks, subjects in the experimental group were administered Deanol, while subjects in the control group were administered a placebo—small sugar pills that were identical to the drug in appearance. Subjects participating in the experiment did not know whether they were receiving the drug or the placebo. At the end of the third week and at the conclusion of the experiment, subjects were given different forms of the *SCAT* in order to determine whether differences developed among the experimental and the control groups. As the study turned out, no significant differences were found.

Most difficulties that occur in the application of the pretest-posttest control group design with matching revolve around the matching procedure. The first question that must be solved by the research worker is to determine what variable or variables to use for matching. Matching on a number of variables that are correlated with the dependent variable will reduce errors more than matching on a single variable that is less highly correlated. In attempting to match on more than two variables, however, a difficult problem often comes up because of the impossibility of finding individuals who are reasonably well matched on several variables. Under these conditions the research worker must discard many subjects for whom satisfactory matches cannot be obtained.

Another related problem is to determine how closely to match the subjects on the matching variable or variables. For example, matching individuals within three or four points on IQ leads to a more precise matching than if a difference of ten points were allowed between pairs. This close matching, however, although leading to gains in precision, increases the number of subjects who cannot be matched. Many statisticians seriously question the value of any matching procedure that results in losing subjects because such a procedure may seriously change the nature of the sampling and lead to sampling biases. In the case of matching for IQ, for example, close matching of subjects at the high and low extremes is most difficult because there are far fewer cases at the extremes and therefore greater differences between adjacent scores. Thus, matching on normally

---

[15] John G. L. Yang, *The Effect of Deanol on Intellectual Efficiency and Experience* (Unpublished Master's thesis; Utah State University, 1961).

distributed variables often leads to losing a disproportionate number of extreme cases, thereby reducing the variability, restricting the range, and making the sample less comparable to the population from which it was chosen.

A method of matching that many statisticians favor is to place all subjects in rank order on the basis of their scores on the matching variable. After subjects have been placed in rank order, the first two subjects are selected (regardless of the difference in their scores on the matching variable) and by random means, such as flipping a coin, one subject is assigned to the experimental group and the other to the control group. The next two subjects on the rank list are then selected, and again one is randomly assigned to the experimental group and the other to the control group. This procedure is continued until all subjects have been assigned. The principal advantage of this procedure over the previous two is that it provides a more random group and no cases are lost because of inability to match. Matching, of course, will be less precise than would be the case in close person-to-person matching, but the advantages of not losing subjects outweigh the disadvantages of the less precise matching.

Posttest-only control-group design

This design is similar to the pretest-posttest control-group designs, except that pretests of the dependent variable are not administered to the experimental and control groups. The steps involved in the posttest-only control group design are as follows: (1) randomly assign subjects to the experimental and control groups, (2) administer the treatment to the experimental group but not to the control group, and (3) administer the posttest to both groups.

This design is recommended when it is not possible to locate a suitable pretest or when there is a possibility that the pretest may have an effect on the experimental treatment. However, in choosing this experimental design, the researcher should consider three possible disadvantages of not administering a pretest of the dependent variable. First, we must consider the fact that random assignment is used in order to eliminate initial differences between the experimental and the control group. If initial differences exist, then any differences found on the posttest can be attributed to them rather than to the effect of the experimental treatment. Although random assignment usually cancels out initial differences, there will be some exceptions. When random assignment fails to control for initial differences, then the researcher can use the pretest scores as a covariate in analysis of covariance; thus the initial differences are controlled statistically. In the posttest-only control-group design, pretest scores on the dependent variable are not available and therefore cannot be used to control for initial differences. This design thus relies primarily on random assignment to equate the experimental and the control group. Since random assignment is most effective in equating groups when large numbers of subjects are involved, the posttest-only control-group design is best employed when the researcher has a large pool of subjects available for study. A second disadvantage of not administering a pretest of the dependent variable is that the researcher cannot use these scores to form subgroups to determine whether the experimental treatment has a different effect on subjects at different levels.[16] The third disadvantage occurs when there is differential attrition during the course of the experiment. For example, if subjects in the control and the experimental group drop out of the experiment before it is over, then one can argue that any differences on the posttest are due to differential drop-out characteristics of the two groups, rather than due to the effect of the experimental treatment. The administration of a pretest of the dependent variable makes it possible to examine the validity of the differential attrition hypothesis. Thus, the posttest-only control group design should not be used when it seems likely that there will be considerable attrition of subjects during the course of the study.

Statistical analysis

The data yielded by this experimental design can be analyzed simply by doing a t test comparison of the mean posttest scores of the experimental and the control group. If more than two groups have been studied, then the mean posttest scores can be analyzed using analysis of variance. If the scores depart radically from the normal distribution, then a nonparametric test should be done.

Solomon 4-group design

The posttest-only control-group design enables the researcher to rule out a possible interaction between the pretest and the experimental treatment. Thus, the research findings can be generalized to groups that have not received the pretest. Suppose, though, that the researcher is interested in studying the actual effect of the pretest on the experimental treatment. This effect can be studied by using the Solomon 4-group design.

Let us consider a research problem that might be studied using this experimental design. Suppose that an experiment is planned to test the effect of an instructional film concerning population control on students' attitudes toward this social problem. To measure attitude change, a pretest and a posttest of attitudes toward population control are to be administered. However, the researcher suspects that administration of a pretest might influence subjects' perceptions of the film. For example, the pretest might sensitize them to attend to aspects of the film that convey

[16] The student may refer back to the data of Table 21 to see how subgroup analysis sometimes reveals significant differences between the experimental and the control groups.

attitudes toward population control. To measure this effect, a total group of subjects is randomly assigned to four groups which vary as follows: (1) the first group receives the pretest, the experimental treatment (i.e., the instructional film), and the posttest; (2) the second group receives the pretest and posttest, but not the experimental treatment; (3) the third group receives the experimental treatment and the posttest, but not the pretest; (4) the fourth group receives only the posttest.[17]

To illustrate the statistical procedures used to analyze the data resulting from the Solomon 4-group design, let us work with some hypothetical data. The following are mean scores obtained from four groups corresponding to those just described:

Group	Pretest	Treatment	Posttest
1	12	X	25
2	12		12
3		X	17
4			12

The data are analyzed by doing an analysis of variance of the posttest scores. A special form of analysis of variance is required, which we will discuss later in this chapter under the heading of "factorial designs." For the present we will consider the data analysis in a nontechnical manner. Let us arrange the posttest means using a two-way classification:

	No Treatment	Treatment	Row Means
Pretested	12	25	18.5
Unpretested	12	17	14.5
Column Means	12.0	21.0	

If we look at the row means, we find that the two pretested groups earn a higher posttest mean score (18.5) than the two unpretested groups (14.5). If we look at the column means, we find that the two groups that viewed the instructional film earn a higher posttest mean score (21.0) than the two no-treatment groups (12.0). Thus, it appears that both pretesting and the experimental treatment have an effect on the posttest measures of attitude toward population control. However, let us look at the data more closely. Considering only the two no-treatment groups, we find that it does not matter whether they are pretested or not. Both groups earn posttest mean scores of 12. But it *does* matter whether the two treatment groups were pretested. The mean posttest score of the pretested experimental group (25) is enhanced by 8 points over the mean posttest score of the

[17] Although they do not receive the experimental treatment, groups two and four could be administered a placebo treatment, such as an instructional film on the physical sciences.

unpretested experimental group (17). Thus, it appears that there is an interaction between pretesting and the experimental treatment.[18] The practical implication of this hypothetical finding is that when the instructional film is shown to other groups, who presumably will not be pretested, one should expect a modest attitude change rather than the more dramatic change obtained when pretesting is done.

The Solomon 4-group design enables the researcher to make several other statistical analyses. For example, the effect of the experimental treatment can be determined in four different ways. The pretest and posttest means of group one (12 versus 25) can be compared to determine the actual change brought about by the experimental treatment. Second, the posttest scores of the two pretested groups can be used to compare the experimental treatment with the control group treatment (25 versus 12). Third, the same analysis can be done on the two unpretested groups, one of which received the experimental treatment and the other of which served as a control (17 versus 12). A final way to determine the effect of the experimental treatment is to compare the pretest scores of group one and group two with the posttest score of group three (12 versus 17, and 12 versus 17). Thus, the effect of the experimental treatment can be replicated over four different comparisons.

The Solomon 4-group design is a powerful experimental design. Its main drawback is that it requires a rather large sample and much researcher effort. The effort is justified if there is a high probability that pretesting will have an effect on the experimental treatment *and* if the researcher wishes to measure this effect. Otherwise the use of the pretest-posttest control-group design or the posttest-only control-group design would be the preferred choice.

QUASI-EXPERIMENTAL DESIGNS

Introduction

As we have already discussed, random assignment of subjects to the experimental and control groups is a very important feature of experimental design. However, it sometimes happens in educational research, particularly in field studies, that random assignment is not possible. Under such circumstances it is still possible to do an experiment having adequate internal and external validity. Such experiments have been termed "quasi-experiments" by Campbell and Stanley [19] to indicate the fact that random assignment has not been used. Although quasi-experiments are quite legiti-

[18] As we shall point out later in our discussion of factorial designs, analysis of variance can be used to determine the statistical significance of interaction effects and of differences between row means and between column means.

[19] Campbell and Stanley, op. cit.

mate, the researcher should be aware of the special problems that may arise when subjects are not assigned randomly to groups.

Static-group comparison design

The static-group comparison design is similar to the posttest-only control-group design except in the way that subjects are assigned to groups. Random assignment of subjects to the experimental and control groups occurs in the latter, but not in the former design. The steps involved in the static-group comparison design are as follows: (1) one group of subjects is administered the experimental treatment and is then posttested, and (2) another group of subjects is given the posttest only. The main source of internal invalidity affecting this design is that posttest differences between groups can be attributed to characteristics of the groups as well as to the experimental treatment. For example, suppose teachers in one school are given the experimental treatment and posttest, and teachers in another school are given only the posttest. If differences on the posttest are found, it can be argued that they are due to differences between teachers in the two schools rather than to the effect of the experimental treatment. In this situation where random assignment cannot be used, it is preferable to use the nonequivalent control-group design discussed next. This design is similar to the static-group comparison design except that both groups are given a pretest, which can be used to determine whether the two groups are equivalent even though they have not been formed by random assignment.

Another possible source of internal invalidity in this design is differential mortality. To illustrate this problem Campbell and Stanley discuss a hypothetical experiment comparing first-year and fourth-year college women.[20] This experiment can be considered a static-group comparison since the fourth-year women have received the experimental treatment (i.e., a college education) but not the first-year women, and the two groups have not been formed randomly. Now suppose it were found that the first-year women received significantly higher ratings of beauty than fourth-year women. Would we conclude from these results that college education has a "debeautifying" effect on women? The finding can be explained more plausibly in terms of differential mortality. Although the first-year women are an intact group, many fourth-year women have dropped out of college during the course of the treatment. We could argue, then, that the differences between groups are caused by the more beautiful women leaving college to be married. Thus, the findings are explained more plausibly in terms of mortality in the experimental group rather than in terms of effects of the experimental treatment.

[20] Op. cit., pp. 182–183.

The static-group comparison design is a relatively weak experimental design. The researcher planning to use it should consider carefully the feasibility of administering a pretest to his subjects. If he can make this simple addition to his experiment, he has created in effect a nonequivalent control-group design. This design enables the researcher to make stronger inferences concerning the effect of the experimental treatment on the posttest.

Statistical analysis

The data yielded by this experimental design can be analyzed simply by doing a t test comparison of the posttest mean scores. If the scores deviate considerably from the normal distribution, then a nonparametric test (most probably the Mann-Whitney U test) would be used instead.

Nonequivalent control-group design

Probably the most widely used quasi-experimental design in educational research is the nonequivalent control-group design. To illustrate the steps involved in setting up this design, suppose that the researcher has available for his experiment six classrooms in each of two schools. Because of administrative considerations he must assign all the classrooms in a given school to either the experimental or control group. The first step in the nonequivalent control-group design is to administer a pretest to each student in all the classrooms. Next, one set of six classrooms is assigned to the experimental treatment group, and the other set is assigned to the control group. Third, after the treatment has been administered, all students in both groups are administered the posttest.

Let us now consider an example of a common situation in educational research that makes use of this quasi-experimental design necessary. Suppose that a researcher is interested in testing the effect of an educational practice or product in the public schools. This practice or product is such that it must be administered to an entire classroom or not at all. For example, the researcher might be interested in whether a series of instructional films in social studies has an effect on student achievement. To answer this question suppose he sets up two groups: an experimental group that receives the treatment variable (the instructional films) in addition to conventional instruction in social studies and a control group that receives only the conventional instruction. Now, it is hard to imagine how the researcher can assign students randomly to these two conditions, unless he can wait until the next term and assign pupils at random to different social studies sections. A teacher cannot easily arrange to have half the students in his classroom view the films and the other half not view them. Although the researcher might ask to have the control students leave the classroom while the films are being shown, this procedure would probably have a disruptive effect on the teacher's classroom. In addition, the researcher would need to arrange a special learning situation to occupy the time of the control students while they were out of the classroom. Faced with these difficulties, the researcher had best assign all the students in a given classroom to either the experimental or the control group. Of course, this procedure involves nonrandom assignment, since each student does not have an equal chance of being in either the experimental or control group.

The main difficulty with nonrandom assignment is that the experimental and control groups may differ in some characteristic, thus confounding the interpretation of the experiment. For example, suppose that the researcher was able to recruit six teachers in two schools to participate in the study. The classrooms of three of the teachers are chosen to view the instructional films; the other three classrooms are to serve as the control group. Assuming 30 students per classroom, there will be 90 students in each group. It may be that the experimental and control classrooms differ in some vital respect. Suppose that teachers in the experimental group are drawn from one school and control teachers are drawn from another school. Under these circumstances differential achievement gain might be attributed to characteristics of the schools rather than to the experimental treatment. (For example, the teachers in the experimental group may work in an urban school, whereas the control teachers work in a rural school.)

Most of these problems can be avoided if the researcher can achieve random assignment of subjects to conditions. However, when this is not possible, there are several alternatives from which the researcher can select to lessen the initial differences between treatment groups that may arise due to nonrandom assignment.

First, the researcher should attempt to do preliminary matching to equalize the treatment and control groups as much as possible. In the preceding example, if four of the teachers are male and two are female, the researcher should try to have two males and one female in each group rather than all males in one of the groups. If it is necessary to administer the same treatment to all the classrooms in one school, the researcher should try to select a school to serve as a control that has similar characteristics, for example, similar location, socioeconomic status, organization, and instructional program.

Second, if he cannot randomly assign students in a classroom to groups, the researcher should consider the possibility of assigning *classrooms* randomly to groups instead. In the preceding example, suppose the researcher can obtain 20 classrooms for his study. Assuming that there are no external restrictions on his assignment of particular classrooms to the treatment and control groups, he can do the assigning on a random basis. For example, the researcher can put identification names for the 20 classrooms in a hat. The first classroom drawn from the hat is assigned to the experimental group, the second to the control group, the third to the experimental group, the fourth to the control group, and so on. Thus, true randomization is achieved. However, instead of using the scores of individual students, the researcher uses the mean score of all the students in a given classroom. Thus, instead of having about 600 individual scores (assuming 30 students in each of 20 classrooms), the researcher has 20 mean scores. To determine whether the experimental and control groups differ on the pretest or posttest, the mean of the mean scores for each group can be computed and these two mean scores compared.[21] If the researcher can achieve random assignment of classrooms to groups and if he analyzes the data accordingly, then his design would be essentially a pre-post control-group design.

A third method to compensate for initial differences between experimental and control groups is the analysis of covariance technique. Analysis of covariance reduces the effects of initial group differences statistically by making compensating adjustments of the final means on the dependent variable. Matching could also be used to achieve the same effect, since subjects having comparable pretest scores are selected for inclusion in the statistical analysis of experimental and control-group means. However, in covariance analysis no subjects are lost and the laborious process of matching, which is often difficult to achieve under field conditions in education, is dispensed with. Also, the process of matching under these circumstances is likely to bring about the regression effect, which would confound the interpretation of the research results. Because much educational research must be done on groups that are already in existence, covariance analysis is an extremely valuable tool for use by educational research workers. As an example of this method, let us say that we wish to compare the effectiveness of three different techniques for teaching algebra. Upon visiting the local junior high school, we find several algebra teachers who are willing to cooperate to the extent of using the three techniques in different sections they teach. However, the pupils have already been assigned to algebra sections, and these sections are probably not equal in terms of average algebra aptitude. In this case covariance analysis would be employed. A preliminary test such as the Iowa Algebra Aptitude Test would be administered to each section to determine initial group differences in algebra aptitude. Then, the different teaching techniques would be applied to different sections, and at the end of the period of the experiment, an algebra achievement test would be administered. The mean achievement scores for each group could then be adjusted for initial group differences

---

[21] Statistical techniques for analyzing means of mean scores are presented in E. F. Lindquist, *Design and Analysis of Experiments in Psychology and Education* (Boston: Houghton Mifflin, 1953), pp. 172–189.

in aptitude before making final comparisons of achievement between groups learning under the different teaching techniques.

Time series design

In the time series design a single group of subjects is measured at periodic intervals. The experimental treatment is administered in between one of these time intervals. The effect of the experimental treatment, if any, is indicated by a discrepancy in the measurements before and after its appearance. For example, a researcher might count the mean attendance of college students at six consecutive lectures in several different courses. Suppose that the mean attendance at the first three lectures is 100, 115, 104 (out of the mean total enrollment of 175 students). Between the third and fourth classes, all enrolled students are informed that the professor will conduct a question-and-answer session instead of giving a lecture. The attendance at the fourth class session subsequently increases to a mean of 160 students. For the fifth and sixth class sessions the professor again gives lectures, and the attendance falls back to a mean of 112 and 107 students, respectively. These hypothetical results suggest quite strongly that the use of a question-and-answer session leads to increased student attendance.

If one refers to Fig. 16, it can be seen that the time series design is similar to the one-group pretest-posttest design. Both designs involve the study of a single group, and both designs involve a measurement before and after the experimental treatment. However, the use of *additional* measurements preceding and following the experimental treatment makes the time series design more powerful than the other design. These additional measurements enable the researcher to rule out maturation and testing effects as sources of influence on shifts from pretest to posttest. In the example already given, suppose that the researcher had only counted attendance at the third class (the pretest) and the fourth class (the posttest), this being the occasion of the question-and-answer session. The shift from a mean attendance of 104 students to 160 students could be attributed to the experimental treatment. However, one could argue that the study was carried out early in the school term, during the first four class sessions, and an increase in attendance is natural as the term gets under way. This argument relies on the maturation effect to explain the findings. Also, one can argue that the presence of a researcher counting class attendance (even if unobtrusive) sensitized students to think that the professor planned to stress attendance in evaluating their performance in the course; as a result, nonattendees decided that they had better start coming to class. Here a testing effect is used to explain the findings. Had he used a time series design instead and obtained the findings given above (i.e., class attendance of 100, 115, 104, 160, 112, and 107 students over six class ses-

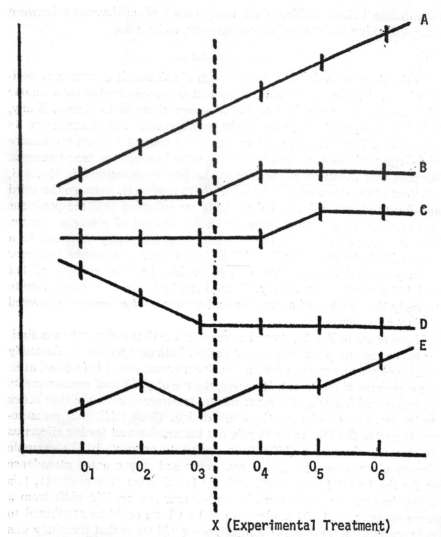

Fig. 16. Possible outcomes of a time series design.

sions), the researcher could safely eliminate maturation and testing as possible sources of influence on the data.

The time series design is quite useful when it is not feasible to form a control group and when subjects can be measured periodically with the same instrument. It seems particularly appropriate for field research where the experimental treatment is a naturally occurring event, such as a change in school administrative policy or teaching method. However, the researcher should be aware that one source of internal invalidity of this experimental design is history. Even if a shift in the measurements is found as expected, it could be attributed to another event occurring at the same time as the experimental treatment (the effect of history). In the example just given, suppose that students were told during the third class session that they would be given a test following the fourth class session (the experimental treatment). The imminence of the test rather than the use of a question-and-answer teaching approach could account for the dramatic increase in class attendance. Thus, in using a time series design, the researcher should attempt to introduce the experimental treatment at a time when no other event could be reasonably expected to affect subjects' performance on the measuring instrument. If the experimental treatment is a naturally occurring event over which the researcher has no control, he should keep note of extraneous events which might also account for any obtained shifts in the measures.

Statistical analysis

Unlike other experimental designs we have discussed, the time series design does not yield data that are amenable to straightforward statistical analysis. Figure 16 presents some possible outcomes of a time series design. Let us suppose that the measuring instrument (O) is an attitude scale assessing favorableness of attitudes toward teaching. This scale is administered to a sample of preservice teachers at one-month intervals on six occasions. Between the third and fourth months, the teachers are given a series of lectures designed to encourage positive attitudes toward the teaching profession. One approach to data analysis would be to use the t test to determine the significance level of the difference between mean attitude scores at O_3 and O_4. We find in Fig. 16 that times series A, B, and E yield the same size shift from O_3 to O_4. However, even if this shift is statistically significant in each time series, we would not conclude that the experimental treatment in time series A and E caused the shift in attendance. For example, although there is a shift in attitude from O_3 to O_4 in time series A, there are similar shifts at other intervals when the experimental treatment was not administered. The shift is plausibly explained as part of a general trend of increasing favorableness toward teaching by preservice teachers, rather than as due to the experimental lectures. In the case of time series E, the shift from O_3 to O_4 cannot be attributed to the experimental treatment in view of the generally erratic pattern that emerges over the six occasions on which teachers' attitudes were measured.

The ineffectiveness of using a simple t test to evaluate time series data can be demonstrated further by examining time series C and D. In time series C there is no immediate effect of the experimental treatment (O_4-O_3), but there does appear to be a delayed effect a month later (O_5-O_4). Of course, the explanation in terms of a delayed effect is tenable only if it has been hypothesized in advance of data collection. Otherwise the "delayed effect" could be attributed to one of many events that occurred between O_4 and O_5. In the case of time series D, there is also no shift from O_3 to O_4. However, the experimental treatment does seem to have an effect here. Whereas teachers' favorableness of attitude had been declining over a period of months, the lectures appear to have had the effect of at least halting the downward trend. (Of course, this interpretation must be evaluated in view of the possibility that teachers' attitudes had reached their lower limit on the scale by O_3, and further decline was not measurable.)

The proper analysis of time series data depends on the particular pattern of findings obtained. Generally analysis of variance or a special type of correlation, called "trend analysis," is used to determine the statistical significance of time series data. The student planning to use time series data should be prepared to consult an expert in research methodology and an advanced statistics textbook.[22]

Counterbalanced designs

Counterbalanced designs are those in which the experimental variables are such that all the different experimental treatments may be administered to the same subjects. The counterbalanced design generally is used when several experimental treatments are to be tested. In effect, it involves a series of replications of the control-group design with random assignment. In each replication, the experimental groups are shifted so that at the conclusion of the experiment, each group has been exposed to each experimental situation. The order of exposure to the experimental situation differs for each group, although the sequence is usually the same. For example, let us examine an experiment designed to test the effects of alcohol and a tranquilizer upon verbal inhibitions.[23] The design of this experiment followed the pattern shown in Table 22. It will be noted that there are five different treatment levels. The first treatment (which was administered to group A in replication 1) involves administration of a placebo followed by measurement on the dependent variable, in this case, a word association test including a number of socially taboo words. The second treatment involves consuming one ounce of alcohol 30 minutes prior to administration of the word association test. The other treatments involve

[22] One such textbook is A. F. Mood, *Introduction to the Theory of Statistics* (New York: McGraw-Hill, 1950). See also Wayne H. Holtzman, "Statistical Models for the Study of Change in the Single Case," in Chester W. Harris (ed.), *Problems in Measuring Change* (Madison, Wis.: University of Wisconsin Press, 1967).

[23] Ruth Southwick, "The Influence of Small Amounts of Alcohol upon Perceptual Inhibitions," (Unpublished Master's thesis; Utah State University, 1960).

consuming larger quantities of alcohol, the tranquilizer, and the two in combination.

Each row in Table 22 represents one replication. It will be noted that

TABLE 22

EXAMPLE OF A COUNTERBALANCED DESIGN

Replication	Placebo	1 Ounce Alcohol	2 Ounces Alcohol	T*a*	2 Ounces Alcohol + T
			Treatment		
1	Group A	Group B	C	D	E
2	E	A	B	C	D
3	D	E	A	B	C
4	C	D	E	A	B
5	B	C	D	E	A
	Overall mean	Overall mean	Overall mean	Overall mean	Overall mean

a T = tranquilizer.

for each replication the groups are shifted so that group A first receives the placebo, then one ounce of alcohol, then two ounces of alcohol until, by the end of the fifth replication, each group has received each treatment. Each box would contain the mean score on the dependent variable for the group, treatment, and replication indicated after the testing was completed. The average mean for each column would give the performance of all five groups on the dependent variable under the treatment represented by the column. For example, in the third column each box would give the mean performance of a group after consumption of two ounces of alcohol, with the overall mean performance for this treatment given at the foot of the column.

Steps

The steps in carrying out the counterbalanced design are as follows:

1. Randomly assign available subjects to the number of experimental and control groups needed.
2. Expose each group to a different experimental treatment, including administration of a placebo to one group.
3. Measure all groups on the dependent variable.

4. Shift groups so that each group is exposed to a different experimental treatment.
5. Measure all groups on the dependent variable.
6. Repeat steps 4 and 5 until every group has been exposed to every treatment.

An experiment of this nature could be carried out as a regular control-group design by randomly assigning each subject to one of the five treatment groups; the experiment would be complete after the first administration of the dependent variable (step 3). At the conclusion of the counterbalanced design experiment, each of the experimental groups will have been exposed to each of the experimental conditions, thus giving results comparable to several replications of control-group design. The principal advantage of the counterbalanced design over the control-group design with random assignment is that, when working with appropriate variaables, it increases the sensitivity of the statistical analysis. This is because, upon completion of the experiment, each of the experimental treatments has been administered to all subjects and therefore subject differences cannot exist except for changes that may have occurred in the subjects during the period required to carry out the experiment. The main limitation of the counterbalanced design is that it may only be used when the experimental treatments are such that exposure to each will have no effect on subsequent treatments. (Earlier in this chapter we designated this threat to the external validity of an experiment "multiple treatment interference." In the previous example, sufficient time was allowed between replications of the experiment so that the effects of the alcohol would have completely disappeared by the time the next replication was carried out. Unfortunately, there are relatively few educational experiments that may be adapted to counterbalanced design. Let us consider, for example, a study in which we are concerned with the efficiency of four different methods of learning poetry. One method might involve memorization of each single phrase followed by combining the phrases into lines, then into stanzas, then into verses, and finally into the entire poem. Another method might involve the line as the smallest unit to be memorized, the next method the stanza, the next method the verse, and finally the entire poem would be memorized as a single unit. This experiment could not be carried out using counterbalanced design because teaching the subject one of these methods of memorization would almost certainly influence his behavior when the later memorization methods were taught.

Statistical analysis

The statistical analysis of data from counterbalanced designs can be quite complex. Generally a modified analysis of variance is used. If he is planning to do an experiment involving a counterbalanced design, the student should consult an expert on research methodology and an advanced statistics textbook.[24]

FACTORIAL DESIGNS

The classic single variable experiment aims at holding all elements of the experimental situation constant except the experimental treatment. However, in most educational situations the experimental treatment cannot realistically be considered in isolation from other factors. For example, using the classic single variable design, a researcher might test the effectiveness of a new reading program (the experimental treatment) by administering it to a large sample of third, fourth, and fifth-grade classrooms. If the mean achievement gain is significantly greater for this sample than for a sample receiving a conventional program (the control group), the researcher would conclude that the reading program is effective. However, further statistical analysis might reveal that the reading program leads to greatly superior achievement gains in the third grade, but not in the fourth or fifth grades. Thus, we cannot consider the effect of the reading program independently of the effect of grade level; the two variables *interact*.

Single variable designs and the statistical techniques used to analyze them (primarily the *t* test) do not permit the researcher to investigate interaction effects. It is necessary to use a factorial design in order to manipulate several variables in the same experiment and to test the statistical significance not only of each variable by itself, but of the interaction effect between variables. There are a variety of factorial designs that the researcher can use, depending on the number and types of variables that are to be manipulated in the experiment.

An example of a simple factorial design experiment is provided by Rotter and Portugal's comparative study of individual and group problem solving.[25] The purpose of their experiment was to test the hypothesis that a combination of individual and group brainstorming would be more effective than either individual or group brainstorming alone.[26] To test the hypothesis, three different variables (individual versus group brainstorming, type of problem, and sex of subject) were manipulated. First, four experimental treatments (called conditions by the authors) were de-

---

[24] See annotated references.

[25] George S. Rotter and Stephen M. Portugal, "Group and Individual Effects in Problem-Solving," *Journal of Applied Psychology*, 53(4) (1969), 338–341.

[26] Brainstorming is a problem-solving technique in which an individual or group tries to think of as many problem solutions as possible without regard to their correctness or quality.

vised: individual brainstorming (I), group brainstorming (G), I followed by G (I-G), and G followed by I (G-I). Thirty-two students were assigned to each treatment and asked to produce as many solutions as possible to a given problem. This design made it possible to determine whether treatments I-G and G-I were more effective than I or G. However, Rotter and Portugal were also interested in determining whether the effectiveness of the treatments depends on the type of problem being solved. Therefore, they manipulated this variable by having half the subjects within each treatment (N = 16) solve a tourist problem (T) and the other half solve an educational problem (E). The researchers also wished to manipulate a third variable, sex of subject. Thus, within each treatment × problem combination, half the subjects were male (N = 8) and half were female. The factorial design can be depicted in the following form:

	I		G		I-G		G-I	
	Problem Problem		Problem Problem		Problem Problem		Problem Problem	
	T	E	T	E	T	E	T	E
Male students	8	8	8	8	8	8	8	8
Female students	8	8	8	8	8	8	8	8

Total N = 128

The preceding table illustrates how three different variables can be manipulated in a single experiment. This particular factorial design is sometimes designated as a $4 \times 2 \times 2$ experiment, because four levels of one variable (treatments I, G, I-G, G-I), two levels of a second variable (problems T and E), and two levels of a third variable (male and female students) are being manipulated. The simplest factorial design is a 2×2 experiment. Rotter and Portugal would have had a 2×2 experiment had they decided to only manipulate two treatments (e.g., I and G) and sex of subject (male versus female).

How does one analyze the data obtained in a factorial design? A statistical technique called "analysis of variance" is used.[27] The mathematical derivation of this technique is quite complex and beyond the scope of this book, but we can present a nontechnical description of it here. In Rotter and Portugal's study, the 128 problem-solving scores varied; the subjects did not all earn the same score. Part of the score variance can be attributed to the fact that the subjects received different treatments. Other parts of the score variance can be attributed to sex differences and differences in the difficulty of the two problems. Still other parts of the score variance are due to interaction effects between these variables (the

[27] The student will recall that analysis of variance was discussed previously in Chapter 12.

meaning of an interaction effect is explained later). Finally, there is residual variance that is due to differences between subjects aside from any effect that the treatments and so forth have on their performance. The contribution of the analysis of variance technique is that it enables the researcher to determine how much of the total score variance can be attributed to each of the variables already mentioned.

Table 23 presents the results of an analysis of variance of the problem-solving data from Rotter and Portugal's study.[28]

TABLE 23

FACTORIAL ANALYSIS OF VARIANCE
OF NUMBER OF IDEAS

Source	df	MS	F
Conditions (A)	3	585.875	5.02*
Problems (B)	1	50.000	
Sexes (C)	1	990.125	8.49*
A × B	3	390.917	3.35*
B × C	1	13.500	
A × C	3	53.208	
A × B × C	3	186.417	1.60
Error	16	116.688	

* $p < .05$.

Looking at Conditions (A) first, we find that there is a statistically significant F ratio. The F ratio is similar in meaning to the t ratio; it indicates that there is a significant difference between the treatment means. Since there were four treatment means (I, G, I-G, G-I), it is necessary to next do t tests to determine which pairs of treatment means differ. It was found that the two mixed treatments (I-G and G-I) produced more solutions than the group problem-solving condition (G). Contrary to the researchers' expectations, individual problem-solving (I) produced significantly more problem solutions than the two mixed conditions. The F ratio for the problems was statistically nonsignificant, meaning that one problem did not elicit more solutions than the other. The significant F ratio for sex can be traced to the fact that males produced more problem solutions than females (see Table 24).[29] Finally, there is a significant interaction between the problems and the conditions. The meaning of this

[28] G. S. Rotter and S. M. Portugal, "Group and Individual Effects in Problem-Solving," *Journal of Applied Psychology*, 53(4) (1969), 339. Reprinted by permission of G. S. Rotter, S. M. Portugal, and the American Psychological Association.
[29] G. S. Rotter and S. M. Portugal, op. cit. Reprinted by permission of G. S. Rotter, S. M. Portugal, and the American Psychological Association.

interaction can be clarified by referring to the mean scores of students in each treatment group shown in Table 24.

TABLE 24

MEAN PRODUCTION OF IDEAS UNDER CONDITION,
SEX, AND PROBLEM TYPE

Con-dition	Tourist problem			Education problem		
	Male	Female	$\overline{X}$	Male	Female	$\overline{X}$
I	78.0	52.0	65.0	61.5	63.5	62.5
G	37.0	34.0	35.5	58.0	42.5	50.2
I-G	52.0	40.5	46.2	71.0	47.0	59.0
G-I	66.5	57.5	62.0	48.0	46.0	47.0

It can be seen that the G-I condition was more effective than the I-G condition (62.0 versus 46.2 ideas) when solving the tourist problem. However, just the reverse is true for the education problem: the G-I condition is less effective than the I-G condition (47.0 versus 59.0 ideas). Thus, we cannot conclude that one of these mixed conditions is more effective than the other without considering the type of problem to be solved. In other words, there is a conditions by problems interaction.

Interactions between two or more variables are a common occurrence in educational research. An experimental treatment may be effective in one type of school but not in another; it may be effective for one type of student but not another; it may be effective only when used under certain conditions of administration. The factorial design is particularly appropriate for investigating interaction effects, since several variables are manipulated at the same time in the experiment.

In discussing Rotter and Portugal's study, we stated that three variables were manipulated. Strictly speaking, only the type of brainstorming group and problem was "manipulated." One cannot manipulate the sex of the subject; it is a given of the situation (i.e., the experimenter cannot manipulate subjects to make them male or female). Campbell and Stanley have provided a useful classification of the types of independent variables that might appear in an educational experiment along this dimension of manipulability:[30]

1. Manipulated variables, such as teaching method, assignable at will by the experimenter
2. Potentially manipulable aspects, such as school subject studied, that

[30] Campbell and Stanley, op. cit., p. 200.

the experimenter might assign in some random way to the pupils he is using, but rarely does

3. Relatively fixed aspects of the environment, such as community or school or socioeconomic level, not under the direct control of the experimenter but serving as explicit bases for stratification in the experiment

4. "Organismic" characteristics of pupils, such as age, height, weight, and sex

5. Response characteristics of pupils, such as scores on various tests.

As Campbell and Stanley point out, the experimenter's primary interest is usually in the class-one variable. Variables in classes three to five are used to group subjects in order to determine how generalizable the effects of manipulated variables are. For example, the researcher's primary independent variable may be a new teaching method. He might also group students by intelligence level (a class five variable, since intelligence is usually determined by a test score) in order to determine whether the teaching method is effective for students of all intelligence levels or just for students of a particular intelligence level.

The design and analysis of factorial experiments is a complicated matter. There are many types of factorial designs depending upon the number of independent variables, the type of independent variables (see classes one to five already mentioned), whether there are unequal numbers of subjects in each treatment group, the scale and distribution properties of scores on the dependent variables, and the need for a covariate to compensate for initial differences between treatment groups. It is useless to develop a sound research hypothesis and to carefully execute the experiment unless the proper factorial design has been chosen. The student who is planning a factorial experiment is well advised to consult a reference textbook on this subject [31] and to consult an expert in the area of experimental design and statistical analysis.

OTHER EXPERIMENTAL DESIGNS

In this chapter we have presented the main designs used in experimental research. However, our presentation is by no means exhaustive. There are many factorial designs that we have not considered here. Also, Campbell and Stanley discuss additional experimental designs which have application to some educational research problems.[32] These designs are

[31] See annotated references.
[32] Campbell and Stanley, op. cit.

essentially variations on designs presented in this chapter. For example, the equivalent time samples design uses a single group of subjects who are measured repeatedly; sometimes the experimental treatment is presented before the measurement, and other times it is not. In an experiment using this design, a researcher compared the effect of 56 days of music on industrial production with 51 days of no music.[33] Essentially, this design is the same as the times series design except for the repeated introduction of the experimental treatment.

It should be apparent to the student at this point that there is a wide range of experimental designs that can be used in educational research. In selecting a design, he should consider its internal and external validity carefully. The main objective is to select a design that will give the clearest picture of the effect of the experimental treatment, unconfounded by the effect of other variables, such as history, maturation, and so forth. Another important objective is to select a design that will yield results that can be generalized to other situations in which one is interested. This is not an easy task. Therefore, the student should consider a range of experimental designs before selecting one to use in his research project.

MEASUREMENT OF CHANGE

All experiments are attempts to determine the effect of an independent variable on a dependent variable. In educational research the independent variable is often a new educational practice or product, and the dependent variable is a measure of student achievement, attitude, or personality. If it has an effect, the independent variable should be reflected as a *change* in students' scores on the measure that was administered before (the pretest) and after (the posttest) the experimental treatment. Thus, an important aspect of experimental design is the measurement of change from pretest to postest scores.

To measure change one might think it sufficient to subtract a student's pretest score from his posttest score. For example, if the student's initial score on a measurement of achievement was 50, and his score rose to 65 after the administration of the experimental treatment, the change score—also called the "gain"—would be 15. However, it is very important for the researcher to realize that there are serious difficulties regarding the legitimacy of change scores as psychometric variables.

These difficulties can be illustrated by considering a published study of achievement gains from the beginning to the end of the freshman year of

[33] W. A. Kerr, "Experiments on the Effect of Music on Factory Production," *Applied Psychology Monographs*, 1945, No. 5.

college.[34],[35] Table 25 lists gains made by students in nine colleges on various tests of achievement.[36] The gain scores are presented separately for subgroups formed on the basis of their pretest scores on each test. It is evident that there is a strong inverse relationship between pretest score and achievement gain. For example, on the test Critical Thinking in Social Science, the students whose scores were lowest at the beginning of the

TABLE 25

AVERAGE GAINS OF STUDENTS ON POSTTESTS, CLASSIFIED
ACCORDING TO PRETEST STANDING

Test	Low Group	Low Middle Group	Middle Group	High Middle Group	High Group
Critical Thinking in Social Science	6.89	5.48	3.68	4.20	2.26
Science Reasoning and Understanding	6.26	5.16	2.93	2.04	0.31
Humanities Participation Inventory	18.00	5.05	4.94	1.39	−2.07
Analysis of Reading and Writing	5.33	2.89	1.81	1.22	0.25
Critical Thinking	6.68	4.65	3.47	2.60	1.59
Inventory of Beliefs	9.09	5.31	4.65	3.32	1.01
Problems in Human Relations	3.19	1.67	1.31	1.51	−0.36

year made considerably larger gains (6.89 points) than the students whose scores were initially highest (an *average* gain of 2.26 points). How are we to interpret such data? Do they mean that students with low initial achievement are likely to learn more (as measured by their change scores) than students with initially high achievement? Although this interpretation is conceivably accurate, it is much more likely that the inverse relationship between pretest scores and achievement gain scores is due to the peculiar psychometric attributes of change scores.

First, scores on many educational tests are subject to a ceiling effect. The concept of ceiling effect means that the range of difficulty of the test items is limited; therefore, the test does not measure the entire range of achievement possible on the dimension being measured. For example, if a student answers 90 items correctly on a 100-item pretest, it is only pos-

[34] P. L. Dressel and L. B. Mayhew, *General Education: Explorations in Evaluation* (Washington, D.C.: American Council on Education, 1954).

[35] The discussion of these data here to illustrate the limitations of change scores is based in part on Diederich's discussion (1956) of the same data (see annotated references).

[36] Adapted by P. B. Diederich, "Pitfalls in the Measurement of Gains in Achievement," *School Review,* 64 (1956) 60, from Paul T. Dressel and Lewis B. Mayhew, *General Education: Exploration in Evaluation* (Washington, D.C.: American Council on Education, 1954). Reprinted by permission of the *School Review,* Paul L. Dressel and Lewis B. Mayhew.

sible for the student to improve his score by 10 points on the posttest. By contrast, a student with a score of 40 on the pretest can make a potential gain of 60 points. Thus, the ceiling effect places an artificial restriction on the distribution of gain scores across levels of initial ability. It is possible that the tests used in Dressel and Mayhew's study were subject to a ceiling effect. Students in the high middle and high groups may have scored near the ceiling of the pretest; thus, they could only earn a minimal gain score when they took the posttest.

The interpretation of gain scores is also confounded because of regression toward the mean. The regression effect means that students who earn a high score on the pretest will earn a somewhat lower score on the posttest, whereas students with a low pretest score will earn a somewhat higher score on the posttest.[37] The regression effect occurs because of errors of measurement in the pretest and posttest and because the tests are correlated with each other. To explain the regression effect in nonstatistical terms, suppose that a student earns a very high score on a multiple-choice achievement test. This is probably not his "true" score; at least one determinant of his high score was probably the operation of chance factors. For example, he may have made lucky guesses on some of the multiple-choice items of which he was unsure; or the test by chance may have included a high proportion of items that he knew. Now it is unlikely that the student will have the same good luck when he next takes a parallel form of the test (equivalent to a posttest in an experiment). Thus, he will likely earn a somewhat lower score. The reverse situation applies to the initially low scorer. This student has probably earned his low score in part because of exceptionally bad luck. Because of the laws of probability, it is likely that his luck will improve when the posttest is administered; thus, he will earn a somewhat higher score. We can see now that gain scores are distorted in part because of the regression effect. In Table 25 the students with initial low achievement have regression working for them to produce a larger gain score, whereas the students with initial high achievement have regression working against them.

A third problem with gain scores is that they assume equal intervals at all points of the test. For example, on a 100-item test, a gain in score from 90 to 95 is assumed to be equivalent to a gain in score from 40 to 45. This assumption is almost never valid for educational measures. In fact, it is probably much harder to make a gain of 5 points when one's initial score is 90 (because of ceiling and regression effects) than when one's initial

[37] The student may recall that on page 366 the regression effect was discussed as a threat to the internal validity of an experiment. It is possible to get significant achievement gains in an initially low-achievement group of students because of the regression effect, even if the experimental treatment has no effect.

score is 40. If the test measures knowledge of word definitions, for example, a student whose initial score is 45 can perhaps earn 5 points by learning the meaning of easy, frequently used words, whereas the student with the initial high score may have to learn the meanings of difficult, rarely used words to improve his score. The problem of equal intervals in test scores is further complicated by the fact that, with the exception of factorially pure tests, a given score on a test may reflect different levels of ability for different students. For example, a mathematics achievement test may include a variety of subtests in addition, subtraction, verbal reasoning problems, algebra, and so on. Two students may earn the same score on the test, although this score may reflect a different pattern of strengths and weaknesses (e.g., student one is weak in subtraction, whereas student two is strong in subtraction but weak in verbal problems). After a period of time, the two students may earn the same gain score because they overcame their respective deficiencies. Thus, the gain score for student one reflects improvement in subtraction skills, whereas the same score for student two reflects improvement in verbal problem solving. Since they are not equivalent in meaning, it is questionable whether the gain scores can be compared statistically.

The fifth difficulty with change scores is that they are not reliable. The higher the correlation between pretest and posttest scores, the lower the reliability of the change score. Also, the reliability of the change score is affected by the degree of unreliability of the pretest and posttest themselves.

We find then that there are many factors that adversely affect the meaning and reliability of change scores, yet some measure of change is necessary if the researcher is to compare the effects of different experimental treatments. Although the limitations of change scores cannot be overcome entirely, there are certain statistical procedures that can be used to overcome some of the limitations. First, we may consider the situation in which the researcher is interested in the change scores of individual students. For example, the researcher may want to know why, in Table 25, some freshman college students showed more gain in Critical Thinking in Social Science (abbreviated here CTSS) than other students. The researcher may hypothesize that the gain scores will be correlated with the students' high school grade-point average (GPA). To test this hypothesis, the researcher should not simply correlate GPA with the CTSS gain scores. Since there is a negative correlation between a student's initial score on CTSS and his gain score (due to regression and ceiling effects), any obtained correlation of GPA with gain scores can be interpreted two ways: the correlation may mean that GPA is related to students' college learning potential, or it may mean that GPA is only related to students' initial achievement score. It is necessary, therefore, to use partial correlation.[38] In partial correlation GPA is correlated with change scores adjusted statistically so that initial score is held constant.

The other situation in which change scores are used is the analysis of mean change. Suppose a researcher administers an achievement pretest to two groups—one group is to receive an experimental treatment and the other is to serve as a control group. If they have been randomly assigned to the two groups, subjects should have equivalent means on their pretest scores. If this is the case, then the researcher can use t tests to determine the statistical significance of the mean change scores. However, occasionally the mean pretest scores will differ significantly by chance even when subjects have been assigned randomly to treatment groups. Also, pretest means may differ when quasi-experimental designs are used. To adjust for initial differences in pretest means, analysis of covariance should be used. Covariance analysis is a statistical technique that permits the researcher to attribute mean change scores to the effect of the experimental treatment rather than to differences in initial scores. For example, covariance analysis could be applied to the data of Table 25. By using this statistical technique, we could compare the mean achievement gain scores of each of the five subgroups *as if* they had all earned the same mean achievement score at the beginning of the freshman year.

MISTAKES OFTEN MADE BY GRADUATE STUDENTS

1. Student selects an experimental design that is inappropriate for his research problem.
2. Does not consider confounding variables, such as history, maturation, regression, and so forth, which might have brought about changes attributed to the experimental treatment.
3. Does not use a factorial design when possible in order to study the effects of several independent variables at once on the dependent variable.
4. When using a control-group design, matches his subjects on variables that do not correlate sufficiently with the dependent variable.
5. In analyzing experimental data, attempts to work with simple change scores when it might be more appropriate to use partial correlation or analysis of covariance.
6. Attempts to use counterbalanced design even though each treatment tends to alter performance on subsequent treatments.
7. Does not take into account the limitations of his experimental design in generalizing his findings to other situations.

[38] The technique of partial correlation is discussed on page 388. The particular form of partial correlation to be used with change scores is discussed in Carl Bereiter, "Some Persisting Dilemmas in the Measurement of Change," in C. W. Harris (ed.), *Problems in Measuring Change* (Madison, Wis.: University of Wisconsin Press, 1963).

ANNOTATED REFERENCES

1. Cox, D. R. *Planning of Experiments*. New York: Wiley, 1958. This text provides a comprehensive treatment of the principles of experimental design. Such basic designs as randomized block designs and Latin squares are treated in the first section of the book, while the latter section deals with factorial designs, incomplete block designs, fractional replication, and other advanced topics. Although the author has attempted to avoid statistical and mathematical technicalities, the average graduate student in education will find this text difficult. It is recommended for students with a strong statistical background who wish to learn more about some of the complex experimental designs. Many of these designs are appropriate for educational research but are not widely used at this time.

2. Ray, William S. *An Introduction to Experimental Design*. New York: Macmillan, 1960. Prepared primarily for psychologists, this text is a useful reference for research workers in education and the other behavioral sciences as well. Single-variable experiments are treated along with factorial designs. The first ten chapters provide the student with a somewhat more thorough treatment of elementary research design than is possible in a textbook in educational research methods, while the later chapters introduce the student to more advanced designs and require a higher level of statistical sophistication. This text is less technical than Cox (see reference 1) and provides the interested student with a foundation that will make transitions to the more advanced textbooks easier.

3. Stanley, Julian (ed.). *Improving Experimental Design and Statistical Analysis*. Chicago: Rand McNally, 1967. The papers in this book are the result of a Phi Delta Kappa symposium on educational research. Some of the papers are fairly technical in nature and are beyond the grasp of the student without extensive training in mathematics. However, the papers by Julian C. Stanley, Frank B. Baker, and Donald T. Campbell should provide the student with insight into the role of experiments in educational research; also, they provide a good discussion of the problems associated with educational experimentation.

4. Harris, Chester W. (ed.). *Problems in Measuring Change*. Madison, Wis: University of Wisconsin Press, 1963. This collection of papers addresses itself to one of the main problems facing the experimenter—the measurement of change from pretest to posttest. Many of the papers require a rather sophisticated understanding of mathematics and statistics. However, the paper by Carl Bereiter ("Some persisting dilemmas in the measurement of change") can be read by students with an elementary statistical background. The paper by Frederic Lord ("Elementary models for measuring change") offers practical suggestions that the student can use in analyzing data from an experiment.

5. Wodtke, K. H. "On the Assessment of Retention Effects in Educational Experiments," *Journal of Experimental Education*, 35 (1967), 28–36. The author discusses a special problem in the measurement of change: the measurement of learning retention. Most experiments use a single posttest, but to assess retention effects, several posttests must be measured. The author presents several statis-

tical procedures that can be used to measure and to test the significance of these retention effects.

6. Diederich, Paul B. "Pitfalls in the Measurement of Achievement Gains," *School Review*, 64 (1956), 59–63. This article provides the student with a nontechnical introduction to the difficulties of measuring changes in achievement.

7. Campbell, Donald T., and Stanley, Julian C. "Experimental and Quasi-Experimental Designs for Research on Teaching," in N. L. Gage (ed.). *Handbook of Research on Teaching*. Chicago: Rand McNally, 1963. This chapter has also been published as a separate title by Rand McNally, 1966. This discussion of experimental designs has become a classic in the field of educational research. Students should read it carefully to supplement our discussion of designs in this chapter.

CHAPTER 16

Educational Research and Development[1]

WHAT IS EDUCATIONAL RESEARCH AND DEVELOPMENT?

Educational research and development (sometimes called "research-based development") appears to be the most promising strategy we now have for improving education. Because research and development is relatively new in education, we will define the term and show how it differs from educational research, which in the past was considered by many to be the best method for improving our schools.

Educational research and development (R & D) is a process used to develop and validate educational products.[2] The steps of this process are usually referred to as "the R & D cycle," which consists of studying research findings pertinent to the product to be developed, developing the product based on these findings, field testing it in the setting where it will be used eventually, and revising it to correct the deficiencies found in the field testing stage. In more rigorous programs of R & D, this cycle is repeated until the field test data indicate that the product meets its behaviorally defined objectives.

In contrast, the goal of educational research is not to develop products, but rather to discover new knowledge (through basic research) or to answer specific questions about practical problems (through applied research). Of course, many applied research projects involve development of educational products. For example, in a project concerned with comparing the effectiveness of two methods for teaching reading, the researcher may develop materials that incorporate each method because suitable materials are not available. Typically, however, these materials are developed

[1] Based on material from *The Minicourse: A Microteaching Approach to Teacher Education* by Walter R. Borg, Marjorie L. Kelley, Philip Langer, and Meredith Gall by permission of Macmillan Educational Services, Inc. Copyright 1970 by the Far West Laboratory for Educational Research and Development.

[2] Our use of the term "product" includes not only material objects, such as textbooks, instructional films, and so forth, but is also intended to refer to established procedures and processes, such as a method of teaching or a method for organizing instruction.

413

and refined only to the point where they can be used to test the investigator's hypotheses. For this reason it is very rare for applied educational research to yield products that are ready for operational use in the schools. Although they have many important contributions to make to education, basic and applied research are generally poor methodologies for developing new products that can be used in the schools. In applied research particularly, the researcher often finds himself comparing poorly designed, unproven, or incomplete products to determine which is less inadequate. This methodology generally produces negative or inconclusive results, and at best brings about improvement in education at a slow rate. Even when they are obtained, positive findings are usually significant only in a statistical sense and have no practical significance for the regular classroom. Another deficiency of many basic and applied research studies is that the situations they study are too removed from the typical classroom to have much direct effect upon educational practice. It is true, of course, that basic and applied research produce the findings that are eventually used to improve educational practice. However, the gap between these findings and educational practice is often so great that many scholars have devoted a lifetime to worthwhile basic and applied research problems without improving the schools one whit.

Educators and researchers have been seeking a way to bridge the gap between research and practice for many years. This is precisely the contribution of educational R & D. It takes the findings generated by basic and applied research and uses them to build tested products that are ready for operational use in the schools. We should emphasize here, though, that educational R & D is not a substitute for basic or applied research. All three research strategies—basic, applied, and R & D—are required to bring about educational change. In fact, R & D increases the potential impact of basic and applied research findings upon school practice by translating them into usable educational products.

THE R & D CYCLE

In the remainder of this chapter we shall discuss each of the major steps in the R & D cycle. The specific R & D cycle which will be presented was developed by the staff of the Teacher Education Program at the Far West Laboratory for Educational Research and Development, with which the authors are affiliated. The Far West Laboratory is one of 10 regional laboratories funded by the U.S. Office of Education to bring about educational improvement through R & D.[3] The Teacher Education Program develops products called "minicourses," which are designed to improve teachers' use of specific classroom skills.

[3] For more information about the regional laboratories, see Chapter 19.

Since we will be using the development of our first minicourse to illustrate the R & D cycle, we will briefly describe here the characteristics of this product. Each minicourse involves about 15 hours of teacher training in either the preservice or inservice setting. During this time, the teacher being trained is introduced to a number of specific classroom skills. These skills are first described and illustrated in an instructional film. The trainee then sees the skills demonstrated in a "model film," that is, a film of a brief classroom situation conducted by a model teacher. Then the trainee plans a short lesson in which he attempts to apply the skills that have been presented, teaches the lesson to a small group of pupils, and records the lesson on videotape. Immediately after the lesson, the trainee views the videotape, focusing his attention on the specific skills he is attempting to learn.

This lesson is called a "microteach lesson" because the regular classroom situation is scaled down in time and number of pupils. Having seen and evaluated the videotape recording of his lesson, the teacher then replans the same lesson and reteaches it the following day to another small group of pupils. This lesson is also recorded on videotape, and he again views and evaluates his performance immediately after the lesson is completed. The teacher then proceeds to the next sequence of instructional lesson, model lesson, microteach and reteach.

The major steps in the R & D cycle used to develop minicourses are as follows:

1. Research and information collecting—Includes review of literature, classroom observations, and preparation of report of state of the art.
2. Planning—Includes defining skills, stating objectives, determining course sequence, and small scale feasibility testing.
3. Develop preliminary form of product—Includes preparation of instructional materials, handbooks, and evaluation devices.
4. Preliminary field testing—Conducted in from 1 to 3 schools, using 6 to 12 subjects. Interview, observational and questionnaire data collected and analyzed.
5. Main product revision—Revision of product as suggested by the preliminary field test results.
6. Main field testing—Conducted in 5 to 15 schools with 30 to 100 subjects. Quantitative data on subjects' precourse and postcourse performance are collected. Results are evaluated with respect to course objectives and are compared with control group data, when appropriate.
7. Operational product revision—Revision of product as suggested by main field test results.
8. Operational field testing—Conducted in 10 to 30 schools involving

40 to 200 subjects. Interview, observational and questionnaire data are collected and analyzed.

9. Final product revision—Revision of product as suggested by operational field test results.

10. Dissemination and distribution—Report on product at professional meetings and in journals. Work with publisher who assumes commercial distribution. Monitor distribution to provide quality control.

This sequence of ten steps, if followed properly, yields an educational product based on research, which is fully ready for operational use in the schools. Although each of the ten steps will be discussed in detail, we should point out here that most of these steps are also included in many educational research projects. This is particularly true of step 6, main field testing, in which quantitative data are collected to determine whether the product meets its performance objectives. This part of the R & D cycle is essentially the same as an applied research project. Thus, many of the skills learned in educational research are useful in conducting R & D projects.

PRODUCT SELECTION

Before the educational R & D process can be applied, it is necessary to describe as specifically as possible the educational product that is to be developed. This description should include (1) an overall narrative description of the proposed product, (2) a tentative outline of what the product will include and how it will be used, and most important, (3) a specific statement of the objectives of the product. In the case of a course of study such as the minicourse, the objectives should state the specific performance levels to be achieved by teachers completing the course, that is, the number of times they will demonstrate each skill within a given time period.

In most cases the nature of the product will change substantially during the development process. This does not mean, however, that the initial planning should be taken lightly. This planning provides the foundation upon which later revisions are built. Without careful planning at the start, the likelihood of building a good product is much reduced.

Since very few well-developed products are available in education, the developer has an almost unlimited range of possible products that he can develop. However, there are a number of criteria that he can apply in selecting an area to work in. The criteria for product selection used at the Far West Laboratory include the following:

1. Does the proposed product meet an important educational need?
2. Is the state of the art sufficiently advanced so that there is a reasonable probability that a successful product can be built?
3. Are personnel available who have the skills, knowledge, and experience necessary to build this product?
4. Can the product be developed within a reasonable time?

It was apparent to the staff of the Teacher Education Program that there was a pressing need to develop effective products for inservice teacher education. School districts generally provide very little inservice education, and what is available is generally poor. Conventional teacher education programs have four serious weaknesses: (1) the teacher is told what to do most of the time, rather than being given the opportunity to practice good teaching techniques; (2) most training programs provide teachers with vague generalities, such as "individualize your instruction," but fail to train them in specific, behaviorally defined classroom skills; (3) student teachers lack effective models to emulate; and (4) conventional training programs provide little or no feedback to the teacher on his classroom performance. The minicourse was designed to overcome these weaknesses of existing teacher training programs.

LITERATURE REVIEW

Once the nature of the educational product has been tentatively identified, a literature review is undertaken to collect research findings and other information pertinent to the planned development. As in basic or applied research, one purpose of the literature review is to determine the state of knowledge in the area of concern. However, in R & D projects, the researcher must also be concerned with how this knowledge can be applied to the product he wishes to develop.

A preliminary review of the literature on teaching methods suggested that questioning techniques in classroom discussions would be a good choice for our first minicourse. The title eventually given to Minicourse 1 was "Effective Questioning—Elementary Level." Since Minicourse 1 was the first product developed by the Teacher Education Program, it was necessary to conduct two literature reviews. The purpose of the first review was to locate research that could be used to develop a basic instructional model for training teachers. Research in four areas was studied: microteaching, learning from films, feedback in learning, and modeling in learning. Through this review we were able to identify several instructional techniques that improve learning. For example, it was found that providing the teacher with videotape feedback of his teaching performance is an effective technique for developing new classroom skills. Another effective technique is to provide a model of the skills to be learned. Interestingly, research findings indicate that the presence of a supervisor is not necessary to bring about teacher improvement when modeling and videotape feedback are provided.[4] In fact, Tuckman and Oliver (1968)[5] found that supervisor feedback led to a change in teachers' rated behavior over a 3-month interval in the direction *opposite* that recommended by the supervisor. Yet many educators believe that the supervisor is a necessary element in training teachers. This example demonstrates that opinion and prevailing practice are often poor guides for developing educational products that work as they are intended to.

Our second literature review was concerned with questioning and discussion skills. We found that research in this area extended back to Stevens' (1912) study of high school classrooms.[6] Stevens found that two thirds of teachers' questions required students to recall facts rather than to think about facts. Furthermore, teachers talked two thirds of the discussion time, thus allowing students to participate only one third of the time. Similar findings have been obtained in more recent studies.[7, 8, 9] It appears that even though they have known about the prevalence of such undesirable teaching practices for a long time, educators have not succeeded in bringing about needed improvements in teachers' classroom skills. We decided that major goals of Minicourse 1 would be to reduce teacher talk and correspondingly to increase student talk, and to increase the percentage of teachers' thought questions.

In the next phase of the literature review, it was necessary to identify specific techniques that teachers could use to accomplish these goals. Although a few research studies were pertinent, it was also necessary for us to give considerable attention to the opinions and experience of practitioners. For example, Groisser advocates several teaching strategies which were included in Minicourse 1, but he presents no evidence on their

---

[4] M. E. Orme, "The Effects of Modeling and Feedback Variables on the Acquisition of a Complex Teaching Strategy" (Unpublished doctoral dissertion; Standard University, 1966).

[5] B. W. Tuckman and W. F. Oliver, "Effectiveness of Feedback to Teachers as a Function of Source," *Journal of Educational Psychology* (August 1968), 297–301.

[6] R. Stevens, "The Question as a Measure of Efficiency in Instruction," *Teachers College Contributions to Education*, 48 (1912).

[7] A. A. Bellack, H. M. Kliebard, R. T. Hyman, and F. L. Smith, Jr., *The Language of the Classroom* (New York: Teachers College Press, Columbia University, 1966).

[8] N. Flanders, "Teacher Influence in the Classroom," in E. Amidon and J. B. Hough (eds.), *Interaction Analysis: Theory, Research, and Application* (Palo Alto, Calif.: Addison-Wesley, 1967), pp. 103–118.

[9] W. D. Floyd, "An Analysis of the Oral Questioning Activity in Selected Colorado Primary Classrooms" (Unpublished doctoral dissertation; Colorado State College, 1960).

effectiveness.[10] Since our later field experience with Minicourse 1 indicated that most of the strategies bring about improved class discussion, they were included in the final form of the course. Interviews and direct field observations have also been useful supplements to the research literature in providing us with a foundation of knowledge upon which to develop a given educational product. For example, in Minicourse 5, which is concerned with mathematics tutoring skills, we could find no research findings regarding what occurs between pupil and teacher in the typical tutoring sequence. In order to partially fill this gap, the laboratory sent observers into a number of classrooms to study tutoring interactions between teachers and pupils. We learned from these observations that the usual tutoring contact between the teacher and the individual pupil was very brief, averaging only 15 seconds. The content of these tutoring contacts suggested that the teacher typically gave the pupil an answer or pointed out his error and then moved on. Efforts to guide the pupil toward the identification of his errors or to develop understanding of mathematical concepts and problem-solving procedures were rare. Although they were not collected in a tightly controlled research setting, these data did provide us with basic information about the nature of mathematics tutoring in the intermediate grades and suggested to us that teachers could profit from learning a tutoring sequence in which the pupil is guided toward discovery of his errors and understanding of mathematical concepts and problem-solving procedures.

In developing an educational product using the R & D approach, the researcher will often have certain questions that cannot be answered by referring to pertinent research. Thus, the researcher will find it helpful to carry out one or more small-scale studies prior to developing the product. Also, as we shall point out in the next sections, the R & D cycle permits several opportunities to collect research data and to revise the product. These phases of the R & D cycle can be used to answer pressing research questions involved in the construction and use of the product.

PLANNING

Once he has completed his review of the literature and collected other pertinent information, the investigator proceeds to the planning step of the R & D cycle.

Perhaps the most important aspect of planning a research based educational product is the statement of the specific objectives to be achieved by the product. A frequent criticism of existing educational practices is

[10] P. Groisser, *How To Use the Fine Art of Questioning* (New York: Teachers Practical Press, 1964).

that no objectives or criteria are available to judge their effectiveness. New curriculum programs are often recommended for their content, format, educational philosophy, and acceptance by teachers and students. Yet what is missing is a statement of the program's objectives in terms of student outcomes. For example, an objective of a social studies program might be stated as, "At least 75 percent of the students who complete the program will earn a score of 90 or better on a test measuring various map skills." Such student-based objectives enable educators to determine in quantitative terms whether the program "works." Objectives also provide the best basis for developing an instructional program, since the program can be field tested and revised until it meets its objectives. Precise specification of educational outcomes—or behavioral objectives, as they are also called—requires considerable skill on the part of the developer.[11] In some ways developing a behavioral objective for an educational product is similar to developing a good criterion in a research study.

During the planning phase, behavioral objectives are usually stated somewhat loosely. For example, in the initial planning of Minicourse 1, one of our objectives stated that after the course most teachers would increase their use of thought questions in a discussion situation. We did not have sufficient knowledge in the planning phase, though, to specify the percentage of thought questions that we would expect teachers to ask in order for the course to be considered effective. As we proceeded through the R & D cycle and accumulated research data, we were able to refine the statement of the behavioral objective so that it took the following form: "Given a 20-minute discussion lesson, at least half of all questions asked by teachers will be classified as thought questions. This criterion will be met by at least 75 percent of teachers who complete Minicourse 1."

Another important element of the planning phase is estimation of the money, manpower, and time required to develop the product. Generally ample resources are needed to carry out a single R & D project. Our experience has been that the cost of developing a single minicourse, which provides about 15 hours of instruction, is in excess of $100,000. A major curriculum project will cost several million dollars. Manpower needs are considerable, too. The development of a minicourse requires an average of 104 man-weeks of professional work, 50 man-weeks of clerical work, and 50 man-weeks of production work. (In contrast, most research projects involve small sums of money, often less than a thousand dollars, and the efforts of a single investigator with perhaps a few part-time graduate assistants.) In R & D work, unless careful planning is done, the investigators may find that their resources have run out before the

[11] A good source of information about behavioral objectives for the beginner is Robert F Mager, *Preparing Instructional Objectives* (Palo Alto, Calif.: Fearon, 1962).

product has been fully developed. Planning is necessary in order to anticipate needed materials, professional help, and field test sites. Consideration of the field test sites is particularly important when testing is done in the schools, which generally are receptive to testing only at certain times of the year. For example, if the product is ready for testing in June, one may have to wait until September or October unless the product can be tested during a summer school session. Also school administrators generally require a few months prior notice before agreeing to have their schools serve as a test site.

Although the R & D specialist must devote a considerable amount of time to initial planning, the planning function is never really ended. As work progresses he is likely to discover several areas in which initial planning was insufficient or in error. Replanning must then be done. Nonetheless it is wise to devote major effort to building a sound initial plan. A good plan can help the investigator avoid much wasted work during later phases of the R & D cycle.

DEVELOPMENT OF THE PRELIMINARY FORM OF THE PRODUCT

After the initial planning has been completed, the next major step in the R & D cycle is building a preliminary form of the educational product that can be field tested. In the case of Minicourse 1, this involved a wide range of tasks. Scripts describing the specific skills that teachers are to learn were written for each instructional sequence. The scripts were then produced on videotape and edited to include clips showing the skills being used in classroom situations. Prospective model teachers were located, observed, and trained to conduct model lessons designed to further illustrate the minicourse skills. The model lessons were then recorded on videotape and edited. A teacher handbook designed to supplement the videotaped instructional lessons was drafted, revised, and printed. A set of forms for the teacher to use in self-evaluation of his microteach and reteach lessons was developed and printed. Questionnaires and interview guides to be used in the preliminary field test were developed, and laboratory staff members were trained in their use. An important principle that should be observed in developing the preliminary form of an educational product is to structure the product so as to permit obtaining as much feedback as possible from the field test. Thus, the preliminary form should include many more procedures for evaluation than will be included in the final product.

The reader who has attempted a major educational R & D effort will realize that these steps, stated so simply, are far from simple to carry out. The investigator must expect many false starts and setbacks in developing a new educational product. However, since the actual procedures involved in product development vary greatly depending upon the nature of the product, there is little specific guidance that can be given in this phase of the R & D cycle. However, one point that applies to most R & D work in education is that the investigator should strive from the outset to develop products that are fully ready for use in the schools. Partially developed products force the local practitioner to make additions and changes in order to use the product. Since few schools are equipped to make such adjustments, a partially developed product cannot be used effectively and is often badly misused.

PRELIMINARY FIELD TEST AND PRODUCT REVISION

The purpose of the preliminary field test is to obtain an initial qualitative evaluation of the new educational product. For the minicourse this evaluation is based primarily upon the feedback of a small group of teachers who take the course plus the observations of laboratory personnel who coordinate the field test. As a rule, from four to eight teachers have been sufficient for the preliminary field test, since the emphasis of this evaluation is upon qualitative appraisal of course content rather than quantitative appraisal of course outcomes.

In all phases of the R & D cycle involving product evaluation, it is important to establish field sites similar to those in which the product will be used when it is fully developed. If a different type of field site is used, the investigator faces the problem of generalizing findings obtained in one setting to another. For example, Minicourse 1 was designed to be used by elementary school teachers during their regular school day. Therefore, the preliminary field test was carried out with six teachers from two elementary schools. Instead of this procedure, we might have invited the teachers and some of their students to our laboratory to take the course, perhaps on a speeded-up basis. The major problem with this procedure is that we might have obtained a very unrealistic impression of the course. Elements of the course that raise no problem in a laboratory setting might create havoc when used in the schools, causing an adverse effect on the course outcomes.

Throughout the preliminary field test of Minicourse 1, two field representatives from the laboratory worked closely with the six teachers in order to obtain as much teacher feedback and observational data as possible. Each teacher was interviewed individually three times during the field test. These interviews focused upon specific problems and course deficiencies as well as suggestions for improvement. At the end of the course, each teacher completed a questionnaire regarding the course and participated in a group discussion with laboratory personnel. In addition to these formal contacts, each teacher had informal contacts with one of the laboratory representatives each day.

The need to obtain extensive feedback from teachers during the preliminary field test can create a problem. Obtaining the necessary feedback results in the teacher's receiving a great deal of attention from the investigators. This attention can produce a Hawthorne effect, which will lead the developer to overestimate the effectiveness of his product.[12] Thus, the developer must strive toward a delicate balance in which feedback is obtained without giving the participating teachers an undue amount of attention.

Observing the participating teachers near the end of the preliminary field test of Minicourse 1 revealed that the teachers were generally unable to use the course skills effectively either in their regular classrooms or in their microteach lessons. Thus, from the standpoint of bringing about specific changes in the classroom behavior of these teachers, the preliminary form of the course was a failure. End-of-course interviews and questionnaires obtained from these teachers, however, indicated that they perceived the course as being very effective and as providing them with a great deal of help in improving their teaching. These responses suggest that teachers as a group are not highly critical and are likely to be charitable in their evaluation of new educational practices. More generally, we have found that global ratings are of little value in evaluating specific educational objectives. Furthermore, they can be detrimental to educational development since they might mislead the investigator into believing that an educational product meets its objectives and is ready for use when actually it is not. In the case of the minicourse, favorable testimonials are perhaps in part a result of the extremely poor quality of most previous inservice teacher education programs which teachers use as a standard of comparison. Nevertheless, our experience has made clear the danger of making user judgment the basis for measuring the success of an educational product. Educational products should have objectives that are couched in terms of terminal behaviors and should be evaluated on the basis of their success in bringing about these terminal behaviors. However, although we put little trust in global teacher evaluations, we rely heavily in the preliminary field test upon specific teacher feedback in helping to develop and improve our educational products. We obtained many specific criticisms and suggestions during the preliminary field test of Minicourse 1 that led directly to changes and improvements in the course structure. In fact, throughout the development cycle, our main

[12] The Hawthorne effect is discussed in Chapter 4.

source of information for revising a minicourse is the classroom teachers who participate in the field tests.

After the preliminary field test of Minicourse 1, all data were compiled and analyzed. The development team used these results to replan the course and then went on to make the revisions called for.

MAIN FIELD TEST AND PRODUCT REVISION

The purpose of the main field test in the minicourse R & D cycle is to determine whether the educational product under development meets its performance objectives. Generally an experimental design is used to answer this question. In the case of Minicourse 1, a single-group, pre-post design was used to determine whether teachers would significantly increase their use of discussion skills. About 50 teachers participated in the experiment. Shortly before the course began, each teacher was asked to conduct a 20-minute discussion in her regular classroom, and this discussion was videotaped. After the course was completed, each teacher again conducted a 20-minute videotaped discussion. Each videotape was viewed by trained raters who made quantitative observations of teachers' use of the skills and behavior patterns presented in the minicourse. Since each videotape was coded and given to raters in random order, the raters did not know which were pretapes and which were posttapes. Table 26 presents the major findings of this experiment to determine the effectiveness of Minicourse 1. Most of the changes in teacher and student behavior brought about by Minicourse 1 are not only statistically significant, but are also significant in their implications for educational practice. Although a control group was not used in the main field test, subsequent studies have indicated that teachers who take the course make substantially larger gains than teachers who either do not have the course or who receive some form of minimal treatment.

In addition to the primary purpose of the main field test, which is to determine the success of the new product in meeting its objectives, the secondary purpose is to collect information that can be used to improve the course in its next revision. Therefore, questionnaire and interview data should be obtained from all participants in the main field test.

If the main field test findings indicate that the new product falls substantially short of meeting its objectives, it is necessary to revise the product and conduct another main field test. This cycle of field testing and revision would continue until the product meets the minimum performance objectives set for it. In practice the product would probably be abandoned if substantial progress were not made in the second main field test.

TABLE 26

MAIN FIELD TEST RESULTS FROM MINICOURSE 1 (N = 48)

Behavior Compared	Pretape Mean	Posttape Mean	t	Significance Level
Increase considered desirable				
1. Number of times teacher used redirection.	26.69	40.92	4.98	.001
2. Number of times teacher used prompting.	4.10	7.17	3.28	.001
3. Number of times teacher used further clarification.	41.17	6.73	3.01	.005
4. Number of times teacher used refocusing.	0.10	0.02	0.00	NS[a]
5. Length of pupil responses in words (based on 5-minute samples of pre- and posttapes).	5.63	11.78	5.91	.001
6. Length of teacher's pause after question (based on 5-minute sample of pre- and posttapes).	1.93	2.32	1.90	.05
7. Proportion of total questions that call for higher cognitive pupil responses.	37.30	52.00	2.94	.005
Decrease considered desirable				
8. Number of times teacher repeated his own questions.	13.68	4.68	7.26	.001
9. Number of times teacher repeated pupil answers.	30.68	4.36	11.47	.001
10. Number of times teacher answered his own questions.	4.62	0.72	6.88	.001
11. Number of one-word pupil responses (based on 5-minute samples of pre- and posttapes).	5.82	2.57	3.61[b]	.001
12. Frequency of punitive teacher reactions to incorrect pupil answers.	0.12	0.10	0.00	NS
13. Proportion of discussion time taken by teacher talk.	51.64	27.75	8.95	.001

[a] Not significant.

[b] Means would have been approximately four times larger if entire tape had been analyzed; t test would have been higher.

OPERATIONAL FIELD TEST AND FINAL PRODUCT REVISION

The purpose of the operational field test is to determine whether an educational product is fully ready for use in the schools without the presence of the developer or his staff. In order to be fully ready for operational use, the package must be complete and thoroughly tested in every respect. In the case of the minicourse, all materials needed to coordinate the course are normally tried out during the preliminary and main field tests. However, since these field tests are conducted by laboratory personnel, a satisfactory test of how well the total course package works "on its own" cannot be obtained. The operational field test is set up and coordinated by regular school personnel and should closely approximate regular operational use. Feedback from both the coordinators and teachers taking the course are collected by means of questionnaires which are mailed in to the Laboratory. The main use of these data is to determine whether the course package is complete. Interviewers focus on parts of the course that fail to do their job or on materials that are needed in order to make the operation of the course easier or more effective. Precourse and postcourse videotapes are not obtained during the operational field test.

After the operational field test is complete and the data have been analyzed, a final revision of the total course package is carried out. In the case of the minicourse program, the Laboratory makes a final revision of all scripts and printed materials and turns these over to a commercial publisher for final production. The course is then sold or rented to schools for operational use in their inservice training programs.[13] During operational use of the course, the publisher supplies course coordinators with evaluation questionnaires and interview forms so that the Laboratory can maintain a continuous appraisal of the course's effectiveness and can identify new problems that arise in its operational use. The final step, however, is essentially a quality control procedure and would not be regarded as further field testing of the course.

PROBLEMS AND ISSUES IN EDUCATIONAL R & D

Since there was virtually no guidance available on the educational R & D process when the Far West Laboratory started its programs in 1966, it was necessary for us to develop our procedures as we went along. In so doing we uncovered several problems and issues that are basic to the R & D approach. Since these issues are likely to be faced by other investigators who do educational research and development, we will describe some of them.

Learning versus polish

The first problem concerns how far the educational developer should go in building the preliminary form of a product involving an expensive

---

[13] Minicourse 1 is being marketed commercially by Macmillan Educational Services, Inc., Front and Brown Streets, Riverside, New Jersey.

component, such as instructional films or tapes. The development of the preliminary form of Minicourse 1 presented us with an interesting dilemma. On the one hand, it was desirable to spend as little money as possible on initial development, since the feedback obtained from the preliminary field test would almost surely call for extensive revision. On the other hand, a poorly developed set of materials might produce poor results even though the ideas underlying the development were sound. The most defensible resolution of this dilemma is to put most of the initial development effort into a simple product that makes maximum use of learning principles, that is, a theoretically sound product. Little or no effort should be devoted to such activities as correcting minor errors in narration, building attractive charts where crude ones would serve the purpose, or reshooting motion picture footage because of poor camera work. In summary, our strategy calls for giving the essentials our best effort and doing everything else as cheaply and quickly as possible. In effect, this approach amounts to a logical application and extension of findings of May and Lumsdaine (1958) and other researchers who have studied the learning outcomes of audiovisual media.[14]

Our experience indicates that the educational developer will not find this an easy road to follow. Media specialists on the development team, such as artists, actors, and television production personnel, may apply great pressure to improve the nonessential aspects of the product. If these pressures are not controlled by the educational developer, he will see an increasing proportion of his resources going into unnecessary polish.

A more subtle reason for resisting efforts to apply polish during the development cycle is that if the developer yields to this pressure, he may well create a monster he is unable to destroy. It is very difficult to scrap a polished product even if field test data indicate that it is not achieving its objectives. First, the developer has spent a great deal of money which he does not want to admit has been wasted. Second, the product looks good and he knows that most consumers of educational products are not very concerned with hard evidence on effectiveness. Finally, even though an educational product fails to achieve its objectives, it is easy to rationalize that it is probably better, or surely no worse, than the competing materials currently in use.

Realism versus pertinence

The second question of development strategy has only recently been resolved in the minicourse program. This question concerns the extent to which educational developers should work with "real" teachers in "real" classrooms who are teaching "real" lessons. Our work with model lessons

[14] M. A. May and A. A. Lumsdaine (eds.) *Learning from Films* (New Haven: Yale University Press, 1958)

in the minicourse instructional model brought us face to face with this problem. Since the use of model teachers seems to offer a great deal of promise as a method of helping other teachers develop effective classroom skills, our experience in developing model lessons during Minicourse 1 seems well worth reviewing.

Initially, we were devoted to the idea that our model lessons would have to be as realistic as possible. We felt that if we could set up video-tape equipment and record the teacher and his pupils without their awareness of what was happening, we would be approaching the ideal model lesson. In practice we found that this idea was often incompatible with the purposes for which model lessons were to be used in the minicourse. In the minicourse model lessons have two main functions. The first is to provide clear-cut examples of the desired skills within the context of a lesson. The second is to give the learner who is taking the minicourse practice in identifying these skills and discriminating among the skills that are being studied. In our initial efforts to develop model lessons, we started by selecting teachers who were reported to have outstanding teaching skills by principals and supervisory personnel. We then worked individually with each teacher, describing the skills that were to be displayed in the model lesson and discussing in general terms methods for fitting these skills into a lesson and modeling them effectively. We then brought videotape recording equipment into the classroom, and teachers conducted the lessons that they had planned.

The typical outcome of these early efforts was a very long model lesson that contained very few examples of the skills that we wished the teacher to model. For example, one of our first model lessons ran for a full hour. During this time the specific skills that the teacher was to model were demonstrated less than five minutes. Though providing a realistic picture of typical classroom teaching, this model was extremely inefficient in terms of the objectives we had set up for the model lesson. Furthermore, if this realistic lesson had been edited to reduce the amount of time that the viewer was required to watch irrelevant behavior, the lesson would have become highly unrealistic, since large segments would have been removed. It became increasingly apparent that if the model lesson were to provide numerous examples of the skills to be learned and contain a minimum of nonpertinent teaching behavior, it would be necessary to plan the model lesson very thoroughly with the model teacher. Thus, although the model lessons for Minicourse 1 were not scripted (the teacher and pupils went through the lesson using their own words), they presented a less natural situation than one finds in the typical classroom. In developing other minicourses, we have found it necessary on occasion to prepare complete scripts so that the model lessons would provide enough clear-cut examples of the skills to be learned within a reasonable period of time. As we have increased our sophistication in working with teachers during the planning and recording of model lessons, their length has gradually been reduced while the number of examples of the skills being modeled has increased.

The idea of creating a less realistic classroom situation in order to gain clarity and save time is a difficult one for many educators to accept. In Minicourse 5, which trains the teacher to use a specific strategy to tutor pupils in mathematics, we found it necessary for teachers to work from a complete script in order to provide a clear illustration of the tutoring strategy. The question then came up: Should we use teachers or actors to play the teaching role in the model lessons? As a compromise we used teachers in two model lessons and actors in the other two. In the main field test of this course we asked the participating teachers whether actors or teachers should be used. (These teachers did not know the identity of the model teachers.) Of the 27 responding, 18 said that only actual school teachers should be used. However, in rating the model lessons, the two done by actors were consistently rated higher than those done by teachers. These findings clearly question the necessity of using "real" teachers in "real" classrooms, teaching "real" lessons for the purpose of teacher training.

Other lessons

Our experience in developing Minicourse 1 also taught us other lessons about educational research and development. First, we learned that the rule so often stated by researchers—if anything can possibly go wrong in a research project, it will—seems to be equally true of research and development. For example, during the preliminary development of Minicourse 1 in 1966, portable videotape equipment was still at a rather primitive level of development. Since we were building a product that relied very heavily upon the use of this equipment for presenting instructional and model lessons and providing feedback during the microteach and reteach sessions, the limitations in the equipment were very important. It was necessary, therefore, for us to put a major effort into developing procedures that would reduce the degree to which our plans could be disrupted by deficiencies or failures in the videotape recording equipment.

Finally, we began to see that developing an educational product was a far more difficult and time-consuming task than we had anticipated. Major development work in education requires a large and competent professional staff and significant long-term financial support. Our experience to date indicates that a large amount of money and labor is required to carry a minicourse through the entire development cycle. Yet we frequently encounter local school administrators who want to develop their own minicourses. There are probably very few school districts that have the resources to attempt a development task of this magnitude. It appears at this time that major educational development programs should be left to organizations such as the regional laboratories and research and development centers, which have the personnel, equipment, and financial support for such work.

OPPORTUNITIES TO DO EDUCATIONAL R & D

We have already discussed the considerable resources required to carry out even a single educational R & D project. It is highly unlikely that a graduate student will be able to find the financial and manpower support to complete a major R & D project. In fact, educational R & D is beyond the abilities of most school districts; it is being realized increasingly that most educational R & D efforts are economical only when a new product is developed at one place and then distributed nationally.[15] There are a number of ways, though, that the student can participate in the R & D process. The student might define a very limited product to develop, particularly if it does not involve expensive materials and requires no more than an hour or two of instruction. For example, a small team of graduate students might develop a new game to improve pupils' skill in using number systems other than base 10. If proven effective, such a product would probably have a much greater impact upon education than the typical doctoral dissertation. Perhaps more feasible, the student might locate a product that has already been developed and use it in a basic or applied research project. For example, the development of the minicourse has raised a number of research problems. One research project in progress is concerned with whether audiotape feedback is as effective as videotape feedback in skill training. Also, much research is needed to determine the effects of teaching skills on student behavior. For example, if teachers are trained to ask more thought questions, what effects will this change have on student behavior? The graduate student could use all or part of a minicourse to investigate such questions.

In the last chapter we shall discuss organizations involved in educational R & D. If he finds an organization developing a product in which he is interested, the student might be able to arrange with the organization to use the product in a research project. Not only might the developers help the student formulate his project, but the student may be able to help the organization answer a pressing research problem.

[15] R. L. Bright and H. D. Gideonse, "Research and Development Strategies: The Current Scene," *The Journal of Experimental Education*, 37 (1968), 139–145.

ANNOTATED REFERENCES

1. Klausmeier, Herbert J., and O'Hearn, George T. (eds.). "Research and Development Toward the Improvement of Education," *Journal of Experimental Education,* 37 (1968), 1–163. This volume contains several articles by researchers working on large-scale research and development projects. These projects include a self-instructional program in productive thinking skills, the mathematics curriculum of the School Mathematics Study Group, the science curriculum of the AAAS Commission on Science Education, and a computer-based instructional system. The volume also contains articles describing basic and applied research that could be used as the foundation of an R & D program.

2. Proceedings of the AIRLIE HOUSE Conference, "The Public Interest vis à vis Educational R & D," *Journal of Research and Development in Education,* 2 (1969), 1–90. In this journal issue, six social scientists discuss the role of R & D in bringing about educational improvement. Hilgard's report deals in part with the relationship between basic research, applied research, and R & D; he illustrates these interrelationships using test development as an example. Chase's report is of particular interest since he discusses a systems analysis approach to developing educational innovations. The student is recommended to study the ten steps characterizing the systems analysis approach and compare them with the R & D approach described in this chapter.

3. Schutz, Richard E. "Developing the 'D' in Educational R & D," *Theory into Practice,* 6 (1967), 73–76. The author describes the R & D process used by the Southwest Regional Laboratory for Educational Research and Development. The six elements of their R & D process are instructional design, test of prototype, production, quality verification, instructional technology, and staff training. The student interested in R & D should compare the process described by the author with that presented in this chapter.

4. Turner, Loyd L. "R and D—In Industry and in Schools," *Educational Leadership,* 25 (1967), 234–237. The author discusses the major role of R & D in industry and how industry is beginning to use R & D to bring about educational improvement. He uses computer-based instruction as an example of how industrial R & D technologists and the educational community can collaborate to improve instruction. Also, the author presents interesting data on relative expenditures on R & D in industry and education.

CHAPTER 17

Processing Research Data

INTRODUCTION

After research data have been collected, it is necessary to process these data into a form that permits easy analysis. Tests must be scored, and scores must often be converted to standard form. Biographical data must be coded, and all data must be recorded in such a way that the analysis may be carried out rapidly and with minimum chance of error.

An important point for the student to remember in processing his data is that a systematic, well-planned procedure is necessary in order to avoid errors and get the most out of the research data.

STEPS IN SCORING STANDARD TESTS

The first step in scoring standard tests used in research is to restudy the test manual and the test in order to be completely familiar with the test content and scoring procedure. Keys are provided with standard tests, and the key should be checked carefully against the test items to be sure that it is correct. Often the handscoring keys supplied with standard tests are less convenient to use than a window key that the research worker can prepare for himself. After keys have been prepared, a definite scoring routine should be set up. In some tests scoring may be done more quickly by scoring the first page of all tests before turning to the second page. On other tests it is more feasible to score each test in its entirety before going to the next. The student can usually arrive at a satisfactory scoring routine by examining the test and answer sheet. When the graduate student is faced with a lengthy test-scoring job, it is usually advisable to work for periods of one or two hours rather than attempt to complete the entire job at one sitting. After an hour or two, most people become tired and bored, which leads to making mistakes. If he alternates periods of study or creative work with periods of test scoring and other clerical work, the graduate student will find the work less fatiguing and will make fewer errors. After all the copies of a test have been scored, the student should select every tenth copy for rescoring. When rescoring, he should tally each error, indicating its size and direction and, if possible, the item on which the error was made. After completing the rescoring of ten percent of the tests, the student must examine the error distribution and decide whether sufficient errors have been found to necessitate rescoring all copies of the test. A few small errors are usually found, and these have relatively little effect upon the research results. After all the copies of a given test have been scored and checked, the tests should be packaged and labeled, giving the date of the testing, the subjects tested, and other pertinent information that may be needed later to identify the data.

MACHINE SCORING OF STANDARD TESTS

Many colleges and universities have test scoring machines available and can supply test scoring services at a low cost. The test scoring machine saves the research worker a great deal of time and should be used to score standard tests whenever the student's finances permit. Some universities will permit the student to score his own tests on the machine during off-hours. If this is permitted, the student should do so because it provides him with valuable experience. Many test scoring machines are also equipped with a graphic item counter that permits item analysis of the test with very little extra work. Item analysis is usually called for if the student has developed his own measure or if he is using a measure which has not been subjected to this analysis. The first step in using the IBM test scoring machine is to check carefully all answer sheets to see that electrographic pencil marks are heavy and to erase random pencil marks that might cause the machine to give an incorrect score. The IBM key should then be checked and the test scored on the machine. Test scoring machines can make errors, so it is advisable to hand score ten percent of the tests and analyze the errors. One-point errors are often made by the person reading the score from the machine. Larger errors can be due to internal difficulties with the machine.

SCORING UNSTRUCTURED OR SELF-DEVELOPED MEASURES

In many educational research projects, the research worker must develop some of his own measuring devices. Occasionally, he uses projective techniques, such as the *Rorschach Inkblot Test* or the *Thematic Apperception Test*, and must adapt the scoring procedures to the specific objectives he wishes to accomplish with these measures. Under these circumstances the scoring procedures should be fully developed during a pilot study or a preliminary tryout of the measurement tools. The usual method of setting up scoring procedures for a new measure is to try out the measure on a number of subjects similar to those who will be used in the main study. During this tryout the research worker can make whatever changes in his scoring techniques seem appropriate, and he may also make changes in the measure itself to correct deficiencies found in the administration and scoring of the preliminary form. After a scoring procedure has been developed, it is usually necessary to administer the measure to another preliminary group in order that an item analysis may be conducted. A measure should not be administered to a research sample until the research worker is fully satisfied with the scoring procedure and has completed the item analysis. Once the scoring of the measure for the research sample has been started, the scoring procedure must remain the same. In many cases the graduate student does an inadequate job of developing scoring procedures, and then, during the scoring of the research data, he discovers changes that should be made. At this point, however, changes cannot be made because this would result in some subjects being scored on one basis and others on another basis. The alternative of rescoring all subjects on the new basis is also questionable unless the measure is highly objective, because his previous scoring may affect the graduate student's perception of the subjects' responses.

The greatest difficulties in developing scoring methods for exploratory measures are encountered in using measures that are somewhat unstructured, such as interview data, observational rating forms, and responses to projective tests. If one of these techniques is used, it is usually necessary that the measure be scored independently by two individuals. This will reduce the likelihood that the biases of a single observer will unduly influence the results, and it also permits the calculation of interrater reliability.

It is extremely important to keep detailed records of the scoring procedure used with self-developed tests or with any test for which the usual scoring procedure is not followed. This information should then be included in the research report so that anyone reading the report can understand the scoring procedure in evaluating the results or replicating the study. The research worker, in developing a scoring system for such measures, should write down his procedure as a series of definite steps to be followed. He should also establish rules and definitions concerning the scoring procedure that will help him score the same responses in the same manner on all his tests. During the actual scoring of the measures, he should refer back to his written scoring procedure frequently, or there may be some tendency to drift away from this procedure as his experience with scoring increases.

RECORDING RESEARCH DATA

After all the measures have been scored and raw scores have been converted when necessary to standard scores, the data should be entered on a record card that lends itself to the planned analysis. In studies involving relatively few cases, such as those usually attempted by graduate students, the hand data card is generally the most efficient method of recording the research data. As a rule, a separate hand data card is prepared for each subject in the study. The hand data card contains all information concerning the subject. A sample hand data card with a key describing each entry is shown in Fig. 17. The research worker can usually have the format mimeographed on 3×5-inch or 4×6-inch note cards at relatively little expense. He then writes in the pupil's name or identification number and copies the research data from the various tests, biographical forms,

I. D.	—————————	Ach 9/60	—————————
Sex	—————————	Ach 5/61	—————————
D. B.	—————————	SSHA	—————————
School	—————————		—————————
Group	—————————		—————————
F. O.	—————————		—————————
IQ	—————————		—————————

Fig. 17. Sample hand data card and key.

I. D.	Pupil's identification number
Sex	1 = Boy; 2 = Girl
D. B.	Date of birth: first two digits give month, second two year (Example: 0250 = February, 1950)
School	1 — Harrison; 2 — Washington; 3 = Horace Mann
Group	1 = Experimental; 2 = Control
F. O.	Level of Father's Occupation using Warner scale
IQ	Total IQ on *California Test of Mental Maturity, 1957 Edition*
Ach 9/69	Achievement score on *STEP Science Test,* level 3, form A, administered 9/69
Ach 5/70	Achievement score on *STEP Science Test,* level 3, form B, administered 5/70
SSHA	Brown-Holtzman *Survey of Study Habits and Attitudes,* Raw Score

Other blanks may be used to record additional data.

school records, and other sources. When he is finished, each card contains all of the information collected about one individual in the study. This method is usually superior to listing the data on summary sheets. With the summary sheet method, the students' names are usually listed alphabetically in the left-hand column of the sheet, and score entries are usually made in the row opposite the student's name. There is a greater chance of error in reading scores from such a sheet than in reading them from the hand data card because it is easy to read the entry from the incorrect row or column on the summary sheet. Hand data cards also simplify analysis in studies where the subjects are to be divided into a number of subgroups for different analytical approaches. With hand data cards, the cards for a given subgroup can quickly be pulled from the deck and data taken directly from them. These cards can then be returned to the deck for analysis of other subgroups or analysis of the overall sample.

The hand data card is too small to permit a complete description of each entry. Therefore, a key sheet describing exactly what is contained in each entry of the card is necessary. The student should use a hand data card large enough to permit a few more blanks than he expects to need because he frequently will encounter information that he wishes to add in the course of the study.

Test scores may often be recorded directly from the test answer sheet to the hand data card. Much of the material collected in educational research, however, must be coded in order to make it readily adaptable to analysis procedures. Descriptive data, such as sex, social class, homeroom teacher, and school attended, are much easier to record if code numbers are assigned. For example, the key for Fig. 17 contains a number code (1, 2, 3) to represent the three schools in the study.

USE OF THE COMPUTER IN DATA PROCESSING

Coding and quantifying of information also permits the research worker to adapt his data to IBM cards for analysis by electronic data processing equipment with little additional effort. If the data on the hand data card are to be transferred to IBM punch cards, the column numbers are given on the hand data card instead of the abbreviated identification. For example, in Fig. 17, instead of I. D., the first entry would be identified as columns 1-3. This would indicate to the key-punch operator that the 3-digit entry in this column would be punched in the first three columns of the IBM card. If the data were to be transferred to IBM cards, the first identification number would be 001, because each column required must be accounted for.[1] Instead of "sex" the next entry would be identified as

[1] Three digits would be required if more than 100 and fewer than 1,000 subjects were used.

column 4 because only one digit would be required to record this information. Date of birth would be identified as columns 5-8 because four digits are required to record the month and year. Eighty digits can be punched on the standard IBM punch card, and a single card will be sufficient to record the data collected in most small studies.

Once data have been readied for the machine by punching on cards or entering on paper or magnetic tape, several steps are required before the electronic equipment can carry out the analysis procedures. Martin and Hall list the following steps that are necessary when a computer is used to solve a problem:

1. The problem must be defined in logical or mathematical terms.
2. This logical or mathematical formulation must be translated into an arithmetical procedure. (The translation from a mathematical statement into an arithmetical procedure is the subject matter of numerical analysis.)
3. An explicit series of instructions to the computer (the program) must be prepared to direct the computer through each step necessary to solve the problem.
4. The input data must be recorded in a form that the machine can read. (Readable media are punched cards, punched paper tape, and digital magnetic tape.)
5. Finally, the problem must be run, and the computer produces answers.[2]

If the student is using a common statistical tool, such as a t test or analysis of variance, it is likely that a program is available that takes care of steps 1, 2, and 3. The student should check with his department or the university computer center to determine which statistical programs are available. If a suitable program cannot be located, then the student can write his own if he has had the necessary training. Otherwise it may be necessary to consult a professional computer programmer who can write a program that will carry out the desired statistical analysis.[3]

If an established computer program is used to perform the statistical analyses, the student should learn the requirements of the program *before* punching the IBM cards and submitting them to the computer center. Some programs require that the cards be punched in a certain format; for example, the program may require that only the first 72 columns on the card (an IBM card has a total of 80 columns) be used. If the student ignores this requirement, the computer will not be able to use the program to perform the statistical analysis. Also, programs usually have certain limits on the number of subjects and variables that can be analyzed. If the student's data exceed these limits, the program cannot be used.

[2] E. Wayne Martin, Jr. and Dale J. Hall, "Data Processing: Automation in Calculation," *Review of Educational Research*, 30 (1960), 523.

[3] The student is also advised to do a literature search to determine whether a computer program meeting his needs has been published (see annotated references).

Assuming that an established program is available for the statistical analysis, the student need only submit the input data (step 4) and control cards to the computer center. The control cards are standard IBM cards that contain such information as number of subjects, number of variables, name of the program, and card format (that is, how many variables are on each card and how many columns each variable occupies). Generally, for established computer programs there is a handbook that describes how these control cards are to be punched.

Although it happens infrequently, it is possible for the computer center to misplace one's IBM cards. This means that all the cards must be re-punched, a costly procedure. Therefore, the student is advised to make a duplicate set of all IBM cards that are submitted to the computer center for analysis. Most computer centers have a duplicating machine that can reproduce a large deck of IBM cards in a few minutes. These few minutes of precaution can save many hours of repeat key punching should the cards be misplaced.[4]

In some studies in which computer analysis is planned, a mark-sense card (see Fig. 18) can be substituted for the regular hand data card. Scores are recorded on the mark-sense card using an electrographic pencil. These scores may then be transferred to a regular IBM punched card without employing a key punch operator, thus greatly reducing cost. In using measures where each response must be transferred to an IBM punched card, such as information on a biographic inventory, a mark-sense card can often be used as an answer sheet. In this case the raw data can be made ready for analysis with very little clerical work. The research worker should take caution when using mark-sense cards to obtain raw data from elementary school children. A study by Thomas Culhane and Quentin Stodola determined whether students at the lower grade levels could follow the instructions for using mark-sense cards with reasonable accuracy.[5] Students in grades one through eight were asked to express their opinions about a new school schedule on mark-sense cards. There were 13 items to be marked. The research results are presented in Table 27, which shows the number of students in each grade, the number of errors caused by making two marks for a single item, and the number of marks too light for machine scoring. It can be seen that double marks are very infrequent at all grade levels; on the other hand, light marks

---

[4] If he plans to do many statistical analyses by computer, the student is advised to learn about other computer machines that may facilitate his work. For example, there is a machine that prints out on a sheet all the data contained in one's IBM cards (a helpful method to check for errors in key punching). Also, there is a machine that automatically counts and sorts IBM cards.

[5] T. Q. Culhane and Q. C. Stodola, "Use of Mark-Sense Cards with Elementary School Children," *Educational and Psychological Measurement*, 27 (1967), 184. Reprinted by permission of *Educational and Psychological Measurement*.

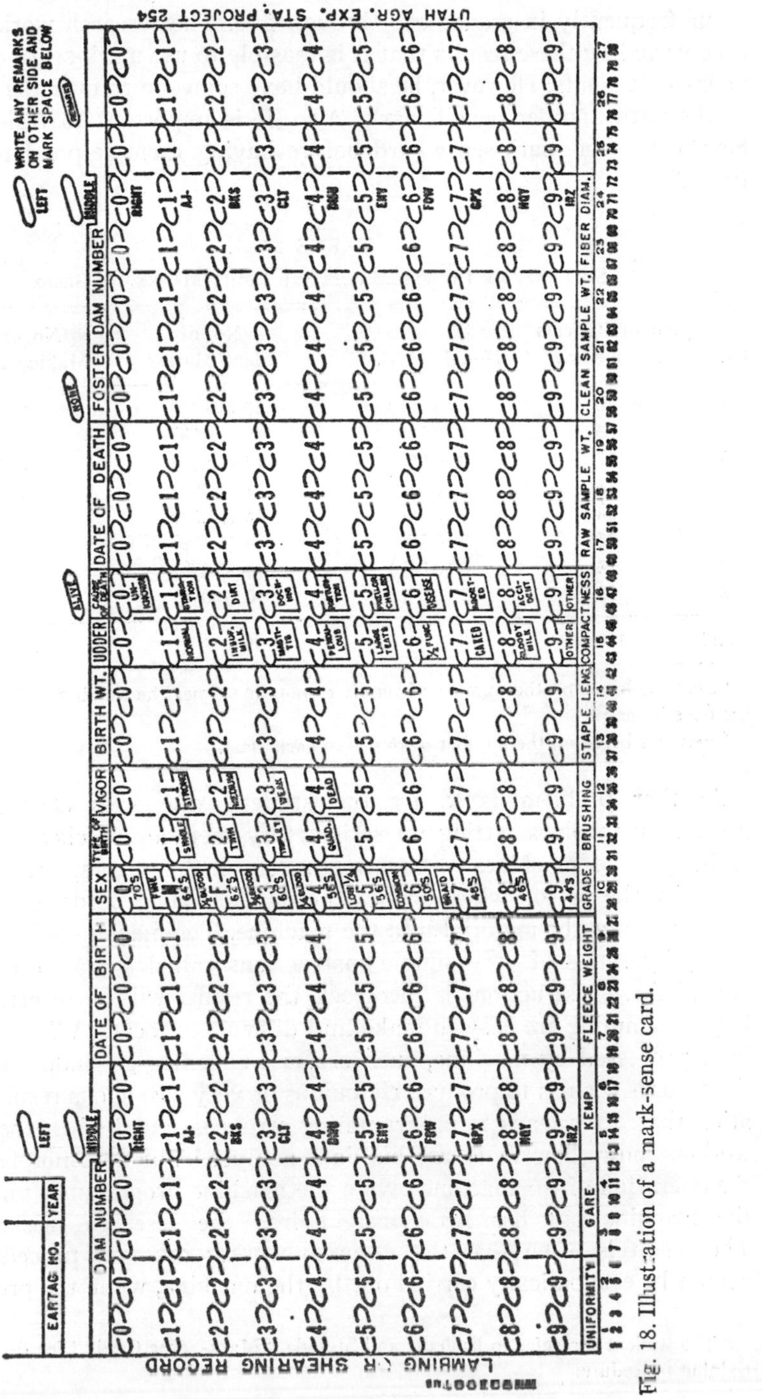

Fig. 18. Illustration of a mark-sense card.

occur frequently in grades one through five. The research worker can be encouraged by these results that it is feasible to use mark-sense cards with younger students. However, he should have someone go over the children's marks with another pencil mark. Also, it is important to train children how to use the mark-sense card before having them respond to the test items.[6]

TABLE 27

SUMMARY OF DOUBLE MARKS AND LIGHT MARKS, BY GRADE

Grade	No. of Students Responding	Double Marks[a]	No. of Light Marks[a]	No. of Students Making Light Marks[b]
1	20	3 (1.2%)	26 (10.0%)	8 (40.0%)
2	23	2 (0.7%)	19 (6.4%)	6 (26.1%)
3	17	0 (0.0%)	13 (5.9%)	2 (11.8%)
4	28	2 (0.6%)	1 (0.3%)	1 (3.6%)
5	24	1 (0.3%)	36 (11.5%)	9 (37.5%)
6	23	2 (0.7%)	4 (1.4%)	1 (4.3%)
7	24	0 (0.0%)	0 (0.0%)	0 (0.0%)
8	23	0 (0.0%)	0 (0.0%)	0 (0.0%)
Total	182	10	99	27

[a] Percents based on the number of pupils responding times the number of items (13) on the questionnaire.

[b] Percents based on the number of pupils in each class.

Another problem faced by the student who uses electronic data processing involves setting up satisfactory methods of checking results. Although the machines themselves rarely make errors, errors can be made by the person who punches the data on IBM cards or the person who programs the material into the machine. The machine merely follows a lengthy series of very simple instructions called a "program," and if any of these instructions is incorrect, the results will be in error. Errors in programming are easy to make and difficult to locate. When data have been processed by machine, such errors frequently go undetected unless the error is such as to produce ridiculous or very suspicious results. A situation that often leads to programming errors is found when the research worker knows how he wants his data analyzed but does not understand the operation of the machine, while the machine programmer understands the machine but has little insight into the research worker's data. The result is often that the research worker asks for procedures that cannot be economically carried out by the machine, while the programmer

[6] The student can refer to Culhane and Stoloda, "Mark-Sense Cards," for details of their training procedure.

suggests procedures for which he already has programs but that do not fit the requirements of the research.

A great many universities have electronic computers and offer courses in their use. Often, if he can prepare his own program for the computer and can operate the computer, the student is permitted to use the equipment without charge. The student who plans a career in educational research should get such training, if available, at his university, even if electronic equipment is not called for in his graduate research project. At present virtually all analysis of major educational research is being done with electronic equipment.

There is some doubt whether it is advisable for the student to turn his data over to the processing center of his university if he is not able to participate actively in the data processing. The student who processes his own research data on a desk calculator has a much better insight into what his data indicate—a better "feel" for the data. This insight often leads to discoveries that would be lost if the data were analyzed by electronic equipment under the supervision of a statistician who may know little about the nature of the data he is processing. The value of electronic data processing for studies involving large numbers of correlations or a complex analysis procedure cannot be overestimated. This method of data processing has opened the door to many research problems that never could have been attacked at all using other methods. The aforementioned precautions are given mainly to make the student aware of the fact that electronic equipment does not provide a panacea. Each research task should be evaluated carefully to determine what form of data processing is the most efficient for that task.

In the next section we shall discuss when it is appropriate to use the desk calculator and when it is appropriate to use a high-speed electronic computer. Whichever of these machines is used, the results should be checked to ensure accuracy. When using the desk calculator, a series of checks at different points in the calculation may usually be made. Some desk calculators now provide a printed tape record of operations that is valuable in checking procedure. Most, however, do not have this feature, and the student must write down the results obtained at key points in his analysis in order to simplify checking. If such checks are not practical, it is advisable to make all calculations twice. Rechecking a major analysis procedure *in toto*, however, is a frustrating procedure because there are many places where an error may be made, and the graduate student who is not highly skilled in the use of a desk calculator may make a different error on each repetition, thus never obtaining a satisfactory check of his results. Checking the work of an electronic computer is usually much more difficult because the student has no data on intermediate steps. He can usually check the program by working out one example on a desk calculator. For example, if the computer has calculated a large number of correlations, he may work one of the correlations on a desk calculator to check the computer program. Generally, if the correct data are entered and the program is correct, the answer given by the computer will be correct.

WHEN TO USE THE COMPUTER FOR STATISTICAL SOLUTIONS

The use of electronic data-processing machines saves a great deal of time and effort in studies involving large numbers of cases or complex analysis procedures. As a rule, the bigger the research job the more is gained by use of electronic data processing. A student can calculate a product-moment correlation involving 100 pairs of scores in about an hour by hand. If he has a desk calculator, this time can be cut to 20 or 30 minutes. Some of the most recent electronic computers can calculate hundreds of product-moment correlations per minute. In fact, high-speed computers can carry out up to 15 million operations per minute. Even though the charge for using such computers is about 300 dollars an hour, the student may be able to carry out all his statistical analyses in only a few minutes' time. At the rate of about five dollars per minute, the cost of using a computer is quite reasonable. This figure, however, does not include the expense involved in setting up the computer program and putting the material in a form the computer can use. Program libraries and exchanges have been set up so that much statistical work can be done at little programming cost. Some adaptation of existing programs is usually necessary, however, to fit the specific problem.

Small studies or studies involving relatively simple analysis can often be done most efficiently using a desk calculator. This is because the cost of programming small studies involving a few subjects is the same as programming the same operations for a great many cases. Inasmuch as programming costs are high, the use of IBM for small studies is often inefficient. A study, for example, involving a number of breakdowns of the research groups into small subsamples followed by comparisons of the mean scores of these subsamples with the t test, is often easier and cheaper to do with a desk calculator than with an electronic data-processing system because of the small number of cases involved and the large amount of programming required to obtain the necessary information by machine.

In deciding whether to use the computer or desk calculator for statistical analyses, the student needs to consider a variety of factors: the number of cases, the number of variables, the complexity of statistical analysis, the number of analyses to be done, and the availability of a suitable computer program and consultant who is familiar with the program. Let us consider a situation that might arise in a research project. A researcher has investigated whether differences in vocational interests and personality traits exist between those high school students who plan to go to junior college (JC) and those who plan to attend a regular 4-year college (RC). Vocational interest and personality inventories, yielding a total of 15 variables, are administered to 30 JC students and 30 RC students. A t test is used to determine whether the two groups differ on any of the variables. If the researcher plans to use the t test on only a few of the variables, the desk calculator would probably be the best method to do the analysis. If the researcher plans to analyze all 15 variables and a computer program is available, the computer would be the method of choice. If the researcher plans subgroup comparisons (e.g., male students versus female students) after the main analysis is completed, a computer is even more desirable, because once the IBM cards are punched and the initial t tests completed, it is usually a simple matter of punching a few new control cards (to give new instructions to the computer) in order to allow further statistical analyses of the same data.

Since many factors are involved in data analysis, the student should consult a person knowledgeable about computer applications in the behavioral sciences before making the decision to use a computer program. However, we can say here that there are at least two types of statistical analyses that are almost always best done by means of a computer program. These are factor analysis and item analysis (used to select items for new tests). Both types of analysis involve hundreds of complex computations, even when the number of cases and variables is not large. Also, the student is advised to consider seriously the use of a computer program when a complex analysis of variance or covariance must be done, or when a regression equation is developed to predict a criterion in a prediction study.

STORING RESEARCH DATA

After he has completed his analysis, the student should file his hand data cards, analysis data, computations, and raw data, labeling all material in such a way that he can easily locate items he wishes to check.[7] In the process of the analysis, he will often wish to refer back to the raw data to check a particular score that seems doubtful. Also, retaining the raw data may make it possible for him to carry out future research in which these data will be used. Sometimes he will hit upon an idea for reanalyzing his data after he has completed the original study. The reanalysis may yield new and interesting information that would be lost if the raw data had been destroyed at the end of the original analysis. If any

[7] Raw data are test answer sheets, observation forms, recording of interviews, and other research material as initially received from subjects.

of his results are challenged, the raw data provide the only fully satisfactory source for rechecking these results.

The process of checking will be greatly simplified if the student records his steps neatly and systematically and labels each step for future reference. The time consumed in keeping systematic records and labeling is well spent because the student will save the time of deciphering forgotten figures and reworking those that he cannot figure out.

MISTAKES OFTEN MADE BY GRADUATE STUDENTS

1. Student fails to set up a systematic routine for scoring and recording data.
2. Does not record details and variations in scoring procedures when scoring data and is then unable to remember what was done when called upon to describe procedure in his thesis.
3. Does not check scoring for errors.
4. Changes his scoring procedure when in the process of scoring his research data.
5. Does not label his data so that he can locate them easily and accurately.
6. Uses the computer to analyze his data when it might be more efficient to use a desk calculator, particularly when only a few statistical analyses are needed.

ANNOTATED REFERENCES

1. Gregory, Robert Henry, and Van Horn, Richard L. *Automatic Data Processing Systems: Principles and Procedures.* Belmont, Calif.: Wadsworth, 1960. A comprehensive discussion of electronic data processing systems and their use. Written primarily to introduce the layman to electronic computers and their applications. The first three chapters provide a brief orientation that will be sufficient for most graduate students. Later sections describe specific equipment, programming, and other topics for the student requiring a reasonably thorough understanding of the subject.
2. Nett, Rogers, and Hetzler, Stanley A. *An Introduction to Electronic Data Processing.* Glencoe, Ill.: Free Press, 1959. Provides the reader with an introduction to electronic computer systems, how they work, programming and machine language, and computer application. Written at a level that can be understood without special training in mathematics or knowledge of computer jargon.
3. Wrigley, Charles. "Electronic Computers and Psychological Research," *American Psychologist,* 1957, 12, 501–508. A brief introduction to electronic computers, tracing their development, describing their operation, and discussing their advantages and disadvantages when applied to research in the behavioral sciences.
4. Lindquist, E. F. *The Impact of Machines on Educational Measurement.* Bloomington, Ind.: Phi Delta Kappa International, 1969. The author discusses how the electronic test scoring machine has speeded up the scoring process and thus greatly increased the use of tests by the public. At the same time the machine has caused test developers to place undue reliance on multiple-choice items. The

author presents some important new developments in electronic machines that permit more flexible item format.

5. Flanagan, John C. "Data Processing in a Large-Scale Research Project," *Harvard Educational Review*, 31 (3) (1961), 250–256. The author discusses the use of the computer in Project TALENT, a large-scale educational research project involving the testing of 450,000 students. The author's delineation of six steps in computerized data processing should prove helpful to the student when he plans his own data analysis.

6. Many computer programs are described in educational and psychological journals. *Educational and Psychological Measurement* regularly includes reports of this type, for example:

Nash, Allan J. "A Generalized One-Way Analysis of Variance Program in Fortran II," *Educational and Psychological Measurement*, 26 (3) (1966), 703–705.

Miller, C. Dean, Doig, Marilyn, and Milliken, George. "Scoring, Analyzing, and Reporting Classroom Tests Using an Optical Reader and 1401 Computer," *Educational and Psychological Measurement*, 27 (1) (1967), 159–164.

Wuebban, Paul L., Timmermans, Gretchen B., and Timmermans, Perry T. Data Processing of Machine Scored Questionnaires," *Educational and Psychological Measurement*, 27 (1) (1967), 195–196.

CHAPTER 18

Preparing the Research Report

INTRODUCTION

The purpose of this chapter is to give the graduate student a general guide for preparing his thesis, dissertation, or research article. The emphasis will be upon general principles of organization and presentation. Errors and weaknesses commonly found in theses and dissertations will be discussed. No attempt will be made to present detailed information on format. Most colleges and universities have established rules on style and format that must be followed closely, and for this reason, specific information on format in a book of this type is of little value to the student.

THE THESIS OR DISSERTATION

Introduction

In carrying out your review of the literature, you will observe that all research articles are organized in essentially the same manner. Theses and dissertations follow this same organizational pattern, but because they are less restricted in length, some topics are covered more thoroughly than in the published research article. Figure 19 is an outline giving the usual organization of the thesis or dissertation. Some variations in this outline will be found in the requirements of different universities.

When he is ready to start writing his thesis, the student should obtain, from his research committee chairman or from the dean of the graduate school, specific information concerning the format required at his university. Some universities prepare a style manual for graduate students; others refer the student to one or more of the published style manuals. It is often wise for the student to ask his committee chairman to refer him to two or three outstanding theses in education recently completed at his school. An examination of these theses along with the prescribed style manual will give the student most of the information he needs to meet the style and format requirements. A study of the organization, method of presentation, and language used in these theses will also give him some

Preliminary Materials

    1. Title page
    2. Preface and Acknowledgments
    3. Table of contents
    4. List of tables
    5. List of figures

Body of the Paper

Chapter 1.   Introduction

    a. General statement of the problem
    b. Statement of the hypotheses
    c. Definition of terms

Chapter 2.   Review of the Literature

    a. Review of previous research
    b. Pertinent opinion
    c. Summary of the state of the art

Chapter 3.   Method

    a. Description of subjects
    b. Description of measures employed
    c. Research design and procedures

Chapter 4.   Findings

    a. Analytic techniques
    b. Description of findings pertinent to each hypothesis
    c. Other findings

Chapter 5.   Summary and Conclusions

    a. Summary of hypotheses, method, and findings
    b. Conclusions
    c. Implications

Reference Materials

    1. Bibliography
    2. Index

Fig. 19. Organization of the thesis.

idea of the sort of thesis that his chairman considers superior. As his own thesis will probably be subjected to the same criteria used by his chairman to evaluate previous theses, this information can be very helpful in preparing his report.

Preliminary materials

Preparing the preliminary materials (title page, preface, table of contents, list of tables, and list of figures) is essentially a matter of following the accepted format. In selecting a title, the student should attempt to be brief while giving a specific description of what his study does. Let us say, for example, that he has done a study comparing the achievement gains of sixth-grade pupils who had taken a course in American history through closed-circuit television with the achievement gains of a matched group of sixth-grade pupils who took the same course through regular classroom instruction. An appropriate title might be "Regular versus Televised Instruction in Sixth-Grade American History." This title is reasonably brief and yet gives the reader some clue as to what the study does. Another title might be "A Study Comparing the Achievement of Sixth-Grade Students Instructed in American History through Closed-Circuit Television and Regular Classroom Procedure." This title tells what the study does but is too long. It also starts out with "A Study," which is superfluous. A third title for the aforementioned study might be "Teaching With Television." This title fails in that it does not tell what the study has done but merely identifies the broad area of the research. In doing your review of the literature, you will find such brief titles to be exasperating. They tell so little that it is necessary to check the article even though the majority will have nothing to do with the area of your review. Many reference books such as *Education Index* list only the title of research reports, and a general title that does not give the reader an idea of what the study has done is misleading and often is not indexed properly.

In preparing the table of contents and the headings for tables and figures, the main point that the student must remember, aside from the usual format requirements, is that such materials should follow parallel grammatical construction. In other words, chapter titles, headings, and titles of tables and figures should be prepared so that they are consistent and comparable in their wording and grammatical construction.

General considerations in preparing the thesis

Students often wait until all data have been collected and all analysis has been completed before starting to write their thesis or dissertation. It is much more efficient for the student to prepare some portions of his research report much earlier. It seems to be an almost inevitable feature of research that the student encounters some periods when he is extremely busy and some periods when he must sit and wait. These lulls in the research routine can be used profitably by the student to prepare drafts of the first chapters of his thesis.

Most students find that the easiest way to prepare a well-organized research report is to outline carefully each section before starting to write the report on that section. This outline may start merely as a listing of all major joints that the student wishes to discuss in the section. These major points may then be placed in what appears to be the most logical order, and finally the subtopics to be discussed under each point can be added to the outline. This detailed outline helps the student a great deal in achieving a logical organization. It helps him identify and think through each point and usually provides him with subheadings for the section he is writing. If he has followed good procedure in planning and carrying out his study, he will have many guides that will help him organize his paper. For example, the outline of his research project, which is prepared early in the research sequence, will contain a detailed statement of the problem and hypotheses that can quickly be filled out to become part of the introductory chapter of his thesis. A well thought out set of subheadings helps the reader a great deal in understanding the organization of the paper and makes the paper more readable.

The introductory chapter

The introductory chapter usually starts with a general statement of the problem area, which has as its aim the general orientation of the reader. This statement should help the reader develop an appreciation for the problem, its place in education, and its importance and pertinence. The next section in this chapter is usually a specific statement of the objectives or hypotheses of the study. These may usually be taken directly from the research plan that the student developed prior to his data collection. The third section of the introductory chapter is devoted to definition of terms. This section is very important because educational terms such as "under-achiever," "gifted child," "core curriculum," and many others are defined differently by different educators. A specific definition of the term as it applies to the reported research is therefore necessary in order that the reader will fully understand the meaning of the report and its significance.

The student can often prepare a reasonably complete rough draft of the introductory chapter early in the conduct of his study. Most writers find that if they prepare a rough draft and then set it aside for a week or two before revising it, they will see weaknesses that would not have been apparent if immediate revision had been attempted. Also, new points or different approaches often occur to the writer during the intervening weeks that can improve the report. If he waits until he has collected and analyzed all his data before drafting any of his paper, the student usually does not have sufficient time to lay each section aside for this period of germination. Another advantage of drafting the early chapters of the thesis while carrying out the research is that a less demanding schedule of writing may be followed. Many people find it difficult to write steadily for any period of time. It is much easier for them to write a few pages and then put the work aside and do something else. Such a procedure is often not possible if the student waits too long to start preparing his report.

Review of the literature

The chapter reviewing the literature is meant to give the reader an understanding of the previous work that has been done in the area of the thesis so that he will better understand the thesis and will be able to fit its findings into an overall picture. In preparing to write this chapter, the first step is to make a rough outline.

The coding system applied to the student's note cards during his review of the literature is often useful as a basis for preparing the first outline. After a rough outline has been prepared covering the major topics of the review, the student should read all his note cards and sort them into the topics contained in the outline. He must then decide upon the order in which these topics will be presented. After ordering his topics, he should review the cards dealing with the first topic until he is thoroughly familiar with their contents. Usually in the process of rereading the cards, he will get some additional ideas on how the topic should be presented. He can also organize the cards for the given topic into the order that he will present them and can decide which studies in this area are to be emphasized. Often he will find two or three studies in each topic that, being more pertinent and carefully done, can serve as the foundation of his review. The student may find several other studies that have been done in essentially the same manner and have produced similar findings. In this case the student should pick out the best studies and describe them in some detail. The other studies are often only summarized by saying "findings of the above studies have been largely supported by a number of other studies that have employed essentially the same approach." These supporting studies may then be referred to in a footnote or referenced using whatever system the student has adopted for his thesis. This procedure has the advantage of presenting the pertinent findings and letting the reader know what other studies support these findings without laboriously discussing each study in detail.

The student should repeat the aforementioned procedure for each of the topics he wishes to cover in his review of the literature. The review of the topics can then be combined in a rough draft of the chapter that is well organized and that gives the reader a brief yet reasonably complete picture of the status of research in the area reviewed.

A more difficult task in preparing the review of the literature is to pull together all the findings under the various topics discussed into an organized picture of the state of knowledge in the area reviewed. The process of combining and interpreting the literature is much more difficult than merely reviewing what has been done. In doing the review, the student should have gained some insights into his field that are not apparent to a person not carrying out a thorough review. These insights should be shared with your reader because they can make a significant contribution to his understanding of the field. This final section of the review is by far the most difficult to write, because it requires that you have a thorough understanding of the research you have read.

A well-organized review of the literature followed by an insightful interpretation is not only of great value to the reader, but its preparation greatly helps the research worker to develop his own understanding of the previous knowledge in his field. If the graduate student's schedule permits, a rough draft of the review of literature chapter should be prepared immediately after completing the review and prior to the start of data collection. At this time the material is most fresh in the student's mind, and the insights that he will gain by preparing his draft and interpreting the previous research may well lead to new ideas and improvements in his research design.

The student is cautioned against an article-by-article presentation in his review of the literature. Many students do little more than prepare an abstract of each article they wish to discuss, and then string these abstracts together without any attempt at continuity or logical organization. Such a review is excessively long and fails in its purpose of giving the reader an understanding of the field. Another pitfall the student should avoid in preparing his review of literature is that of presenting each study in essentially the same way. It is not uncommon, for example, to find reviews of literature in which the student treats each article in a separate paragraph and starts each paragraph with the name of the researcher who has written the described report. Often the student using this approach also devotes the same amount of space to each study he reports, without regard to its importance or pertinence to his topic. Such a stereotyped coverage of the literature, even if well organized, is boring and tiresome to read.

Another error commonly made in preparing the review of the literature is excessive use of quotations. Generally a research report can be made more interesting if quotations are used only when the material quoted is especially well written and can be inserted without spoiling the continuity of the presentation. Nothing is more tiresome or difficult to follow than a review of the literature that is merely an accumulation of quotations, each linked to the next with a sentence or two by the person preparing the review. Inasmuch as each quotation comes from a different context and has a different style, this technique invariably results in a report that is disjointed, poorly organized, and difficult to read.

Research procedures

The chapter on research procedures contains descriptions of the sample, of the measures used, and of the steps taken in carrying out the project.

It usually starts with a detailed description of the sample. This description is needed by the reader to determine the degree to which the research sample is representative of the population and is comparable to other samples to which he may wish to apply the research results. The specific information given in describing the sample varies with the nature of the study, but often includes such information as the age range of the subjects, proportions of each sex if both males and females are used, IQ distribution, scores of the experimental and control groups on variables where comparability is important, urban-rural nature of subjects, education of parents, and so forth. The population from which the sample was drawn should be defined, and the method of selecting the sample should be described in detail. If random sampling was employed, a detailed description of the procedure for selecting cases should be given. If a matching system was used, the matching criteria, why these criteria were selected, the number of cases lost because of inability to obtain a satisfactory matching, and the possible effect of the loss should be discussed in detail. In matching studies some evidence of the comparability of matched groups, that is, an indication of the success of the matching, also should be given. If stratified sampling was used, the criteria for identifying cases at each of the strata or levels should be described, and the method for selecting the cases from those available in each level should also be described. If the study involves comparison of two large groups that are later broken into subgroups, the criteria for establishing the subgroups should be discussed. In most educational studies, it is desirable to describe in considerable detail the schools from which the sample was drawn. This might include descriptions of the curriculum, the socioeconomic groups served by the school, the experience of teachers participating in the study, the performance of the school or district on standardized achievement measures, and the special characteristics of the school or of the geographical area that may tend to make the sample different in some respect from samples drawn from other areas.

The next section of this chapter should include a description of all measures used to collect data in the research project. If well-known standard measures such as the *California Psychological Inventory,* the *STEP Achievement Tests,* or the *SRA Youth Inventory* are used, this description can be quite brief. With well-known measures of this sort, a description of the scores obtained and what they purport to measure, a brief discussion of the evidence of reliability and validity, and the relationship of each measure to the hypotheses are usually sufficient.

If new or little-known measures are used or if measures have been developed especially for the research project, a much more detailed description is required. This should include a description of the types of items used in the measure, reliability data, evidence of validity (with particular emphasis upon construct validity), findings of other studies (if any) in which the measure has been used, and any other material necessary to give the reader a thorough understanding of the measure. If a measure has been developed for the study, a detailed description of how the measure was developed and standardized should be provided. Very often, unless the measure is of a routine nature, such as a biographical data sheet, a separate chapter in the thesis is devoted to the development of the measure. Measures are normally administered either to test one of the hypotheses of the study or to obtain descriptive data concerning the sample that may assist in the selection or description of the sample. In either case the writer should explain in the discussion of each measure the reasons why the measure was selected and the specific purpose that it is to serve in the research.

In using new or locally developed measures or when the scoring procedures of a standard measure have been changed to meet the needs of the study better, a description of scoring procedures is necessary. This description should be sufficiently detailed so as to make it possible for the person reading the description to use the scoring system if he so wishes. In most cases the scoring procedure, keys, a copy of the measure, item-analysis results, and other standardization data on new measures are included in the appendix of the thesis.

In the final section of this chapter, the writer should describe his research procedures, usually starting by identifying the type of experimental design that he has employed, such as descriptive questionnaire study, causal-comparative design, or correlational design. He then should discuss how this basic design was applied in his study, in enough detail that another research worker reading the report could set up an identical study. The description of the research procedures usually reviews the steps taken to collect the data, including any occurrences that may have influenced the results, such as changes in the schedule for administering tests, disturbances during the testing situation, or unexpected subject reactions. This section should also include a discussion of any steps taken to establish controls or reduce errors in the study, such as administering measures to all groups simultaneously or at the same time of day, attempts to equate teacher ability, standardization of the testing situations for different groups, procedures employed to obtain makeups on students absent in the initial testing, methods of avoiding contamination, or controls employed to reduce observer bias. If in carrying out the study the researcher has become aware of any flaws that might have affected the results, these should be discussed so that the reader may consider them in his appraisal of the research findings and so that future research workers may avoid the same mistakes. For example, if measures or techniques are employed that are found to be impractical or inappropriate for the sample, these should be discussed even though the research worker may have discarded the results obtained from them.

Research findings

The next chapter in the thesis or dissertation is concerned with the research findings. If a single analytic technique such as the t test has been employed, this technique and the reasons for using it are usually discussed at the beginning of the chapter on findings. If, on the other hand, the research is such that different techniques have been employed for testing different hypotheses, the description of and reasons for using each technique are usually included with the findings obtained from the use of the technique. Perhaps the best method to obtain clarity in the discussion of the findings is to organize this section of the paper around the hypotheses. After a brief introduction, the writer repeats the first hypothesis as it appears in Chapter 1 and then presents all findings pertinent to this hypothesis. This same technique is then repeated for each hypothesis and has the advantage of focusing the reader's attention on the hypothesis immediately before he reads the pertinent results. The writer should be careful to use the appropriate language in describing each result and the hypothesis that it tests. A research result (defined here as the result of a statistical significance test applied to a correlation coefficient, difference between mean scores, and so forth) does not *prove* or *disprove* a particular hypothesis. Since the test of statistical significance is based on the null hypothesis (see Chapter 11), the writer can only say that his research results *support* or *do not support* a particular hypothesis. Raths has pointed out that many journal publications contain this error of terminology.[1] Although the use of the term "support" rather than "prove" may seem like a small point, Raths argues that it alerts readers to the limitations of the null hypothesis method and increases the likelihood that readers will draw the proper conclusions from the research results.

An approach that many investigators use in preparing the results chapter is to first put the results in tabular form. Then they study the tables carefully, noting the most important results. Then, using the tables as a basis for organizing the chapter, they prepare the text. Tables and figures are useful in describing the research results and in showing trends that have emerged from the analysis. A table or figure can present the overall picture of the data more clearly and more economically than would be possible if each specific fact were discussed in the text. By using tables and figures, the writer is relieved of presenting a tedious recitation of all findings obtained and, instead, can emphasize those aspects of the results that seem to be most important or noteworthy. Students who are inexperi-

[1] James Raths, "The Inductive Process: Implications for Research Reporting," *Educational Leadership*, 24 (1967), 357 ff.

enced in writing research papers often make the mistake of preparing a table and then discussing every entry in the table whether significant or not. This approach results in a boring paper and defeats the purpose of using tables and figures.

The most important task of the researcher in writing the results chapter is to identify and interpret the major findings. He should discuss possible reasons why these results occurred, fit them into the findings of previous research, suggest field applications, and make theoretical interpretations. Because the person doing the study has usually developed a deeper insight into his research problem than will be the case for most of the persons reading the study, his interpretations usually have greater depth than any that most readers would make for themselves. A great deal of thought and careful study is required in interpreting research results. One of the most common weaknesses found in the writing of graduate students is that their reports present important and interesting findings but fail to provide a thoughtful interpretation of these findings. Often the findings obtained from the analysis originally planned by the student will suggest other analytic procedures to the student that will either provide additional data concerning his hypotheses or will yield interesting information not related to his initial hypotheses. In either case the further analysis should be done. Sometimes research workers may be surprised to find that the most important results of their research are unrelated to their original hypotheses.

Summary and conclusions

The summary and conclusions chapter usually includes a brief restatement of the problem, a description of the main features of the method omitting most of the details concerning subjects and measures, a listing of the main findings, and the writer's conclusions based on these findings. The summary should be as brief as possible consistent with a clear presentation of all important information concerning the problem, method, and findings. Findings are often listed by number with each major finding summarized in one or two sentences. The same method suggested for presenting the findings of the previous chapter may be used, that is, each hypothesis may be listed, immediately followed by a very brief summary of the findings related to the hypothesis. The conclusions are usually presented in somewhat more detail. The student should be especially careful to draw all conclusions directly from the findings and to avoid speculations or assumptions totally unsupported by the findings because this is looked upon by most research workers as a sign of immaturity and lack of scientific objectivity.

It is often desirable to add a section on implications. In this section the writer can present interpretations, speculations, and ideas that would be out of place in the conclusions. Possible applications of the findings to the public schools or other field situations may also be discussed; in fact, such a discussion can be of great help to teachers and administrators in the field who may not have sufficient training to discover these applications for themselves.

Inasmuch as this final chapter is the one most often read by other persons, the writer should make every effort to make it clear and concise while covering all the main features of the study.

Reference materials

The usual reference materials in a thesis or dissertation include the bibliography and appendix. The bibliography must list all references that have been referred to in footnotes or otherwise cited in the study and may also include pertinent references not cited.[2] The format of the bibliography should be decided upon when the student starts reviewing the literature so that the data on his bibliography cards will be recorded in the correct format. If this has been done, compiling the bibliography is a very simple matter because it merely requires selecting the bibliography cards that have been cited, placing them in alphabetical order, and copying the bibliographic data onto a sheet. If the bibliography cards have been carelessly compiled, the student will find it necessary to spend a considerable amount of time checking each card and making the changes necessary in order to get the reference in the accepted format. The most common fault found in the bibliographies of theses and dissertations is inconsistent format. The method of referencing a particular type of source should be consistent down to the last comma. Common errors include failure to use the same punctuation marks in different bibliographic entries, the use of the author's first name in some entries and initials only in other entries, the abbreviation of some journal titles while not abbreviating others, and the use of different abbreviations for the same journal title. Each bit of information, however, offers the opportunity to make a mistake, and many mistakes will be made in a bibliographic reference unless the student exercises a great deal of care in preparing his bibliography.

Most theses and dissertations require one or more appendices for presenting items that may be of interest or importance to some readers but are not sufficiently pertinent to be included in the body of the paper. Materials commonly placed in the appendix include (1) tables that are very long or that contain material not essential to understanding the study, (2) locally developed research aids, such as forms and instruction sheets, (3) copies of the data-gathering instruments used in the study, (4) item-analysis data and other materials pertinent to measures, (5) scoring protocols and procedures, and (6) lengthy quotations that may be of interest

---

[2] Some universities require that the bibliography be limited to references actually cited in the study.

to some readers, particularly if the source containing the quotations is not readily available.

PREPARING A RESEARCH ARTICLE

The graduate student has much to gain by preparing one or more research articles based on his thesis or dissertation immediately after he has completed it. At this time all phases of the research are fresh in his mind, and he can prepare the article for publication much more easily than if he puts aside this task and does it later. Most persons who employ holders of graduate degrees in education are interested in their publications; and if the graduate student is able to list one or two publications, he will have an advantage over many of his colleagues.

The first step in preparing a research article is to decide what journal is most likely to publish work in your area. Journals that are likely to accept your article can easily be identified by checking the bibliography of your thesis to determine which journals have published articles pertinent to your research topic. Usually one or two journals will be found that have published most of the articles closely related to your research, and these are the ones most likely to accept your article. A factor that sometimes should be considered in selecting a journal to which the research article will be submitted is the publication lag. If the graduate student plans to seek a position in which research publication is especially important, such as an assistant professorship at a university, it may be to his advantage to submit his article to a journal that provides for early publication. Most journals in education have publication lags ranging from six months to two years. Some journals, however, will publish an article with almost no lag if the author pays an early publication fee. This fee is generally quite high, in some journals, about thirty dollars per page.

Once you have decided upon the journal in which you wish to publish, you should examine several recent issues in order to gain some insight into the format and usual length of articles accepted.

Although it follows the same format as the thesis, the research article is much shorter. Brevity is essential in articles for publication in professional journals because the available space is very limited and the editor usually wishes to include as many studies as possible. In preparing a research article for publication in a journal, the general statement of the problem is usually shortened to a paragraph and is often omitted completely—the article then starting with a statement of the specific hypotheses. The review of the literature is also shortened a great deal, with brief reference made only to those studies that are very closely related to the research being reported. The section on procedure is also shortened to some extent, usually giving only a brief description of the design, sample, and measures used. If, however, some of the procedures or measures employed are new or unusual, they should be covered in some detail. The section on findings makes up a considerably larger proportion of the research article than of the thesis, this section being shortened less when revised for publication. Even in the findings section, however, some shortening of the treatment as it was prepared for the thesis is usually in order. Tables are used extensively because they can present the findings in briefer form. Only the most important findings are discussed at any length in the text. The summary and conclusions should be presented as briefly as possible in the thesis, consistent with clarity, and this section can thus be transferred with little change to the research article. The length of the bibliography is usually not restricted in research articles, and in preparing this section all important sources should be listed. A complete bibliography is, of course, of great help to future researchers who wish to carry out a review of the literature in the same area or wish to learn more about the topic dealt with in your study.

In some cases a thesis or dissertation deals with a subject that can be logically divided into more than one article, and such division usually makes it possible to prepare shorter articles that have a better chance of being accepted for publication. For example, if he were doing a study of the characteristics of successful and unsuccessful nursing school students, a student may have collected some data dealing with personality characteristics and other data concerning vocational aptitudes, interests, and intelligence. In this case, if sufficient important findings were obtained, it may be advisable to prepare two articles for publication—one dealing with personality characteristics of successful and unsuccessful nursing students and the other comparing vocational aptitudes, interests, and intelligence of the two groups.

After preparing a satisfactory draft of a research article, the student should have three or more copies typed (double-spaced) in the format of the journal to which he plans to submit his article. Some journals provide publication manuals that will be of considerable help to the student in preparing an article in acceptable format. If he has decided to submit his article to one of the journals published by the American Psychological Association, he should purchase a copy of the APA publication manual.[3] Usually, however, an article meeting the format requirements of the journal can be prepared without a publication manual if the student carefully follows the format of articles published in a recent issue of the journal. He should be particularly careful to convert the form of his bibliography to the accepted format for the journal he has selected. The manuscript as submitted to the journal should be thoroughly checked at least two or

[3] Available by sending $1.50 to the American Psychological Association, 1200 17th Street, N.W., Washington, D.C. 20036.

three times to be certain that no further changes are needed and no errors are present.

After the final manuscript has been prepared, the author may check a recent issue of the journal to find out where his manuscript should be sent. A brief covering letter should be written, and stamps should be included for the return of the manuscript if it is not accepted for publication. Most journals require that two or three copies of the manuscript be submitted so that copies may be sent to different persons on the editorial board. After the editor receives the manuscript, a postcard is usually sent to the author acknowledging receipt, and the manuscript is sent to members of the editorial board who are most familiar with the topic covered by the article. There is usually a considerable lag before the author is informed whether the article is accepted, and after receiving this information, it may be a year or more before he receives the galley proofs. The galley proofs of an article are set up in type as it will appear in the journal. It is necessary that the author check the galley proofs very carefully and correct any errors discovered.

If the student's manuscript is rejected by the first journal to which it has been submitted, this rejection will usually be accompanied by a statement of the reasons for the rejection. The article, however, may be revised and submitted to another journal. The fact that it has been rejected by one journal does not necessarily mean that it is unsuitable for publication. Many factors operate in the evaluation of an article, such as changes in editorial policy, a particularly heavy backlog of accepted articles, or personal biases of editorial board members, any of which can result in an article's being rejected even though it has merit.

Recently Frantz did a study of the criteria used by journal editors to evaluate manuscripts, and his findings may be helpful to the student who plans to submit a research report for journal publication. Frantz asked members of the editorial boards of six journals (*Personnel and Guidance Journal, Journal of Counseling Psychology, Journal of Educational Psychology, Journal of College Student Personnel, School Counselor,* and *Journal of Educational Research*) to rank a list of criteria commonly used in evaluating manuscripts to determine whether they should be accepted by the journal. The average rank of each criterion is shown in Table 28.[4] It can be seen that the most important criterion is the research report's contribution to scientific knowledge. The student is advised, therefore, to briefly state in the introduction of his report how his research builds upon or goes beyond existing educational theory and previous research findings. The second most important criterion is the design of the study. Journal

---

[4] Thomas T. Frantz, "Criteria for Publishable Manuscripts," *Personnel and Guidance Journal,* 47 (1968), 384–386. Table reprinted by permission of the *Personnel and Guidance Journal.*

editors are concerned about the researcher's choice of subjects, design of treatments, selection of test measures, and control of possible confounding effects.

TABLE 28

SUMMARY OF 14 CRITERIA FOR EVALUATION OF
MANUSCRIPTS RANKED IN IMPORTANCE BY 55
MEMBERS OF THE EDITORIAL BOARDS OF SIX
JOURNALS

Criteria	Mean Rank	SD
1. Contribution to knowledge	1.8	1.2
2. Design of study	3.5	2.1
3. Objectivity in reporting results	4.7	2.3
4. Topic selection	5.5	2.9
5. Writing style and readability	5.7	2.7
6. Practical implications	6.4	3.3
7. Statistical analyses	6.5	2.5
8. Theoretical model	7.0	2.7
9. Review of literature	7.2	2.3
10. Clarity of tabular material	8.1	2.3
11. Length	10.2	1.6
12. Punctuation	11.5	1.9
13. Reputation of author	12.6	1.9
14. Institutional affiliation	13.5	0.9

It is interesting that the editors' third highest ranked criterion was the researcher's objectivity in reporting findings. Before submitting an article for publication, the student should have a colleague read it critically to ensure that the article deals primarily with the research data (rather than the researcher's subjective impressions), and that undue importance is not attributed to the findings, particularly if the absolute size of the correlation coefficients, mean score differences, and so forth is not large. Although ranked fifth in importance, writing style and readability was cited by more editors than any other criterion in their criticisms of manuscripts submitted to them. Experienced researchers usually write many drafts of an article (four or five drafts are not uncommon) and ask their colleagues to criticize the readability of each draft; new researchers would do well to follow the same practice. The new researcher should also be somewhat assured to learn that the journal editors assigned the reputation and institutional affiliation of the author the lowest ranks of the 14 criteria.[5]

[5] Some journal editors make it a practice to omit the name and affiliation of the author before submitting a manuscript for editorial review.

PREPARING A RESEARCH PROPOSAL FOR A FUNDING AGENCY

Educational researchers generally rely on government agencies or private foundations for funding of their projects. In order to obtain funding, researchers need to prepare proposals describing the proposed project, its financial requirements, and its potential contribution to education. The writing of the proposal is very important, since this document is usually the sole means by which the funding agency will decide to support or reject the proposed research project. Although guidelines for preparing a proposal will vary depending upon the agency, there are some guidelines that are generally applicable. In discussing proposal writing, we will use the Regional Research Program of the U.S. Office of Education as an example.

Prior to the actual writing of a research proposal, you should attempt to determine which funding source is most likely to support work on your proposed research study. Federal agencies and foundations often identify a few high-priority problem areas and channel most of their funds into support of projects in these areas. Such priorities are sometimes stated in the agency's literature. In the case of foundations, such information can be found in the *Foundation Directory*.[6] If the priorities of the agency or foundation are not stated in their literature, they may be known to experienced researchers in the field. It is wise to check with your more experienced colleagues on the most likely source of funding for the proposed research. In selecting a funding agency, you should also note that they differ greatly in their preferences for research rigor in the proposed project. For example, the USOE Bureau of Research is most likely to fund proposals that attack a limited and carefully defined problem, using rigorous research procedures. On the other hand, some foundations support loosely stated, innovative attempts to deal with major educational problems.

Thus, your success in obtaining financial support often depends more upon your skill in selecting an appropriate funding source and in writing a proposal that meets its special requirements than in the intrinsic worth and research rigor of your project. Since the interests, biases, and idiosyncrasies of funding agencies shift as new problems become popular in education and new staff members administer the programs, it is important that the researcher get as much current information as he can. It is unfortunate that "grantsmanship" plays a significant role in many decisions on funding of research projects. However, since such is the case, the researcher is wise to learn these biases so that they work for him rather than against him.

[6] Marianna O. Lewis (ed.), *Foundation Directory*, 3rd ed. (New York: Russell Sage Foundation, 1967).

Once you have selected an appropriate funding source, you should write the organization for materials that will help you prepare a proposal. For example, the Regional Research Program issues a bulletin entitled *Guidelines for Preparing a Proposal* which lists the program's goals, resources, eligibility requirements, and types of research funded.[7] Two limitations of their program are that the amount of requested funds cannot exceed $10,000 and the project must be completed within a period of 18 months. Their guidelines also specify types of educational research that they are willing to sponsor. These are primarily research on the learning process and curriculum development. Before submitting a proposal to an agency, the researcher should make sure that it meets all the requirements set forth by the agency; otherwise the proposal will probably be rejected, even though it may be well written and contain good ideas. It is particularly important that the researcher adhere to deadlines for submitting proposals. Although the Regional Research Program will process a proposal whenever it is received, many funding agencies accept proposals only at certain times of the year.

The research proposal is the main document that the researcher will transmit to the funding agency. This document presents the design and budget for the proposed research project. The research proposal is usually given by the funding agency to a panel of reviewers. Since this is the only contact that the reviewers will have with the project, the proposal must contain all the pertinent information about the design of the project. The researcher should not leave anything to be assumed. In preparing the proposal, the researcher should keep in mind that proposed projects are generally evaluated in terms of four criteria:

1. Educational significance. What contribution will the proposed project make to the improvement of education?
2. Soundness of the research design.
3. Adequacy of personnel and facilities.
4. Economic efficiency. Does the proposed project achieve its objectives economically?

Before submitting a proposal, the researcher should evaluate it critically on the basis of these criteria.

There are a few general considerations to keep in mind while writing the actual proposal. First, the proposal should be written clearly, concisely, and in nontechnical language. Generally review panels will have one or more nonspecialists on them; they will rapidly form a negative impression of the proposal if it uses terms that they do not understand.

[7] This bulletin can be obtained by writing any branch of the Regional Research Program. A list of the regions served by this program and addresses of regional offices can be found in Appendix D.

An unclear and unnecessarily long proposal can also cause panel members to form an unfavorable impression. A second general consideration is to make sure the submitted proposal is typed and neat in its appearance. If many copies of the proposal must be submitted, it is probably worth the additional expense to have them multilithed. The physical appearance of the research proposal is a small point, but it can influence some review panel members, particularly since they must rely solely on the proposal to form their impression of the researcher and the worth of his project.

The Regional Research Program recommends that the body of the proposal be divided into four parts. Although they may wish the researcher to use a different organization, other funding agencies will probably need the same types of information. First, there is a statement of the problem and objectives. The statement of the problem should be written in such a manner as to convince the funding agency that your research project is important and likely to make a contribution to education. It is particularly important that the problem be clearly delimited. If the problem is too broadly stated, the funding agency will probably conclude that the project is unwieldy and that you have not thought through the problem deeply enough. The statement of objectives can be in the form of the research hypotheses that you wish to test or the research questions that you wish to answer. These should be stated clearly, concisely, and in simple language. This section of the proposal should also contain a review of the literature. Generally an exhaustive review of the literature is not required. However, the review should indicate that you have a command of the research in your area, including recent research findings, if any. Also, it is advisable to discuss those studies most relevant to the proposed project. The review should be tied directly to the statement of the problem and research objectives.

The second part of the proposal describes the research design that will be used. It is advisable to describe the design in considerable detail. Generally at least one review panel member will be a research methodologist. He will be studying the proposal for flaws and weaknesses in the design. The statement of the research design includes a description of the sample, measures to be administered, and experimental treatments, if appropriate. The research design should be tied directly to the research problem and objectives. The description of the sample is particularly important, because the type of sample selected will affect the generalizability of the research findings. Funding agencies are inclined to fund projects that are likely to yield generally applicable findings rather than projects that deal only with a local problem. The researcher should also build a sound rationale for the size of the sample he has chosen, since sample size often affects the amount of funding required. Even though he may wish to study an entire defined population because it is available, the researcher should probably study a sample drawn from it in order to reduce the cost of the project. The researcher's plans for analyzing the data should also be described in this section. If computer services are needed to analyze the data, he should state how he plans to obtain them. Finally, he should provide a tentative time schedule for completion of the project.

The third part of the proposal should describe the potential relevance of the findings. The researcher must state clearly the new knowledge that may be expected to result from the study. If relevant, he should discuss how he proposes to use or build upon this knowledge when the project is completed. Also, the researcher should state how he proposes to disseminate the findings resulting from the project.

Personnel and facilities are described in the fourth part of the research proposal. Generally funding agencies will want information about all personnel associated with the proposed project. The following information is usually requested: name, position, experience, responsibilities within the project, percentage of time committed to the project, and extent to which a commitment has been secured. If the researcher has identified consultants who will be used in the project, they should be identified by name. Letters from consultants stating their willingness to serve on the project are helpful and may be attached as an appendix to the proposal. Research facilities should be described, including public schools if they are to be used in the project. Funding agencies will generally want some statement of assurance that the facilities are available for the project.

The statement of the budget request is usually a separate section of the research proposal. The researcher must make careful estimates of all expenses that are likely to be incurred in carrying out the project. The budget form used by the Regional Research Program contains the following items: personnel salaries, employee benefits, travel expenses, supplies and materials, communications, services (duplicating and reproduction, statistical analysis, testing), final report production, and equipment. Alternative budgets may be prepared if appropriate to the nature of the research project. An important aspect of the budget is the statement of cost sharing to be provided by the institution with which the researcher is affiliated. Many funding agencies require that the researcher's institution, such as a school district or university, share part of the cost of the proposed project. In order to determine cost sharing requirements, the researcher should obtain information from the funding agency and from his sponsoring institution. Generally the institution will have a committee or person, such as a contract officer, who is responsible for making budgetary arrangements with funding agencies. In certain instances, a funding agency will pay for indirect costs. For example, most funding agencies will pay overhead to cover such costs as use of university furniture and space, and necessary bookkeeping in the project. In the case of the Regional Research Program, the application for reimbursement of indirect costs must be submitted at the same time as the research proposal.

The research proposal may contain a number of appendices. We have already mentioned that letters from consultants are included as an appendix. The Regional Research Program requires that the principal personnel include an appended statement describing any current research projects that they are working on and the agency supporting it. If any of the principal personnel have completed a project supported by the Office of Education, they must describe it, too. If agreements with cooperating agencies, such as school districts, are involved in the project, these should be placed in the appendix. Copies of all instruments to be used in the project (e.g., questionnaires, aptitude tests) must be included in the appendix. If the instrument is to be developed later, sample items must be given and an outline of the proposed instrument. It is important to note that all instruments used in research funded by the Office of Education, if administered to ten or more individuals, must be cleared by the specific sponsoring agency. The purpose of the clearance is to determine whether any of the instruments represent intrusive inquiries into a person's religion, sex, politics, or morals or involve self-incriminating disclosures. Parental consent is required if any instrument is to be administered to an individual below college age. It is advisable to prepare all instruments for the clearance procedure well before you are notified whether the research proposal has been cleared for funding. If the proposal is selected for funding, then you will be able to start clearance procedures immediately.

When it is received by the Regional Research Program, a research proposal is assigned an identification number and reviewed by the staff. If it seems worthy and meets the program's requirements, the proposal is submitted to a panel of specialists for review. Four panel members are from the researcher's region, and one is from a state in another region. The panel makes a recommendation on the research proposal, and this is forwarded to the regional director. He then forwards his recommendation for the commissioner's formal approval. Generally the amount of time that elapses between receipt of the proposal and notification regarding its disposition is within two months. If the proposal is accepted for funding, a contractual arrangement will be worked out between the Regional Research Program and the investigator and his institution of affiliation. During the course of the project, the researcher will need to submit progress and expenditure reports. In addition, he is required to submit a comprehensive final report.

The procedures followed by the Regional Research Program illustrate that the preparation of a research proposal is a complicated and difficult matter. At the present time, the Regional Research Program approves one proposal for every five that it receives. The researcher is well advised, therefore, to devote much time and thought to preparing the proposal, since it is the chief basis on which funding decisions are made.

MISTAKES OFTEN MADE BY GRADUATE STUDENTS

1. Student fails to prepare draft copies of information he must later include in his thesis while he still has it fresh in his memory.
2. Puts off all work on his manuscript until his study is finished.
3. Organizes his review of the literature chronologically instead of arranging his research articles into related topics.
4. Treats each study referred to in the review of the literature in mechanical fashion, devoting about the same amount of space to each regardless of pertinence or importance.
5. Fails to integrate the findings of his review of the literature.
6. Uses too many quotations and selects quotations that do not make their point as well as the student could make it using his own words.
7. Provides an inadequate description of the research sample and measures used.
8. Discusses minor findings that can be presented better in a table, and fails to emphasize important findings.

ANNOTATED REFERENCES

1. The following four references will be particularly useful to the research worker in preparing his first article for publication in an education journal:
   Shannon, J. R. "Tips to Writers from Seventy-Five Editors of Educational Periodicals," *Journal of Educational Research,* 44 (1950), 241–268.
   ——. "Art in Writing for Educational Periodicals: The Introduction," *ibid.,* 44 (1951), 599–610.
   ——. "Art in Writing for Educational Periodicals: The Ending," *ibid.,* 46 (1953), 333–345.
   ——. "Art in Writing for Educational Periodicals: The Main Body," *ibid.,* 47 (1954), 489–504.
2. American Psychological Association Council of Editors. *Publication Manual of the American Psychological Association, 1967 Revision.* Washington, D.C.: American Psychological Association, 1967. This manual contains detailed instructions for preparing articles for the journals published by the American Psychological Association. Much of the material presented, except details of format, is equally appropriate as a guide to publishing in other professional journals in the behavioral sciences.
3. Arkin, Herbert, and Colton, Raymond R. *Graphs: How to Make and Use Them.* New York: Harper, 1936. This book presents a thorough and rather formal treatment of the construction of graphs, including a chapter on each major type of graph, with detailed information on the use, construction, and common applications of each.

4. Ball, J., and Williams, C. B. *Report Writing*. New York: Ronald, 1955. Although written primarily as a guide for business men and engineers, this book contains chapters (on organizing facts and ideas, writing and revising, language, style, and the use of visual aids) that have much information pertinent to writing educational research reports. The third section of the book contains a number of brief and very well-selected supplemental readings by other authors that provide the student with a great deal of pertinent and interesting background material.

5. Camp, William L. *Guide to Periodicals in Education*. Metuchen, N.J.: Scarecrow, 1968.
   Lins, L. Joseph, and Rees, Robert A. *Scholar's Guide to Journals of Education and Educational Psychology*. Madison, Wis.: Dembar Educational Research Services, 1965.
   These two books are excellent references for the student writing a research report for publication. Although Camp's book is more recent, Lins and Rees' book includes some journals not mentioned in Camp. Both references provide important information about each journal, such as publisher, audience, number of subscribers, editor and address, style, length and type of manuscripts accepted, and disposition of submitted manuscripts. This information is very helpful to the student both in selecting an appropriate journal for his report and in preparing the manuscript for a specific journal.

6. Emberger, M. R., and Hall, M. R. *Scientific Writing*. New York: Harcourt, Brace, 1955. This text provides a detailed treatment on the subject of scientific writing. Each aspect of the usual research project ranging from definition of the problem to analysis and interpretation is treated, and other topics, such as ways of directing the paper to the reader, scientific style, and format, are also covered. Each chapter is preceded by a brief outline of the chapter content so that the student may locate subtopics with which he is particularly concerned.

7. Guba, Egon G. *Guides for the Writing of Proposals,* in Jack A. Culbertson and Stephen P. Hencley (eds.). *Educational Research: New Perspectives*. Danville, Ill.: Interstate Printers & Publishers, 1963. This article provides detailed instructions for writing the research proposal and should be read by all beginning researchers. The author discusses statement of problem, review of the literature, questions and/or hypotheses, the design, instrumentation, sampling, data collection, data analysis, significance of the project, and the budget.

8. McCann, L. E. "Presenting That Idea in the Professional Journal," *Phi Delta Kappan*, 39 (1958), 173–176. This article provides a useful guide to writing articles for professional education journals. Most of the suggestions are more appropriate for preparing opinion articles than for research articles. Importance of orderly procedure and of a good outline is stressed, and practical hints are given for finding the most appropriate journals to which to submit the article, procedures for submitting manuscripts, and so on.

9. Modley, R., Lowenstein, D., et al. *Pictographs and Graphs: How to Make and Use Them*. New York: Harper, 1952. A well-illustrated and easily read coverage of the use of graphs with particular emphasis on pictographs. Chapter 6, "Cheating With Charts," deals with misleading charts and graphs and is especially recommended for study by the graduate student so that he may detect

deceptive graphing practices in evaluating the work of others and avoid them in his own work.

10. Shaffer, Laurance F. *Preparing Doctoral Dissertations in Psychology*. 5th ed. New York: Teachers College Press, 1967. Although intended primarily for psychology dissertations, this guide contains much information that will be relevant to the education student. The sections on quality and style of dissertation writing, quotations, and preparation of drafts of the dissertation are particularly recommended to the student.

11. Veri, C. C. "How to Write a Proposal and Get It Funded," *Adult Leadership*, 16 (1968), 318–320. The author provides many practical suggestions for preparing a research proposal. Funding terminology, guidelines, proposal writing, expenses, application procedures, and proposal routing are discussed. The article contains a useful bibliography.

CHAPTER 19

Opportunities in Educational Research

EDUCATIONAL RESEARCH—PRESENT AND FUTURE

Introduction

At present educational research is in a period of great expansion. For many years the overwhelming majority of educational research was carried out by individual professors in colleges and universities and was supported largely by the research worker's personal resources or from small grants that usually covered nothing more than the materials and clerical assistance required. The trend in recent years, however, has been toward a great many more research projects and also larger and better financed projects. Later in this chapter we will discuss some of the sources of financial support for educational research that have developed in recent years. The individual research worker is also, to a considerable degree, being supplanted by the research team because the scope of research projects and the breadth of knowledge required make it extremely difficult for a single individual to plan and carry out all phases of the project.

The expansion we are now experiencing in educational research is due to several factors. First, and perhaps most important, it reflects a gradual increase in scientific values within our society. The tremendous gains made in science and technology over the past twenty years have illustrated the power of the scientific method to the average citizen to a degree far overshadowing his previous experiences. The impressive record of the physical sciences and medicine has led to an increased tendency in our society to look to science for the solutions to our problems. This tendency to look for scientific solutions has now expanded to embrace the problems of the behavioral sciences. It is reflected in the attitudes of businessmen who employ psychologists or sociologists to develop advertising programs, space age industries that employ behavioral scientists to design space capsules and study the effects of space travel on the psychology of the individual, and school teachers and administrators who increasingly recognize the need to understand the human being in the educational process and who for the first time are looking to educational research workers and behavioral scientists in large numbers in quest of knowledge and understanding.

The increase in educational problems brought about by rapid technological change has also been an important factor in the expansion of educational research. Both laymen and educators have recognized in recent years that better educational methods and sweeping curriculum changes are needed to meet the educational challenges of a highly technical and rapidly changing society.

Problems of educational research

In many ways our current resources in educational research are unequal to the demand placed upon them by the increased scientific orientation of our society and the need for solutions to our increasingly complex educational problems. Education is still in the process of transition from an art to a science, and the majority of the persons employed in the profession have little background in scientific thinking nor do they consider themselves to be scientists. Education has a number of "growing pains" that can be traced to its present transition from an art to a science. We can identify two groups in the profession: the smaller, containing persons strongly oriented toward research who consider education to be a science and are applying the available scientific tools to educational problems; and the larger, strongly oriented to deal with the problems of day-to-day teaching who are not familiar with educational research and do not regard the methods of education as being adaptable to scientific investigation. Communication has always been difficult between these groups, and this has contributed in turn to the wide gap that exists between educational research knowledge and public school practice.

Because of the lack of emphasis upon education as a science, many educational research workers are poorly trained, and much of the educational research that has been done in the past has been poorly designed and executed. Thus, a major problem for educational institutions is to develop better training programs and to increase materially the output of educational research workers. When compared with almost any other field of endeavor, the percentage of educational resources that goes into research is extremely small. It has been estimated, for example, that business and industry invest at least five percent of their budgets in research. The comparable figure for education in fiscal year 1968 was a surprisingly low one third of one percent. An observation made by the President's Science Advisory Committee in 1962 is still true today:

Education has a national budget second only to that of national defense. Yet only a small fraction of 1 percent of this budget has been spent on research and development. This is one obvious reason for the failure of education to make technical advances comparable to those seen in other aspects of our national life.[1]

Inasmuch as the amount of money has increased more rapidly in recent years than the number of trained research workers, the financial support available is adequate in terms of the personnel available to do research, but from a longterm standpoint, it is far from adequate in terms of the amount of research that should be carried out in education.

The future of educational research depends to a great degree on how successful we are in solving the aforementioned problems. The solution of one of these problems without making comparable gains in the other problem areas will not lead us to the higher quality and greater quantity of research needed in education. Figure 20 illustrates the interdependence of the various steps in the educational research cycle. Each step in the cycle is related to all the other steps so that a gain in one leads to a gain in all. Forces are at work in each step of the cycle that promise to lead to a great acceleration of educational research over the next few years.

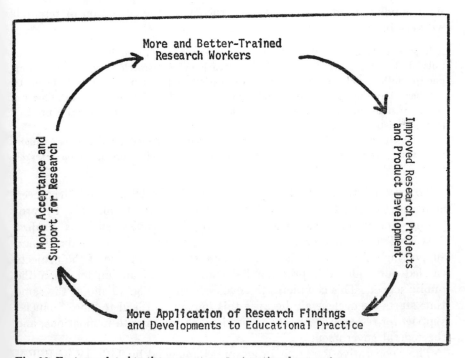

Fig. 20. Factors related to the expansion of educational research.

[1] Behavioral Sciences Subpanel of the President's Science Advisory Committee, "Strengthening the Behavioral Sciences," *Science*, 136 (1962), 240. Reprinted by permission of *Science*.

Although it is difficult to identify all factors that have contributed to the current expansion of educational research, the Cooperative Research Program initiated in 1956 and the Title IV amendments of the 1965 Elementary and Secondary Education Act (ESEA) are considered by many to have provided the initial impetus. Let us examine how this program has accelerated the cycle.

Much of the money made available by the Cooperative Research Program has gone to educational researchers in colleges and universities. This improved the competence of many educational researchers on college faculties by giving them the opportunity to attack significant problems with better designs and more thoroughness than was possible when each faculty member had to rely on spare time and his own financial resources. The more significant studies thus started also contributed to increasing the number of graduate students trained in research, since money for graduate assistantships was made available in the Cooperative Research Program contracts. Students receiving research assistantships also received better training because they were able to participate in more significant projects. As was pointed out in a report concerned with the education of research workers in psychology:

Research training is achieved by doing research in a research environment; details of the procedures used by effective teachers of research vary in detail from one to another, and even the same teacher varies his procedure from one student to another. Only the apprenticeship relation, it seems, has the flexibility to allow for the great individual differences in attitude and procedure that characterize productive scientists.

In conclusion, therefore, we say that research is learned by doing and taught mainly by contagion. Research must first be going on if there is to be research training.[2]

To proceed to the next step in the cycle, better research has been achieved through the Cooperative Research Program, not only by providing money for better and more extensive studies, such as Project TALENT (see Chapter 1), but also by setting up high standards and supporting only research that meets these standards. Some of the projects carried out under this program have already had an impact upon the public schools. This completes the cycle shown in Fig. 20 and at the same time starts the cycle again because this impact will lead to more financial support for research from school districts, states, private foundations, and the federal government.

The Cooperative Research Program, as amended by Title IV of ESEA, also provided the necessary funding for the establishment of research and

[2] American Psychological Association, "Education for Research in Psychology," *The American Psychologist*, 14 (1959), 179. Reprinted by permission of the American Psychological Association.

development centers and regional educational laboratories. The main contribution of the laboratories and centers is their systematic application of research and development technology to the problems that face American education. The R & D programs that they are carrying forth have already produced several major pay-offs. First, they have led to the development of research based products that are significantly more effective than those generally found in the schools. Second, unlike most basic and applied research, the outcomes of research and development are immediately applicable to educational practice. This is the case because one of the steps of the R & D cycle is to develop the product so that it works in the setting in which it is intended to be used. Thus, educational practitioners are likely to adopt products developed by R & D technology. The third pay-off of educational research and development is that it increases support for basic and applied research by showing how knowledge yielded by these approaches can be used to develop more effective products for education. To refer to the cycle shown in Fig. 20, research and development promotes the expansion of educational research since, as research based products are developed and lead to improved school instruction, the government and other funding sources are likely to provide more financial support for this work. Part of these increased resources can be used to train better research workers who, in turn, will be able to carry out more effective research or research and development.

The cycle shown in Fig. 20 not only illustrates factors leading to acceleration of educational research; it also illustrates their interdependence. Ideally, gains must be made in a balanced fashion to get the most out of educational research. For example, if Congress doubled its appropriation for educational research in the next fiscal year, it is doubtful if any great acceleration of research would occur until enough educational researchers had been trained to utilize this money in productive and well designed research programs.

In summary, the future of educational research rests jointly upon the federal government, which is the logical source of funds for research of national significance; the universities, which must bear the burden of training more and better educational researchers; and the interplay among workers in basic research, applied research, and research and development, so that there is an effective chain leading from new research knowledge to improved classroom practice.

SOURCES OF FUNDING FOR EDUCATIONAL RESEARCH

Introduction

Educational research cannot prosper unless it has adequate financial support. Fortunately, educational research has recently come into new prominence, accompanied by greatly increased funding. Table 29 shows U.S. Office of Education (USOE) appropriations for research and training of researchers from 1957 to 1970.[3] Several items of information in this table are worth noting. In 1957 total USOE appropriations for research

TABLE 29

APPROPRIATIONS FOR "RESEARCH AND TRAINING,"
U.S. OFFICE OF EDUCATION, 1957–1970
(In thousands of dollars)

Fiscal Year	Cooperative Research	NDEA Title VI	NDEA Title VII	Vocational Research	Library Research	Handicapped Research	Totals
1970*	88,900	2,500	c	1,100	e	18,000	110,500
1969	76,077	a	b	11,375	d	15,000	102,452
1968	66,467	3,000	4,400	13,550	3,550	11,000	101,967
1967	70,000	3,100	4,400	10,000	3,550	8,100	99,150
1966	70,000	2,800	4,000	17,750		6,000	100,550
1965	15,800	2,250	4,963	11,850		2,000	36,863
1964	11,500	1,800	5,000			1,000	19,300
1963	6,985	1,800	5,000				13,785
1962	5,000	2,000	4,755				11,755
1961	3,357	2,000	4,700				10,057
1960	3,200	4,000	3,000				10,200
1959	2,700	2,500	1,600				6,800
1958	2,300						2,300
1957	1,000						1,000

* requested.
a appropriation included in Cooperative Research in the amount of $2,465,000.
b appropriation included in Cooperative Research in the amount of $4,200,000.
c legislation authorization discontinued.
d appropriation included in Cooperative Research in the amount of $3,000,000.
e appropriation included in Cooperative Research in the amount of $2,200,000.

and training were only $1 million, whereas in 1970 they were $110 million. This represents over a hundredfold increase in just 13 years. Fiscal year 1966 is especially significant, for it was then that USOE made its largest dollar increase in support of educational research—from $36 million to over $100 million.

Although USOE is by far the largest source of funding for educational research, other government and private agencies play an important role, too. Table 30 shows the major agencies' contributions to educational re-

[3] U.S. Office of Education, Bureau of Research, *Educational Research and Development in the United States* (Washington, D.C.: U.S. Government Printing Office, 1969), p. 158. Reprinted by permission of the National Center for Educational Research and Development.

TABLE 30

DOCUMENTED MINIMUM BASE FINANCIAL SUPPORT FOR
EDUCATIONAL RESEARCH AND DEVELOPMENT BY
SPONSORING AGENCY, FISCAL YEAR 1968

United States Office of Education	$101,967,000
National Science Foundation	23,326,000
National Institute of Mental Health	11,860,000
National Institute of Child Health and Human Development	8,377,000
Office of Economic Opportunity	12,800,000
Department of Defense	6,046,000
Other Federal Agencies (Labor, Commerce, Children's Bureau, Agriculture, Social Rehabilitation Service, Food and Drug Administration, Interior, and Endowments for Arts and Humanities)	6,725,000
Private foundations	7,344,000
All other (state agencies, higher education institutions, professional and academic associations, etc.)	13,845,000
Total	$192,290,000

search in fiscal year 1968.[4] The total estimate of $192 million is an impressive figure. Yet as we observed earlier, this figure constituted only one third of one percent of the total education expenditure ($54.6 billion) in fiscal year 1968.[5] Francis Chase, who has made an extensive study of the problem, recommends that support be increased until at least one percent of national expenditures for education are devoted to research and development.[6]

Now that we have a brief overview of recent funding support, let us examine the ways in which government and private agencies sponsor various types of educational research.

National Center for Educational Research and Development

Most of the federal support for educational research is administered by the Office of Education, which is a division of the Department of Health, Education, and Welfare. Various bureaus and agencies within the Office of Education support research activities, but chief among these is the National Center for Educational Research and Development. Until

[4] *Ibid.*, p. 164.

[5] *Digest of Educational Statistics 1968* (Washington, D.C.: U.S. Government Printing Office, 1968), p. 17.

[6] Francis S. Chase, "R & D in the Remodeling of Education," *Phi Delta Kappan*, 51 (1970), 299–304.

recently the functions of the Center were performed by the Bureau of Research. In mid-1969 the Bureau of Research was reorganized and given this new name to reflect the Office of Education's commitment to research and development as an approach to improving American education.

The National Center for Educational Research and Development contains five divisions. The Divisions and their respective branches are shown in Fig. 21.

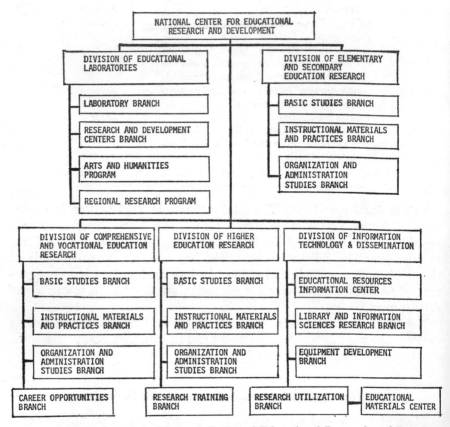

Fig. 21. Organization of the National Center of Educational Research and Development.

1. *The Division of Elementary and Secondary Education Research* administers the funding of research projects related to education at the preschool, elementary, and high school levels. This division contains three branches. The Basic Studies Branch supports basic research related to the learning process. The Instructional Materials and Practices Branch administers projects that produce curriculum guides, texts, programmed

materials, audio-visual aids, and so on. Finally, the Organization and Administration Studies Branch supports research on materials and practices for organizing and administering school programs.

2. *The Division of Higher Education Research* is responsible for all research concerned with college, graduate, and professional education. It also has three branches to administer basic research studies, instructional materials studies, and studies on organization and administration. In addition, this division has a research training branch that administers fellowships to students interested in educational research and development grants to universities for strengthening their research training programs.

3. *The Division of Comprehensive and Vocational Education Research* supports research related to vocational education at the high school and junior college levels. Similar to the divisions already described, it has three branches for basic research, instructional materials studies, and studies on organization and administration. An additional branch, the Career Opportunities Branch, was established to support research concerned with identifying and developing careers in new and growing subprofessional fields.

4. *The Division of Educational Laboratories,* through its Laboratory Branch and the R & D Centers Branch, administers the funding of some 30 educational R & D agencies throughout the nation. We shall have more to say about these agencies later.

5. *The Division of Information Technology and Dissemination* has four branches, each administering a different program. The Educational Resources Information Center Branch is responsible for the national network of ERIC centers for the processing of educational research findings (described in Chapter 3). The Library and Information Sciences Research Branch supports projects aimed at the improvement of libraries and training of librarians. Two new branches, the Research Utilization Branch and the Equipment Development Branch, will support research on educational change and educational technology, respectively. The Research Utilization Branch also administers the Educational Materials Center, a repository for instructional material of all kinds.

Several other programs are administered by the National Center for Educational Research and Development. The Arts and Humanities Program is responsible for research related to instruction in the arts and humanities in schools, museums, cultural centers, and state and local arts councils. The Regional Research Program, which we discussed in Chapter 18, is administered through regional offices and supports educational research projects budgeted at less than $10,000.

The research programs administered by the five divisions of the National Center for Educational Research and Development are funded through several federal acts. The largest of these is the *Cooperative Research Act of 1954*. This act authorized the Office of Education to finance cooperative research projects with universities, colleges, and state education agencies. In 1965 the Elementary and Secondary Education Act (ESEA) broadened the scope of the Cooperative Research Act considerably. The ESEA amendments provided funds for programs to train educational researchers, programs to disseminate research findings, and establishment of regional laboratories and R & D centers. The Vocational Education Act of 1963 authorized funding of research and training programs to improve vocational education. Title VII of the National Defense Education Act of 1958 (NDEA) authorized funding of research, development, and dissemination programs concerned with the educational uses of broadcast media, audio-visual materials, printed and published materials, and related communications media. Title II of the Higher Education Act of 1965 supports research to improve libraries and training in librarianship.

Various individuals and organizations are eligible to apply for project funding from the National Center. Research contracts and grants may be awarded to state departments of education, local school systems, universities and colleges, and various other public and private agencies. To facilitate processing of research proposals, the National Center has developed a standardized application format and procedure. Each proposal is considered under whichever authorization (ESEA, NDEA, etc.) is applicable. The researcher interested in submitting a proposal should write to the National Center for forms and procedures.[7] If he wishes to apply for a small project research grant (discussed in Chapter 18), the researcher should contact the regional research office nearest him (see Appendix E).

Other branches of the Office of Education

The National Center for Educational Research and Development provides the largest amount of research funding within USOE. However, several other branches of USOE provide substantial support for certain types of educational research. The Bureau of Education for the Handicapped, inaugurated in 1967, has a division that supports research projects on educational problems relating to handicapped children. The Bureau of Adult, Vocational and Library Programs supports research and development projects related to vocational education curricula. The Institute of International Studies, Division of Foreign Studies is responsible for administering Title VI of NDEA. This authorization funds research projects concerned with the improvement of instruction in modern foreign languages.

[7] The address is Research Analysis and Allocation Staff, National Center for Educational Research and Development, U.S. Office of Education, Washington, D.C. 20202.

National Science Foundation

The National Science Foundation (NSF), authorized by the National Science Foundation Act of 1950, supports extensive research programs in all scientific fields, including areas relating to education. Four branches of NSF have particular responsibility for educational research and development. The divisions of Pre-College Education in Science and of Undergraduate Education in Science sponsor development of high-quality science and mathematics curriculum materials at the precollege and college levels, respectively. The Office of Computing Activities has particular relevance to education, since it sponsors projects relating to computer-assisted instruction, computer science curricula, and other projects exploring the educational implications of computers. Finally, the Division of Biological and Medical Sciences awards grants to support basic research in learning, including projects concerned with neurophysiological mechanisms in behavior and with complex cognitive processes. As we discussed in Chapter 1, the National Science Foundation has made major contributions to education through its large-scale research and development programs directed at the construction of new science curricula.

Office of Economic Opportunity

The U.S. Office of Economic Opportunity (OEO) administers a number of major programs directed at compensatory education for students considered to be socially, culturally, economically, or educationally disadvantaged. These programs are Headstart, Follow Through, Upward Bound, Job Corps, Parent-Child Centers, and community action programs. OEO provides extensive support for research, development, and evaluation activities aimed at improving the operation of these programs. The OEO Division of Research, Plans, Programs, and Evaluation coordinates these activities and in addition carries out demographic surveys to determine the characteristics and location of disadvantaged people.

Other federal agencies

Several other federal agencies have authorization to sponsor educational research projects that relate to their stated missions. The National Institute of Mental Health (NIMH) was established to bring about improvements in the prevention and treatment of mental illness and in the promotion of mental health. Two branches of NIMH's Division of Extramural Research Programs have responsibility for funding research studies concerned with the relationship between mental health and education. The Behavioral Sciences Research Branch sponsors work in such areas as learning, motivation, and cognitive processes. The emphasis of the Applied Research Branch is on support of research in such areas as learn ing problems of children, especially the emotionally disturbed and retarded, underachievement, dropouts, student stress, and school mental health services.

The mission of the National Institute of Child Health and Human Development (NICHD), broadly stated, is to help individuals achieve a normal healthy life from conception to death. NICHD supports a large program of extramural research in many areas, including some that are education related. For example, NICHD funds studies concerned with the effects of impoverishment on intellectual functions, and studies on language development, dyslexia, attention, memory, and other mental processes.

The Department of Defense supports an extensive program of research, part of which is education related. Funds are available for studies on learning and motivation, and the development of training materials, including computer-assisted instruction. On a much smaller scale, agencies such as the Department of Labor, the National Aeronautics and Space Administration, and the National Endowments for the Arts and Humanities sponsor educational research projects related to their missions.

NSF, OEO, NIMH, NICHD, and the agencies described in this section often designate specific areas in which they wish research to be carried out and then invite scientists to submit proposals. Some of these agencies will also accept unsolicited research proposals related to their stated missions. For more specific information, the researcher should contact the agency to which he is interested in submitting a proposal.

Other sources of funding

In addition to federal support for educational research, research funds are also available through grants and postdoctoral fellowships from foundations, institutional research programs supported by universities, and educational research funds available in state departments of education and local school districts.

The 1967 edition of *The Foundation Directory* lists 6,803 different foundations in the United States.[8] A survey of grants in 1966 revealed that these foundations gave away a total of $661 million that year. A total of $157 million was granted for educational purposes, of which $5 million went directly to support educational research. The foundations most prominent in the support of education are the Ford Foundation, the Carnegie Corporation, the Kettering Foundation, the Danforth Foundation, the Hill Family Foundation, and the Sloan Foundation. The researcher interested in seeking funding from these and similar sources is advised to consult *The Foundation Directory*.

[8] Marianna O. Lewis (ed.), *The Foundation Directory* (New York: Russell Sage Foundation, 1967).

A number of postdoctoral fellowships supported by private organizations and principally aimed at supporting scientists in their research pursuits are listed in the yearly editions of *Fellowships in the Arts and Sciences*.[9] Many universities have institutional research programs supported at least partially by the university budget. Bureaus of Educational Research are found at nearly all the major universities. Some universities have a centralized educational research council to consider proposals from faculty members and/or students. Such funds are particularly helpful to the new faculty member, as they are often made available for pilot studies and small budget studies that would be unacceptable for support under most research programs sponsored by private foundations or the federal government. Such pilot studies, if productive, however, can lead to broader and more sophisticated research proposals that can obtain support from these latter sources. Many state departments of education include a research division, and some state departments also have research funds available to support research projects in the public schools of the state.

Most large school districts now employ research personnel and carry out research programs on problems of special interest to the district. Even smaller districts that do not employ full-time personnel to carry out research in the district are often willing to provide released time and some financial help for teachers or administrators in the district who wish to carry out educational research.

OPPORTUNITIES FOR CAREERS IN EDUCATIONAL RESEARCH

Introduction

In recent years there has been a great increase in appreciation of the potential value of educational research. However, despite this increased appreciation, a shortage of trained personnel has slowed the expansion of educational research. In addition to the growth of educational research in the traditional university setting, the demand for educational research workers has also increased because of many new types of jobs that require this type of training.

Let us review briefly some of the specific job areas in which persons trained in educational research are employed.

Universities and colleges

Twenty years ago nearly all educational researchers were employed by colleges and universities. A majority are still so affiliated. Large universities have, for many years, placed considerable emphasis upon research

---

[9] Robert Quick (ed.), *Fellowships in the Arts and Sciences, 1967–1968*, 10th ed. (Washington, D.C.: American Council on Education, 1966).

productivity in the employment and promotion of faculty members, and this emphasis is now being felt in smaller universities and colleges as well. Many university positions involve part-time research as well as part-time teaching because it has been recognized that adequate programs of graduate training in education cannot be carried out without faculty members who do research. Recent years have also seen the establishment of many new educational research bureaus at colleges and universities and the expansion of the established bureaus at the larger schools. Many university counseling centers also employ educational research workers to carry out local studies concerned with various problems related to counseling. In some universities the Dean of Students Office also employs educational research workers to carry out studies concerning such matters as student dropouts, educational goals, and the validity of student selection procedures.

Regional educational laboratories

The regional educational laboratories were authorized under Title IV of ESEA. There are at present 15 of these laboratories forming a national network. Their mission, broadly stated, is to narrow the gap between educational research and educational practice. Each laboratory serves a different region of the country, and each is governed by members of state departments of education, public and private schools, university departments of education, and industrial and cultural institutions. The governing board is responsible for determining its laboratory's program objectives, policies, personnel, and budget allocation. In effect, each laboratory functions as an independent, nonprofit corporation, funded primarily by Title IV, but also free to seek financial support from other funding sources.

As a result of the manner in which they were set up, regional laboratories have evolved a diversity of research and development strategies and program emphases over the past five years. In Chapter 16 we discussed the research and development strategy of one laboratory, the Far West Laboratory for Educational Research and Development. There we pointed out that research and development involves the construction of an educational product based on pertinent research findings and using a development-feedback-revision cycle to achieve desired objectives. A complete list of the laboratories, including their addresses, regions served, and program emphases, can be found in Appendix F.

Many educators and researchers believe that the regional laboratories offer the greatest promise of bringing about significant improvements in American education. Francis S. Chase, a distinguished educator, recently conducted a survey of R & D centers (see next section) and the regional laboratories. He pointed to several strengths of these institutions not found in other educational research settings:

The importance of the centers and laboratories rests on several bases: First, they supply two essential central links in a chain for moving knowledge and advanced technology into the stream of educational practice. Second, they help to overcome resistance to innovation by establishing collaborative relationships with the producers of knowledge on one side and the users of knowledge on the other, and by offering products of certified performance. Third, they try to assure the effective use of their products by careful specification of the conditions essential to effective performance and by demonstrating how the conditions can be met. In short, the laboratories and centers have undertaken to perform functions not previously performed in education and are beginning to perform these functions in ways that could lead to a toning up of the entire educational enterprise. [p. 303] [10]

The regional laboratories typically commit their resources to large-scale programmatic efforts involving the talents of many specialists. The researcher who joins one of the laboratories is likely to be employed as a member of a research and development team rather than as an individual responsible for one or two small-scale research projects. The larger laboratories employ several hundred persons, and some of them offer graduate assistantships for students interested in learning how to do educational research and development.

Research and development centers

Since 1963 ten research and development centers have been established at major universities throughout the country. A list of all the centers can be found in Appendix G. As we mentioned earlier, these centers are administered by the National Center for Educational Research and Development under the provisions of the Cooperative Research Act of 1963 and the ESEA amendments of 1965. The purpose of the R & D centers is to bring together scholars from several disciplines to work on a significant educational problem. Each center carries out a program of basic research, applied research, and preliminary product development to solve their designated problem. For example, the work of the Stanford Center for Research and Development in Teaching is concentrated on the theory and practice of teaching. The various programs carried on within this center are concerned with such problems as the effect of teachers upon pupils, improvement of teacher training, and the effects of administrative practices on the teacher. As a result of the center's work, a new approach to teacher training, microteaching, was developed. The center has carried out basic and applied research studies on microteaching and has also been engaged in the development of teacher training films.[11]

---

[10] Francis S. Chase, "R & D in the Remodeling of Education," *Phi Delta Kappan,* 51 (1970), 299–304. Reprinted by permission of Francis S. Chase and *Phi Delta Kappan.*

[11] The student will recall that the research and development program described in Chapter 16 (teacher training by minicourses) was derived from microteaching research carried out at the Stanford Center.

Other research and development centers are concerned with such problems as the evaluation of instructional programs (University of California, Los Angeles), the interaction between learning research and school instructional practices (University of Pittsburgh), educational administration (University of Oregon), and higher education (University of California, Berkeley). Two research and development centers were authorized under the Vocational Education Act of 1963 to stimulate national interest in research on vocational and technical education. One of these centers is located at Ohio State University, the other at North Carolina State University. The Vocational Education Act also authorized the establishment of 46 research coordinating units located in state departments of education or on university campuses. The purpose of these coordinating units is to encourage and coordinate research activities among various agencies with an interest in vocational and technical education.

The National Laboratory on Early Childhood Education was established to support research and development leading to the improvement of education of young children. The Laboratory actually consists of a number of institutes. There is a National Coordination Center and ERIC Clearinghouse at the University of Illinois, and six regional R & D Centers located at Gecrge Peabody College for Teachers, the University of Chicago, Syracuse University, the University of Arizona, Cornell University, and the University of Kansas.

In 1968 the Office of Education established two educational policy research centers. One of these centers is located at the Stanford Research Institute, the other at the Syracuse University Research Corporation. Their purpose is to study long-range futures for education and society in order to improve R & D planning. The centers are concerned with such questions as: What demands will society make on schools in the future and how can schools prepare to meet these demands now? What will curriculum objectives and educational technology be like in the future, and what are their implications for schools today?

A number of other research and development centers throughout the country are directed toward improving education for handicapped children. The Comprehensive Research and Demonstration Facility for the Handicapped (Teachers College, Columbia University) and the Center for Educational Research and Development in Mental Retardation (Indiana University) carry out such activities as conducting research, developing curricula, and training research specialists to improve the education of mentally retarded and other handicapped children. There is also a network of 14 Instructional Materials Centers established under the Handicapped Children Act of 1963. These centers have several functions: to disseminate information about curriculum materials for the handicapped to concerned educators, to carry out R & D programs to provide improved teaching materials for the handicapped, and to encourage commercial production of these materials. Instructional Materials Centers are at the following locations: Boston University, New York State Department of Education, George Washington University, University of Kentucky, University of South Florida, Michigan State University, Department of Special Education (Springfield, Illinois), University of Kansas, University of Wisconsin, University of Texas, Colorado State College, University of Southern California, University of Oregon, and the American Printing House for the Blind (Louisville, Kentucky).

The research and development centers just described generally have small full-time staffs. In addition, many of the centers, particularly those located at universities, have part-time professors on their staffs. Similar to the regional laboratories, the R & D centers often provide graduate assistantships for students in education and in the behavioral sciences. These assistantships enable graduate students to receive practical training in research and development and at the same time to make substantive contributions to the center's programs. If he is located near one of these centers, the student is well advised to explore the possibility of receiving research training there.

Public schools

The new enthusiasm for educational research has now infected most of the larger school districts. Many large- and medium-size districts now employ full-time research directors who plan and carry out research projects aimed at evaluating the educational effectiveness of the district and developing and validating new curricula, teaching methods, and educational programs. Some of the very large districts have well-staffed research bureaus that carry out studies in a wide range of educational areas. Smaller districts often employ a school psychologist or pupil personnel director, part of whose time is devoted to educational research projects of particular interest to the district.

Inasmuch as considerable financial support for research and development is available through federal programs and such private foundations as the Carnegie Corporation, educational research workers are often employed to direct a specific research or development project for which the school district has received financial support. In particular, the Elementary and Secondary Act of 1965 requires school districts to conduct evaluation studies on programs instituted under Title I (funds for educationally deprived students) or Title III (innovative and exemplary programs). This requirement has led to the employment of many educational researchers qualified to perform evaluation studies. Such special projects often lead to the district's employing full-time research personnel after the special project has been completed.

State departments of education

The increased interest in educational research has also been reflected in state departments of education where research personnel are increasing rapidly. Federal research support is available to state departments of education through the Cooperative Research Program, and some of the projects currently being carried out indicate that the level of educational research in state departments has improved greatly. A few years ago, the research division in most state departments of education typically carried out no research but merely served as a statistical and record-keeping section concerned with such matters as average daily attendance and pupil cost.

Other career opportunities

There are many opportunities for educational research workers in federal civil service. The Department of Health, Education, and Welfare employs educational researchers to monitor research contract programs and to carry out nationwide surveys of great importance in education. The Department of State also has a number of programs that requires personnel skilled in educational research and development. The military services employ a great many civilian research workers in education and educational psychology. Some of these personnel are employed in centralized research units, such as the Air Force Personnel and Training Research Center, the Personnel Research Branch of the Army Adjutant General's office, and the Naval Research Field Activities. Others are employed to carry out educational research and development in the many schools operated by the armed services. Because the teachers and administrators in these schools are usually military personnel with little or no professional training in education, the need for civilians skilled in educational research and development has long been recognized. Such personnel are often employed as educational consultants or in special research sections, such as the Training Analysis and Development Sections attached to many Air Force training facilities.

There are also a great many research agencies and corporations that employ educational research workers. These organizations carry out educational research tasks under contract with the federal government or with private companies. The American Institutes for Research at Pittsburgh and other locations, the Human Resources Research Office affiliated with George Washington University at Washington, D.C., the Systems Development Corporation at Santa Monica, California, and Educational Testing Service at Princeton, New Jersey are illustrative of the various types of private research organizations that employ educational research workers.

Additional career opportunities for educational researchers are to be found in business and industry. Many large corporations hire educational researchers to organize and administer training and educational programs for their employees. Also, large corporations, such as Xerox and Westinghouse, are starting educational divisions that employ researchers to develop new products for commercial distribution to schools.

FINANCIAL ASSISTANCE FOR GRADUATE STUDENTS IN EDUCATION

Introduction

The amount of financial assistance available for graduate students has greatly increased in recent years. Although undergraduate scholarships are based primarily upon financial need, the emphasis in programs of financial support for graduate students is on academic accomplishment. The amount of financial support is now sufficient so that it is doubtful that any student with a good scholarship record need be deprived of graduate training because of financial considerations.

The usual types of financial assistance include the fellowship, the teaching or research assistantship, and the student loan. In each case these forms of assistance may originate from the university's own income or may be sponsored by a private foundation, industrial organization, fraternal organization, or government agency. The amount of support available under different programs, of course, varies considerably. The fellowship usually does not require that the graduate student do any work or provide any services in return. The teaching or research assistantship requires a certain amount of work from the student, although usually this work is closely allied to his field and constitutes valuable experience. Student loans, which are perhaps expanding more rapidly than other sources of assistance, usually permit repayment over a long period and at low interest rates. Student loan programs sometimes have provisions for canceling part of the loan if the student meets certain conditions.

It is beyond the scope of this book to provide graduate students with data concerning specific fellowships or scholarships. The sources and amounts of assistance, of course, change each year so that such information would quickly become out of date. If, however, he refers to the annotated bibliography at the end of this chapter, the student will find a number of sources that will help him.

Federal and foundation support

Since 1966 USOE has provided support for graduate students in educational research under the Cooperative Research Act, as amended by Title IV of ESEA. In 1969 about 800 graduate students received over $5 million in traineeships under this program. Other sources of federal and foundation support are listed in *Fellowships in the Arts and Sciences,* which is updated annually.[12] We will mention a few of the major sources here:

1. *The National Defense Graduate Fellowship Program.* The purpose of this program is to encourage graduate students to undertake careers as university and college teachers. In 1967 about 6,000 new awards to students were made under this program. To obtain an award the student applies directly to a graduate school participating in the program. The graduate school considers applications and makes its nominations to the Office of Education, which is responsible for making the final awards. The National Defense Graduate Fellowship is normally a 3-year award providing a stipend of $2,000 for the first year, $2,200 for the second, and $2,400 for the third, plus an additional allowance of $400 for each dependent and an optional $400 for summer study.

2. *National Science Foundation Graduate Fellowships.* These fellowships are given in some social sciences, including psychology, but not education. These fellowships are currently being awarded at the rate of 2,500 each year. Although most of the aforementioned fellowships have been awarded to graduate students in the physical sciences, other NSF programs are available for the assistance of teachers and administrators in the public schools. Among these programs are summer fellowships for secondary school teachers in science and mathematics who wish to pursue advanced study in these areas. Tuition fees and a limited travel allowance are paid by the National Science Foundation. The National Science Foundation also supports summer institutes to provide additional training for high school and college teachers in science, mathematics, and engineering. Summer institutes have also been provided for elementary school supervisors and teachers. Inservice institutes for high school and elementary personnel, designed to provide supplemental training in science and mathematics, are offered during the regular academic year. These institutes are offered without tuition or fees, and funds are available for the cost of books and travel, although stipends are not provided.

3. *Woodrow Wilson National Fellowships.* Approximately 1,000 fellowships per year of $1,500 are made to students who wish to enter graduate work in order to prepare for college teaching.

The *Foundation Directory* is also an excellent source for graduate students seeking fellowships. The student should consult the "Field of Interest" index to locate foundations that grant graduate fellowships in his area of interest.

The most extensive source of student loans is the *National Defense Student Loan Program.* In this program both financial need and scholarship

---

[12] Robert Quick (ed.), op. cit.

are considered. Special consideration is given to students who express a
desire to teach in elementary or secondary schools and up to 50 percent of
the loan plus interest is cancelled if the borrower becomes a full-time
teacher in public schools. Students may borrow up to $1,000 a year over
a 4-year period with the repayment plan beginning the year after the borrower ceases to be a full-time student.

Institutional support

A great deal of support for graduate students is provided by educational
institutions themselves in the form of fellowships, loans, and research or
teaching assistantships. Many of these sources of support go unused each
year. In 1963, for example, more than $30 million in nonrepayable stipends
and more than $500 million in low interest rate loans were available to
students, but went unused.[13] Perhaps the essential requirements for obtaining financial aid for graduate work other than good scholarship are that
(1) the student know what aid programs are available, (2) he plan his
own work sufficiently in advance so he can obtain aid when he needs it,
and (3) he be persistent enough to keep checking the available sources
until he receives the financial assistance he needs.

SEEKING A POSITION IN EDUCATIONAL RESEARCH

The résumé

The graduate student who plans to seek a position in educational research should prepare a résumé several months prior to completion of his
graduate work. The résumé should be prepared with considerable care. If
possible, offset process should be used to duplicate the résumé because it
provides a neater copy than either mimeograph or ditto. The employer
tends to judge the applicant not only by the content of his résumé, but the
care with which it is prepared. The résumé usually includes the following
items:

1. *Biographical Data.* A photograph of the individual and a brief biographical sketch including name, address, age, marital status, and so on.

2. *Professional Experience.* A brief chronological description of any professional experience that the student has had.

3. *Educational Record.* This record should include a listing of all college and university courses taken at both the graduate and undergraduate
level. Usually the course title, units of credit, grade, and professor are
given for each course. The student may leave blank the grades for any
courses in his program that he has not yet completed.

[13] Bernard G. Maxwell (ed.), *Current Financial Aids for Graduate Students* (Peoria, Ill.:
College Opportunities Unlimited, 1964).

4. *Professional Affiliations.* It is advisable while still in graduate school for the graduate student to form professional affiliations. Because the majority of educational research workers are currently being trained in educational psychology, membership or student affiliate status in the American Psychological Association is desirable. Another organization that the student should affiliate with is the American Educational Research Association. He should also consider membership in the state education association and the regional psychological association, and should participate in their annual meetings. The early establishment of professional affiliations by the graduate student provides the employer with some evidence of the individual's professional maturity and his identification with the profession.

5. *Publications.* The graduate student usually lists his thesis and/or dissertation as a publication. If he has any other publications or has read any papers at professional meetings, they should be listed. It is also advisable to prepare one or more articles based on the research findings of one's Master's thesis and/or doctoral dissertation as soon as possible and submit these to a professional journal for publication. Because journals publishing educational research have a publication lag, the student may have nothing to list that has actually been published. He should, however, list articles that are in preparation or have been accepted for publication, giving the title of the article and noting its status. Research publications are given a great deal of weight by most employers.

6. *Professional References.* The résumé should also contain the names and current addresses of at least three persons familiar with the student's professional training and ability. For most graduate students, these references are limited to his professors. It is customary to request an individual's permission before listing his name as a reference.

Finding vacancies

The student should register with his university placement office at least six months prior to the time he plans to complete his graduate training. Many universities and public school districts begin looking for employees in December and January to fill vacancies for the following September. The student who is tardy in preparing his résumé and making his availability known will miss many opportunities. In addition to filing his records at the university placement office, there are several other steps the student may take to locate a suitable position.

Some professional placement bureaus specialize in jobs in the public schools or universities. These bureaus often advertise in the professional journals in education and may be located by checking recent issues of these journals. Before registering with a placement bureau, the student should make sure he understands the fees connected with these services.

Some professional organizations, such as the American Psychological Association, provide employment services. The American Psychological Association publishes a monthly *Employment Bulletin* to which the student may subscribe.[14] This bulletin usually lists vacancies throughout the United States and overseas. The student may also, for a nominal fee, place a notice in the *Bulletin* giving his qualifications and indicating his availability. Placement bureaus are operated at the annual meetings of many professional organizations. Employers are present at these meetings to interview applicants. The student is particularly recommended to attend the annual meeting (held each March) of the American Educational Research Association. Also, placement bureaus are often set up at the annual meetings of state educational research associations.

The student may also correspond directly with school districts, universities, or other organizations that employ educational research workers. Such inquiries are usually accompanied by a copy of the individual's résumé. As there are more positions available at present in educational research than there are applicants, the student will often obtain a favorable reply to such direct inquiries.

Many positions calling for educational research workers are available in the various branches of the federal government. The student should check directly with federal installations in the area in which he wishes to work. He may also correspond directly with the Civil Service Commission in Washington, D.C., and may obtain announcements of vacancies from the local post office. Many of the vacancies listed under "Research Psychologist" and "Educational Specialist" require persons with training in educational research.

ANNOTATED REFERENCES

1. Findley, Warren G., and Wittrock, Merlin C. "USOE-Funded Research and Development Centers: An Assessment," *Journal of Research and Development in Education* (1) (1968). This journal issue is devoted to a review of the work of the ten university-affiliated R & D centers. In the first part of the issue, the director or codirectors of each center describes their ongoing programs. These are followed by several articles by distinguished educators who discuss the centers' past performance and future promise.
2. Hjelm, Howard F., and McCann, Richard A. (eds.). "Regional Educational Laboratories: Agents of Change," *Journal of Research and Development in Education*, 3(2) (1970). Contributors to this journal issue describe the programs of the regional educational laboratories and discuss some issues concerning educational research and development. Models of R & D, management and

---

[14] For subscription information, write Editor, *Employment Bulletin*, American Psychological Association, 1200 Seventeenth Street, N.W., Washington, D.C. 20036

operation of the laboratories, dissemination and use of R & D products, and the future of the laboratories are among the topics discussed.

3. Lewis, Marianna O. (ed.). *The Foundation Directory*. New York: Russell Sage Foundation, 1967. (Revised every three years.) This directory includes information on 6,803 foundations with assets over $200,000, making grants of $10,000 per year or more. The directory contains an alphabetical listing of foundations by state, giving the name and address of the foundation, donors, the date established, purpose and activities, and recent assets and expenditures. *The Foundation Directory* also has an index of Fields of Interest in which the student may look up educational research, fellowships, educational aids, student loans, and other topics related to his field of interest.

4. Palmer, Archie M. (ed.). *Research Centers Directory*. 3rd ed. Detroit, Mich.: Gale Research, 1970. This valuable reference book contains information on over 4,500 university-related and other nonprofit research centers located in the United States and Canada. Facts about each research center include name, address, director's name, source of support, composition and size of staff, dollar volume of research, publications, and activities, such as seminars and institutes. The *Directory* lists 299 research centers devoted to various aspects of education. A quarterly publication, *New Research Centers*, reports on newly established centers and changes in existing centers between editions of the *Directory*.

5. Quick, Robert (ed.). *A Guide to Graduate Study*. 4th ed. Washington, D.C.: American Council on Education, 1969. This is a valuable reference for graduate students. It provides a brief general treatment of such topics as the objectives of graduate education, how to select a graduate school, how to gain admission to a graduate school, and how to finance graduate study. This reference also contains a description of graduate schools that offer programs leading to the Ph.D., including information such as when the graduate program was established, library facilities available, residence requirements, and admission requirements. Fees, tuition, cost of room and board in university dormitories, types of housing available, cost of housing, and first-year aid available are also covered. For each field of study offering the Ph.D., a brief description of the program, including the specific area covered, the prerequisites for graduate study, the number of graduate students completing degree programs in recent years, and the number of staff members are given.

6. Quick, Robert (ed.). *Fellowships in the Arts and Sciences, 1967–1968*. 10th ed. Washington, D.C.: American Council on Education, 1966. This directory provides a descriptive listing of predoctoral and postdoctoral fellowships supported by funds outside the universities. It also contains a chapter listing sources of financial support for summer study and another describing loan programs. A new edition is published each academic year, and the student is advised to obtain the latest. For each source of funds, the title of the program is given, the address to which students should mail inquiries, the purpose of the program, the fields in which fellowships are awarded, qualifications of recipients, periods of the award, stipends and other allowances, conditions under which the fellowships are available, application deadlines, and approximate number of awards to be made. The postdoctoral section contains some information on sources of

support for postdoctoral research and study, although a more thorough coverage may be found in *The Foundation Directory*.

7. Renetzky, Alvin, and Kaplan, Phyllis Ann (eds.). *Annual Register of Grant Support*. Los Angeles: Academic Media, 1969. This is a comprehensive directory, revised annually, of all existing forms of grants available for work in the humanities, social sciences (including education), and sciences. Grants offered by government agencies, foundations, and business and professional organizations are all included in this one source. Each entry in the directory contains the name of the organization, its type of grant support, purpose, eligibility, financial data, duration, application information, deadlines, address, and special stipulations, if any. In using the index, the student is advised to look under the headings of education, education research and fellowships, and student aid programs.

8. Simon, Kenneth A., and Grant, W. Vance. *Digest of Educational Statistics*. Washington, D.C.: Government Printing Office, 1968. This publication, revised annually, contains much information that may be of interest to the educational researcher. The statistical data provide many insights regarding the present status, as well as past and future trends, of the American educational system, from kindergarten through graduate school. Information is given on school facilities, personnel, finances, educational attainment, graduation rates, and federal support for education, including research and development.

9. USOE Bureau of Research. *Educational Research and Development in the United States*. Washington, D.C.: U.S. Government Printing Office, 1969. This document provides a wealth of information about the present status of educational research in this country. It includes comprehensive coverage of sponsors and performers of research, present financial and manpower resources, and a discussion of recent USOE policy concerning the use of R & D to bring about educational change.

10. USOE. *Fact Book: Office of Education Programs*. Washington, D.C.: U.S. Government Printing Office, 1968. The *Fact Book*, revised annually, is a useful reference source on all the USOE bureaus and the programs they administer through various education acts. It should be helpful to the researcher or educator interested in the types of financial support available from USOE. Information about each program includes authorizing legislation, purpose, year-by-year appropriations, location within USOE, program officer, application process for receiving an award, and basis for the award (e.g., merit of one's proposal).

ERIC Clearinghouses

1. Adult Education
   Mr. Roger DeCrow, Director
   Syracuse University
   Syracuse, New York 13210
2. Counseling and Personnel Services
   Dr. Gary Walz, Director
   University of Michigan
   Ann Arbor, Michigan 48104
3. Disadvantaged
   Dr. Edmund W. Gordon, Director
   Teachers College, Columbia University
   New York, New York 10027
4. Early Childhood Education
   Dr. Brian Carss, Director
   University of Illinois
   Urbana, Illinois 61801
5. Educational Administration
   Dr. Terry Eidell, Director
   University of Oregon
   Eugene, Oregon 97403
6. Educational Facilities
   Dr. Howard Wakefield, Director
   University of Wisconsin
   Madison, Wisconsin 53703
7. Educational Media and Technology
   Dr. W. Paisley, Director
   Institute for Communication Research
   Stanford University
   Stanford, California 94305
8. Exceptional Children
   Dr. June B. Jordan, Director
   Council for Exceptional Children
   Washington, D.C. 20036

9. Higher Education
   Dr. Lloyd H. Elliot, Director
   George Washington University
   Washington, D.C. 20006
10. Junior Colleges
    Dr. Arthur M. Cohen, Director
    University of California
    Los Angeles, California 90024
11. Library and Information Sciences
    Dr. W. Simonton, Director
    University of Minnesota
    Minneapolis, Minnesota 55404
12. Linguistics
    Dr. A. Hood Roberts, Director
    Center for Applied Linguistics
    Washington, D.C. 20036
13. Reading
    Dr. Edward G. Summers, Director
    Indiana University
    Bloomington, Indiana 47401
14. Rural Education and Small Schools
    Dr. Everett Edington, Director
    New Mexico State University
    Las Cruces, New Mexico 88001
15. Science Education
    Dr. R. Howe, Director
    Ohio State University
    Columbus, Ohio 43221
16. Teacher Education
    Dr. Joel L. Burdin, Director
    American Association of Colleges
       for Teacher Education
    Washington, D.C. 20036
17. Teaching of English
    Dr. B. O'Donnell, Director
    National Council of Teachers of English
    Champaign, Illinois 61820
18. Teaching of Foreign Languages
    Dr. Kenneth Mildenberger, Director
    Modern Language Association of America
    New York, New York 10011
19. Vocational and Technical Education
    Dr. Robert E. Taylor, Director
    Ohio State University
    Columbus, Ohio 43212

Questions to Be Asked by the Student in Planning a Research Project in Education *

A. Scope and Definition of Study
    1. Is your problem being considered broadly enough?
    2. Have you sufficiently limited your problem?
    3. What are the educational implications of your study?
    4. Have you governed your decisions by the experiences of investigators who have preceded you?
    5. How significant psychologically is a socially selected group such as "children who steal," "children who nail bite," "inmates of a correctional institution"?

B. Hypotheses
    1. What are the hypotheses?
    2. Are the hypotheses promising?
    3. Are the hypotheses clearly and precisely stated?
    4. Are the hypotheses stated in a form that permits them to be tested?
    5. Is it better to hazard a hypothesis or to ask a question?
    6. Has the study been restricted to one or a few principal hypotheses to be tested?
    7. Are your hypotheses independent of one another?
    8. Is it better to hypothesize causal factors or merely to hypothesize relationships?

C. Background
    1. Have you made a thorough, careful review of the literature pertaining to your problem?

D. Definitions
    1. Have proper distinctions been made between concepts?
    2. Have concepts been adequately analyzed so as to distinguish between small

* P. M. Symonds, "A Research Checklist in Educational Psychology," *Journal of Educational Psychology,* 47 (1956), 101–109. Reprinted by permission of the Abrahams Magazine Service, Inc., New York, N.Y.

but significant differences in method, materials, subjects, setting, etc.?

3. Is there clear and unequivocal meaning in the use of your terms?
4. Are concepts adequately and accurately defined?
5. Do some of your concepts require restrictive definition?
6. Do the meanings of your terms change with changes in age, sex, socio-economic status, etc.?
7. From what (whose) point of view are you defining your terms?

E. Method of Study

1. Has a decision as to the method of inquiry been made?
2. Is there a relation between the data to be collected and the hypotheses which the study is trying to test?
3. Do you propose to collect your own data or will you make use of published data already gathered?
4. Are you planning to use a "shotgun" approach?
5. If you plan to study individual cases, have you given thought as to how you will go from cases to general conclusions?
6. Are the data necessary for your study available?
7. Are you in a position to secure the data necessary for a successful prosecution of your study?
8. Are there variations in the method whose results would be worth investigating?
9. When more than one investigational approach is available, is it worthwhile to compare the results using different methods?
10. Can you draw conclusions as to cause and effect from evidence as to relationship?
11. To what extent can you generalize from a single experimental situation?
12. Are you planning to draw general conclusions from a study limited in age, sex, social class, race, etc.?
13. Have you considered the desirability of studying the relationships covering the whole range of your population instead of studying contrasting extreme groups?
14. Is the range among your cases sufficient to permit you to demonstrate the relationships in which you are interested?
15. Is it possible that the differences or relationships in which you are interested might be due to differences inherent in the situation (personality differences, for instance) instead of or as well as the experimental factors you propose to study?
16. How do you propose to select your criterion groups?
17. Can you make detailed observations of individual subjects to supplement your mass data?
18. Would it be well to ask questions on both the positive and negative side of an issue instead of just one side?
19. Are you justified in assuming a constant motivation among your subjects?
20. Will your results be influenced by the order or position of your materials?
21. Have you considered the possibility of response sets in your subjects—i.e., a general tendency to respond, which might influence your results?

F. Design

1. Is the design of your study clearly formulated?
2. Have you taken into account the various hidden factors which might influence the results of your study besides the variables that you are specifically planning to study?
3. Have you taken into account the influence of age, sex, school grade, IQ, socioeconomic status, mental set, leakage among subjects, influence of examiner, emotional factors?
4. Have you taken sufficiently into account experiences other than your experimental variables that might intervene between your first and second test?
5. How may the influence of these variables be eliminated?
6. Have you made a decision with regard to whether it is better to control variables experimentally or to test the contribution of variables statistically?
7. Have you given sufficient thought to the necessity of controls?
8. Are you in a position to measure and/or control variables which might influence your results?
9. Does the design of your experiment permit you to randomize variables which you do not want to influence your results?

G. Sampling

1. To what extent will you be able to generalize your findings?
2. What are the criteria for selecting your cases?
3. Is sampling of materials, places, subjects, test items, etc., *adequate?*
4. How do you propose to select subjects for your study?
5. Are your proposed subjects representative of the population to which you intend to generalize your results?
6. What age level and age range do you propose to study?
7. Have you given sufficient attention to the sampling of tasks?
8. What factors may be biasing the selection of subjects?
9. Do you propose to use groups already selected by social processes, or do you propose to select groups by direct testing of the characteristics of individuals?
10. Would your results be more clear-cut if you selected groups which give promise of showing wide differences?
11. How stable will your findings be—that is, will they stand up when made under different conditions—when made with other subjects, materials, instructors, examiners, in other places, etc.?
12. Will you make your selections on the basis of known factors or on the basis of a random sampling?
13. Should you treat as a unit individuals over a wide age, grade, or cultural range?
14. Can you simplify your problem by limiting it to a narrower age range, grade range, geographical range, etc.?

15. Are you taking into account the subgroups in your total population?
16. How do you propose to group your subjects?
17. In studying the differences between two populations, are you sure the populations are differentiated on the variables which you assume differentiate them?
18. Are you determining your sampling, or are you letting others select cases for you?
19. If you depend on voluntary participation for your subjects, have you given consideration to what this will do to your sampling?
20. How do you plan to determine the equivalence of groups?
21. If not all of those whom you solicit return questionnaires, what does this do to your sampling?

H. Studying Personality

1. Are you differentiating between manifest and covert personality trends?
2. To what extent is it possible to consider motives and unconscious purposes?
3. How do you propose to determine the values, attitudes, interests, motives, etc., that you plan to investigate?
4. Will interviews be biased if the interviewer has access to other information about an individual?
5. Can you depend on the subject's report to inform you about his motives, attitudes, problems, etc.?
6. Are you sufficiently aware of the influence of dynamic mechanisms (repression, projection, denial, etc.) in the reports of your subjects?
7. How are you going to ensure that your subjects express their true feelings and attitudes?
8. If you plan to investigate underlying dynamics, are you prepared to establish close relationships with your subjects?
9. Is the questionnaire or testing approach going to permit you to get at the inner dynamics?
10. In a study using tests and other objective data, is it possible to question your subjects further to determine attitudes, beliefs, motives, etc.?
11. Are you assuming that a verbal report of behavior is identical with the behavior?
12. Are you assuming that a verbal report of attitude is identical with the attitude?
13. Are you confounding a verbal report of memory with the actual facts?
14. Is the recall of childhood experiences a safe index of the actual experiences?
15. What is preferable for your study—the questionnaire or interview approach?
16. In a study involving interviewing, have you considered the possibility of securing cooperation and frankness from your subjects?
17. To what extent is the interviewer influencing the answers to questions?
18. To what extent can you depend on self-testimony as compared with the testimony of others?

19. Are you assuming that inner expression of value, interest, and feeling are the same as the judgment of a person made by some other person?

20. Is one justified in attributing dynamic significance to behavior for the purpose of research?

21. Do you prefer the free response type of inquiry (so-called open-ended questions) where the answers to questions must be categorized, or do you prefer recognition type questions where the answers can be directly tabulated?

22. In using observation material, how can you be sure that your observations are representative?

23. Have you made sure that the items which you have selected to represent a given trait are not biased in some other trait?

24. In thinking about personality characteristics, are these general or do they relate to specific situations?

I. Tests and Measures

1. Are you using the appropriate measures?

2. How is the material in your test to be selected?

3. Are your measures independent?

4. Have you taken into account the difficulty level of your test?

5. Do you wish to use a time limit or work limit?

6. Have you considered the relative merits of recall and recognition types of items?

7. Have you given consideration to the best type of score for your test?

8. How will you construct a scale to measure attitude?

9. Do you have a large enough reservoir of items to be able to make a selection of items in terms of difficulty, validity, etc.?

10. How do you propose to make a composite of your measures? What would such a composite mean?

11. In using a questionnaire, do you propose to get a total score or merely to tabulate the answers to separate items?

12. To what extent are the responses of your subjects limited by the examiner or the directions?

13. Can you use a ready-made measuring instrument, or should you construct your own? If the latter, how will you determine its validity and reliability?

14. How valid are your measures?

15. Are there contaminating factors (age, sex, etc.) which might lessen the validity of the test you propose to use?

16. Do you propose testing the validity of your test on a new group?

17. Are your tests sufficiently reliable?

18. Do you propose to test the reliability of your measures?

19. Are you planning to use your time in scale-making, testing validity and reliability when it could more profitably be directed elsewhere?

20. Are there norms with which to compare the findings in the group that you are proposing to study?

21. If you plan to use content material (like the TAT) as a measuring device, have you specified the variables you propose to measure?

22. Have you properly disguised your intentions in the test you propose to use?
23. Should a pretest be given as well as a test at the close of your experiment?
24. Is a pass-fail score on a test item identical with a qualitative score based on a content analysis?
25. Is a point score which is the sum of factors used in the solution to a problem adequate as a measure when there is a possibility that the factors may differ in importance?
26. If you plan to study the extremes on your scale, would it be well at the same time to pay attention to the intermediate points?

J. Use of Judgment
1. If you plan to use judgments, have you specified the basis on which your judgments would be made?
2. In securing ratings, whom will you select as your judges?
3. If you plan to use judgments, are you sure your judges have the necessary intelligence, information, background, and other qualifications to permit them to make the judgments?
4. Can you depend on judgments to serve as a basis for selecting individuals as being mentally deficient, delinquent, schizophrenic, etc.?
5. To what extent will subjective factors enter into judgments that you propose to make (or use), and how can these be avoided?
6. Which is better for your study—the overall judgment or a content analysis?

K. Content Analysis
1. How do you propose to determine your classification scheme?
2. Who is to make the classification scheme?
3. How reliable will the classification scheme be?
4. How do you propose to distribute material into the several classificatory categories?
5. Who is to distribute the items into categories?
6. Have you provided for determining the reliability of your classifications?
7. Have you sufficiently taken into account the subjective factor in analyzing content material?
8. Have you given attention to what sorts of behavior or responses will be included under such general categories as "resistance" or "rejection"?

L. Statistical Handling of Results
1. Do the conditions of your data warrant using the statistics which you propose to use?
2. Do your data satisfy the assumptions on which the statistical constants which you propose to use are based?
3. Have you enough cases to test fairly the significance of your statistical constants?

Checklist for Evaluating Experimental Research in Psychology and Education*

Satisfactory	Unsatisfactory	Questions

		A. The Problem
		  1. Was the problem clearly defined?
		  2. Was a verifiable hypothesis formu-ulated?
		  3. Was the hypothesis one that was logically deduced from some theory (or problem)?
		
		B. The Design
		  1. Was the statistical design employed in the investigation appropriate to the particular experimental methods, conditions, subjects, and hypotheses under test?
		  2. Was the population studied clearly specified?
		  3. Was the method, or methods, of drawing a sample from the population clearly specified?
		  4. Was a control group chosen in the same manner and from the same population as the experimental groups?
		  5 Were the various treatments (including control) assigned at random to the groups?

* Taken from William W. Farquhar and John D. Krumboltz, "A Checklist for Evaluating Experimental Research in Psychology and Education," *Journal of Educational Research*, 52(9) (1959), 354. Reprinted by permission of the *Journal of Educational Research*.

Satisfactory	Unsatisfactory	Questions

		6. Did the experiment include a replication?
		7. Was the level of significance necessary for rejection of the null hypotheses specified before the data were collected and analyzed?
		
		C. The Procedure
		  1. Were the treatments and methods of collecting data described so that an independent investigator could replicate the experiment?
		  2. Were the size and characteristics of the sample adequately described?
		  3. Were the treatments administered so that extraneous sources of error were either held constant for all treatment and control groups or randomized among subjects within all groups?
		
		D. The Analysis
		  1. Was the criterion of evaluation appropriate to the objectives of the study?
		  2. Was any evidence of the reliability of the criterion measure given for the experimental sample?
		  3. Were the statistical assumptions which are necessary for a valid test of the hypotheses satisfied?
		
		E. The Interpretation
		  1. Were the conclusions consistent with the obtained results?
		  2. Were generalizations confined to the population from which the sample was drawn?

Examples of Unobtrusive Measures

The following behavioral situations were designed as unobtrusive measures of student attitudes toward various aspects of school experience.*

Category 1: Student Willingness to Support Nonacademic School Projects

Behavioral situation 1: Student body activities

Procedure: A record will be kept of the number of students who purchase student body cards. If this situation is used, a similar sales campaign should be followed each year so that results will be reasonably comparable from year to year.

Scoring: The score to be applied to the total behavior attitude measure will be the number of students purchasing student body cards divided by the total number of students enrolled at the school. A high score indicates favorable attitude.

Category 2: Student Perception of the Importance of Education and His Identification with the School's Academic Goals

Behavioral situation 2: Educational Television

Procedure: If the school is within range of an educational television channel, the principal will obtain program notes for the month of March and will select two programs offered between 5 and 7 P.M. and two programs offered between the hours of 7 and 10 P.M. that appear to be of good quality and of general interest to high school students. An announcement of each program will be made the day before the program is to be shown and also the day of the program. On the first school day following the program, students of all classes will be given a very brief test and asked to indicate whether they saw the program and, if so, to answer five multiple-choice questions concerning the program.

Scoring: The score on this measure will be the number of pupils indicating they watched the program who also answered at least three of the five objective type questions correctly divided by the total number of pupils in attendance on the day the program was televised. High score is favorable.

Category 3: Student Respect for School Authority and School Property

Behavioral situation 3: Promptness in returning library books

Procedure: During the period of February 1 to February 15 inclusive, a special record will be kept of all books checked out by students. As these books are re-

---

* The situations were taken from Walter R. Borg, *Behavioral Situations to Be Used in Measuring Over-All Student Attitudes* (for the Western States Small Schools Project) (Salt Lake City, Utah: Utah State Department of Public Instruction, 1962).

School _____ Address _____ Name of person completing form _____

From _____ to _____
date   date

boys: _____ girls: _____
Enrollment starting date

boys: _____ girls: _____
Enrollment starting date

Check One *

Pupil's Name	Sex	Days Truant	Cat. 1	Cat. 2	Cat. 3	Other	Remarks

* Category 1 = absent without parent's knowledge
Category 2 = absent with parent's knowledge, but no legitimate excuse
Category 3 = absent with parent's knowledge, excuse doubtful

Fig. 22. Western States Small School Project truancy record form for behavioral situation 4.

turned, the librarian will indicate whether books have been returned on time or are late.

Scoring: The score will be the number of books returned on time divided by the total number of books checked out.

Category 4: Overall Attitudes Toward Teachers and School

Behavioral situation 4: Truancy data

Procedure: Truancy will be defined as any absence of a pupil from school, for which no excuse is given or for which an inadequate or unsatisfactory excuse is given. Using Fig. 22, the school will maintain truancy data during all school days in the month of April. Students returning from absences will be questioned concerning their reasons for being absent. Unless the student has a written excuse from his parent which the school considers genuine, his excuse should be checked with the parent by telephone. After necessary information has been obtained, the number of days and fractions of days truant should be recorded in the proper classification on the record sheet.

Scoring: The score on this item to be applied to the total attitude measure will be the number of days truant divided by the number of pupils in the school.

The Regional Research Program:
Regional Offices

Region 1: Connecticut, Maine, Massachusetts, New Hampshire, Rhode Island, Vermont
Dr. Richard V. McCann
Office of Education
Department of Health, Education and Welfare
John Fitzgerald Kennedy Federal Building
Boston, Massachusetts 02203

Region 2: Delaware, New Jersey, New York, Pennsylvania
Dr. John Sokol
Office of Education
Department of Health, Education and Welfare
26 Federal Plaza
Federal Office Building, Room 1013
New York, New York 10007

Region 3: Kentucky, Maryland, North Carolina, Puerto Rico, Virginia, Virgin Islands, West Virginia, District of Columbia
Mr. John A. Morrow
Office of Education
Department of Health, Education and Welfare
220 Seventh Street, N.E.
Charlottesville, Virginia 22901

Region 4: Alabama, Florida, Georgia, Mississippi, South Carolina, Tennessee
Mr. Theodore Abell
Office of Education
Department of Health, Education and Welfare
50 Seventh Street, N.E.
Atlanta, Georgia 30323

Region 5: Illinois, Indiana, Michigan, Ohio, Wisconsin
Mr. Joseph A. Murnin
Office of Education
Department of Health, Education and Welfare
226 West Jackson Boulevard
Chicago, Illinois 60606

Region 6: Iowa, Kansas, Minnesota, Missouri, Nebraska, North Dakota, South
Dakota
Dr. W. Phillip Hefley
Office of Education
Department of Health, Education and Welfare
601 East 12th Street
Kansas City, Missouri 64106
Region 7: Arkansas, Louisiana, New Mexico, Oklahoma, Texas
Dr. Harold A. Haswell
Office of Education
Department of Health, Education and Welfare
1114 Commerce Street
Dallas, Texas 75202
Region 8: Colorado, Idaho, Montana, Utah, Wyoming
Dr. Lewis R. Crum
Office of Education
Department of Health, Education and Welfare
Federal Office Building
19th and Stout Streets
Denver, Colorado 80202
Region 9: Alaska, Arizona, California, Guam, Hawaii, Nevada, Oregon, Washington
Dr. Walter Hirsch
Office of Education
Department of Health, Education and Welfare
50 Fulton Street, Room 250
San Francisco, California 94102

The Regional Educational Laboratories*

APPALACHIA EDUCATIONAL LABORATORY

Region served: West Virginia and parts of Virginia, Tennessee, Ohio, Kentucky,
and Pennsylvania
Director: Dr. Benjamin Carmichael
Appalachia Educational Laboratory
1416 Kanawha Boulevard
Charleston, West Virginia 25325
Mission: To help rural and isolated schools upgrade their programs through co-
operative relationships and modern technology, including:

A home-oriented preschool program using television and mobile facilities;

A self-instructional vocational guidance system for high school students
using videotapes and microfiche equipment;

An Appalachia-focused reading and language development program with
animated films and television.

CENTER FOR URBAN EDUCATION

Region served: Metropolitan New York and some neighboring cities
Director: Dr. Robert Dentler
Center for Urban Education
105 Madison Avenue
New York, New York 10016
Mission: To create an interaction among universities, public schools, and local
communities that will improve the quality and relevance of urban educa-
tion through:

Instructional materials, curriculum units, and teaching strategies;

* The stated missions of the laboratories were taken from U.S. Department of Health,
Education and Welfare, Office of Education, *Research Centers and Laboratories Supported
by the U.S. Office of Education* (Washington, D.C.: U.S. Government Printing Office, October 1969). Reprinted with permission of the National Center for Educational Research
and Development, U.S. Office of Education.

510 EDUCATIONAL RESEARCH

Community planning and participation techniques to help decentralized schools operate more effectively;

Clearinghouses of materials and information on problems facing urban education.

CENTRAL MIDWESTERN REGIONAL EDUCATIONAL LABORATORY

Region served: Eastern Missouri, southern Illinois, central and western Tennessee, and Kentucky
Director: Dr. Wade M. Robinson
Central Midwestern Regional Educational Laboratory
10646 St. Charles Rock Road
St. Ann, Missouri 63074
Mission: To contribute to the quality and breadth of curriculum and instruction throughout the nation through:

Comprehensive and individualized curriculums in mathematics and aesthetics for all students from kindergarten through high school;

Instructional strategies for teachers of students with special learning problems.

EASTERN REGIONAL INSTITUTE FOR EDUCATION

Region served: New York State (with the exception of metropolitan New York City) and western Pennsylvania
Director (acting): Dr. Milton C. Woodlen
Eastern Regional Institute for Education
635 James Street
Syracuse, New York 13203
Mission: To increase the ability of students to acquire and apply knowledge through curriculums which stress process learning by selecting curriculums, such as the science curriculum developed by the American Association for the Advancement of Science, and revamping, testing, revising, and diffusing these curriculums through a network of elementary schools, colleges and universities, State departments of education, and Supplementary Centers under Title III, ESEA.

EDUCATION DEVELOPMENT CENTER

Region served: New England
Director: Dr. Robert R. Hind
Education Development Center
55 Chapel Street
Newton, Massachusetts 02160

Mission: To create improved systems of inservice education in urban schools through instructional resource teams, trained in social and educational change, that provide background for educators, parents, and community groups in sensitivity, curriculum development, teaching techniques, child development, administration and supervision, and efficient distribution of teaching materials.

THE FAR WEST LABORATORY FOR EDUCATIONAL RESEARCH AND DEVELOPMENT

Region served: Northern California, Utah and Nevada (with the exception of Clark County).
Director: Dr. John K. Hemphill
The Far West Laboratory for Educational Research and Development
Claremont Hotel
1 Garden Circle
Berkeley, California 94705
Mission: To develop educational products and methods which enhance learning including:

Self-instructional training units which provide experienced as well as student teachers with critical teaching skills;

Information systems and training programs to help school personnel modify their organizations and make decisions about adopting educational developments;

Preschool and primary education programs to develop the intellectual abilities and self-concept of youngsters.

MID-CONTINENT REGIONAL EDUCATIONAL LABORATORY

Region served: Eastern Nebraska, western Missouri, eastern Kansas, and central Oklahoma
Director: Dr. Robert J. Stalcup
Mid-Continent Regional Educational Laboratory
104 East Independence Avenue
Kansas City, Missouri 64106
Mission: To improve instruction through inservice and preservice training including:

Instructional processes and classroom arrangements to insure that teachers effectively use the Biological Sciences Curriculum Study materials to foster student inquiry and self-directed learning;

Realistic preservice training in which potential teachers of the inner city live and teach in an inner city and work with community agencies and professionals to upgrade instruction.

NORTHWEST REGIONAL EDUCATIONAL LABORATORY

Region served: Alaska, Idaho, Montana, Washington, and Oregon
Director: Dr. Lawrence D. Fish
        Northwest Regional Educational Laboratory
        400 Lindsay Building
        710 Southwest Second Avenue
        Portland, Oregon 97204
Mission: To develop and disseminate instructional systems meeting selected educational needs:

> To help school administrators and teachers make the teaching-learning process more effective;

> To provide students, teachers, and administrators with experience and understanding in using computers in the classroom and in curriculum development;

> To provide representatives of inner-city, Indian, and migrant groups with skills to plan and implement cooperative educational projects in their communities;

> To broaden and enrich curriculums in small schools through self-instruction in counseling and academic and vocational subjects.

REGIONAL EDUCATIONAL LABORATORY FOR THE CAROLINAS AND VIRGINIA

Region served: North Carolina, South Carolina, and southern Virginia
Director· Dr. Everett H. Hopkins
        Regional Educational Laboratory for the Carolinas and Virginia
        Mutual Plaza
        Durham, North Carolina 27701
Mission: To increase the capability of educational institutions, primarily 2- and 4-year colleges, for self-improvement, initially through:

> A research-based planning and decision-making system using a computerized information system, and training for decision-makers and "educational development officers" who supply information to administrators and serve as catalysts for change;

> Instructional and curricular programs directed toward specific measures of performance and accommodation of different rates of learning;

> Models for diffusion and installation of instructional systems in primary and secondary schools.

RESEARCH FOR BETTER SCHOOLS, INC.

Region served: Delaware, New Jersey, and eastern Pennsylvania
Director: Dr. James W. Becker
      Research for Better Schools, Inc.
      1700 Market Street, Suite 1700
      Philadelphia, Pennsylvania 19103
Mission: To restructure education, with emphasis on learning systems which individualize and humanize, initially through:

Implementation strategies for Individually Prescribed Instruction, including training for school personnel, continued development of materials in schools across the nation, and use of modern technology such as the computer;

Specifications for an instructional program which develops and integrates children's social, intellectual, and emotional skills;

Training programs and materials for school administrators on approaches for adopting new programs.

SOUTHEASTERN EDUCATION LABORATORY

Region served: Alabama, Florida, Georgia
Director: Dr. Kenneth W. Tidwell
      Southeastern Educational Laboratory
      3450 International Boulevard
      Atlanta, Georgia 30054
Mission: To alleviate educational deficiencies in the Southeast through:

Instructional materials in communications skills to overcome the educational and occupational problems which arise from nonstandard speech patterns;

Curriculum materials in interpersonal relations for students, teachers, and parents to facilitate learning and mental health in schools with newly integrated faculties and student bodies;

A mobile program of cultural enrichment and school readiness for rural preschoolers.

SOUTHWEST EDUCATIONAL DEVELOPMENT LABORATORY

Region served: Texas and Louisiana
Director: Dr. Edwin Hindsman
      Southwest Educational Development Laboratory
      800 Brazos Street
      Austin, Texas 78767

Mission: To improve the education of Negro, Mexican-American, and French-American children through products such as:

A mathematics curriculum designed for deprived elementary and junior high students;

Multicultural social education which provides social concepts and skills and an appreciation of cultural diversity for economically deprived and culturally different children;

Bilingual materials and teacher training for preschool through grade six to teach children subject matter in their native language at the same time they learn English as a second language;

Curriculum for ages two through five emphasizing communications and psychosocial development, and involving parents and the community in their children's education.

SOUTHWEST REGIONAL LABORATORY

Region served: Southern California, southern Nevada, and western Arizona
Director: Dr. Richard Schutz
          Southwest Regional Laboratory
          11300 LaCienega Boulevard
          Inglewood, California 90304
Mission: To change the nature of instruction to performance-referenced, computer-managed, and learner-controlled bases, and to develop a technology of instruction, initially through:

Comprehensive computer-managed kindergarten and primary curriculums, which include communications and problem-solving skills and the humanities;

Administrative planning systems, utilizing computer technology and simulation, to assist school administrators in decisions on staff, curriculums, facilities, and instructional procedures.

SOUTHWESTERN COOPERATIVE EDUCATIONAL LABORATORY

Region served: Portions of Arizona, Oklahoma, Texas, and all of New Mexico
Director: Dr. James L. Olivero
          Southwestern Cooperative Educational Laboratory
          117 Richmond Drive, N.E.
          Albuquerque, New Mexico 87106
Mission: To improve the primary education of Indian, Negro, and Spanish-American children, initially through:

A preschool program to develop English oral language skills;

A primary grade program to improve English oral language;

A program to facilitate the transition from oral language to reading.

UPPER MIDWEST REGIONAL EDUCATIONAL LABORATORY

Region served: Iowa, Minnesota, North Dakota, South Dakota, and Wisconsin
Director: Dr. David Evans
Upper Midwest Regional Educational Laboratory
1640 East 78 Street
Minneapolis, Minnesota 55423
Mission: To maximize each student's learning by increasing teachers' skills in managing the learning environment through:

Programs which train educators to analyze behavior, design learning strategies, individualize the curriculum, and reinforce learning according to behavioral principles;

Behaviorally engineered schools with inner-city and Indian children in which these methods are taught and tested.

The Research and Development Centers

Center for the Advanced Study of Educational Administration
Director: Dr. Roland J. Pellegrin
    Center for the Advanced Study of Educational Administration
    University of Oregon
    Eugene, Oregon 97403

Center for Research and Development in Higher Education
Director: Dr. Leland L. Medsker
    Center for Research and Development in Higher Education
    University of California
    Berkeley, California 94720

Center for Research, Development, and Training in Occupational Educational
Director: Dr. John K. Coster
    Center for Research, Development, and Training in Occupational Education
    North Carolina State University at Raleigh
    Raleigh, North Carolina 27607

Center for Research and Leadership Development in Vocational and Technical Education
Director: Dr. Robert E. Taylor
    Center for Research and Leadership Development in Vocational and Technical Education
    Ohio State University
    980 Kinnear Road
    Columbus, Ohio 43212

Center for the Study of the Evaluation of Instructional Programs
Directors: Dr. Erick L. Lindman
    Dr. Merlin C. Wittrock
    Center for the Study of the Evaluation of Instructional Programs
    University of California
    Los Angeles, California 90024

Center for the Study of Social Organization of Schools and the Learning Process
Director: Dr. Edward L. McDill
> Center for the Study of Social Organization of Schools and the Learning
> Process
> Johns Hopkins University
> Baltimore, Maryland 21218

Learning Research and Development Center
Director: Dr. Robert Glaser
> Learning Research and Development Center
> 208 M. I. Building
> University of Pittsburgh
> Pittsburgh, Pennsylvania 15213

National Laboratory on Early Childhood Education
Director: Dr. James O. Miller
> National Laboratory on Early Childhood Education
> 805 West Pennsylvania Avenue
> Urbana, Illinois 61801

Research and Development Center on Educational Stimulation
Directors: Dr. Warren G. Findley
> Dr. J. A. Williams
> Research and Development Center in Educational Stimulation
> Fain Hall
> University of Georgia
> Athens, Georgia 30601

Research and Development Center in Teacher Education
Director: Dr. Robert F. Peck
> Research and Development Center in Teacher Education
> 303 Sutton Hall
> University of Texas
> Austin, Texas 78712

Stanford Center for Research and Development in Teaching
Directors: Dr. Robert N. Bush
> Dr. N. L. Gage
> Stanford Center for Research and Development in Teaching
> Stanford University
> 770 Welch Road
> Palo Alto, California 94304

Wisconsin Research and Development Center for Cognitive Learning
Director: Dr. Herbert J. Klausmeier
> Wisconsin Research and Development Center for Cognitive Learning
> The University of Wisconsin
> 1404 Regent Street
> Madison, Wisconsin 53705

Subject Index

519

Index of Names